READING ROMAN FRIENDSHIP

This book invites us to approach friendship not as something that simply *is*, but as something performed in and through language. Roman friendship is read across a wide spectrum of Latin texts, from Catullus' poetry to Petronius' *Satyricon* to the philosophical writings of Cicero and Seneca; from letters exchanged by the Emperor Marcus Aurelius and his beloved teacher Fronto, to those written by men and women at an outpost in northern Britain. One of the most innovative features of this study is the equal attention it pays to Latin literature and to inscriptions carved in stone across the Roman Empire. What emerges is a richly varied and perhaps surprising picture. Hundreds of epitaphs, commissioned by men and women, citizens and slaves, record the commemoration of friends, a phenomenon as important to the understanding of Roman friendship as Cicero's influential essay *De amicitia*.

CRAIG A. WILLIAMS is Professor of Classics at Brooklyn College and the Graduate Center of the City University of New York, and in 2006 he was awarded Brooklyn College's Leonard and Claire Tow Endowed Professorship. He is the author of the acclaimed *Roman Homosexuality* (second edition, 2010) as well as a commentary on the second book of Martial's *Epigrams* (2004), and numerous articles and reviews on Latin literature and Roman culture.

READING ROMAN FRIENDSHIP

CRAIG A. WILLIAMS

CAMBRIDGE
UNIVERSITY PRESS

CAMBRIDGE
UNIVERSITY PRESS

University Printing House, Cambridge CB2 8BS, United Kingdom

Cambridge University Press is part of the University of Cambridge.

It furthers the University's mission by disseminating knowledge in the pursuit of education, learning and research at the highest international levels of excellence.

www.cambridge.org
Information on this title: www.cambridge.org/9781107003651

© Craig A. Williams 2012

First published 2012

A catalogue record for this publication is available from the British Library

Library of Congress Cataloguing in Publication data
Williams, Craig A. (Craig Arthur), 1965–
Reading Roman friendship / Craig A. Williams.
p. cm.
Includes bibliographical references and index.
ISBN 978-1-107-00365-1 (hardback)
1. Friendship in literature. 2. Latin literature–History and criticism. I. Title.
PA6029.F75W55 2012
870.9´353–dc23   2012016957

ISBN 978-1-107-00365-1 Hardback

Contents

v

Illustrations

Acknowledgments

This book has been long in the coming, and I have been grateful for the opportunity to lecture on some of its many parts at the following institutions: Boston University, Columbia University, Royal Holloway, the University of Reading, Universität Rostock, Universität Trier, Humboldt-Universität zu Berlin. Preparing the lectures and explaining myself in the discussions afterwards invariably helped me both to sharpen the tools I use to read Roman friendship and to think more broadly about the questions of language, literature, and culture with which any discussion like this must grapple.

For their complementarily acute comments on earlier drafts of various parts of my manuscript, I am grateful to John Bodel, Kathleen Coleman, Marco Formisano, David Konstan, as I am to the anonymous readers for the press, whose reports were extraordinarily painstaking and helpful, an author's dream.

The Alexander von Humboldt Foundation has generously supported a series of research stays in Berlin for which I am lastingly thankful. And finally I thank my colleagues in the Classics Department at Brooklyn College, who uncomplainingly let their department chair twice take a semester's leave of absence in order to bring this project to completion.

Abbreviations

Unless otherwise specified, abbreviations of ancient texts used in this book are those found in *The Oxford Classical Dictionary*, ed. Simon Hornblower and Anthony Spawforth, 3rd rev. edn. (2003), and *The Oxford Latin Dictionary*, 2nd edn. (1982).

The following abbrevations are used in the citations of Latin inscriptions in this book.

AE:	*L'année épigraphique* (year and item number)
CIL:	*Corpus inscriptionum latinarum* (volume and item number)
CLE:	Franz Bücheler and Ernst Lommatzsch, *Carmina latina epigraphica*, Leipzig 1930 (item number)
Helttula:	Anne Helttula, ed., *Le iscrizioni sepolcrali latine nell'Isola Sacra*, Rome 2007 (item number)
ILCV:	Ernst Diehl, *Inscriptiones latinae christianae veteres*, Berlin 1925–1967 (item number)
ILS:	Hermann Dessau, *Inscriptiones latinae selectae*, Berlin 1892–1916 (item number)
Inscr. Aq.:	J. B. Brusin, ed., *Inscriptiones Aquileiae*, 3 vols., Udine 1991–1993 (item number)
ISOstiense:	B. E. Thomasson, ed., *Iscrizioni del sepolcreto di via Ostiense. Opuscula Romana* 1, Rome 1954 (item number)
Reali:	Mauro Reali, *Il contributo dell'epigrafia latina allo studio dell'amicitia. Il caso della Cisalpina*, Florence 1997 (item number)

The following standard notation is used in transcriptions:

/	end of line in the text as carved on the stone
//	end of a column or side of the stone

[abc]	reconstruction of text which is missing or illegible on the stone
[---]	missing or illegible letters which cannot be reconstructed
(abc)	expansion by modern editors of text abbreviated on the stone
<abc>	modern editorial additions or corrections to text on the stone
{abc}	modern editorial deletion of text on the stone
[[abc]]	stone carver's deletion of text on the stone

For the dating of Latin inscriptions, most often a matter of approximation, see Chapter 4. If no date can be assigned in a specific case, readers should bear in mind that the great majority of Latin inscriptions were produced between the late first century AD and the beginning of the third century AD; hence the frequency of the label "first–second century AD."

Introduction

> To the Ancients, Friendship seemed
> the happiest and most fully human of all loves;
> the crown of life and the school of virtue.
> The modern world, in comparison, ignores it.
> (C. S. Lewis, *The Four Loves*, p. 69)

In the story of the grand traditions which Western culture proudly anchors in its classical past – democracy and philosophy, for example, or drama and sculpture – Greece is most often the protagonist, with Rome in a distinctly secondary if nonetheless honored role. The Romans were inspired by the Greeks, followed in their footsteps, copied, transmitted and perpetuated; they have been admired for their architecture, roads, military discipline. Friendship is different. Typical is Montaigne's influential essay on friendship (*De l'amitié*, published in 1580) in which he reflects on his dazzling experience of friendship with Étienne de la Boétie. Here the authority of antiquity takes the form not of Homer, Plato or Aristotle but of Cicero, Catullus, Terence, Horace and Virgil. A quotation from Horace – "As long as I am in my right mind, I would compare nothing to a delightful friend" – is prominently placed, and Montaigne evokes the sense of loss he felt after his friend's death through a series of citations from other Latin poets.[1] For his part, Francis Bacon opens his essay "Of Friendship" with a quotation from Aristotle and subsequently cites such Greek thinkers as Pythagoras and Heraclitus, but the concrete examples of friendship he offers are all taken from Roman history – and (in a move that is, as we will see, emblematic) all of them are men.[2]

---

[1] Hor. *Sat.* 1.5.44: *nil ego contulerim iucundo sanus amico.* The other passages quoted are Verg. *Aen.* 5.49–50 (Aeneas on his father's death); Ter. *Haut.* 149–150 (Menedemus on his son); Hor. *Carm.* 2.17.5–9 (Horace on Maecenas); Catull. 65 and 68 (on his brother's death: see Chapter 2). See Screech 2004 for an English translation of Montaigne's essay.
[2] All of Bacon's examples are politically high-ranking figures: Pompey and Sulla, Brutus and Caesar, Augustus and Agrippa, Tiberius and Sejanus, Septimius Severus and Plautianus. See discussion at Korhonen 2006, pp. 287–301.

I

Exploration of Rome's centrality to the history of Western friendship is beyond the scope of this book, but some broadly relevant factors are clear.[3] There has long been an awareness that *amicitia* played a fundamental role in Roman culture, pervading social relations and shaping ethical ideals seemingly even more than did *philia* in the Greek world. But much of the credit goes to a single Roman writer, and one of his texts in particular. Even more than Plato's *Lysis* or the eighth and ninth books of Aristotle's *Nicomachean Ethics*, Cicero's *De amicitia* has offered readers over the centuries a powerfully appealing combination of theoretical reflection and practical advice, and this text played a key role in the transformation of classical into Christian discourses of friendship. Aelred of Rievaulx, for example, begins his *De spiritali amicitia* with an act of homage – reading the *De amicitia* opened his eyes to true friendship – and humanist thought on the question looked back to Cicero more consistently than to Aristotle.[4] In addition to the *De amicitia*, Cicero's letters to his friend Atticus to which we will return in Chapter 3 have left a lasting impression. Several generations later, publishing a corpus of essays in the form of letters to his own friend Lucilius, Seneca predicts that one day the two of them will join the ranks of Epicurus and Idomeneus, Cicero and Atticus, pointedly observing that the name of Atticus is alive not because of his connections to Agrippa or Augustus, but because of his eloquent friend's letters to him. (While the name of Lucilius was and is far less well known than that of Atticus, Seneca's confidence was not entirely misplaced – his *Epistulae morales ad Lucilium* are still being read under that title.) And centuries later, Voltaire gushes: "Céthégus était le complice de Catilina, et Mécène le courtisan d'Octave; mais Cicéron était l'ami d'Atticus."[5]

In the continuous chain of textual reflection on friendship within the Western tradition, then, some of the most important links are Roman. It is all the more paradoxical that when scholars of classical antiquity have written on friendship, they have tended to perpetuate the imbalance regularly occluded by that hybrid concept "Greco-Roman." A monument in the modern study of ancient friendship is Laurent Dugas' *L'amitié antique*

---

[3] For an overview of the history of friendship in the Western tradition see Konstan 1997, pp. 1–23; for some key moments, see Hyatte 1994, Bray 2003, Hermand 2006.

[4] Aelred of Rievaulx, *De spiritali amicitia*, preface: *tandem aliquando mihi venit in manus liber ille quem de amicitia Tullius scripsit; qui statim mihi et sententiarum gravitate utilis et eloquentiae suavitate dulcis apparebat.* See MacFaul 2007, pp. 1–29, for the massive influence of Cicero's *De amicitia* on the English humanists.

[5] Sen. *Ep.* 21.4: *nomen Attici perire Ciceronis epistulae non sinunt. nihil illi profuisset gener Agrippa et Tiberius progener et Drusus Caesar pronepos; inter tam magna nomina taceretur nisi <sibi> Cicero illum applicuisset*; Voltaire, *Dictionnaire philosophique* s.v. "Amitié."

(first edition 1894, second edition 1914). The *antiquité* of his title turns out to be almost entirely Greek, his *Anciens* overwhelmingly philosophers.[6] Decades later, the title of a 1974 monograph by Jean-Claude Fraisse is equally revealing in the equivalence it smoothly establishes: *Philia. La notion d'amitié dans la philosophie antique.* More recently, in a collection bearing the title *Greco-Roman Perspectives on Friendship*, only one out of eleven essays focuses on Latin texts, and they are almost exclusively Ciceronian at that; David Konstan's monograph *Friendship in the Classical World* has a structure typical of thematic studies of classical antiquity (three chapters on Greece, one on Rome, one on early Christianity); and a 2000 bibliographical survey confirms the impression that studies of *philia* far outnumber those of *amicitia*.[7] My book aims to redress this imbalance.

ROMAN IDEALS

Latin literature is full of friends, and Roman idealizing of friendship could be powerful indeed.[8] Not only was *amicitia* inextricably woven into the fabric of social relations in the Roman world, but it could be placed on a pedestal which strikes many modern eyes as surprisingly lofty, extolled in language that perplexes many modern ears. In the preface to

---

[6] Consider the first sentence of the first chapter of the second edition: "Les Anciens donnaient au mot 'amitié' l'extension que nous donnons au mot 'amour'. Ils disaient: l'amitié paternelle, familiale, l'amitié amoureuse (φιλία ἐρωτική)"; on this first page "l'amitié proprement dite" is glossed with φιλία ἑταιρική (Dugas 1914, p. 1). All of this is more or less directly taken from Aristotle, who by synecdoche stands for "les Anciens." Revealingly enough, the qualification found in the title of the 1894 first edition (*L'amitié antique d'après les moeurs populaires et les théories des philosophes*) was tacitly dropped in the 1914 revised edition, simply entitled *L'amitié antique*; but in this second edition, even a chapter devoted to "l'amitié considérée dans les institutions et dans les moeurs" (pp. 11–68) is structured around discussion of Socrates, the Pythagoreans, Epicureans and Stoics. Subsequent studies of friendship in the ancient philosophical tradition include Voelke 1961, Steinmetz 1967 (focusing on Cicero's *De amicitia*), Fraisse 1974 (pp. 388–413 on Cicero's *De amicitia*), Price 1989, Pangle 2003.

[7] Fraisse 1974, Konstan 1997, Fitzgerald 1997; the essay in question is Fiore 1997. The titles of two other essays (David Balch, "Political Friendship in the Historian Dionysius of Halicarnassus, *Roman Antiquities*," and Alan Mitchell, "New Testament Evidence for the Greco-Roman *topos* on Friendship") gesture toward Rome, but each of them begins by declaring a focus on Greek *philia*. Bibliographical review in Devere 2000.

[8] This book reads *amicitia* as it joins individuals, but many of the issues with which we will be engaging also apply to relationships between the Roman Senate and foreign states or leaders, which were often described in terms of both *clientela* and *amicitia*. See Williams 2008 for discussion and bibliography. See Cimma 1976 for the distinction between *socii* and *amici* in the language of inter-state relationships: The former implies the existence of a formal agreement or treaty (*foedus*), the latter does not. Sallust's *Jugurtha* invites being read as a story, among other things, of *amicitia* between a succession of Numidian kings and the Roman people or powerful Romans like Scipio Aemilianus.

his *De amicitia*, which pointedly, indeed insistently presents itself to its readers as a book on friendship written to a friend by a friend (Cic. *Amic.* 5: *hoc libro ad amicum amicissimus scripsi de amicitia*), Cicero explains that he will be speaking to Atticus in the voice of Laelius, meditating upon friendship soon after the death of his friend Scipio in 129 BC. In words to which we will return, Laelius offers this fervent definition:

est enim amicitia nihil aliud nisi omnium divinarum humanarumque rerum cum benevolentia et caritate consensio, qua quidem haud scio an excepta sapientia nihil melius homini sit a dis immortalibus datum. (Cic. *Amic.* 20)

Friendship is nothing other than agreement in all matters, divine and human, joined with goodwill and affection. Besides wisdom, I think the immortal gods have given humanity nothing better.

Giving the credit not to the gods but to Nature herself, Manilius' poem on astronomy makes a similar point: "She has created from herself nothing greater or rarer than the bond of friendship."[9] A poem by Catullus fervently evokes the joys of friendship between men:

> Verani, omnibus e meis amicis
> antistans mihi milibus trecentis,
> venistine domum ad tuos penates
> fratresque unanimos anumque matrem?
> venisti. o mihi nuntii beati!
> visam te incolumem audiamque Hiberum
> narrantem loca, facta nationes,
> ut mos est tuus, applicansque collum
> iucundum os oculosque saviabor.
> o quantum est hominum beatiorum,
> quid me laetius est beatiusve?
>
> (Catull. 9)

> Veranius! Out of all my friends,
> I prefer you to three hundred thousand.
> So you have come back home to your household gods,
> and to your brothers with whom you share heart and soul,
> and to your aged mother?
> Yes, you have come back. Blessed the messengers!
> I shall come see you, safe and sound, and I shall listen to you
> as you tell stories about Spain, its places and events and peoples,
> in your usual way; and I shall cling to your neck

[9] Manil. 2.581–182: *idcirco nihil ex semet natura creavit / foedere amicitiae maius nec rarius umquam.* Cf. Cic. *Fin.* 1.65: *nihil esse maius amicitia, nihil uberius, nihil iucundius* (an element in Torquatus' Epicurean vision of friendship that will, however, have seemed axiomatic to most of Cicero's readers). All translations from Greek and Latin in this book are mine.

and kiss your delightful mouth and eyes.
Of all the happy men there are,
who is more blessed or happier than me?

And, in an overlap to which we will return in Chapter 3, the same poet
not only writes of his relationship with Lesbia in terms that anticipate later
traditions of romantic love – "I loved her like no one else will ever love a
woman" – but describes it as a hallowed friendship (*sancta amicitia*).[10]

In Chapter 2 we will be considering a set of paradigmatic pairs of
friends in the mythic tradition, the most prominent among them being
Orestes and Pylades. Son of the Argive king Agamemnon and his wife
Clytemnestra, Orestes is banished in his youth after his mother has
killed his father and placed her lover Aegisthus on the throne; in exile, he
befriends Pylades, who remains by his side through all of his subsequent
tribulations. These begin with the divine command to kill his mother
in revenge for her murder of his father; continue as he is pursued by the
Furies for having carried out that command; and culminate when he
travels to the land of the Taurians in modern-day Crimea, now on orders
from Apollo to steal a wooden cult image of Artemis. Upon arrival he
not only finds that his sister Iphigenia has ended up in the same place,
but discovers that she has been made priestess of Artemis and given the
duty of sacrificing strangers who arrive on the Taurian shores – including
Orestes and Pylades themselves. This is the scenario depicted in a fresco
painted on the wall of a house in Pompeii in the mid-60s AD (now in the
Naples museum) which gives us a rare opportunity to read friendship in
Roman art (Figure 1).[11] Orestes and Pylades form one point of a triangular arrangement together with the local king Thoas, who sits in front of
them on the other side of a small altar accompanied by an attendant, and
Iphigenia, who stands at the top of a flight of stairs leading to the temple
of Artemis behind them. The composition emphasizes the two friends'
intimacy and unity of purpose. Their hands bound behind their backs,
they stand close together, painted in such a way that the body of one
partially obscures that of the other. Although it is hard to know which is

---

[10] Catull. 8.5 (repeated at 37.12): *amata nobis quantum amabitur nulla* (cf. 87.1–2: *nulla potest mulier tantum se dicere amatam / vere, quantum a me Lesbia amata mea est*); 109.6: *aeternum hoc sanctae foedus amicitiae.*

[11] To be sure, joint burials of two or more individuals were sometimes commemorated by portrait sculptures, and some of the individuals portrayed may have called each other *amici* in life. But unless an accompanying inscription uses the label, such monuments cannot persuasively be read in connection with *amicitia*: joint burials came in a range of configurations, from brothers and sisters to freed slaves and former owners, from masters and slaves to husbands and wives. See Chapter 4 for further discussion.

Figure 1   Fresco depicting Orestes and Pylades before King Thoas, with
Iphigenia in the background.

Orestes and which Pylades, a visual distinction is clearly made. The man
in front is in profile, most of his body bare for us to see, while his companion faces us frontally, most of his body covered by clothing.[12]

The land of the Taurians was the setting of a stirring scene which the-
matizes precisely the difficulty of distinguishing between the two, a scene
frequently and lovingly evoked in stories about the pair. When Thoas
demands to know which one is Orestes so that he may kill him, each
of the two identifies himself as Orestes in order to spare the other. The

---

[12] The cover of this book shows a detail from Benjamin West's 1766 painting of the same scene. The
so-called Orestes sarcophagus, datable to the early second century AD and now in the Museo
Arquelógico Nacional in Madrid (inv. no. 2839; see Prado-Vilar 2011), likewise distinguishes
between Orestes and Pylades in its visualization of this scene: one man appears in three-quarter
profile from behind, the other head-on.

episode was dramatized by the second-century BC tragedian Pacuvius in a scene which proved to be memorable. Pacuvius' play has not survived, but Cicero's Laelius evokes both the scene and its reception, pointedly describing Pacuvius as his own *hospes et amicus*, one with whom he shares the intertwined bond of hospitality and friendship.

itaque si quando aliquod officium exstitit amici in periculis aut adeundis aut communicandis, quis est qui id non maximis efferat laudibus? qui clamores tota cavea nuper in hospitis et amici mei M. Pacuvi nova fabula, cum, ignorante rege uter Orestes esset, Pylades Orestem se esse diceret ut pro illo necaretur, Orestes autem, ita ut erat, Orestem se esse perseveraret! stantes plaudebant in re ficta. quid arbitramur in vera facturos fuisse? (Cic. *Amic.* 24)

And so whenever a friend performs some duty in the form of taking on or sharing danger, who will not extol the deed to the skies? How loudly the entire audience roared at the recent performance of a new play by my guest and friend Marcus Pacuvius, at the scene when the king did not know which of the two men was Orestes, and so Pylades said that he was Orestes in order that he might be killed in his place, but Orestes insisted that he was – as in fact he was – Orestes! The audience rose to its feet and applauded at this fictional scene. What do we think they would have done if it had been real?

The contrast between fictive and real (*res ficta* vs. *res vera*) is intertwined with another which Laelius does not draw out here but which we will see elsewhere – that between Greek and Roman – as we read how a staged scene of two friends vying to die each for the other might bring a Roman audience to its feet in wild applause.[13]

Valerius Maximus' early first-century AD *Facta et dicta memorabilia* ("Memorable Deeds and Sayings"), a thematically organized collection of narratives exemplifying various virtues, well illustrates the ideals and preoccupations of Roman culture and the Latin textual tradition. To the extent, too, that Valerius' was one of the most widely read of Latin prose

---

[13] There is some debate as to which of Pacuvius' tragedies on Orestes contained the scene; possibilities include not only his *Orestes* but his *Dulorestes*, *Chryses*, and *Hermiona*. Elsewhere Cicero refers to the warm reception of the scene by Roman audiences and he may or may not be referring to Pacuvius' play in particular (*Fin.* 5.63–64: *qui clamores vulgi atque imperitorum excitantur in theatris, cum illa dicuntur: "ego sum Orestes", contraque ab altero: "immo enimvero ego sum, inquam, Orestes!"*). For this story see also Cic. *Fin.* 2.79 (*aut, Pylades cum sis, dices te esse Orestem, ut moriare pro amico? aut, si esses Orestes, Pyladem refelleres?*), Ov. *Pont.* 2.6.19–30, 3.2, with Citroni Marchetti 2000, pp. 339–344, 355–364. Nearly two centuries after Cicero, both a polemical contrast between cultures and enthusiastic audience response to stage performances play a central role in Lucian's dialogue *Toxaris, or Friendship*. The title character points out that, whereas Greeks have written and said a great deal in praise of friendship and Greek audiences respond with applause and tears to tragic scenes on the theme (9), his fellow Scythians have preferred deeds to words, erecting an altar and a temple to Orestes and Pylades and worshipping them as gods under the title of *Korakoi*, which he translates into Greek as *philioi daimones* (7).

texts in medieval and Renaissance Europe, it played a key role in shaping later readings of Roman culture too.[14] A look at this text's not coincidentally juxtaposed chapters on conjugal love and friendship (4.6: *De amore coniugali*; 4.7: *De amicitia*) thus promises to be both rewarding and revealing.

The chapter on conjugal love introduces its topic concisely and reverently, if a bit dryly, as "legally sanctioned love" (*legitimus amor*) and proceeds to present eight narratives, divided according to Valerius' usual practice into Roman and foreign: five of the former, three of the latter. These are stirring tales, yet rather briefly told and with only a moderate degree of pathos. All of them illustrate the devotion of husband and wife in connection with motifs related to death which, as we will see, are characteristic of *amicitia* as well, and which I call *contest of death* and *unity in death*. One partner strives to die on behalf of the other and/or the two indeed join each other in death, sometimes physically united. In response to an omen, Tiberius Gracchus forfeits his life in order to spare his wife Cornelia's (4.6.1); Gaius Plautius Numida and Porcia kill themselves after their respective spouses' deaths (4.6.2, 5), as does Marcus Plautius, laying himself on his wife Orestilla's pyre when he does so (4.6.3); Artemisia built her husband's famous tomb and drank a potion containing his ashes (4.6.ext.1); the wives of the Minyae take the place of their husbands, awaiting execution in prison (4.6.ext.3); Julia experiences a miscarriage upon suspecting – falsely, as it turned out – that her husband Pompey had been killed (4.6.4). The only narrative in which death does not figure draws attention to gender: Hypsicratea accompanies her husband Mithridates in exile, giving up feminine luxuries and even her feminine appearance, leading the rough and manly life of a fellow-soldier (4.6.ext.2). Attentive readers may note that all of Valerius' narratives are unidirectional, outstanding cases of devotion by only *one* of the partners. In the Roman stories, the first three focus on a husband's devotion to his wife and the second two on a wife's to her husband; all three foreign narratives focus on wives' devotion.

---

[14] Studies of Valerius Maximus include Bloomer 1992, Skidmore 1996 (who begins by observing that "there are more surviving medieval and Renaissance manuscripts of Valerius Maximus than of any other prose author of the ancient world; a survey of extant monastery library catalogues shows that in the twelfth century virtually every monastery in Western Europe had a copy"), Mueller 2002 (pp. 131–139 on "the rhetorical rituals of friendship"), Lucarelli 2007 (pp. 214–285 on *amicitia*, *fides*, and *gratia*). Valerius Maximus' references to married couples and friends are not, of course, limited to chapters 4.6 and 4.7: consider also 4.2 (on enmities transforming into friendship) and 6.7 (on wives' loyalty to their husbands), and for friends see also 1.7.4, 2.1.9, 2.9.2, 2.10.8, 4.4.7, 5.3.4, 5.8.2, 5.8.5, 6.3.1d, 6.4.4, 7.4.2, 7.4.5, 7.5.4, 7.8.4, 8.8.1, 9.12.6.

Turning to Valerius' chapter on *amicitia*, we immediately see that it is longer – nine pairs of friends are named (seven Roman and two foreign) and most of their stories are told at greater length than those of conjugal love – and as we begin reading it, it quickly becomes perceptibly weightier than its predecessor, more distinctly marked with rhetorical fireworks and pathos. Here are the chapter's opening words.

contemplemur nunc amicitiae vinculum potens et praevalidum neque ulla ex parte sanguinis viribus inferius, hoc etiam certius et exploratius quod illud nascendi sors, fortuitum opus, hoc uniuscuiusque solido iudicio incohata voluntas contrahit. (Val. Max. 4.7.pr.)

Let us now contemplate the powerful, mighty bond of friendship: in no way lesser than the power of blood, in fact surer and more proven to the extent that while kinship derives from the chance of birth, a matter of luck, friendship derives from the free will, undertaken by each on the basis of solid judgment.

Valerius then expands on the thought with remarks that will be familiar to readers of Cicero's *De amicitia*: One lays oneself open to criticism much more for abandoning a friendship than a blood relationship; loyal friends are recognizable in adversity; prosperity is better when shared with a friend than when alone. This leads to the example of Orestes and Pylades, now explicitly marked as foreign:

nemo de Sardanapalli familiaribus loquitur; Orestes Pylade paene amico quam Agamemnone notior est patre – siquidem illorum amicitia in consortione deliciarum et luxuriae contabuit, horum durae atque asperae condicionis sodalicium ipsarum miseriarum experimento enituit. sed quid externa attingo, cum domesticis prius liceat uti? (Val. Max. 4.7.pr.)

No one talks about Sardanapallus' comrades, whereas Orestes is almost better known for his friend Pylades than for his father Agamemnon. After all, friendship with Sardanapallus meant decay in shared decadence and luxury, whereas Orestes' and Pylades' companionship in a rough and difficult situation shone forth all the more because of their experience of misfortune. But why do I mention foreign exmaples, when I can start with Roman ones?

And so, citing – for the only time in his entire text – foreign examples in his introductory paragraph, he proceeds to present his examples in the usual order: first Roman, then foreign.

Focusing on male friendships as he does, and particularly those among men in the upper circles of Roman society, Valerius begins by exploring a theme touched upon in Cicero's *De amicitia*: the tension between the claims of friendship and the claims of politics or more generally the community. His first three narratives are of men who were so entirely devoted to their friends that they tolerated or even committed crimes against the state (Blossius and Tiberius Gracchus, 4.7.1; Pomponius, Laetorius, and Gaius Gracchus, 4.7.2; Reginus and Caepio, 4.7.3). All of this is testimony to the power of friendship, provoking Valerius' grudging, double-edged praise, and the occasional remark revealing of an ethical stance on friends that may have been especially characteristic of the man, his times, or both. Blossius, interrogated as to whether he would have supported his friend Gracchus even in a plan to set fire to the temple of Jupiter Optimus Maximus on the Capitoline, retorts that Gracchus would never have asked him to do such a thing – thereby further alienating his interroga-tors. When the questioners persist, Blossius finally bursts out that, yes, if Gracchus had asked him to do such a thing, he would have heeded his friend's request. Valerius thereupon remarks that no one would have blamed Blossius if he had kept silent, and some might even have thought him wise if he had adjusted his remarks to "the necessity of the situation"; but to an "honorable silence" Blossius preferred the stance of a man loyal to the memory of his friend, no matter how deeply he had fallen into disgrace.[15]

As in his chapter on conjugal love, death is a central theme in Valerius' narratives of *amicitia*. Pomponius and Laetorius protect Gaius Gracchus from his assassins, the former literally over his own dead body (4.7.2: *multis confectus vulneribus transitum super cadaver suum eis, credo etiam post fata invitus, dedit*); Lucius Petronius accedes to his friend Publius Coelius' request and kills him, then immediately joins him in death (4.7.5); Servius Terentius attempts to play Pylades to Decimus Brutus' Orestes, claim-ing that he is Brutus when Furius, sent by Marc Antony, comes to finish him off – but, unlike Orestes, Brutus is killed anyway (4.7.6); and, in a powerful image to which we will return in Chapter 4, Volumnius holds his decapitated friend's head as he offers his own neck to the sword (4.7.4). Valerius uses this as an opportunity to return to the tension between Greek and Roman. The Greeks have the tale of Theseus and Pirithous, but we Romans have examples like this, taken from life – and death.[16]

---

[15] Val. Max. 4.7.1: *quis illum sceleratum putasset fuisse si tacuisset? quis non etiam sapientem si pro necessitate temporis locutus esset? at Blossius nec silentio honesto nec prudenti sermone salutem suam, ne qua ex parte infelicis amicitiae memoriam desereret, tueri voluit.* See Mueller 2002, pp. 80–83. Reading this chapter along with passages from Cicero's *De amicitia* and suggesting that this chapter can be seen to some extent as an "Anti-Laelius," Lucarelli 2007, pp. 245–257, emphasizes that Valerius' choice of exemplary *amici* is biased toward those from the turbulent years of the late Republic and argues that this goes a long way toward explaining the themes he emphasizes: tests of loyalty and risk of death.

[16] Bloomer 1992, pp. 219–221, suggests that these illustrations of *amicitia*, drawing attention to Republican-period heroes, "provide the pretext for much that otherwise would not appear in Valerius' work." This is the only reference to Volumnius and Lucullus in the surviving textual

Valerius' examples of conjugal love bring women to center stage, and five of the seven protagonists are women; the one and only woman to appear on his otherwise masculine stage of *amicitia* plays in an eloquent scene indeed. Having defeated king Darius, Alexander the Great comes to the Persian camp together with his companion Hephaestion. Darius' mother prostrates herself before the pair, but mistakes Hephaestion for Alexander because he is taller and more beautiful. Alexander graciously accepts her profuse apologies; there is no reason for her to be embarrassed, for "Hephaestion is Alexander too (*nam et hic Alexander est*)." And so, Valerius writes, "this most generous king, who had the whole world in his embrace thanks either to military victories or to expectation, now shared himself with his companion by means of a few simple words. The gift of this renowned saying brought honor both to him who gave it and him who received it."[17] Death lurks in the background of this scene, but Valerius draws our attention to two motifs common in Roman idealization of friendship among the living (arguably, as we will see, even more than in idealization of married love): sharing of all that one has, and total identity of the two partners.

As in his chapter on conjugal love, Valerius' narratives of friendship are unidirectional, illustrating the devotion of one partner for the other, and his Roman examples culminate with Laelius and Agrippa, praised for their faithful devotion to Scipio and Augustus respectively.[18] The prominent exception to the pattern is the story of the Greek pair Damon and Phintias, a famous illustration of *mutual* devotion. The tyrant Dionysios condemns Phintias to death but allows him to go home first in order to arrange his affairs – on condition that Damon remain in Dionysios' custody as human collateral. As the time appointed for execution approaches and there is no sign of Phintias, Dionysios and others assume that Phintias is no Pylades: He is indeed going to allow his friend to die in his stead. When, at the last moment, Phintias shows up, ready to give his life, Dionysios is moved not only to spare him but to ask to join his friendship

tradition; Bloomer observes that this "small phase of Roman civil conflict is superseded by the rhetoric of a greater contest, that between Greece and Rome, whose prize is fame."

17 Val. Max. 4.7.ext.2a: *Hephaestione gratissimo sibi latus suum tegente ... Hephaestionemque, quia et statura et forma praestabat, more Persarum adulata tamquem Alexandrum salutavit ... maximi enim animi rex et iam totum terrarum orbem aut victoriis aut spe complexus tam paucis verbis se cum comite suo partitus est. o donum inclitae vocis, danti pariter atque accipienti speciosum!*

18 Val. Max. 4.7.7: *orere igitur ab illa quae sanctorum umbris dicata esse creditur sede, hinc D. Laeli, illinc M. Agrippa, alter virorum, deorum alter maximum amicum et certa mente et secundis ominibus sortiti, totumque beatae turbae gregem, qui vestro ductu veneranda sincerae fidei stipendia laudibus et praemiis onustus peregit, in lucem vobiscum protrahite.*

with Damon as a third party.[19] The tale inspires Valerius to a veritable hymn to *amicitia*.

hascine vires amicitiae? mortis contemptum ingenerare, vitae dulcedinem extinguere, crudelitatem mansuefacere, odium in amorem convertere, poenam beneficio pensare potuerunt. quibus paene tantum venerationis quantum deorum inmortalium caerimoniis debetur: illis enim publica salus, his privata continetur, atque ut illarum aedes sacra domicilia, harum fida hominum pectora quasi quaedam sancto spiritu referta templa sunt. (Val. Max. 4.7.ext.1)

This, then, is the power of friendship! To breed contempt of death, to take away the sweetness of life, to tame cruelty, to turn hatred into love, to exchange punishment for benefit: all of this it has been able to do. Almost as much veneration is due to friendship's power as to ceremonies for the immortal gods: after all, the well-being of the entire people depends on the latter, that of individuals on the former. Just as divine ritual finds its consecrated dwelling-place in temples, the power of friendship takes its abode in trusty human hearts which are, as it were, sanctuaries filled with divine spirit.

Well exploiting the expressive possibilities of the Latin language, Valerius' wording is lapidary, the phrases come in a rolling sequence, and all is balance, contrast, and rhetorical pomp: in honor of *amicitia*, treated almost as a divinity. While Valerius' wording relies on the assumption that *amicitia* did not usually receive cultic ceremonies like those performed for the gods, Tacitus reports that in AD 28 the Senate commissioned an altar to Clemency and another one to Friendship, the latter flanked by statues of Tiberius and Sejanus by way of underscoring the flattering specificity of the gesture. In view of the two men's reputations then and since – Valerius himself seems to denounce Sejanus after his fall from grace and death three years later (9.11.ext.4) – we can only imagine the range of motivations and responses. In any case this seems to have been a one-time gesture and, as far as we can tell, in connection with personified Amicitia there was never anything comparable to the prominent sanctuary and famous cult practices in honor of, for example, Fortuna at Praeneste.[20]

---

[19] See also Cic. *Off.* 3.45, *Tusc.* 5.63, Diod. Sic. 6.243, Iambl. *VP* 234.

[20] Tac. *Ann.* 4.74: *aram clementiae, aram amicitiae effigiesque circum Caesaris ac Seiani censuere.* Pizzolato 1993, p. 179, sees a meaningful statement on the part of the Senate: "non può non suonare come irridente o come una rivincita – purtroppo astratta – delle essenze tradíte." The discussion of the religiosity of Valerius' language of *amicitia* at Mueller 2002, pp. 131–139 (cf. p. 138: "He worships at the altar of friendship") strangely ignores Tacitus' reference to an altar to Amicitia. For references to cultic honors given to Amicitia in the fourth century AD, see Symmachus, *Ep.*. 1.59, 4.59, 5.68, 7.60, 9.149; Auson. *Epicedion in patrem* 2.22, *Eclogae* 1.2.31, with discussion at Pizzolato 1993, pp. 204–213 (seeing an emphasis on *amicitia* as an assertion of continuity with the pagan past in a period of profound transition).

Valerius ends his collection of narratives of friendship with one of the few references to his own life scattered throughout his nine books, citing his *amicitia* with Sextus Pompeius, consul of AD 14 and friend of the poet Ovid as well. The moment is given further emphasis by the fact that Valerius departs from his established structure. After having moved from Roman to foreign examples, he brings us back to Rome with an eloquent tribute to his recently deceased friend, expressing the hope that he will not be too bold if he casts himself as Hephaestion to Pompeius' Alexander. Valerius' description of their relationship is short on detail but charged with key words. Pompeius deserves to be cited among the paragons of lasting and benevolent friendship (*constantis et benignae amicitiae exempla*); his attitude toward Valerius was comparable to that of a father delighting in his son's successes; his friendship brought benefit to Valerius, socially and financially, and he supported Valerius' studies. The chapter ends, however, on a rather ominous note, thereby reminding us that *amicitia* was not always a matter of untempered delight. Valerius' friendship with this powerful man had provoked mutterings of envy, his loss expressions of satisfaction, and Valerius caps off some brief meditations on the terrible power of malevolence with a consolation and threat: The mutability of human fortune will be his avenger.[21]

Valerius' collection of exemplary narratives alludes to a number of ideals, and in the process to a proverbial expression or two. Proverbs on *amicitia* are, of course, particularly significant for a reading of Roman friendship. Many of them have equivalents and some of them their origin in Greek idealizing about *philia*, but as a cluster of ideals they are firmly rooted in Rome and they point to a set of ideals to which we will repeatedly be coming back. One rather cynical saying, attributed to the Greek philosopher Bias, soundly rejected by Cicero's Laelius, but quoted with approval by Aulus Gellius, draws one consequence: It is well to love one's friends in the awareness that one day they may be one's enemies.[22] True

---

[21] Val. Max. 4.7.ext.2b. *cuius in animo velut in parentum amantissimorum pectore laetior vitae meae status viguit ... a quo omnium commodorum incrementa ultro oblata cepi, per quem tutior adversus casus steti, qui studia nostra ductu et auspiciis suis lucidiora et alacriora reddidit. itaque pavi invidiam quorundam optimi amici iactura ... optima vindex insolentiae varietas humanae condicionis viderit.* The only concrete fact we have about Valerius Maximus' life is, as it happens, that he accompanied Pompeius to Asia perhaps in AD 24/25, and that they stopped along the way at Ceos, where he witnessed the suicide of an old woman (Val. Max. 2.6.8). For Sextus Pompeius, cf. Ov. *Pont.* 4.1.

[22] Gellius quotes with approval a line from Publilius Syrus' first-century BC *Mimi* to this effect (*ita amicum habeas, posse ut [facile] fieri hunc inimicum putes*) as one of several *sententiae ... lepidae et ad communem sermonum usum commendatissimae* (Gell. *NA* 17.14.3; also quoted at Macrob. *Sat.* 2.7.11; cf. Gell. *NA* 1.3.30: *hac itidem tenus oderis, tamquam fortasse post amaturus*). The view

friends, as opposed to their fair-weather counterparts, will prove themselves in difficult circumstances.[23] True friendships last forever, while enmities are passing.[24] Friends share everything (*communia esse amicorum inter se omnia*), including their wishes and desires (*idem velle*).[25] Sometimes they even share their home, whether with others or not, full-time or not, whether as *contubernales* or not.[26] Key to idealized *amicitia* was the concept of *fides*, trustworthiness, fidelity, or integrity – of fundamental importance to a wide range of Roman social relations – and the etymologically related concept of the *foedus*, the pact or agreement.[27] Because

is rejected (and the attribution to Bias questioned) at Cic. *Amic.* 59: *negabat ullam vocem inimiciorem amicitiae potuisse reperiri quam eius qui dixisset ita amare oportere, ut si aliquando esset osurus.* Latin proverbs and some of their Greek equivalents are conveniently gathered in Otto 1890, supplemented by Häussler 1968.

[23] Cic. *Amic.* 64 (quoting Ennius): *amicus certus in re incerta cernitur*; similar expressions at Plaut. *Epidicus* 113; Publilius Syrus 42 (*amicum an nomen habeas, aperit calamitas*); Hor. *Sat.* 2.8.73; Petron. *Sat.* 61; Sen. *De moribus* 51 (*amicos secundae res parant, adversae certissime probant*). For the "fair-weather friend" and variants, see Plaut. *Stich.* 521–522 (*si res firma est, <item> firmi amici sunt; sin res laxe labat, / itidem amici conlabascunt; res amicos invenit*); Hor. *Carm.* 1.35.26; Ov. *Tr.* 1.5.27ff., 1.8.10, 1.9.5, *Pont.* 2.3.10 and 23, 3.2.8, 4.3.7; Phaedrus 3.91; Val. Max. 4.7.init.; Petron. *Sat.* 38 (*ubi semel res inclinata est, amici de medio*), 80; Sen. *Ep.* 9.9 (*hae sunt amicitiae quas temporarias populus appellat; qui utilitatis causa assumptus est tamdiu placebit quamdiu utilis fuerit*); Fronto, *Ad Pium* 3 (*numquam ita animatus fui, imperator, ut coeptas in rebus prosperis amicitias, siquid adversi increpuisset, desererem*).

[24] Cic. *Amic.* 32 (*verae amicitiae sempiternae sunt*), *Rab. Post.* 32 (*neque me vero paenitet mortalis inimicitias, sempiternas amicitias habere*), Livy 40.46.12 (*in proverbium venit amicitias immortale, <mortales> inimicitias debere esse*), on *inimicitiae* alone Sen. *Controv.* 5.2, Quint. *Decl.* 9.14.

[25] Ter. *Ad.* 802–803 (*nam vetus verbum hoc quidemst, / communia esse amicorum inter se omnia*; Donatus comments: *inter Pythagoreos ortum dicitur*), Cic. *Off.* 1.16.51 (*in Graecorum proverbio*), Cic. *Verr.* 2.36.89, Sen. *Ben.* 7.4.1, 7.12.1–5, *Ep.* 6.3, 48.2–3, Ps.-Publil. Syr. 203 (*multa cui hominis, illi amici cuncta sunt communia*), Mart. 2.43.1 with Williams 2004 ad loc. According to Asconius Pedianius's *Vita Vergilii*, Virgil quoted the saying frequently (*illudque Euripidis antiquum saepe usurpabat*, τὰ τῶν φίλων κοινά, *communia amicorum esse omnia*). For *idem velle* (sometimes expanded by *atque idem nolle*) see Cic. *Planc.* 2.5; Sall. *Cat.* 20.4, *Iug.* 31.14; Sen. *Ep.* 20.5, 109.16; Sil. Ital. 9.406; Apul. *De dog. Plat.* 2.24; Min. Fel. 1.3. The phrase is particularly common in medieval literature (see Häussler 1968, p. 130).

[26] Cf. Cic. *Amic.* 15 (*et domus fuit et militia communis*), 103 (*una domus erat, idem victus isque communis*); the epitaph for Allia Potestas discussed in Chapter 2 (*CIL* 6.37965.30: *una domus capiebat eos unusque et spiritus illis*); Fronto, *Amic.* 1.1.2 (on Sulpicius Cornelianus, an *amicus* he is recommending): *habitavimus una, studuimus una, iocum seriumque participavimus.* For the phrase *vivere cum* see Chapter 1, p. 109. The term *contubernium* describes a range of more or less formal arrangements in which two men share, for a time, their lives and perhaps their homes, especially in connection with military training (Lendon 2006) or oratorical apprenticeship (Champlin 1980, pp. 45–46). The term also describes the conjugal relationship between a man and a woman who could not or did not wish to enter into full *conubium*; see Chapters 1 and 4.

[27] For *fides* see Hellegouarc'h 1963, pp. 23–40, Freyburger 1986 (especially pp. 177–185), Verboven 2002, pp. 39–41; in connection with Rome's foreign relations, Gruen 1982, Nörr 1991. For *foedus*, cf. Sall. *Iug.* 104 (*foedus et amicitia*), Livy 42.12 (*ad scribendum amicitiae foedus*), Tac. *Ann.* 2.58 (*amicitiam ac foedus memoraturos*). Kent 2009, p. 9, describes a similar pattern in Renaissance Florence: "Economic and business transactions – loans, partnerships, and credit – depended, like friendship, on trust (*fede, fiducia*), and trust depended on the existence of personal ties between the parties."

of this foundation of trust, one can speak to one's friend with complete candor and can count on his frank advice in turn, for he is no empty flatterer.[28] This frankness of friendship might include open expressions of anger (in a self-pitying remark quoted by Suetoniu Augustus was said to have exclaimed, after he had more or less directly driven his friend Gallus to suicide, that he was the only man who could not be as angry with his friends as he wished), but we also find voices urging moderation in this as in all things.[29]

Subsuming and summarizing all of this is one of the most persistent and memorable of ideals about *amicitia*: One's friend is another self (*alter ego, alter idem*).[30] The Latin adjective *alter* ("the other of two") points to a bond that joins precisely two individuals, and in perhaps the grandest of all idealizations, a pair of friends could be imagined as one soul divided between two bodies. Consequently one friend might refer to the other as "part of my soul," "half of my soul," or even "the greater part of my soul," peculiar phrases for many modern readers, who will be inclined to associate them with the relationship between spouses rather than friends.[31]

---

[28] Cf. Cic. *Amic.* 44, 88–100 (91: *monere et moneri proprium est verae amicitiae*), Hor. *Sat.* 1.4.130–133 (*liber amicus*), Sen. *Epist.* 3; Habinek 1990, Fitzgerald 1996, Fürst 1996, pp. 216–222.

[29] Suet. *Aug.* 66.2: *quod sibi soli non liceret amicis quatenus vellet irasci.* Augustus' remark is called "somewhat hypocritical" by Hollis 2007, p. 228, and "somewhat disingenuous" by Cairns 2006, p. 74. Horace ironically alludes to his own tendency to become angry with his friends at *Epist.* 1.8.9 (*fidis offendar medicis, irascar amicis*) and in a poem addressed to Florus (*bono claroque fidelis amice Neroni*) asks him if, as a matter of principle, he is forgiving to his friends (*Epist.* 2.2.210: *natalis grate numeras? ignoscis amicis?*). In a listing of components of the happy life (*vita beata*) Martial juxtaposes a pointedly qualified "careful directness" with "friends who are one's equal" (Mart. 10.47.7: *prudens simplicitas, pares amici*).

[30] Cic. *Amic.* 23 (*verum enim amicum qui intuetur, tamquam exemplar aliquod intuetur sui*), 80 (*tamquam alter idem*); Cic. *Fam.* 7.5.1 (to Caesar): *vide quam mihi persuaserim te me esse alterum*; Cic. *Fam.* 3.6.2 (about L. Clodius, to Ap. Claudius Pulcher): *hominem ita tibi coniunctum ut mihi cum illo cum loquerer tecum loqui viderer*; *Att.* 3.15.4, 4.1.7; Val. Max. 4.7.ext.2a (Alexander and Hephaestion): *et hic Alexander est.* Cf. Arist. *EN* 9.4.6 ἔστι γὰρ ὁ φίλος ἄλλος αὐτός.

[31] Cic. *Amic.* 81 (*paene unum ex duobus*), 92 (*unus quasi animus fiat ex pluribus*); *Off.* 1.56; Hor. *Carm.* 1.3.8 (of Virgil): *animae dimidium meae* (much quoted in medieval literature, see Sutphen 1901, p. 134); *Carm.* 2.17.5 (of Maecenas): *meae partem animae* (with Porphyrio ad loc.: *ex illa amicitiae definitione, qua dicunt amicitiam animam unam esse et duo corpora*); Ov. *Met.* 8.406 (Theseus to Pirithous: *o me mihi carior pars animae meae*; *Anth. Lat.* 443 SB (*nunc pars optima me mei reliquit, / Crispus, praesidium meum, voluptas … / plus quam dimidium mei recessit*); Rut. Namat. *De reditu suo* 1.178–179: *invitum tristis tandem remeare coegi; / corpore divisos mens tamen una manet* (Rutilius invokes a few more ideals in his description of this friend, Rufius Volusianus, at 1.425–428: *exornent virides communia gaudia rami: / provecta est animae portio magna meae. / sic mihi, sic potius, placeat geminata potestas: / per quem malueram, rursus honore fruor*; and describing yet another friend, he writes at 1.493–494: *Victorinus enim, nostrae pars maxima mentis, / congressu explevit mutua vota suo*); Aug. *Conf.* 4.6.11 (*nam ego sensi animam meam et animam illius unam fuisse animam in duobus corporibus*); and elsewhere. A scholiast on Lucan 5.768 notes the similarity to the language of erotic and conjugal relations: *antiqui dicebant duos amicos sive coniuges invicem amantes unam habere animam.* Ovid's Narcissus, burning with

Not only, as we will see in Chapter 3, does the poet Horace use this language to describe his friend and supporter Maecenas, but the two illustrate the kinds of eloquent deeds that might accompany grandiose words about friendship. Suetonius' biography records that, as he neared death, Maecenas commended Horace to Augustus with a phrase that appealed to the ideal of *alter ego* ("Be mindful of Horace as you are of me") and that when, less than three months later, Horace followed his friend, the two found their final resting-places in adjacent tombs on the Esquiline in Rome.[32] We will be seeing that this famous pair of friends was hardly exceptional.

In short, a set of textual and cultural practices endowed Roman friendship with a value that it is hard to overestimate. Indeed, it is a commonplace of historical narratives that in Roman as in Greek cultural traditions, personal friendship occupied the central, honored position in idealizing discourse that later, Christian phases in the Western tradition gave to universal human love (*agape* or *amor proximi*) on the one hand, romantic love within the context of a married couple on the other.[33] How, then, does friendship compare to other bonds within the Latin textual tradition? In Laelius' enthusiastic words quoted above, the gods have given us no greater blessing than friendship: not marriage, not children. What indeed of kinship, that quintessential *relationship*? As we have seen, Valerius Maximus introduces his exemplary narratives of friendship – coming directly after those illustrating conjugal love – with the assertion that the bond of *amicitia* is in no way inferior to that of blood, and that friendship even surpasses kinship to the extent that it is a matter of choice. And what of marriage, that building-block of social structure? The social function of Roman marriage – quite independently of how people may have lived it – was to create legitimate children, transmit property to the

---

passion for his own image, and thus a striking incarnation of the ideal of the *alter ego*, exclaims: *nunc duo concordes anima moriemur in una* (Ov. *Met.* 3.473).

[32] Suet. *Vita Hor.: Maecenas quantopere eum dilexerit satis testatur illo epigrammate … sed multo magis extremis iudiciis tali ad Augustum elogio: "Horati Flacci ut mei esto memor" … humatus et conditus est extremis Esquiliis iuxta Maecenatis tumulum.* West 1998, p. 128, suggests that Horace was "perhaps … like Sir Albert Moreton's wife in Wotton's epitaph: *He first deceas'd; she for a little tri'd / To live without him; liked it not, and di'd.*"

[33] Overviews of early Christian ideals of friendship, especially in contrast with Greek and Roman traditions, include Lombardi Vallauri 1974, pp. 81–170 (contrasting "il primato dell'amicizia" in the Greek and Roman world and "il primato della carità" in the Christian world), Pizzolato 1993, pp. 215–338, Fitzgerald 1996, Konstan 1997, pp. 149–173. An incisive formulation from Aelred of Rievaulx (*De spiritali amicitia* 289) offers a suggestive contrast to the Roman idealization of the pair of friends: *ecce ego et tu, et spero quod tertius inter nos Christus sit.* The presence of a third party in an idealized friendship – and one who is divine at that – would have struck most Romans as incomprehensible.

next generation, and forge links between families. Marriage was not trad-itionally described as the unique locus of a special type of love between two individuals: that was a function of, precisely, friendship.[34] Indeed, there is a noticeable tendency throughout the Latin textual tradition to idealize friendship more highly than marriage, and in doing so to use imagery familiar from later celebrations of romantic love and marriage. The motif of the friend as *alter ego*, for example, corresponds to modern idealizing of one's spouse or partner as "my other half" (or the even more self-effacing "better half"), yet nowhere in surviving ancient texts is it applied to husbands and wives. On the other hand, remarks to the effect that two people are "just friends," or on the contrary "more than friends," so frequently heard today, find no equivalent in the Latin textual trad-ition. The implicit devaluation of friendly as opposed to romantic or mar-ried love would have struck most Romans as perverse; and what could be *more* than friendship?

THE PROBLEM OF DEFINITION

Roman friendship, then, was represented as one of the most richly reward-ing and deeply meaningful of interpersonal relationships, capable of being valued and idealized more highly than marriage or kinship. But what exactly was it? Scholars have long debated whether, for example, *amici-tia* was in essence a politically or otherwise useful connection with no necessary emotional content, or else an emotionally significant relation-ship based on affection whose language could euphemistically be *applied* to political alliances or other interpersonal relationships openly based on utility and advantage. I will be arguing below that such antitheses are false, and in any case the undeniable fact is that relationships given the label *amicitia* can and do include both types, but there is a larger point at stake. What does it mean to ask what friendship means?

The first chapter of Derrida's *Politics of Friendship*, reading Montaigne reading Cicero, observes that the problem of "naming, enumerating, counting" has vexed Western philosophizing on friendship from the beginnings. It is easy to understand why. Since friendship neither neces-sarily flows from nor is determined by biology, marriage or membership in some predetermined social group, anxieties of definition recur: Who

---

[34] Typically enough, Cicero refers to marriage as the *prima societas* among human beings, but describes it as being based not on affection or love but on the tendency of living things to repro-duce themselves (*Off.* 1.54). For a thorough study of Roman marriage, see Treggiari 1991.

is a friend? Who are *my* friends? Philosophers, psychologists, sociologists, anthropologists, and historians have formulated definitions and minimum standards, but none has found universal acceptance.[35] And so there have been attempts at definition by exclusion; if one cannot arrive at a satisfactorily comprehensive description of what friendship is, one can insist on what it is not. It is not the love between spouses; not sexual love; not the love between parents and children; not the undifferentiated love of their fellow humans that Christians are called to; not mere companionship.[36] Derrida's own response is to appeal to paradox and aporia, structuring his reflections around an often-quoted saying: "O my friends, there is no friend." Where does the phrase come from? Derrida cites Montaigne, who (in a sentence added only to his third edition of his essay on *Amitié*) describes the phrase as "le mot qu'Aristote avait très familier" – citing, however, not Aristotle himself but Erasmus, and in fact the phrase is nowhere found in the extant Aristotelian corpus. Instead, we find the philosopher quoting with approval a saying to the effect that "he who has many friends has no friend" as part of his argument in favor of restricting the best kind of *philia* to a small number of friends.[37] At some point in the tradition, it would seem, the key adjective "many" dropped

---

[35] Consider the selection offered by Fehr 1996, p. 7. Although these are implicitly proposed as definitions with a potentially universal validity, interrogation of their key terms reveals the contingency and partiality of each, and the remarkable range itself illustrates the difficulty of the very undertaking of definition. (1) "People who spontaneously seek the company of one another; furthermore, they seek proximity in the absence of strong social pressures to do so"; (2) "Voluntary interdependence between two persons over time, that is intended to facilitate social-emotional goals of the participants, and may involve varying types and degrees of companionship, intimacy, affection, and mutual assistance"; (3) "Someone who likes and wishes to do well for someone else and who believes that these feelings and good intentions are reciprocated by the other party"; (4) "A relationship involving voluntary or unconstrained interaction in which the participants respond to one another personally, that is, as unique individuals rather than as packages of discrete attributes or mere role occupants"; (5) "An intimate, personal, caring relationship with attributes such as reciprocal tenderness and warmth of feeling; reciprocal desire to keep the friendship; honesty and sincerity; trust; intimacy and openness of self; loyalty; and durability of the relationship over time."

[36] This last contrast informs the rhetoric of an unlikely pair of thinkers: Compare Nietzsche, *Also sprach Zarathustra*, "Vom Freunde" ("Es gibt Kameradschaft: möge es Freundschaft geben!") with Lewis 1960, p. 78 ("Many people when they speak of their 'friends' mean only their companions").

[37] In his biography of Aristotle (21), Diogenes Laertius reports that Favorinus says that Aristotle frequently said … what? The main manuscripts of Diogenes indeed give the words "O friends, there is no friend (ὦ φίλοι, οὐδεὶς φίλος)," but already in the sixteenth century Casaubon emended this to the equally paradoxical but crucially different "He who has friends has no friend (ᾧ φίλοι οὐδεὶς φίλος)," and Marcovich's 1999 Teubner takes the next step by inserting an adjective: "He who has *many* friends has no friend (ᾧ πολλοὶ φίλοι οὐδεὶς φίλος)." Marcovich justifies the further emendation by pointing out that, as Diogenes Laertius himself notes, in the seventh book of "the Ethics" (i.e. the *Eudemian Ethics*) we find Aristotle citing with approval a saying to the

out and, by means of a minor but crucial change in the Greek text, from "he who has many friends has no friend" arose the saying "O friends, there is no friend" as well as its evidently false attribution to Aristotle. And so, Derrida writes, "like a renowned filiation, an origin thus nicknamed seems, in truth, to lose itself in the infinite anonymity of the mists of time," and his own sometimes misty reflections on the paradoxical phrase contribute to the continued survival of this elusive evocation of the impossibility of defining friendship.[38]

Still, one might object, some Roman writers do offer definitions of *amicitia*, and they must have known what they were talking about. Yet – a point to which we will return – it is an axiom of interpretive anthropology that observations on a culture's workings by members of the culture itself are often skewed, sometimes downright misleading. And, as it happens, those few attempts at definition found in surviving Latin texts are all demonstrably partial, responding to specific argumentative strategies or philosophical commitments. In one of his early works of rhetoric, for example, Cicero cites *amicitia* as an example of "that which contains an element of utility (*utilitas*) but which we nonetheless call honorable (*honestum*)," and proposes a concise definition:

voluntas erga aliquem rerum bonarum illius ipsius causa, quem diligit, cum eius pari voluntate (Cic. *Inv.* 2.166)

[Friendship is] the goodwill that one feels toward someone, for the benefit of the person for whom one has affection, joined with an equal goodwill on his part.

Yet this definition is accompanied by the acknowledgment that there are different types of *amicitia* and varying understandings among Romans of its benefits:

effect that he who has many friends has no friend (1245b20–21: καὶ τὸ ζητεῖν ἡμῖν καὶ εὔχεσθαι πολλοὺς φίλους, ἅμα δὲ λέγειν ὡς <u>οὐθεὶς φίλος ᾧ πολλοὶ φίλοι</u>, ἄμφω λέγεται ὀρθῶς).

[38] Montaigne, *De l'amitié*, citing Erasmus, *Apophthegmata* 7, *Aristoteles Stagirites* 28; Derrida 1997, p. 2. Further complicating the story is the playfully vague attribution placed in the mouth of Johnson by Boswell in his *Life of Johnson*: "An old Greek said, He that has *friends* has no *friend*." The saying is characteristically overturned by Nietzsche, *Menschliches, Allzumenschliches* 1.376: "'Freunde, es gibt keine Freunde!' so rief der sterbende Weise; / 'Feinde, es gibt keinen Feind!' ruf ich, der lebende Tor." Pizzolato 1993, p. viii, begins with "l'impossibilità del mondo antico di pervenire a una definizione comune, per quanto minimale, dell'amicizia." Similarly, MacFaul 2007 begins his discussion of male friendship in Shakespeare with a quotation from *As You Like It* ("Most friendship is feigning") and the following remarks: "The aphorism contains a deeper truth – that friendship is a *fictional* relationship, artificial rather than natural, despite Humanist attempts to make it into the most natural of human relationships ... The Humanist ideology of friendship tries to make friendship the most important thing in the world; the fact that it cannot ever really be the centre of the world – after all, it can hardly even be defined – enables the emergence of a new way of looking at individuality in the literature of this period."

ne forte qui nos de omni amicitia dicere existimant reprehendere incipiant. quamquam sunt qui propter utilitatem modo petendam putant amicitiam, sunt qui propter se solum, sunt qui propter se et utilitatem. quorum quid verissime constituatur, alius locus erit considerandi. nunc hoc sic ad usum oratorium relinquatur, utramque propter rem amicitiam esse expetendam. (Cic. *Inv.* 2.167)

I say this so that those who think I am speaking about every kind of friendship may not start criticizing me. There are those who think that friendship is to be sought only on account of its usefulness; others who think it is to be sought only for its own sake; others who think both. The question of which of these comes closest to the truth will be treated somewhere else. For now, though, as far as oratorical practice goes let us leave the matter like this: that friendship is to be sought for both reasons.

This is not a philosophical treatise but a work on rhetoric, and the question of which of these understandings has the greatest claim on truth (*quid verissime constituatur*) is left open. Cicero returns to it years later in the form of the *De amicitia*, where we find Laelius' definition quoted earlier.

est enim amicitia nihil aliud nisi omnium divinarum humanarumque rerum cum benevolentia et caritate consensio, qua quidem haud scio an excepta sapientia nihil melius homini sit a dis immortalibus datum. (Cic. *Amic.* 20)

Friendship is nothing other than agreement in all matters, divine and human, joined with goodwill and affection. Besides wisdom, I think the immortal gods have given humanity nothing better.

Laelius' language is perceptibly extreme, simultaneously totalizing (consider the adjective *omnium* and the polar expression *divinarum humanarumque*) and specific to his own relationship with the recently departed Scipio, whose qualities he summarizes in the texts' climactic moments with language that points back to his earlier definition.[39] Furthermore, when Laelius assigns friendship second place among the gods' blessings *after wisdom*, he reveals his cards. He is philosophizing, and indeed his stepson Fannius praises him as a man uniquely qualified to be called *sapiens*, on a par with Socrates himself (7). Throughout this text, Laelius' argumentative strategy is distinctly polemical, insisting on its version of *vera amicitia* and firmly rejecting others, especially Epicurean (e.g. at 56–60).[40]

---

[39] Cf. Cic. *Amic.* 103: *equidem ex omnibus rebus, quas mihi aut fortuna aut natura tribuit, nihil habeo quod cum amicitia Scipionis possim comparare: in hac mihi de re publica consensus, in hac rerum privatarum consilium, in eadem requies plena oblectationis fuit. numquam illum ne minima quidem re offendi, quod quidem senserim; nihil audivi ex eo ipse, quod nollem.*

[40] The bibliography on Cicero's *De amicitia* is vast; especially relevant are Steinmetz 1967, Fraisse 1974, pp. 388–413, Heldmann 1976, Habinek 1990, Powell 1990, 1995.

Finally, another definition of *amicitia* comes from a very different context indeed, that of jurisprudential writing. The *Digest* quotes the following from the second book of the *Sententiae* of Paulus:

amicos appellare debemus non levi notitia coniunctos, sed quibus fuerint [in] iura cum patre familias honestis familiaritatis quaesita rationibus. (*Digest* 50.16.223.1)

We should not call *amici* those who are connected by a superficial acquaintance, but rather those who have privileges in connection with one's *paterfamilias*, acquired through honorable means of association.

This too is an explicitly prescriptive attempt at limiting actual usage (*appellare debemus*) and does not attempt to cover the entire range of relationships which in real life were called *amicitia*. Indeed, as the reference of a connection with the *pater familias* suggests, Paulus' words probably were part of a discussion of the guardianship (*tutela*) of minors and the role of friends.[41]

These attempts at definition remind us of a larger methodological point as we read Roman friendship. We must always be sensitive to distinctions between prescriptive and descriptive language, between ideal and practice, and we must always keep in mind the unique status of philosophical inquiry, with its frequent self-authorizing claims on truth. In her discussion of the differences between philosophical doctrine and popular ethics, Teresa Morgan cites the example of friendship: "For an Aristotelian, for instance, friendship comes in three kinds – that of pleasure, use and virtue – and only the last is really good. In popular sayings and stories, all kinds of friendship count as good."[42] Yet there is a long tradition in classical scholarship of privileging philosophy. A remark from a Ciceronian courtroom speech is, for example, dismissed as hyperbolic and oversimplified, and it is claimed that texts like these, conditioned by the argumentative

---

[41] For discussion of this difficult passage see Rundel 2005, pp. 201–203. The manuscript reading *in iura* is hard to construe and Mommsen proposed emending to *vincula*; Michel 1962, pp. 530–531, argues for deleting *in*, and notes that chapters 27–30 of the second book of Paulus' *Sententia* have to do with *tutela*. For *amicitia* and Roman law, see Albanese 1962 and 1963, Michel 1962, Lombardi Vallauri 1974, Palma 1988. For the possibility of inheriting an *amicitia* from one's father, see Michel 1962, pp. 531–532.

[42] Morgan 2007, pp. 334–335. For reasons that will become clear, I prefer emphasizing the distinction between types of *text* to positing distinctions in social standing. In recent scholarly writing the latter is often expressed by means of the contrast between "elite" vs. "non-elite" (e.g. Burton 2004 on *amicitia* in Plautus), but the imprecision of the terms is at times pressing. Slaves, one might think, were distinctly "non-elite," but can one really say that of Cicero's slave Tiro? Among those who dedicated epitaphs commemorating *amici* – as we will see, they range from slaves to consuls – where do we draw the line between "elite" and "non-elite"? Arguably the very fact that they commissioned epitaphs places all of them in an "elite" category. And what about those who *read* these epitaphs, or the varied audiences to whom Plautus' comedies spoke?

needs of the moment, must be approached with greater caution than those which, like *De amicitia*, are the fruit of "deeper philosophical reflection."[43] Yet philosophical treatises can be just as partial, tendentious, and conditioned by specific needs as are courtroom speeches. Indeed, another scholar evaluates the difference between Cicero's *De amicitia* and his letters in precisely the opposite way, arguing that because the former is not concerned with the varied day-to-day realities of interpersonal relationships, it never attains a certain "depth of analysis."[44] In short, as we read *amicitia* in and across the range of surviving Latin texts, there is *a priori* no reason to assign more interpretive weight to any single writer or genre, not even philosophy. Texts like Cicero's *De amicitia*, Valerius Maximus' *Dicta et facta memorabilia*, or Seneca's *Epistulae morales*, or poetic celebrations of the joys of friendship such as those found in Catullus, all make for impressive and memorable reading, but they are only one part of a larger, more varied and nuanced picture.[45]

Although I am urging skepticism about the possibility of knowing what *amicitia* "really was," there clearly were relationships which could be described with the word and which were capable of the kinds of idealization described above, and those which were not. In the surviving textual tradition an identifiable cluster of words and concepts, many of which could also be associated with other kinds of interpersonal connection (such as patronage), gravitate toward *amicitia* and suggest some characteristic qualities. Along with the proverbial expressions surveyed above, the following motifs point to *amicitia* and have the potential of functioning as a synecdoche for it: trustworthiness or faithfulness (*fides*), a self-perpetuating cycle of favors given and owed and influence dispensed (*beneficia, officia, merita, gratia*), goodwill and affection (*voluntas, bene*

---

[43] Rundel 2005, p. 179 (referring to Cic. *Planc.* 5: *vetus est enim lex illa iustae veraeque amicitiae quae mihi cum illo iam diu est, ut idem amici semper velint, neque est ullum amicitiae certius vinculum quam consensus et societas consiliorum et voluntatum*): "Allerdings ist auch hier Vorsicht geboten gegenüber der Übertreibung und Pauschalisierung dieser komprimierten Definition, die im Rahmen einer Prozessrede sicher nicht das Ergebnis einer eingehenden philosophischen Reflexion darstellt."

[44] Combès 1993, p. xlviii: in the letters, "c'est toute une gamme de relations humaines et de sentiments que le traité ne fait qu'entrevoir, parce qu'il se place au-dessus de ces préoccupations et qu'il n'atteint jamais à cette profondeur dans l'analyse."

[45] The point is formulated as a self-evident truth in a study of the notion of friendship in ancient philosophy, but nonspecialists in philosophy do not always recognize its truth. Cf. Fraisse 1974, p. 21: "Le sens d'un mot ne tient pas, en effet, au décret de tel philosophe, et il faut bien de la naïveté pour croire qu'à en forger de nouveaux l'on se fera mieux comprendre. Les Grecs n'avaient pas cette naïveté, et leurs philosophes puisaient dans le répertoire des poètes, des orateurs ou des historiens, qui n'était autre, au départ, que celui de tout le monde."

velle, amor).[46] Since such relationships did not automatically derive from and were not constituted by citizenship, kinship, or marriage, they can be described as chosen or achieved rather than inborn or ascribed. In short, relationships described with the language of *amicitia* came with the presumption of a minimal degree of goodwill and implied the possibility of benefit for one or both parties. They were, finally, opposed to relationships of open enmity or hostility. *Amicitiae* thus invite being read as existing in a dialectical tension with *inimicitiae*; the one kind of relationship is what the other is not, and the presence of one signifies the absence of the other.[47]

GENDER AND SOCIAL STATUS

A recurring motif in the idealizing of Roman friendship is that of *similarity*. Cicero presents it to a jury as a self-evident truth that "similarity in pursuits and nature (*studiorum ac naturae similitudo*)" is a powerful force in the creation of friendship, and a few generations later, writing about Cicero's own relationship with Publius Clodius Pulcher, Velleius Paterculus observes that their enmity was only to be expected. How could two men like these, so dissimilar from each other, ever be friends?[48] The question is natural enough in view of the ideal according to which *amicitia* is one soul in two bodies, the one the *alter ego* of the other. On a rather less lofty level, the notion of similarity regularly expressed itself in terms of gender on the one hand, social ranking on the other. Chapter 1 will consider the role of gender in *amicitia*, but here it will suffice to observe that in Cicero's *De amicitia* friendship is a matter for men alone, and men of the upper classes at that: those who are in the comfortable possession not only of horses and sheep, but of slaves and expensive clothes (55, 62),

---

[46] For discussion of these and related terms see Hellegouarc'h 1963 (*officium* and *beneficium* at pp. 152–170, *gratia* at pp. 202–221), Michel 1962 (*gratia* in Roman law and society; pp. 502–577 on its association with *amicitia*), Moussy 1966, Gelzer 1969, pp. 65–69, Saller 1982, pp. 15–22, Brunt 1988, Konstan 1997, pp. 122–131, Verboven 2002, pp. 35–48. For *amicitia* and *amor* see Chapters 2 and 3 below.

[47] A formal renunciation of friendship (*amicitiam renuntiare*) usually implied a declaration of enmity (*inimicitias denuntiare*): see Hellegouarc'h 1963, pp. 186–187, and Kierdorf 1987. Valerius Maximus 4.2 reports examples of the opposite movement, from *inimicitiae* to *amicitia*. Epstein 1987, citing the "uselessness of any simplistic dictionary definition" of *inimicitiae* (p. 2), points to "certain behavioural patterns among *inimici*" which were "reasonably consistent," central among them "demonstrations of hostility, whether by action or declaration" (p. 3).

[48] Cic. *Clu.* 46: *iam hoc fere scitis omnes quantam vim habeat ad coniungendas amicitias studiorum ac naturae similitudo*; Vell. Pat. 2.45: *quid enim inter tam dissimiles amicum esse poterat?* For Greek idealizing of ὁμοιότης and ἰσότης in connection with φιλία, see Fürst 1996, pp. 236–242.

those for whom the holding of political office and *imperium* is a real pos-sibility, even a birthright (63) – like, of course, Laelius and Scipio them-selves.[49] In other words, in formulations of the opinion that the best kind of friendship exists "between good men (*in bonis* or *inter bonos*)," most influentially in the words of Cicero's Laelius, the generic masculine is not only generic, while the adjective comes with not only ethical but social connotations, as a self-designation for the "better" classes of men.[50]

Ideals of similarity and of friendship "between good men" conspire to locate the idealized form of *amicitia* firmly amongst men of high social status. What of the other end of Roman social structure, the slaves? We will see in Chapter 4 that the speech genre of epitaphs makes ample room for friendship amongst slaves, and even between slaves and free persons. In the various genres of the literary tradition, however, or in the private correspondence of a Cicero, friendship amongst slaves (like marriage and practically any other kind of relationship amongst slaves) barely receives notice, whereas friendship between a slave and his master appears as something of a shocker or even an outright impossibility. Congratulating his brother on having manumitted his loyal slave Tiro, Quintus implies that, for him at least, one cannot normally consider one's slave to be one's *amicus*: "You have preferred that he be our friend rather than our slave" (Cic. *Fam.* 16.16: *nobis amicum quam servum esse maluisti*). Quintus' view does not seem to have been idiosyncratic. The understanding that a mas-ter and slave cannot be *amici* underlies a rhetorical question Pliny poses in his panegyric of Trajan, looking back at the impossibility of establish-ing *amicitiae* in the poisoned environment of his imperial predecessors: "In the emperors' palace only the name of friendship was left, empty

---

[49] Laelius gives advice on how to respond to separation from one's friend when "important affairs" require it (75: *saepe incidunt magnae res ut discedendum sit ab amicis*) and warns that it is difficult to achieve his version of *vera amicitia* amongst those who seek and hold political office: *itaque verae amicitiae difficillime reperiuntur in iis qui in honoribus reque publica versantur. ubi enim istum invenias qui honorem amici anteponat suo?* (64). The very warning is suggestive of the social setting which the text takes for granted; note the "generic" use of the second person.

[50] Cic. *Amic.* 18: *sed hoc primum sentio, nisi in bonis amicitiam esse non posse*; 65: *amicitiam nisi inter bonos esse non posse*; cf. Cic. *Off.* 1.55: *cum viri boni moribus similes sunt familiaritate coniuncti.* See discussion at Hellegouarc'h 1963, pp. 45–46, Narducci 1989. The thought is by no means unique to Cicero. For Greek precedents idealizing *philia* among the *agathoi*, see Plato, *Lysis* 214c–d; Xenoph. *Mem.* 2.6.16; Aristotle, *EE* 7.1235a, *EN* 8.1157a16. In the longest surviving fragment of Lucilius' satires, the speaker explains that key to valor (*virtus*) is being the *amicus* of "good men and good ways" while being hostile (*inimicus*) to bad men and bad ways (Lucil. 1326–1328 Marx: *hostem esse atque inimicum hominum morumque malorum, / contra defensorem hominum morumque bonorum, / hos magni facere, his bene velle, his vivere amicum*). Varying the thought, Sallust has the tribune of the plebs C. Memmius harangue his audience about the ills of noble factions: *eadem cupere, eadem odisse, eadem metuere ... inter bonos amicitia, inter malos factio est* (Sall. *Iug.* 31.14–15 where, pointedly, *mali* refer to Roman nobles).

and scorned. For what friendship could exist betwen them, since some of them considered themselves masters and the others slaves?"[51] By contrast, Seneca's deliberately controversial remarks about slaves in *Epistulae morales* 47 include the suggestion that an upper-class Roman man might look for a friend (*amicus*) not only in the forum and senate house but at home, in other words amongst the slaves of his household too.[52] The suggestion is clearly meant to be surprising, counterintuitive, disturbing. Just as *amicitia* among free men was fundamental to the structures of Roman society, slavery was indispensable for its functioning, and the two must be kept apart.

Co-existing with ideals of similarity, parity, and friendship between the good is, however, an equally longstanding tradition of acknowledging *amicitia* between social unequals.[53] In fact, the existence of such relationships is always and everywhere taken for granted – the question, for those who posed it, was how best to respond to the difference, how best to treat one's socially inferior or superior friend. Some lines from Ennius' *Annales* evoking the friendship between the nobleman Servilius Geminus (probably the consul of 217 BC who fought and died at Cannae) and a man of lower social rank were cited several centuries later by Gellius, held up as being more valuable than any philosophers' words, and praised as being, despite their antiquity, a good guide to the right observance of "the ancient and hallowed principles of friendship" in Gellius' own day.[54]

---

[51] Plin. *Pan.* 85.1–2: *etenim in principum domo nomen tantum amicitiae, inane scilicet inrisumque remanebat. nam qui poterat esse inter eos amicitia, quorum sibi alii domini, alii servi videbantur?*

[52] Sen. *Ep.* 47.16: *non est, mi Lucili, quod amicum tantum in foro et in curia quaeras: si diligenter attenderis, et domi invenies.*

[53] Reali 1997 aims among other things to chart the extent to which "parità" or "dipendenza" characterizes the instances of *amicitia* commemorated in inscriptions from Cisalpine Gaul. His summary (p. 229) reminds us of the fuzziness often characterizing such distinctions: out of 161 inscriptions, he concludes, 77 "alludono ad una parità, vera o presunta," while 25 "fanno pensare alla disparità" (for a sample of 165 inscriptions from the rest of Italy apart from Rome, he reports figures of 82 and 28 respectively).

[54] Gell. *NA* 12.4: *... quo ingenio, qua comitate, qua modestia, qua fide ... amicum esse conveniat hominis genere et fortuna superioris. eos ego versus non minus frequenti adsiduoque memoratu dignos puto quam philosophorum de officiis decreta. ad hoc color quidam vetustatis in his versibus tam reverendus est, suavitas tam inpromisca tamque a fuco omni remota est, ut mea quidem sententia pro antiquis sacratisque amicitiae legibus observandi tenendi colendique sint.* The lines from Ennius (*haece locutu' vocat quocum bene saepe libenter / mensam sermonesque suos rerumque suarum / inpertit ...*; *Annales* 234ff. Vahlen = 268ff. Skutsch) proved to be influential: cf. Hor. *Sat.* 1.3.63ff., 93ff. (Horace and Maeceneas); Hor. *Sat.* 1.5.44; Verg. *Aen.* 11.822; Plin. *Ep.* 2.13.5; Claud. *Stil.* 2.163ff. Gellius reports a tradition of reading the lines as being about Ennius himself in his own relations with social superiors; Skutsch ad loc. takes this to mean M. Fulvius Nobilior in particular. Holford-Strevens 2003, p. 13, and Keulen 2009, pp. 215–221, see another layer of self-referentiality whereby Gellius, too, is casting himself as *amicus minor* or *inferior*, and Keulen suggests one *amicus superior* in particular: Marcus Aurelius' designated successor Commodus.

Cicero's Laelius, for his part, offers advice on how *inferiores* and *superiores amici* should treat each other concluding that it is always an excellent thing to treat one's socially or otherwise inferior *amici* as one's equals while the inferior should not hold his friend's superiority against him.[55] Nearly two hundred years later, one of Fronto's letters gives us a glimpse at how an asymmetrical relationship between high-ranking men might be sympathetically represented. Fronto writes to the Emperor Lucius Verus of his relationship with the younger, junior senator Gavius Clarus. The latter, Fronto explains, performed the duties normally performed by one's *clientes* and freedmen, going so far as to feed Fronto while he was sick. But this, Fronto assures the emperor, was a matter of mutual affection and genuine love (*mutua caritas, amor verus*) and what was a risk on both sides of such socially unequal relationships was, he emphasizes, decidedly not at play: haughty arrogance (*insolentia*) here, unbecoming submissiveness (*adulatio*) there.[56] Here, then, we see an openly asymmetrical relationship proudly described as *amicitia* and distinguished from *clientela* even as it has some of its features, and there is every reason to think Fronto's language typical.

WRITING ABOUT ROMAN FRIENDSHIP: *FAUX AMIS*

I return to the question posed above and deliberately left unanswered: What does it mean to ask what friendship means? What exactly are we aiming to describe and understand: sentiments, actions, expectations, or something else? Is this a matter for history, sociology, psychology, or yet other disciplines?[57] And what are we doing when we *write* about friendship? And when we are writing in English about ancient Roman friendship, do the distances in time, language, and culture make the

---

[55] Cic. *Amic.* 69: *sed maximum est in amicitia parem esse inferiori*; 71: *inferiores non dolere se a suis aut ingenio aut fortuna aut dignitate superari.*

[56] Fronto, *Ad Verum* 2.7: *a prima aetate sua me curavit Gavius Clarus <u>familiariter</u> non modo iis officiis, quibus senator aetate et loco minor maiorem gradu atque natu senatorem probe colit ac promeretur; sed paulatim <u>amicitia</u> nostra eo processit ut neque illum pigeret nec me puderet ea illum oboedire mihi quae clientes, quae liberti fideles ac laboriosi obsequuntur: nulla hoc aut mea insolentia aut illius adulatione, sed mutua <u>caritas</u> nostra et <u>amor</u> verus ademit utrique nostrum in officiis moderandis omnem detrectationem.*

[57] See Konstan 1997, pp. 1–23, for an overview of approaches to the study of ancient friendship; his own subject is "the *history* of the relationship we call friendship in the classical world," whereby "the emphasis ... will fall on *social* aspects of friendship, but account will be taken where possible of alterations in what may be called the *structure of feeling* characteristic of the relationship" (p. 8, emphases added). For his part, Pizzolato 1993, p. ix, describes his undertaking as "un'indagine *storica* su fatti umani costitutivi" (emphasis added), and he periodically appeals to reconstructed or imagined biography: see below, n. 92.

enterprise fundamentally different from writing about friendship, say, in nineteenth-century English novels or contemporary American films? Interpretive anthropology famously distinguishes between two perspectives on culture: one in which we more or less directly reproduce the conceptual and symbolic systems of the culture being studied, speaking to the extent possible in the terms used by its members; and one in which we take a greater distance, using terms and categories meaningful in the first instance to ourselves as external observers and to other members of our own culture. The two perspectives have been given various names: inside vs. outside, first person vs. third person, phenomenological vs. objectivist, cognitive vs. behavioral, emic vs. etic. Clifford Geertz adopts terminology proposed by the psychoanalyst Heinz Hohut: experience-near vs. experience-distant. Classicists and historians often claim to be speaking from an inside or experience-near perspective; symptomatic is the stated goal of interpreting texts "in their own terms," cultures according to their "inner logic."[58] Not only, however, are we not Romans and can never speak or think entirely like them, but it is an anthropological truism that inside, first-person, or experience-near perspectives on a given culture cannot give the whole picture and are sometimes positively misleading. On the other hand, however much they aim to reproduce an internal perspective, scholarly analyses inevitably also appeal to words, concepts, and categories which are not native to Latin literature or Roman culture. Geertz has argued that the difference between the two perspectives is one of degree, not polar opposition, and that modulating back and forth between them is a necessary part of the process of reading and interpreting a culture's scripts.[59] What is crucial, of course, is awareness of the process.

But the methods of interpretive anthropology are applicable to the study of *amicitia* only up to a point, since no one can speak to or observe living Romans, ask them about their ideas of friendship or chart their behaviors. Furthermore, our ability to apply those methods is limited by the body of material available to be read as representing or performing friendship: almost exclusively texts, and texts which represent some

---

[58] E.g. Bray 2003, p. 6: "My task as a historian is to let the past speak in its own terms, not to appropriate it to those of the contemporary world"; p. 83: "The aim of this chapter is to be attentive to those terms: to attempt to recover the inner logic of this language, from within as it were and in its own concerns." Very few analyses of Roman friendship have explicitly appealed to the model outlined above; one exception is Verboven 2002, p. 62 ("emic" and "etic").

[59] Cf. Geertz 1983, p. 57: The challenge is "to produce an interpretation of the way a people lives which is neither imprisoned within their mental horizons, an ethnography of witchcraft as written by a witch, nor systematically deaf to the distinctive tonalities of their existence, an ethnography of witchcraft as written by a geometer."

small portion of the original production in antiquity. We can make of this necessity a virtue, however, by focusing our interpretive energy on *reading texts* rather than on aiming to reconstruct a culture or recreate (let alone understand) individual experience. Consequently, my readings of Roman friendship are inextricably bound up with the specificity of the Latin language, with words like *amicus, sodalis, necessarius,* and *familiaris.* A semiological approach thus suggests itself: approaching *amicitia* as a system of culturally specific signs to be interpreted rather than as a set of social practices from the past to be reconstructed or personal relationships and emotions to be deciphered. In his book *The Friend,* Alan Bray distances himself from what he calls "the historian's judgment … on what consitutes the real facts of the matter and what can be dismissed as mere rhetoric," and proposes instead "to take each of the sources of evidence from the past alike, precisely as rhetoric, and to look for the traces in them – often in the most material sense – of the practice that once produced them."[60] I would go further. The rhetoric of friendship is itself a fact, meaningful from both an experience-near and an experience-distant perspective, and my interest lies less in finding evidence for "the practice that once produced" utterances than in the utterances themselves. And so, unlike Bray, I do not propose to answer such questions as why one person chose to be buried with another, and unlike many of those who have studied Latin inscriptions commemorating friends, I do not aim to get at the "reality" that is "hidden" behind the term *amicus* or explain the "origin" of specific instances of friendship.[61] Rather than dwelling on questions about the nature of the relationship between language and experience, and hypothesizing about the relationship between words and "ultimate reality," of interpersonal relationships or in general, I set myself a more modest and, I would argue, more attainable goal. Instead of trying to get behind the rhetoric, I stay *with* it and examine its workings: always alert to the non-textual, non-linguistic environments in which these texts arose, circulated, and had their meaning, but keeping my focus firmly on language. In short, rather than setting ourselves the goal of deciding what terms like *friend, amicus,* or *amica* mean, not to mention the even trickier abstracts *amicitia* and *amor, love* and *friendship,* or proceeding as if the answer to that question were already agreed upon, I begin

---

[60] Bray 2003, pp. 76 and 204.
[61] Cf. Caldelli 2001, p. 26: "Quale realtà si nasconde allora dietro il termine *amicus/-a,* ammesso che non rimandi alla sfera dell'amicizia?"; Gregori 2001, p. 34: "Difficile spiegare l'origine dell'*amicitia* che aveva unito il console del 154 M. Nonius Macrinus a M. Caecilius Privatus."

with the assumption that such terms, whether in English, Latin, or other languages, are historically and linguistically contingent.

Since I am writing and you are reading in English, and none of us has Latin as a native language, we must also ask the difficult but important questions regarding words, concepts, and experience which lie at the heart not only of post-structuralist and new historicist readings of texts and cultures, but also of the thriving discipline of translation studies.[62] Are we talking about friendship, about *amicitia*, or both? For there is certainly a difference. It has been a principle of linguistics at least since Saussure that the semantic field of any given word in any given language is almost never entirely commensurable with that of the most closely corresponding word in any other language; and it is a post-structuralist axiom that no word in a given language can ever be entirely the same as another in any other language, since each word necessarily contains traces of others in the same language. Problems of "sameness" and "equivalence" across languages are central to the theory and practice of translation, and it has long been recognized that "exploration of the *differences* constitutes one of the most essential contributions of the translator as a mediator between the surface appearance of a word and its semantic, etymological, and cultural weight." In a much-quoted formulation Edward Sapir argues: "No two languages are ever sufficiently similar to be considered as representing the same social reality. The worlds in which different societies live are distinct worlds, not merely the same world with different labels attached."[63] The so-called "Sapir–Whorf hypothesis" has been deeply controversial,[64] but it is worth noting that Sapir himself refers specifically to *social* reality. When the issue at stake is language as it describes neither visible, tangible things like water or trees, nor biological relationships like those between mother and child, but relationships like friendship, the cultural specificity of language clearly plays a significant role. In a far more than superficial sense, *amicitia* cannot be "the same as" friendship, and an *amicus* is not exactly a friend.

One telltale sign of linguistic uniqueness is what theorists of translation call a *lacuna*, the absence in the target language of a direct equivalent

---

[62] English-language overviews include Biguenet and Schulte 1989, Munday 2001, Bassnett 2002, Venuti 2004.

[63] Quotations from Biguenet and Schulte 1989, p. xiv (emphasis added) and Sapir 1956, p. 69. For a brief introduction to "equivalence," a central and unresolved problem in translation, see Bassnett 2002, pp. 30–36.

[64] The validity of Whorf's method and data has been persuasively challenged, and oversimplified versions of the hypothesis have proven to be easy targets, for example the argument that

to a word or expression in the source language. I have already alluded to
a significant lacuna in the Latin language of friendship as compared to
that of English and many other modern languages: There is no trace in
the Latin textual tradition of a phrase comparable to *just friends*, with its
devaluation of friendship in comparison to, say, erotic love. This lacuna
does not mean that no Roman ever valued another relationship more
highly than friendship, but it does reveal a great deal about the linguistic
and conceptual framework available to Roman writers as they represented
interpersonal relationships. Another noticeable lacuna is that there is no
Latin equivalent to the phrase *my best friend*. Again, we can hardly conclude that no Roman ever considered one person in particular to be the
most important or most intimate of those whom he called his *amici*; what
it does suggest is that those writing Latin had no readily available term
to describe such a person. The formula *optimus amicus*, found, as we will
see in Chapter 4, in a number of inscriptions, means not "the best of all
my friends" but rather "the best possible kind of friend," an excellent or
outstanding friend; the closest comparisons are with the equally formulaic *optima coniunx* – not, of course, "best of all my wives" but "best of
wives," or with the phrase *optimus pater*, "my excellent father."[65] Cicero
and Atticus constitute a pair to whom, if to any, the term *best friends*
invites being applied. How did they describe the bond that joined them?
Of course we do not have access to the entire range of labels the two
used to describe each other between themselves or to others, but in surviving letters we find Cicero assuring Atticus that he loves him "like a
brother," and he makes the same point when writing to someone else
about Atticus.[66] As we will see in Chapter 2, this use of the language of
fraternal love is neither idiosyncratic nor insignificant.

It might be argued that there is a denotative core to words like *amicus* and *friend* which is the same across languages and cultures, and that

---

languages actively limit how their speakers conceive reality. Recently, however, a qualified version of this approach to language has been persuasively re-argued. Building on Roman Jakobson's
suggestion that "languages differ essentially in what they *must* convey and not in what they *may*
convey" (Jakobson 1959, p. 236), Deutscher 2010, p. 152, argues that "if different languages influence their speakers' minds in varying ways, this is not because of what each language allows
people to think, but rather because of the kinds of information each language habitually obliges
people to think *about*."

[65] Cf. Cic. *Fam.* 14.4 (Cicero to Terentia from exile): *fidissima atque optima uxor*; Hor. *Sat.* 14.105:
optimus pater.

[66] Cic. *Att.* 1.5: *cura ut valeas, et nos ames et tibi persuadeas te a me fraterne amari*; Cic. *Fam.* 13.1.5:
Pomponium Atticum sic amo ut alterum fratrem. See Konstan 1997, pp. 124–128, and Citroni
Marchetti 2000, pp. 17–24, 193–204, for overviews of their relationship as reflected in their
correspondence.

it is only the words' connotations and associated social configurations which vary. Perhaps. But I am skeptical that the denotation of such words is *entirely* the same (not least because, as we have seen, it is difficult if not impossible to identify a stable and consistent denotative core at all), and in any case the very fact that connotations do vary across languages and cultures means that the words do not "mean" exactly the same thing and thus in an important sense *are* not the same.[67] In this sense, English *friend* is not the same as, for example, German *Freund*, and neither of them is the same as Italian *amico*. The Italian term can be applied to a person with whom one has a loyal and intimate relationship of long standing, but also to a person whom one has only met a few times, but in such a way as to suggest goodwill and some degree of mutual desire to see more of each other. German *Freund* and *Freundin* are significantly weightier, their range of application narrower. The message sent by using these labels is that the relationship is of some duration, highly valued, built on an assumption of mutual loyalty, and is one of a small number, in contrast to the wider circle of *Bekannte*, itself a far less distancing term than English *acquaintances* or Italian *conoscenti*, the distinction between *Freunde* and *Bekannte* being structural to many utterances.[68]

The corresponding adjectives are revealingly different from each other in yet other ways. The adjective *freundlich* may be translated as *friendly* when referring to a person, but not in the phrase *ein freundlicher Tag*, common in weather reports, neither anthropomorphic nor potentially kitschy as *a friendly day* would be in English, but more like *a pleasant day*. Similarly, the letter-closing formula *mit freundlichen Grüßen* cannot be translated *with friendly greetings*. Instead, like *yours sincerely* or *yours truly*, it is fairly high on the scale of formality; indeed one generally does not use the formula with those whom one calls one's *Freunde*, and it frequently

---

[67] See Lyons 1995 for discussion of denotations, connotations, and what it means to identify what a word "means."

[68] Entirely typical is an article in the Berlin *Tagesspiegel* of May 3, 2004, in which one reads that a woman was standing on a certain street "mit zwei Freundinnen und einem Bekannten." Presumably the reporter made the distinction on the basis of the woman's identification of her companions (if not, yet other interesting questions are raised), but the most salient point is that the distinction is natural and important for author and readership of this newspaper article; an English-language article would much more naturally speak of "three friends" than of "two friends and an acquaintance." To be sure, there are far more possibilities in German than the simple dichotomy *Freund/Bekannter* suggests (terms like *(gut) befreundet sein* create a space between the two); and, when pressed to make distinctions, many Italian speakers will narrow the range of *amico*. But the crucial point is that Italian usage begins with a broad concept of *amico* which can, if necessary or desired, be made more specific, whereas German usage begins with a distinctly narrower concept of *Freund*.

closes a letter to someone one has never met. On the other hand – a point to which we will return in Chapter 1 – in certain syntactic or social contexts German *Freund* and *Freundin*, unlike contemporary English *friend* or Italian *amico*, have been lexicalized as utterly non-ironic terms denoting partners in a stable erotic relationship apart from marriage.

I have dwelt on these examples by way of illustrating a point to which many scholarly treatments of *amicitia* pay lip service but whose implications are rarely pursued. In addition to the commonly acknowledged historical and cultural specificities of the concept of friendship, we must always be aware of the *linguistic* factor. However significant any semantic overlaps may be, *amicus* is not and cannot be entirely coextensive in meaning with any word in any other language. This in turn means breaking with the long tradition of more or less explicitly and usually rather unquestioningly equating Latin *amicitia* with Greek *philia*. Classicists have long been aware that the Homeric use of the adjective *philos* (modifying body parts in phrases like "his *philon* heart," translatable not as "dear" but as "one's own") has no parallel in Latin, and that Aristotle uses *philia* to describe a wide range of relationships, some of which, such as that between parent and child, neither Cicero nor any other Latin philosophical writer ever described as *amicitia*.[69] Typical, however, is Fraisse's study *Philia. La notion de l'amitié dans la philosophie antique*. While duly drawing attention to the problem of translation and the specificity of each language, he nonetheless proceeds to use the Greek word as his master term – even in his reading of Cicero's *De amicitia*. But *amicitia* is not the same thing as *philia*. The two words do not have the same set of associations and resonances, let alone denotative range. *Amicitia*, in short, is as uniquely and quintessentially Roman as such concepts as *patria potestas*, *clientela*, or *pietas*.[70]

---

[69] Konstan 1997, p. 9, 67–72, draws attention to the difference between the abstraction *philia* and the concrete noun *philos*, arguing that the latter is much closer to English "friend" than the former is to "friendship"; see pp. 28–31 for the adjectival use in Homer.

[70] Fraisse 1974, pp. 19–20, vs. pp. 393–394: "la fonction conférée à la *philia*, celle de faciliter et d'agrémenter la vie, de lui ménager les plus nombreux et les plus grands avantages, *plurimas et maximas commoditates*" (Cic. *Amic.* 23). To be sure, Cicero's text places itself firmly within, and responds to, a long tradition of Greek philosophizing on *philia*. Yet Fraisse's focus on the philosophical at the expense of the linguistic leads him to a surprising claim: "Il est remarquable cependant que la langue latine ait transposé, en parlant d'*amicitia*, ce que la langue grecque entendait par *philia*, *sans rien ajouter qui provînt de son génie propre*" (p. 441, emphasis added). Attention to the uniqueness of each linguistic system means that my discussion will not devote much attention to Greek-language texts referring to *philia* amongst Romans, from Plutarch to Dio Cassius to inscriptions from the city of Rome in honor of *philoi* (for which see Moretti, ed., IGUR ii.268, 534, 608, 611, 613, 737, 783, 817; iv.1679 [prose]; iii.1143, 1181, 1222, 1274, 1299, 1355, 1358, 1369, 1482; iv.1567 [verse].) I also generally exclude Greek writers like Plutarch and Lucian,

In short, as we exchange linguistic representations of linguistic representations of interpersonal relationships in a cultural tradition other than our own, we must be particularly attentive to language. The words of scholarly readings necessarily come with their own penumbrae of associations, and these are *not exactly* the same as those of the Latin texts being analyzed, or of scholarship written in other languages. When an essay written in German appeals to the "modern sensibility" about "the actual concept of friendship," the unanswered question is whether that "actual concept" – whatever exactly it might be – and the "sensibility" are modern *tout court* or specific to German *Freundschaft.*[71] When an English-language commentary on the *De amicitia* assures its readers that Cicero's "ideal of friendship, affectionate but without misplaced sentiment … contains nothing which a twentieth-century reader would regard as outdated or unfamiliar," that reader would appear to be just as culturally specific as C. S. Lewis' lovers and friends: "Lovers," he writes, "are always talking to one another about their love; friends hardly ever about their friendship"; and "lovers are normally face to face, absorbed in each other; friends, side by side, absorbed in some common interest."[72] Although they invite being read as universally valid statements, formulations like these in fact speak to a specifically English male experience of friendship – taciturn, understated, indirect, shy – which in some other cultural spheres would seem peculiar at best, barely worthy of the name of friendship at worst. Then there is that tempting first-person plural. When scholars argue that *amicitia* is different from "friendship as we know it today,"[73] "friendship as we conceive it" or "in our sense,"[74] "unser Verständnis von Freundschaft,"[75] "quella realtà che noi intendiamo per amicizia,"[76] "l'amitié au sens où nous l'entendons aujourd'hui";[77] when they claim that "we find it difficult to think of them as truly friends"[78] or

---

as much as they have to say about *philoi* and *philia*; by contrast, they figure prominently in Pizzolato's chapter on "l'amicizia nel mondo romano" (Pizzolato 1993, pp. 187–194).

[71] Treue 1972.422: "Für modernes Empfinden gehören derartige Beziehungen kaum unter den eigentlichen Begriff der Freundschaft."

[72] Powell 1990, p. 1; Lewis 1960 p. 73. Cf. Burton 2004, p. 218: "By nature friendships require (particularly at the beginning) constant nurturing by frequent contact and intimacy between the partners." This may or may not be true of "friendship," but is certainly not always true of all relationships between those whom, for example, Italians might call their *amici.*

[73] Kleijwegt 1998, p. 25.   [74] Price 1989, p. 131.

[75] Rundel 2005, p. 163: "das mit unserem Verständnis von Freundschaft wenig korrespondierende Verhältnis römischer *amicitia.*"

[76] Pizzolato 1993, p. 133: "Dai poeti Tibullo e Properzio non viene cantata quella realtà che noi intendiamo per amicizia."

[77] El Murr 2001, p. 29; cf. p. 34: "ce qu'on entend par amitié."

[78] White 1993, p. 13.

that *amicitia* is "a relationship sometimes closer to our notion of political alliance than the affective bond we label friendship,"[79] a question urges itself: Who are "we," speaking in which language and living where?

Unlike many, then, this study consciously avoids drawing contrasts between Roman friendship and "our" understanding of the relationship. For not only the wording of scholarship, but its very methods are at stake. A typical procedure in discussions of ancient friendship is to start with the relevant term in the language in which one is writing and then turn to the ancient material, looking for signs of that to which the modern term refers – duly noting differences between ancient and modern concepts, to be sure, but not taking into account the contingency and particularity of the modern term. An essay on Martial, for example, lays down criteria for "friendship," albeit without specifying the basis on which it does so: "mutual fondness, shared interests and the pleasure of being in each other's company," along with "commitment." Then, reading Martial's poems to or about any given man, the question is posed whether or not "friendship" is at stake in each case, regardless of whether or not Martial calls the man in question his *amicus*. If the relationship does not meet the stated criteria for "friendship" but uses the language of *amicitia*, the "obvious" conclusion is that Martial "deliberately misdirects" his readership. In short, we are told that "allusions to *amicitia* … may not be the product of friendship *per se*" – as if the meaning of "friendship *per se*" were patently clear.[80] To the extent that words like *friendship*, *Freundschaft* and *amicizia* are themselves just as culturally specific as *amicitia*, analyses like these are locked into circularity, perhaps even doomed to failure.[81]

Of course, the problem cannot be entirely circumvented as long as we write in a language other than Latin, and even if we were to write in Latin we would be doing so for a readership whose cultural experiences and memories could not possibly be those of a Cicero or a Martial. But there are ways out of the apparent impasse. One technique is to refrain entirely from translating the nouns *amicitia* or *amicus*, as is widespread practice with a few other terms referring to uniquely Roman social roles, like *princeps*. Another is to render the Latin nouns with "friendship" and "friend"

---

[79] Miller 2004, p. 27.   [80] Kleijwegt 1998, p. 263.

[81] Kent 2009, p. 12, notes the same issue in the scholarly analysis of *amicizia* in Renaissance Florence. Oschema 2007, p. 11, generalizes the point: "Anstatt die Beziehungen der Vergangenheit an einem idealtypisch konstruierten Freundschaftsbegriff zu messen, erscheint es aufschlussreicher, dem diskursiven Gebrauch der Freundschaftsterminologie und den damit verbundenen Praktiken nachzugehen."

but to imply quotation marks around the term on every occasion.[82] In what follows, not least for ease of reading, I combine the two methods: I sometimes leave *amicus* and *amicitia* untranslated but often translate or paraphrase with English "friend" and "friendship" – but always with the implied scare quotes and urging a constantly monitored linguistic self-awareness. Exploring these problems as they relate to *sophia*, *episteme*, and *scientia*, by no means *the same as* "wisdom," "knowledge," and "science" respectively, G. E. R. Lloyd writes:

> Neither modern nor even ancient categories will do precisely for all our purposes. I have argued that in general ancient ones are preferable to modern, but also that it would be absurd to think that we can use the ancient ones entirely to replace our own. Any search for an entirely neutral language in which to report and discuss ancient ideas is, in any case, bound ultimately to fail. But that does not mean that we cannot discuss those ideas at all. Rather, it means that whatever terms we use must be treated as provisional and revisable.[83]

Provisional and revisable – and, I would add, specific to the language in which we are writing.

GENRES AND SPEECH GENRES

Alertness to the polyvalence of language is fundamental to a reading of representations of interpersonal relationships, and one way of managing the deceptive clarity of words is to be attentive to the type of utterance in which they are used. Readings of Latin literature have long done so by appealing to the concept of *genre*. On what basis the genres of that literature are to be defined is a contested question, but generally used labels combine those which we find within the ancient textual tradition itself (such as "epic") with those which we do not (such as "didactic"), making reference to criteria having to do with both form and content. Since my readings of Roman friendship are not limited to the literary tradition, a more fundamental categorization of Latin textuality on the basis of original form suggests itself. Two broad categories emerge. (1) Texts originally written on papyrus rolls or wax tablets and surviving today in manuscript copies. These include the whole range of literary genres, from epic to drama to elegiac poetry, along with the correspondence of

---

[82] The problem persists even when writing in English about nineteenth-century texts written in English. Cf. Luftig 1993, p. ix: "Throughout this book, I could put the word 'friendship' in quotation marks nearly every time I use it; for my object of study is almost always the word 'friendship', rather than some supposed social, historical, or psychological fact it might denote."

[83] Lloyd 1992, p. 576.

figures like Cicero or Pliny, subsequently gathered and circulated; a sub-set particularly relevant to a reading of *amicitia* are the letters written on wooden tablets by soldiers and their wives at the camp at Vindolanda in northern England and still surviving in their original form. (2) Texts carved on bronze tablets or stones set up at tombs, statue bases, building facades and elsewhere ("inscriptions" of a formal nature, announcing laws or commemorating individuals, living or dead), as well as more informal texts painted or scratched on walls and other surfaces ("graffiti," which very often have the functions of sending the message "I was here," or engaging in gossip or dispensing praise).[84]

Does the language of inscriptions bring us closer to historical real-ities or even to "the truth" about Roman friendship than, say, Cicero's *De amicitia* or Catullus' poetry? Or is it the other way around? Mikhail Bakhtin's concept of *speech genres* offers one way of responding to the ques-tion. Responding to the Saussurean concept of the *parole* as freely chosen, individual communication, more or less endlessly permutable recombina-tions of elements within the larger system of the *langue*, Bakhtin argues that individual utterances, whether oral or written, are themselves con-strained by what he calls speech genres: "forms of combination of forms" which are marked in both content and style, by lexical, phraseological, and grammatical means and in their compositional structure. Bakhtin's examples include the following: "short rejoinders of everyday dialogue, everyday narration, writing (in all its various forms), the brief standard military command, the elaborate and detailed order, the fairly variegated repertoire of business documents (for the most part standard), and the diverse world of commentary (in the broad sense of the word: social, pol-itical)" as well as "the diverse forms of scientific statements and all literary genres (from the proverb to the multivolume novel)."[85]

Bakhtin distinguishes between *primary* speech genres of "unmediated speech communion" (e.g. "genres of salon conversation about everyday, social, aesthetic and other subjects, genres of table conversation, intimate conversations among friends, intimate conversations within the family, and so on") and *secondary* or complex speech genres such as "novels, dra-mas, all kinds of scientific research, major genres of commentary." Texts

---

[84] See the Cambridge University Press Online Resource Centre for a collection of photographs of Latin inscriptions commemorating friends in a variety of configurations (www.cambridge.org/gb/knowledge/textbooks/resourcecentre).

[85] See Bakhtin 1986. One challenge in learning to speak a new language is, precisely, acquiring mastery of a range of speech genres: Someone who can read scholarship and give an academic lecture in a foreign language may have great difficulties ordering a meal in a restaurant or nego-tiating a basic telephone conversation.

participating in a secondary speech genre sometimes imitate or reproduce a primary genre, but by virtue of occurring in secondary-genre texts they are no longer primary-genre utterances. The point is illustrated by the informal conversations in Plautine comedy or the distinctly non-literary Latin used by many characters of Petronius' *Satyricon*. These certainly point toward primary speech genres, but the very fact that these are characters in literary texts (the Plautine characters are, after all, speaking in verse) makes these secondary-genre utterances.[86] In the case of Latin, the primary genres of unmediated speech in all its individual and social variety are lost to us, and we can only speculate about the representation of interpersonal relationships in utterances within these genres. Instead, we have access to a wide range of secondary speech genres, from the traditional literary genres (comedy, tragedy, elegy, epic, epistolography, history, oratory, and so on) to the inscriptional texts. The key point is that no one of these speech genres brings us any closer "the truth" about Roman friendship than any other; each gives us a partial view, and precisely for that reason a reading across various speech genres suggests itself and we must be careful not to generalize on the basis of any one genre. As we will see in Chapter 4, for example, freedmen are distinctly overrepresented in Latin epitaphs commemorating *amici*, but we cannot conclude on this basis that friendship was more prevalent or significant to Roman freedmen than it was to others.

Another speech genre important to a reading of Roman friendship is that of the private letter. We will be considering the role of *amicitia* in the the correspondence of Cicero, Pliny, Fronto, and men and women living at Vindolanda in northern England at the beginning of the second century. The letters from Vindolanda remind us of the risks of oversimplifying if we speak of *the* speech genre of, say, "private letters"; much depends on who is writing the letters, to whom, when, and where. The language of the letters of a Cicero or Pliny is significantly different from that of letters written by people living at Vindolanda, some of whom may not have been native speakers of the language (many were Batavians, serving at this outpost on the edge of the Empire). In any case, the Latin of these letters blends literary and poetic features with syntax, vocabulary,

---

[86] Cf. Bakhtin 1986, p. 62: Secondary genres can "absorb and digest various primary (simple) genres that have taken form in unmediated speech communion," but the primary genres are "altered and assume a special character when they enter into complex ones. They lose their immediate relation to actual reality and to the real utterances of others." The English term "*speech* genre" is misleading to the extent that these are not always or only spoken; but the adjective serves to distinguish this concept from the traditional "genres" of literary texts.

and orthography at times radically different from what we find in the literary tradition. Still, thanks to some ancient writers' reflections on letter-writing, we have glimpses at some of the generally valid principles of this speech genre.[87] For example, letters were generally expected to reflect the way one spoke in person (*sermo quotidianus*), their language was to avoid excessive adornment, brevity was a virtue, and their tone was to be adapted to their recipient.[88] A distinction could be made between *epistulae familiares* or *privatae* on the one hand and *epistulae negotiales* or *publicae* on the other (the distinction roughly corresponds to the question of whether the letter was intended to be read just by its recipient or by others as well) and the former type, as the very label *familiares* implies, suggested and was often associated with *amicitia*.[89]

In what ended up being the final phase of their relationship, Cicero charges Marcus Antonius with a violation of a basic principle of both letter-writing and friendship by making public a letter Cicero had sent him privately: letters, Cicero reminds his audience, are "conversations with absent friends" (Cic. *Phil.* 2.7: *amicorum colloquia absentium*; see below, Chapter 3).[90] Even person-to-person conversations, however, are not always transparently truthful, let alone those conducted by means of letters; and while their language may often reflect that of everyday speech

[87] For the role of friendship in Greek and Latin theorizing on letter-writing see Fleury 2006, pp. 16–18, 23–31; for studies of ancient letters see Cugusi 1983, Stowers 1986, Morello and Morrison 2007, Corbinelli 2008, and for an anthology of Greek and Latin letters see Trapp 2003. For the Vindolanda letters, see Bowman and Thomas 1994, 2003, and the internet resource http://vindolanda.csad.ox.ac.uk.

[88] Cic. *Q Fr.* 2.10.1 (*quem ad modum, coram cum sumus, sermo nobis deesse non solet, sic epistulae nostrae debent interdum alucinari*), Sen. *Ep.* 75.1 (*qualis sermo meus esset si una desideremus aut ambularemus, inlaboratus et facilis, tales esse epistulas meas volo, quae nihil habent accersitum nec fictum*), Cic. *Fam.* 9.21.1 (*quid tibi ego videor in epistulis? nonne plebeio sermone agere tecum … epistulas vero cotidianis verbis texere solemus*), Plin. *Ep.* 7.9.8 (*volo epistulam diligentius scribas… pressus sermo purusque ex epistulis petitur*), Quint. *Inst.* 9.4.19 (*est … oratio alia vincta atque contexta, soluta alia, qualis in sermone <et> epistulis …*), Sen. *Ep.* 45.13, Plin. *Ep.* 2.5.13, 3.9.27, Fronto, *M. Caes.* 4.3.8, Julius Victor (*Rhetores latini minores* ed. Halm p. 448.16: *epistola si superiori scribas ne iocularis sit; si pari, ne inhumana; si inferiori, ne superba; neque docto incuriose, neque indocto indiligenter, nec coniunctissimo translatitie, nec minus familiari non amice*). See Cugusi 1983 for a thorough overview and discussion.

[89] See Cugusi 1983, pp. 105–135 for nuancing of these and other distinctions. Cicero's correspondence for one makes it clear that some letters, even though addressed to an individual, were circulated more generally with the letter-writer's approval (Cic. *Att.* 7.17.2, 8.2.1, 8.9.1–2), while others were very much meant to be private. In general, it was recognized that there were *multa genera epistolarum*: Cic. *Fam.* 2.4.1 (to Curio), 4.13.1 (to Figulus), 6.10.4 (to Trebianus).

[90] The concept was clearly not unique to Cicero or his day. In the fourth century AD, the Christian bishop Ambrose writes in one of his own letters that letters can effect the mingling of friends' souls (*Ep.* 47.4: *in quibus (sc., epistolis) inter absentes imago refulget praesentiae et collocutio scripta separatos copulat, in quibus etiam cum amico miscemus animum et mentem ei nostram infundimus*).

(Bakhtin's "unmediated speech communion"), by virtue of being a text written within a defined tradition, a "form of a combination of forms," a letter by definition belongs to a secondary speech genre.[91] To be sure, it is tempting to read a private letter of Cicero's, and especially one from Vindolanda, as more "immediate" and more revealing of the writer's feelings and thoughts than, say, a Horatian ode or a passage from the *Aeneid*, and many readers have precisely that experience.[92] My own readings, however, aim not at a reconstruction of what, for example, Cicero really thought or felt about his friends, but at a reading of what he wrote to and about them.

Scholarly readings of Roman friendship have not made use of Bakhtin's concept of speech genre, but they have generally placed a broader concept of genre at the very center of their analysis. For there is a long tradition of interpreting the Latin literary tradition on the one hand, and the considerable body of epigraphical texts referring to *amici* and *amicae* on the other, in more or less complete isolation from one other, or else of placing one in the center of attention and citing the other by way of comparison or contrast.[93] In what follows, I will be reading these types of Latin textuality *with* rather than against each other, in order to both broaden and complicate prevalent narratives of Roman friendship. To anticipate just one example, we will see in Chapter 1 that the inscriptions use the terms *amicus* and *amica* across distinctions in gender in ways that we would not expect from reading the literary texts alone. Here – quite unlike what we find in the literary tradition – we see women fully integrated into *amicitia*, not only being commemorated in public texts, meant to last, as the friends of other women and of men but arranging burials for and commissioning inscriptions commemorating themselves and others: their husbands, children, freed slaves, but also their friends, both male and female. We will be returning to a remarkable poetic epitaph from Rome, in which

---

[91] See Rosenmeyer 2001 and Gunderson 2007 on the illusion of "epistolary immediacy."

[92] Pizzolato 1993 regularly appeals to a speculative reconstruction of how individual writers personally experienced friendship. Typical are his pages on Virgil's poetry (p. 129: "In realtà ci sono validi motivi per sostenere che l'animo di Virgilio fosse portato ad avvertire l'intensità dell'amicizia") and his contrast between Ovid and Seneca (p. 153: "Se lo si paragona a Seneca, si vede che Ovidio non ha mai realmente interiorizzato o verificato la sua amicizia"). More subtle formulations corresponding to what is essentially the same reading practice appear throughout the pages of scholarship on Greek and Roman friendship.

[93] The essays in Bodel 2001 represent an important step toward bridging the gap between the specialist work of epigraphers and literary, historical, and cultural studies of classical antiquity. On the question of Roman friendship in particular, Brunt 1988, Pizzolato 1993, Konstan 1997, Verboven 2002 make little mention of inscriptions, while Reali 1997 and Caldelli 2001 refer to the literary tradition only in passing, with a strong bias toward philosophical texts.

a certain Aulus Allius commemorates his freed slave Potestas, passionately evoking her loyalty and physical beauty as well as his own devotion
to her: He keeps a portrait of her which will accompany him when he,
one day, joins her in the afterlife (*CIL* 6.37965). This text invites being
read as presenting Allius and Potestas as an erotically bonded couple, like
those who in elegiac poetry are, as we will see, described as consisting of
an *amicus* and his *amica*. Yet the epitaph itself uses none of those labels,
and when it evokes ideals of *amicitia*, it does so in order to describe the
bond that joined two men, one of them probably Allius himself, as part of
a triangle of which Potestas was the apex.

LABELS

One point on which the language of the speech genre of inscriptions seems
sharply distinct from that of the other speech genres to which we have
access is that of vocabulary. We find a set of other terms denoting interpersonal relationships across the Latin textual tradition, and some of them
seem nearly synonymous with each other and with *amicus* and *amicitia*.
But of course there are differences among them. The etymologies themselves suggest distinctions in nuance and connotation: *familiaris* evokes
a sense of belonging to a domestic group (cf. *familia*); *sodalis* suggests a
rather more formal collectivity (cf. *sodalicium, sodalitas*); *necessarius* suggests an obligation incumbent upon both parties (cf. *necesse*); *comes* points
to companionship and shared travels (cf. *co-ire*); and *amicus* itself hints at
an underlying affection (*amor*). While these and other connotational penumbrae always came with the respective words, in speech genres other than
inscriptions these nouns' denotations frequently approach synonymy.[94]

Plautus' comedies and Martial's epigrams, for example, speak of *sodales*
and *amici* often without any obvious distinction, sometimes using the
two words in the same sentence or verse, and *comes* comes close to being a
synonym of *amicus* as well. In a Horatian lyric poem inspired by Alcaeus,
the Greek term *philoi* becomes *sodales* rather than *amici,* and another of
Horace's odes, opening with a ringing celebration of Pompeius as first

---

[94] See Hellegouarc'h 1963, pp. 68–80, on *familiaritas, necessitudo,* and *consuetudo* as "parmi les sub-
stituts les plus courants du mot *amicitia*"; pp. 82–90 for *socius,* pp. 109–110 for *sodalis,* and pp.
56–62 for *comes* (a term around which, he argues, the conceptual distinction between *amicus* and
cliens collapses). For a detailed study of the terms *socius* and *societas* see Wegner 1969, and see
Deniaux 1993, especially pp. 75–108, 135–161, for analysis of Cicero's vocabulary of interpersonal
relationships in the letters of recommendation. Relevant discussions of the mechanisms of synonymy by linguists include Lyons 1995, pp. 60–65, and Murphy 2003.

among his *sodales*, ends with the oft-quoted phrase "it is delightful to go crazy when an *amicus* has returned."[95] Ovid's exile poetry speaks of men, both *amici* and *sodales*, whom he loved like brothers and whose friendship he evokes by means of mythic paradigms to which we will return in Chapter 2.[96] As for *familiaris*: Cicero writes letters of recommendation for men whom he calls *familiares* but whom he describes as being linked to himself in *amicitia*, and Augustus, in letters to the poet Horace quoted by Suetonius, appeals to the notion that they share an *amicitia* and asks (perhaps teasingly, certainly prophetically) whether the poet is afraid of what will happen to his reputation if posterity knows that he was the emperor's *familiaris*.[97] Even in the philosophical prose of Cicero's *De amicitia*, where one might expect to find terminological distinctions, the abstractions *amicitia* and *familiaritas* are used apparently interchangeably, and the same is true of the concrete nouns *amicus* and *familiaris*.[98] On the other hand, the two terms could be distinguished from each other, juxtaposed in phrases in which the connotational differences come to the foreground. Lucilius describes one and the same man as someone's *amicus et familiaris*, and Gellius writes of a man's *amici et familiares*.[99] Finally,

---

95 Plaut. *Cas.* 581–582: *verum hic <u>sodalis</u> tuos, <u>amicus</u> optumus, / nescioquid se sufflavit uxori suae*; Mart. 1.54: *nam sunt hinc tibi, sunt et hinc amici / … / tu tantum inspice qui novus paratur / an possit fieri vetus <u>sodalis</u>*; Hor. *Carm.* 1.37.1–4: *nunc est bibendum … / <u>sodales</u>*; 2.7: *recepto / dulce mihi furere est <u>amico</u> (comes*: Mart. 5.19.7–10; 14.122). For *amicitia* in Plautus, see Raccanelli 1998, Burton 2004.

96 Ov. *Tr.* 1.3.15: *adloquor extremum maestos abiturus <u>amicos</u>, / qui modo de multis unus et alter erat*; 65–66: *quosque ego dilexi <u>fraterno amore sodales</u>, / o mihi Thesea pectora iuncta fide*.

97 Cic. *Fam.* 13.58: *L. Custidius est tribulis et municeps et <u>familiaris</u> meus … ut libente et impetret sentiatque meam sibi <u>amicitiam</u>, etiam cum longissime absim.* Suet. *Vita Hor.: neque enim si tu superbus <u>amicitiam</u> nostram sprevisti, ideo nos quoque* ἀνθυπερηφανοῦμεν *… an vereris ne apud posteros infame tibi sit, quod videaris <u>familiaris</u> nobis esse?*

98 Cic. *Amic.* 4 (chiastically arranged): *cum enim saepe mecum ageres, ut de <u>amicitia</u> scriberem aliquid, digna mihi res cum omnium cognitione tum nostra <u>familiaritate</u> visa est … cum accepissemus a patribus maxime memorabilem C. Laelii et P. Scipionis <u>familiaritatem</u> fuisse, idonea mihi Laelii persona visa est quae de <u>amicitia</u> ea ipsa dissereret.* See also Cic. *Amic.* 38–40: *videmus Papum Aemilium Luscino <u>familiarem</u> fuisse … tum et cum iis et inter se <u>coniunctissimos</u> fuisse M'. Curium, Ti. Coruncanium memoriae proditum est. igitur ne suspicari quidem possumus quemquam horum ab <u>amico</u> quidpiam contendisse.* That there is no inherent privileging of *amicitia* over *familiaritas* in this text is shown by Laelius' contrast between the *familiaritates* of "the wise" and the *amicitiae* of "the common type" (76: *iam enim a sapientium familiaritatibus ad vulgares amicitias oratio nostra delabitur*).

99 Gell. *NA* 17.10.2: <u>*amici familiaresque*</u> *P. Vergilii*; 9.15.1: <u>*amici familiaresque*</u> *eius*; Lucil. 953 Marx *homini <u>amico et familiari</u> non est mentiri meum*; related usages are illustrated by Sall. *Iug.* 7.7 (*quibus rebus sibi multos ex Romanis <u>familiari amicitia</u> coniunxerat*) and Gell. *NA* 15.28.1 (*Cornelius Nepos et rerum memoriae non indiligens et M. Ciceronis ut qui <u>maxime amicus familiaris</u> fuit*). Pliny uses the adjective *familiaris* as a way of vaguely but suggestively distinguishing between degrees or kinds of *amicitia*: cf. *Ep.* 4.17.2 (on Clusinus Gallus): *est quidem mihi cum isto, contra quem me advocas, non plane familiaris sed tamen amicitia*.

the word provides a concrete illustration of how formal factors may influence the vocabulary characteristic of speech genres. The metrical shape
of *familiaris* precludes its use in dactylic verse, and so it is absent from
entire genres of Latin poetry and nowhere to be found in Virgil, Ovid, or
Martial.

When we turn to the speech genre of Latin inscriptions and the constraints which its formulaic language places on it, a striking point emerges
which has received little notice and less discussion. I cite the respective
number of occurrences of terms in a few geographically defined samples from the online *Epigraphische Datenbank Clauss–Slaby*, a databank
of over 404,000 Latin inscriptions (www.manfredclauss.de). Because
this database occasionally fails to consolidate duplicate citations of the
same inscription, its absolute numbers are not always entirely accurate;
but searching this database nonetheless gives a generally reliable idea of
broad distribution patterns. A search for *amic-* in its more than 404,000
inscriptions yields 1,922 hits, and the geographically defined samples in
Table 1 show some clear patterns. This body of material includes inscriptions of all kinds, ranging from dedications of statues in honor of friends
to the epitaphs which are the subject of Chapter 4 and which constitute
the great majority of surviving inscriptions. But the pattern is clear and
consistent; in this speech genre, *amicus* and *amica* are the labels of choice.
Particularly striking is the near-total absence of the nouns *necessarius*
and *familiaris* from Latin inscriptions: A search of Clauss–Slaby's massive databank yields only a handful of instances of the two nouns. The
plural *necessarii* occurs only twice, and the only instance of the singular
(excluding such usages as the title *necessarius Augustorum*) I have found
in the database comes from an epitaph found in Rome, commemorating
the 4-year-old Fausta as the *necessaria* of the woman who commissioned
the inscription.[100] As for the noun *familiaris*, so widespread as a near-synonym of *amicus* throughout the various genres of the literary tradition
and private letters, a search of the database yields only two attestations of
the singular.[101] In yet other speech genres now lost to us – such as direct

[100] *CIL* 6.41062, the so-called *laudatio Turiae* from Rome: *cum plurumis necessariis*; *CIL* 10.1401
(a decree from Herculaneum referring to the *necessari Alliatoriae Celsillae uxoris Atilii Luperci
ornatissimi viri*); *CIL* 6.17775 (Rome): *D(is) M(anibus) / Faustae / quae vixi(t) / annis IIII /
mensib(us) X / d(iebus) XXVIII Li/via Delphis / necessari/ae suae / fecit.*
[101] *AE* 1994, 866 (Mérida): *Petronia / Agilis / h(ic) s(ita) e(st) / Aponia Serana / familiari suae /
locum sepultur[ae] / et hoc [m(onumentum?) f(ecit?)]*; *CIL* 11.4433a (Amelia in Umbria, Regio
VI): *Verran[...] A(uli) l(iberta) / sibi et / Antho familiari / Statiae Enisaema* [sic; for *Enaesima*];
CIL 5.3619 (Verona): *Q(uintus) Gaesius Secundus / Q(uinto) Gaesio Lucano loci et familiaribus*;
CIL 12.5233 (Narbonne): *Vibia Vari l(iberta) Tertia / sibi et / Q(uinto) Asellio Gemello / viro et*

Labels

Table 1. *Friendship terms in samples from the online Epigraphische Datenbank Clauss–Slaby*

	amicus/amica	sodalis	necessarius/necessaria	familiaris
Rome	672[a]	67 (15)[b]	1[c]	–[d]
Etruria (Regio VII)	21	2	–	–
Transpadana (Regio XI)	51	7	–	–
Apulia et Calabria (Regio II)	18	4 (4)	–	–
Aemilia (Regio VIII)	27	6 (3)	–	–
Gallia Narbonensis	71	21 (1)	–	1
Lusitania	22	1	–	1
Hispania citerior	85	15 (5)	–	–
Africa proconsularis	53	7 (3)	–	–
Numidia	46	3 (1)	–	–

[a] Figures in this column exclude attestations of the adverb *amice*, the proper name *Amicus*, adjectival phrases such as *amica tellus*, the title *a cura amicorum*, and inscriptions with explicitly Christian language.
[b] Figures in parentheses are the number of attestations of *sodalis* included in the total figure which, usually in the plural *sodales*, probably refer to members of an association known as a *sodalicium* or *sodalitas* (closer to English "colleague" than to "friend"). Both figures exclude occurrences of the word in titles like *sodalis Augustalis, Flavialis,* or *Hadrianalis*, as well as the proper name *Sodalis*.
[c] Figures in this column exclude titles like *necessarius Augustorum* and adjectival uses.
[d] Figures in this column exclude expressions like *res familiaris, Lares familiares,* and the proper name *Familiaris*.

verbal communication across the whole range of speakers of Latin, potentially differentiated for class, status, gender, and other factors – we simply cannot know the different tonalities and valences of terms like *amicus* or *familiaris* or others which have not survived in the textual record.

Precisely in its generically conditioned formulary, the language of epitaphs – especially those in prose – can help us see things that are easily obscured in the sometimes elaborate flourishes of literary Latin. The repertory of labels that could be attached to individuals by way of publicly identifying a relationship in texts of this speech genre was fairly limited: above all, terms referring to relations of kinship (*mater* and *pater*,

familiari[b(us)]; *CIL* 10.3980 (an epitaph, probably from Capua, for the 22-year-old Scantia Redempta): ... *matrimoni(i) fuit t[alis] / ut contemneret iuventutem, nam maritus am[-avit? –isit?] / co(n)iugem familiarem, salutis et vitae suae nut[ric(em)]*. Because the sample is so small, the temptation to place interpretive weight on the fact that they refer to men or women in relation to a woman is probably to be resisted. See below, p. 92, for *familiaris* used of a woman in relationship to a man in such speech genres as letter-writing and history.

filius and *filia, frater* and *soror,* and so on) or marriage (*uxor, maritus, vir, coniunx*), as well as terms associated with the institutions of slavery and manumission (*libertus* and *patronus, servus* and *dominus*). The labels *amicus* and *amica* stand out. There was no fact of birth, no legally recognized or religiously sanctioned act such as a wedding or the purchase of manumission of a slave, which existed independently of the labels used to describe the relationship.[102] And so we come back to the question of definition. What makes someone an *amicus?* One answer to the question suggested by the language of inscriptions is this: being *called* an *amicus.* Commemorating someone in an inscription as an *amicus* or *amica* made it so for as long as the stone lasted, however the individuals named may actually have experienced, construed, or identified their relationship. Just as when one person says "I forgive you" to another in front of a third, the utterance itself carries out the relevant social act whether or not the individuals involved subjectively experience forgiveness, it can be argued that identifying someone as one's friend in an inscription is performative in a way that identifying one's spouse, parents, or children is not. And *amicitia* can be performative in another way. As in many languages, addressing a person one barely knows, or even a stranger, as "my friend" can perform a lack of hostility, positive goodwill, or the desire to make a connection or forge an alliance, and, in some instances the verbal equivalent of demonstratively open arms, it can cast the speaker in the role of a person experienced in the ways of friendship.[103] How far can the point be generalized? The question will remain an active one throughout this study.

PATRONAGE, POLITICS, AND "REAL FRIENDSHIP"

I am suggesting, then, that we read any given use of the language of *amicitia* as, in the first instance, the application of linguistically and

---

[102] The argument of Albanese 1963 that *amicitia* constituted a legal institution marked by formal acts of creation and dissolution has convinced few. But it is clear that the formal ending of an *amicitia* could be a socially significant move marked by certain traditional signs: see Suet. *Calig.* 3.3 (*ac ne tunc quidem ultra progressus, quam ut amicitiam ei more maiorum renuntiaret*), Tac. *Ann.* 6.29.2, Kierdorf 1987. For further discussion see Palma 1988, pp. 13–15; Caldelli 2001, pp. 22–25; Ricci 2001, pp. 46–47; Rundel 2005, pp. 201–203. There is no persuasive evidence for a Roman equivalent to the "sworn brotherhood" of medieval Western Europe, entered into with formal acts of swearing oaths, or to the Christian rites for "making brothers" discussed in Boswell 1994 and Bray 2003; see Shaw 1997.

[103] At Phaedrus, *Fabulae* 3.7 a dog and a wolf meet by chance and begin a conversation; at one point the wolf notices the marks of the dog collar on the dog's neck and asks *unde hoc, amice?* (v. 17); at Phaedrus, *Fabulae* 4.9.8, a fox who has fallen into a well calls up to a goat who happens to come by: *descende, amice! tanta bonitas est aquae.* In Chapter 4 we will consider examples of this

culturally meaningful labels rather than as a transparent window on to biographical or psychological truths. If we do so, a problem that has long exercised scholars of Roman friendship essentially disappears. The Latin textual tradition is pervaded by a distinct tension between the fervently described ideals of the friend as one's equal – an *alter ego* with whom one shares everything from material goods to thoughts, with whom one aspires to be united in life and death, to whom one is joined in *amor* – and the realities of the entire range of linguistic usage. *Amicitia* often subsists not only, as we have seen, between individuals whose social inequality is clearly marked, but is often explicitly a matter of exchanging favors and establishing alliances, participants and observers openly speaking of the benefits one or both parties might seek and obtain. Mutual affection is secondary in importance at best, at worst empty pretence or not even pretended. The language of favors and gifts (*gratia, beneficium, munus*) lies at the heart of the discourse of *amicitia*, and the fact that the terms often have a concretely financial sense is by no means euphemized or politely ignored. One analysis even concludes that "*amicitia* can be seen as a system of social exchange generating various resources," "a form of human capital yielding an irregular interest" consisting of gifts, inheritances, legacies, or services.[104]

How are we to reconcile these apparent contradictions? We may invoke the distinction between ideals and reality, and while that will go far towards explaining many instances as a matter of historical and biographical inquiry, it is important to note that the contrast between ideals and reality itself forms a traditional part of both Greek and Roman theorizing and description of the relationships called *philia* and *amicitia*.[105] In the Latin textual tradition, the possibility of concrete benefits of one kind or another in connection with *amicitia* was always recognized: by many voices rejected but always recognized as a possibility. One such benefit was being named as an heir in a will. The speaker of Juvenal's twelfth satire,

---

usage in Latin epitaphs. For performative language, see Austin 1975 and consider Judith Butler's description of gender as performative, "that is, constituting the identity it is purported to be" (Butler 1990, p. 34).

[104] Verboven 2002, p. 341; see also Rauh 1986. Cf. Saller 1982, pp. 13–14: "The fundamentally instrumental nature of Roman friendship was a corollary of the underdevelopment of rational, impersonal institutions for the provision of services." For favors, gifts, and benefits (*gratia, munus, beneficium*, etc.) in connection with *amicitia* see Michel 1962, Hellegouarc'h 1963, pp. 152–170, 202–221.

[105] See Fürst 1996 for the tension between ideals and reality in what he calls the *Freundschaftslehre der Antike*, focusing on the issues of dissension between friends and the ending of a friendship as represented in idealizing and prescriptive texts, ranging from popular maxims to philosophical treatises.

for example, rejoices in his friend Catullus' recent escape from death at sea, contrasting his friendship with that of many others who would consider Catullus a *sterilis amicus*, in other words, unlikely to produce any fruit because he has three healthy young heirs (Juv. 12.93–98). The speaker scorns the view, but it was clearly a common one. Concrete benefit of various kinds was a real possibility in connection with another type of interpersonal relationship which, alongside and often overlapping with *amicitia*, is equally structural to Roman society and pervading the textual tradition. In English traditionally called "patronage," this relationship joined two men of openly divergent economic, social, or political status in a mutually beneficial connection in which the higher-status man could be called a *patronus*, his dependant his *cliens*.[106] Any reading of *amicitia* must also read *clientela*; not only do we find men in a relationship of hierarchical dependency being called *amici* in many Latin texts, but the two share many core practices, ideals, and terminology. Most prominent among the ideals is that of a mutually bonding trust or trustworthiness (*fides*), and key among the overlapping terms is "companion" (*comes*), suggesting not only the company one might offer a friend on his travels but also the public support one might provide to one's patrons in their public appearances, to a Roman provincial official as part of his *cohors*, or even to the emperor in connection with the title *amicus Caesaris*.[107]

The question, then, becomes one of distinguishing between the two kinds of relationship. But how might one do so, on what basis, and why? One common response, advocated by Richard Saller among others, is to conclude that if a given relationship comes with markers signaling a personal relationship of reciprocal exchange between men of unequal social status, the open exercise of power, or if phrases like *in fidem recipere* are used, we are justified in describing it as one of "patronage," regardless of

---

[106] See Hellegouarc'h 1963, pp. 41–62, Saller 1982 and 1989, Freyburger 1986. A related but different phenomenon is the interdependent relationship between poets and their powerful, wealthy supporters, also usually called "patronage" in the language of scholarship, although *patronus* and *cliens* are absent from the poetry itself. Discussions include White 1975, 1978, 1993 (especially pp. 27–34), 2007, Gold 1987, Wiseman 1987, Konstan 1997, pp. 135–137 and 141–145, Nauta 2002, Spisak 2007, pp. 35–51.

[107] The terms *amici Caesaris* or *amici principis* referred to courtiers who regularly attended *salutationes*; those who publicly appeared with the emperor as a council supporting his judgments; and/or those (also described with the formal title *comites Caesaris*, attested from the time of Claudius on) who formally accompanied him on other occasions. But of course those who were called, or called themselves, *amici* of the emperor were hardly limited to men who played these roles. See Crook 1955, pp. 86–89, Millar 1977, pp. 110–122, Champlin 1980, pp. 94–117, Gaudemet 1982. In Juvenal's parody of a *consilium* called by Domitian in order to debate what to do with a giant fish, we find the terms *amicitia*, *consilium*, and *comes* (Juv. 4.73, 75, 84; cf. Epictetus, *Disc.* 4.1.47ff.).

whether the Latin texts in question use the language of *clientela, amicitia*, both or neither.[108] In other words, when we find expressions like *dives amicus, potens amicus*, or *magnus amicus* in Latin literature, emphasizing significant difference in status from the implicitly poorer, less powerful, less grand friend, we are seeing a relationship of "patronage" being described as one of "friendship."[109] The method, driven by the historian's desire to understand and describe the past, at the same time appeals – implicitly or openly – to the distinction fundamental to cultural anthropology as described above. When Latin texts speak of a *potens amicus* or describe a man's *amici* accompanying him on his way to the forum, from an internal or experience-near perspective what is at stake is *amicitia*, from an external or experience-distant perspective it is patronage.

So far, so persuasive. Some scholarly readings, however, have taken a crucial step further: denying that such relationships are "friendship" at all and concluding that, whether "by courtesy" or as a "euphemism" or "mask" or an act of "concealing" or "covering up," the terms *amicus* and *amicitia* are being applied to relationships that are not actually friendship but something else; more strikingly still, some formulations make use of the Latin term, arguing that in certain cases what we are seeing, even if it is described with the language of *amicitia*, is not really *amicitia* and the men involved are not truly *amici*.[110] It is one thing for us today, on the other side of a gulf in time and culture, to argue that a relationship which calls itself *amicitia* is not really friendship, but quite another to claim that it is not really *amicitia*. Such responses perpetuate, of course,

---

[108] Saller 1982, p. 15: "Where the term *amicus* occurs with respect to a friendship between men known to be of unequal status, we can assume a patronage relationship"; cf. Saller 1989, p. 57: *amici inferiores* "can appropriately be analysed under the heading of patronage." Similarly, Deniaux 1993, p. 36 argues that the phrase *in fidem recipere/accipere* in Cicero's correspondence signals the existence of patronage. See Freyburger 1986 on *fides*, pp. 149–159 for *recipere in fidem* in connection with patron–client relationship.

[109] Examples include Hor. *Epist.* 1.18.24 (*dives amicus*), 44 (*potens amicus*), 73 (*venerandus amicus*), 86 (*potens amicus*); Hor. *Carm.* 2.18.11–13; Mart. 3.7, 3.36, 3.41, 3.46; Juv. 1.33 (*magni delator amici*), 3.57 (*a magno semper timearis amico*), 5.14 (*fructus amicitiae magnae cibus*).

[110] Rouland 1979, p. 463: "Le langage n'est donc ici qu'un masque, et les assimilations entre *clientela* et *amicitia* semblent bien n'avoir trompé personne"; Serrano Delgado 1987–1988, p. 227: "la aparición de *dedicationes amico optimo* y similares … ocultan … auténticas relaciones de dipendencia o clientela"; Brunt 1988, pp. 360–361: "Many who belonged to the governor's *cohors*, or who paid morning visits of respect to the great houses, were *amici* only by courtesy. More accurately, some were clients, but this was an appellation resented like death by all with any pretensions to rank or affluence"; Verboven 2002, p. 51: "it is beyond doubt that the terms *amicus* and *amicitia* served as euphemisms to cover up relations of factual dependence"; Hellegouarc'h 1963, p. 56: "il ne s'agit pas d'authentiques *amici*"; cf. Spisak 1998, p. 246: "Martial clearly shows that he himself is quite aware of the sometimes subtle distinction between an actual *amicus* and a *cliens*" and Peachin 2001, p. 7: "what we would recognize as real *philia*."

the scholarly love of distinction found already in Porphyrio's remark that although Horace refers to himself as Maecenas' *amicus* in the first *Epode*, in the interests of decency he really ought to have called himself Maecenas' *cliens*.[111] On a deeper level, however, they are in effect accepting the claim on truth asserted by Cicero's Laelius, who contrasts *vera et perfecta amicitia* with that which he dismisses with the qualifications *vulgaris et mediocris, communis*, or *levis*,[112] or by Seneca, who reproaches Lucilius for mistaking the "meaning of true friendship (*vim verae amicitiae*)" if he considers someone a friend but does not trust him as much he trusts himself – in other words, if he does not enact the ideal of the *alter ego*.[113] Likewise, in his *De beneficiis* Seneca laments a practice among higher-status Romans that he traces back to Gaius Gracchus. In receiving visitors at home (men whom many modern scholars, not unreasonably, would call "clients"), they distinguish between *amici primae admissionis* and those *secundae admissionis*. Seneca himself denies them the status of "true friends (*veri amici*)," but he is obviously responding to the reality that these men go by the name of *amici*.[114]

As I have suggested, texts like these operate in idealizing and philosophizing modes which as part of their self-authorizing strategies assert a

---

[111] Porphyrio ad Hor. *Epod.* 1.2: *non videtur verecundiae Horati convenire, ut amicum se Maecenatis dicat, cum clientem debeat dicere.* White 1993, p. 32, sees this as evidence for a "change of perception" between Horace's and Porphyrio's time related to a simultaneous "inflation" and "pullulation of honorific formulas" from the second century AD onwards. Konstan 1997, p. 144, suggests that "Porphyrio is conscious that at the writing of this early poem Horace has not yet achieved the familiarity implied by the word *amicus*."

[112] Cic. *Amic.* 22: *neque ego nunc de vulgari aut de mediocri [sc., amicitia], quae tamen ipsa et delectat et prodest, sed de vera et perfecta loquor, qualis eorum qui pauci nominantur fuit.* The contrast implicitly structures the entire text and surfaces here and there, e.g. 76: *iam enim a sapientium familiaritatibus ad vulgares amicitias oratio nostra delabitur*; 77: *loquor ... non de sapientium, sed de communibus amicitiis*; 100: *ab amicitiis perfectorum hominum, id est sapientium ... ad leves amicitias deflexit oratio.*

[113] Sen. *Ep.* 3.2: *si aliquem amicum existimas cui non tantundem credis quantum tibi, vehementer erras et non satis nosti vim verae amicitiae.* Discussions of friendship in Seneca's writings (the *Epistles* above all) include Fraisse 1974, pp. 424–433, Pizzolato 1993, pp. 157–177, Clark and Motto 1993, Korhonen 2006, pp. 234–242.

[114] Sen. *Ben.* 6.33.4–34.2: *non sunt isti amici, qui agmine magno ianuam pulsant, qui in primas et secundas admissiones digeruntur. consuetudo ista vetus est regibus regesque simulantibus populum amicorum discribere, et proprium superbiae magno aestimare introitum ac tactum sui liminis et pro honore dare, ut ostio suo propius adsideas, ut gradum prior intra domum ponas, in qua deinceps multa sunt ostia, quae receptos quoque excludant. apud nos primi omnium <C.> Gracchus et mox Livius Drusus instituerunt segregare turbam suam et alios in secretum recipere, alios cum pluribus, alios universos. habuerunt itaque isti amicos primos, habuerunt secundos, numquam veros.* For differentiated *amici*, see also Sen. *Tranq.* 12.6–7, *De Brev. Vitae* 14.3, Plin. *Ep.* 2.6 (a host offers different qualities of food and wine to his guests in a tripartite division: *maiores amici, minores amici, liberti*), 7.3 (*amicitiae tam superiores quam minores*) with White 1978 and Saller 1989.

totalizing claim on the truth in which we need not acquiesce; they give us only one perspective on *amicitia* and invite being read as part of the entire range of Latin textuality. Moreover, it is worth emphasizing that not even Cicero or Seneca deny – how could they? – that relationships quite different in nature from their idealized form of *amicitia* commonly went by that name. Seneca's vehement wording comes in response to common practice; in another letter he advises Lucilius (whom he elsewhere urges to a restrictive, philosophically correct view of "true friendship") how to respond to the social reality that some people seek the *amicitia* of the more powerful, others of the less powerful, others of their social equals.[115] As for Cicero, we have already seen that in one of his earliest extant writings (*De inventione* 2.166–167), he describes various perspectives on *amicitia*. Some think friendship desirable for the benefits it offers, others consider it desirable in and of itself, still others argue for a blend of the two motivations; for the purposes at hand, Cicero adopts the third of these perspectives, saving the question of which has the greatest claim on truth (*quid verissime constituatur*) for another time and another discussion – which ends up being *De amicitia*, years later. Meanwhile, in a private letter to his friend Atticus to which we will return in Chapter 3, Cicero himself distinguishes between their own intimate *amicitia* and the relationships he has with his supporters in the forum. Although he describes the latter as being far less meaningful to him than his relationship with Atticus, he does not exclude them from the realm of *amicitia*. He qualifies the noun with adjectives (they are *ambitiosae* and *fucosae*, adorned for display and effect), but he does not deny its ultimate applicability, nor does he conceal the fact that these other friendships bring him some benefit.[116]

Modern readerly responses to relationships described in ancient texts as *amicitia* but amenable to analysis in modern terms as "patronage" often turn on a cluster of concepts which they may or may not openly cite: utility, benefit, advantage. It is undeniably true of the relationship we call

---

[115] Sen. *Ep.* 94.14: *alia enim dare debemus feneranti, alia colenti agrum, alia negotianti, alia regum amicitias sequenti, alia pares, alia inferiores amaturo.*

[116] Cic. *Att.* 1.18: *nam illae ambitiosae nostrae fucosaeque amicitiae sunt in quodam splendore forensi, fructum domesticum non habent.* The adjective *fucosae* means "painted up," "overly adorned," "for show," hence slightly but significantly different from "unreal" or "fake": cf. *Priapeia* 50.2 (*quaedam, si placet hoc tibi, Priape, / fucosissima me puella ludit*) and *Comment. pet.* 35 (*minutatim ex communibus proprii, ex fucosis firmi suffragatores evadunt*). Perhaps influenced by Cicero's words to Atticus is a remark from Seneca's fragmentarily preserved text *Quomodo amicitia continenda sit: hoc sibi quisque proponat, quo minus facile fucatis capiatur officiis: rara est amicitia, <non> vulgaris aut exposita, ut inplere totas domos possit, <ut> vulgo sibi homines persuasere.* A few paragraphs from this text were found in a palimpsest and first published by B. G. Niebuhr in 1820; printed in Fürst 1996, pp. 242–244.

"patronage" and Romans describe with the terms *cliens* and *patronus* that those in such a relationship expected to derive benefit from it. Indeed, that was arguably its very reason for being. Under the influence of later ideological traditions including Christian idealizing of selflessness and otherworldliness, however, many modern readers are evidently inclined to understand the highest or "true" form of friendship as something that cannot be described in terms of utility, and thus to conclude, implicitly or openly, that relationships between social unequals which openly aim at obtaining benefits cannot be "true friendship." Furthermore, under the direct or indirect influence of idealizing utterances about *vera amicitia* in Cicero and Seneca, we have seen that not a few modern readers take the further step of concluding that such relationships are not even "real *amicitia*." But a closer look at the most influential of these idealizing texts shows that on the key point of utility the step is too hastily taken. Even Cicero's Laelius accepts the benefits and uses (*utilitates, opportunitates, fructus*) that can come from friendship – in fact, he claims that the usefulness (*utilitas*) of friendship is one thing on which "everyone agrees": but he insists that this is not the *reason* for which "true friendships" arise. His own friendship with Scipio, for example, led to *utilitas* but was not led by it, and he concludes that "we" seek friendship not because we hope for material gain but because we know that the true benefit (*fructus*) friendship brings consists in the affection (*amor*) that lies at its heart. It is one of the central arguments of Cicero's *De amicitia*, in other words, that *vera amicitia*, precisely because it nurtures *virtus*, is in fact profoundly beneficial.[117] We must never forget, however, that the passionate argument comes in response to, and aims to transcend, social and linguistic realities which were widespread among Cicero's readership and actively at work elsewhere in Cicero's own writings, most vividly in the letters of

---

[117] Cic. *Amic.* 31: *amicitiam non spe mercedis adducti, sed quod omnis eius fructus in ipso amore est, expetendam putamus.* Cf. 22: *talis igitur inter viros amicitia tantas opportunitates habet quantas vix queo dicere. principio qui potest esse vita "vitalis", ut ait Ennius, quae non in amici mutua benevolentia conquiescit? quid dulcius quam habere quicum omnia audeas sic loqui ut tecum? qui esset tantus fructus in prosperis rebus, nisi haberes, qui illis aeque ac tu ipse gauderet?*; 30: *sed quamquam utilitates multae et magnae consecutae sunt, non sunt tamen ab earum spe causae diligendi profectae*; 51: *non igitur utilitatem amicitia, sed utilitas amicitiam secuta est*; 86: *una est enim amicitia in rebus humanis de cuius utilitate omnes uno ore consentiunt*; 100: *virtus, virtus, inquam, C. Fanni et tu Q. Muci, et conciliat amicitias et conservat.* Hymning the *amicitia* experienced by Laelius and Scipio, Agrippa and Augustus, Valerius Maximus cites the enjoyment of the fruit born by one's friends' virtues (Val. Max. 4.7.7: *harum rerum uberrimos fructus*). See Saller 1982, p. 14, for Seneca's take on the question at *Ben.* 7.31.1: "The Stoic wise man should not form *amicitiae* for the purpose of *utilitas*, yet *utilitas* inevitably results from *amicitia*: how can that *utilitas* not enter into the wise man's thoughts? The answer: What virtue does not have *utilitas* as a by-product?"

recommendation. Among those realities are the open acknowledgment that *amicitia* can be, and often is, undertaken because of the entire range of benefits it brings, and that these are hardly limited to affection and companionship and the pursuit of virtue.[118]

The explicit acknowledgment of utility and concrete benefits also characterizes relationships which some scholars call "political friendship," contrasting it not only with "personal friendship" but with "true friendship," thereby making the same move we have seen in the case of "patronage" (the parallel is not coincidental, of course, since *amicitia* between political allies is itself susceptible of being described as "patronage" when there is a clear distinction in rank between the partners and the higher-ranking man holds, or is a candidate for, political office).[119] No doubt in many cases, as lived by the parties involved and perceived by observers, there were crucial differences between these relationships and those between, say, two social equals who had no political ambitions and consistently performed mutual affection in word and deed. Yet the texts describing these relationships just as consistently call them *amicitia*, with no qualifying adjective comparable to English "political." Laelius' distinction between *vera et perfecta amicitia* and other kinds emphatically does not correspond with that between "personal" and "political," not least because he and Scipio were themselves political allies. At most, we find description of and meditation on the differences, as in Cicero's remarks to Atticus in the letter cited above, contrasting *illae ambitiosae fucosaeque amicitiae* with what he has with Atticus (*Att.* 1.18). What can justifiably be called the *locus classicus* on so-called

---

[118] Cf. Powell 1990, p. 22: "Cicero's relations with some of his contemporary politicians could well exemplify his category of *vulgares amicitiae*." See Spielvogel 1993 for detailed study. For the speech genre of the letter of recommendation (*commendationes* or *epistulae commendaticiae*) see below Chapter 3, n. 94. The following remarks on Renaissance Florence equally apply to ancient Rome: "To most modern historians, patronage obtained from friends, interceding with friends of friends to help one another, equals graft or corruption and is incompatible with what they recognize as 'true' or 'sincere' friendship; thus, they are apt to dismiss many Renaissance friendships as 'mere patronage.' For Florentines, their relationships with patrons and the particular group of friends who depended upon them were an essential form of close friendship" (Kent 2009, p. 7).

[119] In a much quoted remark, Ronald Syme observes that "*amicitia* was a weapon of politics, not a sentiment based on congeniality" (Syme 1939, p. 12). Powell 1990, pp. 21–23, notes that, "like some other sayings of that great historian," this is "no more than an epigrammatic half-truth"; for Powell, *amicitia* "refers *properly* to a personal relationship involving genuine feelings of goodwill and affection on both sides" (emphasis added), and "political alliances were *claimed* to be instances of personal friendship" (emphasis original). Cf. Rawson 1978, pp. 4–5: Cicero's need for "real friendship," associated with "personal warmth," is distinguished from the "'friendship'" between Cicero and Pompey which was "for the most part ... created, maintained and destroyed by purely political factors" (inverted commas in the original). By contrast, Hellegouarc'h 1963, pp. 41–90, speaks of "différentes formes de l'*amicitia*"; for him, "les relations politiques fondées sur la *fides*" include both *amitié* and *clientèle*.

"political friendship" is a passage from the *Commentariolum petitionis*, a text purporting to be Quintus Cicero's advice to his famous brother on how to run his electoral campaign.

> sed hoc nomen amicorum in petitione latius patet quam in cetera vita; quisquis est enim qui ostendat aliquid in te voluntatis, qui colat, qui domum ventitet, is in amicorum numero est habendus. sed tamen qui sunt amici ex causa iustiore cognationis aut adfinitatis aut sodalitatis aut alicuius necessitudinis, iis carum et iucundum esse maxime prodest ... deinde sunt instituendi cuiusque generis amici ... (*Comment. pet.* 16–18)[120]

> During an electoral campaign the term *amici* is used more broadly than in other times in life: anyone who shows you even a little goodwill, who cultivates an association with you, who visits you frequently at home is to be considered one of your *amici*. Yet in the case of those who are your *amici* for a sounder reason – a relation of blood or marriage, shared membership in some group, any kind of close bond – it is particularly beneficial to be affectionate and pleasant.... You should make friends of every kind ...

The writer makes no distinction between "true" and "political" (let alone "false") friends. He is not claiming that in the context of electoral campaigns one refers to as *amici* men who in fact are nothing of the kind. Rather, he observes that in this context and for this purpose some men are both called and socially treated as *amici* (note both *nomen* and *in numero est habendus*) who would not otherwise be given the label. For, as he notes with breathtaking clarity, when you are campaigning for office you can initiate *amicitia* with anyone you want, something you cannot normally do.[121] In other words, rather than the application of a term to a reality which it does not properly designate – a process of metaphor or transfer – this writer sees a process of semantic expansion (*hoc nomen amicorum latius patet*). And so there are different types (*genera*) of friendships and of friends, some of whom are *amici* "for a sounder reason (*ex causa iustiore*)." The phrase is revealing. The question is not whether such men actually are one's *amici* or not, but what the reason for the relationship's existence is, and the comparative *iustiore* suggests that a range of possible reasons existed.[122]

---

[120] It is generally accepted that Quintus Cicero did not in fact write the *Commentariolum* but that whoever the author was, he was "well versed in the manners of the age" (Brunt 1988, p. 360). See further discussion in Laser 2001.

[121] *Comment. pet.* 7: *potes honeste, quod in cetera vita non queas, quoscumque velis adiungere ad amicitiam, quibuscum si alio tempore agas ut te utantur, absurde facere videare, in petitione autem nisi id agas et cum multis et diligenter, nullus petitor esse videare.*

[122] Hellegouarc'h 1963, pp. 55–56, comments on the *amici* of this passage: "Il ne s'agit pas d'authentiques *amici*." Yet the author of the *Commentariolum* does not speak of *amici iusti* or

The specific case of campaigns for elected office can stand, *mutatis mutandis*, for many others. Instead of denying that "real friendship" exists in any given case we find in the Latin textual tradition or, more drastically, denying that two men were "real" or "actual *amici*" even when they are identified with precisely that word, I am advocating a skeptical stance toward the self-authorizing claims on truth characteristic of such influential prescriptive texts as Cicero's *De amicitia*, and urging that we stay with the language of the texts, considering the possibility that words like *amicus* and *cliens* are projecting and representing relationships rather than transparently and truthfully identifying their essence: in short, that they are linguistically and socially meaningful labels that can be applied, removed, and reapplied as rhetorical, social, and other needs required. The Latin textual tradition in general identifies a set of roles that a man's dependants might play. A particularly detailed catalogue appears in Cicero's request for Atticus' help in obtaining a private library that had been bequeathed to him – *amici, clientes, hospites, liberti, servi* – but the pairing of *amici* and *clientes* in particular frequently appears.[123] The terms represent two distinct ways of describing one's relationship to a dependant and one's proper behavior in connection with him. Fronto asserts, for example, that when a man dies, his freedman, *cliens*, and *amicus* each mourn differently.[124] More generally, the term *cliens* suggests a relation of dependence and the very fact of using it places a man in a hierarchical constellation, while *amicus* suggests a voluntarily established relationship between men on more or less equal footing, and underscores the goodwill at least ideally uniting them.[125] Another point worth emphasizing is that

amici iustiores and, significantly enough, neither of those collocations is attested in the texts included on the Packard Humanities Institute website. For the phrase *iustior causa*, cf. Cic. *Div. Caec.* 61 (*nullam neque iustiorem neque graviorem causam necessitudinis posse reperiri quam coniunctionem sortis, quam provinciae, quam offici, quam publici muneris societatem*), Cic. *Phil.* 8.12 (*quae causa iustior est belli gerendi quam servitutis depulsio?*), Sen. *Ben.* 2.22.1 (*iusta enim causa laetitiae est laetum amicum videre, iustior fecisse*).

[123] Cic. *Att.* 1.20: *si me amas, si te a me amari scis, entiere per amicos, clientes, hospites, libertos denique ac servos tuos ut scida ne qua depereat.* Cf. Cic. *Fam.* 5.8.5 (*amici, hospites, clientes*), Cic. *Verr.* 2.4.140 (*Syracusani haec faciunt, istius clientes atque amici*), Sall. *Cat.* 26.4 (*circum se praesidia amicorum atque clientium occulte habebat*), Livy 38.51.6 (*citatus reus magno agmine amicorum clientiumque per mediam contionem ad rostra subiit*), Tac. *Ann.* 16.32.3 (*P. Egnatius … cliens Sorani, et tunc emptus ad opprimendum amicum …*); cf. Mart. 2.74.6 (*amici et greges togatorum*). See Hellegouarc'h 1963, pp. 54–56.

[124] Fronto, *M. Caes.* 1.6.8: *sciat familia, quemadmodum lugeat: aliter plangit servus manumissus, aliter cliens laude vadatus, aliter amicus legato honoratus.*

[125] In a much quoted phrase, Cicero claims that men who think of themselves as wealthy and fortunate "consider it to be like death" to become dependent upon another's patronage and to be called *clientes* (Cic. *Off.* 2.69: *patrocinio vero se usos aut clientes appellari mortis instar putant*); cf. Sen. *Ben.* 2.23.3, Brunt 1988, pp. 394–395. Pliny never describes any of his protégés as *cliens*, and

these labels are not mutually exclusive, nor are the categories to which they refer watertight; someone called *amicus* or *familiaris* in one context might be called *patronus* or *cliens* or *hospes* in another, to other effects. To the extent that the act of applying labels like *amicus* and *cliens* performs a relationship in its socially meaningful aspect, one kind of performance does not exclude others.[126]

In short, in what follows I make a heuristically naïve assumption. If writers of Latin texts refer to a relationship as *amicitia* or describe a person as someone's *amicus*, then, in the absence of any explicit indication that the words are being used in a transferred, metaphorical, or nonliteral sense, it is *amicitia* and they are *amici*, regardless of what else they might be.[127] We find all different kinds of *amici*, some of them implicitly or explicitly said to have a stronger claim on the title than others, but the fact of usage is that they are all given the label, and with it a set of potentially wide-reaching rights and responsibilities. We should, in short, resist the temptation of seeing only some of these relationships as "the real thing," not allowing ourselves to be won over by the lofty proclamations of a Cicero or the decisive assertions of modern scholars which urge an either/or view, no matter how weighty their self-authorizing rhetoric or how seductive their claims on absolute truth may be.

VARIATIONS IN TIME AND PLACE

Although this study does not aim to offer a history of Roman friendship, nor even a history of the word *amicitia*, questions of diachronic and

---

Seneca's and Tacitus' uses of the term are more or less openly disparaging (Sen. *Brev. Vitae* 19.3, Tac. *Hist.* 1.81, 3.73–74, 3.86, *Ann.* 4.2, 4.34). In the language of inscriptions, however, we not infrequently find the labels *patronus* and *cliens*, mostly in inscriptions dedicated by men in the client position. The term *patronus* in this sense (as opposed to "legal advocate," "patron of community," or "former master of a freed slave") is found quite rarely in the literary tradition, presumably because "the language of social subordination may have seemed arrogant when used by the patron, a tactless advertisement of his superiority and the relative weakness of his client" (Saller 1982, p. 10). Two examples from Cicero's correspondence seem to confirm the principle: at *Fam.* 7.29.2, Manius Curius deferentially addresses Cicero as *patrone mi*, and at *Att.* 1.16.10, Cicero disparagingly calls Clodius the *patronus* of C. Scribonius Scribo.

126 Val. Max. 9.4.3 (L. Septimuleius as *familiaris* and *cliens* of C. Gracchus), Cic. *Fam.* 7.29 (Manius Curius to Cicero: both *patrone mi* and *amice magne*), *CIL* 6.14672, 13.3162; cf. White 2007, p. 196: "In principle, nothing prevents a friend from occupying the position of a patron or a client at the same time."

127 Such indications include Tacitean phrases like *species amicitiae* ("the appearance of friendship"): *Agr.* 24.4 (*Agricola expulsum seditione domestica unum ex regulis gentis exceperat ac specie amicitiae in occasionem retinebat*), *Hist.* 4.80.5 (*unde paulatim levior viliorque haberi, manente tamen in speciem amicitia*), *Ann.* 1.10.2 (*sed Pompeium imagine pacis, sed Lepidum specie amicitiae deceptos*) 2.3.4 (*ob scelus Antonii, qui Artavasden regem Armeniorum specie amicitiae inlectum, dein catenis oneratum, postremo interfecerat*).

geographical variation must be addressed. I have been speaking of Roman friendship as a uniform and implicitly unchanging phenomenon, yet the texts in which *amicitia* figures range across not only speech genres but time and place: from the second century BC through the third century AD, from Spain to Asia Minor. On the point of diachronic change it is my argument that various shifts and upheavals in Roman political and social structures, above all those accompanying the transition from Republic to Principate, no doubt led to changes in *practice* (for example, whose *amicitia* was sought or advertised, or what social effects any given friendship might have) but that there is no sign of any significant change in the vocabulary available for *representing* these relationships in language, nor in the core of associated concepts and ideals. However variously Roman friendship may have been lived out in different times, the texts we have consistently associate *amicitia* with concepts like *fides, officium,* and *amor,* and ideals such as that of the *alter ego* are always ready to be exploited.[128]

Assertions of changes in Roman friendship, especially in the transition from Republic to Principate, invite closer scrutiny. A study of friendship in Cicero's letters and Ovid's exile poetry claims that "friendship has changed" over the intervening decades, and not only because of the passage of time but because "power relationships have changed."[129] The latter point is undeniably true, but the argument for deeper change in friendship itself – whatever precisely that might mean – turns out to rest only on the two bodies of textual material under investigation: the letters of a leading political figure negotiating his way through complex networks of power, and the poetry of a man who had been exiled precisely because he had run afoul of power. In all their specificity, Cicero's letters and Ovid's exile poetry are not a persuasive basis for broad claims about change in Roman friendship. Likewise, a reading of Cicero's letters together with those of Pliny shows that while political structures had radically changed in the intervening 150 years, the language, rhetoric, and ideology of *amicitia* at the highest levels of Roman society – which is precisely where we might expect to find traces of those changes – have not. The mechanisms of how men acquired political office were different, but

---

[128] Cf. Saller 1982, p. 12: "The ideals concerning *amicitia* changed very little in the transition from the Republic to the Principate: Seneca's views differ little from Cicero's"; p. 30: "There is no evidence that the importance of the reciprocity ethic as described by the language of *beneficium* and *gratia* diminished in private relationships in the Principate." For similar arguments about different but related areas of Roman social life, see Saller and Shaw 1984, p. 136 (family), Kaster 2005, p. 11 (emotions), Williams 2010a, pp. 11–12, 257–258 (masculinity and sexuality).

[129] Citroni Marchetti 2000, p. vi: "L'amicizia è cambiata … Non è cambiata per uno scorrere neutro del tempo quanto perché sono cambiati i rapporti di potere."

the key language used and ideals invoked behind the scenes remained the same: *beneficium, officium, gratia*, all under the banner of *amicitia*.[130]

To be sure, changed social and political structures might well be reflected in the themes or emphases of any given text. It has been argued, for example, that Valerius Maximus' focus on narratives of *amicitia* set in politically turbulent times and illustrating issues of conflicting loyalty is not coincidental, writing as he did under Tiberius during the period of Sejanus' power and downfall. But the language Valerius uses to narrate *amicitia* and the ideals of *amicitia* which his narratives illustrate are the same as those we find across the textual tradition.[131] And while a remark by Valerius Maximus on the importance of being cautious in choosing one's *amici* has been read as specifically reflecting the situation of his day, when intrigue and denunciation were rife, it is worth noting that the topic was traditional in reflections on *amicitia*, as Cicero's *Laelius* amply demonstrates.[132] At most, I would argue, we can read a contemporary relevance *into* or *behind* Valerius' words, but his words themselves reflect and respond to ideals and social practices that are not anchored in any particular period in Roman history. Likewise, the tradition of formally "renouncing a friendship" (*amicitiam renuntiare*) attested in the Republican period persisted. The Emperor Tiberius wrote a letter to the Senate announcing that his rupture with Pomponius Labeo was nothing other than such a renunciation, taking the form of declaring an end to one's "favor" (*gratia*) and excluding the other from one's home (*interdicere domo*).[133] Of course, *amicitia* with Tiberius was not like any other. After Augustus, the social ramifications of enjoying (or losing) an *amicitia* with the *princeps* were qualitatively different from other kinds of *amicitia*, for example with powerful men of the Republic. But the form and above all the language remained the same, and that is my primary interest.

---

[130] Focusing on the letters of recommendation, Pani 1993 hypothesizes that changes in the social context in which they were circulated had an effect, but does not actually show that the language and ideals were any different.

[131] Lucarelli 2007, pp. 214–285.

[132] Val. Max. 4.7.pr. (*tam necessarium subsidium temere adsumi non debet, semel autem recte adprehensum sperni non convenit*) with Pizzolato 1993, pp. 155–156: "Ciò potrebbe rispecchiare anche la situazione dell'epoca, in cui erano d'attualità intrighi e delazioni." Cf. Cic. *Amic.* 60: *illud potius praecipiendum fuit, ut eam diligentiam adhiberemus in amicitiis comparandis, ut ne quando amare inciperemus eum quem aliquando odisse possemus*; 78: *ne nimis cito diligere incipiant neve non dignos.*

[133] Tac. *Ann.* 6.29.2: *disseruit morem fuisse maioribus, quotiens dirimerent amicitias, interdicere domo eumque finem gratiae ponere: id se repetivisse in Labeone.* See Rogers 1959 and Kierdorf 1987, with references to other instances of *amicitiam renuntiare.*

In short, the chronologically arranged thematic chapter headings of Luigi Pizzolato's *L'idea di amicizia nel mondo antico classico e cristiano* (for example, "l'amicizia arcaica tra sentenziosità ed esperienza"; "l'amicizia nella tormentata età di Cesare"; "tra la nobiltà dei principî e i compromessi del quotidiano: l'amicizia nell'età dei Flavi") certainly give us glimpses at characteristic emphases of specific texts or periods, but the diachronic narrative they construct runs the real risk of oversimplifying and over-schematizing, not least because of the chronological unevenness in the amount of textual material that survives.[134] Nor does the speech genre of inscriptions, absent from Pizzolato's analysis, offer much by way of support for any narratives of change. The overwhelming majority of Latin inscriptions date to the first and second centuries AD – in other words, after the political and social transformations from Republic to Empire had been completed – and within the surviving material it is hard to see any diachronic shifts in the formulaic language of inscriptions which commemorate friends.

A more persuasive case can be made for geographical variation. Not to mention the range of local cultural traditions and languages through-out the Roman Empire, even within the Italian peninsula we can detect some regional variations. Some of these, to be sure, are of limited sig-nificance. In inscriptions from Cisalpine Gaul, for example, *optimus* is the most common of epithets modifying *amicus*, followed by *carus* and *bene merens*, whereas in the rest of Italy *bene merens* is the most common, followed by *optimus* and *carus*.[135] Other differences may be more mean-ingful. The percentage of surviving funerary inscriptions which men-tion *amici* is, for example, distinctly higher in the city of Rome and in Cisalpine Gaul than in the rest of Italy, in other words in the two most urbanized and prosperous areas of the peninsula – and, in the case of the

---

[134] Pizzolato himself admits, for example, that the apparent prevalence of sententious sayings about *amicitia* in texts from the archaic period may largely be an effect of the fragmentary nature of what survives (Pizzolato 1993, p. 93). As for the arguments that Romans in Seneca's lifetime were in particular need of "personal solidarity at an existential level" as a means of resisting imperial power (Pizzolato 1993 p. 157), or that in the Empire "political life was entrusted to the logic of personal relations" (p. 180): When were these things not true among Romans of the pol-itically active class?

[135] Reali 1997, pp. 195, 211. Specifically, 55 inscriptions from Cisalpine Gaul attach epithets to the noun *amicus/amica*: 22 of these are *optimus/-a*, 13 *carus/-a*, 9 *bene merens*; in south-central Italy (excluding the city of Rome) there are a total of 92 such inscriptions: 35 with *bene merens*, 32 with *optimus/-a*, 12 with *carus/-a*. Reali's attempts to distinguish among these epithets (*optimus* and *bene merens* belong to an "ethical" sphere and *carus* to an "affective" sphere) are not convin-cing, and he himself notes that such distinctions cannot be rigidly insisted upon in any case (p. 196).

city of Rome, the home of a disproportionately high number of soldiers and veterans without spouses or families. The greater presence of textual traces of *amicitia* in urban contexts says little or nothing about the role of *amicitia* in social life in rural contexts, but a great deal about the far greater opportunities for *representing* interpersonal relationships in the denser social networks of cities and in the epitaphs which clustered in the cemeteries at their outskirts.[136] Another geographical variation has to do with gender. Women are underrepresented yet quite distinctly visible as both dedicators and honorees throughout the corpus of inscriptions surviving from around the Roman Empire, but in two regions they figure more prominently than elsewhere. The proportion of women among those who dedicate epitaphs is higher in the material surviving from the Iberian peninsula than from any other region in the Roman Empire; and, within the sample of inscriptions commemorating *amici*, the percentage of women among named individuals is distinctly higher in Cisalpine Gaul than in the rest of the Italian peninsula (one out of four and one out of seven respectively). It has been tentatively but not implausibly argued that we may be seeing here the influence of the Celtic cultural traditions prevalent in these two areas.[137]

It would be interesting to compare the discourse of *amicitia* in Latin texts with comparable discourses in other languages of the Roman Empire but the paucity (or, in most cases, sheer absence) of relevant texts apart from the special case of Greek generally frustrates any such attempt.[138] But what of Latin inscriptions from, say, Gaul or North Africa? The extent to which the act of setting up inscriptions in Latin was a statement of Roman "identity" or a sign of "Romanization" is an open question,

---

[136] The respective proportions are 1 out of 80 in Rome and the urbanized areas of Cisalpine Gaul, as opposed to 1 out of 200 in Italy, Sicily and Sardinia as a whole. See discussion of this and related issues at Reali 1997, pp. 219–241, 259–260.

[137] For the relative prominence of women in inscriptions from Cisalpine Gaul and the Iberian peninsula, see Chevallier 1983, Saller and Shaw 1984, pp. 138–139 (citing Strabo 3.4.18 with its hint at matrilineal inheritance in local cultures), Morris 1992, p. 160, Reali 1997, pp. 177, 201–202. In a powerful illustration of the general underrepresentation of women among individuals named in Latin epitaphs, Hasegawa 2005, p. 65, compiles statistics from inscriptions from columbaria in the city of Rome: Of a total of 1,799 named individuals, 63% are male, 36% female, and 1% of uncertain sex.

[138] We do have a few glimpses, provided for example by the so-called hospitality tablets found in Spain inscribed in the Celtiberian language. One of these, in the form of two joined hands, has a text reading *Caisaros Cecciq(om) k(a)r Arcailo* (*CIL* 2.5762, from Paredes de Nava, Palencia). Noting that *kar*, which appears frequently in such tablets, is cognate with Latin *carus* and "the nearest Celtiberian equivalent to Latin *hospitium*," Curchin 1994 translates "Caisaros of the Ceccici (has the) friendship of Arcailos"; he translates another tablet reading *kar Arcobriga Co[...]cidos(i)q(om)* as "friendship (between) Arcobriga (and) Co ... of the ... cidosici." The slide from *carus* to *hospitium* to "friendship" begs a few questions.

not least because the meaning of those terms is not universally agreed upon.[139] But I would argue that the very fact of commissioning an epitaph memorializing someone, in Latin, as an *amicus* or *amica* located such a text within the semiotic system I am exploring in this study, and Latin epitaphs from all over the Roman Empire will be discussed alongside those from Rome itself in Chapters 1 and 4. Discourses and ideals of friendship among, say, Latin-speaking Celts, and the nuances of their use of the language of *amicitia*, may well have been different from those of native Latin speakers born and raised in the city of Rome; yet when we today read inscriptions from Spain or Gaul referring to *amici* and *amicae*, these differences almost entirely elude our vision.

We will be reading quite a few epitaphs from the western parts of the Empire in particular which memorialize individuals in Latin yet with unmistakably Celtic names, and to those of us familiar with the nomenclature dominating the literary tradition, many of these look and sound distinctly foreign. But we must keep in mind that we are looking at artefacts of a cultural mix whose precise workings elude us. So much is suggested by the very fact that those who commissioned the inscriptions chose Latin as the language (for there was a tradition, albeit less robust, of setting up inscriptions in local languages), and the fact that the great majority of these individuals bear a combination of Roman and non-Roman names. Typical is the combination in men's names of Latin praenomen and nomen and, say, Celtic cognomen, which suggests that either he or one of his paternal ancestors had acquired the Roman citizenship and with it had taken the family name of a Roman *gens*. Even farther from our knowledge are the cultural and linguistic traditions for representing interpersonal relationships, including those which in Latin are called *amicitia*, among those individuals and peoples who have left no textual material for us to read. Stephen Greenblatt's remarks on sixteenth-century European responses to the linguistic otherness of the peoples of the Americas give food for thought. "Reality for each society

---

[139] Woolf 1998, p. 78 (emphases added): "Latin inscriptions in Gaul thus provide evidence for the adoption of Roman *cultural practices* and for the spread of Roman *social structures*, but were not designed or understood by contemporaries primarily as symbols of Roman *identity*"; Häussler 2002 sees the use of Latin in inscriptions precisely as "expressing Roman identity." Hingley 2005, esp. pp. 94–102, uses models from post-colonial studies to suggest that Latin may have been strategically used by members of local cultures even while keeping their own cultural identity. For issues of interactions between Roman and other cultures around the Empire, especially as they relate to the problem of identity, see Woolf 1997 and 1998; Webster and Cooper 1996; Keay and Terrenato 2001; Dench 2005; Wallace-Hadrill 2008 (esp. pp. 3–37); Mattingly 2011 (esp. pp. 203–245); and, with special attention to language, Parca 2001, Adams 2003.

is constructed to a significant degree out of the *specific* qualities of its language and symbols. Discard the particular words and you have discarded the particular men. And so most of the people of the New World will never speak to us. That communication, with all that we might have learned, is lost to us forever."[140]

READING ROMAN FRIENDSHIP

This book, then, does not ask the kinds of questions which have tended to dominate discussion of Roman friendship. What it was like to be a friend in ancient Rome? What *was* Roman friendship? Was it about affection or utility? When, under what circumstances, and why did individual friendships arise? Could slaves and free men be friends? Instead, I approach "Roman friendship" as a case study in problems of language and culture, reading *amicitia* as a system of labels and categories to be interpreted more than as a set of relationships and events to be reconstructed. This means that we cannot assume that we always have direct access to the realities and subtleties of interpersonal relationships among Romans – though these sometimes come through – but what we do have may be even richer in possibilities: texts ready to be read, systems inviting interpretation.

I hope to persuade my readers that reading Roman friendship can teach us a great deal not only about how discourses of friendship or the language of *amicitia* could work, but also more generally about Latin literature and Roman culture. My readings are organized around the following sets of questions, which structure the book's four chapters. Roughly speaking, Chapters 1 and 2 consider recurring themes, questions, and problems, while Chapters 3 and 4 offer focused readings of a selection of texts in various genres, literary and inscriptional respectively; gender is a guiding category throughout.

What is the relationship between friendship and gender? Montaigne bluntly asserts that "there is no example yet of woman attaining to it and by the common agreement of the ancient schools of philosophy she is excluded from it," and Derrida's reflections on friendship are inspired by what he calls its canonically androcentric structure in the long sweep of Western culture. Chapter 1 will consider the rather more complex picture of the intersection between discourses of *amicitia* and gender that is visible

---

[140] Greenblatt 1990, p. 32. These remarks seem to underestimate the extent to which indigenous languages and anti-colonial perspectives have survived among the native peoples of the Americas to this day, but the argument is persuasive to the extent that it describes the *historical* moment of the first wave of European colonization.

in the Latin textual tradition. Alongside prescriptive male-authored texts which represent friendship as a masculine prerogative are others – inscriptions commissioned by and for women around the Latin-speaking world, a precious handful of letters sent by one woman to another at Vindolanda in northern England, and some male-authored literary texts as well – which configure women as linked to each other by interpersonal bonds, and many of them use the language of *amicitia*. And what of friendships between the sexes? It is well known that in Latin literature the feminine *amica* denotes a man's sexual partner, and the very possibility of *amicitia* between the sexes is a contested and in any case faint feature of the cultural landscape visible in literary texts. But we will see that here too the language of inscriptions complicates the picture considerably. Men and women commemorate each other as *amici* and *amicae* without, I will be arguing, thereby denoting a sexual relationship.

What is the relationship between friendship and love? Across languages and cultures, the two terms, evocative as they are elusive, often stand in an unresolved tension: sometimes an intertwined pair (friendship is a type of love), seemingly more often oppositional dyad (friendship is contrasted with love, the latter implicitly qualified as sexual or erotic, whatever precisely those words might mean). In heteronormative cultural settings, generally speaking, love is construed as that which joins the two sexes, while friendship is for members of the same sex; any variations from this principle are troublesome at best, unnatural at worst, sometimes even unthinkable. Once again, matters are not so straightforward in the Latin textual tradition, since intimacy and desire between males are an unproblematic feature of the cultural landscape it both reflects and makes visible. Chapter 2 will explore the complexities of *amicitia* and *amor* in the Latin textual tradition, and here too gender will be a central term of analysis. Textual representations of relationships between women, between women and men, and between men negotiate the tension between *amicitia* and *amor* in different but interrelated ways. We will then turn to triangular configurations in the interpersonal relationships of Latin texts, and will end by considering the implications of Latin writers' use of the language of brotherly and sisterly love to describe pairs who in contemporary English would be called both friends and lovers. Chapter 3 offers readings of a representative selection of texts from various genres of the literary tradition, from Catullus' poetry to the letters of Cicero and Fronto, with attention to the shifting interplay of *amor* and *amicitia*.

What is the relationship between friendship and death? Derrida and others have seen an intimate, even definitive connection between friendship and the act of commemorating the dead. Chapter 4 will consider a point that is rarely noted outside of specialist studies of epigraphy, its implications even more rarely pursued. Along with spouses, children, kin, and freedmen, friends were not infrequently included in Roman group burials, and in hundreds of surviving epitaphs named individuals are commemorated with the label *amicus* or *amica*. Inscribed in stone and meant to last, epitaphs perpetuate by their continued existence the relationships they name, and anchor them in one of the most concrete of individual and social realities: burial of the dead. In this chapter most of all, we are vividly reminded that *amicitia* is not *only* a semiotic system; in addition to the language of epitaphs commemorating the dead there is also the physical fact that ashes and bones were put to rest with each other. This gesture, too, can be "read" in a broad sense of the term – interpreted, deciphered, as part of a larger system of signs – yet in its irreducible individuality, the disposition of men's and women's remains reminds us that our reading of Roman friendship is not only a matter of language. The epitaphs allow us, moreover, to hear more fully and more consistently than elsewhere the voices of slaves and freedmen as well as of knights and senators, of women as well as of men. Because they poignantly blend the singularity of individual lives and deaths with the generic and formulaic language of Latin inscriptions, and because the people whom they name and in whose voices they speak are almost always otherwise unknown and unknowable to us, these texts can speak to us in a particularly powerful way about the flexible durability of *amicitia*.

CHAPTER I

Men and women

Are you a slave? Then you cannot be a friend.
Are you a tyrant? Then you cannot have friends.
All too long a slave and a tyrant were hidden in woman:
that is why woman is not yet capable of friendship;
she knows only love.

(Nietzsche, *Thus Spoke Zarathustra*)

In *A Room of One's Own*, Virginia Woolf reminds her readers that, despite what the history of Western literature until Jane Austen might suggest, "sometimes women do like women." Woolf's sharply ironic remark comes in response to a long history of denying or ignoring friendships among women – or else exoticizing them. "Although examples of such friendships are rarer," Rousseau writes in his *Confessions*, "they are also more beautiful." Similarly, women's friendships with men have long been the locus of anxious debate, the very possibility of their existence sometimes denied. In short, the Western tradition is characterized by a persistently recurring belief that, while women may have intimate relationships with each other and with men, these cannot constitute friendship in its fullest or truest form, because that is reserved for men.[1] Montaigne lays bare with breathtaking clarity the misogynistic assumptions often implicit in this view of friendship:

Women are in truth not normally capable of responding to such familiarity and mutual confidence as sustain that holy bond of friendship, nor do their souls seem firm enough to withstand the clasp of a knot so lasting and so tightly

---

[1] Among the many studies of friendships between women in the European literary tradition see Todd 1980, Faderman 1981, Haggerty 1998, Kim 2003, Vicinus 2004, Marcus 2007; for friendships between men and women see, among others, Mauser and Becker-Cantarino 1991, Luftig 1993, Hermand 2006, pp. 67–84, Korhonen 2006, pp. 321–356, Thomas 2009, pp. 198–214. Jacques Derrida's *Politics of Friendship* begins with the consideration that "the canonical structure of friendship" in the Western tradition is androcentric, assimilated to the model of brotherhood.

drawn ... There is no example yet of woman attaining to it and by the common agreement of the ancient schools of philosophy she is excluded from it.[2]

A rather less well-known text, Jordan Simon's 1767 *Dorians Briefe von der Freundschaft an eine vornehme Freundin*, takes it as axiomatic that friendship is a "masculine virtue," and so it comes as no surprise when the noble woman of the title promises to be "a manly, not a womanly friend" to Dorian. On this model, women may participate in friendship, but only on the condition that they effectively renounce their gender.[3] Even when the possibility of friendship between women and men is granted, suspicion and anxiety are frequently not far behind:

When the two people who thus discover that they are on the same secret road are of different sexes, the friendship which arises between them will very easily pass – may pass in the first half-hour – into erotic love. Indeed, unless they are physically repulsive to each other or unless one or both already loves elsewhere, it is almost certain to do so sooner or later.[4]

There are a number of questionable assumptions here: that all human beings are by default irresistibly attracted to the opposite sex and thus that erotic love inevitably lurks around the corner whenever men and women become close; that the erotic is reducible to the physical; that love is or should be limited to one other person alone. Questionable as they are, however, they are hardly unique to Lewis, nor a matter of the past. The risks, limitations, and sheer possibility of friendship between men and women are a major theme of the popular-philosophical musings of Epstein's *Friendship: An Exposé*, for example, and provide seemingly endless fodder for humor, a sure sign of cultural preoccupation. In the world of American television, whose popularity is hardly limited to the United States, it is enough to think of *Seinfeld* or, precisely, *Friends*.

---

[2] Screech 2004, pp. 6–7. Montaigne's absolute language ("no example yet") is as remarkable as the oversimplification about ancient philosophy (added only in the essay's third edition): At least one major school of ancient philosophy, the Epicureans, did seem to have allowed for women's participation in friendship. In a posthumously published essay Montaigne observes that the young Marie de Gournay may one day be capable of "the perfection of that hallowed friendship" about which "we read" that no woman has yet been able to achieve it (*Essays* 2.17, *De la presumption*: "Si l'adolescence peut donner presage, cette âme sera quelque jour capable des plus belles choses, et entre autres de la perfection de cette tressaincte amitié, où nous ne lisons point que son sexe ait peu monter encores"). These words may signal some rethinking on Montaigne's part, or might have been added by de Gournay herself, who edited the version of his essays in which the remark appears: see Korhonen 2006, pp. 279–285.
[3] Simon, *Dorians Briefe* 11.332: "eine Tugend, die männlich, und nicht weibisch kann seyn"; 11.335: "eine männliche und nicht weibische Freundinn." See the introduction to Mauser and Becker-Cantarino 1991.
[4] Lewis 1960, pp. 80–81.

In this chapter we will read *amicitia* as it is found in various combinations of gender across the full range of surviving speech genres of the Latin textual tradition, from Cicero's eloquent philosophizing to elegiac poetry to simple prose epitaphs marking burials. The questions I ask are not whether men and women could be friends in ancient Rome or whether Roman women could be friends with each other; phrased in those terms, these questions are easily answered in the affirmative. Instead, I consider how *amicitia* is inflected for gender in Latin texts, aiming to explore the interactions between semiotic systems of masculinity, femininity, and interpersonal relationship.

AMICITIA: MEN ONLY?

In certain key moments in the Latin literary tradition, *amicitia* is portrayed as both quintessentially male experience and masculine prerogative. Lucretius' poetic Epicurean anthropology, for example, locates its origins in a primordial pact between men, who agreed to refrain from harming each other, their children, and womenfolk.[5] Valerius Maximus' chapter on *amicitia* discussed in the introduction (Val. Max. 4.7), in which he names nine Roman pairs, two foreign pairs, then culminates with himself and Pompeius, refers exclusively to male friends; women figure in the preceding chapter on conjugal love (Val. Max. 4.6). For his part, Cicero lauds friendship in his *De officiis* as a bond linking "good men of similar character (*viri boni moribus similes*)" and, as we have seen, his Laelius proclaims, with more than a little complacency, that "friendship can only exist amongst the good."[6] The parallel from *De officiis* suggests that the masculine gender of *boni* is not simply generic; and Laelius proceeds to cite a series of men from the upper levels of Roman society as illustrations of the sort of people he is talking about – all of them *viri boni* (19) – and not a single woman. After reviewing another roster of great men (Paulus, Cato, Galus, Scipio, Philo), Laelius hymns the benefits and joys of friendship:

---

[5] Lucr. 5.1011–1013: *tunc et amicitiem coeperunt iungere aventes / finitimi inter se nec laedere nec violari, / et pueros commendarunt muliebreque saeclum.*

[6] Cic. *Off.* 1.55: *sed omnium societatum nulla praestantior est, nulla firmior, quam cum viri boni moribus similes sunt familiaritate coniuncti; illud enim honestum, quod saepe dicimus, etiam si in alio cernimus, tamen nos movet atque illi, in quo id inesse videtur, amicos facit.* Several generations of scholars have disputed the authenticity of this paragraph or argued that it was transposed from somewhere else in Cicero's work; see Dyck 1979 for arguments in favor of authenticity. Even if the passage is not Ciceronian, it voices a common perspective.

talis igitur inter viros amicitia tantas opportunitates habet quantas vix queo
dicere. principio qui potest esse "vita vitalis," ut ait Ennius, quae non in amici
mutua benevolentia conquiescit? quid dulcius quam habere quicum omnia
audeas sic loqui ut tecum? qui esset tantus fructus in prosperis rebus, nisi haberes qui illis aeque ac tu ipse gauderet? ... nam et secundas res splendidiores facit
amicitia et adversas partiens communicansque leviores. (Cic. *Amic.* 22)

This kind of friendship between men has such great advantages that I can barely
name them. First of all, to quote Ennius, how can there be a "livable life" unless
it rests upon the reciprocal goodwill of a friend? What is more pleasurable than
to have someone with whom you do not hesitate to say whatever you want, as
if you were talking to yourself? Would the enjoyment of prosperity be so great
if you did not have someone who took pleasure in it as much as you do? ...
Friendship makes favorable circumstances even more magnificent, and by distributing the burden of unfavorable circumstances it makes them easier to bear.

Like Cicero himself, nearly all of the men participating and named in
this text were married, but men's wives apparently do not count as the
perfect partners with whom they share life's joys and pains, with whom
they speak as freely and openly as if to themselves.

Throughout the *De amicitia*, in fact, faceless, anonymous wives and
mothers remain in the background as their menfolk contemplate the joys
of their relationships with each other. This text mentions not one woman
by name. Laelius' opening eulogy of his beloved friend Scipio praises
him for his treatment of his mother and sisters (11), but it is of course
his friendship with Laelius that inspires and dominates the entire text.
Otherwise, women appear in this text as potential obstacles to masculine friendship. In one passage we read that young men have sometimes
broken off friendships in a dispute over a marriage match (34), and the
only other mention of women in conjunction with friendship in this text
is rather brutally dismissive.

itaque, ut quisque minimum firmitatis haberet minimumque virium, ita amicitias appetere maxime; ex eo fieri ut mulierculae magis amicitiarum praesidia
quaerant quam viri et inopes quam opulenti et calamitosi quam ii qui putentur
beati. o praeclaram sapientiam! (Cic. *Amic.* 46–47)

And so they say that the less solidity and strength one has, the more one will
look for friendships, and that this is why womenfolk seek the protection provided by friendships more than men, the poor more than the rich, and those
who have suffered disasters more than those who are considered fortunate. Such
glorious wisdom!

The exclamation is deeply ironic: Laelius is rejecting an Epicurean view
of friendship as based on need and weakness rather than on spontaneous
affection. And he uses Roman discourses of gender to parody it. Women

are weak and needy (note the disparaging diminutive *mulierculae*) and thus seek friendship out of desperation, while men (unqualified *viri*) are strong and self-sufficient and thus enter into friendships not out of need but out of affection and attraction. Laelius thereby admits in passing what could not be denied – that women *do* have friendships – even as he coolly keeps them distinct from the ideal type of *amicitia* that is his concern.[7]

No doubt under the influence of Cicero and Valerius Maximus, more than one scholar has come to the conclusion that Roman friendship was a "civic inter-male relationship," or that "for the ancients there was no true friendship between man and woman."[8] The matter seems clear enough. Yet other texts, ranging from Pliny's elegant epistles to epitaphs memorializing the deceased found everywhere Latin inscriptions were being commissioned to letters written by a woman at the fringes of the Roman world, suggest that that clarity is illusory, the perspective partial, the ideal an ideal only for some. In short, reading Roman friendship with attention to codes of both gender and speech genre shows us a far more richly variegated landscape of interpersonal relationships than the complacently masculinist idealizations of Cicero or the matter-of-fact androcentrism of Lucretius' anthropology.[9]

FRIENDSHIP BETWEEN WOMEN IN LITERATURE
AND LETTERS

The Latin literary tradition frequently describes relationships between women without using the word *amica* but in such a way as to activate discourses of friendship, for example by using terms like *familiaris* or *amor* or by appealing to the motif of *alter ego*. Sometimes, too, there is no single word or set of words associated with *amicitia* but a narrative which anchors two women's intimacy in the body, in embraces and kisses. In the course of Trimalchio's banquet in Petronius' *Satyricon*, the host's wife Fortunata joins the party and takes her place next to Scintilla, wife of

---

[7] When we elsewhere read that adulation and charming flattery (*blanditia*) are incompatible with *amicitia* in its ideal form, the cultural coding of *blanditia* as feminine comes to mind: see Cic. *Amic.* 91 (*sic habendum est nullam in amicitiis pestem esse maiorem quam adulationem, blanditiam, assentationem*) and Dutsch 2008, pp. 49–91, 196–198. For the contrast between the flatterer and the friend, see Introduction, p. 15.

[8] Kroll 1989 ad Catull. 109.6: "wirkliche Freundschaft zwischen Mann und Weib gab es für die Alten nicht"; Gibson 1995: 75: "a civic inter-male relationship."

[9] Kent 2009, p. 13, notes a comparable situation in fifteenth-century Florence: "Friendship was seen as a male prerogative and pleasure," yet there is "rich evidence of friendships not only among women but also between women and men in the sixteenth century."

one of Trimalchio's guests, greeting her with a kiss and a polite salutation (Petron. *Sat.* 67.5: *osculataque plaudentem: "est te" inquit, "videre?"*). The two women proceed to show off their jewelry to each other, and as the wine flows, tongues loosen and things get physical.

interim mulieres sauciae inter se riserunt ebriaeque iunxerunt oscula, dum altera diligentiam matris familiae iactat, altera delicias et indiligentiam viri. dumque sic cohaerent, Habinnas furtim consurrexit, pedesque Fortunatae correptos super lectum immisit. "au! au!" illa proclamavit aberrante tunica super genua. composita ergo in gremio Scintillae indecentissimam rubore faciem sudario abscondit. (Petron. *Sat.* 67.11–13)

Meanwhile the women were pretty tipsy, laughing amongst themselves and exchanging drunken kisses; the one went on about what a hardworking lady of the house she was, the other about how capricious and lazy her husband was. While they were wrapped up in each other like this, Habinnas got up without their noticing, grabbed Fortunata's feet and hoisted them up on to the couch. Her tunic slipped up above her knees as she shouted "Hey! Hey!" and then, nestling in Scintilla's lap, she hid her unflatteringly blushing face in her kerchief.

The gossiping about their husbands foreshadows an ugly turn of events. Soon thereafter Trimalchio kisses a slave boy, Fortunata calls him a lecherous dog (*canis*), and he throws a cup in her face, whereupon Fortunata turns to Scintilla for comfort, hiding herself once again in her embrace (Petron. *Sat.* 74.12). Throughout this narrative Fortunata's and Scintilla's bodies are comfortably contiguous, even intertwined (*cohaerent*), and parallels with some of the male *amici* of Latin poetry suggest themselves. Like Catullus and Veranius, the two women exchange kisses of delight and repeated embraces as they meet again; like Propertius and Gallus, they take tearful comfort in each other's embrace when one or both are mistreated by their partners.[10]

Some texts describing relationships between women use words other than *amica*, such as the near-synonym *familiaris*. Tacitus' bloodcurdling narrative of Nero's attempt to kill his mother Agrippina by rigging a shipwreck begins by setting the stage: Agrippina is on board the ship with two *familiares*, one male and one female (Crepereius Gallus and Acerronia), the latter at Agrippina's feet as she reclines on a couch. As the ship begins to sink, Acerronia shouts out that *she* is Agrippina in a desperate attempt to save herself which perverts the example of the paradigmatic *amici*, Orestes

---

[10] Catullus 9.8–9 (*applicansque collum /iucundum os oculosque saviabor*; see above, p. 4); Prop. 1.5.29–30 (*sed pariter miseri socio cogemur amore / alter in alterius mutua flere sinu*; see below, p. 202). Boehringer 2007, pp. 314–321, describes Scintilla and Fortunata as joined in "une relation sexuelle," but it is not clear on what basis the adjective is used.

and Pylades, each of whom claims to be Orestes in order that the other may be saved (see above, p. 6). This imprudent speech act leads to Acerronia's being killed on the spot; Agrippina escapes in a wiser silence.[11]

Not infrequently we find the relationship between two women invoked in connection with their menfolk. Pliny's panegyric on Trajan celebrates the relationship between the emperor's wife Plotina and his sister Ulpia Marciana.

suspiciunt invicem, invicem cedunt, cumque te utraque effusissime diligat, nihil sua putant interesse utram tu magis ames. *idem utrique propositum, idem tenor vitae, nihilque ex quo sentias duas esse.* (Plin. *Pan.* 84.4)

They respect each other and yield to each other. Since both of them love you so abundantly, they do not think it matters which one of them you love more. The two have one purpose, one aim in life – in fact, there is nothing to make you even think there are *two* of them.

In these carefully constructed sentences we may read a hint that the women had no great affection for each other; the emphasis is entirely on their equal respect and affection for Trajan. Placing no label on the women's relationship with each other, Pliny skilfully appeals to ideals associated with *amicitia* – "wanting the same thing (*idem velle*)," "one soul in two bodies," "another self (*alter ego*)" – without naming it.[12] For his part, Statius gives another name – *amor* – to the relationship between his wife and Priscilla, recently deceased wife of Flavius Abascantus, freedman secretary in the emperor's household, even as he advertises the bond that joins him to Abascantus as *amicitia*.

uxorem enim vivam amare voluptas est, defunctam religio. ego tamen huic operi non ut unus e turba nec tantum quasi officiosus adsilui. *amavit enim uxorem meam Priscilla et amando fecit mihi illam probatiorem*; post hoc ingratus sum, si lacrimas tuas transeo. praeterea latus omne divinae domus semper demereri pro mea mediocritate conitor. nam qui *bona fide* deos colit, amat et sacerdotes. sed quamvis propiorem usum *amicitiae tuae* iampridem cuperem, mallem tamen nondum invenisse materiam. (Stat. *Silv.* 5.1.pr.)

It is a pleasure to love one's wife while she is alive, it is a sacred obligation to do so after her decease. I took up this task [of writing a poem of consolation] not as one of a nameless crowd, nor even from a sense of duty. Rather, Priscilla had great

---

[11] Tac. *Ann.* 14.5: *duobus e numero familiarium Agrippinam comitantibus, ex quis Crepereius Gallus haud procul gubernaculis adstabat, Acerronia super pedes cubitantis reclinis paenitentiam filii et recuperatam matris gratiam per gaudium memorabat ... verum Acerronia, imprudentia dum se Agrippinam esse utque subveniretur matri principis clamitat, contis et remis et quae fors obtulerat navalibus telis conficitur.* I thank Kathleen Coleman for reminding me of this passage.

[12] See Carlon 2009, pp. 143–145, for discussion of Trajan and Plotina in the *Panegyricus*.

affection for my wife and through her affection commended my wife all the more to me. Consequently I would be an ingrate if I were to pass over your tears in silence. Besides, I always try to oblige every aspect of the divine house as far as my limited ability allows: whoever worships the gods in good faith loves their priests too. But, while I long yearned for a closer enjoyment of your friendship, under the circumstances I wish I had not yet been given the occasion to do so.

In this textual negotiation of men's relationships with each other, whatever may actually have joined the two women is irrecoverable, but what the text portrays is suggestive enough. The *amor* between Priscilla and Statius' wife co-exists with and is a prop in Statius' performance of *amicitia* with Abascantus – and, lurking unmentioned behind both of them, with the Emperor Domitian, the divinity whose faithful priest (*bona fide*) Statius here plays.[13]

Among the private letters written on thin wooden tablets which have been found at the site of Vindolanda near Hadrian's Wall and date to the early second century AD are several sent by Claudia Severa to Sulpicia Lepidina. In a configuration comparable to that evoked by Statius, though in a very different social context, these women's husbands –Aelius Brocchus and Flavius Cerialis respectively, the latter holding the title of Prefect of the Ninth Cohort of Tungrians – were themselves on intimate terms, writing to each other as *frater* in correspondence to which we will return in Chapter 2. For our reading of friendship between women, Severa's letters to Lepidina are invaluable. Here we have woman-authored texts that give us glimpses at how a relationship between two women might be performed in words shared privately.

[*outside*] Sulpiciae Lepidinae Flavii Cerialis a Severa.

[*inside*] Cl(audia) Severa Lepidinae suae salutem. III Idus Septembres, soror, ad diem sollemnem natalem meum rogo libenter facias ut venias ad nos, iucundiorem mihi diem interventu tuo factura si venies. Cerialem tuum saluta. Aelius meus et filiolus salutant. [*in another hand*] sperabo te, soror. vale – soror, anima mea, ita valeam, et karissima – et have. (Bowman and Thomas 1994, 291)

[*outside*] To Sulpicia Lepidina, wife of Flavius Cerialis, from Severa.

[*inside*] Claudia Severa sends greetings to her dear Lepidina. On the occasion of the celebration of my birthday on 29 August I kindly ask you the favor, sister, of coming to us. You will make the day all the more delightful for me if you come.

---

[13] For Statius and Abascantus (and behind them Domitian), see further Gibson 2006 ad loc. and Nauta 2002, pp. 193–194, 233–234. See Chapter 3 below, p. 254, for an affectionate relationship between women at the highest levels of Roman society – Marcus Aurelius' mother Domitia Lucilla and Fronto's wife Cratia – described in terms of *amor* and kisses and intertwined with the friendship between their menfolk.

Greetings to your (husband) Cerialis. My (husband) Aelius and my little son send their greetings too. [*in another hand*] I will be waiting for you, sister. Take care, sister darling – I swear it! – and dearest to me, and be well.

Another letter gives us a glimpse – but just that – at the relationship between Severa and her husband and its potential impact on that between the two women: Severa tells Lepidina that she has asked for and obtained her husband's *permission* to visit her.

ego, soror, sicut tecum locuta fueram et promiseram ut peterem a Broccho et venirem at te, peti, et respondit mihi <i>ta corde semp[er li]citum una... [*in another hand*] [val]e m[.] soror karissima et anima ma (*sic*) desideratissima ... (Bowman and Thomas 1994, 292)

Dear sister: Just as you and I had discussed, and I had promised that I would ask Brocchus and come to you, I have asked him, and he answered that I was always freely allowed ... [*in another hand*] Farewell, dearest sister and most precious darling.

Comparable formulae of affection appear in a partially surviving letter of Severa's (635: *Aelius meus te et filiolus sal[utant] ... vale mi soror [karis]-sima*), and a fragment of yet another, written in the same hand as the closures of 291 and 292, is addressed to a *soror karissima*, who may well be Lepidina yet again (293).

These are quite literally a woman's words, and in more than one sense. Following common practice, Severa seems to have dictated the body of the letter to a secretary but added the concluding phrases in her own hand.[14] The precise tonalities of her words to Lepidina must of course elude us. The wide variations in the use of terms of address within a single language, not to mention between languages, discourage dogmatism or generalization. Consider the regionally and socially varying tonalities of phrases like "dear," "honey," "love," or "mate" in English as it is spoken around the world today. Still, the affectionate quality of Severa's language to the woman she addresses as *soror* – a term to which we will return – seems clear enough. Less clear is whether we can or should place much weight on the fact that in the surviving correspondence Severa nowhere addresses Lepidina as *amica* (and none of the surviving fragments of letters between the women's husbands uses the vocative *amice*). This might possibly reflect the idiolect of the individuals involved or the usage of

---

[14] The body of Severa's first letter quoted below is written in what has been called a "very refined cursive," the closing words in a "hesitant, ugly and unpractised hand but very elegant Latin" (Bowman 1994, p. 124). As one of the anonymous readers for the press points out, the judgment "very elegant Latin" may not withstand scrutiny.

the Latin-speaking community at Vindolanda; it might tell us something
about the contours of these particular relationships; or it might not be a
phenomenon at all, since now-lost letters may well have contained phrases
like *mi amice* and *mea amica*.

Do Severa's letters give us a glimpse at a specifically feminine language
of interpersonal relationships? Any attempt to answer the question is
hampered by the paucity of material with which to compare it. Women's
writings in classical Latin are exiguous, other examples of private correspondence in Latin from one woman to another nonexistent.[15] We might,
then, compare Severa's language to Lepidina with that found in men's
letters from Vindolanda or more generally with men's addresses to each
other in the textual tradition. The results are not overwhelming. Neither
the phrase *Lepidinae suae* nor the vocative *carissima* is marked as specifically feminine in style. The use of the possessive adjective and the adjective
carus or its superlative are perfectly standard in letters and inscriptions
commissioned and composed by men, whether to men or to women. Nor
is the use of the phrase *anima mea* specific to women's writing: Cicero
addresses letters to his wife and daughter with the phrase *animae meae*,
and in Roman comedy *mi anime* is found in the mouths of both men and
women.[16] In short, no single lexical item in Severa's letter seems to inflect
her message for gender. On the other hand, the cumulative effect – the
repetitions of *soror*, the rapid succession of terms of endearment (*soror,
soror, anima mea, karissima*), and the rather breathless pileup, probably
written in Severa's own hand, at the end of letter 291 – might possibly be
signs of a style marked as feminine, for a remark by Donatus in his commentary on Terence suggests that the frequent use of appellatives like *mea*
and *amabo* were considered characteristic of (but not limited to) women's
speech, along with flattering language, self-pity, and longwindedness.[17]

[15] For women's writings in Latin see, for example, Dixon 2001, Farrell 2001, pp. 52–83. See Bagnall
and Cribiore 2006 for a commented collection of women's autograph letters from Egypt, in both
Greek and Coptic.

[16] For *carissima* see Dickey 2002, pp. 315 ("a general term of mild affection, especially for friends
and acquaintances of equal or lower status") and for the use of the possessive adjectives *mi* and
mea see pp. 214–224. For *animae meae* see Cic. *Fam.* 14.14, 14.18. Adams 1995 counts twelve
occurrences of *mi anime* in Plautus and Terence, nine of them in the mouths of women, three
spoken by men (twice addressing women, once addressing a male slave); *anima mea* does not
occur at all in comedy. As Adams notes, however, attempts to find significance in the relative
order of possessive adjective and noun are not persuasive. For further discussion of women's language in Latin, see Adams 1984, Fögen 2004, Dutsch 2008.

[17] Don. Ter. *Eun.* 656.1: *mea et mea tu et amabo et alia huiuscemodi mulieribus apta sunt blandi-
menta*; cf. Don. Ter. *Ad.* 291.4: *proprium est mulierum, cum loquuntur, aut aliis blandiri … aut se
commiserari*; ad *Hec.* 741.5: *senile et femineum tardiloquium*. See discussion at Dutsch 2008, pp.
4–12, 49–58.

What of Severa's use of the term *soror*? The practice of addressing a female friend as "sister" seems to reflect a widespread usage, analogous to the use of *frater* to be discussed in Chapter 2 and presumably, like the latter, characteristic of a wide range of speech genres. We find it, for example, not only in the private correspondence of a woman at Vindolanda but in the loftiest of the Latin poetic genres. Virgil's narrative of the Italian warrior-princess Camilla evokes a tight network of feminine relationships. In a flashback narrative to one of her nymphs, the goddess Diana describes her *amor* for Camilla; and after being fatally wounded, Camilla addresses her dying words to a female companion of her own.

> tum sic exspirans Accam ex *aequalibus* unam
> adloquitur, *fida* ante alias quae sola Camillae
> *quicum partiri curas*, atque haec ita fatur:
> "hactenus, Acca *soror*, potui ..."
> (Verg. *Aen.* 11.820–823)

> Thus, breathing her last, she spoke to Acca, one of her fellows,
> uniquely faithful to Camilla, beyond all others,
> one with whom she shared her burdens. Thus she spoke:
> "I have done what I could, sister Acca ..."

Acca is a passing but memorable figure. As far as we can tell, she is (like Camilla herself) an invention of Virgil's, and she exists in this text only in her connection with Camilla, her only other appearance being when she complies with Camilla's final request by bringing the news of the Vulscians' defeat and Camilla's death to Turnus at the very end of Book 11.[18] But Camilla's dying words to Acca make an impression. When she calls her *Acca soror*, readers of the *Aeneid* may recall another memorable pair of women in this poem: Dido and her sister, whom she addresses at the opening of Book 4 as *Anna soror* (Verg. *Aen.* 4.9); some attentive readers may even note the similarity between the two names. In Chapter 2 we will return to the considerable overlaps among discourses of brother and sister love, the passionate love associated with Venus, and the love between friends, and will see among other things that in no Latin text surviving from antiquity is the label *soror* or imagery of sister-love used in connection with homoerotic desire between women. But Virgil's brief evocation of Camilla's relationship with Acca – lines which may have been influenced by Ennius' description of Servilius Geminus' *amicus minor* (see

---

[18] V. *Aen.* 11.537–538 (Diana to Opis about Camilla): *cara mihi ante alias; neque enim novus iste Dianae / venit amor*; V. *Aen.* 11.896–900 (Accius brings the news to Turnus). Servius has nothing to say about Acca.

Introduction, p. 25) – does arguably activate the discourse of *amicitia* by means of the term *aequales*, the invocation of *fides*, and the motif of a leader sharing burdens with a comrade (*quicum partiri curas*).[19]

None of the preceding texts uses the label *amica*. But, although Cicero's *De amicitia* ignores and almost succeeds in obscuring the fact, relationships between women who are described as *amicae* are a distinct feature of the Latin textual tradition across a range of genres. A scene in Plautus' *Casina* brings together two neighbors, Cleustrata and Myrrhina, in a brief but vivid evocation of their relationship. Cleustrata flatteringly tells Myrrhina that she loves no other neighbor more deservedly (*amo*) and proceeds to unload her burden. Her husband is in love with Cleustrata's slave-girl Casina (*amat*); the polyvalence of *amor*, to which we will return in Chapter 2, is here particularly eloquent. And so the distressed wife seeks advice from her neighbor. Rather to Cleustrata's distress, Myrrhina not only counsels wifely submission, but suspiciously wonders how Cleustrata came into possession of the slave-girl and how she can claim sole possession at that: Surely "whatever is yours is your husband's too"? We may note the invocation of the ideal of sharing, characteristic both of marriage and, precisely, of *amicitia*; for her part, Cleustrata reminds Myrrhina of their own friendship, which *ought* to have meant that she was on her side. Instead, as she exclaims in exasperation, "everything you say goes against your friend (*tuam amicam*)!"[20]

The scene dramatizes some lasting stereotypes as they play out in the Latin textual tradition's images of women's friendships: the wiley wife seeking assistance from a female friend as she strategizes against her husband, and the decently submissive wife thwarting her plans. Another recurring stereotype is that of the married woman slipping out of her home in order to meet a lover – on the pretext of visiting a sick female friend (*amica*) who is actually in perfect health.[21] Fearfully masculinist stereotypes aside, a social background made the commonplace possible.

---

[19] Surprisingly, neither Diana/Camilla nor Camilla/Acca appear in Rabinowitz and Auanger 2002 or Boehringer 2007. See Matter 2006 for sisterly love and the homoerotic in medieval texts and Haggerty 1998, pp. 73–119, for discussion of sisterly love, romantic friendship, and desire between women in late eighteenth-century English literature.

[20] Plaut. *Cas.* 182: *nam vicinam neminem merito amo magis quam te*; 196: *ipsus eam amat*; 202: *hoc viri censeo esse omne quicquid tuomst*; 203: *tu quidem advorsum tuam amicam omnia loqueris*. Dutsch 2008, pp. 30–39, discusses this scene with attention to the possibility of a specifically feminine discourse of friendship.

[21] Lucil. 993–934 Marx: *aut cum iter est aliquo et causam commenta viai / aut apud aurificem, ad matrem, cognatam, ad amicam*; Ov. *Am.* 2.2.21: *ibit ad adfectam, quae non languebit, amicam*; Ov. *Ars am.* 3.641–642: *cum, quotiens opus est, fallax aegrotet amica, / et cedat lecto quamlibet aegra suo*; Mart. 11.7.7: *aegram simulabis amicam?*

Roman women were connected with each other by the bonds of *amicitia* and could, for example, make provision for their *amicae* in their wills.[22] Friendships between women could, as we have seen, at least partially be lived out in physical and other kinds of space distinct from that of their relationships with their husbands; and these *amicitiae* were easily imagined to involve physical intimacy. In one of his poems on Cynthia to which we will return in Chapter 2, meditating on the power of jealousy and suspicion, Propertius expresses fear of any and all who may have physical contact with Cynthia. He fears her mother's kisses, her sister, and the *amica* with whom she might sleep.[23]

Women's relationships with their *amicae* sometimes form the background or provide the fuel for misogynistic remarks. In Petronius' *Satyricon*, Oenothea's excuse to Encolpius for coming back home later than expected is that she had gone to visit a female friend (*amica*) who insisted that she stay longer over drinks (136.11). The stereotype of the bibulous female already activated by her name (Wine Goddess) is at stake here, but the existence of friendships among women and the fact that they spend time with each other apart from men is not itself being ironized. Martial brings the misogyny right to the surface in a version of the "take my wife – please" joke:

> omnes quas habuit, Fabiane, Lycoris *amicas*
> extulit: uxori fiat *amica* meae.
>
> (Mart. 4.24)

> All of the female friends Lycoris has ever had, Fabianus,
> she has buried. She should be my wife's friend!

Elsewhere Martial writes of a woman who surrounds herself with old or ugly *amicae* in order to make herself seem that much more young and beautiful, and of Phyllis, who uses any number of techniques to take advantage of his finanical resources: compelling him to buy expensive fish, for example, on the excuse that a wealthy female friend (*amica*) is coming to dinner.[24]

---

[22] Cf. *Digest* 34.2.40.2: *mulier decedens ornamenta legaverat ita: "Seiae amicae meae ornamenta universa dari volo."* See Gardner 1986, pp. 163–204, for women, inheritances, and bequests, and Verboven 2002, pp. 183–223, for inheritances, legacies, and guardianships in connection with friendship.

[23] Prop. 2.6.11–12: *me laedet, si multa tibi dabit oscula mater, / me soror et quando dormit amica simul.*

[24] Mart. 8.79.1–2: *omnes aut vetulas habes amicas / aut turpes vetulisque foediores*; 11.49.9–10: *nunc ut emam grandemve lupum mullumve bilibrem, / indixit cenam dives amica tibi.*

Friendships between women are an integral part of the complex urban landscape of Juvenal's satires, above all in the sixth satire, spoken in the voice of a man dissuading another from marrying by running through a catalogue of misogynistic stereotypes. Even less than Petronius' *Satyricon* or Martial's epigrams is this poem a historically reliable report on Roman women's relationships with each other; but it does show us what an angry, misogynistic man in a literary text might be imagined to imagine about female friendships. He complains that a wasteful, showy woman goes to the games with rented clothing, cushions, and seat – but also rented slaves and even "rented friends" (*conducit … amicas*, 6.352–354)! He grumbles that the overly learned woman should direct her criticism of grammatical mistakes at her female friends rather than at her husband (6.455–456: *opicae castiget amicae / uerba: soloecismum liceat fecisse marito*). And, scandalized, he describes how one woman has her slaves mercilessly beaten while she herself casually chats with her women friends (*audit amicas*: 6.48).[25]

FRIENDSHIP BETWEEN WOMEN IN INSCRIPTIONS

Although underrepresented in terms of absolute numbers, women were distinctly noticeable participants in the widespread practice of commissioning dedicatory and funerary inscriptions. Reading these texts opens up for us a world in which women publicize their friendships with each other, using the same formulaic language as do men; in Chapter 4 we will focus on the wide range of configurations in which *amicitia* is commemorated in epitaphs in particular. In inscriptions of all kinds commissioned by and for women in honor of their female friends, just as in those commissioned by and for men, the label of choice is *amica* rather than *familiaris* or *necessaria*.[26]

Several surviving dedicatory inscriptions, marking statues or other publicly visible signs of honor given to women, were commissioned by other women. An inscription found along the Via Appia outside of Rome reads as follows:

[25] We will return in the next chapter to Juvenal's voyeuristic depiction of women's drunken intimacy, which takes Encolpius' narrative of Fortunata and Scintilla several steps further (Juv. 6.306–313).
[26] No overall statistic is available, but in his compilation of individuals identified as *amici* in inscriptions throughout Italy apart from the city of Rome, Mauro Reali reports that 610 are male, 118 are female, and 33 of undeterminable gender or a generic plural *amici* (Reali 1997, pp. 177 and 201). For discussion of the dating and interpretation of Latin inscriptions, see Chapter 4.

Caeciliae verissimae / clarissimae memoriae / sanctissimae feminae, / Atilia Rufina clariss(ima) fem(ina) / et Caesonia Victorina / *amicae incomparabili*. (*CIL* 6.1363; Rome)

To Caecilia, truest and most respectable lady of honorable memory. The noble lady Atilia Rufina and Caesonia Victorina [commissioned this] for their incomparable friend.

The arrangement of the words on the stone adds to the impact of the message. The text begins with the deceased Caecilia's name and a pileup of superlatives and honorific phrases suggesting high social status (especially *clarissima*), all of them ending in -*ae*. We then read the names of the two women who honor her memory, one of whom commemorates herself with her own honorific superlative (again *clarissima*), and finally the eloquent final line, honoring Caecilia not in terms of status but as a friend. Less exuberant, but powerful precisely in its spareness, is this inscription found at Lodi (ancient Laus Pompeia) in northern Italy, whose formulae carefully specify that both Viria Severa and the woman who honors her, her friend Annia Quintula, were freeborn Romans:

In memoriam / Viriae M(arci) f(iliae) / Severae / *amicae optim(ae)* / Annia Corelli f(ilia) / Quintula / [imp]ensa sua / [fecit]. (*CIL* 5.6391 = Reali 134C; Lodi, first–second century AD; see Figure 2)[27]

In memory of her excellent friend Viria Severa, daughter of Marcus. Annia Quintula, daughter of Corellius, erected this at her own expense.

Here too the arrangement of the words in short lines on the stone is expressive, but in this case the two words commemorating the bond which joined the two women and motivate the very existence of this inscription come not at the end but in the center of the text: *AMICAE OPTIMAE*.

As we will see in Chapter 4, the great majority of surviving Latin inscriptions are epitaphs, marking the burial of an individual or group, commemorating the deceased by name and often locating him, her, or them in one or more social networks: as spouse, child, freed slave, former owner, or friend. Among the wide range of configurations advertised is that between *amicae*. Epitaphs like the following, commissioned by one woman in honor of another, not only memorialize the departed but publicize the generosity of their *amicae*. In most cases the nomenclature suggests, without explicitly communicating the fact, that the women were freed slaves who had acquired enough means to dedicate epitaphs, tombs,

---

[27] A slightly different version of the text was earlier published as *CIL* 2.1250 and erroneously identified as coming from Seville.

Figure 2 Stele with an inscription commissioned by Annia Quintula in memory of her
friend Viria Severa (*CIL* 5.6391, first to second century AD). Lodi, Museo Civico.

and altars; we will see in Chapter 4 that the distinctive presence of freed
slaves is typical of Latin epitaphs.

D(is) M(anibus). / Titiae Ter/tylinae. / Vetulena / Dorcas / *amicae* / *b(ene)*
m(erenti) f(ecit). (*CIL* 5.3050; Padua, late first century AD)[28]

D(is) M(anibus). / Settidi/ae Calli/tyche. po/suit aram / *amicae caris(ssimae)* /
Aeli[a] Chre/ste. (*CIL* 5.232 = Reali 6C; Pola, second–third century AD)

D(is) i(nferis) M(anibus). / Avianiae Amandae. / *amicae suae* / *fecit bene merenti* /
Livia Lauris. (*CIL* 6.12881, 12882; Rome)

---

[28] This inscription, missing from Reali 1997, is carved on a marble urn in which was found a coin
dating to the reign of Vespasian (69–78 AD).

D(is) M(anibus). / Corneliae / Saturninae. / Aetronia / Filumene / *amic(a)e opt(imae).* (*AE* 1995.1065; Nîmes, third century AD)

To the spirits of the departed. For Titia Tertylina. Vetulena Dorcas commissioned this for her well-deserving friend.

To the spirits of the departed. For Settidia Callityche. Aelia Chreste erected this altar to her dearest friend.

To the spirits of the departed below. For Aviania Amanda. Livia Lauris commissioned this for her well-deserving friend.

To the spirits of the departed. For Cornelia Saturnina. Aetronia Filumene dedicated this to her excellent friend.

An inscription on a plaque found along the Via Appia outside Rome, originally located in one of the columbaria lining that road and commemorating a woman's four *amicae*, is of interest not only because of the all-female group it memorializes but because of its final word.

Agrilia Piste, quae et / Pompusidia, f(ecit) Valeriae / Trophime et Vi(c)toriae / Erotario et Muciae / Ianuariae *amicabus / optimis*, et sibi et / posterisq(ue) eorum. (*CIL* 6.7671; Rome)

Agrilia Piste, also called Pompusidia, commissioned this for Valeria Trophima, Victoria Erotarion, and Mucia Januaria her excellent friends, and for herself, and for their descendants.

The open-ended reference to descendants implies that some or all of these women are or expect some day to be married and produce children. But no men are named, a point which is underscored by the unusual use of the feminine dative plural *amicabus*; most inscriptions, even those naming women, use the form *amicis*. All the more noticeable, then, is the final phrase providing for unnamed descendants: not the feminine *posterisque earum* but the masculine *posterisque eorum*. We can explain this – along with the clumsy double conjunction *et posterisque* and just possibly the dative form *Erotario*[29] – as a stonecutter's error, but this does not quite explain it away. The error, as usual, invites us to consider the prevailing linguistic and conceptual habits which might have made it that much more "natural" of a mistake to make. In this case we might point to the formula *posterisque eorum* characteristic of the speech genre of inscriptions, as well as to the use of the so-called generic masculine plural in Latin of all speech genres to describe groups of mixed gender; neither usage is coincidental in a patriarchal social structure and male-dominated textual tradition. Whether we call it an error or not, the masculine *eorum*

---

[29] Solin 2003 cites the nominative of this name as *Erotarion*.

in the inscription commissioned by Agrilia Piste reminds us that, while women are a clear and constant presence in the speech genre of texts commemorating the dead and meant to last, all-female groups are rare, just as the feminine *amicabus* reminds us that they are by no means impossible.

AMICI AND *AMICAE* IN LATIN LITERATURE

Women, then, could and did use the language of *amicitia* to describe their relationships with each other, both in literary texts written by men and in inscriptions that they themselves commissioned. What about their relationships with men? We begin with an asymmetry familiar to any experienced reader of Latin literature. In genres ranging from drama to epigram to courtroom speeches, when a woman is linked with an *amicus* or a man is said to have an *amica*, what is not merely connoted but directly denoted is a sexual relationship apart from marriage. We will return below to the difficult question of tone. Were *amicus* and *amica* in this sense like contemporary German *Freund* and *Freundin*, a neutrally descriptive lexical item found in a wide variety of stylistic registers from everyday speech to journalistic prose? Or more like contemporary English *friend* or Italian *amico/amica* which, when referring to a sexual partner, are in most usage patterns ironic or coy, endowed with implied quotation marks? Or something in between?[30] What is clear is that *amicus* and *amica* in the various genres of Latin literature – quite unlike, as we will see, the speech genre of inscriptions – denote one thing when used of same-sex pairs, and another when used between the sexes.

In elegiac poetry, the poet's lover is famously called his *puella* or his *domina*. The opposition between the terms' respective implications (youthful feminine subordination or woman in control, owner of slaves) captures the tension around which so much of the poetry is built. But she is also his *amica* and he her *amicus*, a term whose connotations suggest yet other qualities, among them fidelity (*fides*) and affection (*amor*).

[30] The scholarship gives a contradictory picture of the denotative and tonal range of *amica*. Cf. *TLL* s.v. *amica* 1912.58 (*paelex, concubina, scortum*, the third proposed synonym noticeably swerving from the first two), *Oxford Latin Dictionary* (*OLD*) s.v. 2 ("mistress, sweetheart, courtesan"), Dickey 2002, p. 310 ("complimentary term used by a male lover to his beloved, or the (female) object of his desire"), Wray 2001, p. 70 (*amica* means "girlfriend," "but not a nice word for it"). Following Adams 1983, pp. 348–350, Dickey 2002, p. 150, argues that "the referential meaning of *amica* changed between the time of Plautus and that of Cicero, so that by the classical period it meant 'prostitute'." The range of usage illustrated below suggests that this use of *amica* comes with no single tone, nor is there clear evidence for unidirectional diachronic change. For fluctuations in the usage of English *friend* to refer to sexual relationships between men and women, see *OED* s.v. and Luftig 1993, pp. 93–127.

We will look more closely at this language in the poetry of Catullus and Propertius in Chapter 3; here a few illustrations from Ovid will make the point. Referring to the motif of the *exclusus amator*, Ovid writes that whereas a soldier besieges cities and their gates, a lover (*amans*) lays siege to the home of his *amica* and its door; separated from his woman, a lover may complain that even the doorkeeper is now sleeping with his own *amica*, while he himself is alone. For the lover, Ovid writes elsewhere, the birthday of his *amica* is a holy day, and – in more cynical vein – blessed is he whose *amica* can truthfully claim "I didn't do it!" The usage is found across the range of literary genres. Characters in Plautine comedy, some of them referring to the relationship between a man and a female prostitute, juxtapose the terms *amica* and *amans*, playing off the assonance in the process. And in one of his *Epistulae morales* to Lucilius, listing frivolous reasons that have led people to kill themselves, Seneca cites the case of a man who hanged himself in front of his *amica*'s door.[31]

Not infrequently we find a man's *amica* being contrasted with his wife. Ovid urges his student in love to treat his *amica* with care. With his wife he can expect to quarrel – "fighting is a wife's dowry" – but a sure way to lose his *amica* is to argue with her, and a sententious line from an epigram attributed to Annius Florus proclaims in language that sounds proverbial that an *amica* outside is just as bad as a wife at home.[32] Rather more expansively, Petronius' poet Eumolpus announces the theme of the forbidden fruit: *vile est quod licet, et animus errore laetus iniurias diligit* (What is permitted is of low value, and a mind rejoicing in its error loves wrong). He then recites a poem meditating on the point with illustrations from the realm of sensual pleasures: food, flowers, and women.

> Ales Phasiacis petita Colchis
> atque Afrae volucres placent palato,
> quod non sunt faciles; at albus anser

---

[31] Ov. *Ars am.* 1.417–418: *magna superstitio tibi sit natalis amicae*; Ov. *Am.* 2.5.9–10: *felix, qui quod amat defendere fortiter audet, / cui sua "non feci!" dicere amica potest*; Plaut. *Bacch.* 193–194: *animast amica amanti: si abest, nullus est; / si adest, res nullast: ipsus est — nequam et miser*; Plaut. *Merc.* 972–973: *nam te istac aetate haud aequom filio fuerat tuo / adulescenti amanti amicam eripere emptam argento suo*; Pseud. 672–673: *hic doli, hic fallaciae omnes, hic sunt sycophantiae, / hic argentum, hic amica amanti erili filio*; Ov. *Am.* 1.9.19–20: *ille graves urbes, hic durae limen amicae / obsidet; hic portas frangit, at ille fores*; Ov. *Am.* 1.6.45–46: *forsitan et tecum tua nunc requiescit amica: / heu, melior quanto sors tua sorte mea*; Sen. *Ep.* 4.4: *alius ante amicae fores laqueo pependit.*

[32] Ov. *Ars am.* 2.155–156: *dos est uxoria lites: / audiat optatos semper amica sonos*; *Anth. Lat.* 244.4 SB: *tam malum est foris amica quam malum est uxor domi*. Elsewhere Ovid urges his reader to refrain from writing like an orator to his *amica* so as not to bore her (*Ars am.* 1.465–466: *quis, nisi mentis inops, tenerae declamat amicae? / saepe valens odii littera causa fuit*).

> et pictis anas renovata pennis
> plebeium sapit. ultimus ab oris
> attractus scarus atque arata Syrtis
> si quid naufragio dedit, probatur;
> mullus iam gravis est. *amica vincit*
> *uxorem.* rosa cinnamum veretur.
> quicquid quaeritur, optimum videtur.
>   (Petron. *Sat.* 93.2)

The bird from far-off Colchis
and African fowl are pleasing to the palate
because they are not easy to get. The snowy goose
and the duck, ever new with its colorful feathers:
they taste plebeian. Taken from distant shores,
the parrot-wrasse fish, and whatever the furrowed gulf of Syrtis
provides through shipwrecks: that's what people like.
By now the mullet is considered heavy.
The *amica* wins out over the wife;
the rose must fear cinnamon.
Whatever has to be sought
is thought to be the best.

A man's *amica* is comparable to exotic foodstuffs from far-off places; she has the allure of the exotic, possibly the expensive, the not quite licit. The implication is that a wife – like goose, duck, mullet, and roses – should be a source of delight and satisfaction, but that in today's decadent world all of these pleasurable things are seen as ordinary, too easy, and thus underappreciated. Like peacock or cinnamon, an *amica* is enticing precisely because she comes with some difficulty (*non sunt faciles*); she has to be sought elsewhere (*quicquid quaeritur*); she is not just lying around at home.[33]

Other references to men's *amicae* anchor their relationship quite unambiguously in the body – of the man, the woman or both. Ovid contrasts the kisses that an *amica* gives to her lover with those which a sister gives to her brother (in the former – as in those exchanged by the archetypical pair of divine adulterous lovers, Venus and Mars – there are tongues),[34] and the same poet elsewhere writes in the voice of a man frustrated by the failure of another body part:

---

[33] See Connors 1998, pp. 64–65, for this poem, and Rimell 2002 for a reading of the *Satyricon* with attention to imagery of food and the body. For the motif *vile est quod licet*, see Otto 1890 s.v. *licet* 1.

[34] Ov. *Am.* 2.5.25–26: *qualia non fratri tulerit germana severo, / sed tulerit cupido mollis amica viro.* Aulus Gellius quotes two lines from Cn. Matius' *Mimiambi* which vividly evoke the kisses of one's *amica: sinuque amicam refice frigidam caldo, / columbulatim labra conserens labris* (Gell. *NA* 20.9.2).

a, pudet annorum: quo me iuvenemque virumque?
nec iuvenem nec me sensit amica virum!
(Ov. *Am.* 3.7.19–20)

I'm ashamed of my age! What is the point of being young and a man?
My *amica* found me neither young nor a man.

Again in the *Ars amatoria*, explaining that men are repelled by excessively dour women, Ovid cites the mythic examples of Andromache and Tecmessa, perpetually in mourning.

odimus et maestas: Tecmessam diligat Aiax;
  nos hilarem populum femina laeta capit.
numquam ego te, Andromache, nec te, Tecmessa, rogarem,
  ut mea de vobis altera *amica* foret.
credere vix videor, cum cogar credere partu,
  vos ego cum vestris *concubuisse* viris.
(Ov. *Ars am.* 3.517–522)

We also dislike gloomy women. Let Ajax love his Tecmessa,
but we men are a cheery folk; a happy woman captivates us.
Neither you, Andromache, nor you, Tecmessa,
would I ever ask to be my *amica*.
I can hardly believe – though I have to, since you gave birth –
that you ever slept with your husbands.

The parallelism is clear, and it is the verb *concumbere* which provides the link between the two categories of woman active in this passage: *amica* and *uxor*. Likewise, an epigram of Martial's speaks in the voice of a young man asserting his maturity to his *tutor* (11.39: "My *amica* will tell you I'm a man now!") and another catalogues the various kinds of bodies the speaker finds attractive in his *amicae* (11.100).

Not surprisingly, we find *amica* functioning as a near-synonym of *concubina*, a term whose etymology, like that of the related verb *concumbere*, points to the bed. In a scene from Plautus' *Miles Gloriosus* the sexual partner of a slave's owner is called "Master's *amica*" (122, *amica erilis*) and in another scene of the same play "Master's concubine" (508, *concubina erilis*). Generations later and writing in a very different genre, Quintilian underscores how important it is that parents model propriety both in rhetorical style and in their behavior:

nec mirum: nos docuimus, ex nobis audierunt; nostras *amicas*, nostros *concubinos* vident; omne convivium obscenis canticis strepit, pudenda dictu spectantur. fit ex his consuetudo, inde natura. (Quint. *Inst.* 1.2.7–8)

No wonder. We taught our children, they heard it from us. They see our *amicae*, our male concubines. Every banquet resounds with disgraceful songs, things that are shameful to say are put on display. From all of this arises habit, and from habit nature.

Taking the existence of male and female sexual companions for granted, Quintilian's disapproval emphasizes what others – children in particular – see and hear (*audierunt, vident, strepit, spectantur*), and the parallelism in his formulation is revealing: *amica* is the female equivalent of *concubinus*.[35]

The verbs of which *amica* can be the object are equally revealing. The joke in an epigram of Martial's to which we will return in the following chapter hinges on the normative usage of *amica* as object of *futuere*, the primary obscenity for vaginal penetration: Philaenis rightly calls her *amica* the woman whom she fucks.[36] Other, less coarse verbs in the language of Plautine comedy include *ducere* or *ductare* ("take out, bring along" – whether for payment or for free) and *parare* ("acquire, buy").[37] The language of buying an *amica* is found in the polemical description in the *Commentariolum petitionis* of two of Cicero's rivals for the consulship, Gaius Antonius Hybrida and Catilina. As an illustration of Hybrida's lechery, the author witheringly observes that, while praetor, he had bought a woman on the slave-market to be his sexual partner (*amicam de machinis emit*) and set her up openly in his home. The scandal is not the purchase itself, but Hybrida's intent of setting her up openly as his partner at home.[38] The writer of the *Commentariolum* is not indulging in a witty neologism or cleverly inventive pun. Making *amica* the object of the verb *emere* was clearly a possibility in respectable registers of Latin prose.

Cicero exploits the flexibility and polyvalence of the term *amica* in his brilliantly malicious attack on Clodia:

[35] For a father cavorting with his *amica* in his son's presence, cf. Plaut. *Asin.* 862–863: *qui quidem cum filio / potet una atque una amicam ductet, decrepitus senex.* In the opening scene of Terence's *Self-Tormentor*, the title character describes to his friend Chremes (to whom he is joined in *amicitia*, 57) the beginning of his woes: His son had treated his *amica* almost like a wife (Ter. *Haut.* 104: *amicam ut habeas prope iam in uxoris loco?*). For the parallel between *amica* and *concubinus* or *puer* as bedmates see also Petron. *Sat.* 58, 113; Plin. *HN* 35.141; Mart. 1.71.3.

[36] Mart. 7.70: *recte, quam futuis, vocas amicam.* For *amica* as the object of *futuere*, compare two nearly identical graffiti from the Palatine in Rome: *Crescens / [q]uisque meam futues rival/[li]s amicam, illum se/cretis mont[ibus] / u[rsu]s eda[t]; Cresces / quisque meam futuit rivalis / amicam, illum secret[i]s montibus / ursus edat* (*CLE* 50, 954 = Castrén and Lilius 1970: 283, 286).

[37] *Amicam ducere/ductare*: Plaut. *Asin.* 863 (quoted above), *Poen.* 867–868, *Stich.* 425–426; *amicam parare*: Plaut. *Merc.* 341.

[38] *Comment. pet.* 8: *competitores ambo a pueritia sicarii, ambo libidinosi, ambo egentes ... in praetura competitorem habuimus amico Sabidio et Panthera, cum ad tabulam quos poneret non haberet; quo tamen in magistratu amicam quam domi palam haberet de machinis emit.* Robert Harris' historical novel *Imperium* uses this incident to build its unflattering portrayal of Hybrida (p. 315: "buying a beautiful young slave girl at an auction and living openly with her as his mistress"; p. 332: "the drinker who kept a slave girl for a wife" [*sic*]).

quod quidem facerem vehementius, nisi intercederent mihi inimicitiae cum istius mulieris viro – fratrem volui dicere; semper hic erro. nunc agam modice nec longius progrediar quam me mea fides et causa ipsa coget. neque enim muliebres umquam *inimicitias* mihi gerendas putavi, praesertim cum ea quam omnes semper *amicam* omnium potius quam cuiusquam *inimicam* putaverunt. (Cic. *Cael.* 32)

I would do this [sc., defend Caelius] even more vigorously were it not for my enmity with this woman's husband – I meant to say "brother"; I always make that mistake. Instead, I will proceed moderately and will go no further than my role as advocate and the case itself require. After all, I never thought I would have to become involved in enmities with women, least of all with one whom everyone has always thought to be everyone's *amica* but no one's enemy.

With breathtaking speed and characteristically skillful manipulation of the possibilities of the sound and meaning of Latin words, Cicero insinuates first that Clodia was her own brother's lover (we will return to the ambiguities of *frater* in the following chapter) and then that she had been widely generous with her favors: everyone's *amica*.

This passage brings us to the important but difficult question of tone. Of course we cannot know the entire range of tonality with which the word was used (we have, above all, little access to the primary speech genres of direct verbal communication in particular), but there are a few indications in the textual tradition. The *Digest* quotes from the first-century AD jurist Masurius Sabinus by way of terminological clarification:

libro memorialium Masurius scribit *pellicem* apud antiquos eam habitam quae, cum uxor non esset, cum aliquo tamen vivebat; quam nunc vero nomine *amicam*, paulo honestiore *concubinam* appellari. (*Digest* 50.16.144.pr.)

In his *Liber Memorialium* Masurius writes that the ancients used the term *paelex* for a woman who lived with a man without being his wife. Such a woman is now called, to use a straightforward word, *amica* – or, to use a slightly more honorable one, *concubina*.

Like Quintilian's parallel between *amicae* and *concubini*, Masurius' remarks suggest that *amica* could be a straightforward term (*vero nomine*) more or less synonymous with the slightly more honorable *concubina*. To be sure, the lawyer has no more authority to speak for the entire range of linguistic usage than does, say, the philosopher (see Introduction, p. 21). But that *concubina* could be considered a more "honorable" label than *amica* is confirmed by its usage as a label in the formulaic language of Latin epitaphs, and concretely reminds us of the unpredictability of tone, even in linguistic borrowings and cognates. English "concubine," for example, is distinctly more disparaging than "girlfriend" or "mistress."

In fact, the appearance of the term *concubina* in Latin inscriptions shows that it was not only not shameful, but a respectable label that could be used in epitaphs.[39] As for *amica*, just as a woman might make a bequest to a female friend in the dryly descriptive language of wills (*Digest* 34.2.40.2, above p. 75), the jurisprudential writings gathered in the *Digest* specify that a man might make provision for a woman he identifies with the label.[40] In short, we probably cannot perceive the full range of tonalities and connotations in Cicero's phrase *amica omnium*, but what we hear is powerful enough. An *amica* is a woman who can be placed on a pedestal, to be courted and treated well lest she run away; but she can also be a man's bedmate and little more, giver of passionate kisses, subject of verbs like *concubere* and synonym of *concubina*, object of verbs like *emere* and *futuere*. An epigram by Martial and a poem from the *Corpus Priapeorum* use the bodily associations of the term *amica*, together with the grammatical fact that the Latin word for "hand" (*manus*) is feminine, as fuel for a wry joke: Sometimes a man's best friend is his hand – or his hand is his *amica*.[41]

Just as an *amica* could denote a man's sexual partner, a woman's sexual partner could in some speech genres be called her *amicus*, with all of the connotational range the word came with; sometimes we find a man cast in the roles of a woman's – or boy's – *amicus* and *amator* at once.[42] An

---

[39] For discussion of the term *concubina* in literary and inscriptional texts, see Treggiari 1981, Friedl 1996. Some epitaphs were commissioned by a man to commemorate a *concubina* along with himself (*CIL* 3.2157, 6.5036), his sons, daughters, and mother (*CIL* 5.936, AE 1978.20), his patron (*CIL* 11.849), an *amicus* and a colleague in the office of *augustalis* (*CIL* 9.2368). Others were commissioned by women who commemorate themselves in the role of *concubina*: see *CIL* 6.6962, 6.26556, 6.32734 (along with her male partner's sister-in-law), 10.4918, 10.6177 (commemorating her male partner's mother). In one epitaph a Vestal Virgin commemorates her father's *concubina* (*CIL* 11.17170). Yet others commemorate a man's wife and his *concubina* together: Examples include *CIL* 1.2527a, 5.1918 (with portrait statues of the man flanked by the two women), 6.1906 = 32292, 6.23210, 9.2255, 10.1267. Treggiari 1981, pp. 69–71, argues that these refer to temporally distinct relationships, but see pp. 77–78, for the extra-legal possibility of a man's having a wife and a *concubina* simultaneously.

[40] *Digest* 34.2.35.pr.: *Titiae amicae meae, cum qua sine mendacio vixi, auri pondo quinque dari volo.* We will see below that *vivere cum* does not necessarily signify sharing a home – it often means something like "share one's life with" – and indeed no surviving text suggests that a woman could be called a man's *amica* only if she shared a home with him. Aulus Gellius confirms the older usage of *paelex* in a definition that speaks of a lasting connection (Gell. *NA* 4.3.3: *paelicem autem appellatam probrosamque habitam, quae iuncta consuetaque esset cum eo in cuius manu mancipioque alia matrimonii causa foret*).

[41] *Priapeia* 33.5–6: *sed ne tentigine rumpar, / falce mihi posita fiet amica manus*; Mart. 9.41.1–2: *Pontice, quod numquam futuis, sed paelice laeva / uteris et Veneri servit amica manus.* The joke may ultimately derive from Lucilius 307 Marx (*at laeva lacrimas muttoni absterget amica*) or else, more likely, it was a common, even proverbial witticism.

[42] Ter. *An.* 717: *summum bonum esse erae putavi hunc Pamphilum, / amicum, amatorem, virum in quovis loco / paratum*; Lucilius 902 Marx: *favitorem tibi me, amicum, amatorem putes* (perhaps,

erotic pairing typical of comic plots – prostitute and customer, besotted but still paying – can be described as consisting of a woman variously called *meretrix* ("prostitute"), *scortum* ("whore"), or *amica* and her *amator* or *amans* ("lover") or her *amicus*. The assonance and sound-play made possible by the use of *amicus*, especially if paired with *amica*, is not infrequently exploited in lines from comedy. A character in Caecilius Statius' *Synephebi* makes this comical complaint: "A prostitute (*meretrix*) refuses to take cash from her loving friend (*ab amico amante*)!" while a character in a Plautine play expresses outrage at the kiss his rival gives to their shared object of desire, as if she were a street whore – "That an *amicus*, standing, should give a kiss to his *amica*, standing!" – as he pushes them apart, adding an alliteration to the assonance for good measure.[43]

The opening scenes of Plautus' *Truculentus* well illustrate the ways in which comic language can play with its *meretrices* and *amicae*, its *amatores* and *amici*. In love with the prostitute Phronesium, Diniarchus casts himself in his opening monologue in the role of *amans* and *amator*, the woman as *scortum* (24–25, 40, 45–46, 56); in the lively, flirtatious conversation with her maid Astaphium that follows, we hear Astaphium describing a scene at Phronesium's house, with a young man kissing his *amica* (102), and Diniarchus bitterly asks if Phronesium has a new *amator* (135). After a brief and bawdy debate on the relative merits of women and boys (149–157), Astaphium berates Diniarchus. Previously considered to be Phronesium's greatest lover, he now comes to see his "friend" bringing nothing but complaints (166–167: *qui antehac amator summus / habitu's, nunc ad amicam venis querimoniam deferre*). Diniarchus defends himself, first parroting Astaphium's pairing of *amator* with *amica* and then strategically casting himself not in the role of *amator* but in that of *amicus*, explicitly contrasting the two.

DIN. vestra hercle factum iniuria, quae properavistis olim:
rapere otiose oportuit, diu ut essem incolumis vobis.
AST. *amator* similest oppidi hostilis. DIN. quo argumento [est]?
AST. quam primum expugnari potis [est], tam id optimum est *amicae*.

---

as Marx suggests, inspired by Terence); cf. Petron. *Sat.* 113.8 (*neque Tryphaena me alloquebatur tanquam familiarem et aliquando gratum sibi amatorem*). See also Lucilius 269–270 Marx (*qui te diligat, aetati[s] facieque tuae se / fautorem ostendat, fore amicum polliceatur*). Marx takes *amicus* to be synonymous with *amator* and suggests that these are the words of a woman or pimp encouraging a girl or boy to begin a career in prostitution.

[43] Caecil. Stat. fr. 214 Ribbeck (quoted at Cic. *Nat. D.* 1.13) *ab amico amante argentum accipere meretrix non volt*; Plaut. *Stich.* 765–766: *prostibilest tandem? stantem stanti savium / dare amicum amicae?* Cf. Naev. *Palliata* fr. 90: *numquam quisquam amico amanti amica nimis fiet fidelis / nec nimis erit morigera.*

DIN. ego fateor, sed longe aliter est *amicus* atque *amator*:
certe hercle quam veterrimus, tam homini optimust *amicus*.

(Plaut. *Truculentus* 168–173)

DIN. Well, this happened because *you* did wrong; you were in too much of a
hurry. You should have taken your leisure as you took me, so that I could have
remained intact longer. AST. A lover (*amator*) is like an enemy town. DIN. How
so? AST. The sooner captured, the better for his *amica*. DIN. I'll grant you that.
But a friend (*amicus*) is one thing, a lover (*amator*) quite another: after all, the
longer someone is a friend, the better friend he is.

Astaphium takes him at his word: If he is to play the role of Phronesium's
amicus, he should not stay in front of her home like a stranger (*pro ignoto
alienoque*), but should go in; he is, after all, hardly an outsider to this
place (*haud alienus tu quidem es*). Though she does not use the word, this
amounts to saying that he is a *familiaris*, and to say that a man is not
an *alienus* to a woman amounts to casting him as "hers": her husband,
lover, or relative (see below, pp. 91–92). After Diniarchus goes off stage,
acknowledging that he is being being lied to but is incapable of resisting
because he is still in love (190–192, *amamus*), Astaphium then has her
own monologue. She reveals that her mistress sees Diniarchus, the man
who loves her (*huic homini amanti*, 213), as a friend to be consulted rather
than used (*magisque adeo ei consiliarius hic amicust quam auxiliarius*, 216),
the military metaphor suggesting that she does not plan to engage in the
battles of the bed with him.[44] The ambivalence of *amicus* is especially
pointed in these scenes. Diniarchus is, as he admits, still very much in
the throes of Venus, still Phronesium's *amator* or *amans*; in the language
of this speech genre, he still sees her as his *amica*. At the same time he is,
or wants to be, her *amicus* in more sense than one – but she plans to treat
him as an *amicus* in a rather more limited sense than he hopes.

This usage of the terms *amicus* and *amica* brings with it, of course, a
distinct asymmetry, noticeable to us but in the various speech genres of
Latin literature evidently so naturalized that it goes unnoticed. If a man is
joined to his *amicus* by *amicitia*, what joins him to his *amica*? Pondering
the paradoxical blindness that we so often show to flaws in those close to
us, not to mention ourselves, Horace writes of a male lover (*amator*) and
his *amica* on the one hand, a man and his male friend (*amicus*) on the
other.

illuc praevertamur, *amatorem* quod *amicae*
turpia decipiunt caecum vitia aut etiam ipsa haec

---

[44] See *OLD* s.v. *alienus* 1b, *auxiliarius*, and *consiliarius*.

delectant, veluti Balbinum polypus Hagnae.
vellem in *amicitia* sic erraremus et isti
errori nomen virtus posuisset honestum.
ac pater ut gnati, sic nos debemus *amici*,
siquod sit vitium, non fastidire.
(Hor. *Sat.* 1.3.38–44)

Let's think about this: the blinded lover
is taken in by the ugly defects of his *amica*.
Sometimes they even attract him,
like Hagna's nasal polyp did Balbinus.
I wish we made this mistake in friendship.
I wish virtue had given this mistake an honorable name.
Like a father with his son, with our friend we should
not criticize whatever faults he may have.

The complexities of *amor* and *amicitia, amici* and *amicae,* will be the subject of the following chapters. Here we see that the relationship between an *amator* and his *amica* can be contrasted with *amicitia,* which refers to the bond of friendship between men and is revealingly compared to the foundational patriarchal relationship, that between father and son.

Regardless of any linguistic and conceptual asymmetry, the contrast between a man's *amica* and his *amicus* can be quite pointed indeed. A character in a Plautine comedy pairs the terms in order to put *amicae* in their place:

cape sis virtutem animo et corde expelle desidiam tuo
in foro operam *amicis* da, ne in lecto *amicae,* ut solitus es.
(Plaut. *Trin.* 650–651)

Be valorous of mind, drive out laziness from your heart.
Dedicate yourself to your friends in the forum,
not to your *amica* in bed, like you've usually done.

A line from a Terentian comedy exploits the same eloquent juxtaposition to different effect:

nam istaec quidem contumeliast,
hominem *amicum* recipere ad te atque eius *amicam* subigitare.
(Ter. *Haut.* 566–567)

That's an insult all right: to take in a friend (*amicus*)
and screw his girlfriend (*amica*)!

The contrast between a man's *amica* and his *amicus* frames the first of Horace's poetic *Epistles.* Towards the beginning of the poem we find

the image of a man waiting in vain for his untruthful *amica* (Hor.
Epist. 1.1.20: *ut nox longa quibus mentitur amica*), and at the end Horace
describes himself as the loyal and dependent *amicus* of Maecenas (105: *de
te pendentis, te respicientis amici*). An epigram by Martial on the theme of
the stingy friend plays off a set of contrasts between the way Lupus treats
his male friends (chief among them the poet himself) who are joined to
Lupus in *amicitia*, and his *amica*, who is joined to him by something
quite different.

> Pauper *amicitiae* cum sis, Lupe, non es *amicae*
> et queritur de te mentula sola nihil.
> illa siligineis pinguescit *adultera* cunnis,
> *convivam* pascit nigra farina tuum.
> incensura nives *dominae* Setina liquantur,   5
> *nos* bibimus Corsi pulla venena cadi;
> empta tibi nox est fundis non tota paternis,
> non sua desertus rura *sodalis* arat;
> splendet Erythraeis perlucida *moecha* lapillis,
> ducitur addictus, te futuente, *cliens*;   10
> octo Syris suffulta datur lectica *puellae*,
> nudum sandapilae pondus *amicus* erit.
> i nunc et miseros, Cybele, praecide cinaedos:
> haec erat, haec cultris mentula digna tuis.
>
> (Mart. 9.2)

You are cheap with your friends, Lupus, but not with your girlfriend;
only your dick has no complaint to make about you.
Your married mistress fattens herself on fine cunt-shaped cakes;
dark grain is fodder for your dinner guest.
Setine wine, ready to warm up the shaved ice, is being strained for your lady;
we drink black poison from a Corsican vat.
You pay for just part of a night out of your father's estates;
your abandoned friend plows fields not his own.
Your mistress gleams with jewels from the Red Sea;
while you have a fuck, your client is led off to debtor's prison.
Your girlfriend gets a litter borne by eight Syrian slaves;
your friend will be the unadorned weight carried by a stretcher.
Go ahead and castrate unfortunate *cinaedi*, Cybele –
but *this* was a dick that deserved your knives.

The poem is structured around a contrast between the women on whom
Lupus lavishes his attention and resources and the men he is ignoring or
mistreating – a masculine collectivity with which Martial identifies himself by means of the passing *nos* and which, in a revealing act of abstraction, Martial begins by calling simply *amicitia*. The woman is Lupus'

adultera, domina, moecha, puella, amica; the man is his *conviva, sodalis, cliens, amicus*. Whereas he receives skimpy rewards, she has generous use not only of Lupus' riches but also of his *mentula*, the salient point with which the poem begins and – drastically – ends.

MEN AND WOMEN: FRIENDSHIP WITHOUT FRIENDS?

Amicae, then, appear in the pages of Latin literature as the subjects of idealizing and objects of male desire. But if the feminine noun can denote a man's bedmate, and the masculine *amicus* a prostitute's client, by what linguistic means might men and women be represented as friends without automatically evoking a genitally expressed relationship or erotic bond? Was such a relationship even a representational possibility? One might be inclined to think it was not. A number of texts give the impression that the only roles a Roman woman might normally play in connection with a freeborn man were three: his relative by blood or marriage; his wife; his lover. The adjective *alienus* ("belonging to someone else, not one's own") modifies *vir* ("man") in a few suggestive textual moments. Attempting to portray herself as beyond suspicion, Plautus' Cleustrata reassures her husband that it is for prostitutes, not married ladies, to be overly familiar with men who are "not hers" (Plaut. *Cas.* 586–587: *non matronarum officiumst, sed meretricium, / viris alienis, mi vir, subblandirier*). Narrating the tale of king Servius Tullius' two daughters, married to two Tarquinius brothers, and insinuating that the elder sister had an affair with the younger's husband, Livy describes her as a woman "accustomed to the private conversations of a man not hers" (Livy 1.46.7: *secretis viri alieni adsuefacta sermonibus*). Here, then, *vir alienus* suggests another woman's husband. Cicero's much-admired *prosopopoiia* of Clodia's venerable ancestor Appius Claudius Caecus builds up to a strategic use of the phrase *alieni viri*.

mulier, quid tibi cum Caelio, quid cum homine adulescentulo, quid cum alieno? … cum ex amplissimo genere in familiam clarissimam nupsisses, cur tibi Caelius tam coniunctus fuit? cognatus, adfinis, viri tui familiaris? nihil eorum. quid igitur fuit nisi quaedam temeritas ac libido? … ideone ego pacem Pyrrhi diremi, ut tu amorum turpissimorum cotidie foedera ferires, ideo aquam adduxi, ut ea tu inceste uterere, ideo viam munivi, ut eam tu alienis viris comitata celebrares? (Cic. *Cael.* 34)

Woman! What are you doing with Caelius? What are you doing with this young man, not even of your family (*alieno*)? … Coming from such an impressive background, you married into a renowned family: so why were you so intimate with Caelius? Was he a kinsman, an in-law, a friend (*familiaris*) of your husband's?

No, none of those things. So what was it, then, if not some kind of wantonness and lust on your part? … Did I overturn the peace with Pyrrhus so that you might make daily pacts of disgraceful lust? Did I bring water to the city so that you might use it to clean up after your filthy deeds? Did I build that great road so that you might travel on it surrounded by menfolk not your own (*alienis viris*)?

In this powerful evocation of the *mos maiorum*, the categories of men with whom a respectable Roman woman could acceptably have a public relationship are limited to three: her blood-relatives, her relatives by marriage, and her husband's friends. All other men were, it seems, off-limits. And so we appear to have a rule of thumb.

Or perhaps not. Speaking through the grandly censorious Appius Claudius Caecus, Cicero is oversimplifying, exaggerating, on a rampage; for her part, the Plautine wife is talking about flirtation (*subblandirier*), not mere association. In fact, other texts make it clear not only that respectable women could have friendly relationships with men that were distinct from kinship and not shaped by a sexual bond, but that they could be openly acknowledged. But with what language? Near-synonyms of *amica* which did not run the risk of denoting or even connoting a sexual relationship provided one way of describing friendships between men and women: for example the term *familiaris*, with its vague but respectable connotations of belonging to a group. In a letter to Atticus, Cicero describes Servilia as *tua familiaris*, and Pliny, too, uses the word in connection with a woman's friendship with a man, observing that his correspondent's father had been a *familiaris* to Pliny himself, his uncle, but also to his mother.[45]

Nowhere in his surviving letters does Cicero use the noun *amica* to describe any woman connected with himself, and the noun occurs only once in his entire correspondence, referring with evident scorn to women accompanying Marcus Antonius' mistress in a scandalous entourage (*Att.* 10.10.5; see below, pp. 114–115). In fact, Cicero's letters refer quite rarely to his own relationships with women other than his wife and daughter. One exception is the older, wealthy Caerellia, whom he recommends to Publius Servilius Isauricus, proconsul in Asia, asking that he look out for her properties and buiness interests (Cic. *Fam.* 13.72). Avoiding the

---

[45] Cic. *Att.* 15.11.2: *tua familiaris*; Plin. *Ep.* 1.19: *pater tuus et matri et avunculo meo, mihi etiam quantum aetatis diversitas passa est, familiaris*. Writing in another genre, Tacitus reports that a woman named Silia was exiled by Nero on suspicion of having revealed details about the emperor's sex life to her friend Petronius, almost certainly the author of the *Satyricon* (Tac. *Ann.* 16.20: *Petronio perquam familiaris*).

all too polyvalent *amica*, Cicero introduces her as *necessaria mea*, a term whose connotations point away from affection and toward obligation. Yet Cicero's enemies, drawing upon what was always a ready weapon, used his relationship with Caerellia against him. According to Dio Cassius, the tribune Quintus Fufius Calenus, defending Marcus Antonius against Cicero's attacks made in the *Philippics*, accused him of a sexual affair with Caerellia (*emoikheusas*), pointing out that the difference in ages between her and Cicero was the same as that between Cicero and his new young wife Publilia. In the same speech, Fufius turns another one of Cicero's relationships with a woman – his daughter Tullia – against him, directing the accusation of incest at Cicero just as the latter had done to Publius Clodius Pulcher and his sister.[46]

One has the impression that, in many circles at least, practically any intimate relationship between man or woman outside of marriage could, in accordance with rhetorical, political, or other needs, be depicted as suspect. In a discussion of evidence that requires further substantiation before it can be taken as persuasive (in Greek *eikota*, in Latin *signa non necessaria*), Quintilian warns about the dangers of going too far. If we take a woman's going to the baths with men as proof that she is an adulteress, we might as well conclude the same thing on the basis of her going to dinner parties with young men or enjoying a close friendship (*amicitia*) with a man – both practices, he implies, being innocent in themselves.[47] But some Romans, less scrupulous or more tendentious than Quintilian, might draw precisely that conclusion when it suited them. Tacitus refers to a letter written by the emperor Tiberius in which a generally phrased criticism of men's "friendships with women" (*amicitiae muliebres*) in fact constituted a specific if indirect attack on the consul Fufius, who enjoyed Livia's favor; adding his own insinuation, the historian observes that Fufius was "skilled at enticing ladies' minds."[48] Remarks like these derive their insidious force from potentially anxious ambivalences in the linguistic representation of male–female relationships not definable in terms of

---

[46] For Caerellia, see Austin 1946 and Deniaux 1993, pp. 473–474. She was interested in philosophy and obtained a copy of Cicero's *De finibus* from Atticus' scribes (Cic. *Att.* 13.21, 22); Cicero borrowed some money from her on at least one occasion (Cic. *Att.* 12.51.3, 45 BC; 15.26.4); the two evidently corresponded on political subjects (Quint. *Inst.* 6.112). For Fufius' speech see Dio Cassius 46.1–28. For Cicero and Tullia see also [Sall.] *Cic.* 2.1.

[47] Quint. *Inst.* 5.9.14: *sed vereor ne longe nimium nos ducat haec via. nam si est signum adulterae lavari cum viris, erit et convivere cum adulescentibus, deinde etiam familiariter alicuius amicitia uti.* See further discussion of this passage at Williams 2010, pp. 208–209.

[48] Tac. *Ann.* 5.2: *quin et parte eiusdem epistulae increpuit amicitias muliebris, Fufium consulem oblique perstringens. is gratia Augustae floruerat, aptus alliciendis feminarum animis.*

marriage or kinship. And so we come back to Cicero's malevolent puns
regarding his own enmity – regrettable, as he would have us believe –
with Clodia (Cic. *Cael.* 32). Never did he think he would engage in *inimicitiae muliebres*, least of all with a woman who has the reputation for
being no one's enemy and everyone's friend (*amicam omnium*).

Some texts, however, do refer to *amicitia* between men and women in
such a way as to keep it clearly distinct from the realm of Venus. Ovid's
poetic advice to men on the prowl for women refers to the possibility of
amicitia with a woman while contrasting it with *amor*.

> nec semper Veneris spes est profitenda roganti:
> intret *amicitiae* nomine tectus *amor*.
> hoc aditu vidi tetricae data verba puellae:
> qui fuerat *cultor*, factus *amator* erat.
> (Ov. *Ars am.* 1.719–722)

Mentioning your hopes of Venus as you make your plea is not always advisable!
Let love make its entrance concealed under the name of friendship.
I have seen an unyielding girl tricked by this approach.
He started out her devoted follower; he became her lover.

This clever lover begins by playing what is evidently a respectable role: He
is out not for the joys of Venus but instead for *amicitia* with the woman.
Ovid deftly avoids the tricky nouns *amicus* and *amica*. The man first plays
the role of a man interested in cultivating a friendly relationship (*cultor*),
and the woman is called *puella*; when things take a different turn and the
man ends up in the woman's bed, he is her *amator*.[49] This is the playfully
cynical world of Ovidian poetry. Quite another approach to friendships
between men and women is found in the sober language of the letters of
Pliny the Younger. A reading of his letters shows that in the upper levels
of Roman society from which they came and in which they circulated,
relationships between men and women which in English would be called
friendships not only existed but were freely talked about. Here too, as in
Ovid, the nouns *amica* and *amicus* are avoided, but we find the abstract
amicitia:

fuerat alioqui mihi cum Helvidio *amicitia* ... fuerat cum Arria et Fannia (Plin.
Ep. 9.13.3)

---

[49] Elsewhere Ovid naughtily suggests that his student should strive to be an *amicus* – not of the
woman he wants, but of her current male partner (Ov. *Ars am.* 1.579–580: *sint etiam tua vota,
viro placuisse puellae: / utilior vobis factus amicus erit*). In view of the lively debates, ancient and
modern, about the role of *utilitas* in men's friendships, the irony is sharp. For *cultor* see OLD s.v.
4 and 6; in connection with *amicitia*, see Livy 25.28.8 (*Romanae amicitiae cultor*), Mart. 9.84.4
(*ille tuae cultor notus amicitiae*), and cf. Martial 2.55 with Williams 2004 ad loc.

erant quidam in illis [sc., coheredibus meis], quibus obici et Gratillae *amicitia* et Rustici posset (Plin. *Ep.* 5.1.18)

I enjoyed a friendship, moreover, with Helividius … and with Arria and Fannia too. My fellow heirs included some men who were subject to criticism for their friendship with Gratilla and Rusticus.

In addition to the abstract *amicitia*, Pliny exploits the flexibility created by the conveniently masculine "generic" plural *amici*. Memorializing a group of men and women, he avoids the potential awkwardness of referring to a woman as his *amica* by calling them all – both men and women – his *amici* (Plin. *Ep.* 3.11.3: *septem amicis meis aut occisis aut relegatis, occisis Senecione Rustico Helvidio, relegatis Maurico Gratilla Arria Fannia*). As often, *amicitia* gives us glimpses into various social and political networks – in the case of Arria and Fannia, for example, those associated with a Stoically inflected resistance to imperial power – but what is especially interesting for our purposes is to observe that men and women equally participate.[50] And, as usual, we may ask whether some or all of these *amicitiae*, whether with men or with women, also had the nature of a patron–client relationship. To be sure, that a richer or higher-status woman might play the role of *patrona* to a man was certainly possible. Martial places a few women in the role, including the poet Lucan's widow Polla Argentaria and the Spanish lady Marcella. But, avoiding the tricky *amica*, he uses the respectful terms *regina* and *domina*, directly parallel to the masculine *rex* and *dominus*, honorific titles for men's patrons.[51]

Pliny's delicate avoidance of the feminine *amica* stands in illuminating contrast with his disparaging reference to an unnamed sexual partner of the proconsul Caecilius Classicus as *amicula quaedam*.[52] Not only

---

[50] See Carlon 2009, pp. 58–64, for the role of women in the so-called Stoic opposition to the Principate as it appears in Pliny's letters. The Gratilla mentioned in *Ep.* 5.1 is probably to be identified with Verulana Gratilla, wife of Arulenus Rusticus, mentioned in *Ep.* 3.11 and Tac. *Hist.* 3.69; see Carlon 2009, pp. 32–33. Another important woman in Pliny's correspondence is Corellia Hispulla, daughter of his mentor and supporter Quintus Corellius Rufus: although Pliny nowhere in the surviving correspondence uses the word to describe his relationship with her, it was arguably an *amicitia* inherited from her father. Cf. Plin. *Ep.* 3.3 with Carlon 2009, pp. 68–99, and for friendships inherited from one's father see Plin. *Ep.* 6.3.3 (*est mihi cum illo non sane paterna amicitia, neque enim esse potuit per meam aetatem*) with Bütler 1970, p. 95.

[51] Polla Argentaria: Mart. 7.21, 7.23, 10.64 (*regina*); Marcella: Mart. 12.21, 12.31 (*domina*). For discussion of women as *patronae* see Dixon 2001, pp. 89–112, Osiek 2008, pp. 255–264; for *rex* and *dominus* see Mart. 2.18.5 and 2.32.8 with Williams 2004 ad loc. See Chapter 3 below for Fronto's relationship with the empress Domitia Lucilla; writing in Greek, he casts himself as her *philos* (Front. *M. Caes.* 2.3.1).

[52] Plin. *Ep.* 3.9.13: *miserat etiam epistulas Romam ad amiculam quandam iactantes et gloriosas.* Prosecuting Classicus for corrupt practices in connection with his proconsulate in Baetica, Pliny made use of an incriminating letter which Classicus had sent to the woman.

the diminutive suffix but the noun itself conveys the message that the kind of relationship this woman had with her powerful male *amicus* was nothing like Pliny's *amicitia* with Arria, Fannia, or Gratilla. His language crisply illustrates the asymmetry; although he shared *amicitia* with those ladies, for reasons of decorum he does not describe them in his letters as *amicae*. At the same time, he and many Romans like him would not have described the relationship between Classicus and his *amicula* as *amicitia*. That was something else: *amor* if one approved, *libido* if one did not.

AMICI AND AMICAE IN INSCRIPTIONS

In stark contrast to the language of *amici* and *amicae* in literary texts, that of the speech genre of inscriptions uses the terms symmetrically. Although the point has gone largely unnoticed in the pages of scholarship, its implications unexplored, the body of surviving inscriptions makes it clear that men and women – slaves, freed, and freeborn – could and did commission texts commemorating both men and women as their *amici* and *amicae* with no hint of denotative distinction among the various configurations of gender.[53]

Here a reminder of the aims and methods set out in the Introduction may be in order. I read inscriptions, like other texts, less as windows onto biography than as illustrations of the workings of a system of linguistic signs. However any given relationship commemorated in an inscription may have been experienced by the participants or perceived by observers – whether it was deeply intimate or distantly respectful, whether it consisted of one *alter ego* paired with another, a patron paired with his or her client, or two individuals joined in an erotic relationship to which genital pleasures belonged – the labels *amicus* and *amica* themselves did not have the function of locating the relationship anywhere in particular within that continuum of possibilities. That was the function of terms like *uxor, contubernalis* or *concubina, maritus* or *patronus*.[54] In other words, it

---

[53] Lexicographers have noted the meaning of *amica* in inscriptions – see *TLL* s.v. *amica* 1913.43–50 (*in titulis sepulcralibus, ponentibus tam viris quam mulieribus*) – but scholars of Latin literature have generally ignored it, and there have been no systematic attempts to theorize the divergent usages in literary and inscriptional texts. In this chapter I focus on the words *amicus* and *amica*; the labels *sodalis* and *sodalia* appear in a small number of inscriptions commemorating relationships between men and women. See, for example, *CIL* 11.654 (Faenza), 11.922 (Modena), 11.1096 (Parma).

[54] For *concubina* see n. 39 above. For *contubernalis*, denoting an opposite-sex partner in a conjugal relationship which does not have the legal status of full marriage or *conubium*, see Treggiari 1981, Friedl 1996, pp. 75–85.

is my argument that when a woman is identified in an inscription as a man's *amica*, the label in itself – quite unlike what we have seen in the speech genres represented in Latin literature – no more signifies a sexual bond than does *amicus* in an inscription in which one man memorializes another. Independently of how a relationship to which the label *amica* or *amicus* was applied was lived or perceived, and whatever polyvalent associations those words had, their primary denotation in texts participating in the genre of inscriptions is not "girlfriend" and "boyfriend," "mistress" or "lover." A feature of contemporary German usage, mentioned in the Introduction, suggests itself as a partial parallel. In many utterances the nouns *Freundin* and *Freund* have a primary denotation comparable to that of English "girlfriend, boyfriend, partner," but in others not. How does one tell the difference? In this case the criteria have to do not so much with speech genre as with syntax (*ein Freund von mir*, for example, sends the message that this is *not* an erotic or romantic bond, whereas *mein Freund* can do precisely that) and social clues (when a married woman of a certain age and traditional sexual morality speaks of *mein Freund* or *meine Freundin*, she would not be taken to be speaking of her sexual partner). Opportunities for misunderstanding and ambiguity certainly arise, but the principles of usage are as a whole quite clear.

As we will see in Chapter 4, women figure prominently among those named and commemorated in Latin inscriptions in general and in epitaphs in particular, where they are often the protagonists, providing for individual or group burials – their own and others' – and commissioning the texts which commemorated them in stone. Many of these announce a woman's provision of burial for herself along with her husband, any children who may have predeceased her, along with her freed slaves and their descendants, a provision marked by the formula *libertis libertabusque posterisque eorum*, widespread in epitaphs of all kinds. Some epitaphs also include in the burial group a man whom the woman who commissioned the inscription commemorates for posterity as her *amicus*.

Clodia (mulieris) lib(erta) / Mineme sib(i) et / M(arco) Rustio Severo / contubern(ali) et / T(ito) Octavio Severo fil(io), / VIvir(o) aug(ustali), *et /* C*(aio)* *Rantulan(o) Mionid[i] /* amico. (*CIL* 5.4409 = Reali 82C; Brescia; first–second century AD; see Figure 3)

[D(is)] M(anibus). Manilia Nice fecit sibi et Ser(gio) / [...]o Amiantho coniugi carissimo cum quo sine ulla fraude vixit / [...] pluribus *et T(ito) Flavio Idaeo amico optimo* et L(ucio) Aquilio Onesimo, / [itum] ambitum, et libertis libertabusque suis posterisque / [e]orum. ne de nomine nostro exsiat. (*CIL* 6.21925; Rome)

Figure 3 Altar with inscription commissioned by the freedwoman Clodia Mneme
for her spouse Marcus Rustius Severus, her son Titus Octavius Severus, and her
friend Gaius Rantulanus Mionides (*CIL* 5.4409, first to second century AD).
Brescia, Civici Musei d'Arte e Storia.

D(is) M(anibus) / [---] Volusio Dextro. / [V]olusia Successa / [pa]trono et coniu/
[gi] b(ene) m(erenti) fecit, item *Dio/[ge]ni amico karo,* / [si]bi et suis libertis / [lib]
ertabusque pos/[te]risque eorum f(ecit). (*CIL* 6.29527; Rome)

Ducenia Thallusa / sibi et / Ti(berio) Claudio Epagatho / coniugi et / Claudiae
Honoratae f(iliae) / et libertis libertabusq(ue) / omnium posterisque / eorum *et /
T(ito) Terentio Epaphrae amico optimo.* (Reali 74It = Ferrua 1972; found between
Paliano and Serrone in Lazio)

Clodia Mneme, freedwoman of a woman, dedicated this to herself, to her spouse
Marcus Rustius Severus, to her son Titus Octavius Severus the *sevir augustalis,*
and to her friend Gaius Rantulanus Mionides.

To the spirits of the departed. Manilia Nice made this for herself and for Sergius (…) Amianthus, her dear husband with whom she lived without deceit for many [years?], and for Titus Flavius Idaeus her excellent friend, and for Lucius Aquilius Onesimus – both the approach to the tomb and the area around it – and for her freedmen and freedwomen and their descendants. The tomb shall not be separated from our family name.

To the spirits of the departed. To […] Volusius Dexter. Volusia Successa dedicated this to her patron and deserving husband, likewise to Diogenes her dear friend, to herself and her freedmen and freedwomen and their descendants.

Ducenia Thallusa [dedicated this] to herself, to her husband Tiberius Claudius Epagathus, to her daughter Claudia Honorata, to all of their freedmen and freedwomen and their descendants in turn, and to her friend Titus Terentius Epaphra.

The epitaph commissioned by the freedwoman Mneme implies a story or two, such as the following. Originally the slave of a woman named Clodia, Mneme had a son named Titus by a man named Octavius, with whom she may or may not have had a relationship of *contubernium*; subsequently she entered such a relationship with Marcus Rustius Severus (the fact that her son by Octavius also bore the cognomen Severus may or may not be a coincidence). At some point Mneme received her freedom, and subsequently she commissioned an epitaph for herself, her spouse Marcus and her son, along with a male friend whose cognomen suggests that he, too, was a freed slave.[55] Attentive readers of the epitaph commissioned by Manilia Nice may notice that she commemorates Lucius Aquilius Onesimus without attaching any relational label to his name at all; we will return to cases like this in Chapter 4. But what of her commemoration of Idaeus? And Successa's of Diogenes, Thallusa's of Epaphra, and Mneme's of Mionides? Inscriptions like these are honorific texts chiseled in stone, meant to last, and they both embody and perpetuate for the future the newly acquired status of these women, all of them either explicitly or implicitly identified as freed slaves. In view of the formality of their language and the respectability they are performing, and in view of traditional Roman sexual and conjugal paradigms, with their insistence on women's *pudicitia* (which came down to the principle that a respectable woman should have sexual relations only with her husband), it is quite unlikely that these texts are communicating the message that the women who commissioned

---

[55] The stone's MINEME is either a carver's error or else reflects the pronunciation of the well-attested Greek slave name *Mneme*: see Solin 2003, p. 1335, and cf. *Claudia Mneme* in *CIL* 6.8889. Solin has no listing for the cognomen *Mionides, Myonides*, or anything similar.

them are buried with, and are commemorating for posterity, not only their husbands, children, and freed slaves, but also their lovers.[56] In the language of this speech genre, women's *amici* are directly analogous to their *amicae*.

Traditional paradigms governing the relationships a Roman man might respectably advertise were different but complementary. It was perfectly acceptable, even expected, that a man, whether married or not, might have sexual relations with his own slaves and might have a female partner who could be called his *paelex* or *concubina* (above, p. 85). In many speech genres, as we have seen, such a woman could also be called his *amica*, but in the formulaic language of inscriptions that message was communicated by such labels as *uxor, coniunx,* or *concubina* and not, I would argue, by *amica*. Consider this epitaph from Padua, marked by an especially careful sequence of labels.

V(ivus) f(ecit). / L. Cosius Donatus / sibi et / Cosiae Erotice / uxori carissim(ae), / C. *Clodio Metrodor(o)* / *amic(o),* / Clodiae Fortunatae / uxori eius, / *T. Vario Verecundo* / *amico,* / Variae Iustae / uxori eius, / *Asconiae Amabili amicae,* / *Asconiae Florae amicae,* / A. Plotio Prhonimo (*sic*), Plotiae / Severae, et Diadumen(o) / liberto. / in fr(onte) p(edes) XLIIII ret(ro) p(edes) LX. (*CIL* 5.2937 = Reali 59C; Padua, second century AD)

While still alive, Lucius Cosius Donatus dedicated this to himself and to his dear wife Cosa Erotice; to his friend Gaius Clodius Metrodorus and Clodia Fortunata his wife; to his friend Titus Varius Verecundus and Varia Justa his wife; to his friend Asconia Amabilis; to his friend Asconia Flora; to Aulus Plotius Phronimus; to Plotia Severa; and to his freedman Diadumenos. 44 feet wide, 60 feet deep.

The lack of verbal or visual distinction between the *amici* and the *amicae* commemorated on this stone is emblematic. The epitaph commissioned by Donatus is not communicating to its readers his commemoration of his wife, two male friends and their wives, one of his freed slaves, and two of his mistresses. However the various relationships memorialized on this stone were lived or perceived (including Donatus' relationship to Phronimus and Severa, given no label at all), what joined Donatus to Amabilis and Flora is being commemorated for posterity just as his relationship with Metrodorus and Verecundus is: as *amicitia*. This way of reading men's *amicae* in the language of inscriptions is also suggested by an inscription found in Brescia.

---

[56] For *pudicitia* especially as it relates to women's sexuality, see Langlands 2006; for the double standards which become visible when comparing the ideal as it relates to women and to men in general, wives and husbands in particular, see Williams 2010, pp. 50–59.

L. Lucreti / Ephori VIvir(i) / aug(ustalis). *amico cariss(imo)* / et Statiae Verae / *coniuge (sic) huius, domin(a)e / meae sanctissimae et / amicae carissim(a)e.* his / aram posuit / [– I]uventius Eros *amicis. (CIL* 5.4438 = Reali 83C; Brescia, second or perhaps third century AD)

The tomb of Lucius Lucretius Ephorus, sevir augustalis. For my dearest friend and his wife Statia Vera, my noble lady and dearest friend. [..] Juventius Eros erected this altar for them, his friends.

The labeling is once again both insistent and clear. Independently of the unanswerable questions regarding what kinds of relationships subjectively or objectively joined these individuals, that the word *amica* should in this context denote a concubine, mistress, or sexual partner seems impossible – unless we read this as Eros' commemoration not only of Ephorus *as his friend* but of Ephorus' wife Vera *as his own mistress,* in an inscription prominently honoring Ephorus! Instead, as the final word suggests, verbally embracing both, Vera is Eros' *amica* just as Ephorus is his *amicus.*

Epitaphs in which an individual, man or woman, is jointly commemorated by a male–female pair as their friend clearly imply a symmetrical use of the terms *amicus* and *amica.*[57]

Diis Manibus. / C(aius) Poppaeus Vale(n)s et / Poppaea Ilias fecerunt / sibi et Avianiae Charidi / *amicae suae carissimae. (CIL* 6.39780; Rome)

D(is) M(anibus). / Sentio / Celeri. / Dom(itia) Aphro/disia et Vir(ius) / Stephanus / *amico* b(ene) m(erenti) p(osuerunt). *(CIL* 3.2522; Salona)

To the spirits of the dead. Gaius Poppaeus Valens and Poppaea Ilias dedicated this to themselves and to Aviania Charis their dear friend.

To the spirits of the dead. To Sentius Celer. Domitia Aphrodisia and Virius Stephanus erected this monument to their deserving friend.

Conversely, we find inscriptions in which a man and woman are jointly commemorated as the *amici* of the individual, man or woman, who commissioned the memorial. Here too the implication is that, across configurations of gender, the man is the *amicus* of the dedicator just as the woman is his or her *amica.*[58]

---

57 Other examples of a man and a woman jointly commemorating an *amicus* include *CIL* 2.3763 (Valencia), 6.4532 (from the *monumentum Marcellae* in Rome), 6.13761 (Rome), 6.13895 (Rome), 11.7778 = Reali 154It (Capena); a man and a woman jointly commemorate an *amica* in *CIL* 6.7648 (from a columbarium along the Via Appia outside Rome).

58 Other examples include *CIL* 5.3395 = Reali 63C (Verona: a man commemorates himself, his wife, and a man and woman as his *amici*) and 3.4913 = 3.11515 (Sankt Georgen am Längsee, Austria: a woman commemorates a man and woman as her *amici*).

[image of Ganymede and the eagle, flanked by two sea lions] / V(iva) f(ecit). / Appia P(ubli) libert(a) / Faventina sibi / et P(ublio) Valerio Nilo / marito suo VIvir(o) / et augustali et / P(ublio) Appio Nigrino, / Favori, Hermione, / Helpidi, Cale, / Iucundae, Iucundinae / libertis suis / et C(aio) Atilio Prosdocimo / et Litaniae Secundae / *[empty space]* / *amicis*. CIL 5.6516 = Reali 136C (Novara; first century AD; see Figure 4)

D(is) M(anibus). / M(arcus) Ulpius Aug(usti) lib(ertus) / Herma a cura amicor(um) / fecit sibi et Ulpiis / Pythe Agathopo Successo, / et Nicandro Caes(aris) n(ostri) ser(vo), et / lib(ertis) libertab(usque) poster(is)q(ue) eor(um), et / Aerario Soteri et Setriae / Iulian(a)e *amicis bene / merentibus*. (*CIL* 6.8799; Rome)[59]

While still alive, Appia Faventina, freedwoman of Publius, dedicated this to herself and Publius Valerius Nilus her husband, *sevir augustalis*, and to Publius Appius Nigrinus, Favor, Hermione, Elpis, Cale, Jucunda and Jucundina her freedmen, and to Gaius Atilius Prosdocimus and Litania Secunda her friends.

To the spirits of the departed. Marcus Ulpius Herma, freedman of Augustus in charge of his friends, dedicated this to himself and to Ulpia Pythe, Ulpius Agathopos, and Ulpius Successus, and to Nicander, slave of our emperor, and to his freedmen and freedwomen and their descendants, and to Aerarius Soter and Setria Juliana his well-deserving friends.

The epitaph commissioned by Appia Faventina for herself, her husband, six former slaves, and a male and female friend (Figure 4) is framed by two elements which visually stand out because of their larger size: the formulaic abbreviation V.F. ("while still alive") and first elements in Faventina's name at the beginning, and the single word AMICIS at the end. Together these bring home the message that Faventia has provided for friends while she is still alive; the noticeable space separating AMICIS from the body of the text may have been designed as spill-over to receive the names of any other eventual recipients of Faventina's favor, subtly reinforcing the image of Faventina as generous friend of those who could be called both her *amici* and her *amicae*.

Illustrating an even broader network of *amicitia* is an epitaph from Aquileia which was commissioned by two men and a woman in order to jointly commemorate themselves along with a man and a woman, both of whom they memorialize as their friends.

59 For the title *a cura amicorum* see also *CIL* 6.604, 630, 8795–8799, 30557, with *RE* 4.1773 (s.v. *cura*): Mommsen, Marquardt, and Mau hypothesize that the function of such an official was to keep a list of the emperor's *amici* and to collaborate with the *nomenclator ab admissione*; Friedlaender suggests that he had the specific duty of overseeing the meals served to the emperor's friends. As Courtney 1995, p. 357, points out, it may not be coincidental that in a dedication to the god Priapus commissioned by an imperial freedman holding this office, the god is invoked, rather unusually, with the language of *amicitia* (*CIL* 14.3565, vv. 33 and 47, from Tivoli: *o Priape potens amice, salve*).

Figure 4 Stele with an inscription commissioned by the freedwoman Appia Faventina for herself, her husband, six of her freedmen and freedwomen, and her friends Gaius Atilius Prosdocimus and Litania Secunda (*CIL* 5.6516, first century AD). Novara, Museo Civico.

Q(uintus) Etuvius / Q(uinti) l(ibertus) Felix / et Cassia Nice / et L(ucius) Ovius Privatian(us) / v(ivi) f(ecerunt) sibi *et / M(arco) Claudio Nicostrato / et Oviae Primulae / amicis bene merent(ibus).* / h(oc) m(onumentum) h(eredem) n(on) s(equetur). (*CIL* 5.1197 = Reali 29C; Aquileia, first–second century AD; see Figure 5)

Quintus Etuvius Felix, freedman of Quintus, and Cassia Nice and Lucius Ovius Privatianus, while still alive, dedicated this to themselves and to Marcus Claudius Nicostratus and Ovia Primula, their deserving friends. This tomb will not pass into the possession of the heirs.

Figure 5 Altar with an inscription commissioned by Quintus Etuvius Felix,
Cassia Nice, and Lucius Ovius Privatianus for their friends Marcus Claudius
Nicostratus and Ovia Primula (*CIL* 5.1197, first to second century AD). Aquileia,
Museo Archeologico Nazionale.

Epitaphs like these not only draw attention to the generosity of those
who commissioned the texts and memorialize their devotion to their
friends, but suggest that in the language of this speech genre the relationship between, for example, Felix and his *amicus* Nicostratus or Nice and
her *amica* Primula are not substantially different from that between Felix
and his *amica* Primula or Nice and her *amicus* Nicostratus.

So much is suggested, too, by epitaphs commemorating married couples not only as each other's spouses but as the friends of the men who
commissioned them. The wife, then, is *amica* of the dedicator as the husband is his *amicus*.

Caecia C(ai) l(iberta) Eulimene / C(aio) Caecio C(ai) l(iberto) Philaristo viro suo / et sibi fecit. / D(ecimus) Cornelius Hilarus *amicus* / locum ollarum duarum dedit donavitque. (*CIL* 6.13871; Rome)

[D(is)] M(anibus). / T(ito) Vaternio Basso / et / Mariae Marcellinae / uxori eius. / Q(uintus) Vedius Paederos / *amicus*. (*CIL* 11.8095 = Reali 131It; Fano)

D(is) M(anibus). / L(ucio) Naevio / Allio vivo et / Naeviae Severin(ae). / L(ucius) Titius Onesimus / senior VIvir *amic(is)*, / et L(ucius) Naevius Iustinus / VIvir parentibus. (*CIL* 5.8295 = Reali 21C; Aquileia)[60]

Caecia Eulimene, freedwoman of Gaius, dedicated this to herself and to her husband Gaius Caecius Philaristus, freedman of Gaius. Their friend Decimus Cornelius Hilarus gave and donated the niche for the two urns.

To the spirits of the dead. To Titus Vaternius Bassus and his wife Maria Marcellina. [Dedicated by] Quintus Vedius Paederos, their friend.

To the spirits of the departed. To Lucius Naevius Allius, while still alive, and to Naevia Severina. Dedicated by Lucius Titius Onesimus, senior *sevir*, to his friends, and by L. Naevius Justinus, *sevir*, to his parents.

The rules of the speech genre seem clear enough: The bonds between *amicus* and *amicus*, *amica* and *amica*, and *amicus* and *amica* are directly comparable to each other, the labels perfectly symmetrical in denotation. A statue base found in southern Spain contains an inscription in honor of the man whose image originally surmounted it: Publius Magnius Rufus Magonianus, military tribune and *procurator Augusti*.[61] The text communicates to those who can read it that the statue was commissioned by a woman whose name, Acilia Plecusa, suggests that she is a freed slave. But while the inscription carefully specifies Magonianus' status as freeborn Roman citizen, it says nothing about hers; her name signals that if she is a freedwoman, she did not earlier belong to Magonianus but to a man named Acilius or a woman named Acilia. What the text directly communicates to its readers is that Magonianus has treated the provincials well, and that he was Plecusa's *amicus*. Whatever kind of relationship the two may have had or have been thought to have had, the highly formal language of this inscription is not memorializing them as a conjugal couple but as friends.

Inscriptions naming only two people, man and woman, and using the label *amicus* or *amica* and little else, draw attention to their language precisely in their spareness. Because they commemorate a relationship between a man, a woman, and no one else, they urge questions regarding

---

[60] The Clauss–Slaby transcription expands AMIC to *amico* but Reali 1997 more persuasively suggests *amicis*.

[61] *CIL* 2.2029 (Villanueva de la Concepción, Málaga): ... *Acili(a) Plec(usa) amico optimo / et bene de provincia / semper merito d(onum) d(at)*.

the labels used to commemorate interpersonal relationships in this speech genre with particular intensity.

D(is) M(anibus). / Betutia Pri/ma viva si/bi *et P(ublio) Popilio / Victori ami/co.* (*CIL* 12.3472; Nimes, second century AD)

Iuliae / Chreste / A[g]a[t]ho / *amicae / bene / merenti.* (*CIL* 3.2387; Salona)

To the spirits of the departed. Betutia Prima, while still alive, dedicated this to herself and to Publius Popilius Victor her friend.

To Julia Chreste. Agathon to his well-deserving friend.

Presumably under the influence of the language of Latin literature, scholars have generally assumed that the combination *amicus–amica* in such epitaphs is fundamentally different from the combinations *amicus–amicus* and *amica–amica*; and so, although sometimes duly noting the impossibility of knowing for certain, they conclude that the pairs commemorated in epitaphs like these were conjugal couples or united in a sexual relationship.[62] To be sure, a few such epitaphs make that conclusion somewhat less than obvious. An inscription from Rome announces that Marcus Clodius Zosimus, whose name suggests he is a freedman, is commemorating himself along with his *amica carissima* Fabia Ionis, carefully identified as freeborn daughter of Lucius Fabius and 14 years old at her death; and an epitaph from Nimes commissioned by Gaius Terentius Anicetus (likewise probably a freedman) memorializes himself along with his *amica optima* Sammia Severina, identified as freeborn daughter of Quintus Sammius and as priestess in the cult of Augustus.[63] Ionis' age does not in itself preclude a conjugal relationship (see Chapter 4, n. 25), but what is highly unlikely is that these men, freed slaves or not, would commission joint epitaphs for themselves and unmarried women, carefully identified as daughters of citizens, in which the latter are called the men's mistresses. In that case these inscriptions, carved on stone and marking the burial place of both man and woman, would be announcing relationships liable to moral sanctions and, after Augustus at least, legal penalties as *stuprum.* Instead, these inscriptions are memorializing them as devoted friends.

---

[62] Other examples of this configuration include *CIL* 2.4448 (near Tarracona, Spain), 6.13329 and 6.29409 (Rome), 13.2075 (Trion). Caldelli 2001, p. 25, remarks that in many cases "non è facile ... stabilire se si tratta di amicizia o di un legame di tipo matrimoniale," but "pare improbabile leggervi l'indicazione di una relazione sessuale passeggera"; similarly Rawson 1974, pp. 299–300 with n. 66.

[63] *CIL* 6.17607 (Rome): *D(is) M(anibus) / Fabiaes L(uci) f(iliae) / Ionidi[s] / vixit ann(is) XIIII / mens(ibus) IIII dieb(us) V / M(arcus) Clodius / Zosimus / amicae carissimae / fecit et sibi. CIL* 12.3269 (Nimes): *D(is) M(anibus) / Sammiae Q(uinti) fil(iae) / Severinae / flamin(icae) Aug(ustae) Nem(ausensis) / C(aius) Terentius / Anicetus amicae / optimae et sibi / v(ivus) p(osuit).*

On my reading, then, the words of epitaphs like those just quoted communicate nothing more nor less than the words of epitaphs like these:

D(is) i(nferis) M(anibus). / Avianiae Amandae / *amicae suae* / *fecit bene merenti* / Livia Lauris. (*CIL* 6.12881, 12882; Rome)[64]

Q(uinto) Annio Apto, / vix(it) ann(is) XXXV. / C(aius) Antonius Herma / *amico bene merenti* / *fecit.* (*CIL* 6.11704; Rome)

To the spirits of the dead below. Dedicated to Aviania Amanda, her well-deserving friend, by Livia Lauris.

To Quintus Annius Aptus, who lived 35 years. Gaius Antonius Herma to his well-deserving friend.

The combined weight of traditional models for relations between the sexes in Western culture and of the linguistic usage pervading Latin literature understandably enough encourages the assumption that if a woman is called a man's *amica* she is his mistress. But texts which signaled their participation in the speech genre of inscriptions by being inscribed on stone and erected near burials, on statue bases, and elsewhere, and by their use of a standard repertory of abbreviations and formulae, used the Latin language in a specific way, and invited and invite being read as such. An inscription commissioned by a woman in honor of her *amicus* communicated nothing more nor less than one she might have commissioned in honor of an *amica*. Nothing more nor less, that is, than *amicitia*.

COMBINATIONS AND HYBRIDS

As I suggested in the Introduction, one way of describing and at least temporarily pinning down the polyvalence of language, the deceptive clarity of words, is to apply the concept of the speech genre as a way of locating an utterance within a specific code. The denotations of *amicus* and *amica*, then, are suggested not by the lexical items themselves but by various contextual clues, principal among them the speech genre in which the relevant utterance is made. In general, those who composed and read Latin prose inscriptions used and understood the words in one way, the writers and audiences of staged comedies, lyric poetry, or courtroom speeches in another. But of course the readers and composers of Latin inscriptions were also fluent in other speech genres, and the readers and writers of elegiac poetry, in which a man's *amicus* is one thing and

---

[64] The text is carved twice, once on each side of a marble tablet identified as originating from Rome, but now located in Fossombrone (Forum Sempronii). The version on one side (6.12882) emphasizes the key label by placing a drawing of a dish (*patera*) between AMICAE and SVAE.

his *amica* quite another, read and composed prose epitaphs in which the terms *amicus* and *amica* are symmetrically used. Do we find any signs of interference? Bakhtin's concept of a "hybrid construction" offers one way of describing what happens when words become particularly hard to pin down.[65]

A formula typical of inscriptions commemorating married couples specifies how long they lived together and sometimes adds the stereotypical phrase that they never quarreled, thereby evoking the conjugal ideal of *concordia*. A search of any database or index of inscriptions for the nouns *coniunx, uxor, maritus,* or *vir* together with the phrase *cum quo/qua vixit ___ annis* will yield hundreds of examples like the following:

Diis Manibus / M(arci) Numisi Glypti. / Numisia Parthenio / fecit coniugi bene / merenti, *cum quo* / *vixit sine querella* / *annis XX.* et ipse vixit / annis XXXVII. / sit tibi terra levis. (*CIL* 6.23115; Rome)

To the spirits of the deceased Marcus Numisius Glyptus. Numisia Parthenio dedicated this to her well-deserving husband, with whom she lived for 20 years without quarrel; he himself lived 37 years. May the earth lie lightly upon you.

Pairs of men and women who are not identified as husband and wife but placed in some other relationship are also commemorated with the formula, such as this epitaph commissioned by a freedwoman for her former master:

D(is) M(anibus). / C(aio) Iulio Pacato. / vix(it) an(nis) L. / Iulia Restituta / lib(erta) patrono b(ene) m(erenti), / *cum quo v(ixit) a(nnis) VI.* (*CIL* 6.20170; Rome)

To the spirits of the departed. For Gaius Julius Pacatus, who lived 50 years. Julia Restituta [dedicated this] to her well-deserving patron, with whom she lived for 6 years.

Sometimes the phrase appears in commemorations of male–female pairs whose relationship is given no label at all:

D(is) M(anibus). / Alfio Salbio. / Seia T[y]che. / *cum quo bixit* / *annis XXVII* / *mense uno* / *d[iebus] tri(bus).* b(ene) m(erenti) f(ecit). (*CIL* 10.6247; Fundi)

To the spirits of the departed. For Alfius Salbius. Seia Tyche, who lived with him for 27 years, 1 month, 3 days, dedicated this to him; he deserved it well.

Do such inscriptions have the function of commemorating the deceased *as a couple*, for example in a relationship that could be called *contubernium*,

---

[65] Bakhtin 1981, p. 305: "The same word will belong simultaneously to two languages, two belief systems that intersect in a hybrid construction – and the word has two contradictory meanings, two accents."

or in an arrangement like that commemorated by Aulus Allius of Rome in his epitaph for his freedwoman Potestas (see Chapter 2, pp. 146–148)? It is hard to know, but one thing is clear. The formulaic phrase "lived together for X years" in itself does not necessarily signal a sexual or conjugal relationship. Tellingly enough, it appears in commemorations of pairs of men configured in those two most significant male relationships within a patrilineal kinship system: father–son and brother–brother.

D(is) M(anibus). / Philetus f(ilius) cum / Niphade matre fec(it) / Epio patri pientis/simo et b(ene) m(erenti), *cum / quo vix(it) an(nis) XLIII. (CIL* 6.24098; Rome)

D(is) M(anibus). / Ti(berio) Claudio Miz/oni. fratri bene m/erenti fecit Ti(berius) Cl(audius) / Micus, *cum quo vi/xit annis LV mens(ibus) / duobus, sine ulla / querela vixit,* et / C(aius) Statius Eutychus, / Boionia Hospita. *ISOstiense* 105

To the spirits of the departed. His son Philetus, together with his mother Niphas, dedicated this to Epius: his most devoted and well-deserving father with whom he lived for 43 years.

To the spirits of the departed. To Tiberius Claudius Mizon, his well-deserving brother: dedicated by Tiberius Claudius Micus, who lived with him for 55 years and 2 months, and lived with him without any quarrel, and by Gaius Statius Eutychus and by Boionia Hospita.

I have found no inscriptions in which the *cum quo vixit* formula is applied to two men identified as each other's *amici*. If such commemorations existed, they were rare.

Regardless of the configurations commemorated with the formula, the inscriptions just quoted remind us of an important point. Unlike English "to live with," Latin *vivere cum* does not necessarily signify living under the same roof; it may mean more generally "to spend time with," or to share one's life but not necessarily one's home with someone, and when accompanied by an adverb, the phrase describes the kind of relationship one has (for example, *familiariter vivere cum aliquo,* "to be on familiar terms with someone").[66] To be sure, the specification of length of time may make a crucial difference: "to be on familiar terms with someone" is one thing, "to spend forty years with someone" is arguably another. Yet

---

[66] Cf. Cic. *Amic.* 2: *quocum coniunctissime et amantissime vixerat*; 76: *nihil enim est turpius quam cum eo bellum gerere quocum familiariter vixeris*; 89: *aliter cum tyranno, aliter cum amico vivitur*. When Laelius uses the phrase to describe his own friendship with Scipio, he adds that they also shared a home for a time, which suggests that *vivere cum* in itself does not make the point (15: *quia cum Scipione vixerim, quocum coniuncta cura de publica re et de privata fuit; quocum et domus fuit et militia communis*; cf. 103: *una domus erat, idem victus, isque communis*). Among inscriptions, cf. *CIL* 8.22914 from Hadrumetum in proconsular Africa: *omnes amici et amatores cum quibus semper b{a}ene vixi.*

is Tiberius Claudius Micus really communicating that he shared a home
with his brother for 55 years?

What, then, of inscriptions such as the following, carved in a marble
tablet found in Rome?

D(is) M(anibus). / Iuliae P[a]/ternae / *amicae san/ctissimae, / cum qua vi/xit ann(is)
LVII /* mens(ibus) VI. fecit Oc/tavius verna. (*CIL* 6.38513; Rome)

To the spirits of the departed. To Julia Paterna his most honorable friend, with
whom he lived for 57 years, 6 months. Dedicated by Octavius, home-born slave.

Octavius carefully records his own status as a slave, whereas Julia Paterna's
name signals that she is either a manumitted slave or perhaps even freeborn. What does the inscription commissioned by Octavius communicate about his relationship with her? According to the rules of this speech
genre, I am arguing, neither the label *amica* nor the formula *cum qua vixit*
in itself signifies the existence of a relationship of concubinage or *contubernium*. And yet, as we have seen, the jurist Masurius notes that *amica*
could be synonymous with *concubina*, referring to "a woman who lived
with a man without being his wife" (*quae, cum uxor non esset, cum aliquo
tamen vivebat, Digest* 50.16.144.pr), and elsewhere in the *Digest* we read a
fictitious but realistic provision in a man's will: "I wish for five pounds
of gold to be given to my *amica* Titia, with whom I shared a life without
lies" (*Digest* 34.2.35.pr.: *Titiae amicae meae, cum qua sine mendacio vixi,
auri pondo quinque dari volo*). By combining the label *amica* with the formula *cum qua vixit*, inscriptions such as that commissioned by Octavius
for Julia Paterna may be signifying the kind of relationship described by
the jurists. If so, however, it is worth emphasizing that a specific combination of linguistic usage and speech-genre rules sends the message, not
any single lexical element.

Inscriptions in verse constitute an arguably different but closely related
speech genre, drawing not only on the formulaic language of prose
inscriptions but also on the richer, more varied, but equally formulaic
language of Latin poetry. How to read *amici* and *amicae* in texts like the
following epitaph found at Piglio, site of the ancient town of Capitulum
Hernicorum?

> D(is) M(anibus).
> h(ic) iacet in tum[ulo Cir]/ce *carissima ami[ca*
> *quam]* / mihi di dederant, si [non ta]/men invidi fuissent.
> hae[c e]/go cum dicto lacrimis fle/tuque dolens,
> pluria si potu/isse(m) in hoc titulo proscribe/re laudes,
> ut scirent plures / qualis illa fuit.

qu(a)e vixit annis / XXIIII, m(ensibus) V, d(iebus) XII.
Lupercus *amic(a)e / merenti* fecit memoratus amorem.
(*CIL* 10.5958 = *CLE* 596 = Reali 73It; Piglio)

To the spirits of the deceased.
Here lies in her tomb Circe, the dearest friend
whom the gods had given me: if only they had not been so spiteful!
As I dictate these words, grieving with tears and weeping:
if only I had been able to write up more in her praise in this inscription,
that more might know what kind of person she was.
She lived 24 years, 5 months, 12 days.
Lupercus dedicated this to his deserving friend, recalling their love.

The poem commissioned by Lupercus for his beloved Circe (the names suggest that they are slaves or freed slaves but the inscription does not specify status), framed by prose formulae, is in rough but recognizably dactylic meter. There may be a stonecarver's error or two, and at times the meter and syntax depart from what we might expect, but in general the message is loud, clear, and effective, conveyed with repetition and balance (*hic iacet in tumulo ... in hoc titulo ... pluria si potuisse ... ut scirent plures*). But how clear is the key term *amica* in the poem's first verse and in the closing prose formula? If we were reading a Latin poem transmitted in the manuscript tradition, we would probably understand the message sent by the phrase *carissima amica / quam mihi di dederant* in one way;[67] yet as an element in a prose epitaph, I have argued that the closing dedication *amicae merenti* denotes something else, no more nor less than a dedication *amico merenti*. The climactic appeal to *amor* adds no clarity. In the following chapter we will explore the interplay between *amicitia* and *amor*, the latter as elusive and polyvalent as English "love." In its entirety, Circe's epitaph seems to be inviting both readings of *amica* at once in an illustration of how a hybrid construction might work.

Valerius Maximus' narrative of a rather squalid affair (which he describes as fairly well known in his day) gives a glimpse at other possibilities. A man named Gaius Visellius Varro had what Valerius decorously but unambiguously calls a "relationship based on lust (*commercium libidinis*)" with a married woman named Otacilia; seriously ill, Varro took a significant loan from her, reckoning that if he died, his heirs would take care of things. Unexpectedly – and rather against Otacilia's hopes – Varro

---

[67] With *quam mihi di dederant* we might compare a couplet from Sulpicia's poetry: *illum Cytherea ... / attulit in nostrum deposuitque sinum* ([Tib.] 3.13.34–35). I thank one of the anonymous readers for the parallel.

survived, and she promptly sued him for the money: "Having previously played the role of the obliging friend (*amica obsequenti*)," Valerius caustically comments, "she now took on that of the demanding money-lender."[68] The key phrase is pointedly ambivalent. The reference to *commercium libidinis* suggests that Otacilia was *amica* to Varro in the way Cynthia was to Propertius, but she also played the role in the way a male *amicus* might have done: Financial assistance in times of need was one of the most traditional benefits of *amicitia*.[69] An epitaph commissioned by Varro, commemorating Otacilia as his *amica bene merens* or himself as her *amicus*, would hardly be unthinkable. The adjective *obsequens* ("obliging, compliant") raises a few questions too. Are we hearing an echo of Otacilia's complacent self-description, the reported observations of others who knew the pair, or an ironic comment on the part of the narrator himself? And how significant is it that in the language of inscriptions *obsequens* is an epithet commonly attached to husbands and wives, sisters and brothers, sons and daughters, freedmen and freedwomen – but almost never to *amici* and *amicae*?[70]

The freedman Niceros, guest at Trimalchio's banquet in Petronius' *Satyricon*, tells a gripping tale of how, when still a slave, he had an encounter with a werewolf.

cum adhuc servirem ... *amare coepi* uxorem Terentii coponis; noveratis Melissam Tarentinam, pulcherrimum bacciballum. sed ego non mehercules corporaliter aut *propter res venerias* curavi, sed magis quod benemoria fuit. si quid ab illa petii, nunquam mihi negatum; fecit assem, semissem habui; in illius sinum demandavi, nec unquam fefellitus sum. huius contubernalis ad villam supremum diem obiit. itaque per scutum per ocream egi aginavi, quemadmodum ad illam pervenirem: nam, ut aiunt, in angustiis *amici* apparent. (Petron. *Sat.* 61.6)

While I was still a slave ... I fell in love with the wife of the innkeeper Terentius. You knew her – Melissa from Taranto, a cute little thing. God knows I wasn't interested in her for her body or for sex; no, it was because she was so well-behaved. If I asked her for anything, I always got it; if she earned an *as*, I got half of it. I hid things in her pocket and never regretted it. Anyway, her companion

---

[68] Val. Max. 8.2.2: *ne quod (sc., iudicium) relatu<ru>s sum quidem obliteratum silentio... ex amica obsequenti subito destrictam feneratricem agere coepit.* Valerius adds that the judge rejected Otacilia's suit, but Varro was then tried (and implicitly condemned) for *adulterium* before another court.

[69] See Verboven 2002.

[70] Reali 1997, pp. 195 and 211, reports that among ninety-two inscriptions from central and southern Italy which accompany the noun *amicus/amica* with an adjective, only one has *obsequens* (the most common epithets are *bene merens*, *optimus*, and *carus* in that order); and that among fifty-five such inscriptions from Cisalpine Gaul, none has *obsequens* (most common are *optimus/a*, *carus/carissimus*, and *bene merens* in that order).

passed away at the villa. So I went through hell and high water in order to get to her. After all, as the saying goes, it's when the going gets rough that you know your friends.

The phrase *amare coepi* and the potential double meaning of the phrase *in illius sinum demandavi*, not to mention the tenor of Niceros' narrative as a whole, suggest the realm of Venus. To Niceros' coy protest that he was not interested in Melissa for sex but because of her character we may compare Trimalchio's unconvincing attempt at self-defense to his wife later in the evening. When Niceros describes his condolence visit to Melissa after her spouse (*contubernalis*) had died as an act of friendship, citing a proverb about *amici*, and soon thereafter refers to Melissa as his *amica*, his language teasingly activates two senses of *amicus* at once.[71] Later in the *Satyricon*, Eumolpus narrates an invented scenario in which he and his two "slaves" – roles played by Encolpius and Giton – had been at a party hosted by a female "friend in common" (105.3: *apud communem amicam*). That here too there is a playful double meaning seems clear, but what we cannot know is whether the use of *amica* by these two characters in the *Satyricon* reflects generically or socially conditioned linguistic patterns that would have been recognizable as such to Petronius' ancient readership. These moments may stand for many, and remind us of what we do not know: the full denotational, connotational, and tonal range of words like *amicus* and *amica* across all speech genres of Latin as spoken and written by men and women of all social backgrounds.

I end with the pointed juxtaposition of *amici* and *amicae* in a private letter of Cicero's to his own *amicus* Atticus regarding the shocking behavior of Marcus Antonius. Here – typically of his correspondence, as we will see in Chapter 3 – we have glimpses at the ways in which men's *amicitia* could be played out as a matter of allegiances and alliances at the highest levels of Roman society. Writing from Cumae on May 3, 49 BC, after Caesar's crossing of the Rubicon, Cicero is waiting to leave Italy and eventually to join Pompey; he gives Atticus the background story. He had

---

[71] Petron. *Sat.* 62.9: *donec ad villam amicae meae pervenirem.* For *amare coepi*, cf. Plaut. *Merc.* 13 (*amare occepi forma eximia mulierem*), Pompon. *com.* 174 (*porcus est, quem amare coepi, pinguis, non pulcher puer*); for *sinus* see OLD s.v.; for Trimalchio's protest see Petr. *Sat.* 75.4 (*puerum basiavi frugalissimum non propter formam, sed quia frugi est*). For proverbs of the type *in angustiis amici apparent* see Otto s.v. *amicus* 6. Smith 1975 tries to explain how and why Niceros uses the term *contubernalis*: "The word is probably used accurately here: Melissa is the *contubernalis* of the unnamed slave whose death is described in the story; later she becomes the *uxor* of Terentius … The alternative is to assume that *contubernalis* represents the absent-mindedness of Niceros, an ex-slave himself, in referring to the death of Terentius." Rather than being absent-minded, perhaps Niceros is speaking the language of a speech genre otherwise unknown to us.

written to Antony, who at the time held the position of tribunus plebis,
assuring him that he had no intention of acting contrary to Caesar's
interests, for he was mindful of his son-in-law Dolabella and mindful of
amicitia (by the latter he seems to be referring to his fragile alliance with
Caesar, though he writes in the abstraction, underscoring his commitment to the principle). Cicero then quotes from Antony's written reply: "I
am sure Caesar will grant what you request, especially since you promise
that you will be taking into account your friendship."[72]

After sharing with Atticus the next steps he plans to take, Cicero adds
a few bitter words about Antony's recent behavior in connection with his
mistress, the mime-actress Volumnia Cytheris.[73]

hic tamen Cytherida secum lectica aperta portat, alteram uxorem. septem
praeterea coniunctae lecticae *amicarum; et sunt amicorum.* <vi>de quam turpi
leto pereamus et dubita, si potes, quin ille, seu victus seu victor redierit, caedem
facturus sit. (Cic. *Att.* 10.10.5; text of Shackleton Bailey)

He is taking Cytheris with him in an open litter, like a second wife. Seven litters of *amicae* have joined the group, too – and litters of *amici* as well! Look at
how disgraceful a death we are dying and doubt, if you can, that regardless of
whether Caesar comes back victor or vanquished, he will start a massacre.

The text is disputed. Whatever Cicero wrote, his words caused some
confusion among later scribes, at least partly, I would suggest, because
of his play with the already slippery language of *amicitia*. The manuscripts give implausible or impossible readings of the italicized words
(*amicarum, eae sunt amicorum; amicarum, hae sunt amicorum; amicarum
esse sunt amicorum;* or simply *amicarum sunt amicorum*) and the solution
most commonly accepted until Shackleton Bailey's edition was Dubois'
emendation *amicarum, an sunt amicorum*: "seven litters of *amicae* – or
are they *amici?*" If Cicero wrote this, his remark was explicitly drawing attention to the point of gender; but how exactly? Some understood
Cicero to be doubting whether the entourage consists of female or male
companions, the latter being male prostitutes. Carcopino, understanding

[72] Cic. *Att.* 10.10.1: *meminisse me generi mei, meminisse amicitiae;* 10.10.2 (quoting Antony's letter):
cum praesertim te amicitiae vestrae rationem habiturum esse pollicearis. Shackleton Bailey proposes
emending the universal manuscript reading *vestrae* to *nostrae.*

[73] Cytheris was the former slave of Antony's friend Volumnius Eutrapelos. In a letter to L. Papirius
Paetus, Cicero tells of a dinner-party hosted by Eutrapelos at which both Cicero and Cytheris
were present (*Fam.* 9.26). For Eutrapelos' connection with Antony see Cicero's sarcastic words
at *Phil.* 13.3: *addite illa naufragia* Caesaris amicorum, *Barbas Cassios, Barbatos, Polliones; addite
Antoni conlusores et sodales, Eutrapelum, Melam, Pontium.* For Antony's scandalous entourage
see also Plut. *Ant.* 9.4–5: ὃ (i.e. Cytheris) δὴ καὶ τὰς πόλεις ἐπιὼν ἐν φορείῳ περιήγετο, καὶ τὸ
φορεῖον οὐκ ἐλάττους ἢ τὸ τῆς μητρὸς αὐτοῦ περιέποντες ἠκολούθουν.

the traveling companions to be not Antony's but Cytheris' "friends," proposed two different ways of reading the remark. Either the masculine *amici* are "pretty boys," or they are actually women, whom Cicero disparagingly masculinizes, implying that they are sexual partners for Cytheris herself. More recently, however, Shackleton Bailey's text as printed above has won acceptance. On this reading, Antony's traveling companions are both female and male, and the implication is that both groups contained potential sexual partners for him.[74]

Judging by the usual meaning of the feminine in the genres of literary Latin and by the avoidance of the noun in Cicero's and Pliny's letters (see above, pp. 94–95), at least some of Antony's *amicae* could also be called his *concubinae*, supplementing Cytheris as she herself supplements Antony's wife. What of his *amici*? The parallelism between masculine and feminine urges the conclusion that if Antony's *amicae* are his *concubinae*, the *amici* are his *concubini*. In other words, by means of the pointedly symmetrical pairing of *amicae/amici*, Cicero is alluding to the same configuration which Quintilian describes by means of the asymmetrical pairing *amicae/concubini* (*Inst.* 1.2.7–8). Yet we have seen that in the speech genres of literary Latin, *amicus* and *amica* are precisely *not* parallel. If Cicero is indeed describing Antony's sexual partners as his *amici*, he is pushing the envelope, not least because some of them may have been Antony's slaves who could otherwise be called his *concubini*, like the slave-boy of Catullus' wedding-hymn (61.123, 125, 130, 133). Whether in an *ad hoc* pun or inspired by some usage to which we no longer have access, his words may be suggesting that Antony is a man whose relationships, even *amicitia*, too easily end up in the bedroom. In all its compression, and whatever precisely Cicero may have written to Atticus, the implicit question seems to be: Who are the *amici* of a man like this?

---

[74] Cf. Tyrrell and Purser ad loc., quoting an older Latin commentary: *dubitat Cicero utrum illae lecticae amicas Antonii contineant an exoletos*; Carcopino 1947, vol. I p. 143 with n. 1: "sept autres litières garnies d'amies et d'amis de la comédienne"; "des mignons d'Antoine ou des lesbiennes, ou les deux à la fois"; vol. II, p. 55: "sept autres litières suivent, remplies de petites amies et de trop jolis garçons." In his 1993 Budé edition, Jean Beaujeu translates: "avec les petites amies; et il y a celles des petits amis"; Shackleton Bailey translates "seven other litters are attached, containing mistresses; and there are some containing *friends*" (emphasis original). In the *Second Philippic* written five years later, Cicero stages a similar scene but configures Antony's entourage somewhat differently: Cytheris is his *amica* and the only males present are pimps (Cic. *Phil.* 2.58: *sequebatur raeda cum lenonibus, comites nequissimi; reiecta mater amicam impuri filii tamquam nurum sequebatur*). The scene he stages in this public attack on Antony may or may not be relevant to a reading of his words in a private letter to Atticus.

CHAPTER 2

Love and friendship: questions and themes

Friendship is far more tragic than love. It lasts longer.
(Oscar Wilde, "A Few Maxims for the Instruction of the
Over-Educated")

I want your love – I don't want to be friends!
(Lady Gaga, "Bad Romance")

The complexities of writing about friendship become even more acute when we couple it with love. Referring to relationships which are both stereotypical and intensely unique, the very words *love* and *friendship* are notoriously polyvalent, and issues of linguistic and conceptual trans-latability become that much more urgent when we try to read love and friendship *between* languages. Even if we think we know, more or less, what "love" and "friendship" mean, can we say the same of *amour* and *amitié*, *Liebe* and *Freundschaft*, *amor* and *amicitia*, and how closely can we align any of these pairs with any other?

The very act of pairing such terms, in whichever language, raises another troubling question. Do love and friendship stand in a relationship of opposition, or of whole to part or genus to species? Is the conjunction joining them disjunctive or copulative? Here too there is no easy answer. On the one hand, the idea that friendship is a kind of love has a long his-tory, and C. S. Lewis crystallizes much Western thinking on the matter when he describes four kinds of love: Affection, Friendship, Eros, and Charity.[1] "Friendship" and "eros," then, are distinct from each other, yet both of them are embodiments of "love." And so we find revealing linguis-tic usages – as we will see, in some languages the very words for "friend" sometimes denote a sexual partner – along with some equally revealing and sometimes anxious questions: Can one's friend be one's lover, or one's

---

[1] Lewis 1960. Several centuries earlier, von Ramdohr 1789 had distinguished *Freundschaft* from *Geschlechtszärtlichkeit*, roughly equivalent to the second and third of Lewis' four loves respect-ively: The former is possible across all combinations of gender, the latter only between men and women. See Tobin 2000 for further discussion.

lover or spouse one's friend?[2] Accompanying and feeding such questions, however, is an impulse to demarcate and delineate which stands in direct contrast with the idealization of friendship as love. On this view, friendship is one thing, love quite another. The contrast is structural to a long line of texts in the Western tradition, from a maxim of La Rochefoucauld ("the reason why most women are hardly touched by friendship is that it is a bit flat after one has been touched by love"), to Nietzsche's harshly ironic words quoted at the opening of the previous chapter ("woman is not yet capable of friendship; she knows only love"),[3] to the differently ironic but equally representative words of Oscar Wilde and Lady Gaga quoted at the beginning of this chapter, to common utterances to the effect that "they're just friends" (not, implicitly, *something more*, something that involves "love"), formulaic in contemporary English but, as we have seen, quite alien to the Latin textual tradition.

Yet even in some of the very texts in which friendship and love are contrasted with each other we find traces of the understanding that friends are united by, precisely, love. Three very different texts from a span of more than four centuries illustrate the tension: Montaigne's *De l'amitié*, an early novel by Jane Austen, and a recent "exposé" on friendship that reveals much that is typical of contemporary American popular culture. In his influential 1580 essay on friendship, inspired by his experience with Étienne de la Boétie, Montaigne insists on a distinction between *amitié* and *amour* – the former is a "general, universal warmth," the latter "a mad desire for what escapes us" – while arguing that Platonic relationships were, at their best, instances of love which ended up as friendship ("un amour se terminant en amitié"). In the same essay, however, Montaigne writes in much quoted words that if he is pressed to say why he *loved* his friend ("pourquoi je l'aimais"), he can only reply: "Because it was him, because it was me."[4] A little over two hundred years later, the 14-year-old Jane Austen's epistolary novel *Love and Friendship* (1790) bears the maudlin subtitle *Deceived in Friendship and Betrayed in Love*. "Friendship"

---

[2] For the questions raised by these conceptual overlaps see, for example, Foucault 1994, Weeks *et al.* 2001, pp. 51–76, Halperin 2002, Weeks 2007, pp. 178–183.

[3] La Rouchefoucauld, *Maximes* 440: "Ce qui fait que la plupart des femmes sont peu touchées de l'amitié, c'est qu'elle est fade quand on a senti de l'amour"; Nietzsche, *Also sprach Zarathustra*, "Vom Freunde": "Deshalb ist das Weib noch nicht der Freundschaft fähig: es kennt nur die Liebe."

[4] Montaigne, *De l'amitié*: *amitié*, "c'est une chaleur générale et universelle, tempérée au demeurant et égale," whereas *amour*, "ce n'est qu'un désir forcené après ce qui nous fuit"; "si on me presse de dire pourquoi je l'aimais, je sens que cela ne se peut exprimer qu'en répondant: parce que c'était lui; parce que c'était moi." Screech 2004, p. 5, translates *amitié* in the first passage as "the love of friends" and *amour* as "sexual love."

suggests that which the two female protagonists share with each other, "love" that which they experience with men and which ideally culminates in marriage, but the narrative itself tells a more passionately interwoven story.[5] And in his recent *Friendship: An Exposé*, Joseph Epstein reflects conceptual and linguistic habits widespread in the contemporary United States when he proclaims it as a self-evident truth that "friendship is different from love," and resolutely excludes sex from friendship; yet warmly affirms that he "loves" his friends and describes his wife, with whom he implicitly "makes love," as his "best friend."[6] Linguistic and conceptual tensions like these provide seemingly endless fuel for contemporary negotiations of relationships between men and women in particular, ranging from the anxious to the farcical. It is enough to watch a few episodes of popular television series like *Seinfeld* or, precisely, *Friends*.

The language of scholarship, too, often shows the effects of implicit definitions and unresolved tensions, even scholarship dedicated precisely to reading love and friendship in the textual tradition. Laurent Dugas opens the 1914 second edition of his study *L'amitié antique* by observing that he was moved to write a revised edition precisely because of his changed thinking about the relationship between *amitié* and *amour*. The latter term clearly corresponds to Greek *eros* in general, pederasty (*amour grec*) in particular. More recently, the editor of Cicero's *De amicitia* in the Budé series notes that Greek and Roman society, being "essentially masculine," tended to confuse the two categories "until it gave women a true position". Here, too, *amour* points toward the body but in this case it is associated with women rather than with the young men of the Greek pederastic tradition.[7] For his part, the author of a monograph entitled *Love*

---

[5] The narrator Laura's description of the moment she met Sophia is typical in its lush exaggeration (Austen 2003, p. 13): "A soft languor spread over her lovely features, but increased their beauty. It was the characteristic of her mind: she was all sensibility and feeling. We flew into each other's arms, and after having exchanged vows of mutual friendship for the rest of our lives, instantly unfolded to each other the most inward secrets of our hearts. We were interrupted in the delightful employment by the entrance of Augustus, Edward's friend, who was just returned from a solitary ramble. Never did I see such an affecting scene as was the meeting of Edward and Augustus. 'My life! my soul!' exclaimed the former. 'My adorable angel!' replied the latter, as they flew into each other's arms. It was too pathetic for the feelings of Sophia and myself – we fainted alternately on a sofa."

[6] Epstein 2006, pp. xiii, 13, 21; 129; 30; 49.

[7] Dugas 1914, pp. vii–viii. Combès 1993, p. xlii: "Le problème de l'amitié revêt pour la pensée antique une importance qu'il a perdue aujourd'hui. La société est alors essentiellement masculine et confond longtemps *amitié* et *amour*, jusqu'à ce qu'elle fasse à la femme une place véritable." Fraisse 1974, p. 27, criticizes Dugas for neglecting the "clear distinction" betwen the terms ("Cela l'amène, en particulier, à négliger complètement la distinction, pourtant si nette, entre amour et amitié") but he only cites Dugas' first edition and does not add clarity on what the distinction is.

and Friendship in Plato and Aristotle consistently uses the first term of his title as a gloss for *eros*, the second for *philia*, yet notes that "a central question for any philosophical theory of friendship is what it is to love an individual for himself."[8] An entire body of work on Shakespeare deploys the terms "love and friendship" as a more or less self-evident antithesis which informs a great deal of scholarship: "love" quickly slides into "romantic love," "erotic love," and "love of women," while "friendship" is reserved for relationships between men, even as Shakespeare's poetry – above all his sonnets to a young man – famously meditates precisely on "love" between men who are called each other's friends (see below).[9] Sometimes the implications of transhistorical or cross-cultural validity become explicit, as when one scholar responds to a formulation of Eve Kosofky Sedgwick's by asserting that "no one, in our society or Shakespeare's, feels much personal stake in 'a sum of male power'."[10]

Such tensions are as pervasive as they are powerful, and can only partially be resolved by distinguishing between, say, the verb "to love" as tending to be broader and the noun "love" narrower, or by appealing to the notion of shorthand, whereby "love" refers to a specific *kind* of love. The very facts that the shorthand exists and that it is so often taken for granted invite questioning. *Why* does "love" (or, in a widespread contemporary usage, "a relationship") so easily imply the qualifiers "sexual" or "erotic" or "romantic," terms whose own slipperiness we will next consider? Why is that qualified love so often contrasted with friendship? And whatever distinctions we make or labels we use, are they valid across cultures, languages, history? Proposing answers to questions like these is beyond the scope of this book, but they always lurk. My readings of Roman friendship, with or without love, presuppose such questions but focus on the language of Latin texts, beginning and ending with the

---

[8] Price 1989; quotation from p. 103.

[9] The opposition between "love and friendship" in Shakespeare and contemporaries is axiomatic in, among others, MacCary 1985, Parker 1987, Bloom 2000, MacFaul 2007, pp. 65–90. Thomas 2009, p. 212, more carefully speaks of "the conflict between male bonds and marriage," but when he rephrases the contrast as that between "male friendship" and "falling in love with a woman," there is a rapid slide from social act (marriage) to sentiment (falling in love). Smith 1991, pp. 225–270, uses "desire" as his key term, thus avoiding the messiness of "love"; see below for Sedgwick 1985 and the concept of the homosocial. The problem is well illustrated by scholarly analyses written in languages other than Shakespeare's own. A recent German study of *die Sprache der Liebe* in Shakespeare's comedies (Biewer 2006) carefully explores the meanings and semantic fields of words like *passion* or *body/bawdy* in Shakespeare without doing the same for *love* itself: It is taken as axiomatic that the English word corresponds to German *Liebe*, which itself is narrowed down to *Leidenschaft* in the book's subtitle.

[10] MacFaul 2007, p. 3.

polyvalence of words, both within and across languages. As Stephen Orgel puts it in his study of Shakespeare, the language of love "implies everything and nothing,"[11] and the same is true of the language – or rather, the languages – of friendship.

TROUBLE WITH TERMINOLOGY: PINNING THINGS DOWN

With what language, then, might we attempt to describe, if not pin down, the languages of love and friendship? A set of adjectives has been put into service by way of describing, distinguishing, and limiting love and friendship – "romantic," "erotic," or "sexual," for example – but these usually end up being as elusive as the nouns themselves. Lillian Faderman's 1981 study of "romantic friendship" between women, like Adrienne Rich's influential concept of the "lesbian continuum," deliberately refrains from establishing the presence of genital acts or even a conscious desire for them as a criterion. The hallmarks of Faderman's "intimacy" are kissing, fondling, and verbalizations of faithfulness and union in death that are "in no way different from the language of heterosexual love," a formulation which raises without answering the question of what "heterosexual love" is.[12] In Janet Todd's 1980 study *Women's Friendship in Literature*, "erotic friendship" is set apart from four other types – sentimental, manipulative, political, and social – by the fact that it "requires physical love," a term whose meaning is illustrated by passages from Cleland's *Fanny Hill* and Diderot's *The Nun* which make unmistakable reference to genital organs and orgasm.[13] In his 1998 study of women in late eighteenth-century English fiction, George Haggerty uses the adjective "sexual" to suggest genital contact, with emphasis on penetration, the noun "desire" to suggest a wide range of experience that can include genital contact, and "love" as the broadest and most flexible of all.[14] And Keith Thomas' 2009 study of Shakespearean culture uses the phrase "sexual dimension" in such a way as to appeal to the legal category of sodomy and thus to the act of anal intercourse.[15]

[11] Orgel 1996, p. 42. For some thoughts on the inevitable open-endedness of the Latin language of *amor*, see Gunderson 1997, pp. 222–229, sparked by a reading of Pliny's *Ep.* 3.3.
[12] Faderman 1981, p. 16; for "romantic friendship" see also Oulton 2007.
[13] Todd 1980, pp. 4, 69–131. For the German-language category "erotische Freundschaft" see the discussion of Elfriede Friedländer's 1920 *Sexualethik des Kommunismus* at Hermand 2006, pp. 106–121.
[14] Haggerty 1998, pp. 75, 90.
[15] Thomas 2009, p. 204: "Male friends could dance with each other, kiss each other, and share a bed without arousing suspicion … without implying any sexual dimension to their relationship."

Like Haggerty, Sharon Marcus uses the term "desire" to describe a broad range of relationships in her 2007 *Between Women: Friendship, Desire, and Marriage in Victorian England*, and genital contact is the implicit criterion for distinguishing between "sexual and nonsexual intimacies" between women.[16] As Marcus points out, however, Victorian women's writings are as a rule extremely reticent about describing such acts – even indirectly, even when experienced with their husbands – and the language of "love" is particularly rich and polyvalent in Victorian English writings. Apart from the rare exception, then, how can we establish whether a given relationship was "sexual"? Or, as Marcus puts it: "Given that 'friends' was used to describe women who were lovers and women who were not, how can we tell when 'friends' means more than just friends?" Her answer is this:

Declarations of love are as insufficient to prove a sexual relationship between Victorian women as lack of evidence of sex is to disprove it. But in iterated, cumulative, hyperbolic references to passion, exclusivity, idealization, complicity, private language, and mutual dependence, we can locate a tipping point that separated Victorian women's ardent friendships from the sexual relationships they also formed with one another.[17]

And so, rather like those scholars who assert that some Roman men who identify each other as *amici* were nonetheless "not really *amici*" but something else (usually "patrons"), and who establish criteria for distinguishing between the two that are ultimately independent of the language of the Latin texts themselves, Marcus argues that Victorian women's lifewritings give us a glimpse at interpersonal relationships which are "often confused with friendship, indeed often called friendship, but significantly different from it."[18]

In much scholarly language on love and friendship in literary texts, then, the concepts of the "sexual" and the "erotic" are grounded in genital stimulation; there is a distinct tendency to use the two terms interchangeably or with a slight difference in nuance, "erotic" being less tightly bound to specific physical acts than its Latinate equivalent and thus all the more hazy.[19] But what of textual relationships in which genital acts play no role, not even indirectly, yet which can be read as evoking or hinting at desires for unnamed acts? What words do scholars use to describe various points along the continuum of desire? In his 2003 monograph *The Friend*, Alan

---

[16] Marcus 2007, pp. 25, 44.   [17] Marcus 2007, pp. 50, 54.   [18] Marcus 2007, p. 44.
[19] See, for example, Smith 1991, pp. 54–55: Shakespeare uses "erotic imagery" and "sexual images" to describe "male bonding."

Bray argues passionately against the kind of historical analysis which reduces "what we recognize today as being sexual to the narrow question of sexual intercourse"; but it is hard to know what precisely he means with the term "sexual kisses" – unless these are kisses exchanged by two people whose relationship includes genital contact, desired or consummated. And Martha Vicinus' 2004 *Intimate Friends* links the adjective of its title to "an emotional, erotically charged relationship between two women," making room for desires not carried out in acts, but leaving unanswered the question of what counts as an "erotic charge."[20]

Behind all this trouble with language lurk a number of interrelated questions. In the absence of explicit or implicit descriptions of acts, how can we ever know whether any given relationship described in a text, ancient or modern, has, or is imagined to include, genital stimulation as a feature? Does one act suffice to make the relationship "sexual"? Must it be a regular occurrence? How regular? Is it enough that genital acts are *assumed* to be a regular part of a relationship, even if they rarely occur? What happens if genital contact ceases but the relationship continues? And which acts count anyway? An act can readily be called "sexual" when there is penetration or genital stimulation – but penetration of which orifices? By a penis only? Do the genitals of both parties need to be stimulated, or is one enough? What of acts that involve the genitals of neither party, such as a mouth and a nipple? What if there are no acts at all, but only desire? What if only one party experiences desire? What if the desire is not consciously felt but nonetheless detectable to others? The insistent series of questions is intended to provoke another one, relevant not just to a study of Roman friendship. Why is it important to know? Here I adopt the stance that it is not; more generally, as in Eve Kosofky Sedgwick's *Between Men*, "what, historically, it means for something to be 'sexual' will be an active question."[21] For me the question remains active not only in a historical sense.

AMOR AND AMICITIA: A BRIEF OVERVIEW

In Marcus' formulation quoted above, the knowing euphemism "more than just friends" is aligned with "lovers," and both imply genital stimulation. That is the language of contemporary Anglophone culture

---

[20] Bray 2003, pp. 268–269, 316 (on the pair of friends Anne Lister and Ann Walker in nineteenth-century Yorkshire; Lister's diaries make direct and indirect reference to genital contact with Walker and other women); Vicinus 2004, p. xxiv.
[21] Sedgwick 1985, p. 2.

as it informs scholarship on texts written in English. How to write in English about relationships in texts written some two thousand years ago in Latin? Generations of scholars have tried without success to pin things down. Readings of Catullus' poetry, to which we will return in the next chapter, have often slapped some label or other on the various relationships it describes (from "fondness" to "a supra-sensual kind of affection," from "sensual love" to "love" itself), to determine whether these relationships are "ordinary friendship" or "sexual," or to assert the impossibility of doing so, even as their language tends to reify the distinction itself.[22] To the extent possible, I avoid making such qualifications and distinctions in my readings of *amicitia*, keeping my focus on the language of the Latin text, above all on the shifting interplay between *amor* and *amicitia*. At the same time I urge alertness to the tempting assumption that we know exactly what those and similar Latin words "mean."

Especially risky is the assumption that *amor* and *amicitia* directly correspond to English *love* and *friendship*, Greek *philia* and *eros*, or any other comparable pair in another language. Even a superficial attempt to map the Latin words onto Greek shows the uniqueness of each language's terminology and the corresponding impossibility of establishing one-to-one equivalence (see Introduction, p. 32). In particular, the Greek lexicon contains two items, *philia* and *eros*, which are both often translated by Latin *amor* and, as it happens, English *love*. While the denotative and connotative meanings of *philia* and *eros* and the differences between them are periodically contested in the Greek textual tradition, not least in philosophy, their very existence allowed speakers and writers of Greek by the use of single words to point to one of two spheres of experience that are not distinguished by comparable lexical means in Latin. Roughly speaking, while *philia* suggests connections and bonds of all kinds (for example, between parent and child or between friends), *eros* suggests the desire to possess and enjoy. In Homeric usage, one may experience *eros* for food and drink, but in the speech genres accessible to us from subsequent periods of Greek literature, *eros* is primarily directed at other human beings, their bodies in particular. Just as roughly speaking, Latin

---

[22] See for example Thomson 1998 on Catull. 50.9 (*miserum*): "implying a degree of affection tantamount to love"; 72.8 (*bene velle*): "ordinary friendship" as opposed to "being fond of"; 72.3 (*dilexi*): "a supra-sensual kind of affection" (the verb is said to have "an earthier connotation" at 6.5); and Kroll 1989 on 72.3 (*dilexi*): "kann auch von sinnlicher Liebe gesagt werden, wie *amare* von Freundschaft." Newman 1990, p. 319, comments that Catullus 100 "shows how impossible it is to separate *ordinary friendship* from sex" (emphasis added).

amor can denote everything that both Greek *philia* and *eros* denote, and *amicitia* is often the equivalent of *philia*, thus seemingly a subset of *amor*. If we ponder how the two Greek terms might be – and were – translated into Latin, the issue becomes particularly clear. *Philia* is usually *amicitia*, yet no Latin writer uses *amicitia* to refer to the relationship between parent and child, which in the Greek textual tradition appears as an example of, precisely, *philia*. For its part, *eros* could be translated by Latin *cupido*, but the latter also renders Greek *epithumia* (which itself can be translated as *libido*), and the personified god Eros has two names in Latin: Cupido and Amor.[23]

More fruitful than attempting to map Latin terms onto those of any other linguistic and cultural system is an investigation of the internal workings of the Latin semiotic system, with attention to the interactions of words and phrases and the boundaries between them, however permeable and shifting they may be. The latter is certainly true in the case of *amor* and *amicitia*. On the one hand, we find *amicitia* represented as a type of *amor*. Cicero's *Laelius* reminds us of the etymological relationship between the words which points, he argues, to deeper truths: *Amor* is a fundamental principle drawing living beings to each other, *amicitia* is one of its results, and the two nouns are suggestively intertwined and powerfully embodied in Laelius' own relationship with the recently deceased Scipio.[24] Neither Laelius nor Cicero is using language idiosyncratically. We will see below that in Cicero's correspondence as, generations later, in Fronto's, *amare* can function as the verb corresponding to the noun *amicitia*. In one of Ovid's allusions to the paradigmatic pair of *amici* Orestes and Pylades, he does not even name the latter; it is enough to describe him as Orestes' "companion from Phocis, a pattern of true

[23] Among many discussions of *eros* and *philia* see Dover 1978, Price 1989, Ludwig 2002. For *amor* and *amicitia* in relation to *philia* and *eros*, see the brief but illuminating discussion at Fraisse 1974, pp. 441–445; for *amor*, *cupido*, and *libido*, see Fischer 1973 and Fliedner 1974. Konstan 1997, pp. 67–72, persuasively argues for attention to the distinction between *philos* and *philia*; but while *philos* more closely corresponds to *amicus* than *philia* does to *amicitia*, there are still some significant gaps, e.g. in the Homeric usage of the adjectival *philos* (Konstan 1997, pp. 28–31).

[24] Cic. *Amic.* 26: *amor enim, ex quo amicitia nominata est, princeps est ad benevolentiam coniungendam*; 100: *virtus, virtus, inquam, C. Fanni et tu, Q. Muci, et conciliat amicitias et conservat … ex quo exardescit sive amor sive amicitia; utrumque enim dictum est ab amando*; 102: *virtutem enim amavi illius viri, quae exstincta non est.* Modern etymologies likewise see a relationship between *amor* and *amicitia* but explain the meaning of the common root divergently. Ernout and Meillet 2001 point to physical acts and desires ("faire l'amour"); Walde and Hofmann 1938, followed by Fliedner 1974, emphasize affection or inclination, comparing phrases like *ita me di ament* or the expressions of polite request *amabo te* and *si me amas*. For *amare, amans, amator*, and other expressions of affection (*diligere, caritas, benevolentia*) in connection with *amicitia* see Hellegouarc'h 1963, pp. 142–151.

love (*exemplum veri amoris*)."[25] In Valerius Maximus' narrative of another paradigmatic pair, Damon and Phintias, the tyrant Dionysios not only revokes his decision to kill Phintias, but asks to join his paradigmatic *amicitia* with Damon, and in Valerius' hymn to *amicitia* that this narrative inspires, we read that it has the power of converting "hatred" to "love" (*odium in amorem convertere*, Val. Max. 4.7.ext.1, above p. 12).

On the other hand, we often find *amor* referring to what Greek writers would describe not as *philia* but as *eros*. Given the flexibility of *amor* (and even of *libido* or *cupido*, which denote desire for a wide range of acts and objects, hardly limited to human beings or genital stimulation), how do Latin texts unambiguously signal that the word is referring to that which in Greek is called *eros*? Most unambiguous are allusions to the body and its beauty, to embraces and kisses, and – in speech genres making room for such directness – to genital acts; there is the imagery of burning and flames; and there is the name of Venus. Two very different texts illustrate the possibilities. In the first book of Virgil's *Aeneid*, Venus sends her son (called both *Cupido* and *Amor*: 1.658, 663) to Dido in order to afflict her with a consuming passion for Aeneas. The result is powerfully evoked in the opening lines of the fourth book with the imagery of wound, flame, and anxiety (*vulnus, ignis, cura*: 4.1–2). To quite different effect, a passage from Petronius' *Satyricon* narrates how Chrysis' old slave-woman tries various means to revive Encolpius' drooping member. She prepares a place Encolpius describes as *dignus amore locus*, and the physical implications of *amor* in this phrase are brought out by the constant focus on Encolpius' penis throughout the scene.[26]

And so we find *amor* openly contrasted with *amicitia*. Ovid, as we have seen, urges his male readers to feign interest in *amicitia* with a woman when their real aim is *amor* (Ov. *Ars am*. 1.719–722, above, p. 94), and more generally on the stage of the elegiac lover's life we find two players: Here his beloved *domina* or *puella* or *puer*, there his male *amici* to whom he confides, who tease him or encourage him or try – unsuccessfully – to help him out in his difficult experience of, precisely, *amor*.[27] And, philosophizing to his *amicus* Lucilius, Seneca proclaims

---

[25] Ov. *Tr*. 4.4.71: *comes exemplum veri Phoceus amoris*; cf. Ov. *Pont*. 3.2.69–70: *par fuit his aetas et amor, quorum alter Orestes, / ast Pylades alter: nomina fama tenet*.

[26] Petron. *Sat*. 131.8. In the next scene preserved by the manuscript tradition, Encolpius experiences both *venus* and *amor* amongst intertwined bodies, slurping kisses, and wandering hands (Petron. *Sat*. 132). In another allusion to sexual impotence, an epigram attributed to Apuleius concretely figures the problem in terms of blocked access to *amor* (Courtney 2003, p. 394 [Apuleius fr. 7, vv. 4–5]: *quos Venus amavit, facit amoris compotes; / nobis Cupido velle dat, posse abnegat*).

[27] Hor. *Epod*. 1.23–28, Prop. 1.1.25–26, Ov. *Am*. 1.7.1–4; see further below, pp. 197–214.

that *amicitia* is always beneficial, whereas *amor* is sometimes damaging.[28] Yet some attempts to keep *amor* and *amicitia* safely distinct simultaneously give glimpses at the difficulty of doing so. Seneca himself ponders the notion that the passion experienced by those in love (*amantes*) is an unhealthy type of friendship (*insana amicitia*), while Apuleius commends to his readers Plato's insistence that so destructive a passion as *amor* must not be called *amicitia*. Prohibition, as usual, implies practice to the contrary.[29]

What of the substantivized participle *amans* and the agent noun *amator*, usually translated with English "lover"? Although in their morphology none of these terms is specifically anchored in the body, when used in connection with interpersonal relationships (as opposed, say, to phrases like "coffee lover") they generally point to the realm of *eros*, Venus, and the body. In the first of Horace's poetic *Epistles*, for example, the *amator* is invoked at the culmination of a list of qualities which, along with envy, irascibility, and drunkenness, bespeak a lack of self-control and which can be tamed by the influence of learning; Virgil's gnomic question "Who could possibly deceive a lover (*amantem*)?" comes as a comment on Dido's intuition that all is not as it seems in her affair with Aeneas; and one of the best-known Ovidian poems in the collection entitled, precisely, *Amores* begins with a famously incisive proclamation: "Every lover (*amans*) is a soldier; Cupid sets up his camp." In short, when the grammarian Priscian describes *amans* as synonymous with *amator* and gives *erastes* as the Greek equivalent to both, he is reflecting long-standing Latin usage.[30]

Yet sometimes "lover" would be a serious mistranslation of *amator* or *amans*. In a public speech, Cicero describes a Roman knight's old friend as his *amicus* and *amans*, and in private letters he uses *amans* and *amator*

---

[28] Sen. *Ep.* 35.1: *amicitia semper prodest, amor etiam aliquando nocet.* See also Sen. *Ep.* 81.12: *deinde idem admiratur cum dicimus "solus sapiens scit amare, solus sapiens amicus est"; atqui et amoris et amicitiae est pars referre gratiam, immo hoc magis vulgare est et in plures cadit quam vera amicitia* (for the contrast between *vulgaris* and *vera amicitia*, see introduction, p. 48).

[29] Sen. *Ep.* 9.11: *non dubie habet aliquid simile amicitiae affectus amantium; possis dicere illam esse insanam amicitiam*; Apul. *De dog. Plat.* 2.13 (on *qui vulgo amor dicitur*): *eiusmodi calamitates animarum amicitias idem appellari vetat, quod nec mutuae sint nec reciprocari queant.*

[30] Hor. *Epist.* 1.1.38–40: *invidus, iracundus, iners, vinosus, amator, / nemo adeo ferus est ut non mitescere possit, / si modo culturae patientem commodet aurem.* Verg. *Aen.* 4.296: *quis fallere possit amantem?* Ov. *Am.* 1.9.1: *militat omnis amans et habet sua castra Cupido*; cf. *Ars am.* 1.729, *palleat omnis amans.* Prisc. *Inst.* 11.550.22 *("amans illum" participium est … "amans" autem "illius" nomen ut "amator illius")*; 111.148.21 *(amans* ὁ ἐραστής*)*; TLL 1957.79–1958.53 with numerous examples. Writing in philosophical mode, Cicero asserts a distinction between *amator* and *amans* that is hard to detect in many other genres (Cic. *Tusc.* 4.27: *aliud … est amatorem esse, aliud amantem*).

to refer to men who support him or are on his side in a political issue.[31] In the language of inscriptions we find the noun *amator* used in such a way as to suggest near-synonymy with *amicus*. An epitaph from Vienne in southern France memorializes the departed as one who loved his friends (*amicorum amator*); an inscription from northern Africa speaks of "all my *amici* and *amatores*"; an epitaph from Pozzuoli, datable to the late second or early third century AD, announces that the *amatores* of the deceased have commissioned the memorial; and a dedicatory inscription from Pesaro honors a man as *patronus* and speaks in the name of his *amici et amatores*.[32] Participating in yet another speech genre, a voting recommendation painted on the walls of Pompeii commends a candidate for office as *vester amator*, and in another such recommendation a man publicizes himself as the *amator* of the candidate whom he supports. In cases like these, "lover" would be a serious mistranslation; words like "admirer" or "supporter" or phrases like "he cares for you" would be more appropriate.[33] Yet people walking down the streets of Pompeii also saw graffiti in which *amator*, like *amans*, referred not to the realm of campaigns and political office but to that of Venus.[34] The flexibility of the agent noun and participle bring us back to that of *amor* itself. The same Cicero who in his encomium of friendship lauds *amicitia* as inspired by *amor* elsewhere speaks of the consuming, destructive passion "that is commonly called *amor*." His formulation hints at dissatisfaction with an insufficiently nuanced word.[35]

---

[31] Cic. *Rab. Post.* 43: *equitem Romanum, veterem amicum suum, studiosum, amantem, observantem sui... excepit*; *Att.* 1.18.7 (on Cato): *miseros publicanos quos habuit amantissimos sui tertium iam mensem vexat*; *Att.* 1.14.6: *nostri laudator, amator, imitator*; cf. *Att.* 1.20.7, *Fam.* 9.15.4. As Hellegouarc'h 1963, p. 143, observes, in these instances *amator* is nearly synonymous with *fautor*; but he collapses the distinction between denotation and connotation when he concludes: "Dans une telle phrase *amans* est, de toute évidence, l'équivalent exact d'*amicus*."

[32] *CIL* 12.1982 (Vienne): *D(is) M(anibus) / M(arcus) Magius / [S]otericus / signo / Hilari / amicorum / amator / [v]ivus sibi / fecit ut / esset / memoriae / [bo]num iter / [...]cibus feliciter*; *CIL* 8.22914 (Hadrumetum): *omnes amici et amatores, cum quibus semper b{a}ene vixi / et {i}stater(a)e pondus lib(e)re <d>edi, / valete*; *AE* 1983.188 (Pozzuoli): *D.M. / Munio Puteol/ano, qui vixit / annis XXVII /mensibus XI die/bus XXII, amator/es (h)uius fecerunt / merenti*; *CIL* 11.6362 (Pesaro): *cives amici / et amatores eius quorum / nomina inscripta sunt ob / eximiam benignamq(ue) erga / omnes cives suos adfectio/nem sinceramq(ue) et inconpa/rabilem innocentiam eius / patrono dignissimo.*

[33] *CIL* 4.45b: *amator(em) vest(rum) / faciat(is) aed(ilem) M(arcum) / Ma(rium)*; *CIL* 4.9926: *M(arcum) Cerrinium Vatiam / [rogat Gr]anius amator.*

[34] *CIL* 4.1950: *quisquis amator erit, Scythiae licet ambulet oris, / nemo adeo ut feriat barbarus esse volet*; 4.1658: *Vetti vere amator coctor*; 4.1649: *alliget hic auras si quis obiurget amantes, / et vetet assiduas currere fontis aquas*; 4.1893: *surda sit oranti tibi ianua laxa ferenti / audiat exclusi verba receptus amans*; 4.5296: *sic Venus ut subito coniunxit corpora amantum*; 4.4509: *(quis)quis amare vetat, / (quis)quis custodit ama(n)tes.*

[35] Cic. *Tusc.* 4.68: *totus vero iste, qui volgo appellatur amor – nec hercule invenio, quo nomine alio possit appellari –, tantae levitatis est, ut nihil videam quod putem conferendum.*

DESCRIBING CONTRASTS

In the face of such tensions in the Latin language itself, what words are *we* to use as we read, write, and talk about love and friendship in Latin texts? It is common practice to imply or assert a direct alignment of the pairing *amor* and *amicitia* with *love* and *friendship*, *Liebe* and *Freundschaft*, *amour* and *amitié*, and so on, the first term being sometimes expanded by adjectives like "erotic" or "sexual" but often, tellingly enough, not. And scholarly formulations often move easily *between* languages. We read of "the transference of *amicitia* to the erotic sphere"; of the ways in which Catullus and the elegists "superimpose *amicitia* on an erotic relationship"; and of "the cross-fertilization of friendship by sexual love, *amicitia* by *amor*, in the poetry of Tibullus, Propertius, and Horace" which involves "the contamination of *amor* by *amicitia*."[36] The term "contamination" recalls *contaminatio*, a hostile description of Terence's blending of Greek plays as he created his Latin comedies; literary history aside, what are the implications of using the English word to describe the relationship between *amor* and *amicitia*? Another scholar uses an almost directly opposed metaphor: "In Catullus's hands, *amicitia* and related terms came to designate those aspects of his relationship with Lesbia that transcend the *more purely* sexual realm denoted by the term *amor*."[37] Not only, however, have we seen that within the Latin textual tradition *amor* and *amicitia* are not consistently in opposition to each other, but we might well ask whether texts like these represent *amor* in terms of *amicitia*, the other way around, or both at once.[38] And what is "more purely sexual"?

One way out of the impasse is suggested by Dale Kent's recent study of *amicizia* in Renaissance Florence. Rather than seeking to analyze the relationship between "friendship" and "love" as antithesis, synecdoche, or in some other way, Kent begins by positing two basic oppositions: *friendship/enmity* and *love/hatred*.[39] As we read Roman friendship there is much to be gained by attending to the antitheses *amor/odium* on the one hand, *amicitia/inimicitiae* or *amicus/inimicus* on the other, fundamental and recurring throughout the textual tradition. The opposition between

---

[36] Newman 1990, p. 320; Gibson 1995, p. 63; Oliensis 1997, p. 155 with n. 16. Cf. Pizzolato 1993, p. 133: "negli elegiaci la realtà dell'*amore* è espressa con la *terminologia* dell'amicizia" (emphases original; on p. 134 the first term is expanded to the compound *amore-passione*).

[37] Miller 2004, p. 28 (emphasis added).

[38] Compare the thought-provoking discussion in Kennedy 1993 of the language of love and *amor* (p. 25: "Translatability is an issue not only *between* languages but *within* a language as well").

[39] Kent 2009, p. 14.

amor and *odium*, for example, famously informs a Catullan two-line poem ("I hate and I love," *Odi et amo*, Catull. 85) and, less intensely but just as clearly, the language of social relations in Cicero's letters, where, just as *amor* is more flexible and less heartfelt than English "love," *odium* is rather less virulent than "hate."[40] For its part, the opposition between *amicitia* and *inimicitiae*, signaled by etymology, is distinctly more transparent on the lexical level than the comparable antithesis in many other languages, such as English "friendship" vs. "enmity." A witty graffito from Pompeii, painted in careful letters at the entrance to a house along with several other messages, is particularly suggestive of how the contrast might be exploited: "I would rather my friends (*amici*) suck me than my enemies (*inimici*) face-fuck me."[41] The graffito invites being read less as making statements about the role of sex in friendship than as as toying with antithesis on the lexical level (*fellare* vs. *irrumare*, *amici* vs. *inimici*) and playing with traditional concepts of interpersonal relations by metaphorizing them in terms of sexual acts. To draw out the implications of the metaphor – one would not normally want to put one's friends in a subordinate or shameful position, but this would be preferable to being put in that position oneself by one's enemies.[42] A saying of the elder Cato's quoted in Cicero's *De amicitia* plays off the opposition in a different and, of course, eminently respectable way. Sharp-tongued enemies (*inimici*) are preferable to sweet-speaking friends (*amici*) to the extent that the former always tell the truth, the latter never.[43]

---

[40] Thus Shackleton Bailey translates Cic. *Fam.* 4.8a.3 (*homo peramans nostri semper fuit nec mihi umquam odio*) as "he was always extremely friendly to me and I never had anything against him" and 15.15.2 (*reginam odi*) as "I dislike Her Majesty." For the language of *amor* and *amicitia* in Cicero's letters, see below, pp. 218–238.

[41] *CIL* 4.10030 (Reg I, Ins. 12, n. 3): *malim me amici fellent quam inimici irrument*. Just to the left is found a message (*CIL* 4.10031) which seems to make some similarly sententious remark: *an dedecet vitare malum quam cre(berrime?)*. Other graffiti from the same entryway include an image of a rooster with a phallus; the rude message *Valeria, fel(l)as* (4.10033a); and an image of a gladiator with the inscription *Faustioni felic(iter)* (4.10035). For discussion of Greek and Latin graffiti with sexual content see Williams (forthcoming).

[42] The joke is either based on a proverb for which no other attestations have survived, or else it wants to sound like one; in any case, there were no doubt other similar jokes in circulation. Consider the vulgar Sicilian saying *isti pi futtiri e fusti futtutu* ("You went to fuck but got fucked instead"): To quote this exuberantly alliterative saying is not so much to make a statement about sexual practices or desires as it is to offer sardonic commentary on a failed strategy, to engage in witty play with the possibilities of language, and to apply the metaphor of "fucking" as using or taking advantage of. Consider also the fifteenth-century Florentine saying: "One enemy can harm you more than four friends can help you" (Kent 2009, p. 191).

[43] Cic. *Amic.* 90: *scitum est enim illud Catonis, ut multa: melius de quibusdam acerbos inimicos mereri, quam eos amicos qui dulces videantur: illos verum saepe dicere, hos numquam.*

Here and elsewhere, then, the basal contrast is not between *friend-ship* and *love*, let alone between *friendship* and *sex*, but between *friends* and *enemies*. In what follows, my readings of textual representations of interpersonal relationships in Latin will not be looking for – let alone positing – an antithesis between *amor* and *amicitia*, but will describe a range of combinations and recombinations, configurations and constel-lations. Once again gender is an organizational principle: beginning with that most thinly represented of interpersonal combinations in the Latin textual tradition – *amor* and *amicitia* between women; then turn-ing to relationships between men and women; and finally considering the configuration which dominates by far the textual tradition – *amor* and *amicitia* between men. The chapter will conclude with a paradigm which effectively ties together many of the threads that have preceded, that of brotherly love.

AMOR AND *AMICITIA* BETWEEN WOMEN

Inquiry into the interplay of *amor* and *amicitia* among women is ham-pered by the paucity of relevant texts. As we have seen in the previous chapter, wherever Latin inscriptions were being commissioned and set up, women recorded for posterity their participation in friendships with each other, honoring *amicae* in dedicatory and funerary inscriptions; but *amor* is not a perceptible element in the formulaic language of this speech genre. There is every reason to believe that in other genres of written and spoken communication, Latin-speaking women used the language of both *amicitia* and *amor* to describe and express their rela-tionships. As it happens, in one of the few surviving examples of a text written by and to women this is not the case. Claudia Severa's letters to Sulpicia Lepidina at Vindolanda use, as we have seen, neither the language of *amicitia* nor that of *amor* (see above, pp. 70–72), but use other linguistic means to express affection: accumulations and terms of endearment like *anima mea, carissima*, and – a key term to which we will return below – *soror*.

These letters and fragments are so brief, and represent so small a por-tion of the original body of textuality written by women, that we cannot draw any conclusions about how women used the language of *amor* and *amicitia*: the range of denotations, connotations, and tonalities in vari-ous speech genres. In male-authored texts, however, we have more to go on, and in the previous chapter we saw some examples. We have seen that women's *amicae* appear both in Latin inscriptions and in various genres of the literary tradition, from comedy to satire, from elegy to epigram, and that jurisprudence recognized that a woman might leave an inheritance to an *amica* in her will. Plautus' *Casina* stages Myrrhina as Cleustrata's *amica* and object of her *amor*; Virgil's Camilla addresses Acca as her *soror* and is joined to her by *fides*, while the goddess Diana evokes her own *amor* for Camilla herself; Tacitus refers to a female *familiaris* of Nero's mother Agrippina; Statius prominently memorializes the *amor* shown by friend's deceased wife Priscilla for his own wife, while reserving the language of *amicitia* for his own relationship with Priscilla's husband Abascantus.[44]

The denotations and connotations which the term *amica* might have in connection with relationships between men and women in the literary tradition invite us to consider whether any descriptions of friendships between women in the Latin textual tradition play with the noun's ambivalence on the point of physicality. Encolpius' narrative of Scintilla and Fortunata in Petronius' *Satyricon*, joined in embraces and drunken kisses (Petron. *Sat.* 67, 74, above, pp. 67–68), refrains from doing so, as do nearly all surviving Latin texts referring to sexual desire or practices between women – a noticeable silence that is reflected in the scholarship.[45] Surviving references to sexual acts between women (in now lost acts of textual and verbal communication, and in speech genres to which we have little or no access, things may have been different) are cast not in terms of *amicitia*, but in terms of the hierarchically gendered model of penetration which dominates Roman textual representations of sex. One of the women is imagined to play the masculine role, sometimes explicitly called "the man" or said to penetrate her partners, and the latter, tellingly enough, are imagined as either female or male. At the heart of the issue lies not homoerotic desire but practices which violate gender-bound expectations.[46]

The only use of the language of *amicitia* in connection with sexual acts between women known to me seems to play with *double entendre*.

> Ipsarum tribadum tribas, Philaeni,
> recte, quam futuis, vocas *amicam*.
> (Mart. 7.70)

---

[44] Plaut. *Cas.* 182–203; Verg. *Aen.* 11.537–538, 820–823, Tac. *Ann.* 14.5, Stat. *Silv.* 5.1.pr.

[45] Neither "friendship" nor *amicitia* appears in the index of Brooten 1996; the only essay in Rabinowitz and Auanger 2002 which discusses friendship concerns Egyptian monasticism (Wilfong 2002); and friendship is not a prominent theme in Boehringer 2007.

[46] "The man": Sen. *Controv.* 1.2.23; phallic female: Phaedrus 4.16; penetrating males and females: Sen. *Ep.* 95.21 (*viros ineunt*), Mart. 7.67.

Philaenis, tribad of the tribads,
you are right to call the woman you fuck your *amica*.

The precise workings of the humor are tantalizingly elusive, not least because of the poem's compression and knowing allusiveness, but the immediate joke seems clear enough. Philaenis is "right" to describe her sexual partner as her *amica* because that word can be used by men to refer to women who are, precisely, the object of the verb *futuere* (see above, p. 84): simultaneously a masculinization of Philaenis and a voyeuristic exposure of what is imagined to be going on between her and her female friend. The ironic adverb *recte* invites further thought too. Is the point that Philaenis herself uses *amica* as women regularly do, to describe female friends without denoting a sexual bond, but the speaker of the epigram is exposing the deeper truth of her language? Is Philaenis' use of the word being represented as a personal idiosyncrasy, or is this a real or imagined usage pattern among women called *tribades*?[47] And to what extent do anxieties or fantasies about *all* women's friendships fuel this joke?

One exception to the tendency to conform sexual practices between women to a gendered penetrative paradigm comes in the prolonged, passionate attack on women and marriage in Juvenal's sixth satire. This poem is anything but an objective or historically reliable report of what Roman women might do with each other, but illustrates what an angry, misogynistic man might be imagined to imagine women doing. And that is scandalous indeed. At nocturnal all-female get-togethers they urinate on the statue of the goddess Chastity and "ride each other" under the watching and no doubt scandalized eye of the moon. Neither the language of *amicitia* nor that of *amor* lends its dignity to this voyeuristically scandalized narration of women's bodies joining in filth and darkness – in horrified contrast with one of their husbands who, apostrophized by the speaker, is imagined to step in the puddles of his wife's urine the next morning on his way to visit his powerful friends (*magni amici*), a phrase which arguably diminishes him by casting him in the role of client, but

---

[47] For *tribas*, see Brooten 1996, Halperin 2002, pp. 48–80, Boehringer 2007 passim (pp. 292–293 on this epigram), Williams 2010, pp. 233–239. I understand the term to denote a woman who is imagined to play the role coded as dominant and masculine in sexual relations with other women or with men; Boehringer argues that it denotes a woman who engages in sexual relations with other women. One of the readers for the Press points out that Martial's phrase *tribadum tribas* might be playing on two senses: "tribad of the very tribads" or "most choice of all tribads" on the one hand, a "'she does them, they do her' mutuality" on the other.

which in any case grants him the dignity of participation in *amicitia*, even as his wife's urine makes its own comment.[48]

AMOR, AMICITIA, MARRIAGE

Even though it has been persuasively argued that the primary function of Roman marriage is to join bloodlines and produce legitimate offspring to whom property can be passed on, *amor* is closely associated with marriage. It may not necessarily be its cause or purpose, but it ideally arises within it. Epitaphs commemorate *amor* between spouses; Ovid's poetry from exile includes stirring lines to his wife, whom he misses more than all else and whose *amor* for him, he imagines, causes her great grief; Statius pompously observes that "it is a pleasure to love one's wife (*uxorem amare*) while she is still alive, and once she has passed away it is a sacred duty"; and Pliny the Younger's three letters to his young wife Calpurnia have long struck readers for their expressions of affection and intimacy, *amor* and *desiderium*.[49]

But to what extent is *amicitia* an ideal or even a possibility within Roman marriage? Contemporary Western discourses allow for and more recently have positively encouraged friendship in marriage – as sentimental praise of one's spouse as "my best friend" attests – regardless of the potentially messy conceptual consequences.[50] But Montaigne's dismissive differentiation between the friendship he so exalts and marriage (the latter

---

[48] Juv. 6.309–314: *micturiunt hic / effigiemque deae longis siphonibus implent / inque vices equitant ac Luna teste moventur. / inde domos abeunt; tu calcas luce reversa / coniugis urinam magnos visurus amicos.* See Boehringer 2007, pp. 328–330, for further discussion.

[49] See *CIL* 6.1341, 6.30125, 6.41321 (just a few among many epitaphs praising conjugal *amor*); Ov. *Tr.* 3.3.15–18, 4.3.27–28; Stat. *Silv.* 5.pr. (*uxorem enim vivam amare voluptas est, defunctam religio*); Plin. *Ep.* 6.4, 6.7, 7.5 (Sherwin-White 1966, p. 407, notes that these three letters "blend together, for the first time in European literature, the role of husband and lover"). Discussions of love between spouses in these and other Roman texts include Dixon 1992, pp. 83–90, Treggiari 1991, pp. 183–261, Carlon 2009, pp. 157–175.

[50] On one and the same page, Epstein 2006, p. 49, complacently declares "I resemble my father in having, as my best friend, my wife" and asserts that "where there is sex, there is not friendship." Since, however, "husbands and wives obviously make love," how can his wife be his best friend? If we consider the earlier remark that "real friendship between husbands and wives sets in after courtship is done" (p. xiii), the implication would seem to be that once courtship is over, sex between spouses ends! The issues are hardly idiosyncratic to Epstein or characteristic of the early twenty-first century. Within the English literary tradition we find Samuel Richardson's Clarissa describing marriage as "the highest state of friendship" (letter 59) and Edward Bulwer Lytton proclaiming both that "a man's best female friend is a wife of good sense and good heart" and that "pure friendships" are "those in which there is no admixture of the passion of love, except in the married state" (quoted at Luftig 1993, p. 22 with n. 12). See Thomas 2009, pp. 214–220, for an overview of the models of companionate marriage and friendship in early modern England.

is a "contract entered into for other reasons") corresponds to much of what we read in Latin literature. The central aim of Roman marriage was the creation of legitimate offspring (*liberorum quaerundorum causa*), and two nouns reveal with exemplary clarity the conceptual underpinnings of the institution. Legitimate marriage (*matrimonium*) places a woman in the role of *mater*, enabling her husband to become a *pater* who will pass on the property (*patrimonium*) to the children she gives him. These concerns place marriage in a unique category, in its goals and prime social purpose quite distinct from *amicitia*. Yet there are some significant overlaps in the imagery and ideals associated with Roman marriage and friendship: above all, the related concepts of *fides* (fidelity, trustworthiness) and *foedus* (pact, agreement) along with the formal gesture of joining right hands (*dextrarum iunctio*), a potent symbol of the bonds of hospitality, of *amicitia*, and of marriage.[51]

In the surviving textual tradition, however, the terms *amicus* and *amica* themselves are applied to married couples very rarely indeed, and even indirect invocations of the discourse of *amicitia* – by means, for example, of the image of "one soul in two bodies" or of the "other self" – are hard to find in connection with husband and wife.[52] To be sure, in texts and speech genres now lost to us, *amicitia* may have been invoked in conjunction with marriage more frequently, or in ways we might not have expected, but the rarity with which the connection is made in the surviving textual tradition is in itself noteworthy. Among the thousands of surviving epitaphs commemorating spouses, only a handful use the language of friendship, such as this one from Rome in which a slave memorializes his wife:

D(is) M(anibus) s(acrum). / Cestius Clarus / Severin(a)e *conservae* / *sodali et amic(a)e coniugi* / <b>ene merenti et inco(m)para/bili fecit / et sibi / posterisque eorum. (*CIL* 6.14697; Rome)

Sacred to the spirits of the deceased. Cestius Clarus dedicated this to Severina his fellow-slave, companion, friend, well-deserving and incomparable wife, and also to himself and their descendants.

---

[51] See Treggiari 1991, pp. 1–13, for the traditional purposes of marriage and the phrase *liberorum quaerundorum causa*. For *fides/foedus* and marriage, see Treggiari 1991, pp. 237–238; for the *dextrarum iunctio* see Freyburger 1986, pp. 167–176 (marriage), 177–185 (*amicitia*), 185–193 (*hospitium*).

[52] The dying Chrysis' commendation of the young Glycerium to Pamphilus at Ter. *An.* 295 *te isti virum do, amicum tutorem patrem* (you will be her husband, her friend, her guardian, her father) invites being read with Andromache's words to Hector at *Iliad* 6.524–525 ("you are my brother, you are my parents") and Propertius 1.11.23 (*tu mihi sola domus, tu, Cynthia, sola, parentes*). If we pursue the parallelism, the young man is no more expected to be his future wife's *amicus* than her *tutor* or *pater*. See Chapter 3, p. 229, for Cic. *Fam.* 14.1.

And a lengthy fourth-century AD verse inscription commissioned by Vettius Agorius Praetextatus in honor of his wife Paulina praises her in fulsome terms as displaying not only the ideal qualities of mother, spouse, sister, and daughter, but also "that trustworthiness which joins us to our friends (*quanta amicis iungimur fiducia*)."[53] In the literary tradition we find Statius' poem to Pollius Felix on his villa at Sorrento, which ends with verses lauding his marriage with Polla: "Torches from your hearts have lastingly mingled; your unsullied love observes the laws of pure friendship (*sanctusque pudicae / servat amicitiae leges amor*)." Here we see the torch, traditional poetic image both for erotic passion and for weddings, is blended with an invocation of *amicitia*, strikingly modified by the adjective *pudica* ("pure, chaste"), all under the aegis of that elusive term *amor*.[54]

BETWEEN MEN: THE CONCEPT OF THE HOMOSOCIAL

Among the rich variety of paradigms for relationships between men in the Western textual tradition, one is embodied by pairs like Gilgamesh and Enkidu, Jonathan and David, Achilles and Patroclus. Two inseparable but hierarchically distinguished friends fight or travel together, the subordinate partner dies, and the survivor's mourning is monumental. Their love is intense and unshakable, favorably contrasted with the love of women and (a point to which we will return) compared to that between brothers. Other lasting paradigms for male intimacy show similarities to this ancient narrative pattern. Christian rites for "making brothers" existed in both eastern and western Europe for centuries; French fictions of the twelfth and thirteenth centuries narrate chivalric friendship in terms of both *amistié* and *amor* and sometimes assimilate it to the *fine amor* that joins man and woman; in England, a range of textual and

---

[53] *CIL* 6.1779 = *CLE* 111, vv. 46–50: *munus deorum qui maritalem torum / nectunt amicis et pudicis nexibus, / pietate matris, coniugali gratia, / nexu sororis, filiae modestia / et quanta amicis iungimur fiducia*. A fragmentarily preserved epitaph from Narbo (*CLE* 2106) contains a line which begins *tu dominus coniunx*; guesses as to how the line ended include *patronus me decorasti* and *fidus mihi semper amicus*. Likewise at *CIL* 6.29131 (– *ami]co sodali viro optimo M. Ulpio Adaucto fecit Flavia Gemella / cum quo vixit annis XXXXVI sine lite ulla*) the application of the term *amicus* to a husband is only conjectural.

[54] Stat. *Silv.* 2.2.143–145: *quorum de pectore mixtae / in longum coiere faces sanctusque pudicae /servat amicitiae leges amor*. Van Dam 1984 ad loc. describes *pudicae amicitiae* as "a striking expression for marriage." If we read this together with Catullus' ringing celebration of *aeternum hoc sanctae foedus amicitiae* (Catull. 109.6), quite distinctly *not* in the context of married love, the placement of the adjective *sanctus* points to an important distinction. In Statius' verses on husband and wife, the adjective modifies *amor*, in the Catullan poem it describes a special kind of *amicitia*.

cultural practices from the eleventh through the late eighteenth centuries was available for celebrating the love of "sworn" or "wedded brothers"; and Shakespeare's sonnets to a young man ("Lord of my love," "the master-mistress of my passion") contain some of the most renowned expressions of love in the English literary tradition: "Shall I compare thee to a summer's day?" Nineteenth-century North American paradigms of cowboy and sidekick or "partner," together and alone on the forefront of exploration and conquest, or of Anglo-American adventurer and Native companion, each partly separated from his home culture, also invite being studied for their powerful blend of friendship and love between men.[55]

The term *homosocial* has often been applied to such relationships. Introduced into scholarly discourse above all by Eve Kosofsky Sedgwick's 1985 study *Between Men*, the term describes a broad continuum of desire and love in relationships ranging in nature from the passionately genital to the intensely physical to the sublimely but not physically erotic to the openly homophobic. As a matter of description and analysis, to describe a bond between men as homosocial is precisely to avoid posing questions about the specific ways in which it is given bodily expression.[56] As a matter of historical development, however, such questions certainly pose themselves in various times and places. Generally speaking, as anxieties about sexual practices of all kinds and about intimacy and desire between men in particular became more and more deeply rooted in Western cultures after antiquity, the need to draw lines and assert distinctions became more pressing. The glorious friendship that only two men can share may be the most rewarding and satisfying human relationship imaginable, surpassing anything they might experience with women – but we find strategically repeated, well-placed reminders that there is one thing such a friendship is *not*. One of the Christian rites for blessing male pairs, for example, contains two prayers with an insistent negative: The men are joined *"not in bodily love but in faith and in the love of the Holy Spirit."*[57] Montaigne

---

[55] For the ancient paradigm see Halperin 1990, pp. 75–87; for chivalric friendship in French medieval literature ("sweeter than woman's love") see Hyatte 1994, pp. 87–136; for "sworn" or "wedded brothers" see Bray 2003 passim; for the rites for "making brothers" see Boswell 1994 with Shaw 1997; for Shakespeare and contemporaries, see Smith 1991, Orgel 1996, MacFaul 2007; for Anglo-American cowboy/explorer and Native sidekick (e.g. Hawkeye and Chingachgook or the Lone Ranger and Tonto), see Packard 2005. Such patterns are hardly limited to the Western tradition: see Schalow 2007 for the poetry of Heian Japan (AD 794–1185).

[56] There is a distinct reluctance among scholars to apply the term "homosocial" to relationships among women: see Sedgwick 1985, p. 2, Haggerty 1998, pp. 74–75, 90, Marcus 2007, p. 4.

[57] From the *Ordo ad fratres faciendum* found in a fourteenth-century manuscript now in the library of the church of St. John in Trogir, Croatia (quoted and translated at Bray 2003, pp. 132–133): *non dilectione carnali sed fide et dilectione Spiritus Sancti* (not in fleshly love but in faith and the

distinguishes the glorious friendship he experienced with Étienne de la Boétie from marriage on the one hand, from "that alternative license of the Greeks" which is "rightly abhorrent to our manners" on the other.[58] In Shakespeare's poetry, too, just when things get interesting, lines are drawn. Sonnet 20 opens with an avowal of attraction to ambiguity and mixture ("A woman's face with nature's own hand painted, / hast thou, the master mistress of my passion") but ends on a note of demarcation and refusal:

> Till Nature, as she wrought thee, fell a-doting,
> and by addition me of thee defeated,
> by adding one thing to my purpose nothing.
> But since she prick'd thee out for women's pleasure,
> mine be thy love and thy love's use their treasure.

The famous pun in the final couplet brings home the point in all its defensiveness. His friend's "prick" is "to my purpose nothing," something for women's "use" just as "thy love" shall be mine.[59]

Such distinctions have been insisted upon in certain times and places more than in others, and of course there was no clean chronological break. Acknowledgments that men might love each other more intensely and rewardingly than they love women show up at sometimes surprising moments in the textual tradition.[60] Expressions of anxiety seem to have become particularly intense, sometimes downright shrill, as the discipline of sexology established itself at the end of the nineteenth century, and with it the notion that all people could be – must be – defined as either "heterosexual" or "homosexual," with "bisexual" being the uneasy solution for intractable cases. Once homosexuality became a universally applicable category, and especially when it was seen as innate disposition,

---

love of the Holy Spirit), *non colligatos carnali consuetudine sed fide et Spiritu Sancto* (not joined in the manner of the flesh, but in faith and by the Holy Spirit). Bray's translations ("not through the bonds of birth, but through faith and by the love of the Holy Spirit"; "not united by the bonds of birth but through faith and the Holy Spirit") mistake the sense of *dilectio* and *consuetudo* and obscure the effect of the key adjective *carnalis*. This is all the more unfortunate as Bray criticizes Boswell's 1994 *Same-Sex Unions* for its "inadequate grasp of the Greek and Slavonic liturgical texts" (Bray 2003, p. 316).

[58] Screech 2004, p. 7.

[59] Cf. Sedgwick 1985, pp. 34–35: "As elsewhere in the Sonnets, 'nothing' denotes, among other things, female genitals." For further discussion see Smith 1991, Bray 2003, pp. 138–139, MacFaul 2007, pp. 30–47.

[60] Consider these lines from Badger C. Clark's cowboy poem "The Lost Pardner," published in 1917: "We loved each other in the way men do / And never spoke about it, Al and me, / But we both *knowed*, and knowin' it so true / Was more than any woman's kiss could be." See discussion at Packard 2005, pp. 6–13, and Katz 2001 for other examples.

disease, or sin, the risk of being put into the category provoked all manner of anxious reaction, including what Sedgwick has called "homosexual panic."[61] C. S. Lewis' reflections on what he calls "the four loves" are typical of much twentieth-century thinking on male intimacy.

This is not to say that Friendship and abnormal Eros have never been combined. Certain cultures at certain periods seem to have tended to the contamination. In war-like societies it was, I think, especially likely to creep into the relation between the mature Brave and his young armour-bearer or squire. The absence of the women while you were there on the warpath had no doubt something to do with it. In deciding, if we think we need or can decide, where it crept in and where it did not, we must surely be guided by the evidence (when there is any) and not by an *a priori* theory. Kisses, tears and embraces are not in themselves evidence of homosexuality. The implications would be, if nothing else, too comic. Hrothgar embracing Beowulf, Johnson embracing Boswell (a pretty flagrantly heterosexual couple) and all those hairy old toughs of centurions in Tacitus, clinging to one another and begging for last kisses when the legion was broken up … all pansies? If you can believe that you can believe anything.

These are jarring words in a text lauding charity as the greatest of all loves, written by one who preaches a religion which asks its adherents to believe a number of remarkable things.[62] Equally surprising is the elision of the most obvious, indeed pressing paradigms for erotic relationships among males in the Western tradition. Instead of ancient Greece, Lewis darkly cites unnamed "certain cultures at certain periods," contrasting them in turn with a staunchly heterosexual England and Rome. More recently, to the shrill denials of a Lewis correspond the quiet erasures of an Epstein, who, citing Achilles and Patroclus along with Orestes and Pylades as admirable examples of classical ideals of friendship, strangely describes the former as a pair of brothers-in-law, passing over in silence the fact that the two were and are represented in many texts, both ancient and modern, as joined by the bonds of eros. Epstein raises the possibility

---

[61] Haggerty 1998 discusses "the codification of gender and the increasing pathologization of love between men" in eighteenth-century English texts. For "homosexual panic" see Sedgwick 1985, pp. 83–96. A cartoon in a 1907 German periodical illustrates the concept quite incisively. Depicting a staute of Goethe and Schiller standing hand in hand, the caption reports Schiller's words to his sculpted friend: "Panic in Weimar! 'Wolfgang, let's not hold hands any more; Dr. Magnus Hirschfeld is coming!'" (*Jugend* 11.18 [19 November 1907], 1089: "Panik in Weimar. 'Wolfgang, lassen wir die Hände los! Der Dr. Magnus Hirschfeld kommt!'"). Hirschfeld was a key figure in the new discipline of sexology and in the movement to decriminalize homosexual acts. See Tobin 2000.

[62] Lewis 1960, p. 75. Lewis lets drop a comparably uncharitable remark elsewhere: "Those who cannot conceive Friendship as a substantive love but only as a disguise or elaboration of Eros betray the fact that they have never had a Friend" (p. 73).

of pederastic relationships only in connection with Sparta, and only to add the rather misleading qualification that the question is "among scholars, still in the flux of controversy." As for Rome, he offers the examples of Cicero and Atticus, Pliny and his correspondents. No hint of eros there![63]

Anxious or evasive reactions like those of a Lewis or an Epstein are hard to find in Latin texts, and the nervousness about the physical expression of masculine intimacy detectable across northern Euro-American cultures in particular finds no equivalent in Roman representations of friendship. In *Roman Homosexuality* I argue that the paradigms of masculinity informing the Latin textual tradition are structured not around the distinction between heterosexual (normal) and homosexual (abnormal) but instead around those between masculine and feminine, penetrating and penetrated, free and slave. Roman men were regularly cast and cast themselves in the role of the penetrating sexual partner of male slaves or prostitutes, and sexual relations with freeborn young men were open to criticism not because of the young men's sex but because of their freeborn status. Sexual *practices* between men, in other words, were a freely available option – subject, like all sexual practices, to various protocols – and sexual *desire* between males was simply taken for granted, neither questioned nor stigmatized, but assumed to be a part of human and animal nature. In such a cultural environment, there was no need to hermetically seal off the erotic from the affectionate or the friendly when representing, describing, and perhaps even living intimacy between men. To be sure, prevailing paradigms for representing relationships involving genital acts were rather resolutely structured around a gendered distinction between the masculine insertive role and the feminine receptive role, but *amicitia* came with associations of reciprocity and its very language avoided making hierarchical distinctions. Whereas the term *puer* implies as male partner a *vir*, the label *amicus* implies another *amicus*. In short, as David Halperin puts it, in Rome and elsewhere "the friendship tradition provided socially empowered men with an established discursive venue in which to express, without social reproach, sentiments of passionate and mutual love for one another."[64] Catullus' poem to Veranius quoted in the Introduction is typical of the hearty, bodily expression of affection between men throughout the Latin textual tradition, where we frequently find scenes of male friends embracing, kissing, and reclining in each other's bosom with casual but intense affection, the embodiment of *amicitia* and *amor*.

---

[63] Epstein 2006, pp. 57–58; cf. n. 135 below.   [64] Halperin 2002, p. 121.

AMOR AMICITIAE

Most textual performances of *amor* and *amicitia* between men, as we will see, do not speak directly to the question of physical and particularly genital expression. But there was one paradigm for masculine intimacy which unmistakably had genital acts and the desire to perform them as a characteristic feature: relationships between citizen men and younger freeborn males on the model of Greek pederasty. What language do Latin texts use when referring to these relationships? Not surprisingly, *amor* is a key term, in this connection a close equivalent to Greek *eros*, but what of *amicitia*? It is, as it turns out, rarely named in connection with Greek-style pederasty.[65] One example comes in Cicero's discussion of the deleterious effects of strong emotion in the fourth book of his *Tusculan Disputations*.

quis est enim iste *amor amicitiae*? cur neque deformem adulescentem quisquam *amat* neque formosum senem? mihi quidem haec in Graecorum gymnasiis nata consuetudo videtur, in quibus isti liberi et concessi sunt amores. bene ergo Ennius: "flagiti principium est nudare inter civis corpora." qui ut sint, quod fieri posse video, pudici, solliciti tamen et anxii sunt, eoque magis, quod se ipsi continent et coercent. atque, ut *muliebris amores* omittam, quibus maiorem licentiam natura concessit, quis aut de Ganymedi raptu dubitat, quid poetae velint, aut non intellegit, quid apud Euripidem et loquatur et cupiat Laius? (Cic. *Tusc.* 4.70–71)

After all, what is the so-called love of friendship? Why does no one love an ugly youth or a beautiful old man? It seems to me this custom arose in the Greek gymnasia, where such love affairs are freely allowed. Ennius put it well, then: "The root of disgrace is for citizens to strip in each other's presence." I grant that these affairs can be chaste, but even so, they are full of worry and anxiety, all the more so because one must restrain and constrain oneself. Leaving aside for the moment affairs with women, to which nature has granted more freedom: Who has any doubts what the poets mean when they speak of the rape of Ganymede? Who does not know what Euripides' Laius is talking about, or what he desires?

The demonstrative in Cicero's phrase *iste amor amicitiae* implies that the phrase was just as well known, in Cicero's circles at least, as Euripides'

---

[65] Nepos, pr. 4: *laudi in Graecia ducitur adulescentulis quam plurimos habuisse amatores*; Nep. *Alcib.* 2: *ineunte adulescentia amatus est a multis more Graecorum* (for the alternate reading *amore Graecorum* see Williams 1995); Cic. *Tusc.* 5.58: *haberet etiam more Graeciae quosdam adulescentis amore coniunctos*. For Greek pederasty see especially Dover 1978, Winkler 1990, Halperin 1990 and 2002; see Williams 2010a, pp. 67–102, for differences between Greece and Rome. The combination of *amicus* and *amatus* at Gell. 16.9.4 (*eum Arionem rex Corinthi Periander amicum amatumque habuit artis gratia*) may or may not signal a pederastic relationship; Holford-Strevens 2003, p. 106 n. 47, assumes that it does, concluding that the phrase "means that Arion was a favourite of Periander's, not merely an official φίλος or *amicus*."

Chrysippus, probably even more so. The conjunction of those two nouns draws attention to itself. What does "love of friendship" mean, and what kind of genitive is *amicitiae*? Cicero's skepticism is aimed at a specifically Stoic version of pederasty. Since, according to Diogenes Laertius, Stoics held that *eros* should aim not at intercourse (*sunousia*) but at *philia*, the Latin *amor amicitiae* seems to be a calque of Greek *eros philias*. Thus *amor* corresponds to *eros*, *amicitia* to *philia*, and the genitive is objective: "love of friendship" refers to the desire for friendship rather than for the body. In that case, Cicero's *iste* takes on a further role, ironizing the phrase so as to suggest that while such relationships describe themselves as not being aimed at genital pleasures, in fact "everyone knows" that, like Zeus and Ganymede or Laius and Chrysippus, they often end up in bed.[66]

The denotation of the phrase *amor amicitiae* in Cicero's *Tusculanae* is clear enough. The same cannot be said of what seems to be the only other example of this juxtaposition of the two nouns in surviving Latin. Gellius' summary of a section of his *Attic Nights* which itself no longer survives reads as follows:

cum post offensiunculas in gratiam redeatur, expostulationes fieri mutuas minime utile esse, superque ea re et sermo Tauri expositus et verba ex Theophrasti libro sumpta, et quid M. quoque Cicero de *amore amicitiae* senserit, cum ipsius verbis additum. (Gell. *NA* 8.6)

When good relations are restored after minor offences, it is quite useless to indulge in mutual recrimination. On this subject Taurus' words are explained and a quotation is taken from Theophrastus' book, as well as Cicero's opinion on the love of friendship, along with his own words.

It is worth emphasizing that this is Gellius' summary of a now-missing chapter. The latter may or many not have even used the key phrase *amor amicitiae*.[67] That said, one way of reading the phrase is to understand the

---

[66] Reporting a Stoic definition of *amor* as "the attempt at creating a friendship (*amicitia*) on the basis of a beautiful outward appearance," Cicero implies that such lofty ideals were often excuses for rather more corporeal versions of *amor* (Cic. *Tusc.* 4.72: *Stoici vero et sapientem amaturum esse dicunt et amorem ipsum "conatum amicitiae faciendae ex pulchritudinis specie" definiunt*). A few generations later, Seneca perpetuates this suspicious attitude, not speaking of *amicitia* but using the language of *amor* alone (Sen. *Ep.* 123.15: *illos quoque nocere nobis existimo qui nos sub specie Stoicae sectae hortantur ad vitia. hoc enim iactant: solum sapientem et doctum esse amatorem ... "quaeramus ad quam usque aetatem iuvenes amandi sunt." haec Graecae consuetudini data sint*). See Bartsch 2006, pp. 57–114 for further discussion. For *eros sunousias* see Diog. Laert. 7.129–130 (ἔρωτα... μὴ εἶναι συνουσίας ἀλλὰ φιλίας) and see Nussbaum 2002 for Stoics and eros, especially in pederastic configurations.

[67] Gellius' titles and the corresponding chapters sometimes show subtle differences in wording. At *NA* 12.4, for example, the title speaks of a *homo minor* and his *amicus superior*, but the chapter text of the *amicus* of a *homo genere et fortuna superior*.

genitive not as objective (as it is in the passage from Cicero's *Tusculanae*) but as characteristic: "the kind of *amor* which one experiences in *amicitia*." In that case the most obvious Ciceronian text for Gellius to cite would be *De amicitia*, presumably a passage where the *amor* that is associated with *amicitia* is the topic.[68] Holford-Strevens, however, vigorously argues that rather than *De amicitia,* Gellius was citing the passage from the *Tusculanae* quoted above – "so disturbing a passage of so well-known a work," and one which gives us a "Ciceronian sense" of the phrase *amor amicitiae*. Holford-Strevens concludes that Gellius too is referring to Greek-style pederasty, and he further argues that Gellius is obliquely referring to his own relationship with Favorinus, "presented as an equal friendship."[69] The entwined assumptions – not only that a single sentence in the *Tusculanae* established a "Ciceronian sense" of a phrase (especially a phrase using the terms *amor* and *amicitia*, so susceptible to slippage) but that Gellius would have expected his readership to recall it – are questionable in themselves; and how disturbing is, or was, that passage anyway, to whom, and why? The connection with Favorinus is just as tenuous. Holford-Strevens argues that Gellius "would have been a fool not to foresee that readers would think of Favorinus, with whom he had exchanged information only four chapters previously and who is portrayed throughout with no hint of either impropriety or discomfort."[70] The argument that Gellius would expect readers (some or all?) to think of Favorinus simply because he had appeared four chapters earlier does not persuade. Quite a bit of text has intervened, and not all readers read the *Attic Nights* sequentially anyway.

---

[68] E.g. Cic. *Amic.* 36: *id primum videamus, si placet, quatenus amor in amicitia progredi debeat* (introducing a discussion of how much a man can justifiably ask his friend to do – even set fire to the Capitoline?). Note that Gellius devotes a long chapter (*NA* 17.5) to Cicero's *De amicitia*, quoting a passage in which precisely *amor* is at stake: *sic amicitiam non spe mercedis adducti, sed quod omnis eius fructus in ipso amore inest, expetendam putamus* (Cic. *Amic.* 31). Gellius elsewhere cites Theophrastus and Cicero together, the latter specifically in connection with the *De amicitia*, and mentioning Favorinus as well (*NA* 1.3). Fürst 1996, p. 126, likewise suggests that Gellius cited some unspecified passage from the *De amicitia*. Holford-Stevens 2003, p. 105 n. 40, argues that if Gellius were referring to the *De amicitia*, the most likely candidate would be a passage on the theme of broken friendship (e.g. 85, *cum iudicaris diligere oportet, non cum dilexeris iudicare*).

[69] Holford-Strevens 2003, p. 106: "It would be perverse to suppose either that Cicero had changed the sense of *amor amicitiae* in some lost work and not in *De amicitia*, or that Gellius employed the expression in a non-Ciceronian sense when quoting him; on the one hand he can hardly have forgotten, or expected the reader not to recall, so disturbing a passage of so well-known a work, on the other he could have expressed 'the love proper to friendship' by the hendiadys *amore et amicitia*" (which is how Franz Skutzsch emended the text of Gellius). For the pairing *amor et amicitia* Holford-Strevens cites as parallels Sen. *Ep.* 81.12, Gell. *NA* 15.28.5 and 16.9.4, but hendiadys is not at stake in any of these passages.

[70] Holford-Strevens 2003, p. 106

Like Holford-Strevens, Wytse Keulen also sees the passage from the *Tusculanae* as well as Favorinus in the background, but he reads Gellius' implicit message in precisely the opposite way. Whereas Holford-Strevens asserts that "only one thing is morally impossible, that Gellius should have taken a less than positive view of his relations with Favorinus, the warmest friendship of his life," Keulen sees Gellius as "integrating figures like Favorinus as inadequate, controversial, or subversive elements into his Roman cultural world, casting them as ambiguous contemporary role-models, against which the reader is invited to pit the unassailable heroes of Gellius' admired Roman past, in particular Cato the Elder."[71] That there are such divergent readings is understandable enough, since our text of Gellius gives us so little to go on. In fact, while these and other scholars make assertions about the importance of "friendship" and *amicitia* to Gellius in general and in connection with Favorinus in particular, it is worth noting that, while Favorinus is clearly a key figure for Gellius, valued as a *philosophus*, Gellius never uses words like *amicus* or *familiaris* to refer to their relationship.[72]

TRIANGLES

Sedgwick's influential discussion of the homosocial begins with one of the most famous triangles of English poetry – the poet, the fair youth, and the dark lady of Shakespeare's sonnets – suggesting that the most characteristic configuration of the homosocial, and with it of the "traffic in women," is a triangle consisting of two men and a woman with whom one or both are joined by erotic desire, whether consummated or not. The bond between the two men shapes and is given expression through their shared desire for a woman, and may itself be erotically colored to varying degrees; and, although Sedgwick's own reading does not bring the point out, the Shakespearean triangle sometimes uses the intertwined language of love and friendship.[73] In the Latin textual tradition we not infrequently

---

[71] Holford-Strevens 2003, p. 107; Keulen 2009, p. 315 (cf. pp. 131–132).

[72] Cf. Beall 2001, p. 101: Favorinus was Gellius' "special friend," and the two form an "'odd couple'" (scare quotes in the original); Lakmann 1997 speaks of a "close connection," "respect," and "admiration" (p. 234: "einer seiner glühendsten Verehrer"; p. 236: "enge Verbundenheit mit dem Lehrer"). The closest Gellius actually comes to placing a label on his relationship with Favorinus, apart from the rather elastic phrase *Favorinus noster*, comes in his narration of a dinner-party at which he was present (*NA* 2.22.1, *apud mensam Favorini in convivio familiari*): here Gellius represents himself as one among a number of Favorinus' *familiares*.

[73] Cf. Shakespeare, Sonnet 42: "If I lose thee, my loss is my *love's* gain, / And losing her, my *friend* hath found that loss." Sedgwick 1985 passim, esp. pp. 21–27. Studies subsequent to Sedgwick

find the mingled discourses of *amor* and *amicitia* constructing erotic triangles which invite being read through the lens of the homosocial. By
way of prelude to the following chapter's readings of a selection of Latin
texts in which various kinds of triangulations appear, in what follows I
here offer some introductory remarks on the role of *amor* and *amicitia* in
textual configurations of two men and a woman.

Sometimes we find the discourses of *amor* and *amicitia* being kept distinct in order to forestall an unwanted triangle. Ovid recommends that
his male readers refrain from pursuing their friends' women: *Amor* with a
woman, metonymized by the bed, disturbs the equilibrium of masculine
amicitia (Ov. *Ars am.* 1.741–746). A poem by Propertius explores the same
tension as he narrates a drunken pass at his girlfriend made by his friend
Lynceus. The poem opens with the following couplets (terms referring to
Propertius' relationship with the woman are underlined, those referring
to his relationship with Lynceus are in italics).

> Cur quisquam faciem <u>dominae</u> iam credat *amico*?
> sic erepta mihi paene <u>puella mea</u> est.
> expertus dico, nemo est in <u>amore</u> *fidelis*:
> <u>formosam</u> raro non sibi quisque petit.
> polluit ille deus cognatos, solvit *amicos*,
> et bene concordis tristia ad arma vocat.
>
> (Prop. 2.34.1–6)

Why should anyone entrust his mistress' beauty to a friend any more?
My girl was nearly stolen away from me.
I speak from experience: no one is trustworthy when it comes to love.
Rare it is that a man is not out to find a beautiful woman.
The god [Cupid] besmirches kin, dissolves friends,
and summons to grim conflict those previously of one mind.

The opening couplet introduces the players: a generic *domina* on the one
hand, an *amicus* on the other, both quickly given first-person specificity
(*mihi … puella mea*).[74] The second and third couplets make a strong statement indeed, *amor*, anchored in the woman's beauty (*formosam*) is not
always compatible with *fides*. The word's metonymical hint at *amicitia* is

---

include Smith 1991, Orgel 1996, Shannon 2002, and MacFaul 2007. The concept of the "traffic in
women" derives from the work of Claude Lévi-Strauss.

[74] The manuscripts of the first line read *iam credat amori* but, following a pre-1600 emendation,
most modern editors correct the text to *iam credat amico*. The implications of the textual uncertainty are worth drawing out. If Propertius wrote *amico*, something about the poem led a scribe
or scribes to make the change to *amori*; if he wrote *amori*, something has led modern editors to
emend to *amico*. See Cairns 2006, pp. 295–319, for a reading of the poem which hypothesizes
that Lynceus is a pseudonym for the epic and tragic poet L. Varius Rufus.

made explicit in the third couplet: The god – unnamed here, but known as *Cupido* or, precisely, *Amor* – can break the bond which unites *amici*. As the poem continues, it invokes one of the grandest ideals of masculine friendship ("*amici* share everything") by way of asserting a limit.

> te socium vitae, te corporis esse licebit,
>   te dominum admitto rebus, *amice*, meis:
> lecto te solum, lecto te deprecor uno:
>   rivalem possum non ego ferre Iovem.
>   (Prop. 2.34.15–18)

> You can share in my life, my body;
> I make you, my friend, master over my affairs.
> Only in bed – in the bed alone I do not want you.
> Not even Jupiter can I put up with as a rival there.

In texts like this a clear distinction is maintained. On one side a man's *amicitia* with another man, on the other side his or his friend's *amor* with a woman.

On the other hand, we find graffiti in Pompeii and Herculaneum in the voice of men, boasting of sexual accomplishments achieved in the company of other men whom they call their "pals" (*sodales*). A cluster of messages of the type "So-and-so had a fuck here with his pals (*hic futuit cum sodalibus*)" has been found on the walls of a building near the theaters in Pompeii, evidently a hotspot for rendezvous,[75] and another cluster on the walls of the Thermae Maritimae at Herculaneum tell similar stories, the first of them in rather wordy if not entirely clear detail.

duo sodales hic fuerunt et cum diu malum ministrum in omnia haberent nomine Epaphroditum, vix tarde eum foras exigerunt. consumpserunt persuavissime cum futuere HS CV s(emissem). (*CIL* 4.10675)

Apelles cubicularius Caesar(is) cum Dextro pranderunt hic iucundissime et futuere simul. (*CIL* 4.10677)

Apelles Mus cum fratre Dextro amabiliter futuimus bis bina(s). (*CIL* 4.10678)

Two pals were here. Long having had a terrible servant named Epaphroditus to help with everything (?), they got rid of him with great difficulty. They happily went through 105 sesterces and half an *as* on a fuck.

---

[75] *CIL* 4.3935: *Festus hic futuit com sodalibus*; 4.3938: *Iarinus hic cum Atheto futuit* (cf. 4.3934: *Iarinus cum Atheto hic*); 4.3942: *Ampliatus Afer hic futuit cum suis sodalibus* (cf. 4.3941: *Ampliatus cum suis sodalibus hic*). See also *CIL* 4.2192 (*XVII K(alendas) Iul(ias) Hermeros cum Philetero et Caphiso hic futuerunt*), 2249 (*Hyginus cum Messio hic*), 4816 (*Chryseros cum Successo hic terna(s) futuimus*).

Apelles the imperial chamberlain together with Dexter had a very nice lunch here and fucked together.

Apelles Mus with Dexter his brother had a lovely fuck with two women twice.[76]

In some speech genres, as we have seen, *sodalis* is a near-synonym of *amicus*, and we will return to the polyvalent *frater* at the end of this chapter. As it happens, none of the graffiti alluding to group sexual encounters uses the term *amicus*, the term of choice in formal inscriptions and above all epitaphs. The sample of relevant graffiti is too small to justify building an argument, but the distinction is worth noting nonetheless. It is also worth noting that these graffiti do not speak of *amor*; this is about what Catullus calls *fututiones* (Catull. 32.8).

In Chapter 4 we will consider the wide range of commemorative configurations using the language of *amicitia* in Latin epitaphs, but an unusual epitaph found in the *sepulcretum Salarium* in Rome is worth citing here because of the triangular configuration it describes, vividly if elusively. The poetic epitaph for the freed slave Potestas of Perugia was commissioned by her former owner Aulus Allius; its date is unknown, but suggestions range from the first through the fourth centuries AD (*CIL* 6.37965).[77] The poem strikingly joins powerful expressions of grief – Allius has not replaced Potestas in his affections (*nulla cui post te femina visa proba est*, 38) and expects to join her in the afterlife (*cumque ad te veniam*, 46) – with praise of her moral and especially physical qualities expressed with a frankness that has struck many readers. She did not think too highly of herself or ever forget her servile origins; her breasts were snowy white, her nipples small, her thighs like those of Atalanta.[78] Equally striking are the following lines:

> mansit et infamis, quia nil admiserat umquam.
> haec duo, dum vixit, iuvenes ita rexit *amantes*
> exemplo ut fierent similes *Pyladisque et Orestae*:
> una domus capiebat eos unusque et spiritus illis.

---

[76] In the Latin both of literary texts and of graffiti, *futuere* is normally transitive, almost always taking a woman as its direct object. Although according to the rules of grammar-book Latin *binas* would signify that each man had two partners, these graffiti seem to be communicating that there were two simultaneous pairings of the two named men with two unnamed women, i.e. one each. The tone of the phrase *amabiliter futuimus* is hard to hear, but there is almost certainly a humorous contrast between the adverb and the obscene verb to which it is juxtaposed.

[77] See Horsfall 1985 for commentary on the inscription, and Rizzelli 1995 for the history of interpretation of the lines quoted below. Horsfall describes Allius as the "author" of these verses, but it is of course also possible – indeed more likely – that he commissioned a poet to write them.

[78] *CIL* 6.37965, 16: *haec sibi non placuit, numquam sibi libera visa*; 20–21: *pectore et in niveo brevis illi forma papillae; / quid crura? Atalantes status illi comicus ipse.*

post hanc nunc idem diversi sibi quis(que) senescunt:
femina quod struxit talis, nunc puncta lacessunt.
aspicite ad Troiam quid femina fecerit olim;
sit precor hoc iustum exemplis in parvo grandibus uti.
hos tibi dat versus lachrimans sine fine patronus ...

(*CIL* 6.37965, lines 27–35)

Her reputation remained unblemished, for she never committed any offense.
While she was alive, she exercised such a rule over two young lovers
that they became like the famous example of Pylades and Orestes.
One home sheltered them, one spirit was theirs.
Now that she is gone, they grow old apart from each other.
What such a woman had built up, picks now tear down.
Consider what a woman once did at Troy:
I pray it may be right to use grand examples on small scale.
These verses your patron dedicates to you, weeping without end ...

It is noticeable that Allius does not memorialize his beloved Potestas with the label *amica*, a silence which draws attention to the particularity of inscriptions in verse. To what speech genre(s) might we assign them? Their language is in general that of the poetic genres we find in the Latin literary tradition, but they are carved in stone just like (often on the same stone as) prose inscriptions, whose formulaic language uses the terms *amicus* and *amica*, as we have seen, so differently from, say, elegiac poetry.

What about the relationship between the two young men (*duo iuvenes*), and how to read the key term *amantes*. Does it mean "her lovers," or "loving each other"? That is, does the *amor* evoked here join the two men to each other, or each of them to Potestas, or does its very elasticity evoke a triangle? Most recent readings indeed see a triangle, and one that is characterized by the erotic, and some have used the label *ménage*, even *à trois*. But the French noun raises another question: Does this epitaph literally commemorate a *household*, and if so, consisting of how many? The motifs of "sharing a home" and "one spirit in two bodies," combined as they are with the citation of Orestes and Pylades, suggest the ideals of *amicitia* between precisely two men. The pronouns referring to those who shared a home and a spirit (*eos, illis*) seem to refer to the two men alone, though the imagery of course need not compel any particular reading of who actually lived with whom. And who are these two men anyway? Various possibilities have been suggested since the epitaph was first published in 1914 (they are Allius' sons; they are Allius himself and another man; they are two other men; and so on), but it is most likely that one of them is Allius, briefly narrating his experience in the third person just as he commemorates himself in the third person as Potestas' *patronus* immediately afterwards (v. 35). The other young man remains a cipher.[79] However we read the details, the epitaph as a whole is commemorating a triangular relationship of some kind joining Potestas (*haec*) and two young men (*duo iuvenes*); the triangle is viewed in such a way that a woman stands at its apex, and an erotic charge is palpable throughout the poem. Potestas, subject of the evocative if imprecise verb *rexit*, is compared to the mythic figure of Helen, herself a deeply ambivalent figure but indubitably suggestive of the power that a woman favored by Aphrodite can exert over men, and the tragic consequences it can have.

MYTHIC PARADIGMS

Within the massive body of Greek mythological narrative adopted and adapted by Roman culture, Orestes and Pylades, invoked in Allia Potestas' epitaph and memorably brought to stage by Pacuvius in the scene so glowingly recalled by Cicero's Laelius (Cic. *Amic.* 24), can justly be called *the* mythic paradigm for friends in the Latin textual tradition. Not surprisingly, then, we find the pair represented as an exemplary embodiment of *amor* and *amicitia*. Ovid describes them "in their bodies two, one in mind," and Pylades as an "example of true love (*exemplum veri amoris*)"; after describing the bond of friendship (*foedus amicitiae*) as the greatest of Nature's creations, Manilius cites Orestes and Pylades as his sole illustration; and we have seen that Valerius Maximus writes that Orestes is almost better known as Pylades' friend than as Agamemnon's son.[80] Indeed, Pylades' very name could be a metonymy for *amicus* – the speaker in one of Juvenal's satires asks who is "such a Pylades" that he will accompany you outside of the city in order to support you in a legal complaint against

---

[79] Horsfall 1985, p. 266, assumes that all three lived together and sees the only question as being whether one of the *duo iuvenes* of v. 28 was Allius himself; he concludes that he was. For two men (as it happens, twin brothers) described as each other's *amantes* see *CIL* 6.7426: *Zetes et Calais / duo fratres / gemelli obierunt / amantes.* An alternative translation of vv. 28–29 would be "she ruled them by her example, so that they became like Pylades and Orestes," but, as Horsfall notes, it is not clear how Allia might serve as an *exemplum* to the two men. Much depends on the meaning of the verb *rexit*. See Horsfall 1985, p. 268, for various ways of interpreting *puncta lacessunt* in v. 32.

[80] Ov. *Tr.* 4.4.71–72: *et comes exemplum veri Phoceus amoris, / qui duo corporibus, mentibus unus erant*; cf. Ov. *Pont.* 3.2.69–70: *par fuit his aetas et amor, quorum alter Orestes, / ast Pylades alter: nomina fama tenet*; Manil. 2.583–585: *unus erat Pylades, unus qui mallet Orestes / ipse mori; lis una fuit per saecula mortis, / alter quod raperet fatum, non cederet alter*; Val. Max. 4.7.pr: *Orestes Pylade paene amico quam Agamemnone notior est patre.*

a soldier? – and in the visual artistic tradition, both Greek and Roman, Pylades appears exclusively in the company of his friend; we never see him alone.[81] The pair are exemplary in a long, interconnected series of texts in the Western tradition, from Augustine's *Confessions* and Dante's *Purgatorio* through Racine's *Andromache* to Gluck's *Iphigénie en Tauride* and Goethe's *Iphigenie auf Tauris*,[82] up to twentieth-century popularizing reflections on friendship like C. S. Lewis' *The Four Loves* and Joseph Epstein's more recent *Friendship: An Exposé*; and they are repeatedly associated with ideals like the *alter ego*, fidelity, and desiring the same thing.

But Orestes and Pylades are by no means the only mythic paradigms of *amicitia* in the Latin textual tradition. Often they are cited in combination with one or more other pairs: Theseus and Pirithous, Achilles and Patroclus, and – after Virgil – Nisus and Euryalus.[83] These four pairs play a special role in Ovid's exile poetry, reflecting on friendship in general and his own *amici* in particular. One poem, as we have seen, invokes Pylades as *exemplum veri amoris* and in another, a personified letter brings a message to a friend in Rome whom Ovid calls "his Patroclus, his Pylades, his Theseus and his Euryalus." Here the mythic figures are paradigmatic even on the lexical level.[84] Sometimes, too, these paradigmatic pairs have been invoked as a means of highlighting the gap between idealized *then* and lamented *now*. Voltaire opens his entry on "Amitié" in the 1764 *Dictionnaire philosophique* with a poem entitled *Temple de l'amitié*.

> En vieux langage on voit sur la façade
> Les noms sacrés d'Oreste et de Pylade,
> Le médaillon du bon Pirithoüs,
> Du sage Achate et du tendre Nisus,

[81] Juv. 16.26–27: *quis tam Pylades, molem aggeris ultra / ut veniat?* The next sentence shifts from the proper name to the noun it metonymizes (27–28: *lacrimae siccentur protinus, et se / excusaturos non sollicitemus amicos*). For the visual arts, see *LIMC* 7.1 (1994): 603: "Pylades, dont la tradition antique fait l'ami fidèle et le compagnon d'Oreste, n'apparaît dans l'iconographie que comme tel, dans le cadre de l'Orestie."

[82] Aug. *Conf.* 4.4–9; Dante, *Purgartorio*, Canto 13 ("i' sono Oreste"); Racine's *Andromache* opens with Orestes' joyful reflection on his reunion with his friend ("Oui, puisque je retrouve un ami si fidèle …"); Gluck's *Iphigénie en Tauride* includes a famous aria on Orestes and Pylades' friendship and imminent union and death ("unis dès la plus tendre enfance, / nous n'avions qu'un même désir").

[83] In the fourth century, Ausonius adds the historical Roman pair Scipio and Laelius to the list of Nisus–Euryalus, Pylades–Orestes, Theseus–Pirithous, Damon–Phintias (*Ep.* 23 and 24); Cicero's *De amicitia* almost certainly lies behind this. See Knight 2005 for a reading of Ausonius' poetry of "eroticized friendship."

[84] Ov. *Tr.* 1.5.21: *ut foret exemplum veri Phoceus amoris*; Ov. *Tr.* 5.4.25–26: *teque Menoetiaden, te, qui comitatus Oresten, / te vocat Aegiden Euryalumque suum*. Discussions of the theme of friendship in Ovid's exile poetry include Williams 1994 (especially pp. 100–153) and Citroni Marchetti 2000 (especially pp. 295–368).

Tous grands héros, tous amis véritables:
Ces noms sont beaux; mais ils sont dans les fables.

In ancient language are seen on the facade
The sacred names of Orestes and Pylades,
The medallion of goodly Pirithous,
Wise Achates and tender Nisus:
All of them great heroes, all of them true friends.
These names are beautiful – but they exist in tales.

The heroic, true friendships of the wistfully invoked past are embodied in four paradigmatic pairs, two Greek (Orestes and Pylades, Theseus and Pirithous) and two Latin (Achates and Aeneas, Nisus and Euryalus): Orestes and Pylades are first on the list, and they are the only pair of whom both members are explicitly named. The late sixteenth-century essayist Saint-Evremond writes that passionate friendships like those of Orestes and Pylades "are things we read, and see represented, which are not to be found in the commerce and practice of the world," and nearly four centuries later we find C. S. Lewis invoking the pair as the sole example from Greece or Rome to make the same suspiciously recurring contrast. Orestes and Pylades, in short, not only illustrate the central role of friendship in long-term narratives of Western culture, but they have also performed both functions of mythic narrative that Jan Assmann describes in his influential study of cultural memory: foundational and contra-present.[85]

It is both emblematic and significant that there are no comparable mythic paradigms for friendships between women, and that, in the speech genre of epitaphs at least, one of these paradigmatic male pairs could be invoked as paradigm not only for relationships between two men. A poetic epitaph from Rome for Rhodanthion and his wife Victoria uses intertextual means to activate the paradigm of Nisus and Euryalus:

> haec est sancta fides, haec sunt felicia vota: /
> amplexus vitai reddere post obitum. /
> fortunati ambo! si qua est, ea gloria mortis: /
> quos iungit tumulus iunxerat ut thalamus.
> (*CIL* 6.25427 = *CLE* 1142, lines 23–26)[86]

---

[85] Assmann 2011, pp. 62–66; Lewis 1960, p. 69: "Tristan and Isolde, Antony and Cleopatra, Romeo and Juliet, have innumerable counterparts in modern literature: David and Jonathan, Pylades and Orestes, Roland and Oliver, Amis and Amile, have not."

[86] The verses recall not only the epitaph for Nisus and Euryalus (Verg. *Aen.* 9.44–45: *fortunati ambo! si quid mea carmina possunt, / nulla dies umquam memori vos eximet aevo*) but other Virgilian details as well. Compare *si qua est, ea gloria mortis* (25) with Verg. *Aen.* 7.4 (*si qua est ea gloria, signat*) and *hunc coniunx talem nimio dilexit amore* (9) with Verg. *Aen.* 9.430 (*tantum infelicem nimium dilexit amicum*).

This is hallowed trust, these are successful prayers:
to requite the embraces of life after death.
Blessed pair! This, if any exists, is glory in death:
they are united by the tomb as the bedchamber had united them.

Commemorating the joint burial of Probatia and her granddaughter
Concordia, a verse inscription from Spoleto not only evokes the ideal of
unanimitas (also associated, as we will see, with brothers, friends, and
spouses) but invokes Nisus and Euryalus, joined in death.[87]
  It may not be coincidental that Nisus and Euryalus are the only one
of the four paradigmatic pairs who are not Greek, and who are closely
associated with one Latin text in particular, and one of the most influential of all Latin texts at that: Virgil's *Aeneid*, whose narrative of the pair is
the only one surviving and which may well have been the first. They are
introduced on two separate occasions in the epic.

> Nisus et Euryalus primi,
> Euryalus forma insignis viridique iuventa,
> Nisus *amore* pio pueri;
> (V. *Aen.* 5.294–296)

> et iuxta comes Euryalus, quo pulchrior alter
> non fuit Aeneadum Troiana neque induit arma,
> ora puer prima signans intonsa iuventa.
> his *amor unus* erat pariterque in bella ruebant.
> (V. *Aen.* 9.179–182)

Nisus and Euryalus first of all:
Euryalus remarkable for his beauty, his fresh youth,
Nisus for his devoted love of the boy.

Next to him was his comrade Euryalus. None of Aeneas' followers,
none who had shouldered Trojan armament, was more beautiful than he:
a boy with the first bloom of youth on his unshaven face.
These two shared one love and rushed into the fighting side by side.

Virgil's narrative blends themes of manly military valor (*virtus*) with
those of friendship and eros, *amicitia* and *amor*.[88] Both times Euryalus

---

[87] *CIL* 11.4978 = *CLE* 1848: *hic aviam neptemque locus post fata recepit, / quosque dies olim fecerat unanimes. / evolat ad superos mentis quoque gratia simplex, / sa[rcophag]um dup[p]lex corpora nunc sociat. / alternis praestant votis: sic lumine vero / tunc iacuere simul Nisus et Eurialus ...* For other echoes of Nisus and Euryalus in epitaphs, see *CLE* 753 (*hic iacet Heraclius nimium dilectus amicus*) and *CIL* 6.34083 = *CLE* 502 (mother to son: *si quid mea carmina possunt*). Virgil is the poet most often alluded to in Latin verse inscriptions: see Cugusi 1985, pp. 173–184, Milnor 2009.

[88] See, for example, Makowski 1989; Hardie 1994 ad loc.; Fowler 2000, pp. 95–99, Dupont and Éloi 2001, pp. 59–82; Williams 2010, pp. 126–130. The phrase *amor unus* is readable as referring

is presented as a *puer* with the classic tokens of youthful desirabil-
ity (beardlessness, fresh youth, beauty: *forma, viridi iuventa, pulchrior,
intonsa iuventa*) and both times the pair is described as joined by
amor, but Virgil's poetry just as emphatically portrays them as *amici*.
Euryalus wins a footrace after Nisus slips and falls in some blood and
then trips up the frontrunner Salius. Nisus is "mindful of Euryalus, his
love (*amorum*)" who wins the race thanks to "his friend's gift (*munere
amici*)". Later, when planning the exploit which ends up being their last,
Euryalus addresses his *amicus* Nisus; later still, when Nisus has lost track
of Euryalus, it is his *amicus* he seeks. Finally, distraught when Euryalus
has been captured by the enemy, Nisus exclaims that the young man is
not at fault, the only thing he has done is to "love his unhappy friend
(*infelicem amicum*) too much."[89] The narrative voice then describes the
climactic moment as Nisus, mortally wounded, flings himself upon his
Euryalus' lifeless body:

> tum super exanimum sese proiecit *amicum*
> confossus, placidaque ibi demum morte quievit.
>   (Verg. *Aen*. 9.444–445)

> He flung himself on top of his lifeless friend,
> pierced by countless wounds, and there at last found rest in death.

Their death scene invites comparison with Valerius Maximus' improv-
ingly gory narrative of Lucullus, who held his friend Volumnius' severed
head in his hands as he met his own death (Val. Max. 4.7.4, above p.
10), and has been fittingly described as an "elegiac union" of "lovers in
death."[90] Virgil's epitaph for the two is as renowned as it is stirring.

> fortunati ambo! si quid mea carmina possunt,
> nulla dies umquam memori vos eximet aevo,

---

to their love for each other and/or for glory in battle: Hardie ad loc. comments, "probably 'common love [for each other]' rather than 'shared passion [for war]'" but adds that "erotic and martial passion are difficult to disentangle." A question Nisus poses to Euryalus also invites being
read in military and erotic terms at once: *dine hunc ardorem mentibus addunt, / Euryale, an sua
cuique deus fit dira cupido?* (9.184–185) The phrase *dira cupido* echoes and blends Lucretius 4.1046
(*dira libido*, describing men's urge to ejaculate) and 4.1057 (*muta cupido*).

[89] Verg. *Aen*. 5.334: *non tamen Euryali, non ille oblitus amorum*; 5.337–378: *emicat Euryalus et munere
victor amici / prima tenet*; 9.198: *simul his ardentem adfatur amicum*; 9.389: *et frustra absentem
respexit amicum*; 9.430: *tantum infelicem nimium dilexit amicum*. For his part, Servius worries
about the seeming contradiction between the phrases *amore pio pueri* (5.296) and *non ille oblitus
amorum* (5.334) since for him the plural *amores* can only mean "something disgraceful" (*plural-
iter non nisi turpitudinem significant*).

[90] See Lyne 1987, p. 235 ("elegiac union as lovers in death"), citing Prop. 2.20.18 and Tib. 1.1.59–62.

dum domus Aeneae Capitoli immobile saxum
accolet imperiumque pater Romanus habebit.
(Verg. *Aen.* 9.446–449)

Blessed pair! If my poetry has any power at all,
you will never be blotted out from the memory of the ages,
not as long as the house of Aeneas shall dwell
on the unmoving Capitoline rock
and the Roman father hold sway.

Like the couple themselves, these lines quickly became paradigmatic and
eminently quotable – not only in literary texts but also, as we have seen,
in inscriptions marking burials, and not just burials of men.[91]

The presence of Nisus and Euryalus and, even more strikingly, of
Achilles and Patroclus in Roman rosters of paradigmatic *amici* illustrates the difficulty of neatly categorizing intimate relationships between
men in the Latin textual tradition. Like most *amici*, they embody both
amicitia and *amor*; but what kind of *amor* joins these pairs in particular? Virgil gives the *amor* of Nisus and Euryalus a decorously but discreetly erotic coloring, while Achilles and Patroculs appear in a range of
Greek texts openly described as exemplars not only of *philia* but also of
eros.[92] In Latin texts, we sometimes find one or both names functioning
as a synecdoche for *amicitia*. A verse epistle by Statius addressed to his
friend Vitorius Marcellus culminates with an invocation of mythic paradigms of *amicitia*: Heracles, Theseus, and "he who dragged Priam's son
around Troy's walls in consolation for his slain friend." Neither Achilles
nor Patroclus is named; the poem's final word, *amico*, tells us all we need
to know.[93]

What of *amor*, exemplified, as we have seen in Ovid's words, by
Pylades (*exemplum veri amoris*)? In the case of Achilles and Patroclus,

[91] Virgil's lines are all the more memorable because this is "the most emphatic authorial interven-
tion in the epic and the only explicit reference to the power of his own poetry" (Hardie 1994 on
9.446–449). Later allusions to this passage in the literary tradition include Sen. *Ep.* 21.5.

[92] The two were portrayed as sexual partners on the Athenian stage in Aeschylus' *Myrmidons* (fr.
135–137 Nauck), and oratory (Aesch. 1.33, 141–150) and philosophy (Pl. *Symp.* 180a–b) suggest
that in fourth-century BC Athenian they were widely conceived as *erastes* and *eromenos*. The
Symposium passage shows that there was some debate as to which played which role, but the
assumption that they were a pederastic couple is unquestioned.

[93] Stat. *Silv.* 4.4.101–105: *iamque vale et penitus voti tibi vatis honorem / corde exire veta. nec enim
Tirynthius, almae / parcus amicitiae cedet tibi gloria fidi / Theseos, et lacerum qui circa moe-
nia Troiae / Priamiden caeso solacia traxit amico.* The reading of v. 103 is contested (I follow
Shackleton Bailey), but in any case there is clearly a reference to *amicitia*. The otherwise unparalleled addition of Heracles to the list of paradigmatic friends alludes to his friendship with
Telamon (Coleman ad loc., cf. Stat. *Theb.* 9.68). At *Silv.* 4.4.105, Statius refers to Patroclus, without naming him, as Achilles' "slain friend" (*caesus amicus*).

the polyvalence of *amor* and absence in Latin of a lexical equivalent to Greek *eros* become particularly piquant. How, for example, might we read Statius' evocation of the young Achilles and Patroclus on Scyrus in his epic *Achilleid*, "joined in a great love (*magno amore*)"?[94] Using the exuberantly obscene language of epigram, Statius' contemporary Martial dispenses with ambiguity.

> Deprensum in puero tetricis me vocibus, uxor,
>   corripis et culum te quoque habere refers.
> dixit idem quotiens lascivo Juno Tonanti!
>   ille tamen grandi cum Ganymede iacet.
> incurvabat Hylan posito Tirynthius arcu:
>   tu Megaran credis non habuisse natis?
> torquebat Phoebum Daphne fugitiva: sed illas
>   Oebalius flammas iussit abire puer.
> Briseis multum quamvis aversa iaceret,
>   Aeacidae propior levis *amicus* erat.
> parce tuis igitur dare mascula nomina rebus
>   teque puta cunnos, uxor, habere duos.
>   (Mart. 11.43)

You caught me with a boy and let me have it, wife,
with some rough words. You have an ass, too, you say!
How often has Juno said just that to Jupiter –
but he still goes to bed with his big Ganymede.
When Hercules put down his bow it was Hylas he bent over –
you think his wife Megara didn't have a behind?
Daphne tormented Apollo as she ran away; but
the boy Hyacinth put out that flame!
However much Briseis offered him her backside,
closer to Achilles was his smooth friend.
So stop giving masculine names to your business,
and think of it this way: you, my wife, have got two cunts.

Rather than being in the company of Orestes and Pylades as inspiring models of masculine *amicitia* and *amor*, Achilles and Patroclus are here simultaneously elevated to the company of the gods and brought down with a bang to the bodily, as an example of a specific copulatory

---

[94] Stat. *Achil.* 1.174–177: *insequitur magno iam tunc conexus amore / Patroclus tantisque extenditur aemulus actis, / par studiis aevique modis, sed robore longe, / et tamen aequali visurus Pergama fato.* The emphasis on their similarity in age and interests and delicate allusion to their shared destiny of dying at Troy paint a portrait of heroic *amici*, but the phrase *magnus amor* opens up further possibilities of meaning. Heslin 2005, pp. 54–55, contrasts Statius' "significant ambiguity" with *Achilles in Scyrus*, "a merry and ribald piece of homosexual pornography" from the early twentieth century in which the relationship between Achilles and Patroclus is expressly sexual.

configuration. The epigram reiterates the theme of anal intercourse in several couplets both by key words (*culum, natis, aversa*) and by citing the figure of "the boy (*puer*)," which itself can be a metonymy for the act.[95] Like Martial's *puer*, with whom he shares the attribute of a satisfying orifice (*culum*, line 2), Patroclus is unnamed. He is Achilles' "smooth friend (*levis amicus*)," a compressed allusion which draws attention to the noun in a powerfully irreverent way, inviting a parallel with the widespread usage of the feminine *amica*. Is this a one-off joke on Martial's part, or is he appropriating a usage to which we do not otherwise have access? It is hard to know.

And so we come to the complication. If Achilles and Patroclus and Nisus and Euryalus were thinkable not only as model *amici* but also as bonded by desire, cited in the earthy discourse of Latin epigram as illustrations of the pleasures of anal intercourse, to what extent is there a penumbra of eros or hint of bodily pleasure in *any* text that names them? To what extent does this possibility extend to the other pairs with whom they are commonly listed? Such questions have rarely been asked in scholarly readings. Commentaries on the Ovidian lists, for example, leave the impression that Achilles and Patroclus were in no way different from Orestes and Pylades.[96] I am hardly arguing that Latin texts which invoke these paradigmatic pairs without suggesting any distinctions among them are thereby representing all of these mythic men – let alone the real Romans to and for whom they are offered as models and parallels – as actual or potential partners in genital pleasures. But I am proposing that we look in these texts for traces of fire and desire of all kinds, of the various sorts of *ardor* and *cupido* associated with *amor*, and that we see the overlaps as suggestive, not so much of a presence (say, of eros in friendship) as of a significant absence: of uncrossable lines, impermeable boundaries, anxious distinctions.

---

[95] See Williams 2010, pp. 204–206.

[96] In the Greek textual tradition, Lucian's *Toxaris* gives us a glimpse at the kind of slippage that can occur in connection with these paradigmatic pairs. Unlike Achilles and Patroclus, Orestes and Pylades are rarely if ever described as being joined by *eros*, but that is precisely what the Scythian title character does in this text (7: τὸ ἀληθὲς καὶ βέβαιον τοῦ πρὸς ἀλλήλους ἔρωτος; the same speaker elsewhere [44] uses the related verb *eramai* to describe a man's desire for a woman whom he seeks to marry). In the Latin textual tradition, the comparison of Maecenas and Augustus to both Theseus and Pirithous and Achilles and Patroclus at Propertius 2.1.35–38 has attracted editorial attention: some have posited a lacuna, and Heyworth 2007, p. 109, even thinks the couplet an interpolation by some later poetaster (see Fedeli 2005 ad loc. for further discussion). Arguments have circled around the impression that the couplet does not fit its immediate context, but it is also possible that some other kinds of readerly anxiety lurk here.

BROTHERS AND SISTERS

The bond joining sister to sister plays a remarkably small role in the surviving Latin textual tradition – even so powerful a paradigm as that of Antigone and Ismene does not find much resonance[97] – but one of the few sisterly pairs we find is memorable indeed. Caught in the dilemma of her passion for Aeneas, Virgil's Dido confides first in her sister Anna, whom the narrator introduces to readers with an epithet to whose significance we will shortly return: *unanima*, "of one mind." And Anna begins her reply with a variation on a motif found in expressions of intimacy between male friends in Latin poetry: "I love you more than my own life."[98]

The bond between brothers, for its part, played a central role not only in Roman social relations but in a range of cultural identity-making practices. Romans traced the foundation of their city back to the twin brothers Romulus and Remus – or more precisely to Romulus, who was said to have killed his brother in a fit of envy or fear, by this primal act of fratricide bringing a blood-curse upon generations of Romans to come, plagued by generations of civil war.[99] The love that ideally joins brother to brother was assigned a high symbolic value indeed. Virgil's catalogue of sinners punished in the Underworld places those who had been hostile to their brothers at the top of the list, and Valerius Maximus' collection of paradigmatic narratives of fraternal love (brothers only, no sisters) is introduced by a paragraph urging that affection for one's brother not be overshadowed by any other interpersonal bond: not with wife or children or relatives by marriage, not even with friends.[100] Not surprisingly, then,

---

[97] See Goldhill 2006 for some reflections on Antigone and Ismene. It would be interesting to know how the theme of sister love shaped Accius' lost tragedy *Antigona*.

[98] Verg. *Aen.* 4.8: *cum sic unanimam adoquitur male sana sororem: / "Anna soror, quae me suspensam insomnia terrent!"*; 4.32: *o luce magis dilecta sorori.* Ovid's poetic letter from Dido to Aeneas echoes and amplifies the Virgilian line (Ov. *Her.* 7.191: *Anna soror, soror Anna, meae male conscia culpae*). In alternative versions recorded by Varro, it was not Dido but Anna who fell in love with Aeneas and eventually killed herself (Serv. ad *Aen.* 5.4 and Serv. auct. ad *Aen.* 4.82; see Hexter 1992). There is something both powerful and elusive about Anna and Dido as paradigm for sibling love: Although its Latin title quotes Dido's first words to her sister at *Aen.* 4.9, Marguerite Yourcenar's novella *Anna soror* explores the theme of incestuous love between brother and sister. Explaining the title as a reference to the Latin epitaph composed for her brother by the Anna of her fiction, Yourcenar says not a word about Dido (postface, p. 97). The occlusion of Virgil is striking, as is an imprecision in Yourcenar's own explanation: She describes *Anna soror* as the "deux premiers mots de l'epitaphe" but the epitaph actually begins ANNA DE LA CERNA Y LOS HERREROS / SOROR.

[99] See Hor. *Epod.* 7.17–20 with Watson 2003 ad loc. Discussions of brothers in the Latin textual tradition see Wiseman 1995, Mencacci 1996, Bannon 1997.

[100] Verg. *Aen.* 6.608 *quibus invisi fratres*; Val. Max. 5.5.pr.: *cara est uxor, dulces liberi, iucundi amici, accepti adfines, sed postea cognitis nulla benevolentia accedere debet quae priorem exhauriat.*

we find the language and imagery of brotherly love repeatedly recurring in textual representations of intimate relationships between men who were not biological siblings as a way of lending value and prestige to them; there are numerous overlaps with the language and imagery of *amicitia*. This is part of a long, complex story in the Western tradition. Montaigne invokes the eloquent "name of brother" as he describes his incomparable friendship with La Boétie, and when writing of the latter's death he reaches back not to Cicero's *De amicitia* but to Catullus' verses on the death of his brother; centuries later, Derrida sees the enduring model of brother love as key to understanding the androcentric model of Western friendship.[101] In the Roman textual tradition the overlap between brothers and friends, *fratres* and *amici*, and the bonds that join them is as insistent as it is recurrent, and has the effect of lending prestige and value to the relationships described. Sometimes this takes the form of parallels. When Cicero's Laelius approvingly notes how Scipio, though socially superior to his friends, always treated them as his equals, he adds the example of how Scipio treated his own brother, who was also his inferior; generations later, Aulus Gellius quotes some words of wisdom from Favorinus on the question of strife between brothers or friends.[102]

Across speech genres, we find explicit comparisons and the occasional metonymic identification. A man loves his *amicus* like a brother, or a man's friend *is* his brother. An epitaph from Padua memorializes the deceased as *amicus, frater* and *sodalis* of the man who commissioned it in his honor, and in honor of his friend's parents as well (all of them embraced in the phrase *amici bene meriti*); and an epitaph for an imperial freedman from Rome announces that it was commissioned by the deceased man's son and two *amici*, one of whom he had "loved like a brother."[103] As we have

---

Perhaps inspired by this passage, Bannon 1997, p. 89, generalizes: "Friends can only play at being brothers; their relationship does not have the security of traditional *pietas*." This underestimates both the power of *amicitia* and the extent to which male friendship and brotherly love could overlap.

[101] Catull. 65, 68, 101; Screech 2004, p. 4: "The name of brother is truly a fair one and full of love: that is why La Boétie and I made a brotherhood of our alliance"; Derrida 1997. For friends and brothers in Shakespeare and contemporaries, see MacFaul 2007, pp. 48–64. It is emblematic that the cover of the 1985 edition of Cicero's *De amicitia* in the *Biblioteca Universale Rizzoli* series is adorned with a second-century AD Fayyum mummy portrait of two brothers.

[102] Cic. *Amic.* 69; Gell. *NA* 2.12.5–6.

[103] *CIL* 5.2903 = Reali 58C (Padua): *D(is) M(anibus). / L. Axio Charist[o] / amico fratri / sodali, qui vicsit / annis XXI, diebus / LIIII, item parentibus / eius L. Axio Cresce[n(ti)], / Axiae Tyche poste/risque eorum. M. / Calvisius Claudius / Victor amicis / bene meritis*; *AE* 1957.127 (Rome): *D(is) M(anibus). / Petroniano Aug(usti) lib(erto). / Iulius Tannonius ami/cus, quem fratris / loco*

seen, Cicero assured his own friend Atticus, and asserted to others, that he loved him like a brother. It is thus all the more poignant to read Cicero's textual negotiations of what seems to have been a serious conflict between his brother Quintus and Atticus, a situation which, he explains in a letter to Atticus, thanks to his great *amor* for both causes him great suffering.[104] The image is so symbolically potent that Cicero uses it in praise of his client Plancius' relationship with his *father* – he loved him "like a friend, a brother, an age-mate" – and in a letter written in the second half of 56 BC, the previous year's consul Q. Metellus Nepos informs Cicero: "I think of you as being a brother to me."[105] In a poetic epistle to the young Julius Florus, Horace inquires after his friendship with Munatius, invoking the "brotherly bond (*fraternum foedus*)" so as to encourage them to nurture their relationship.[106] One of Ovid's poems from exile appeals simultaneously to the model of fraternal love and to the paradigmatic friends Theseus and Pirithous, and several of Martial's epigrams cite the mythic brothers Castor and Pollux as paragons not just of fraternal love but of friendship.[107] And just as a man's friend can be called or compared to a brother, brothers can be paradigmatic *amici*. When Sallust has the Numidian king Micipsa ask Jugurtha, whom he has just adopted in addition to his natural sons Adherbal and Hiempsal: "Who is more of a friend than a brother is to brother?" he is not only speaking the Latin language but invoking Roman ideals. He poses the rhetorical question as part of a manipulative and strategically focused deathbed speech to his newly adopted heir (a kingdom is best maintained not by weapons or money but by one's *amici*, and who could be more of an *amicus* than one's own brother?) and Sallust subsequently comments that Jugurtha knew

---

dilexit, et Cae/cilius Proculus amico / inconparabili et Aure/lius Hermes parenti / dignissimo. qui / vixit annis XLVI / m(ensibus) VII d(iebus) XXIII / s<i>ne macula. A fragmentary epitaph found at Hippo Regius in northern Africa honors the deceased as a friend whose love surpassed a brother's (*AE* 1955.153: *fraternum erga se / amorem supergresso / amico a prima aetate / carissimo*).

[104] Cic. *Att.* 1.5: *cura ut valeas, et nos ames et tibi persuadeas te a me fraterne amari*; *Att.* 9.12.1: *in Epirum vero invitatio quam suavis, quam liberalis, quam fraterna*; *Fam.* 13.1.5: *Pomponium Atticum sic amo ut alterum fratrem*; *Att.* 1.17.1: *qua ex re et molestia sum tanta adfectus quantam mihi meus amor summus erga utrumque vestrum adferre debuit* (see Citroni Marchetti 2000, pp. 17–24, for an overview of this dispute).

[105] Cic. *Planc.* 29: *amat vero ut sodalem, ut fratrem, ut aequalem*; *Fam.* 5.3.1: *te mihi fratris loco esse duco*.

[106] Hor. *Epist.* 1.3.35: *indigni fraternum rumpere foedus*; cf. Hor. *Epist.* 1.10.3–4: *paene gemelli / fraternis animis*.

[107] Ov. *Tr.* 1.3.65–66: *quosque ego dilexi fraterno more sodales / o mihi Thesea pectora iuncta fide*; Mart. 1.36 and 9.51, 5.38, 7.24.

Micipsa's words were full of falsity. Yet their effectiveness was based on the self-evident truth of the axiom about brother love.[108]

Ancient etymologies are often revealing. While one explanation of the origin of *frater* recalls the idealization of the *amicus* as *alter ego* (the noun was seen as a contraction of *fere alter*, "practically another self"), another etymology saw *soror* as a contraction of *seorsum*, "outside": A sister was born to be married off and thus to leave her family of origin. Both etymologies are false by the standards of modern historical linguistics, and even Aulus Gellius, who reports them, calls them "clever" and "elegant" – not necessarily true. None of this diminishes what they reveal about common notions of what brothers and sisters were.[109] Whatever their etymology was thought to be, the nouns *frater* and *soror* were an affectionate and respectful way of addressing individuals who were not biologically one's siblings, and this usage too seems to have characterized a broad range of speech genres. As we have seen, in Virgil's *Aeneid* the dying Camilla addressses a female comrade as *Acca soror* (*Aen.* 11.820– 827), and Severa of Vindolanda writes to Lepidina as her *soror*, while these two women's husbands, like other men in these documents, write to each other as *frater*.[110] Writing in roughly the same period, Martial dedicates a book of epigrams to Toranius, whom he prominently addresses in the preface as *frater carissime*. A few decades later, we find the correspondence of Fronto peppered with the vocative *frater* or *domine frater* as a respectful term of address to men who were not his biological brother.[111]

---

[108] Sall. *Iug.* 10.4–5: *non exercitus neque thesauri praesidia regni sunt, verum amici … quis autem amicior quam frater fratri?*; ibid. 11.1: *ad ea Iugurtha, tametsi regem ficta locutum intellegebat et ipse longe aliter animo agitabat, tamen pro tempore benigne respondit.*

[109] Gell. *NA* 13.10.3–4: *praeterea in libris quos Ad praetoris edictum scripsit (sc., Antistius Labeo) multa posuit, partim lepide atque argute reperta... "soror" inquit "appellata est quod quasi* seorsum *nascitur separaturque ab ea domo in qua nata est in aliam familiam transgreditur." fratris autem vocabulum P. Nigidius, homo impense doctus, non minus arguto subtilique* ἐτύμῳ *interpretatur: "frater" inquit "est dictus quasi fere alter."*

[110] See, e.g. 233, Cerialis to Brocchus: *frater*; 243, Brocchus to Cerialis: *frater*; 248, Niger and Brocchus to Cerialis: *frater* and *domine*; 622, Brocchus to Cerialis: *Severa mea vos [s]alutat. va[le] mi frater k[ari]ssime*; 623, *vale mi frat[er] et domine karissi[me]*). *Frater* is found so often in the Vindolanda correspondence among men of all social levels, including slaves, that one recent study of life at the garrison bears the subtitle *A Band of Brothers* (Birley 2002). The indices to Bowman and Thomas 1994 and 2003 list 73 clear or probable instances of *dominus*, 64 of *frater* or *fraterculus*, and only 8 of *amicus*; see further Adams 1995, pp. 118–120.

[111] Mart. 9.pr.: *have, mi Torani, frater carissime*; Fronto, *Ad amic.* 1.8, 1.9, 1.27, 2.4. The remark by a jurist preserved in the *Digest* to the effect that a man might name as an heir someone whom he calls his *frater*, even though he is not his biological brother, reflects longstanding usage (*Digest* 28.5.59.1: *qui frater non est, si fraterna caritate diligitur, recte cum nomine suo, sub appellatione fratris, heres instituitur*). Boswell 1994 hypothesizes that behind this lay a practice according

Such overlaps occasionally complicate our reading of *fratres* in Latin texts. Consider, for example, the following letter from Vindolanda.

Chrauttius Veldeio suo fratri contubernali antiquo plurimam salutem. et ego te, Veldei frater, miror quod mihi tot tempus nihil rescripsti a parentibus nostris si quid audieris, aut quo [...]m in quo numero sit. et illum a me salutabis{s} verbis meis et Virilem veterinarium, rogabis illum ut forficem quam mihi promisit pretio mittas per aliquem de nostris. et rogo te, frater Virilis, salutes a me Thuttenam sororem, Velbuteium. rescribas nobis cum [...] se habeat. opto sis felicissimus. vale.

[*exterior*] Londini. Veldedeio equisioni cos. a Chrauttio fratre. (Bowman and Thomas 1994, 310)

Chrauttius sends warm greetings to his brother and old comrade Veldeius. Well, brother Veldeius! I must say I am surprised that you never wrote back to me in all this time, if you heard anything from our parents or how many (...) in which unit he is. Be sure to give him my greetings (...) in my own words, and the veterinarian Virilis as well – be sure to ask him if you can send by means of one of our men the shears which he promised to sell me. And please, brother Virilis, do send my greetings to sister Thuttena and to Velbuteius. Write back how he is doing (?). I hope all is well with you. Farewell.

[*exterior*] Written in London. To Veldedeius the governor's groom, from his brother Chrauttius.

We have no external evidence regarding any of these individuals, but on the most straightforward reading of the letter Chrauttius and Veldedeius are brothers, Thuttena is their sister, Velbuteius their brother as well, and Chrauttius is chiding Veldedeius for not having sent news of their parents. But another reading of the terms *frater*, *soror*, and even *parentes* has also been proposed. In their edition of the Vindolanda documents, Bowman and Thomas suggest that Chrauttius and Veldedeius are not literally brothers but fellow-soldiers and comrades; that Thuttena is a common friend, as is the veterinarian Virilis; and that *parentes nostri* are "our elders."[112] In support of the metaphorical reading of the kinship vocabulary, Bowman and Thomas claim that Chrauttius would not have called his brother *antiquus contubernalis* and that one of the two men's names seems to be Celtic but the other Germanic; and Chrauttius' first reference to Virilis as *veterinarius* seems odd if he were his and Veldedeius' brother. On the other hand, there is no obvious reason why two brothers who

___

to which a man might adopt his partner in a sexual and conjugal union; see Shaw 1997 for arguments to the contrary.

[112] Bowman and Thomas 1990 (whose text I give above); see pp. 36–37 for the name of the addressee (*Veldeius* seems to be a syncopated form of the full name *Veldedeius*).

had served in the army together might not also call each other *contuber-nales*,[113] and our knowledge of linguistic usage and onomastic practice on the fringes of the Latin-speaking world is so tenuous as to urge agnosticism. In view of the inherent flexibility of this language, moreover, it is just possible that the kinship terms are being used *both* literally *and* not. For example, Chrauttius and Veldedeius might indeed be brothers, the *parentes* their parents, but the veterinarian Virilis a shared friend, whom Chrauttius addresses as *frater*; and Thuttena might be the sister not of Chrauttius and/or Veldedeius but of Virilis.

Complications of another kind arise when we consider potential overlaps between brotherly and sisterly love on the one hand, the erotic on the other. As Maurizio Bettini has suggested, the imagery and language of sibling love provided an irresistibly appealing model for describing those couples who were joined by eros but not by the institution of marriage precisely as a *pair*, even as the concept of incest placed its stamp of horror on sexual relations between siblings.[114] The resulting tensions are perceptible in a number of texts, perhaps most memorably Ovid's narrative of Byblis, wittily and self-consciously drawing attention to its own language in a way characteristic of this poet (*Metamorphoses* 9.450–665). Byblis desires her twin brother Caunus "not as a sister should her brother" (455–456: *correpta cupidine fratris / non soror ut fratrem, nec qua debebat, amavit*); in the throes of her passion, she avoids calling him *frater* and instead addresses him as *domine*, making it clear that she would prefer that he call her simply *Byblis* rather than *soror* (466–467). When she writes him a letter, she first identifies herself as *soror* but then erases the word, replacing it with *amans* (528–531). She reminds Caunus that she has occasionally given him kisses which, whether he noticed it or not, could be interpreted "not as sisterly ones" (539: *non … sororia*) and desperately points out that, if he accedes to her wishes, they can use the "name of brother" as a cover for their affection (558: *dulcia fraterno sub nomine furta tegemus*). Handing the letter to a slave, she hesitates before using that charged word: "Take this to my … brother" (569–570: "*fer has, fidissime, nostro –*" / *dixit, et adiecit longo post tempore* "*fratri*".). The

---

[113] As a general principle, in inscriptions commemorating soldiers, "*fratres* with different *nomina* may be unrelated comrades" (Phang 2001, p. 162). For the terms *contubernalis, commanipularis*, and *commilito* in soldiers' inscriptions, see Lendon 2006.

[114] Bettini 1992, p. 122. Surveying the theme of brother–sister love in Western literature in the "Postface" to *Anna soror*, Marguerite Yourcenar describes a scene between the sibling lovers Giovanni and Annabella in John Ford's '*Tis pity she's a whore* ("You are my brother, Giovanni. – And you are my sister, Annabella") as "l'une des plus belles scènes d'amour du théâtre" (Yourcenar 1981, p. 98).

recurring emphasis on the words *frater* and *soror* is not only characteristic of Ovidian poetics, with its fine awareness of the power of language, but suggests that for many of Ovid's readers a relationship between a man and a woman described as brother and sister ideally did not belong to the realm of Venus, bodies, and tongue-kisses.[115]

Yet matters are not quite so clear-cut. For one thing, the language and imagery of sibling love, like those of *amor* and *amicitia*, could be associated with a range of experience which could include the erotic. In Hyginus' catalogue of men joined in friendship (Hyg. *Fab.* 257, *qui amicitia iunctissimi fuerunt*) we find, in addition to the usual suspects (Orestes and Pylades, Theseus and Pirithous, Achilles and Patroclus) the Athenian pair Harmodius and Aristogiton, who are identified as joined in friendship "like brothers" (*Harmodius et Aristogiton more fraterno*). The erotic penumbra associated with Achilles and Patroclus discussed above is here especially relevant, for there was a long tradition of describing Harmodius and Aristogiton too as a pair of lovers on the Athenian pederastic model, joined by *eros*.[116] In another, more widespread overlap we find the concept of *unanimitas* or "one-mindedness" periodically invoked in idealizing descriptions of friends, lovers, spouses – and brothers and sisters.[117] The same is true of a motif to which we will return in Chapter 4, which I call the *union in death*. To Valerius Maximus' gory narrative of Volumnius meeting his death as he clutches his friend's severed head to his breast (4.7.4, above, p. 152) we might compare his narrative of Marcus Plautius, who killed himself on top of his wife's body as it lay on the pyre (in a vivid enactment of the intersection of various ideals, the two were then

---

[115] Discussions of Byblis and Caunus include Janan 1991 and Raval 2001, the latter attentive to the role of language in Ovid's narrative but saying little about the words *frater* and *soror* themselves. Ovid contrasts the kisses that a sister gives her brother with those exchanged between a man and his *amica*: In the latter there are tongues (Ov. *Am.* 2.5.23–26: *inproba tum vero iungentes oscula vidi– / illa mihi lingua nexa fuisse liquet– / qualia non fratri tulerit germana severo, / sed tulerit cupido mollis amica viro*).

[116] Thuc. 6.56–59, Aeschin. 1.133–134. To be sure, Thucydides observes that not everyone sees them this way and, for his part, Cicero cites the pair among examples of glorious deaths, but says nothing about the nature of their relationship (Cic. *Tusc.* 1.116). But many readers, ancient and modern, perceive a continuum from Achilles and Patroclus through to Harmodius and Aristogiton.

[117] For *unanimitas* and siblings, see Domitius Marsus' epigram quoted below, as well as Pac. *Trag.* 109, Liv. 40.8.14, Verg. *Aen.* 4.8, 7.335, Stat. *Theb.* 8.668–669; for *unanimitas* and friends, see Plaut. *Stich.* 731 (with a twist, since the two friends love the same woman: *ego tu sum, tu es ego, unianimi sumus, / unam amicam amamus ambo*), Catull. 30.1 (*unanimis false sodalibus*); for lovers and spouses, see Catull. 66.80–81, *CIL* 6.31711 (*Celsino nupta univira unanimis*), 10.7643, 14.1364. That the ideal of *unanimitas* could be applied to yet other interpersonal relations is shown by the epitaph for grandmother and granddaughter which invokes Nisus and Euryalus discussed above (*CIL* 11.4978).

cremated together by Plautius' *amici*; 4.6.3), but also his narrative of a soldier who unwittingly killed his own brother, and upon discovering the fact stabbed himself on his brother's pyre with the sword he had used to kill him, and so met his end on his brother's breast (5.5.4). The related motif of the *contest of death*, whereby one partner hopes or even rejoices to die before the other, informs narratives not only of Orestes and Pylades and other male friends, not only married couples in verse epitaphs and exemplary stories, but also a pair of brothers in Martial's epigrams, and an epigram by Martial on two brothers in turn may have inspired the poet of an epitaph on husband and wife.[118]

The motif of the contest of death appears in Encolpius' narrative of his stormy but lasting relationship with Giton in Petronius' *Satyricon*, a text which exploits the erotic potential of sibling love which Ovid's *Metamorphoses* so emphatically rejects even as it hints at it. Not only is the relationship between Encolpius and Giton, so unmistakably anchored in bodies and the bed, described with the language of *amor* and *amicitia* (see Chapter 3, pp. 214–218), but it is represented as an instance of brother-love. Imagery suggestive of fraternal love periodically recurs, but more strikingly still, the very word *frater*, in the mouths not only of Encolpius as he narrates his adventures but of other characters as well, denotes a sexual partner and invites being translated "boyfriend" or "lover." Of the triangle consisting of Encolpius, Giton, and Ascyltos, each party is the actual or potential *frater* of each of the others, and the language is not limited to men. In one episode Circe proposes configuring herself in yet another triangle: "To be sure," she slyly asks Encolpius, "you have a brother – I was not ashamed to make my inquiries – but what is to stop you from adopting a sister as well?" While it is just possible that Circe's use of the noun *soror* is a witty coinage on analogy to *frater*, and it could be argued that the humor of her remark is partially fueled by her use of an uncommon or less familiar expression, on balance it is more likely that she is not inventing the usage but following established usage patterns which are symmetrical for gender, just as both *mater* and *pater* are attested as respectful terms of address to older people both before and after Petronius.[119]

---

[118] Male friends: Val. Max. 4.7.2, 4.7.6, 4.7.ext.1; Mart. 1.93, 6.18 (with an echo of Hor. *Carm.* 2.17 on Horace and Maecenas); husband and wife: Val. Max. 4.6.1, *CLE* 467, 995, 1034, 1487, 1551c (perhaps echoing Mart. 1.36.6); for the brothers Lucanus and Tullus see Mart. 1.36, 3.20, 5.28, 9.51 and Plin. *Ep.* 8.18. Compare Mart. 1.36.6 (*vive tuo, frater, tempore, vive meo*) with *CIL* 10.7565 = *CLE* 1551C, v. 4 (*"tempore tu" dixit "vive, Philippe, m[e]o"*). The motif is especially common in epitaphs commissioned by parents for their children (Citroni ad Mart. 1.114.4).

[119] Giton and Encolpius and the contest of death: Petron. *Sat.* 94.10; Giton and Encolpius as *fratres*: 9.2, 24.6, 91.2, 97.9, 127.2,3,7 (cf. 79.9); Encolpius and Ascyltos as *fratres*: 9.4, 10.6, 11.3,

This way of using the words *soror* and *frater* is probably not Petronius' own exuberant coinage. There is a self-evident familiarity in the terms' usage throughout his text. Petronius, the "hidden author" who gives life and language to Encolpius, seems to be drawing on a usage familiar to his readership, or at least part of it. A more difficult question is whether this was a usage with a long history, or rather a fairly recent turn of linguistic events, perhaps even fashionably contemporary slang. The narrative of Byblis and Caunus in Ovid's *Metamorphoses*, written only half a century earlier, appeals not only to a conceptualization of brothers and sisters as normatively not being joined by erotic passion but to the very word *frater* as excluding the sexual – when used, that is, precisely by his sister. That the words *frater* and *soror* might indeed mean something like English "lover" may go unnoticed here not because the possibility did not exist in Ovid's day, but precisely because these are the words of a sister caught in her forbidden desire. While it is just possible that the use of *frater* and *soror* we find in Petronius was a recent pattern, one which had taken hold over the few decades separating him from Ovid, a longer and deeper history seems more likely.

So much is suggested by the overlaps in imagery for brotherly and sisterly love, conjugal love, *amor*, and *amicitia* we have seen above, conceptual and linguistic habits which find parallels in other cultural spheres, for example in ancient Egypt.[120] But there are hints at an erotic charge in the very *language* of brothers and sisters elsewhere in the Latin textual tradition too. As early as Plautus' comedies, we find a scene in which a young couple having a fight hurl at each other the terms – usually of endearment – "sister" and "brother" (and even "mother"); Propertius offers to be the "brother and son" that Cynthia does not have; the speaker in a poem by Lygdamus pathetically contrasts the role he currently plays with a woman and what he so desperately desires (they are now *frater* and *soror*, but he hopes one day they will be *coniuges*); and Seneca's Phaedra, suffering from her passion for her stepson Hippolytus, begs him not to

---

13.2; Giton forced to choose either Encolpius or Ascyltos as his *frater*: 80.6; Circe's proposal: 127 (*si non fastidis, inquit, feminam ornatam et hoc primum anno virum expertam, concilio tibi, o iuvenis, sororem. habes tu quidem et fratrem — neque enim me piguit inquirere — sed quid prohibet et sororem adoptare?*) That the terms "brother" and "sister" are used of both same-sex and opposite-sex pairs is one of several arguments against seeing *frater* as slang characteristic of a putative gay subculture (see Williams 2010, pp. 239–245). For *mater* and *pater* see Petron. *Sat.* 7, 98, 100, with Dickey 2002 s.v.

[120] For the Egyptian material see Simpson *et al.* 1973, pp. 205–209, Herman 1959, pp. 75–78, McDowell 1999, pp. 28–32, 152–157.

call her "mother" but rather "sister" or, even better, "slave."[121] Tellingly enough, Martial writes of a mother and her son who call each other *frater* and *soror*, asking why they use these "naughty names (*nomina nequiora*)" and portentously concluding with a barely concealed imputation of incest: "A mother who wants to be a 'sister' takes pleasure in being neither a mother nor a sister."[122]

Read this way, a reference to brothers and sisters in Cicero's speech in defense of Caelius takes on an even sharper point than is usually perceived. Even if the argument that the words *frater* and *soror* could be exploited in this way in Cicero's day is not accepted, his language clearly plays with the overlap between fraternal love and *amicitia*.

quod quidem facerem vehementius, nisi intercederent mihi *inimicitiae* cum istius mulieris viro – *fratrem* volui dicere; semper hic erro. nunc agam modice nec longius progrediar quam me mea fides et causa ipsa coget. neque enim muliebres umquam *inimicitias* mihi gerendas putavi, praesertim cum ea quam omnes semper *amicam* omnium potius quam cuiusquam *inimicam* putaverunt. (Cic. *Cael.* 32)

I would do this [sc., defend his client Caelius] even more vigorously were it not for my enmity with this woman's husband – I meant to say "brother"; I always make that mistake. Instead, I will proceed moderately and will go no further than my role as advocate and the case itself require. After all, I never thought I would have to become involved in enmities with women, least of all with one whom everyone has always thought to be everyone's *amica* but no one's enemy.

The complementary pairs are interwoven with malicious eloquence: *frater* and *soror*, *vir* and *mulier*, *amicitia* and *inimicitia*. Clodia and Clodius are themselves cast in the roles of *vir* and *mulier*, a shocking enough configuration for brother and sister, that much more shocking if *frater* and *soror* can have another sense as well. When Cicero soon thereafter imagines Clodia's glorious ancestor Appius Claudius Caecus reproaching her for taking not the virtues of her ancestors but the vices

---

[121] Plaut. *Cist.* 451–452: ALC. *germana mea sororcula!* SEL. *repudio te fraterculum!* / ALC. *tum tu igitur mea matercula!* SEL. *repudio te fraterculum!*; Prop. 2.18.33–34: *cum tibi nec frater nec sit tibi filius ullus,* / *frater ego et tibi sim filius unus ego*; [Tib.] 3.1.23–27: *haec tibi vir quondam, nunc frater, casta Neaera,* / *mittit et accipias munera parva rogat,* / *teque suis iurat caram magis esse medullis,* / *sive sibi coniunx sive futura soror;* / *sed potius coniunx* (Navarro Antolín 1996 ad loc. glosses *frater* as *amator* and *soror* as *concubina* or *amasia*; Lygdamus' date is debated, but he may well have been a younger contemporary of Ovid); Sen. *Phaedra* 609–612: *matris superbum est nomen et nimium potens:* / *nostros humilius nomen affectus decet;* / *me vel sororem, Hippolyte, vel famulam voca,* / *famulamque potius.*

[122] Mart. 2.4.4: *cur vos nomina nequiora tangunt?* 7–8: *matrem quae cupit esse se sororem,* / *nec matrem iuvat esse nec sororem.* In another epigram Martial strikes back at the effeminate Charmenion: "Stop calling me 'brother' or I'll call you 'sister'!" (Mart. 10.65.14–15: *quare desine me vocare fratrem,* / *ne te, Charmenion, vocem sororem*).

of her brother as a model (*fraterna vitia*), the phrase suggests not only the vices of Clodius himself but their shared vices as *frater* and *soror* – and if the terms have more sense than one, the polyvalence is again sharply pointed. One can only imagine the reactions among Cicero's audience as he then draws a portrait of the young Clodius, afraid of the dark and climbing into bed with his big sister, whom he loves *so* much.[123]

In Catullus' poetry, too, brotherly love stands at the nexus between *amicitia* and *amor* across the entire range of their meanings. His stirring poetic reflections on his brother's death (65, 68, 101) have long attracted readerly attention, and Catullus' brother has been called his "supreme friend."[124] Another poem, in quite another key, is suggestively placed in the collection immediately before one of the poems on Catullus' own brother (see the following chapter for further discussion of juxtaposed poems). Here we find a brother and sister, two men, and Catullus himself in a network of *amor* and *amicitia*; here, too, if *frater* and *soror* can also signify sexual partners, the language is that much more polyvalent.

> Caelius Aufillenum et Quintius Aufillenam
>   flos Veronensum depereunt iuvenum,
> hic *fratrem*, ille *sororem*. hoc est, quod dicitur, illud
>   *fraternum* vere dulce *sodalicium*.
> cui faveam potius? Caeli, tibi: nam tua nobis
>   perspecta ex igni est unica *amicitia*,
> cum vesana meas torreret flamma medullas.
>   sis felix, Caeli, sis in *amore* potens.
>
> (Catull. 100)

> Caelius has fallen for Aufillenus, Quintius for Aufillena:
>   the upper crust of young Verona.
> One for the brother, one for the sister:
>   talk about sweet brotherly comradeship!
> Whom shall I root for? You, Caelius. Your friendship
>   with me and yours alone withstood the test of fire,
> when a flame of insanity roasted my guts.
>   Happiness and success to you, Caelius, in love.

Caelius and Quintius are united in their desire to make a brother–sister pair – in Latin, a pair of *fratres* – their own *fratres* in another sense; and

---

[123] Cic. *Cael.* 34: *cur te fraterna vitia potius quam bona paterna et avita et usque a nobis cum in viris tum etiam in feminis repetita moverunt?*; 36: *minimum fratrem … qui te amat plurimum, qui propter nescio quam, credo, timiditatem et nocturnos quosdam inanes metus tecum semper pusio cum maiore sorore cubitavit. eum putato tecum loqui: "quid tumultuaris, soror? quid insanis?"*; cf. 78: *ne eadem mulier cum suo coniuge et fratre et turpissimum latronem eripuisse et honestissimum adulescentem oppressisse videatur.*
[124] Newman 1990, p. 318; see further Fitzgerald 1995, pp. 185–211.

since the two young men are joined by the bond of friendship (*sodali-cium*) it is no great leap to imagine them calling each other *fratres* themselves. Caelius had earlier demonstrated the solidity of his *amicitia* with Catullus by supporting the poet when he was suffering the flames of passion; Catullus now wishes him success in *amor* – with Aufillenus, *frater* of Aufillena and, if things go well, one day of Caelius too. *Fraternum ... dulce sodalicium* indeed![125]

One of the few surviving epigrams of the Augustan poet Domitius Marsus – supported by Maecenas like Virgil, Horace, and Propertius and an important model generations later for Martial – uses the language of brotherhood to sharpen its gossipy point.

> omnia cum Bavio communia frater habebat,
> unanimi fratres sicut habere solent,
> rura domum nummos atque omnia; denique, ut aiunt,
> corporibus geminis spiritus unus erat.
> sed postquam alterius mulier concumbere <fratri>
> non vult, deposuit alter amicitiam.
> omnia tunc ira, tunc omnia lite soluta,
> <et> nova regna duos accipiunt <dominos>.
> (Domitius Marsus fr. 147 Hollis)[126]

Bavius' brother shared everything with him,
just as like-minded brothers usually do:
a country estate, a city home, money, everything.
As the saying goes, in short, there was one spirit in two bodies.
But after one man's wife refused to sleep with his brother,
the other broke off the friendship.
Then it was all dissolved in anger, a court case too;
there are new kingdoms now, with two lords.

Bavius and his brother live out ideals of *amicitia* – they share everything, including a home; they are joined in *unanimitas*; they are one soul in two bodies – until the scurrilous turn of events changes everything. Although

---

[125] For the plural *fratres* denoting a brother and sister pair, see *CLE* 1355 (Rome: *haec tenet urna duos sexu sed dispare fratres*). The implications of Catullus' phrase *fraternum sodalicium* have been brought out variously. Ellis 1889 ad v. 3 writes that Caelius and Quintius "are *fratres sodales* because they attach themselves to a brother and sister, but it is probable that the notion of brotherhood of profligacy is included," and he raises the further possibility that they were cousins (*fratres patrueles*). Kroll 1989 emphasizes the fact that Caelius and Quintius are in love with siblings ("daß sie sich wie Brüder lieben, zeigt sich in diesem Falle darin, daß sie in Geschwister verliebt sind"). Quinn 1973 ad v. 4 uses the language of grammar to explain the polyvalence: "The joke lies in applying a popular saying in which *fraternum* = the subjective genitive *fratrum* to a situation in which *fraternum* has to stand for the objective genitive *fratrum*." For Newman 1990, p. 319, this poem "shows how impossible it is to separate ordinary friendship from sex." See further Forsyth 1977, Arkins 1982.

[126] For Domitius Marsus and his poetry see Fogazza 1981, Hollis 2007, pp. 300–313.

the precise wording of the third couplet is debatable, it is usually understood as communicating a scenario in which one of the two men sought to apply the grand ideal of sharing everything to the other man's wife; his overture was refused, whereupon the dramatic rupture (*deposuit ... amicitiam*), apparently complete with a legal quarrel over the previously shared property. Another reading, even more scandalous, sees Bavius and his brother as sharing a sexual relationship with each other, *fratres* not only in the biological sense but also in the way Petronius' Encolpius, Giton, and Ascyltos are "brothers" – until one of them slept with a woman, precipitating the rupture.[127] However one reconstructs the sexual gossipmongering in this poem, it is making use of a number of common motifs. Not only might brothers, like friends, be "one soul in two bodies," but they were just as proverbially inclined to strife; and the piquant possibility of extending the friendly-fraternal ideal of sharing to the bedroom appears in a few other Latin texts. Among the many scandalous accusations Cicero makes of Verres is the implication that when he spent a night at the home of a certain Dorotheos, the two men indeed "shared everything," including Dorotheos' wife Callidama; and, anything but scandalized in tone, there is Aulus Allius' epitaph for his beloved Potestas, who held two young *amantes* together, making of them a latter-day Pylades and Orestes configured in a triangle with herself until her lamented death (*CIL* 6.37965).[128] On the other hand, as we will see in the next chapter,

---

[127] See Pangallo 1976 (proposing *sed postquam alterius mulier <vix> concubitum <unum> / novit, deposuit alter amicitiam*, construing *alterius* not with *mulier* but with *concubitum*, and reading an accusation of incest), followed by Fogazza 1981, pp. 29–30, 49–52, and Mencacci 1996, p. 103 n. 114. Neither Courtney 2003, pp. 300–302 (printing *sed postquam alterius <sibi> concubitum <ire>* in v. 5) nor Hollis 2007, pp. 300–308 (text as printed above) consider the possibility that an incestuous relationship is being insinuated. Hollis understands *both* brothers to have wives and thus sees a potential "ménage à quatre"; this is not impossible, but the phrase *alterius mulier* need not imply that both men had wives, and in any case the poem focuses on one woman alone. Hollis translates *lite* in the final couplet as "court-case"; Pangallo 1976 and Fogazza 1981 read *omnia tunc ira, tunc omnia desolata*.

[128] For brothers, like friends, sharing a soul cf. Quint. *Decl.* 321.8 (*quid est aliud fraternitas quam divisus spiritus?*) and for brothers sharing a home, property, and slaves, see Plut., *De frat. amor.* 481d–e. For the theme of *discordia fratrum* see Ov. *Met.* 1.60, Tac. *Ann.* 13.17.2, 4.60.5. For Verres, Dorotheos, and Callidama see Cic. *Verr.* 2.89 (*una nox intercesserat cum iste Dorotheum sic diligebat ut diceres omnia inter eos esse communia, Agathinum* [Callidama's father] *ita observabat ut aliquem adfinem atque propinquum*). The motif of friends who share everything, even wives (though presumably without the implications drawn by Domitius Marsus) informs Montaigne's reflections on *amitié*: "Everything is genuinely common to them both: their wills, goods, wives, children, honour and lives; their correspondence is that of one soul in bodies twain" (Screech 2004, p. 13). See Bray 2003, pp. 172–174, for a tale from the sixteenth-century William Painter's *Palace of Pleasure* about two friends who "not only seemed to be two brethren, but also they appeared in all semblances to be but one man" – until one of them married.

Propertius cuts off the possibility of such sharing by drawing a line in front of the bed (Prop. 2.34.15–17).

Read this way, the epigram is sharply, even venomously pointed enough, living up to the title of the collection in which it was published: *Cicuta*, "Hemlock." But for some readers, past and present, possessing certain information, there is more to it. One piece of information is that a poet named Marcus Bavius was a critic of Virgil and object, together with a certain Mevius, of a passing swipe by Virgil himself. Read with this knowledge, Domitius' epigram is not only indulging in titillating gossip but making its own contribution to an ongoing literary controversy – and perhaps a political one as well, if, as has been suggested, Bavius was a supporter of Antony as Marsus apparently was of Octavian, later Augustus.[129] For some readers there is yet more to this poem. It is preserved for us by Junius Philargyrius in his commentary on Virgil, written in the fifth century or later; Philargyrius understands the other man in Domitius' poem to be none other than Mevius. Nothing in the poem's words prevents such a reading, but if we do read the epigram this way, we must ask in what sense Bavius and Mevius are being called *fratres*. Their names, both of them *gentilicia* or family names, suggest that they are sons of different fathers, and indeed most scholars from Servius and Philargyrius onward have not described the two Virgilian critics as brothers.[130] It would seem, then, that the most plausible reading of Mevius in Domitius' epigram will take the word *frater* to be referring to a bond that is not biological and perhaps, as we have seen, like that joining Encolpius to Giton and Ascyltos. The tendency among modern scholarly readings, albeit not universal, is to disbelieve Philargyrius or else to emend his text so that Mevius is not part of the picture, and in any case to take Domitius' epigram to be telling tales about Bavius and his biological brother.[131]

---

[129] Verg. *Ecl.* 3.90–91: *qui Bavium non odit, amet tua carmina, Mevi, / atque idem iungat vulpes et mulgeat hircos*. This Mevius is generally but not universally understood to be the man by the same name who is attacked in Horace's tenth *Epode*. That Bavius was a supporter of Antony's is suggested by Pangallo 1976 and Fogazza 1981, following up on an earlier suggestion of Rostagni.

[130] Cf. Serv. ad Verg. *Ecl.* 3.90: *nam Maevius et Bavius pessimi fuerunt poetae, inimici tam Horatio quam Vergilio*; Philarg. ad Verg. *Ecl.* 3.90: *duos poetas temporis sui dicit pessimos … ex quibus Bavius curator fuit; de quibus Domitius in Cicuta refert*. One exception is Peter Schmidt's entry on Mevius in *Der neue Pauly*: citing Domitius' epigram, Schmidt identifies him as "*Bruder des Bavius*, mit dem er sich einer Frau wegen zerstritten haben soll" (emphasis added). Courtney's entry on Bavius in the same work makes no mention of Mevius at all.

[131] Courtney 2003, p. 301, speaks of "Bavius A" and "Bavius B," Byrne 2004 of "the two Bavii," and Hollis 2007, p. 207, of "the Bavius brothers." None of these readings mention the name of Mevius, and both Courtney and Hollis raise the possibility that Philargyrius (see previous note) wrote *de quo* rather than *de quibus*. See Fogazza 1981, pp. 49–50, for a brief overview of readings of the poem which take Bavius' *frater* to be Mevius.

The questions about reading practice raised by this poem are not unlike those raised by the figure named "Licymnia" in Horace's *Odes* 2.12 (see below, p. 193). Many readers have taken her to be Maecenas' wife Terentia, even though neither of the latter two names appears in Horace's poem. Reading Terentia in the ode adds, of course, layers of meaning to an already complex poem; yet the poem can also be read without Terentia or Maecenas and still be richly meaningful and in the end, as Gordon Williams reminds us, "the solution of such a historical riddle is not essential to appreciation."[132] Likewise in the case of Domitius' epigram, readers who have no knowledge of who Bavius is, or have never heard the name Mevius, will find more than enough in the text to construct and enjoy meaning. But even for readers who know or suspect more about the two men, the poem's primary effect derives from the naughty blurring of brotherhood, friendship, and sex given expression through the rapid accumulation of key terms: *frater* and *amicitia, omnia communia, unanimi,* and *spiritus unus* juxtaposed with *corporibus,* and of course *concumbere,* with which the turning point comes.

The linguistic and conceptual overlaps among *amor* and *amicitia, fratres* and *sorores,* have some implications that have only rarely been pursued.[133] On the one hand, as we have seen, there is the culturally sanctioned impulse to sharply distinguish the love of biological siblings from *amor* in the sense of *eros.* Cicero's insinuations about Clodius and Clodia and Ovid's juicy narrative of the mythic pair Byblis and Caunus remind us that sexual relations between brother and sister were liable to censure as incestuous by traditional Roman standards. On the other hand, the very fact that, in some speech genres at least, Latin-speaking lovers could and at some point in the history of the language did refer to each other as *frater* and *soror* complicates the picture. Both Cicero's nasty eloquence as he imagines Clodius addressing Clodia as *soror* and Martial's epigrammatic point about mother and son who call each other with the "naughty names" *frater* and *soror* play with these lurking tensions. A scene from Petronius' *Satyricon* does so in a slightly different way. Encolpius tells of how, with a young man at his side, he watched the young man's sister having sex with Eumolpus. Stimulated by what he sees his *soror* doing, this *frater* shows himself more than willing to let his fellow voyeur

---

Encolpius have his way with him, thereby teasing with the role of *frater* in yet another way.[134]

The concept of incest can lay down boundaries: "He loves her like a sister." In the case of homoerotic desire, invocation of the paradigm of fraternal love can serve an additional policing function in cultural contexts in which the impulse to demarcate and deny the homoerotic is particularly strong: "No, it wasn't like *that* – they loved each other like brothers."[135] But in a cultural environment such as that which we find in the Latin textual tradition, where sexual practices between men are a freely available option (subject, of course, like all sexual practices, to various protocols) and sexual desire between males is simply taken for granted, neither questioned nor stigmatized but assumed to be a part of human and animal nature, there is no pressing need to hermetically seal off the erotic from the affectionate or friendly in images of male intimacy, or even to offer consistent and unmistakable definitions of what constitutes the one and what the other. Anxieties around physical intimacy and desire between males, and accompanying impulses to deny or erase, do not form a part of the cultural landscape visible to us in the Latin textual tradition. Furthermore, as will emerge from the discussion of Petronius' *Satyricon* in the next chapter, the language and imagery of fraternal love might have a positive, productive function in the representation of intimate relationships among men in the Latin textual tradition. Most of the labels and categories available for describing sexually bonded couples inevitably cast one of the two partners in a feminized role, in bodily terms in the role of the penetrated. But, suggestively like *amicus*, the label *frater* offered a way of representing intimate relations between males in such a way as both to represent a relationship as meaningful and affectionate, valuable to participants and respected by others, and to sidestep questions of gendered and penetrative hierarchy.[136]

---

[134] Cic. *Cael.* 36; Mart. 2.4; Petron. *Sat.* 140.11: *dum frater sororis suae automata per clostellum miratur, accessi temptaturus an pateretur iniuriam. nec se reiciebat a blanditiis doctissimus puer, sed me numen inimicum ibi quoque invenit.*

[135] Cf. Shakespeare, *Cymbeline* III.vi.70–71 (Arviragus to Guiderius on their sister Imogen, disguised as a young man): "I'll make't my comfort / he is a man. I'll love him as my brother"). Epstein 2006, p. 57, describes Patroclus as Achilles' "brother-in-law and beloved friend"; the former is by no means the first relational label that has come to most readers' minds over the millennia. In a comparable swerve away from the erotic (and from the Greek and Latin textual tradition), Brad Pitt's Achilles in the film *Troy* motivates his fierce wrath with the cry: "He killed my cousin!"

[136] My perspective is thus directly opposite to that of Bannon 1997, p. 80: "In a society where intimacy between men could raise eyebrows, fraternal intimacy was a safe alternative, a positive paradigm for men's love for each other."

Figure 6 "The Sarcophagus of the Two Brothers"

I end by looking beyond the artificial boundary I have set for myself by excluding explicitly Christian material from this study. A sarcophagus with scenes from the Bible, datable to the first half of the fourth century AD, found in the necropolis of Lucina near S. Paolo fuori le Mura in Rome and now in the Vatican's Museo Pio Cristiano, depicts two bearded men in the central shell, in a pose normally reserved for husband and wife (Figure 6). The commemorative configuration is puzzling, even startling, in itself. But the name traditionally given to this sarcophagus and propagated by means of the museum label is all the more intriguing: "The Sarcophagus of the Two Brothers."[137] Since no accompanying inscription naming the two men or identifying their relationship seems to have survived, it would appear that at some point in the history of this sarcophagus the label "brothers" was applied by some of its viewers who, as they responded to the image of two men commemorated together in this way, reached for the most readily available paradigm. And it is by no means

---

[137] Museo Pio Cristiano inv. 31543 (*sarcofago detto "dei due fratelli"*). For husband and wife in the same pose, see among others inv. 31427 (*sarcofago detto "dei due testamenti"*). Readings of potentially ambiguous male pairs readily appeal to brother love. An Augustan-era statuary group of two young men with their arms around each other (Madrid, Prado 28.E), usually taken to be representing Orestes and Pylades, is understood by some to be the mythic brothers Castor and Pollux or Sleep and Death: see *LIMC* 7.1 (1994): 602. An Egyptian tomb for two men, Nianchchnum and Chnumhotep, is variously interpreted as housing friends, a sexually bonded pair, or brothers: see Schukraft 2007, pp. 319–322.

unlikely that these two men called each other *frater* in their lifetimes. But if so, in what sense of the word? We will see in Chapter 4 that Roman commemorative practice over the centuries preceding the dedication of this sarcophagus included double burials of men who were liable to being identified as *fratres*, whether pairs of brothers or pairs of friends. As we consider the Vatican sarcophagus and its museum label, some questions suggest themselves. Were these two men in fact biological brothers? Or were they *fratres* like Martial and Toranius, Chrauttius and Veldedeius of Vindolanda, or even Encolpius and Ascyltos? Does the Christian practice of calling fellow believers *adelphoi* or *fratres* somehow lie behind this label? Whoever these two men were, the label "brothers" has stuck; not only, I would suggest, because it appeals to a prestigious paradigm for male relationships but also because, by hinting at a range of possibilities, it effectively occludes further questions.

CHAPTER 3

Love and friendship: authors and texts

The preceding chapters have considered some of the major themes in Roman friendship as we read it on the pages and stones of the Latin textual tradition: the difficulties of definition, the variety in configurations of gender, the role of triangles, the concept of the homosocial, the intertwining of *amor* and *amicitia*, the resonances of brother-love. In this chapter, attentive to the characteristic preoccupations and themes of certain genres of Latin literature and to the specificity of individual authorial voice, I offer readings of *amor* and *amicitia* in a representative selection of authors. I begin with four poets of the first century BC (Catullus, Horace, Virgil, and Propertius); then consider Petronius' *Satyricon*, a massively creative prose narrative interspersed with poetry in the tradition of Menippean satire, unique in the surviving Latin textual tradition; and finally turn to two examples of the speech genre of private letters, the correspondence of Cicero and Fronto. This is only a selection, meant to illustrate some of the texts in which the thematics of *amor* and *amicitia* are particularly prominent. There are of course many others which appear scattered through this study but which invite being read continuously for their performance of Roman friendship. Obvious examples include Horace's first books of *Epistles* and *Satires*, Ovid's exile poetry, Martial's epigrams, Statius' *Silvae*, and the letters of Pliny the Younger.[1]

CATULLUS

Catullus' poetry is renowned for its play with the complexities of *amor* and *amicitia* across its characteristic range in theme and tone.[2] One poem

---

[1] For *amicitia* in Ovid's exile poetry, Williams 1994 (especially pp. 100–153) and Citroni Marchetti 2000 (especially pp. 295–368); in Martial's epigrams and Statius' *Silvae*, White 1975, Kleijwegt 1998, Nauta 2002, Spisak 2007, pp. 35–52, Augoustakis and Newlands 2007; in Pliny's letters, Bütler 1970, pp. 94–106, Méthy 2007, pp. 255–262.

[2] Relevant discussions of Catullus' poetry include Reitzenstein 1912, pp. 15–36 (influential pages), Lyne 1980, pp. 19–61, Newman 1990, 318–342, Fitzgerald 1995, pp. 114–139, Gibson 1995, Oliensis 1997, Greene 1998, Wray 2001.

uses the asymmetrical language of female *amicae* and male *amici* as it participates in the tradition of invective against women:

> Ameana *puella defututa*
> tota milia me decem poposcit,
> ista turpiculo *puella* naso,
> decoctoris *amica* Formiani.
> propinqui, quibus est *puella* curae,
> *amicos* medicosque convocate:
> non est sana *puella*, nec rogare
> qualis sit solet aes imaginosum.
> (Catull. 41)

Ameana, that fucked-out girl,
asked me for ten whole thousand!
That girl with the ugly little nose,
amica of the bankrupt guy from Formiae.
Note to her relatives: you'd better summon friends (*amici*) and doctors!
The girl is not well. Clearly she doesn't ask
the mirror how she looks.

On the one hand, as the obscene *defututa* of the opening line and the repeated use of *puella* vividly make clear, Ameana is the sexual partner of Caesar's associate Mamurra, the "bankrupt guy from Formiae" elsewhere given the unflattering nickname Mentula ("Prick"), and this is hardly her first experience. She is, to use a Ciceronian hyperbole, *amica omnium* (Cic. *Cael.* 32). On the other hand, in the midst of this scene we find her male relatives (*propinqui*) being urged to seek advice not only from doctors but from their male friends (*amici*) in their attempt to cure her of her insane self-delusion.[3]

Even more than for its personal and political invective, Catullus' poetry is known for its meditations on a relationship with a married woman it calls Lesbia, memorably invoked in a number of poems with the mingled language of *amicitia* and *amor*.

> Dicebas quondam solum te nosse Catullum,
> Lesbia, nec prae me velle tenere Iovem.
> dilexi tum te non tantum ut vulgus *amicam*,
> sed pater ut gnatos diligit et generos.
> nunc te cognovi: quare etsi impensius uror,
> multo mi tamen es vilior et levior.

---

[3] For Mamurra/Mentula see Catull. 29, 41, 43, 57, 94, 105, 114, 115. For the traditional role of *amici* as givers of advice see, e.g., Cic. *Rosc. Am.* 27 and Val. Max. 5.8.2.

qui potis est, inquis? quod *amantem* iniuria talis
cogit *amare* magis, sed *bene velle* minus.

(Catull. 72)

You used to say that you knew only Catullus, Lesbia,
that you would prefer not even Jupiter to me.
I loved you then:
not just like most men love their *amicae*,
but like a father loves his sons and sons-in-law.
I know you now:
and so, though I am burning more intensely than ever,
you are that much cheaper, more worthless in my eyes.
How can that be, you ask?
Because being done wrong like that
makes a lover love more, be fond of less.

Lesbia is, or was, more than the usual *amica* to Catullus – who casts himself in the role not of *amicus* but of *amans*; the poem builds up to the concluding assertion that, now that a rupture has happened, and precisely because of the wrong that she has done him, Catullus feels passion and desire (*amare*) all the more, affection and goodwill (*bene velle*) that much less.[4] Gordon Williams' reading of this poem, picking up on a suggestion made early in the twentieth century by Richard Reitzenstein, draws out some implications of the final couplet. Since *iniuria* and *benevolentia* were key terms in the language of *amicitia* (the former referring to the refusal of an obligation, the latter to the affectionate sentiment characteristic of *amicitia*), "Catullus can make play with this emotive word *amicitia* – with its pleasant ambiguity in the case of a woman – as an alternative framework for expressing his relationship with Lesbia; taken seriously, it supplied the terms of condemnation and she then, as a variant on the erring wife, appeared as the friend who 'let him down'." The poem's final words, then, suggest that Lesbia has missed or ruined a rare opportunity for something more complex than the usual kind of *amor* joining a man and his *amica* in Catullus' world.[5]

---

[4] Even as they try to distinguish between *diligere* and *amare* (often citing Cic. *Fam.* 13.47, *ut scires eum a me non diligi solum verum etiam amari*), commentators acknowledge that any distinction cannot be hard and fast, especially in poetry of this kind. So too with *bene velle*: It is often asserted that the phrase indicates "the sphere of friendship" (Kroll) or "ordinary friendship" (Fordyce), yet it is also used of lovers (e.g. Plaut. *Truculentus* 441: *egone illam ut non amem? egone illi ut non bene velim?*).

[5] Williams 1968, p. 408; cf. Reitzenstein 1912, p. 26. See Lyne 1980, p. 25, for another approach: "It is worth stressing, I think, that there is not really any question here of *metaphor*. Catullus did actually conceive of love or part of love as a form of *amicitia*; he did actually think that love ought to involve the sort of ideals and standards there were inherent or theoretically inherent

It remains a debated question whether the poet himself or some later editor is responsible for the arrangement of the poems within the Catullan corpus; there are in any case a number of juxtapositions which invite being read as such.[6] Directly following upon poem 72, which ends with the words *bene velle minus*, is one whose opening line ends with the sequence *bene velle mereri*. Will this lead into further meditation on Lesbia?

> Desine de quoquam quicquam bene velle mereri
>   aut aliquem fieri posse putare pium.
> omnia sunt ingrata, nihil fecisse benigne
>   <prodest>, immo etiam taedet obestque magis;
> ut mihi, quem nemo gravius nec acerbius urget,
>   quam modo qui me unum atque unicum *amicum* habuit.
>
> (Catull. 73)

> Give up expecting that you'll be paid back for your good deeds,
> give up thinking that anyone is capable of decency.
> There's no gratitude any more; to have done a kindness
> doesn't help, is even considered a regrettable nuisance.
> Look at me! The one who is causing me the most pain and suffering
> is the one who just now had me as his one and only friend.

The verbal echo between the final line of poem 72 and the first of 73 turns out to be as superficial as it is teasing: *bene* here modifies *mereri* rather than *velle*. Yet, like *bene velle*, *bene mereri* is itself an item in the traditional vocabulary of social relations and of *amicitia* in particular; as we will see in the following chapter, *bene merens* is a common epitaph in the commemoration of friends and spouses in epitaphs. And so, as this poem unfolds, we find that the complaint of ingratitude is directed not at Lesbia but at a male friend, one who considered Catullus his *amicus* in a uniquely valued way, much as Catullus had considered Lesbia not an ordinary *amica*.

The first poem of another paired sequence is literally framed by *amor* and *amicitia*.

> Iucundum, mea vita, mihi proponis *amorem*
>   hunc nostrum inter nos perpetuumque fore.

---

in the aristocratic code; and therefore he used that language." My own approach avoids asking questions about what Catullus "actually thought" and interrogates the relationship not between "friendship" and "love," whether in part or whole, but between *amicitia* and *amor*; the linguistic asymmetry of Lyne's formulation draws attention to itself.

[6] Fitzgerald 1995 and Wray 2001 illustrate how one can read meaningful sequences in Catullus' poetry.

di magni, facite ut vere promittere possit,
atque id sincere dicat et ex animo,
ut liceat nobis tota perducere vita
aeternum hoc sanctae foedus *amicitiae.*

(Catull. 109)

Delightful the love you hold out to me, my darling,
and one we will share for ever, you say.
Great gods! See to it that the promise be truthful,
that it be spoken sincerely from the heart,
that we may live our whole lives
in this eternal bond of sacred friendship.

The poem expands the boundaries of *amicitia* to include a passionate erotic relationship – or rather, restates *amor* in terms of *amicitia*. But to whom? The addressee remains unnamed, his or her gender not specified by morphology, and the term of endearment *mea vita* need not be addressed to a woman.[7] And yet, although nothing in the poem's language prevents us from reading it in connection with Catullus' verses to and about, say, the young man he calls Juventius, most readers have taken this poem to be to and about Lesbia, and few have even questioned the reading. To be sure, the temptation to read Lesbia in this poem is hard to resist, not least because of a poem naming her and emphatically entwining the concepts of *fides, foedus,* and *amor,* and because Catullus, writing in autobiographical mode, seems to be participating in the tradition of publishing sequences of poems on one and the same beloved exemplified in the collection of Greek epigrams known as Meleager's *Garland.*[8] Still, read as a self-contained composition, Catullus 109 displays the irremovable feature that its addressee has no name and no sex. Any readers, ancient or modern, are free to read this poem with little or no knowledge of the rest of

---

[7] Cf. Catull. 45.13, *mea vita Septimille*; Courtney 2003, p. 276 (Maecenas fr. 2) = Hollis 2007, p. 315 (fr. 185), addressed to Horace (*mea vita*); Courtney 2003, p. 394 (Apul. fr. 3), addressed to Charinus (*pars in amore meo, vita, tibi remanet*). At *Verr.* 3.27 Cicero speaks of *Apronium, delicias ac vitam tuam*: we need not necessarily conclude from this that Verres actually called Apronius *deliciae ac vita mea*, but, Cicero's sarcasm aside, it was quite possible to address a man as *mea vita*. See Dickey 2002 s.v. *vita* (summarized at p. 365: "term of endearment, normally for lovers, often with *mea*", 28 attestations).

[8] Catull. 87: *Nulla potest mulier tantum se dicere amatam / vere quantum a me Lesbia amata mea est. / nulla fides ullo fuit umquam foedere tanta / quanta in amore tuo ex parte reperta mea est.* See Williams 1968, pp. 469–470, for Catullus' "autobiographical mode"; for Juventius, see below, n. 10. One of the few modern readers to raise the possibility that the addressee of Catullus 109 might not be Lesbia is Newman 1990, pp. 326–327, citing Ov. *Tr.* 2.427–430. To be sure, the manuscript heading makes the connection ("Ad Lesbiam"), but these headings were not written by Catullus himself, as is shown by the fact that some of them are obviously inaccurate. Whoever was responsible for this heading made the same connection that many subsequent readers have made.

Catullan poetry and will still be able to make complex meaning out of it. Central to that meaning is its memorable and grandly worded wish, phrased not in terms of love between men and women but in terms of the intertwined concepts of *amor, amicitia,* and *foedus* ("pact" or "agreement"), the latter suggesting the promises made and implied in marriage, but also the bond of *amicitia.*[9]

The ringing final line of poem 109, climaxing with *amicitia,* which in turn responds to *amorem* at the end of the first line, is juxtaposed with a very different use of this language in the opening of the following poem.

> Aufillena, bonae semper laudantur amicae;
> accipiunt *pretium,* quae facere instituunt.
> tu quod promisti mihi quod mentita inimica es,
> quod nec das et fers saepe, facis facinus.
> aut facere ingenuae est, aut non promisse pudicae,
> Aufillena, fuit: sed data corripere
> fraudando officiis, plus quam *meretricis* avarae
> quae sese toto *corpore prostituit.*
>
> (Catull. 110)

> Aufillena, good *amicae* always get a word of praise;
> they set out to do it, they take the payment.
> But you, like an enemy making a lying promise:
> you don't put out but frequently take. It's a crime!
> An honest woman does what she promises, Aufillena;
> a chaste woman does not make promises.
> To grab what you've been given and to cheat on your duty:
> not even a greedy whore does that,
> one who sells her entire body.

Here we return to the *amicae* of poem 72, those who are loved by the *vulgus*; but this poem's even sharper point is delivered by the language of prostitution accumulated especially at the poem's end, all of it aimed squarely at Aufillena (the language of *amicitia* is underlined above; italics indicate the language of prostitution). She could have been an *amica* of

---

[9] Cf. Reitzenstein 1912, pp. 28–29 (together with Catullus 76), Williams 1968, pp. 23–25, 408, Williams 1980, pp. 216–217, Lyne 1980, pp. 35–38 (translating *foedus amicitiae* as "the marriage-pact of friendship"). For *fides* and *foedus* in connection with marriage, *amicitia,* and hospitality, see Freyburger 1986, pp. 167–193. Fitzgerald 1995, p. 116, reads this poem rather differently: "For me this poem invokes the kind of embarrassed silence that follows a joke that has fallen flat. Like the uproarious laughter of the joketeller at his own wit, the earnest ecstasy of the last couplet seems out of proportion to its occasion." It is striking that Fitzgerald's otherwise sensitive readings of these poems ignore the specificity of their language of *amicitia*: Symptomatic is his translation of Catull. 109.6 (*aeternum hoc sanctae foedus amicitiae*) as "this eternal treaty of holy love."

one kind or another, but is now not only an *inimica*, but worse than the kind of *amica* who is paid for her favors.

In addition to *amicae* like these and the unique Lesbia, and along with the young man named Juventius, object of Catullus' *amor* and recipient of his passionate kisses, Catullus' poetry is pervaded with relationships between men: from the opening dedication to Cornelius Nepos (1) through the enthusiastic invocation of his affection for Veranius, with its kisses and embraces (9), to his *comites* Aurelius and Furius, ready to accompany him wherever he goes (11) but bitterly assaulted with the language of penetrative, macho masculinity when they question Catullus' own masculinity (16).[10] Some of Catullus' poetry to and about men with whom he has intimate relationships constructs triangles, and much of it invites being read in terms of the homosocial. Above all, Catullus' relationship with his fellow poet Gaius Licinius Calvus has drawn a great deal of attention since antiquity. The bond that linked them, both as friends and as poets with similar interests, was and is paradigmatic.[11] One of Catullus' poems is an elegant consolation of Calvus on the death of a woman named Quintilia.

> Si quicquam mutis gratum acceptumque sepulcris
>   accidere a nostro, Calve, dolore potest,
> quo desiderio *veteres* renovamus *amores*
>   atque olim *missas* flemus *amicitias*,
> certe non tanto mors immatura dolori est
>   Quintiliae, quantum gaudet *amore* tuo.
>   (Catull. 96)

> If anything delightful and pleasing can reach the speechless tombs,
> Calvus, coming from our pain,
> a longing by which we renew old loves
> and shed tears for friendships long abandoned,
> Quintilia surely feels pain at her own early death less,
> delights in your love more.

Calvus' relationship with Quintilia (either his wife or his mistress) is, then, both *vetus amor* and *olim missa amicitia*. The parallel syntax of lines 3 and 4 (adjective, first-person verb, noun) places the two nouns in the same

---

[10] See also Wray 2001, pp. 80–87, for Catullus' performance of aggressive masculinity in conjunction with the men of poem 37. Juventius is named in Catull. 24, 48, 81, 99; just as the unnamed *mea vita* of 109 can be read as Lesbia, the unnamed *puer* of 15 and 21 (Catullus' *amores*, desired by Aurelius as well) can be read as Juventius too.

[11] Catullus and Calvus are paired – often in connection with the women they celebrate in their poetry – at Hor. *Serm.* 1.10.16–19, Prop. 2.25.3–4, Ov. *Am.* 3.9.61–62, Ov. *Tr.* 2.431–432, Plin. *Ep.* 1.16.5, Gell. *NA* 19.9.7. Hollis 2007, pp. 58–59, summarizes the "almost identical" range of themes in Catullus' and Calvus' poetry; see also Courtney 2003, pp. 201–210.

position, and the structure of the final couplet aligns *amor* with pleasure (*gaudet*) just as death (*mors*) is aligned with pain (*dolori*). As often in
Roman poetry, moreover, the level of intertextuality and self-referentiality
is higher than a first reading might suggest. Catullus' poem can be read
as referring both to Calvus' relationship to his *poetry* on that relationship,
and *amor* and *amicitia* are structural to these relationships.[12]

Another poem evokes with delightfully polyvalent irony an encounter
with Calvus.

> Hesterno, Licini, die otiosi
> multum lusimus in meis tabellis,
> ut convenerat esse delicatos:
> scribens versiculos uterque nostrum
> ludebat numero modo hoc modo illoc,
> reddens mutua per iocum atque vinum.
> atque illinc abii tuo lepore
> incensus, Licini, facetiisque,
> ut nec me miserum cibus iuvaret
> nec somnus tegeret quiete ocellos,
> sed toto indomitus furore lecto
> versarer, cupiens videre lucem,
> ut tecum loquerer, simulque ut essem.
> at defessa labore membra postquam
> semimortua lectulo iacebant,
> hoc, iucunde, tibi poema feci,
> ex quo perspiceres meum dolorem.
> nunc audax cave sis, precesque nostras,
> oramus, cave despuas, ocelle,
> ne poenas Nemesis reposcat a te.
> est vehemens dea: laedere hanc caveto.
> (Catull. 50)[13]

> Yesterday, Licinius, we had a good time
> with my writing tablets, relaxed
> and agreed we would indulge ourselves.
> We had a good time, each of us writing verses
> sometimes in this meter, sometimes in that,

---

[12] For Calvus' lament on Quintilia and the question of whether she was his mistress or wife, see
Hollis 2007, pp. 68–71; for readings of Catullus' poem in connection with Calvus' fragment, see
Williams 1968, p. 189, Putnam 2006, pp. 104–106.

[13] Readings of Catullus 50 include Pucci 1961, Segal 1970, MacLeod 1973, Burgess 1986, Williams
1980, pp. 212–214, Williams 1988, Fitzgerald 1995, pp. 36–37. Following a suggestion of Syndikus,
Gunderson 1997, p. 203, reads the poem as having "the form of a verse letter." Describing its
recipient as "the orator C. Licinius Calvus Macer" and moving fairly seamlessly from Catullus
to Pliny, Gunderson's reading downplays the poetic and metapoetic qualities of this text.

giving it to each other as we drank and fooled around.
Afterwards I left, Licinius, burning
with your delightfulness, your wit.
Alas! Food gave me no pleasure,
sleep gave my eyes no rest;
frenzied, wild, I tossed and turned in bed,
couldn't wait for the light of day,
to talk with you, to be with you.
My body, drained and exhausted,
practically dead, lay there in bed;
then I wrote you this poem, my sweet,
so you could see my suffering.
Careful! Don't be too cocky! I beg you,
be careful, my dear, not to reject my prayers,
or else Nemesis will take her revenge on you.
She is a harsh goddess – be careful not to insult her.

Imagery traditionally associated with erotic passion pervades this poem. The verb *ludere*, found twice in the first five lines, could be read as hinting at a pair of lovers romping in bed; the verse *ludebat numero modo hoc modo illoc* recalls Catullus' own erotically charged sparrow (*sed circumsiliens modo huc modo illuc / ad solam dominam usque pipiabat*, 3.9–10); and *reddens mutua per iocum atque vinum* suggests a playful exchange of poetic compositions but also an erotic back-and-forth lubricated by the gift of Dionysus. In the evocation of Catullus' nighttime suffering after their tipsy encounter, his inability to sleep or eat, his tossing and turning, his frenzied obsession with seeing Calvus echo commonplaces of erotic passion, and the two following lines (*at defessa labore membra postquam / semimortua lectulo iacebant*) are readable as a description of post-coital exhaustion.[14] And so this poem (*hoc poema*), written to express Catullus' pain and rounded off with a naughty tease to his darling (*ocelle*), ends with a warning not to offend Nemesis: in other words, to give him what he wants. After all this, it is tempting to read significance in the juxtaposition of this poem to the next (51), lyrically narrating the experience of

---

[14] I owe to Quinn 1973 the translation of *ludere* as "have a good time." For an especially vivid illustration of this use of the verb see Petron. *Sat.* 11 (Ascyltus bursts in on Encolpius and Giton in bed together): *invenit me* cum fratre ludentem. Kroll 1989 glosses *me miserum* (v. 9) as "den gewissermaßen Verliebten"; Ellis 1889 ad vv. 9–10 draws the parallel to Achilles mourning for Patroclus in *Iliad* 24, and compares *versarer* in v. 12 to Propertius 1.14.19–21. For post-coital exhaustion see Ov. *Am.* 1.5, Mart. 9.67.3, *Priapeia* 26.1, Suet. *Calig.* 36.1, Apul. *Met.* 8.26. By contrast, Thomson 1998 sees an "almost juvenile delight" which culminates in "sheer over-exhaustion," but comments that *miserum* in v. 9 "impl[ies] a degree of affection tantamount to love (hence the use of an adjective appropriate to lovesickness)."

seeing Lesbia, perhaps for the first time, and ending with a stanza on the deleterious power of *otium*.[15]

But Calvus was not the only man to whom Catullus addressed poetry which passionately mingles the imagery of *amor* and *amicitia*.

Alfene immemor atque unanimis false *sodalibus*,
iam te nil miseret, dure, tui dulcis *amiculi*?
iam me prodere, iam non dubitas fallere, *perfide*?
nec facta impia fallacum hominum caelicolis placent.
quae tu neglegis ac me miserum deseris in malis.
eheu quid faciant, dic, homines cuive habeant *fidem*?
certe tute iubebas animam tradere, inique, me
inducens in *amorem*, quasi tuta omnia mi forent.
idem nunc retrahis te ac tua dicta omnia factaque
ventos irrita ferre ac nebulas aereas sinis.
si tu oblitus es, at di meminerunt, meminit *Fides*,
quae te ut paeniteat postmodo facti faciet tui.
(Catull. 30)

Thoughtless Alfenus, untrue to like-minded comrades!
So you have no pity on your dear little friend – heartless?
So you don't hesitate to betray me, to cheat me – traitor?
The indecent doings of deceitful men find no favor among the gods in heaven.
But you don't care; you abandon me, leave me to suffering.
What, O, what should men do? Tell me: whom should they trust?
You told me to hand over my heart – faithless!
You led me to love, as if everything were fine.
You pull back now and everything you said and did
you now let the winds and mists of the sky carry away
useless. You may have forgotten, but the gods remember,
the goddess of Trust remembers. One day
she will make you regret what you have done.

Whoever Alfenus is, the language of betrayal and bitter disappointment pervading this poem is unmistakable.[16] The first two lines evoke and inflect some of the grand ideals of Roman friendship (note *unanimis sodalibus*,

---

[15] Ellis 1889 describes the reference to Nemesis and the sentiment of the final lines as "almost a common-place of lovers"; Quinn 1973 sees in *ocelle* a "(bantering) use of the language of love poetry"; cf. Dickey 2002, p. 346, for *ocelle* as "term of endearment, normally for lovers." For readings of Catullus 50 and 51 together see Wray 2001, pp. 96–109 (arguing that *hoc poema* in 50.16 refers not to poem 50 but to poem 51 and suggesting that the Lesbia of poem 51 is Sappho herself, but with little to say on the homosocial) and Putnam 2006, pp. 48–54 ("Calvus plays at once the separate roles of Lesbia and Sappho," p. 49).

[16] He is probably Alfenus Varus, addressed in Catullus 22 and *consul suffectus* in 39 BC (see Fordyce 1961 ad loc.). Putnam 2006, pp. 54–58, considers the possibility that he is the Varus of Hor. *Carm.* 1.18, reading the two poems together.

vividly interrupted by the accusing *false*, and *tui dulcis amiculi* with its pathetic diminutive) but the third line, sounding the note of *fides* which pervades the rest of the poem, could just as well come from the mouth of an abandoned lover. Indeed, in what follows Catullus' voice sounds very much like that of an abandoned mistress such as Ariadne in his own poem 64, or Virgil's Dido inspired by her: the unforgiving stream of vocatives (*immemor, false, dure, perfide, inique*), the talk of pity and betrayal (*te nil miseret, me prodere ... fallere*), the invocation of the gods (*caelicolis*), the self-pitying stance and focus on one's own abandonment (*tui dulcis amiculi, me miserum deseris in malis*), the anticipation of divinely sanctioned revenge.[17] How, then, are we to understand the complaints "you bade me give over my soul (*iubebas animam tradere*)" and "you led me to love (*inducens in amorem*) as if everything were safe"? What kind of *amor* was this, and for whom? For Lesbia, Juventius, Alfenus himself, or someone else? If we read the poem as part of the Catullan collection, we might piece together a scenario in which Alfenus had somehow become involved with – or come between – Catullus and Lesbia. But if we read it as a self-contained poetic composition, we observe that the text contains no hints of a third person, let alone Lesbia in particular. On the contrary, this poem concentrates insistently and painfully on two people – Catullus and Alfenus – and what has happened between them, and in doing so it offers a powerful blend of the imagery and language of *amicitia* and erotic passion.[18]

However its workings are described, the "semantic slippage" of Catullus' *amor* and *amicitia* is usually taken to be not only a hallmark of

---

[17] See Ellis 1889 for a compilation of parallels, among them Verg. *Aen.* 4.305–306 (*dissimulare etiam sperasti, perfide, tantum / posse nefas...?*), 308 (*nec moritura tenet crudeli funere Dido*), 360 (*desine meque tuis incendere teque querelis*). Both Catullus 30 and Dido's complaints to Aeneas in *Aeneid* 4 lurk in the background of Ovid's poetic complaint from exile to an unnamed man with whom he has been joined in *amicitia* since their early years: from the opening challenge (*conquerar an taceam? Pont.* 4.3.1) to the description of his own speech as *querela* (3) to the verse-initial *dissimulas etiam* and third-person self-naming (*dissimulas etiam nec me vis nosse videri / quisque sit audito nomine Naso rogas*, 9–10) to the melodramatic statement *ille ego sum qui nunc an vivam, perfide, nescis* (17).

[18] Ellis 1889 summarizes arguments for the various referents of *amor*, inclining toward Alfenus. Kroll 1989 too dogmatically asserts that it can *only* refer to the friendship between Catullus and Alfenus ("wie sollte ihn dieser denn zu einer anderen Liebe (etwa der zu Lesbia) verlocken?") but makes the under-appreciated point that the poem makes no explicit or even indirect allusion to the relationship with Lesbia. Quinn 1973 glosses *amor* as "the affection, i.e. of true friendship," implicitly with Alfenus. More recently, Wray 2001, pp. 101–103, reading this poem along with poem 38 as examples of the "performative outrageousness" of ancient Mediterranean masculinity, sees here "saccharine self-pity and shrill self-righteousness"; Wray concludes that "Alfenus' 'faithlessness', then, has consisted in a lag in the epistolary exchange of poems enjoyed by the two poets, a commerce portrayed by the Catullan speaker as a love affair."

his poetic style but a sign of his striking originality.[19] Yet we cannot be certain that Catullus was not adopting or adapting usage patterns found in earlier Latin poetry now lost, or in other speech genres, including perhaps those of oral communication, about which we have little or no idea. And even if Catullus was being strikingly original on this point, his poetry clearly plays off pre-existing possibilities of language and conceptualization. The nouns *amicus* and *amica* might signify sexual partners, but they might not; *amicitia* might be an idealized mingling of being – two souls in (preferably male) bodies – or it might be something rather less grand; *amor* remained elusive and desirable at once.

VIRGIL

In Virgil's *Aeneid*, as we have seen in the preceding chapters, the imagery of *amor* and *amicitia* is intertwined in the narrative of Nisus and Euryalus, who became paradigmatic for a range of relationships in literary and inscriptional texts, while two pairs of women in this poem (Dido and Anna, Camilla and Acca) are memorable for the language of sisterhood that joins them. As a whole, however, Virgil's epic does not draw sustained attention to *amicitia*. The abstract noun itself only occurs twice in the whole poem, both times describing the bond created between peoples joined by a formal agreement (*foedus*). It can be argued that the muted role of interpersonal *amicitia* reflects the poem's thematic preoccupations with larger questions of destiny and the sweep of history, or reflects the characterization of Aeneas in particular. No interpersonal relationship – not even the passionate *amor* joining him to Dido (which, although poetic precedent lay at hand, is never described with the language of *amicitia*) – can outweigh the imperatives of his destiny and his commitment to the ideal of *pietas*.[20] To be sure, Virgil's Aeneas is by no means

---

[19] For "semantic slippage" see Miller 1994 and 2004. Some have argued that through its use of the language of *amicitia* the Lesbia poetry is making statements about contemporary political issues just as much as, or even more than, private affairs (see Ross 1975, followed by Skinner 1997); others see a more general discourse of aristocratic obligation at stake (see Lyne 1980, pp. 25–26, followed by Fitzgerald 1995, pp. 117–120; see also Vinson 1992).

[20] For some general remarks on *amicitia* in Virgil, see Bellincioni 1984. The relationship between Dido and Aeneas is sparked by Venus' son at her behest (*Aen.* 1.657–722, where he is called both *Amor* and *Cupido*); see also 1.749 (*longumque bibebat amorem*), 4.296 (*quis fallere possit amantem?*), 4.395 (*magno labefactus amorem*), 4.412 (*improbe Amor! quid non mortalia pectora cogis?*). When Dido desperately reminds Aeneas of "the right hand once given" (*Aen.* 4.307, *data dextera quondam*), her words invoke the gesture of *dextrarum iunctio* and, drawing out one implication, Servius ad loc. comments that the phrase *data dextera* signals *foedus amicitiarum*. But the gesture

without comrades and companions, and some of these (Hector, Palinurus, Misenus, Deiphobus, and the older adviser Nautes) are called his *amici*.[21] Achates, Aeneas' most prominent companion in the epic's opening book, his constant comrade throughout, and most likely Virgil's creation, has for many readers embodied the ideal of *fides*, common to both *amor* and *amicitia*; strikingly enough, however, he is nowhere in the epic called Aeneas' *amicus* or described as joined to him in *amor*.[22] Another memorable male pairing in this poem, unlike that joining Aeneas to Achates, which pervades the entire poem, is that joining Aeneas to Evander's son Pallas in the final books. A form of military tutelage or *contubernium* given erotic hints, it too lacks the language of *amor* and *amicitia*.[23]

Amor is certainly present in the *Georgics*, evoking plants' bond with the earth, Virgil's devotion to the Muses' rites, Orpheus' love for his departed wife Eurydice, or the diffuse power of attraction that holds sway over all living things.[24] Neither the abstract noun *amicitia* nor the concrete *amicus*, however, appears in this poem, and the adjectival *amicus* only once, describing the water in which plants delight (Verg. *G.* 4.115: *figat humo plantas et amicos inriget imbres*). Many readers have found significance in this absence, as in that of a key figure in the poetry of Virgil's day. Gaius Cornelius Gallus, together with Virgil apparently supported by Asinius Pollio early in his poetic career, was also friend to the likes of Cicero and Octavian Augustus as well as of poets like Tibullus and, as we will see, Propertius. Gallus' lost collection of poems, almost certainly bearing the title *Amores*, centered on the figure of Lycoris, said by

symbolized and cemented not only the bonds of *amicitia* but also those of marriage and hospitality (see above, n. 9), and it is only the latter two which we find in the language of the *Aeneid* itself. Confiding to her sister Anna at the opening of Book 4, Dido marvels at the new *hospes* (4.10); after she realizes that Aeneas is leaving, she desperately, bitterly notes that, whereas previously she had considered him spouse (*coniunx*) and called their relationship marriage (*coniugium*), the only label she has left now is *hospes* (4.172, 323–324).

[21] For the abstract noun see Verg. *Aen.* 7.546: *dic in amicitiam coeant et foedera iungant*; 11.321–322: *cedat amicitiae Teucrorum et foederis aequas / dicamus leges*). Apart from adjectival uses (*amica verba* and the like), occurrences of the noun *amicus* in the *Aeneid* include the following: 1.486 (Aeneas seeing the painting representing Hector's death): *utque ipsum corpus amici … conspexit*; 2.93 (Sinon referring to Palamedes); 3.82 (king Anius recognizes *veterem amicum* Anchises); 5.452 (Acestes and Entellus); 5.719 (Nautes is Aeneas' *senior amicus*), 5.869 (Aeneas and Palinurus), 6.149 (Aeneas and Misenus), 6.507–509 (Aeneas and Deiphobus).

[22] For Aeneas and Achates (given the epithet *fidus* at Verg. *Aen.* 1.188, 6.158, 8.521, 8.586, 12.384), see Bellincioni 1984 and especially Weber 1988, arguing that Achates makes of Aeneas a coupled hero ("Durch ihn wird die Titelfigur der Aeneis zu einem Paarhelden," p. 9).

[23] For Aeneas and Pallas, see Evander's commendation of his son to Aeneas (Verg. *Aen.* 8.515–517, *sub te tolerare magistro / militiam et grave Martis opus, tua cernere facta / adsuescat, primis et te miretur ab annis*) with Gillis 1983, Putnam 1985, Moorton 1990.

[24] Verg. *G.* 2.301 (*tantus amor terrae*), 2.476 (*quarum sacra fero ingenti percussus amore*), 3.244 (*amor omnibus idem*), 4.464 (*ipse cava solans aegrum testudine amorem*).

Servius to have been a pseudonym for none other than the freed slave Volumnia Cytheris, whose liaison with Marc Antony was the subject of Cicero's scandalized remarks quoted at the end of Chapter 1. Gallus' poetry was deeply influential (he is placed by Ovid at the beginning of a series of four love-poets culminating with himself; *Tr.* 4.10.53–54) and his fall from Augustus' favor soberingly spectacular. Accused of having conspired against Augustus, he committed suicide in 26 BC. What is his connection with Virgil's *Georgics*? Servius reports that Virgil originally ended the poem with a passage in praise of Gallus, but that under pressure from Augustus he replaced those lines with the Aristaeus–Orpheus episode that brings the *Georgics* as we have them to their end. For readers of the *Georgics* who have this knowledge, Gallus' fate illustrates the vicissitudes of high-ranking *amicitia:* from prominent figure at the climax of Virgil's poem to an expunged name whose trace remains only in the tradition of scholarly commentary.[25]

And so there is no Gallus in our *Georgics*. But he remains a prominent presence in two of the *Eclogues*, and with him a dense web of *amor* between men, between the sexes, and between poets. There is a long tradition, reaching back to antiquity, of reading a variety of male friendships in the *Eclogues*, Virgil's earliest surviving poetry. Many of these are either right on the surface of the poetry or just below it – Virgil and Octavian, Virgil and Varus, Virgil and Pollio, and above all Virgil and Gallus – while others have been located between the lines, in allegorical and related kinds of reading. Servius, for example, understands Corydon in the second Eclogue to be standing for Virgil and his beloved Alexis as standing for Octavian (!) – or perhaps for a slave of Virgil's friend Pollio.[26] It comes as something of a surprise, then, to observe that neither *amicitia* nor *amicus*, nor even the semantically more flexible *comes* occurs anywhere in the *Eclogues*, and *socius* only once (referring to Ulysses' companions at

---

[25] See Courtney 2003, pp. 259–270, and Hollis 2007, pp. 219–252, for testimonia and fragments relating to Gallus, and Cairns 2006 for an extensive reading of his influence on Propertius' poetry. For Gallus' friendships, see Servius ad 10.1 (*hic primo in amicitiis Augusti Caesaris fuit: postea cum venisset in suspicionem quod contra eum coniuraret, occisus est. fuit autem amicus Vergilii* …), Suet. *Aug.* 66.2 (Augustus long considered him an *amicus*, but then *domo et provinciis suis interdixit*, a gesture of renunciation for which see Kierdorf 1987, pp. 233–235), Ov. *Am.* 3.9.63–64 (he is imagined joining Tibullus in Elysium – if, Ovid adds, covering his bases, the charge of violating a friendship is false), Cic. *Fam.* 10.32 and perhaps also in 10.31 (Asinius Pollio). For the ending of the *Georgics* see Serv. *Ecl.* 10 intro, *G.* 4 intro (a report whose historicity is generally accepted, though questioned by Hollis 2007, pp. 228–229). A papyrus fragment published in 1978 is almost universally attributed to Gallus, not least because it mentions Lycoris. For a rare voice urging caution in making the attribution see Giangrande 1980.

[26] Serv. ad *Ecl.* 2.1.

Verg. *Ecl.* 8.70). On the other hand, this is very much poetry of *amor*. In the course of the 10 poems and 829 verses making up the book of *Eclogues*, the noun *amor* occurs 28 times and the verb *amare* 12. Beyond statistics, this is a world of shepherds and Romans and their experience of Venus and flames, a world in which *amor* makes life difficult for animals and humans alike (3.101: *idem amor exitium pecori pecorisque magistro*). The configurations of human *amor* are the usual ones in the Latin textual tradition: male–female and male–male couplings, desired or consummated, both of them firmly situated in the natural world amongst plants and animals and an Epicurean-colored *voluptas* (cf. 2.14–16, 35–44; 3.8–9, 64–66).

How does Gallus fit into this world? The sixth poem, a massively creative nesting of songs, begins with Virgil more or less openly adopting the persona of Tityrus, recalling to Varus, with whom he has extratextually been joined in friendship, how he was once approached by Apollo and told to sing a "thinly spun song" (*deductum carmen*, 6.1–12). After an invocation of the Muses, Virgil sings how the mythic figure Silenus was once compelled to sing a song (13–30) and then (31–61) paraphrases Silenus' broadly sweeping poetry, from Lucretian verses on the origins and nature of the world to mythological themes (Hylas briefly singled out, Pasiphae at greater length) to a narrative of Gallus' encounter, located in Hesiod's native Boeotia, with a Muse, Apollo's chorus, and Apollo's son Linus (64–73). The sudden appearance of a contemporary Roman in Hesiodic Greece, his irruption amongst Muses, nymphs, and mythological figures, casts a strong spotlight on Gallus himself, who is introduced quite simply and all the more prominently by means of his bare name, no epithets, no explanations. And yet as much as Gallus is a key figure in the sixth *Eclogue*, the poem's words make no explicit connection between Gallus and Virgil himself, no use of the language either of *amicitia* or of *amor*; and Gallus appears not as poet of his *Amores* or of Lycoris, but as Hesiodic and Callimachean shepherd-poet of learned verse.[27]

The tenth and last of the *Eclogues*, which announces itself as end and culmination of the collection, brings Gallus front and center. Now he is very much a poet of love and poet in love, central figure in a poem which

---

[27] Linus hands Gallus a reed, symbol of poetic authority, and proclaims him to be the successor of Hesiod, and implicitly also of Callimachus and Euphorion, whose poetry, Servius tells us, Gallus himself had rendered into Latin (Serv. ad Verg. *Ecl.* 6.72, 10.1). Relevant readings of the sixth *Eclogue* include Williams 1968, pp. 243–249, Williams 1980, pp. 220–225, Ross 1975, pp. 18–38, Miller 2004, pp. 64–66, Breed 2006, pp. 74–94. On the possibility of reading Tityrus as Virgil, Servius has some cautionary remarks on *Ecl.* 1.1: *hoc loco Tityri sub persona Vergilium debemus accipere; non tamen ubique, sed tantum ubi exigit ratio.*

names *amor* far more often than any other of the *Eclogues*.[28] The opening lines intimately connect him both with Virgil and with the theme of *amor*, repeating his name twice in close proximity to first-person pronouns and possessives.

> Extremum hunc, Arethusa, *mihi* concede laborem:
> pauca *meo* <u>Gallo</u>, sed quae legat ipsa Lycoris,
> carmina sunt dicenda: neget quis carmina <u>Gallo</u>?
> sic tibi, cum fluctus subterlabere Sicanos,
> Doris amara suam non intermisceat undam,
> incipe; sollicitos <u>Galli</u> *dicamus* amores ...
> (Verg. *Ecl.* 10.1–6)

Grant me, Arethusa, this final task:
I must sing a little song to my dear Gallus,
the kind of song Lycoris herself might read.
Who would deny Gallus a song?
If, as you glide underneath the Sicilian waves,
you do not want the salty sea-nymph Doris to mingle her water with yours,
begin now! Let us tell of the troubled loves of Gallus ...

Virgil's theme, then, is Gallus' *amores* or *Amores*, his passion and his poetry, and the core of the poem (31–69) gives us both of these in the form of a monologue by Gallus, who imagines himself in Arcadia and laments his hopeless love now that Lycoris has left him – in words which, according to Servius, were taken from Gallus' own poetry.[29] Two interrelated moments are worth a closer look. First is Gallus' announced intention to carve his *amores* in the bark of trees: an allusion to the practice

---

[28] The noun *amor* occurs twelve times in this poem, seven in the eighth *Eclogue*, and between one and three times in each of the others. Among readings of the tenth *Eclogue*, see Williams 1968, pp. 233–239 (in conjunction with Catullus 68), Williams 1980, pp. 231–236 (seeing a "curious, almost triangular, relationship" joining Gallus, Virgil, and Lycoris in the "primary field" of the poem, while the "secondary field" has to do with poetry itself), Conte 1986, pp. 100–129, Kennedy 1987, Van Sickle 2004, pp. 188–205, Breed 2006, pp. 117–135. Rumpf 1996 is a book-length study of the poem as a *Freundschaftsgedicht*. As we have seen, words like *amicus*, *socius*, or *comes* are nowhere to be found in the poem; Rumpf glosses *amor* in line 73 with *Freundschaft* (p. 186; see pp. 257–264 on the role of *amor* in the poem).

[29] Serv. ad Verg. *Ecl.* 10.46: *hi autem omnes versus Galli sunt, de ipsius translati carminibus*. Since Gallus' *Amores* were presumably composed in elegiac couplets, Virgil's lines cannot be a verbatim quotation; with this caution in mind, Courtney includes Verg. *Ecl.* 10.42–63 as Gallus, fr. 3, in his *Fragmentary Latin Poets* (Courtney 2003, pp. 268–270). Servius claims that Cytheris had left Gallus to accompany her lover Marcus Antonius (whom he pointedly calls Augustus' *inimicus*) on a military campaign in Gaul (Serv. ad Verg. *Ecl.* 10.1: *hic autem Gallus amavit Cytheridem meretricem, libertam Volumnii ... et in Gallo inpatientia turpis amoris ostenditur, et aperte hic Antonius carpitur, inimicus Augusti, quem contra Romanum morem Cytheris est in castra comitata*). See Conte 1986, pp. 100–129, for the relationship between the Virgilian/Gallic verses and Theocritus.

of carving the name of one's beloved in a tree-trunk, but also (since the word *liber*, literally "bark," recalls the substance on which early texts were imagined to have been written) suggesting a metonymy for writing down one's poetry in a book.[30]

> certum est in silvis inter spelaea ferarum
> malle pati tenerisque meos incidere *amores*
> arboribus: crescent illae, crescetis *amores*.
> (Verg. *Ecl.* 10.52–54)

> I've made up my mind: I would rather suffer
> in the woods amidst the dens of beasts,
> and carve my Loves into pliant trees:
> as these grow, you, my loves, will grow.

The second moment is the memorable final line of Gallus' song ("Love beats everything; let us give in to Love as well"; *omnia vincit Amor, et nos cedamus Amori*, 69), which leads into the poem's closing lines.[31] Here Virgil evokes his own *amor*, which is not a destructive *furor* for the likes of Lycoris or Amyntas, but a growing, living love for Gallus himself.

> haec sat erit, divae, vestrum cecinisse poetam,
> dum sedet et gracili fiscellam texit hibisco,
> Pierides; vos haec facietis maxima Gallo,
> Gallo, cuius *amor* tantum mihi crescit in horas
> quantum vere novo viridis se subicit alnus.
> surgamus: solet esse gravis cantantibus umbra,
> iuniperi gravis umbra, nocent et frugibus umbrae.
> ite domum saturae, venit Hesperus, ite capellae.
> (Verg. *Ecl.* 10.70–77)

> It will be enough, O goddesses, for your poet to have sung this
> as he weaves, sitting down, a basket of slender mallow.
> You shall see to it, Muses, that they are worthwhile for Gallus.
> Gallus! My love for him grows hour by hour, just like
> the green alder shoots forth in the fresh springtime.
> Let's get up! The darkness is no good for singers,
> the darkness is no good for the juniper,
> darkness does damage to the crops too.

---

[30] For carving names in trees, see Callim. *Aet.* fr. 73 Pf., Prop. 1.18.22, Ov. *Her.* 5.21–22; for books and bark, see Serv. ad *Aen.* 11.554.

[31] Coleman 1977 and Clausen 1994 suggest that the phrase *omnia vincit amor* might have been the second half of a pentameter in Gallus' *Amores*. Yet there is no reason why it could not have been the opening of a hexameter, as it is in Virgil's poem; or perhaps the entire line is a direct quotation from Gallus. In any case, the phrase *omnia vincit amor* became proverbial (Macrob. *Sat.* 5.16.7).

Go home! You've had your fill.
The evening star approaches; go home, goats!

The repetition of Gallus' name by means of the device of epanalepsis, itself readable as an allusion to the pastoral motif of the echo, draws attention to the name; as in the sixth *Eclogue*, it is unaccompanied by epithet or adjective. Verbal correspondences with the lines from Gallus' own song draw attention to themselves as well. Virgil's love (*amor*) for Gallus grows (*crescit*) like a young tree (*viridis alnus*) in springtime; Gallus himself had sung that his own loves (*amores*) will grow (*crescent, crescetis*) along with the tender trees (*tenerae arbores*) on which they are written. Gallus' unhealthy, destructive, anxious *amor* for Lycoris that informs this poem gives way to Virgil's fresh, growing, healthy *amor* for Gallus himself, and for his poetic *Amores*.[32] Like the first and, as it happens, the sixth *Eclogue*, this poem, and with it the collection as a whole, comes to its end with the approach of nightfall and hints at the danger it brings. Culminating with the satisfied goats who have the last word, these lines remind us that, just as Gallus imagines carving his *amores* into the bark of living trees, the whole range of *amor* in the *Eclogues* – Virgil's for Gallus just as much as Gallus' for Lycoris, Phyllis, Amyntas, and others – is woven into the fabric of nature.

HORACE

Across Horace's varied poetry, *amor* and *amicitia* are prominent themes, from the *Epistles* and *Satires* to the *Epodes* and *Odes*. The first book of the *Satires* and the first book of the *Epistles* in particular invite being read as poetic performances of *amicitia*, as statistics alone make clear. A reader of the first book of *Satires* finds thirty-five occurrences of the terms *amicus*, *amica*, and *amicitia*, and in the twenty poems constituting the first book of *Epistles* the masculine *amicus* occurs nineteen times: from the first poem, addressed to Maecenas and culminating with the image of Horace as that powerful man's loyal, dependent friend (1.1.105: *de te pendentis, te respicientis amici*), to the eighteenth, addressed to Lollius (*amice*, 1.18.106),

---

[32] Gallus' love for Lycoris: *sollicitos ... amores*, 6; *indigno ... amore*, 10; *insanis ... tua cura Lycoris*, 22 (*insanus amor* in line 44 refers either to his passion for warfare – if we read *me* – or Lycoris' for another man – if we read *te*). Servius' reading of Virgil's declaration *amor* for Gallus in line 73 is all the more deserving of quotation because it has gone largely unnoticed: Virgil's love for Gallus is invisible, like the growth of trees, and the discretion is "because of Caesar," i.e., presumably to avoid provoking his jealousy (*amo, inquit, Gallum, sed latenter, sicut arbores crescunt – nam comparatio ista hoc significat – scilicet propter Caesarem*).

giving advice on how to behave with a richer, more powerful friend whom most modern readers would call a "patron" (24 *dives amicus*, 44 *potentis amici*, 73 *venerandi amici*). In what follows, however, I consider the interplay of *amor* and *amicitia* in Horace's relationship with Maecenas, intimate of Augustus and supporter of a number of poets from Virgil to Horace to Propertius, as played out in two *Odes*, two fragments of Maecenas' poetry, and Suetonius' biography.[33]

One of the *Odes*, quoted and adapted centuries later by Montaigne in order to express his grief at the loss of his friend, opens with words meditating on Maecenas' fear of death.

> Cur me querellis exanimas tuis?
> nec dis *amicum* est nec mihi te prius
>   obire, Maecenas, mearum
>   grande decus columenque rerum.
>
> a! te meae si partem animae rapit   5
> maturior vis, quid moror altera,
>   nec carus aeque nec superstes
>   integer? ille dies utramque
>
> ducet ruinam. non ego perfidum
> dixi sacramentum: ibimus, ibimus,   10
>   utcumque praecedes, supremum
>   carpere iter *comites* parati.
>   (Hor. *Carm.* 2.17.1–12)

> Why wear me down with your complaints?
> Neither to gods nor to me is it dear that you first
> should perish, Maecenas, of my affairs
> the great glory and pillar.
> But, ah! If you, half of my soul, should be swept away
> by some premature violence, why should I keep on,
> a remaining half, worth less, surviving
> only in part? That day
> will be the destruction of us both.
> The oath I swore was not in jest. We will go,
> yes, we will go wherever you lead: comrades
> ready to take the final journey.

These opening stanzas evoke *amicitia* by means of the motifs "part of my soul" and "union in death" and the image of Horace and Maecenas as

[33] See Kilpatrick 1986 for a reading of the first book of Horace's *Epistles* through the lens of *amicitia*. The bibliography on Maecenas and Horace is extensive; see Gold 1987, pp. 115–141, and White 2007, pp. 196–200 for a more recent overview. Oliensis 1997, pp. 162–168, argues that Horace provides the "most extensive documentation of the erotics of the patron–client relation."

traveling companions (*comites*); the fairly unusual use of the neuter adjective *amicum* ("it is dear to") takes on a special point in these verses.[34] But the verses also evoke a passionate *amor*. The opening question would sound perfectly natural in the mouth of an exasperated poetic lover (compare Aeneas' words to Dido: *desine meque tuis incendere teque querellis*, Verg. *Aen.* 4.360) and the motifs "part of my soul" and "union in death" are, as we have seen, commonplaces in Roman discourses of both erotic passion and friendship. Horace's verses have been read together with Catullus' poem on his passionate encounter with Calvus (50); the shared journey wherever Maecenas might lead recalls Catullus' poem to his comrades Furius and Aurelius; and the reference to the military oath has invited comparison to Virgil's Nisus and Euryalus, "both warriors and lovers."[35]

Another poem constructs a triangle linking Horace both to Maecenas and to a woman called Licymnia. *Odes* 2.12 opens by dissuading Maecenas from composing lyric poetry on martial or mythological themes and encouraging him to write a prose work on Augustus' military successes.[36] As for Horace himself:

> me dulcis dominae Musa Licymniae
> cantus, me voluit dicere lucidum
> fulgentis oculos et bene mutuis
> fidum pectus *amoribus*.
> (Hor. *Carm.* 2.12.13–16)

> A song of sweet lady Licymnia: the Muse
> has willed me this, has willed me to tell
> of her bright gleaming eyes, her heart
> true to requited love.

Who is Licymnia? At first glance she seems joined to Horace himself in *amor*, a lyric counterpart to the *amicae* of elegy (the juxtaposition of *me*

---

[34] For the neuter *amicum*, likewise in words addressed to an *amicus*, cf. Cic. *Att.* 12.15: *secundum te nihil est mihi* amicius *solitudine*. Discussions of the dynamics of friendship in this poem include McDermott 1982, Oliensis 1997, pp. 167–168.

[35] Catull. 11.1–4: *comites Catulli ... quaecumque feret voluntas / caelitum, temptare simul parati*; Oliensis 1997, p. 171, n. 38 (an "(elegiacally tinged) erotic *queror/querela*"), p. 168 ("warriors and lovers"). Less persuasive is Oliensis' argument that the interjection *a!* is "stylistically effeminate and grammatically feminine" (p. 167).

[36] *Odes* 2.12.1–10: *nolis longa ferae bella Numantiae ... tuque pedestribus / dices historiis proelia Caesaris*. Nisbet and Hubbard 1991 point to an ambiguity in these opening second-person statements: *nolis* is "a courteous potential subjective," the second person "often generalizing ('one would hesitate') and so to some extent here; it is only at 9, *tu*, that Maecenas is clearly identified." Oliensis 1997, by contrast, reads a strong second person and an indirect invocation of the ideal of the *alter ego*: Horace knows Maecenas' wishes better than Maecenas himself does.

and *dulcis* is expressive, whether we take the latter with *dominae* or with *Musa*) and she is kept quite distinct from Maecenas: *You* should write of Augustus, *I* will write of Licymnia (1: *nolis*; 9: *tuque*; contrast 13, 14: *me*). But an ancient commentator claims that Licymnia is, like Lesbia, Cynthia, and others, a pseudonym for a Roman woman – and not just any woman, but none other than Maecenas' wife Terentia Licinia.[37] For readers who make that connection, the two stanzas that bring the poem to a close are especially titillating.

> num tu quae tenuit dives Achaemenes
> aut pinguis Phrygiae Mygdonias opes
> permutare velis crine Licymniae,
>   plenas aut Arabum domos,
>
> cum flagrantia detorquet ad oscula
> cervicem aut facili saevitia negat
> quae poscente magis gaudeat eripi,
>   interdum rapere occupet?
>   (Hor. *Carm.* 2.12.21–28)

> But you: would you exchange
> wealthy Achaemenes' holdings,
> the luxuriant riches
> of Phrygian Mygdonia,
> for Licymnia's hair –
> or the homes of the Arabs replete –
>
> when she turns her neck to meet
> burning kisses, or refuses them
> with light cruelty – delighting more
> when they are taken
> than when she must ask for them,
> sometimes taking them first herself?

Now the focus is not on Horace but on Maecenas. He would not exchange Licymnia's hair, her neck, and the kisses planted on it for all the riches of the East. Whether or not we connect Licymnia to Terentia, her shifting role within the poem calls attention to itself. Many readers have detected a voyeuristic edge in the poem's evocation of the give-and-take of two close

---

[37] Ps.-Acro ad Hor. *Serm.* 1.2.64. The question as to whether an allusion to Terentia is *intended* in *Odes* 2.12 has been debated back and forth by scholars. See Nisbet and Hubbard 1991 and West 1998, pp. 83–86. Emphasizing how unusual this poem's frank language of bodily pleasures is in the context of Horace's *Odes*, Williams 1968, pp. 299–307, argues that it is participating in the tradition of wedding poetry and thus that the wedding of Maecenas and Terentia lies behind it – "though," he crucially adds, "the solution of such a historical riddle is not essential to appreciation" (p. 305).

friends, each the *alter ego* of the other, and even as the two final stanzas shift Licymnia from the role of Horace's lover to that of Maecenas', it is remarkable that no pronouns, no possessives, mark her or her kisses as belonging to either of the two men in particular.[38]

Only fragments of Maecenas' own poetry survive and, as it happens, two of them are addressed to Horace.

> lucentes, mea vita, nec smaragdos,
> beryllos mihi, Flacce, nec nitentes,
> <nec> percandida margarita quaero,
> nec quos Thynia lima perpolivit
> anellos, nec iaspios lapillos.
> (fr. 185 Hollis = fr. 2 Courtney)

> ni te visceribus meis, Horati,
> plus iam diligo, tu tuum *sodalem*
> hinnulo videas strigosiorem.
> (fr. 186 Hollis = fr. 3 Courtney)

Flaccus my dear, I want
neither sparkling emeralds nor radiant beryls,
nor pure white pearls, nor finger-rings
which a Thynian file has polished to the
uttermost, nor pebbles of jasper.

If I do not love you now, Horace,
more than my innermost self,
may you see your friend
skinnier than a young hinny.

Both fragments give us a glimpse at the lushness of imagery and language for which Maecenas had a reputation, for better or worse, and in their evocation of friendship they invite being read together with Catullus. To be sure, we find neither *amor* nor *amicitia* in these fragments, but instead their near synonyms *diligere* and *sodalis* and the emphatic if poly-valent term of endearment *mea vita*, which punctuates, as we have seen, Catullus' grand claim on a lasting *amicitia* (109). In the first fragment, as Ellen Oliensis puts it, "Maecenas's priamel seems to lack only its romantic conclusion: 'All I want is you,'" and the second invites comparison with one of Catullus' poems to Calvus.[39]

---

[38] Cf. Oliensis 1997, p. 164: "However one reads the scene, the 'other man' hovers very close by the entwined lovers. Whoever Licymnia may be, within this poem she triangulates the desires of two men." See Oliensis 1997, pp. 155–157, for a reading of Tibullus 1.1 and 1.5 as triangulating Tibullus with his patron Messalla and his beloved Delia.

[39] Oliensis 1997, p. 165: "Like a good elegiac lover, Maecenas would rather stay home with his beloved Horace than travel the world in quest of exotic riches." Hollis 2007, p. 319, reminds us

Suetonius' biography of the poet configures Horace and Maecenas in a triangle rather different from that linking them with Licymnia. Here it is not fiery kisses, gleaming eyes, and *mutui amores* that are at stake, but *amicitia*, and the third party is not a woman but a man, and none other than Augustus. The biographer reports that, after befriending first Maecenas and then (presumably through him) Augustus, Horace soon ranked high in each man's *amicitia*. In itself this is not an unusual story; but Suetonius then quotes a teasing letter from Augustus to Maecenas in which the former announces his intention to "lure our Horace away from you (*Horatium nostrum a te cupio abducere*)" and put him in charge of his own correspondence with other friends. The first-person plural calls attention to itself. As always, it can simply be an elegant way of saying "*my* friend Horace," but here its plurality makes itself felt as well, for Horace belongs to both Augustus and Maecenas. The narrative continues. Horace refuses Augustus' overture, and in another letter Augustus playfully uses language reminiscent of that of a spurned lover: asserting his own dignity while chiding Horace's haughtiness (*superbia*).[40] And there is more: Suetonius also records that Augustus, even as he gave him generous financial support, jokingly referred to Horace as *homuncio lepidissimus* and *purissimus penis*, "a delightful little guy" and "an absolutely clean penis." Although both denotation and connotation of the latter phrase are lost to us, it incisively illustrates the role that sexual imagery might play in the banter of masculine *amicitia*.[41]

that reading fragments is not always easy: "This could be a preference for the simple life (however much at variance with reality) or a statement that Maecenas values Horace's friendship more highly than all the jewels listed here." West 1998, p. 128, rather more drily notes that "the terms used in addressing Horace are normally the vocabulary of lovers." Courtney comments that "*mea vita* suggests an erotic element in Maecenas' feelings for Horace," but adds that "we have no trace of this elsewhere" (Courtney 2003, p. 277). Commenting on the second fragment of Maecenas quoted above, Courtney compares Catull. 14.1–2 (*ni te plus oculis meis amarem, / iucundissime Calve*), as does Hollis 2007, pp. 306–308, along with Catull. 45.3 (*ni te perdite amo*). For harsh criticism of Maecenas' poetic style and lifestyle at once, see Seneca, *Epistulae morales* 114.

[40] Suet. *Vita Hor.*: *ac primo Maecenati, mox Augusto insinuatus non mediocrem in amborum locum tenuit ... "ante ipse sufficiebam scribendis epistulis amicorum, nunc occupatissimus et infirmus Horatium nostrum a te cupio abducere ... neque enim, si tu superbus amicitiam nostram sprevisti, ideo nos quoque* ἀνθυπερηφανοῦμεν." For *superbia* cf. Prop. 3.8.35–36 (*gaude, quod nulla est aeque formosa: doleres, / si qua foret; nunc sis iure superba licet*). Oliensis 1997, pp. 165–166, cites Augustus' letter in connection with a reading of *Odes* 3.16, in which "Horace confirms his fidelity to Maecenas by rejecting the advances of another, richer man." See Lowrie 2007 for further discussion of Horace and Augustus.

[41] Suet. *Vita Hor.*: *praeterea saepe eum inter alios iocos "purissimum penem" et "homuncionem lepidissimum" appellat, unaque et altera liberalitate locupletavit.* The manuscripts of Suetonius read *purissimum pene* ("quite pure with respect to his penis"), but modern editors have accepted Muretus'

Readings of Horace's entire body of poetry have often noted that Maecenas' presence diminishes over time. At most this suggests a change in the politics of poetic patronage joining the two men; it has been argued that after his return from military campaigns in 20 BC, Augustus played a more direct role in his relationship with his poet friends.[42] But any ups and downs in their poetic relationship seem to have been quite independent of the *amicitia* which joined Horace and Maecenas to their lives' end and beyond. This friendship is legible not only in the language of lyric poetry and the teasing remarks of private letters. Nearing death, Suetonius reports, Maecenas commended Horace to Augustus' care "as if he were me (*Horati Flacci ut mei memor esto*)," and, as we will see in the next chapter, the two ended up in adjacent tombs on the Esquiline hill in Rome.

PROPERTIUS

Famously, Propertius is a poet of *amor*. The noun occurs in every one of the twenty-two poems in his first book, sometimes with noticeable insistence (eight times in 1.9, a poem of thirty-four lines), while the second book opens by prominently positioning Propertius as a poet of *amor*, his book as soft and effeminate (*mollis*).[43] Propertius' *amor* is famously inspired by the woman whose name opens the collection and who brings him suffering and ecstasy – Cynthia, both *puella* and *domina* – and its qualities are summarized by a series of key words that occur throughout this poetry. This is the realm of the divinities Venus (*dea*) and Cupid (*puer, deus*), the body and its beauty (*corpus, forma*), embraces and kisses (*amplexus, complexus, oscula, basia*), nighttime and the bed (*nox, lectus, torus*), delight and pleasure (*laetitia, voluptas*), flames (*ignis, flamma*), slavery and subjection (*servitium, subiectus*), weeping (*fletus*), anxiety and guilt (*cura, culpa*), fear, frenzy and pallor (*timor, horror, pallor, furor*), loneliness and exclusion (*solus, exclusus, desertus*), a rival (*rivalis*), wretchedness (*miser*), and metaphorical or perhaps even literal death (*perire, mori*). This *amor* is so anchored in the body that the very word can be a metonymy for

---

correction of the ablative to the accusative *penem*. As Adams 1982, p. 36, notes, the phrase is *pars pro toto*: Augustus is making an (affectionate) statement about Horace as a person.

[42] Williams 1968, pp. 86–88, Williams 1990 (arguing that, from the beginning, Augustus' relationship with Maecenas was planned to undergo this shift).

[43] Prop. 2.1.1–2: *quaeritis, unde mihi totiens scribantur amores, / unde meus veniat mollis in ora liber* ... The noun *amor* and verb *amare* occur 74, 82, 34, and 6 times respectively in the four books of Propertius' poetry. For an overview of Venus and *amor–Amor–Amores* in Propertius see Landolfi 2008. Except where otherwise noted, I here use the text of Goold (revised Loeb edition 1999).

copulation.[44] And while Propertius' own persona is immersed in *amor* with a woman, the world of his poetry is by no means heteronormative. In a poem to which we will return, first evoking his *amicitia* with a man he calls Lynceus and exulting in his own success as elegiac poet, he cites both male–female and male–male pairs in Virgil's *Eclogues*, both of them happy in *amor*;[45] elsewhere he expresses the wish that his enemy may desire girls (*amet … puellas*) but his friend boys (*gaudeat in puero*), because the latter are easier to deal with;[46] and, as we will see below, in poem 1.20 he offers helpful warnings to his *amicus* Gallus in connection with the latter's love affair with a young man, his *amores*.

As Gallus reminds us, Propertius is also a poet of *amicitia* between men.[47] Often this relationship is kept distinct from the *amor* he experiences with Cynthia and other women. Melodramatically imagining leaving Rome in order to find a cure for his painful passion, Propertius bids a twofold farewell, first to his *amici* and then to his *puella* (Prop. 3.21.15–16: *Romanae turres et vos valeatis, amici! /qualiscumque mihi tuque, puella, vale*). The configuration recurs throughout this poetry: Cynthia here, his friends there, sometimes encouraging, sometimes dissuading him. The two categories can be distinguished from each other in another way too: *amor* for a woman may set two *amici* against each other.[48]

Not surprisingly, however, *amicitia* and *amor* are by no means always opposed to each other in this poetry. The concept of *fides* evokes and may function as a synecdoche for either; and, as usual in Latin poetry, the very language used to describe heteroerotic couples blends the two discourses, thereby creating without resolving a fundamental tension. The male–female couple consists of *amica* and *vir*, or *puella* and *amicus*, but they

---

[44] Cf. Prop. 1.13.21 (*facili pressit amore*) and 2.9.48 (*ille vir in medio fiat amore lapis*).

[45] Prop. 2.34.71–74: *felix, qui vilis pomis mercaris amores! / huic licet ingratae Tityrus ipse canat. / felix intactum Corydon qui temptat Alexin / agricolae domini carpere delicias!*

[46] Prop. 2.4.17–21: *hostis si quis erit nobis, amet ille puellas: / gaudeat in puero, si quis amicus erit … / alter saepe uno mutat praecordia verbo, / altera vix ipso sanguine mollis erit.* The framing of the couplet draws attention to the opposition between *hostis* and *amicus*, in turn aligned with the objects of their respective desire, *puellas* and *puero* (*alter* and *altera*).

[47] Like that of *amor*, the language of *amicitia* is densest in Books 1 and 2 (8 and 16 occurrences respectively of *amicus/amica/amicitia*) and noticeably thinner on the ground in Books 3 and 4 (5 and 1 occurrence respectively). For an overview of *amici* and *amicitia* in Propertius' poetry see Stok 2008; see Gibson 1995 for the language of *amicitia* in connection with motifs like the *servitium amoris*. For various reasons it is hard to agree with Pizzolato 1993, p. 133: "Dai poeti Tibullo e Properzio non viene cantata quella realtà che noi intendiamo per amicizia. Ciò risulta particolarmente strano nell'estroverso Properzio piú che nel riservato Tibullo."

[48] Cf. Prop. 1.1.25–26, 1.11.25–26, 2.8.1–4, 2.34, 3.24.9–12.

are joined in the first instance not by *amicitia* but by *amor*, sometimes metonymized by the bed (*torus*).[49] In a poem invoking *amor* and beds in another configuration, Propertius casts himself as a woman's *amicus* in another sense. Recalling a time when she was desperately ill, Propertius reminds her that he stood by her sick-bed (*lectus*) as one of her friends (*amici*), weeping and praying for her recovery – unlike his current rival for her love, who was nowhere to be seen. Yet although she is no longer his *amica* and is in fact his *inimica*, he for his part will allow no other woman into his bed (*lectus*), while he wishes that her current lover may become paralyzed in the midst of *amor*.[50]

Propertian poetry likewise exploits the ambivalence of the feminine *amica*. Sometimes it is an adjective modifying a grammatically feminine noun, and the level of semantic interference ranges from relatively low ("fickleness is the *amica* of beautiful women") to high (if you were granted the favor of one night, it was "because she was angry [*offensa*] at me, not because she was kindly disposed [*amica*] to you"; "may Venus never be my rival's *amica*").[51] Most often, however, *amica* is a noun describing the female counterpart of the poet-lover who is cast as her *vir* or *amator*. And most often this woman is Cynthia, who, like Catullus' Lesbia before her, is more than the usual *amica*. In one poem she claims that no man other than Propertius has been in her bed, using the language of *adulterium* and thereby casting their relationship in terms of marriage even as she describes herself as his *amica*.[52] Another poem comes to its memorable end with this couplet:

> nos uxor numquam, numquam seducet *amica*:
> semper *amica* mihi, semper et uxor eris.
> (Prop. 2.6.41–42)

---

[49] For *amica* and *vir* joined by *amor* see 1.6.10–12, 2.33.34; for *puella* and *amicus* see 1.13.5–6, 12; 3.20.9–10 (*fortunata domus, modo sit tibi fidus amicus. / fidus ero: in nostros curre, puella, toros!*). At 2.13.51–52 (*tu tamen amisso non numquam flebis amico, / fas est praeteritos semper amare viros*) *amicus* slides into *vir*.

[50] Prop. 2.9.25–28: *haec mihi vota tuam propter suscepta salutem, / cum capite hoc Stygiae iam poterentur aquae, / et lectum flentes circum staremus amici? / hic ubi tum, pro di, perfida, quisve fuit?* 44–48: *te nihil in vita nobis acceptius umquam; / nunc quoque erit, quamvis sis inimica, nihil. / nec domina ulla meo ponet vestigia lecto: / solus ero, quoniam non licet esse tuum. / atque utinam, si forte pios eduximus annos, / ille vir in medio fiat amore lapis!*

[51] Prop. 2.16.25–26: *vulgo / formosis levitas semper amica fuit*; 2.21.2: *tantum illi Pantho ne sit amica Venus*; 3.8.39–40: *cui nunc si qua datast furandae copia noctis, / offensa illa mihi, non tibi amica, dedit.*

[52] Prop. 2.29.31: *"quid tu matutinus"*, ait, *"speculator amicae?"*; 35–38: *apparent non ulla toro vestigia presso, / signa volutantis nec iacuisse duos. / aspice ut in toto nullus mihi corpore surgat / spiritus admisso motus adulterio.* See also 2.6, 2.7.19–20, 2.18.33–34.

No wife, no girlfriend will ever separate us;
always my girlfriend and always my wife: that's what you will be.

The chiastic arrangement of the terms *uxor – amica – amica – uxor*, intertwined with the internal chiasmus of the first line (*uxor – numquam – numquam – amica*) and the interlocking order in the second (*semper – amica – semper – uxor*), heighten the impact of this evocation of Cynthia's uniqueness, drawing attention to and at the same time confounding the distinction between the roles evoked by those two meaning-laden nouns.[53]

The relationships among male *amici* in Propertius' poetry have drawn the attention of many readers, who have noted that Book 1 begins and ends with poems addressed to Tullus, joined to him in *amicitia* and describable as one of Propertius' "patrons" (1.22.1), and that its very structure intertwines the Cynthia affair with various masculine relationships.[54] Chief among these is that between Propertius and a man or men named Gallus who appears in four poems (1.5, 10, 13, 20; we will return below to the question of poems 21 and 22). There is a growing though not universally shared consensus that these poems refer not only to one and the same man, but that he is none other than the poet Gaius Cornelius Gallus, and recent readings of Gallus in Propertius have tended to invoke the categories of the metapoetic and the homosocial. This poetry is read as saying something *both* about Propertius' and Gallus' relationship, at times triangulated with a third party, *and* about the relationship between their poetry.[55] What I add to these readings in the following, taking a cue

---

[53] The couplet appears in the manuscripts as the final and climactic couplet of poem 2.6, and "there is no intrinsic difficulty involved by the acceptance of this couplet as the conclusion" (Butler and Barber 1933). Nonetheless –a sign of its unusual power – some editors have transposed it: Following a suggestion of Luck, Goold 1999 prints the couplet as the opening of 2.7; Heyworth 2007 moves it to a position after 2.7.6.

[54] There is a long scholarly tradition of reading Book 1 on its own, not least because, unlike what is handed down in the manuscripts as Book 2, it clearly constitutes a compositional unit; whether Propertius entitled Book 1 *Monobiblos* (a title found at Martial 14.189 and in some Propertian manuscripts, and used by many contemporary scholars) is not clear. Poems 1, 4, 5, 6, 7, 9, 10, 12, 13, 14, 20, and 22 are addressed to men who are explicitly or implicitly cast in the role of Propertius' *amicus* and are themselves also poets or, in Tullus' case, play the role of Propertius' patron; the other poems of Book 1 (with the exception of 21) are addressed to or centrally thematize Cynthia. See Sharrock 2000.

[55] Discussions of the Galli in Book 1 include Petrain 2000, Janan 2001, pp. 33–34, Pincus 2004, pp. 168–172, Miller 2004, pp. 68–69. Cairns 2006 offers a sustained reading of Propertian poetry as deeply influenced by the poetry of C. Cornelius Gallus. It has by no means always been a consensus that the Galli of Book 1 are one and the same man or that he is C. Cornelius Gallus (Hollis 2007, p. 252: "I continue to doubt (with Syme, *History in Ovid*, 99ff.) whether any of the Galli in Propertius I are to be identified with the poet Cornelius Gallus"). The metapoetic reading of Propertius' poetry on Gallus is concisely summarized at Cairns 2006, p. 222: "Contemporaries

from Gordon Williams' suggestion that we be alive to the power of individual words in Propertius' poetry, is a close and sustained attention to the interwoven language of *amicitia* and *amor* in Book 1.[56]

The first poem of the book, addressed to Tullus, sounds many of the key themes of Propertian poetry: the name Cynthia itself (1), suffering and self-pity (*miserum me*, 1), desire (*cupidinibus*, 2), a girl (*puella*, 5, 15), cruelty (*saevitia*, 10), a mistress or slave-owner (*domina*, 21; the corresponding term *servitium* first appears in 1.4.4), disease (*non sani pectoris*, 26), hard nights (*noctes amaras*, 33), a bed (*torum*, 36), anxiety (*cura*, 36). All of this is *amor* (4, 16, 17, 32, 34, and 36), but Propertius punctuates his brief mythological narration with a *sententia* linking *amor* to two terms central to the idealization of *amicitia* as well: fidelity and benefactions, *fides* and *benefacta* (16). This poem does not directly cast Propertius' relationship with Cynthia as one of *amicitia*: instead, Cynthia and *amor* are here, *amicitia* and men are there, and Propertius asks the latter for "help for an unwell heart."[57]

The opening couplet of poem 5 evokes the theme of love as painful disease by means of four key terms:

> quid tibi vis, *insane*? meos sentire *furores*?
> *infelix*, properas ultima nosse *mala*.
> (Prop. 1.5.1–2)[58]

What are you up to? Are you insane? Do you want to feel my frenzy?
Unhappy man! You are heading toward the ultimate in suffering.

The addressee remains unnamed for most of the poem; whoever he is, Propertius quickly lays out what awaits him: suffering (*miser*, 2, 18), a woman (*illa*, 5), anxiety (*curarum*, 10), sleeplessness (*somnos*, 11), rejection

---

would also have recognized these Propertian fantasies about Gallus' love affairs as a metaphrased version of recent literary history."

[56] Williams 1968, p. 781: Propertius can "select a word which will create, by itself, a maximum appropriate effect in a given context." For readings of Propertian poetry and especially Book 1 through the lens of the homosocial, see Pincus 2004, Miller 2004, pp. 60–94, Keith 2008, pp. 115–128. Oliensis 1997, pp. 157–162, reads Prop. 1.6 as creating a triangle consisting of Propertius, Cynthia, and Tullus and sees a "more intoxicating blend of *amor* and *amicitia*" in the Gallus poems, and Sharrock 2000, p. 270, concludes that "a relationship with Cynthia is a shared relationship between men"; but neither Oliensis nor Sharrock makes use of the concept of the homosocial. See Rosati 2008 for a reading of rivals and triangles as integral to Propertius' poetry, and elegy in general.

[57] Prop. 1.1.16: *tantum in amore fides et benefacta valent*; 1.25–26: *aut vos, qui sero lapsum revocatis, amici, / quaerite non sani pectoris auxilia*. For discussion of Tullus and Maecenas in Propertius' poetry in general, see Gold 1987, pp. 142–172.

[58] The manuscript tradition actually marks this poem as beginning two lines earlier (i.e. with what is now generally taken to be the final couplet of 1.4) but most editions since Enk's of 1946 print

(*contemptus*, 13; *exclusum*, 20), weeping, dejection and fear (*fletibus, horror, timor*, 15–16), enslavement (*tum grave <u>servitium</u> nostrae cogere puellae / discere*, 19–20, words which reveal that the woman in question is none other than Propertius' domineering lover), pallor (*pallorem*, 21): in a word, *amor* (*nec tibi nobilitas poterit succurrere <u>amanti</u>: / nescit <u>amor</u> priscis cedere imaginibus*, 23–24). Recurring to the theme of disease, the poem then comes to its close, revealing for the first time that this man is Gallus.

> non ego tum potero solacia ferre roganti,
>   cum mihi nulla mei sit medicina mali.
> sed pariter miseri socio cogemur *amore*
>   alter in alterius mutua flere sinu.
> quare, quid possit mea *Cynthia*, desine, *Galle*,
>   quaerere; non impune illa rogata venit.
> (Prop. 1.5.27–32)

I won't be able to offer you consolation then, even if you ask:
I have no remedy for my own ills.
Instead, we will be forced by our shared love, equally
desperate each one, to weep in each other's embrace.
So stop asking about my Cynthia's power, Gallus.
If you ask her, she comes with a vengeance.

In an image that memorably embodies the homosocial, Propertius and Gallus tearfully embrace, equally suffering in their *socius amor*, their shared love. For whom? The phrase suggests the men's affection for each other – we might compare the tears and embraces of Catullus and Veranius, Fortunata and Scintilla – but also their (potentially) shared experience of painful passion for the same woman. Indeed, the couplet insists on the imagery of sharing and of a pair (*pariter; socio; mutua; alter in alterius*), foundational elements in ideals of *amicitia*, while the imagery of compulsion subtly underscores the parallel between the two instances of *amor* at stake. Compare *sed pariter miseri socio <u>cogemur</u> amore* (29–30) with *tum grave servitium nostrae <u>cogere</u> puellae / discere* (19–20), both future passives in the same metrical position. The final couplet verbally enacts the intertwining of the actors in this drama, naming all three players in its first verse (*mea; Cynthia; Galle*) and framing them with an alliterative sequence (*quare, quid, quaerere*).[59]

---

this couplet as the first of 1.5. In line 1, Hemsterhuys' emendation of the manuscript reading *meos* to *meae* is printed by Goold 1999, but not by Heyworth 2007.

[59] Oliensis 1997, pp. 158–162, reads this poem together with Catullus 50; Janan 2001, p. 43, describes Propertius and Gallus "swapping tears and sighs over the (missing) body of Cynthia, as if they were amorous twins – or lovers" (see above, pp. 156–173, on the imagery of brother love). Miller 2004, p. 91, suggests that for readers who recognize a Greek intertext in which the beloved is a

The next poem to name Gallus does so in its third couplet, rapidly sketching a scene of *amor*.

> O iucunda quies, primo cum testis *amori*
> affueram vestris conscius in lacrimis!
> o noctem meminisse mihi iucunda voluptas,
> o quotiens votis illa vocanda meis,
> cum te complexa morientem, *Galle*, puella
> vidimus et longa ducere verba mora!
> (Prop. 1.10.1–6)

What a nighttime of delight! I was there with you,
a witness to the beginning of your love, a conspirator in your tears.
What delight, what pleasure, to remember that night!
How often I will invoke it in my prayers!
As you lay dying in your girl's arms, Gallus,
I saw you dragging out your conversation.

This encounter between Gallus and a woman, the beginning of *amor*, Propertius himself witnessed (*vidimus* 6), now recalling it to his own delight (3) and depicting for ours, with more than a touch of voyeuristic pleasure. Is this woman Cynthia? She is not named, and many readers have felt that she *cannot* be Cynthia – even as they are uncomfortably aware of the possibility.[60] Whoever she is, Propertius casts himself first in the role of witness to the encounter (*testis*), then in that of Gallus' confidant. Like the *amici* to whom Propertius himself appeals in the collection's opening poem (1.1.25–26), he offers the cure (*medicina*) which in Poem 5 he had professed himself unable to find either for Gallus or for himself (1.5.27–28).[61] The cure consists of advice, offered and justified

boy (an epigram by Meleager, *Anth. Pal.* 12.72), "the homosocial bond becomes almost explicitly *hom(m)osexuel*." Quite different the reading of Hodge and Buttimore 1977: "The picture in line 30 is faintly ludicrous, with its erotic overtones ... There is a curious strand in Propertius' feelings towards Gallus; one should compare also the oddities of poem 10." The language of the "ludicrous," "curious," and "odd," combined with the "erotic," may make many contemporary readers think of the "queer"; compare Butler and Barber 1933 ad 1.5.25: "Gallus was a gay deceiver."

60 Cf. Janan 2001, p. 35: "The astonishingly intimate knowledge Propertius records of his friend's mistress' nature (not to mention his nervous discouragement of Gallus' too-keen interest in Cynthia, noted in 1.5) suggests that Gallus has filched Propertius' beloved ... Yet the poem's friendly and congratulatory tone pushes us simultaneously *not* to read the beloved as Cynthia: how could Propertius banter so jauntily with Gallus were the latter an intimate traitor?" Here too a metapoetic reading is possible: cf. Cairns 2006, p. 222 ("Propertius 1.10 and 1.13 do not record that Propertius played the voyeur when Gallus was making love to a girl-friend, but rather refer to Propertius having read a poem by Cornelius Gallus in which Gallus described his own love-making") and Keith 2008, p. 120 (this poem "seems to record Propertius' ecstatic response to Gallus' achievement in the genre").

61 Some readers have found a double meaning in the noun *testis*: cf. Oliensis 1997, p. 160 ("as if Propertius had been transformed into an adjunct of Gallus' lovemaking equipment") and

because of what joins Propertius to Gallus: the bond of *amicitia*, based on trust.

> sed quoniam non es veritus *concredere* nobis,
>   accipe commissae munera laetitiae.
> non solum vestros didici reticere dolores:
>   est quiddam in nobis maius, *amice, fide.*
> possum ego diversos iterum coniungere *amantes,*
>   et dominae tardas possum aperire fores,
> et possum alterius curas *sanare* recentis,
>   nec levis in verbis est *medicina* meis.
> Cynthia me docuit semper quae cuique petenda
>   quaeque cavenda forent: non nihil egit *Amor.*
>   (Prop. 1.10.11–20)

But since you were not afraid to confide in me,
here is the reward for sharing your happiness.
I have learned to keep your pain a secret;
but there's something in me even greater than trustworthiness, my friend.
Lovers who have separated – I can bring them back together.
A lady's cruel door shut to you – I can open it.
I can soothe another's fresh distress;
my words contain no feeble remedy.
Cynthia has taught me what everyone should do –
or should avoid. Love has not been ineffective.

Addressing Gallus with the vocative *amice*, all the more powerful because unaccompanied by any adjective, not even the possessive *mi*, Propertius makes the portentous statement that he has something even greater than *fides* (14), and then helps Gallus with advice drawn from his own experience of the two figures whose names frame the last couplet quoted above: *Cynthia* and *Amor*.

The configuration is familiar: trust and *amicitia* between men here, suffering and *amor* for a woman there. The next poem, imagining Cynthia on vacation in Baiae, repeats the set-up, situating his masculine friendships in the midst of his relationship with her, described as *amor* (1.11.6, 18, 30) and metonymized by her name:

Pincus 2004 (who notes that Gallus' name is the same as that of the eunuch priests of Cybele, p. 174). Among texts using the noun *medicina* in connection with *amicitia* is Cicero's *De amicitia*. Reflecting on the recent death of his *amicus* Scipio, Laelius asserts that he has no need of *medicina* because he can console himself with the knowledge that in death no ill has befallen his beloved friend (Cic. *Amic.* 10).

> seu tristis veniam seu contra laetus *amicis*,
> quicquid ero, dicam *"Cynthia* causa fuit."
> (Prop. 1.11.25–26)

> Whether I go to my friends despondent or elated –
> whatever I am I will say: "It's because of Cynthia."

Poem 12 continues the theme of separation: Cynthia is as far from Propertius' bed (*lecto*) as a river in Sarmatia is from one in northern Italy (1.12.1–4). And so there are no more embraces to nurture their *amor* (5), a relationship associated with *fides* in a couplet of perceptibly Catullan quality and memorably reasserted in the poem's final couplet:

> olim gratus eram; non ullo tempore cuiquam
> contigit ut simili posset *amare fide* …
> mi neque *amare* aliam neque ab hac desistere fas est:
> *Cynthia* prima fuit, *Cynthia* finis erit.
> (Prop. 1.12.7–8, 19–20; cf. Catull. 87, above p. 178)

> I was in favor then; never has it befallen anyone
> to love with a trust like that …
> It would be a crime for me to love another, or to stop loving her.
> Cynthia came first, Cynthia will be the end.

The opening couplet of Poem 13 brings us from Cynthia to an emphatic second-person pronoun *tu*. A first-time reader might well wonder: Is this an address to Cynthia? The first line, with no gender markings and its self-pitying stance ("you rejoice at my suffering"), raises the possibility, but the reader quickly learns that it is not Cynthia but Gallus who is being addressed.

> <u>Tu</u>, quod saepe soles, nostro laetabere casu,
>   <u>Galle</u>, quod abrepto solus *amore* vacem.
> at non ipse tuas imitabor, <u>perfide</u>, voces:
>   fallere te numquam, Galle, *puella* velit.
> (Prop. 1.13.1–4)

> As usual, you will rejoice in my suffering, Gallus:
> I'm alone now, abandoned, my love taken away.
> But I will not talk the way you do, traitor.
> May no girl ever seek to deceive you, Gallus.

The familiar set-up again: on the one hand Propertius and Gallus, in earlier poems joined in *amicitia*; on the other hand, each of the two men joined with a woman in *amor*. But the opening couplets make a melodramatic accusation of a perversion of the ideals of friendship. Far from being an *alter ego* joined to Propertius in the lasting bond of *amicitia*, Gallus rejoices in his misfortune in *amor*, delights that Propertius is alone (*solus*). The address to Gallus as *perfide* in the second couplet reminds us of the polyvalence of the discourse of *fides*, applicable both to *amicitia* and to *amor* in all its range, for the adjective *perfidus* is a weapon wielded by abandoned or betrayed lovers of Latin poetry: by Dido against Aeneas, for example, or Propertius himself against Cynthia.[62]

As the poem progresses we learn that Gallus, too, has not always been the faithful lover. Known for a series of affairs with women, a series of disappointments for the latter (*deceptis… puellis*, 5), he is now falling for one who will put an end to all that and who will avenge her predecessors' pain (9–10).

> haec tibi vulgaris isto compescet *amores*,
> nec nova quaerendo semper *amicus* eris.
> (Prop. 1.13.11–12)

> She will put an end to those common loves of yours;
> you will not always be an *amicus*
> looking for something new.

The couplet is framed by a pronoun and a verb referring to the two characters – the new woman (*haec*) and Gallus (*eris*) – and casts Gallus in a role typical of elegiac poetry: an *amicus* to women, joined to them in *amor*. The idea is clear enough. Gallus' varied erotic experiences with women and his inability to stay with just one will come to an end with this new woman. Yet there is a subtle complexity in the Latin, related to how we construe *semper* and whether we understand the gerund *quaerendo* pseudo-participially. The second verse is usually taken to mean: "You will not be her *amicus* for ever if you continue looking for new experiences" (in other words, if you continue to pursue new affairs, this woman will drop you) but it might also be understood with a rather different emphasis: "You will not be a lover (*amicus*) of the kind who is for ever seeking new experiences" (in other words, your philandering will come to an end with this relationship).[63] Whether *amicus* here suggests "her *amicus*" or

---

[62] Verg. *Aen.* 4.305, 366; Ov. *Her.* 7.79, 118; Prop. 1.11.16 (cf. *perfidia* at 1.15.2, 34).

[63] Fedeli 1988 takes the former route ("se andrai cercando nuove avventure non continuerai a restarle a cuore"), Lee 1994 and Goold 1999 the latter, surprisingly omitting the key term *amicus*: "You'll cease to enjoy the search for novelty" (Lee); "Nor will you always be so eager for new conquests" (Goold). Goold and Lee implicitly accept Camps' suggestion that the adjective *amicus* represents an equivalent of a Greek compound beginning *philo-* (Camps 1961 glosses: "and no longer will you be always on the hunt for new adventures"). Heyworth avoids the issue

"an *amicus*," the parallel positioning of *amores* and *amicus* towards the end of each line of this couplet reminds us that *amicus* can be a near-synonym for *amans* or *amator*.

All the more striking, then, is what follows. Echoing some of the language and imagery of poem 10 (compare 1.10.1 *testis* and 1.10.6 *vidimus* with 1.13.14 *teste* and the repeated *vidi ego* at 1.13.14, 15), Propertius vividly describes the physical signs of Gallus' status as *amicus* to this new woman, climaxing with the same bare vocative *amice* found in the earlier poem (1.10.14) but now casting Gallus as "friend" not of the woman, but of Propertius himself.

> haec non sum rumore malo, non augure doctus:
> vidi ego. me quaeso *teste* negare potes?
> vidi ego te toto vinctum languescere collo
> et flere iniectis, Galle, diu manibus,
> et cupere optatis animam deponere labris,
> et quae deinde meus celat, *amice*, pudor.
> non ego *complexus* potui diducere vestros,
> tantus erat *demens* inter utrosque *furor*.
> non sic Haemonio Salmonida mixtus Enipeo
> Taenarius facili pressit *amore* deus,
> nec sic caelestem flagrans *amor* Herculis Heben
> sensit ab Oetaeis gaudia prima rogis.
> (Prop. 1.13.13–24)

I did not learn this from malicious gossip or from a soothsayer.
No, I saw it. I was a witness: how can you possibly deny it?
I saw you languishing, neck wholly clutched,
long bouts of weeping, Gallus, hands in place.
I saw you longing to leave your soul on the lips you desired.
I saw what happened next – but my modesty means silence, friend.
I could not disentangle your embrace:
the insane frenzy joining you was too much.
Not like this, mingled with the Haemonian river Enipeus,
did Poseidon compel Tyro with a welcome love;
nor like this did Hercules' burning love for heavenly Hebe
taste its first pleasures after the funeral pyre on Mount Oeta.

With perceptibly more voyeurism than in 1.10, Propertius associates Gallus' *amor* with bodies, embraces, kisses, and a woman, and his own *amicitia* for Gallus with the *pudor* that keeps him from telling more. And the first of the two mythological allusions draws attention to itself in all

altogether by taking up a proposal of Watt and emending the universal manuscript reading *amicus* to *inultus*; rather unusually, he offers no discussion of the point in Heyworth 2007.

its concision. In order to have his way with Tyro, who was married to Cretheus but in love with the river-god Enipeus, Poseidon took on the latter's form. Propertius' image of one male figure "mingling" (*mixtus*) with another in order to have intercourse with a female figure gives passing but vivid form to the way homosocial triangles may work.[64]

Poem 19 opens by announcing and intertwining two themes that run throughout Propertius' poetry: Cynthia and *amor* (italicized below), and death, in this case his own (underlined below).[65]

> Non ego nunc tristis vereor, mea *Cynthia*, <u>Manes</u>,
> nec moror extremo debita <u>fata rogo</u>;
> sed ne forte *tuo* careat mihi <u>funus</u> *amore*,
> hic timor est ipsis durior <u>exsequiis</u>.
> non adeo leviter nostris *puer* haesit ocellis,
> ut <u>meus</u> *oblito* <u>pulvis</u> *amore* vacet.
>
> (Prop. 1.19.1–6)

> No, I am not afraid of the grim spirits of death now, my Cynthia;
> I am not worried about our final debts to the funeral pyre.
> No: that my funeral should be unaccompanied by your love,
> *that* is more frightful to me than the rites themselves.
> Boy Cupid did not enmesh himself in my eyes so casually
> that my ashes should lie bereft, love forgotten.

The last line quoted brings to the surface a cluster of themes central to this entire collection of poetry – separation and forgetting, the prospect of losing love – at the same time establishing a link with one of the poems to Gallus (cf. 1.13.2: *Galle, quod <u>abrepto</u> solus <u>amore</u> vacem*). After two couplets alluding to the mythic tale of Protesilaus, first to be slain at Troy and allowed to briefly leave Hades in order to see his wife Laodamia (7–10), Propertius imagines himself in the afterlife.

> illic quidquid ero, semper tua dicar imago:
> traicit et fati litora magnus *amor*.
>
> (Prop. 1.19.11–12)

> There, whatever I am, I will always be called *your* spirit.
> A great love crosses over to the other shore of death.

Magnus amor continues to bind even after the separation of death. In the next and final chapter we will consider the performance of *amicitia* in and beyond the grave.

---

[64] See Adams 1982, pp. 180–181, for the verb *misceri* as euphemism for copulation.
[65] See Papanghelis 1987 for *amor*, death, *Liebestod*, and related themes in Propertius.

In its final couplet, poem 19 reiterates the key term, which constitutes a bridge to the opening of the poem that follows.

> quare, dum licet, inter nos laetemur *amantes*.
> non satis est ullo tempore longus *amor*.
> (Prop. 1.19.25–26)
>
> * * *
>
> hoc pro continuo te, Galle, monemus *amore*,
>   quod tibi ne vacuo defluat ex animo:
> saepe imprudenti fortuna occurrit *amanti*.
>   crudelis Minyis sic erat Ascanius.
> est tibi non infra specie, non nomine dispar,
>   Theiodamanteo proximus *ardor* Hylae.
> (Prop. 1.20.1–6)[66]

And so, as long as we can, let us enjoy each other as lovers.
Love never lasts long enough, no matter the time.
* * *
This is my advice to you, Gallus, for longlasting love:
don't let it slip your mind in your reveries!
Misfortune often happens to a careless lover:
the river Ascanius was hard on the Argonauts that way.
No lower on the scale of looks, no different in name,
second to Hylas son of Theiodamas is he, your flame.

In the final couplet of poem 19 we read that *amor* is to be enjoyed as long as possible in this life (*dum licet*, line 25), and the first line of this poem describes it as lasting (*continuo*). But of course this is not quite the same *amor*. In poem 19 the noun refers to Propertius' relationship with Cynthia, whereas in poem 20 it refers to – what? The set-up is familiar (a man dispenses warnings and advice to a friend who is caught in the snares of *amor*) but there is a twist or two. Since Gallus' *ardor* is not for a woman, the homosocial dynamics are complicated by the fact that all three parties are male. And what of the opening appeal *pro continuo amore*? Is this "in the name of our uninterrupted *amor* for each other," or "in the interests of your uninterrupted *amor* for Hylas," or both at once?[67]

---

[66] Goold 1999 adopts Butrica's emendation of the opening word of the poem from the universal manuscript reading *hoc* to *haec*. With most other modern editors, including Heyworth 2007, I print the manuscript reading. I also accept the most obvious implication of the phrase *non nomine dispar*; the alternative – that *nomen* means "fame" rather than "name" – is suggested by Butler and Barber 1933 (cf. 2.20.19, *quod si nec nomen nec me tua forma teneret*). Hylas is a well attested name of slaves and thus also of freedmen; and, as Heyworth 2007, p. 87, points out, an epigram by Crinagoras plays on the theme of a dead boy named Eros (A.P. 7.628.6: οὔνομα καὶ μορφὴν αὐτὸς ἔδωκεν Ἔρως; compare the same poet's epigram on Selene, A.P. 7.633).

[67] The productive ambiguity has been noted by many. Even Heyworth 2007, whose readings tend toward the elimination of inconsistency or ambivalence, observes that the phrase "seems

As the poem continues, Propertius issues a warning to Gallus: Be watchful of your Hylas, lest, like his mythological namesake, he be stolen from you by Italian women. The women are figured as lustful nymphs, driven by *amor* as the nymphs are by *cupido*, and in the subsequent narration of the story of Hercules' beloved Hylas, the latter's physical beauty is evoked, and the unwanted kisses of Zetes and Calais, sons of the North Wind, are described with the noun *oscula*, emphatically repeated at the beginning of two successive verses.[68] In the poem's last couplet Propertius reprises the role of giver of advice.

> his, o *Galle*, tuos monitus servabis *amores*,
> *formosum* Nymphis credere visus Hylan.
>> (Prop. 1.20.51–52)

> Take this advice, Gallus, and watch out for your love:
> it seems you've entrusted the lovely Hylas to some nymphs.[69]

This final couplet invites being read together with the poem's first:

> hoc pro continuo te, *Galle*, monemus *amore*,
> quod tibi ne vacuo defluat ex animo.
>> (Prop. 1.20.1–2)

Each begins with a form of the demonstrative (*hoc*; *his*); each addresses Gallus in its first line with the vocative *Galle* juxtaposed with a personal pronoun or possessive adjective (*te, Galle*; *o Galle, tuos*); each speaks of warning (*monemus*; *monitus*); each raises the notion of continuity (*continuo*; *servabis*). And each ends with the key term *amor*, polyvalent as always. But although there is plenty of that elusive quality in this poem, *amicitia* does not appear; the closest we get is when Hylas is decorously described as Hercules' "companion" (*comes invicti iuvenis*, 23).

---

designed for ambiguity" (p. 100 n. 66). For readings of Prop. 1.20 in metapoetic vein, see King 1980 (suggesting that Hylas evokes Propertius himself), Petrain 2000 (seeing a pun on *hyle*, "subject matter": Gallus is being advised to protect his poetic material from those who might steal it), Pincus 2004, Cairns 2006, pp. 219–249 (noting that Gallus himself almost certainly wrote a Hylas poem). Cornelius Gallus' books of elegiac poetry, like those of Ovid after him, almost certainly bore the title *Amores*.

[68] Prop. 1.20.11–12: *Nympharum semper cupidas defende rapinas – / non minor Ausoniis est amor Adryasin*; 27–28: *oscula... oscula*; 45: *cuius et accensae Dryades candore puellae*; 48: *rapto corpore*; 52: *formosum*.

[69] I give the MS reading, which, as Butler and Barber 1933 observe, yields "perfectly satisfactory sense"; Camps glosses "for it has seemed to me that you ..." or "for I have seen you ..." Goold 1999 prints Palmer's emendation *ni vis perdere rursus Hylan*. Heyworth 2007 intervenes even more drastically, positing a lacuna of two lines between 51 and 52 and printing the last line thus: *formosum nymphis credere rursus Hylan.*

The final two poems of Book 1 form a pair apart. Poem 21, abruptly shifting from erotic themes, speaks in the voice of a soldier who has been killed by unknown hands after having escaped the Caesarian forces in the fighting at Perusia in 41–40 BC; his name is, of all things, Gallus. Poem 22 is in the voice of Propertius himself, addressing Tullus (to whom the opening poem of the collection was also addressed) and making the surprising revelation that he is related to the Gallus of the preceding poem. Poems 21 and 22 thus constitute a tightly bound pair in themselves, the *sphragis* to Book 1, and the closure of a ring composition. Among the many questions raised by these two poems, I begin by drawing attention to the name Gallus. As a point of historical fact, the Gallus of poems 21 and 22 is clearly not the same man of the earlier poems of this book, nor is he Gaius Cornelius Gallus. But as a point of reading, matters are not so easily settled. In a collection of poems so densely and artfully constructed as Propertius' first book, the name Gallus invites scrutiny; at the same time, as I suggest in what follows, the two poems continue the imagery of *amicitia* and *amor* intertwined throughout the book.[70]

Poem 21 opens thus:

> Tu, *qui* consortem properas evadere casum,
>   miles ab Etruscis saucius aggeribus,
> quid nostro gemitu turgentia lumina torques?
>   pars ego sum vestrae *proxima* militiae.
>   (Prop. 1.21.1–4)

You there! In a hurry to avoid a destiny like mine?
A wounded soldier coming from the ramparts of Tuscany,
why do you turn your eyes, bulging with fear at our groans?
I am a part of your army, the closest.

Already some echoes may be heard, for example of the opening couplet of one of the poems to Gallus:

---

[70] For readings that find positive value in considering all of the Galli of Book 1 together, see Nicholson 1999, Sharrock 2000, p. 268, Janan 2001, pp. 33–52, Pincus 2004, Miller 2004, pp. 68–69. Keith 2008, pp. 7–8, separates out the Gallus of the final two poems from the others; Hutchinson 1984, p. 105, suggests that the Gallus of poem 21 is the father of the Gallus of preceding poems; even less persuasive is Heyworth's 2007 suggestion that *Gallum* at 1.21.7 may be a scribal error. It is certainly possible that Propertius happened to have a relative named Gallus who died in the aftermath of the siege of Perusia: the name is common enough. In some recent scholarship the speaker of poem 21 is cleverly called "the dying Gallus," punning on the name of the statue in the Capitoline Museums. Following Williams 1968, pp. 172–185, however, I understand the Gallus of this poem to be *already dead*; like Cornelia in Prop. 4.11, he is speaking from beyond the grave.

<u>Tu</u>, *quod* saepe soles, nostro laetabere <u>casu</u>,
Galle, quod abrepto solus *amore* vacem.
(Prop. 1.13.1–2)

Each opening line is framed by the emphatic pronoun *tu* and the noun *casus*; each follows the pronoun with a subordinate clause (beginning respectively *qui* and *quod*); each contains the motif of separation (*evadere*; *abrepto*). The adjective *proxima*, whose precise sense in this line has been debated,[71] echoes two of the Gallus poems (1.13.29: *cum sit Iove dignae proxima Ledae*; 1.20.6: *Theiodamanteo proximus ardor Hylae*), and the three occurrences of the adjective remind us the kinds of *amor* characteristic of Propertius' poetry. The dead Gallus is *proxima pars* of his comrade's brigade; the living Gallus' new woman is *proxima* to Leda in her beauty; his Hylas is *proximus* to the mythical figure in name and looks.

As poem 21 continues, the speaker reveals his own name, laden as it is.

sic te servato ut possint gaudere parentes
et soror acta tuis sentiat e lacrimis:
Gallum per medios ereptum Caesaris enses
effugere ignotas non potuisse manus;
et, quaecumque super dispersa invenerit ossa
montibus Etruscis, haec sciat esse mea.
(Prop. 1.21.5–10)

Save yourself, so that parents may rejoice
and from your tears a sister learn what has happened:
that Gallus, though he escaped from the very midst of Caesar's swords,
was unable to avoid death at unknown hands.
And whatever bones she may find scattered
over the Tuscan hills, let her know: these are mine.

Who is this sister? "Yours" or "mine"? The Latin text of lines 5–6 has been emended, printed, and interpreted in various ways. Some have understood her to be Gallus' sister (in which case she might be the soldier's wife, close to him as are the *parentes* of the preceding line), while others take her to be the soldier's sister (and Gallus' girlfriend, betrothed, or wife).[72] However we understand the situation, the triangular configuration is clear. Gallus

---

[71] Note the subtle differences among Butler and Barber 1933 ("your close comrade-in-arms"), Williams 1968, p. 173 ("I belong to the same unit and fought at your side"), Goold 1999 ("I am the closest person to you among your comrades-in-arms"), and Heyworth 2007 ("I am the closest part of your army," explaining "I am one of your fellow soldiers, and the closest one to you now"); Camps sees a temporal meaning ("recently, lately").

[72] For various readings of the identity of this sister see Williams 1968, pp. 176–177, Nicholson 1999, Janan 2001, p. 40. Accepting an emendation first proposed by T. T. Sluiter, which would specify the woman's name as Acca, Heyworth 2007 prints *sic te servato possint gaudere parentes: / me soror Acca tuis sentiat e lacrimis*. For another *soror Acca*, see Verg. *Aen.* 11.824 (above, p. 73).

links himself to his fellow-soldier on the one hand, a woman on the other, and these two to each other, in an utterance of pressing intensity. What unites them all is neither *amicitia* nor *amor* but tears and death, his own death (*ossa ... mea*).

The final poem of Book 1 opens with an address to the man who had been addressed in the book's first poem, and invocation of that relationship which has shaped so much of what has preceded even as it has gone unmentioned in the last few of its poems.

> Qualis et unde genus, qui sint mihi, Tulle, Penates,
>   quaeris pro nostra semper *amicitia*.
> si Perusina tibi patriae sunt nota sepulcra,
>   Italiae duris funera temporibus,
> cum Romana suos egit discordia civis
>   (sic mihi praecipue, *pulvis Etrusca*, dolor,
> *tu* proiecta mei *perpessa es* membra propinqui,
>   *tu* nullo miseri *contegis* ossa solo),
> proxima suppositos contingens Umbria campos
>   me genuit terris fertilis uberibus.
>
> (Prop. 1.22)

What my standing, whence my family, Tullus, who my household gods:
all this you ask in the name of our eternal friendship.
If you have heard of the graves of our homeland at Perusia –
Italy's funeral at a dark hour, when Rome's strife afflicted her citizens
(dust of Tuscany, my greatest grief,
you put up with my relative's remains cast upon you;
you fail to cover his bones, the wretch, with earth):
– the closest part of Umbria touching upon the fields that lie below
gave birth to me, fertile with fruitful fields.

The poem foregrounds bonds between men. First there is that between Propertius and Tullus, prominently evoked as *amicitia* in a syntactically ambivalent phrase (does *semper* modify *quaeris* or *amicitia*?) which echoes the differently ambivalent opening of poem 20 (*hoc pro continuo te, Galle, monemus amore*, 1.20.1), which itself, as we have seen, creates verbal links joining Propertius' *amor* for Gallus with his *amor* for Cynthia and Gallus' *amor* for Hylas.[73] The second bond foregrounded by this poem is that between Propertius and the man here described as his *propinquus*, whose name was revealed in the preceding poem to be none other than

---

[73] For a request made *pro nostra amicitia* cf. Cic. *Fam.* 13.51, 13.77 (letters of recommendation), *Att.* 3.18.1, 10.8b.1–2. Confessing that he cannot remember its source, Heyworth 2007, p. 100, records the suggestion that Propertius' line contains a riddling *sphragis (PRO nostra semPER amiciTIa)*.

Gallus. This connection is established in a parenthetical sentence (lines 6–8) which simultaneously has the effect of making this poem's syntactical structure complex if not tortuous, and of binding the poem to its predecessor.

Of particular interest is the way in which the relationship between Propertius and the now-dead Gallus is mediated by a third party, linguistically marked as feminine: not Cynthia or a sister, but the "dust of Tuscany (*pulvis Etrusca*)," practically personified by means of a twofold apostrophe and anaphora of the personal pronoun (*tu ... perpessa es*; *tu ... contigis*), its feminine grammatical gender underscored by the morphology of the first verb form. The poem's final couplet introduces another geographical name (*Umbria*), modifying it with an adjective which reiterates the feminine morphology and creates a further link with poem 21 and, through it, with a man named Gallus: *proxima* (cf. 1.21.4, 1.20.6, 1.13.29). Readers who perceive the links may pause for a moment on the word's range of denotation and connotation. Like *propinquus* itself in line 7, the adjective *proximus* suggests connections, bonds, relationships.[74] And so, with the motifs of proximity and connection and a man named Gallus, and the mediating presence of the feminine in the midst of a masculine world, Propertius places his seal on this book, with its tight weave of passion and death, poetic self-awareness, men and women. What distinguishes Propertius' relationship with his Gallus from that with his Cynthia is clear enough – Cupid, Venus, and the bed; flames, servitude, and suffering – yet the overlaps deserve attention too. In both there is love and affection, constancy and suspicion, trust and its violation, pleasure and pain; in both, in short, there is *amicitia* and there is *amor*.

PETRONIUS

Petronius' *Satyricon*, regularly if imprecisely called an example of the "Roman novel," has a form unique among surviving Latin texts: an extensive first-person prose narrative regularly interspersed with poetry, in the tradition of so-called Menippean satire. Among the panoply of interpersonal relationships narrated by Encolpius, passing and lasting,

---

[74] Other occurrences of the adjective in Propertius are at 1.11.4 (*proxima Misenis aequora nobilibus*), 2.1.75 (*si te forte meo ducet via proxima busto*), 2.24.32 (*discidium vobis proximus annus erit*), 4.6.56 (*proxima post arcus Caesaris hasta fuit*). For *proximi* cf. Cic. *Div. Caec.* 47: *L. Appuleium esse video proximum subscriptorem*; Ter. *Phorm.* 125: *qui sint genere proximi*; Cic. *Verr.* 2.2.48: *sed proximum, paene alterum filium*, 2.3.157 (Verres' freedman Timarchides) *coniunctus ac proximus*; Sall. *Iug.* 80: *regis Bocchi proximos*; 97: *proximos eius donis corrupit*. Val. Max. 4.7.pr. (see Introduction, p. 9) distinguishes one's relations (*propinqui*) from one's friends (*amici*).

of all possible configurations of gender, we find *amor* and *amicitia*
joined with *libido* and physical pleasures openly described, in what is
probably the most richly detailed of masculine triangles in Latin literature: that consisting of Encolpius himself, Giton, and Ascyltos.[75] Giton
is a beautiful *puer* comparable to Ganymede, about 16 years old; he and
Encolpius, called *amantes*, periodically end up in bed, although the
impotence with which Encolpius has been afflicted just as periodically
comes between them.[76] Describing their relationship as far more than a
passing physical connection, Encolpius uses the language both of kinship and of friendship, *sanguis* and *amicitia*,[77] and periodically draws
on imagery traditionally associated with *amicitia*, such as the motifs of
unity in death and the contest of death. Giton passionately swears that
he wants to die before Encolpius (94.10), and the two tie themselves to
each other as they face what they think is imminent death in a storm
at sea (114.8–11). Then there is this brief poetic narration of a scene of
lovemaking:

> qualis nox fuit illa, di deaeque,
> quam mollis torus! haesimus calentes
> et transfudimus hinc et hinc labellis
> errantes animas. valete, curae
> mortales. ego sic perire coepi.
> (Petron. *Sat.* 79.8)

> What a night that was, O gods and goddesses!
> How soft the bed! We clung to each other, hot,
> and with our lips transferred here and there
> our wandering souls. Farewell, anxieties
> of mortals! Thus began my destruction.

From the opening invocation to gods of both sexes to the image of
exchanging souls through a kiss, the poem dwells insistently on duality
and reciprocity, and the phrase *transfudimus ... animas* incarnates the

---

[75] Another, passing triangle arises in the episode on board ship. Encolpius watches as his former
girlfriend Tryphaena and current boyfriend Giton are drawn to each other: as he puts it, "I
couldn't figure out whether I should be more angry at the boy for taking my *amica* from me,
or at my *amica* for corrupting the boy" (Petron. *Sat.* 113: *nec tamen adhuc sciebam, utrum magis
puero irascerer, quod amicam mihi auferret, an amicae, quod puerum corrumperet*).

[76] Giton as beautiful *puer*: 92, 97, 105 (cf. 92.3: Eumolpus praises him as a Ganymede); Giton and
Encolpius as *amantes*: 79.10, 95.1, 99.2; the two of them in bed, interrupted by Ascyltos: 11;
Encolpius' impotence as a disturbance to their relationship: 128–129.

[77] Petron. *Sat.* 80.6: *vetustissimam consuetudinem putabam in sanguinis pignus transisse*; 81.5: *reliquit
veteris amicitiae nomen*; 91.9: *et ut facile intellegeret redisse me in gratiam et optima fide reviviscen-
tem amicitiam, toto pectore adstrinxi*.

ideal of *amicitia* as a single soul in two bodies, giving bodily meaning to the concept of the *alter ego*.[78]

The second side of the triangle consists of Encolpius and Ascyltos. Unlike the *puer* Giton, Ascyltos is Encolpius' age-mate, and both the narrator Encolpius and other characters in his narrative describe their relationship as one of *amicitia* and *familiaritas*.[79] But that is not all. In the fiery encounters which follow Ascyltos' successful attempt to construct the third and final side of the triangle by seducing Giton and eventually luring him away from Encolpius (9, 11, 79), Ascyltos' and Encolpius' angry words reveal that in addition to having been joined in *amicitia*, they had shared physical pleasures as well. In the first of these scenes Encolpius assails Ascyltus as a "whore" who has played "the woman's role" and befouled his mouth in sexual encounters. This might be read as empty macho bluster, but it might also be a mean-spirited recollection of their own experience.[80] When Ascyltos returns the compliment in an outburst of linguistic aggression, he makes direct allusion to an incident from their past:

non taces, nocturne percussor, qui ne tum quidem, cum fortiter faceres, cum pura muliere pugnasti, cuius eadem ratione in viridario *frater* fui, qua nunc in deversorio puer est? (Petron. *Sat.* 9)

Why don't you shut up, you murderer by night! Not even when you were performing with all your strength did you do it with a clean woman. I was your brother in the garden the same way the boy now is in the inn.

Here the term *frater*, which, as we have seen, usually comes with connotations of value and prestige, is used to convey an insult. What is its content? Ascyltus' retort is effective, the insult well sharpened, only if he is invoking the paradigm of penetrative role so important to the Roman discourse of masculine sexuality. Ascyltus' point thus seems to be that – in violation of usual norms whereby older penetrates younger – the *puer* Giton is playing the penetrative role with

---

[78] The motif of kisses as the blending of souls recurs in Encolpius' narrative (cf. 132.1, identified as the manuscripts as narrating an encounter with a boy named Endymion, but some take it to refer to Encolpius and Circe). See also Catulus fr. 1 Courtney (inspired by an epigram of Callimachus) and Apuleius fr. 6 Courtney (inspired by an epigram attributed to Plato) with Courtney 2003, pp. 76, 397. Connors 1998, p. 69, points to the motif of sex as figurative death.

[79] Petron. *Sat.* 79.11: *fides et communis amicitia*; 80.3: *familiaritatis clarissimae sancta; amicitiae sacramentum*; 80.8: *paulo ante carissimum sibi commilitonem fortunaeque etiam similitudine parem .... nomen amicitiae*; 97.9: *per memoriam amicitiae perque societatem miseriarum*.

[80] Petron. *Sat.* 9.6: *muliebris patientiae scortum, cuius ne spiritus <quidem> purus est*.

Encolpius, and that Ascyltus himself had done the same in an earlier, now lost episode in a garden.[81]
But this is hardly the end of the matter. After Giton has left Encolpius for Ascyltus, Encolpius indulges in a soliloquy combining massive doses of self-pity with bitter assaults on both Giton and Ascyltos.

et quis mihi hanc solitudinem imposuit? adulescens omni libidine impurus et sua quoque confessione dignus exilio, stupro liber, stupro ingenuus, cuius anni ad tesseram venierunt, quem tamquam puellam conduxit etiam qui virum putavit. quid ille alter? qui die togae virilis stolam sumpsit, qui ne vir esset a matre persuasus est, qui opus muliebre in ergastulo fecit, qui postquam con-turbavit et libidinis suae solum vertit, reliquit veteris *amicitiae* nomen et – pro pudor! – tamquam mulier secutuleia unius noctis tactu omnia vendidit. iacent nunc *amatores* obligati noctibus totis, et forsitan mutuis libidinibus attriti deri-dent solitudinem meam. sed non impune. nam aut vir ego liberque non sum, aut noxio sanguine parentabo iniuriae meae. (Petron. *Sat.* 81.3–6)

And who was it that has condemned me to this solitude? A young man filthy with all kinds of lust; by his own confession worthy of being exiled; a free man – freeborn at that! – thanks to his debauchery. He put his young self up for sale for a ticket, and he was rented like a girl even by those who thought him a man. And what about that other one? On the day he should have put on his man's toga for the first time, he put on a matron's dress. He let his mother persuade him not to be a man. He played the woman in the slaves' prison. And after he had lost everything and relocated his lust, he abandoned the name of our old friendship and – the shame of it! – sold everything, like some loose woman, for just one night of groping. There they lie now, lovers, wrapped up in each other all night long, and after wearing each other down in lust they probably make fun of me for being alone. But they'll regret it! Either I am no man – no free man at that – or else I will avenge with their guilty blood the wrong they've done me.

Here Encolpius invokes what he had previously had with Giton not as *amor* but as an "old friendship" (*vetus amicitia*), and in his narrative pre-ceding this passage, punctuated by a poem, he had bitterly reflected on Ascyltos' neglect of the *amicitia* he had shared with Encolpius;[82] for their part, however, Giton and Ascyltos are *amatores* joined in a sordid affair by *mutuae libidines*. Rather than aligning one with a masculine role and the

---

[81] It is suggestive that Encolpius makes no attempt at denial, indeed quickly changes the subject, and the quarrel dissolves into laughter. For other scandalized or bemused references to younger penetrating older, in reversal of the normative scheme, see Sen. *Ep.* 47.4, Mart. 3.71, and for per-formances of gender in this and other scenes from the *Satyricon* see Williams 2010.

[82] Petron. *Sat.* 80.8–9: *egreditur superbus cum praemio Ascyltos, et paulo ante carissimum sibi com-militonem fortunaeque etiam similitudine parem in loco peregrino destituit abiectum. "nomen amicitiae, sic, quatenus expedit, haeret; /calculus in tabula mobile ducit opus. / dum fortuna manet, vultum servatis, amici; / cum cecidit, turpi vertitis ora fuga."* For this brief poem see Labate 1995, Connors 1998, pp. 69–70.

other with a woman, Encolpius feminizes them both: Ascyltus was rented like a girl (*tamquam puellam*), Giton played the role of a slave-woman in prison (*tamquam mulier secutuleia*). Imagining the two in bed with each other, Encolpius' words point to the implication: Like two women, neither of them the phallic means to penetrate the other, and so they wrap themselves around each other and finally wear each other out (*obligati, attriti*).

By contrasting the *libido* linking Ascyltos and Giton with his own relationship with Giton, and by constructing the latter not as *amor* but as *amicitia*, Encolpius plays a strong hand. *Amicitia* trumps *amor*, which after all too easily slides precisely into *libido* and can raise uncomfortable questions about who is playing what role. And yet, as we have seen, when narrating their happier moments Encolpius portrays himself and Giton not only as participating in *amicitia* but also as *amantes* whose relationship is not cast in hierarchical terms of penetration, but in terms of mutuality, sharing, exchange. When things are going well, in other words, Encolpius happily ignores any such invidious distinctions in favor of blissful imagery of exchange, friendship, love; when he finds himself betrayed, he reaches for the traditional hierarchical language of masculinity and effeminacy, lust and disgrace. The contrast is revealing, the dynamic hardly limited to this text. Catullus, for example, extols Furius and Aurelius in one poem as his comrades (*comites*) who will follow him wherever destiny may lead, in another subjects them to a memorable poetic assault as *pathici* and *cinaedi*, exploiting to the full the obscene language of penetration.[83] The contrast is typical. Two kinds of masculine voice make themselves heard throughout the Latin textual tradition: the loud voice of a man on the attack, appealing to hierarchical protocols of penetration and gender in order to align his opponent with women; and the softer, more subtle voice of a man recalling or evoking the shared pleasures of *amicitia* with another.[84]

CICERO'S LETTERS

Cicero's surviving correspondence consists of more than 900 letters, gathered and published at some point after his death in a set of compilations: sixteen books of letters to Titus Pomponius Atticus dating from 68 to

[83] Catull. 11.1: *Furi et Aureli, comites Catulli*; 16.1–2: *pedicabo ego vos et irrumabo, / Aureli pathice et cinaede Furi.*

[84] For different styles of masculine performance in Latin literature see Gunderson 2000, Wray 2001, Williams 2010, pp. 170–176.

44 BC; three books to his brother Quintus from 59 to 54 BC; three books of correspondence with Marcus Junius Brutus from the spring and summer of 43 BC in the aftermath of Julius Caesar's assassination; and sixteen books of letters dating from 62 to July 43 BC to and from a variety of men moving at the highest political levels, but also including letters to his wife Terentia (Book 14) and his freedman Tiro (Book 16). This last collection was given the title *Epistulae ad diversos* in some Renaissance manuscripts, *Epistulae familiares* or *Epistulae ad familiares* in others, and the last title has stuck.[85] Since Cicero notoriously negotiated and manipulated a wide range of alliances, relationships, friendships with a wide range of men in the social and political elite of his day, a reading of *amicitia* and *amor* in his correspondence illustrates some of the ways interpersonal relationships might be described and performed in the private communication of such a man. While the surviving corpus contains some letters *to* Cicero (letters from Marcus Caelius Rufus are gathered as Book 8 of *Ad familiares*) the correspondence is overwhelmingly unidirectional. We have no letters *from* Atticus, Terentia, or Tiro. In what follows, then, I read not so much "love and friendship in Cicero's letters" as Cicero's performance of interpersonal relationships in his private correspondence in and through language.

That language is familiar enough. We read of *amici, familiares*, and *necessarii*, of concepts like *benevolentia* and *voluntas*, of the wielding of influence (*gratia*) and the mutually reinforcing, ongoing exchange of *beneficia* and *officia*. The terms *amici* and *amicitia* are especially prominent on the landscape of Cicero's correspondence – a search of the PHI *Classical Latin Texts* database yields 409 occurrences of the two nouns in the letters, along with 265 of *familiaris/familiaritas/familiariter*, and 196 of *necessarius/necessitudo* – and pervading them all is *amor*. It is only a slight oversimplification to say that in the speech genre of letters the verb *amare* signals the existence of *amicitia* just as the verb *odi* signals the existence of *inimicitiae* (we will return to the point below in a reading of Fronto's correspondence). For this reason among others, then, in many cases it would be a serious mistranslation to render *amor* and *amare* in Cicero's correspondence with English "love," which so easily brings readers into the

---

[85] The editions and commentaries of D. R. Shackleton Bailey are fundamental (*Ad Atticum*: Cambridge 1965–1970; *Ad familiares*: Cambridge 1977). Studies include Boissier 1908, Carcopino 1947 (an empassioned and much criticized reading of the correspondence as a massive indictment of Cicero's character), Cugusi 1983, pp. 159–176, Jäger 1986, Deniaux 1993 (focusing on the letters of recommendation but with much to say about Cicero's correspondence in general), Hutchinson 1998, Citroni Marchetti 2000, pp. 3–99, Oppermann 2000, Gunderson 2007, Hall 2009, White 2010.

realm of the romantic or erotic: "affection," "have a liking for," "be fond of," or even "support" are usually more appropriate renderings. When, for example, Cicero reports to Atticus a conversation he had with Caesar and concludes *credo igitur hunc me non amare, at ego me amavi* (*Att.* 9.18), or when he writes of Brutus' *amor* for Atticus and a shared stroll (*Att.* 13.35.3, *de Bruti amore vestraque ambulatione*), Shackleton Bailey's translations are more accurate than any using the English word "love": "I imagine Caesar is not pleased with me, but I was pleased with myself" and "Brutus' affection." Likewise, the agent noun *amator* and participle *amans*, in elegiac poetry usually translatable as "lover," are in Cicero's letters (and, as we have seen, in some inscriptions and graffiti: above, p. 127) often best translated with "admirer" or "supporter" or periphrases like "fond of."[86] Similar caution is called for in the case of the noun *desiderium* and verb *desidero*. Like their Italian derivatives, these words are often much closer in denotation and connotation to English expressions like "missing you" or "wishing I were with you" than they are to that powerful and usually pointed term "desire." An Italian mother might say to her grown child living far away, "ho desiderio di vederti," and Laelius' climactic words in Cicero's *De amicitia* poignantly dwell on his *desiderium* for the recently deceased Scipio, whose *amicitia* he valued more than anything else in his life.[87] (I cite contemporary Italian usage not by way of suggesting a direct correspondence with ancient Latin usage, let alone historical continuity, but as a means of urging alertness to the denotative and connotative possibilities of specific words and as a reminder of the uniqueness of each linguistic and cultural system.)

---

[86] Cf. *Att.* 1.20.7: *L. Papirius Paetus, vir bonus amatorque noster* (Shackleton Bailey: "an honest man and an admirer of mine"); *Att.* 1.19.11: *Cossinius hic, cui dedi litteras, valde mihi bonus homo et non levis et amans tui visus est* (Shackleton Bailey: "a thoroughly good fellow, responsible and fond of you"). Indeed, Shackleton Bailey rarely translates *amor* and *amare* with "love." Instead we find "affection" (*Att.* 1.18.8, 5.18.3, 5.19.3), "caring for" (*Att.* 3.25.1), "warm feelings" (*Att.* 4.16.7), "being fond of" (*Att.* 6.1.12), "have great regard for" (*Att.* 16.6c), or even "being friends" (!) (*Att.* 4.5.2: *qui nihil possunt, ii me nolunt amare* – "the powerless won't be my friends"), while the phrase *Piliae salutem* is rendered "my love to Pilia" (*Att.* 13.22.5, 13.49.1). The risks of "love" are well illustrated by the shifting meanings of the English phrase "to make love to": previously "to court or woo," now "to have sex with." The older Loeb translation of Cicero's letters by W. Glynn Williams renders *Q.fr.* 1.3.8 (*puto per Pomponium fovendum tibi esse ipsum Hortensium*) thus: "I think you should get Pomponius to help you to make love to Hortensius himself." Shackleton Bailey translates: "I think you should conciliate Hortensius himself through Pomponius."

[87] Cic. *Amic.* 104: *quarum rerum recordatio et memoria si una cum illo occidisset, desiderium coniunctissimi atque amantissimi viri ferre nullo modo possem … magnum tamen adfert mihi aetas ipsa solacium. diutius enim iam in hoc desiderio esse non possum; omnia autem brevia tolerabilia esse debent, etiamsi magna sunt.* A letter of the 64-year-old Augustus to his grandson Gaius quoted by Aulus Gellius opens with these words: *Ave, mi Gai, meus asellus iucundissimus, quem semper medius fidius desidero, cum a me abes* (Gell. *NA* 15.7.3).

Cicero's correspondence with and about Lucius Lucceius, praetor in 67 BC and a long-time friend of both Cicero and Atticus, concisely illustrates the way in which the language of *amicitia* and *amor* can be intertwined and manipulated. In a letter from May 45 BC, Lucceius writes to Cicero expressing concern at the latter's departure from Rome. Activating the discourse of *amicitia* by an invocation of the image of the *alter ego*, Lucceius assures him that if Cicero is in pain, so is he. Cicero's warm reply opens with gratitude for Lucceius' *amor* and poses a warmly reassuring rhetorical question: "Longevity, affection (*amor*), familiarity, similar pursuits: what bond, I ask you, is missing from our relationship?"[88] Earlier correspondence reveals some interesting ups and downs in this relationship, and reminds us that the language of hierarchy and power was by no means excluded from talk with and about one's *amici*. In the year of Lucceius' praetorship, Cicero writes in one letter to Atticus about the obvious tension between Atticus and Lucceius, and in another expresses confidence that in the end Lucceius, *noster amicus*, "will act in accordance with his duty and my power (*in officio et in nostra potestate*)." Twelve years later, we find Cicero asking Lucceius to compose a text about Cicero's own accomplishments, with a pointed appeal to *amor noster*. Perhaps, Cicero writes, the affection we have for each other might lead you to write more than you actually believe, perhaps even to bend the truth – just a bit, of course.[89]

Cicero's language of *amor* for his *amici* at times takes on qualities that may surprise modern readers yet that seem to have been a standard part of the speech genre.[90] We may, if we wish, see a metaphorical operation at

---

[88] *Fam.* 5.14, May 45 BC: *sin autem, sicut hinc discesseras, lacrimis ac tristitiae te tradidisti, doleo quia doles et angere*; *Fam.* 5.15: *omnis amor tuus ex omnibus partibus se ostendit in iis litteris... vetustas, amor, consuetudo, studia paria – quod vinclum, quaeso, deest nostrae coniunctioni?* Two years later, Cicero uses similar language in a letter to L. Munatius Plancus, who was to become consul the year after Cicero's death: *me tuorum consiliorum adiutorem, dignitatis fautorem, omnibus in rebus tibi amicissimum fidelissimumque cognosces. ad eas enim causas quibus inter nos amore sumus, officiis, vetustate coniuncti patriae caritas accessit, eaque effecit ut tuam vitam anteferrem meae* (*Fam.* 10.10.2; March 30, 43 BC).

[89] *Att.* 1.8.1, February 67 BC: *ille noster amicus, vir mehercule optimus et mihi amicissimus, sane tibi iratus est*; *Att.* 1.10.1, May 67 BC: *primum tibi de nostro amico placando aut etiam plane restituendo polliceor ... quia nullam video gravem subesse causam, magnopere confido illum fore in officio et in nostra potestate* (Shackleton Bailey translates "as a friend should and as I tell him," noting that this is language "generally used of clients or servants"); *Fam.* 5.12.3, April 55 BC: *itaque te plane etiam atque etiam rogo, ut et ornes ea vehementius etiam quam fortasse sentis, et in eo leges historiae neglegas gratiamque illam ... ne aspernere amorique nostro plusculum etiam quam concedet veritas largiare.*

[90] Cf. Hutchinson 1998, p. 17: "The importance of conveying friendship is indicated by the ardent and affectionate language with which these letters overflow – for all the traditional conception of their authors as tough-minded politicians. Cicero can be more lavish than most (in part because he is so often the older man); but the general type of language is found everywhere."

work in texts like the following, an operation whereby one realm of experience (*amicitia*) is *compared* to another, the kind of *amor* that comes with flames and can be translated with Greek *eros*; but, as I have suggested in the Introduction, to do is to beg a number of questions. Writing Atticus from Formiae in March 49 BC in the aftermath of Pompey's departure from Italy, Cicero describes how Pompey's failure to communicate with him has alienated him and explains why he has not left Italy with Pompey. Cicero describes his internal tensions by means of a simile that evokes, by means of the key Greek term, the realm of the erotic.

sicut ἐν τοῖς ἐρωτικοῖς alienat <quod> immunde, insulse, indecore fit, sic me illius fugae neglegentiaeque deformitas avertit ab *amore*. nihil enim dignum faciebat quare eius fugae comitem me adiungerem. nunc emergit *amor*, nunc *desiderium* ferre non possum, nunc mihi nihil libri, nihil litterae, nihil doctrina potest. ita dies et noctes tamquam avis illa mare prospecto, evolare cupio. do, do poenas temeritatis meae. etsi quae fuit illa temeritas? quid feci non consideratissime? (Cic. *Att.* 9.10.2)

Just as in erotic *affaires*, inelegant, stupid or inappropriate actions can turn you off, the unattractive quality of his escape and of his discourtesy to me blocked my love for him. Nothing he did gave me any reason to join him as he escaped. But now my love has resurfaced; now I cannot endure my longing for him; now I find no solace in books, letters, or learning. And so, like that bird [Plato, *Ep.* 7.348a] who looks out over the sea, day and night I long to fly away. Yes, now I am paying for my rash decision. But actually, what was rash about it? I thought carefully about every step I took.

To be sure, Cicero is using a simile – his experiences with Pompey are *like* those of someone in the snares of Cupid (*sicut ... sic ...*) – but the following sentences, describing *amor* and *desiderium*, are not part of the simile, and are in fact typical of the language of *amicitia* in Cicero's letters.[91] Two letters to Gaius Trebonius, associate of Julius Caesar and consul suffect in 45 BC, supplement the language of *amor* and *desiderium* with that of *cupido*, burning and flames. In a letter from December 46 BC, Cicero makes much of the fact that Trebonius had written a book gathering some of Cicero's own witty sayings; this sends him into veritable spasms of epistolary love.

---

[91] Cf. Hutchinson 1998, p. 162: the evocation of *amor* as a matter of "violent changes from repulsion to affection" has the effect of linking "Cicero's own feeling with a wild, irrational, and volatile type of passion"; Hutchinson compares Cic. *Tusc.* 4.67–76 and rightly emphasizes that Cicero's use of Greek in and of itself "does not indicate any lewdness" (see pp. 13–15 on Greek in Cicero's letters and cf. *Att.* 1.13.4, ἐν τοῖς πολιτικοῖς). For code-switching in Latin texts, with particular attention to Cicero's letters, see Adams 2003, pp. 18–28, 297–415. Perhaps surprisingly, Hutchinson's discussion of the motifs of flames and burning, *desiderium* and *amor*, comes in a chapter dedicated to "humour."

et epistulam tuam legi libenter et librum libentissime; sed tamen in ea *voluptate* hunc accepi dolorem, quod, cum *incendisses cupiditatem* meam consuetudinis augendae nostrae – nam ad *amorem* quidem nihil poterat accedere –, tum discedis a nobis meque tanto *desiderio* afficis, ut unam mihi consolationem relinquas, fore ut utriusque nostrum *absentis desiderium* crebris et longis epistulis leniatur: quod ego non modo de me tibi spondere possum, sed de te etiam mihi; nullam enim apud me reliquisti dubitationem, quantum me *amares*. (Cic. *Fam.* 15.21.1)

I was delighted to read your letter, even more delighted to read your book. As much pleasure as that gave me, however, I also felt pain. For just as you inflamed my desire to get to know you better – nothing could increase the love that was already there – just then you are leaving us, afflicting *me* with such longing that the only consolation you give me is that our mutual longing can be soothed by letters: lots of them and long ones. I can make that promise not only on my own behalf, but also on your yours, because you have left me no doubts as to how great your affection for me is.

After more in this vein, including the exclamation that Trebonius' book constitutes a "declaration of your love" (*liber iste … quantam habet declarationem amoris tui*) and the remark "I cannot imagine that anyone loves himself more than you love me" (*non possum existimare plus quemquam a se ipso quam me a te amari*), along with a recitation of the various ways Trebonius has supported Cicero in the past, Cicero brings his letter to its conclusion:

reliquum est, <ut> tuam profectionem *amore* prosequar, reditum spe exspectem, *absentem* memoria colam, omne *desiderium* litteris mittendis accipiendisque leniam. tu velim tua in me studia et officia multum tecum recordere; quae cum tibi liceat, mihi nefas sit oblivisci, non modo virum bonum me existimabis, verum etiam te a me *amari* plurimum iudicabis. vale. (Cic. *Fam.* 15.21.5)

All that remains is for me to accompany your departure with my love, to hopefully await your return, in your absence to keep your memory alive, to soothe my yearning for you by sending and receiving letters. Please always keep in mind your interest in me, the services you have performed. To be sure, *you* may forget them, but it would be criminal of me to do so. And so you must not only think of me as a decent man, but must realize that you are very much the object of my affection. Farewell.

In a later letter, Cicero again draws on the imagery of flames to describe his affection for Trebonius while at the same time appealing to Trebonius' own unique love for him.

tu, mi Treboni, quoniam ad *amorem* meum aliquantum <olei> discedens addidisti, quo tolerabilius feramus *igniculum desiderii tui*, crebris nos litteris appellato, atque ita, si idem fiet a nobis ... cura ut valeas meque *ames amore* illo tuo *singulari*. (Cic. *Fam.* 15.20)[92]

My dear Trebonius, by your departure you have add a bit of oil to the fire of my love; so that I may better tolerate the burning sting of your absence, please do keep in touch with frequent letters on the understanding that I will do the same... Take care of yourself, and keep on loving me with that unique love of yours.

Amor and flames also make their appearance in a letter to Publius Cornelius Dolabella, Cicero's former son-in-law and recently confirmed consul, written at Pompeii in the aftermath of Julius Caesar's assassination (May 3, 44 BC). Cicero first casts himself as Nestor, elder advisor to Dolabella's king Agamemnon, then changes key, speaking the language of passionate *amor* and placing it on a distinctly higher level than the fondness denoted by the verb *diligere.*

nam cum te semper tantum dilexerim quantum tu intellegere potuisti, tum his tuis factis sic *incensus* sum ut nihil umquam in *amore* fuerit *ardentius*. nihil est enim, mihi crede, virtute formosius, nihil pulchrius, nihil amabilius. semper *amavi*, ut scis, M. Brutum propter eius summum ingenium, suavissimos mores, singularem probitatem atque constantiam; tamen Idibus Martiis tantum accessit ad *amorem* ut mirarer locum fuisse augendi in eo quod mihi iam pridem cumulatum etiam videbatur. quis erat qui putaret ad eum *amorem* quem erga te habebam posse aliquid accedere? tantum accessit ut mihi nunc denique *amare* videar, antea *dilexisse*. (Cic. *Fam.* 9.14.4–5 = *Att.* 14.17a.4–5)

Although I was always very fond of you and you realized it, what you have done now has inflamed me more than any passionate ardor that has ever been. Believe me: nothing is more beautiful, more lovely or more lovable, than valor. As you know, I have always loved Marcus Brutus for his great talents, his delightful character, his unique decency and reliability. But on the Ides of March my love for him increased so much that I was surprised to find there was room for growth in what I had thought long since fully developed. Who would have thought that the love I had for you could ever increase? Well, now it has increased; and now it seems to me that now I love you, whereas previously I was only fond of you.[93]

---

[92] The imagery of "adding oil to the flame" is only at stake if, with Shackleton Bailey, we emend the MS reading *olim* to *olei*; but the imagery of flames is indisputably present in the sentence that follows.

[93] In a letter written six days later, Cicero complains to Atticus that Dolabella has not paid a debt (*Att.* 14.18: *sed totum se a te abalienavit Dolabella ea de causa qua me quoque sibi inimicissimum reddidit*). Later still, we find Cicero writing Dolabella a flowery note of thanks, citing the latter's *singularem erga me amorem* (*Att.* 15.14.2); even later, Cicero writes Atticus that he will gladly publicize his enmity with Dolabella (*Att.* 16.15.1: *ut illum oderim*). So quickly can one go from being the object of winning expressions of *amor* to being called *inimicissimus* and the object of *odium*, and back and forth.

Cicero's 111 letters of recommendation (*commendationes*) gathered as Book 13 of *Ad familiares* are of particular interest. Introducing one of his *amici* to another and commending him – occasionally her – to the latter's protection, these letters, to use Cicero's own metaphor, "open the door to *amicitia*."[94] But the language of *amor* is also used in these letters, generously and no doubt strategically. In a letter recommending Egnatius Rufus to Publius Silius, probably dating from May 51 BC, Cicero reasserts the *amor* that exists between himself and Silius on the one hand, and himself and Egnatius on the other, while carefully noting that Silius' relationship with Egnatius is on a somewhat lower level. In the process he again distinguishes between *diligere* and *amare*.

quid ego tibi commendem eum, quem tu ipse *diligis*? sed tamen, ut scires eum a me non *diligi* solum, verum etiam *amari*, ob eam rem tibi haec scribo: omnium tuorum officiorum, quae et multa et magna sunt, mihi gratissimum fuerit, si ita tractaris Egnatium, ut sentiat *et se a me et me a te amari*; hoc te vehementer etiam atque etiam rogo. illa nostra scilicet ceciderunt: utamur igitur vulgari consolatione: quid, si hoc melius? sed haec coram: tu fac, quod facis, ut *me ames teque amari a me* scias. (Cic. *Fam.* 13.47)[95]

Why should I even recommend someone to you of whom you are already so fond? Still, you should know that I am not only fond of him but have great affection for him, and so I am writing you with the following request. You have shown me the greatest support, and the crowning joy would be if you were to treat Egnatius in such a way that he perceives my affection for him and yours for me. This is my fervent request of you. To be sure, those plans of ours have not worked out, but let us console ourselves with the thought, banal as it is, that this might actually be for the best. More on this in person. Meanwhile, keep on doing what you do, showing affection for me and knowing that I do the same for you.

We occasionally have glimpses at formulaic building blocks that could be combined and recombined as suited the occasions: "Since he thinks that he has my affection (*a me amari*), please let him know that I have yours (*a te amari*)"; "I cannot imagine that anyone has affection for himself more than you do for me (*me a te amari*)"; "you will do me a great favor indeed

---

[94] Cic. *Fam.* 13.10.4 (recommending M. Terentius Varro to M. Junius Brutus): *qua commendatione quasi amicitiae fores aperiantur*. For the letters of recommendation see Cugusi 1983, pp. 111–114, Cotton 1985 and 1986, Rees 2007, and above all Deniaux 1993, with extensive bibliography. Deniaux 1993, pp. 135–161, includes a table listing all of Cicero's *commendati* and the terms with which he describes their relationship; see Rowland 1970 for Cicero's *necessarii*.

[95] See also Cic. *Ad Brut.* 1.1 (recommending L. Clodius): *valde me diligit vel, ut* ἐμφατικώτερον *dicam, valde me amat*. For discussion of *amare* and *diligere* see Hellegouarc'h 1963, pp. 142–146.

if you see to it that he perceives your affection for me (*me a te amari*) to be as great as I think it is."[96]

Another formula appealed to the benefits and pleasures that can come from *amicitia*. A letter from early 44 BC sent to Marcus Acilius Caninus, proconsul in 46–45 BC and recipient of eleven such letters, reads as follows.

M'. Curius, qui Patris negotiatur, ita mihi *familiaris* est, *ut nihil possit esse con-iunctius*: multa illius in me *officia*, multa in illum mea, quodque maximum est, summus inter nos *amor* et mutuus. quae cum ita sint, si ullam in *amicitia* mea spem habes, si ea, quae in me *officia* et studia Brundisii contulisti, vis mihi etiam gratiora efficere—quamquam sunt gratissima—, si me a tuis omnibus *amari* vides, hoc mihi da atque largire, ut M'. Curium sartum et tectum, ut aiunt, ab omnique incommodo, detrimento, molestia sincerum integrumque conserves. et ipse spondeo et omnes hoc tibi tui pro me recipient, ex mea *amicitia* et ex tuo in me *officio* maximum te fructum summamque voluptatem esse capturum. vale. (Cic. *Fam.* 13.50)

Manius Curius, who is doing business at Patrae, is such a close acquaintance of mine that nothing more intimate can be imagined. He has performed many services for me and I for him, and above all we are joined by the utmost mutual affection. And so, if you have any expectations of my friendship for you; if you want to make the services and interest you showed for me at Brundisium even more delightful to me (though, as it is, they are extremely delightful); if you can see that I am the object of all your people's affection; grant me the following. Keep Manius Curius, as they say, safe and sound, intact, protected from every-thing uncomfortable, damaging, or annoying. For my part, I promise – and all your people will vouch for me on this – that from my friendship for you and from your services to me you will have nothing but benefit and pleasure. Farewell.

The language is typical throughout, but the final sentence is especially illuminating –perhaps formulaic not only in letters of recommendation, and not only in Cicero's[97] – in its open appeal to the benefits and pleasures (*fructus* and *voluptas*) that Acilius may draw from Cicero's *amicitia* if he does him this favor and consents to creating a new configuration amongst *familiares* and *amici*. The combination of utility and pleasure the phrase

---

[96] Cic. *Fam.* 13.75 (to T. Titius); *Fam.* 15.21 (to Trebonius); *Fam.* 13.44, 74 (a letter recommending L. Oppius sent in duplicate to Q. Gallius and Q. Philippus respectively). A search of the PHI *Classical Latin Texts* database yields thirty-three occurrences of phrases like *me a te amari, te a me amari*, or *te ab eo amari* in Cicero's letters.

[97] Recommending Marcus Bolanus to P. Sulpicius Rufus, proconsul in 46 BC, Cicero concludes: *promitto tibi te ex eius amicitia magnam voluptatem esse capturum* (*Fam.* 13.77). About 150 years later, Fronto uses a similar phrase in one of his letters of recommendation (*Amic.* 1.1.2, *omnibus modis amicitia nostra et voluptati nobis et usui fuit*).

evokes is fundamental to much Roman writing on *amicitia*. Even Cicero's *Laelius*, in his idealizing, prescriptive remarks on *amicitia* in general and his own relationship with Scipio in particular, admits that numerous *utilitates* arose from their relationship, insisting that this was not the *reason* they entered into it; rather, they understood that the true benefit (*fructus*) lay in affection (*amor*) itself.[98] Laelius, of course, distinguishes his idealized version of *amicitia* from what "most people" do, and one thing they do is "to seek the greatest possible benefit (*fructus*)" from friendship (Cic. *Amic.* 79: *plerique … amicos tamque pecudes eos potissimum diligunt ex quibus sperant se maximum fructum esse capturos*). That, however, is precisely what Cicero smoothly assures his correspondent Caninus he will receive from his own friendship with Cicero in the letter just quoted (*maximum te fructum summamque voluptatem esse capturum*), but this is by no means the only time Cicero's own practice does not quite match his idealizing.

Not only in the letters of recommendation but throughout the correspondence, one element in this florid language of affection and delight, superlatives and extremes, is the assertion "no one is more X," closely related to expressions of the type "nothing is more X," emphatic but clearly not meant to be taken literally, that are found in a number of Latin speech genres and may be related to colloquial speech patterns.[99] We have already seen some examples (*Fam.* 9.14.4–5 = *Att.* 14.17a.4–5: *ut nihil umquam in amore fuerit ardentius; nihil est enim, mihi crede, virtute formosius, nihil pulchrius, nihil amabilius; Fam.* 13.50: *ita mihi familiaris est, ut nihil possit esse coniunctius*) but others abound.[100] To Publius

---

[98] Cic. *Amic.* 31: *omnis eius fructus in ipso amore inest.* The notion that reaping the benefit (*fructus*) – even of pleasures (*voluptates*) – is a normative goal and that *amicitia* can help meet that goal recurs elsewhere in the *De amicitia* (22: *qui esset tantus fructus in prosperis rebus, nisi haberes qui illis aeque ac tu ipse gauderet?* 70: *fructus enim ingenii et virtutis omnisque praestantiae tum maximus capitur, tum in proximum quemque confertur;* 87: *quis tam esset ferreus qui eam vitam ferre posset, cui non auferret fructum voluptatum omnium solitudo?*).

[99] Hofmann 1951, pp. 89–90, 196, Williams 2004 ad Mart. 2.54.5 (*nil nasutius hac maligniusque*). Examples of this kind of expression in connection with *amici* include Plaut. *Poen.* 504 (*tardo amico nihil est quicquam inaequius*), Plin. *Ep.* 2.13.5 (*quid enim illo aut fidelius amico aut sodale iucundius?*).

[100] Hutchinson 1998, p. 27, notes that Cicero uses phrases like "no one ever" with "cavalier freedom," citing this as an example of how Roman writers in general "display their emotions flamboyantly." Examples include *Fam.* 2.3.2 (to C. Scribonius Curio): *mihi te neque cariorem neque iucundiorem esse quemquam;* cf. *Fam.* 1.9.24, quoted above; *Fam.* 6.9 (to Furfanus Postumus): *cum A. Caecina tanta mihi familiaritas consuetudoque semper fuit ut nulla maior esse possit … sic semper dilexi nullo ut cum homine coniunctius viverem; Fam.* 6.17 (to the propraetor Pompeius Bithynicus): *nam sic habeto, beneficiorum magnitudine eos, qui temporibus valuerunt ut valeant, coniunctiores tecum esse quam me, necessitudine neminem; Fam.* 13.26 (recommending L. Mescinius to the former consul Servius Sulpicius Rufus): *itaque eo sic utor ut nec familiarius ullo nec libentius.*

Cornelius Lentulus Spinther, consul in 57 BC, Cicero writes an unusually long letter in December 54, warmly reassuring him of his affection.

me quidem certe *tuarum actionum sententiarum voluntatum rerum denique omnium socium comitemque* habebis, neque mihi in omni vita res tam erit *ulla* proposita quam ut cottidie vehementius te de me optime meritum esse laetere ... existimesque *neminem* cuiquam neque *cariorem* neque *iucundiorem* umquam fuisse quam te mihi, idque me non modo ut sentias, sed ut *omnes gentes* etiam et *posteritas omnis* intelligat esse facturum. (Cic. *Fam.* 1.9.22–24)

You can count on having me as your ally and companion in everything you do, think, and want. For me no purpose in life will surpass my daily increasing delight in our relationship with each other ... You can be sure that no one has ever found anyone to be more valuable, more delightful, than I find you and that I will continue to do so in such a way that not only will *you* realize it, but the whole world, and generations to come, will know it.

The first statement invites comparison with a remark from Cicero's own *De amicitia* written ten years later (*est enim amicitia nihil aliud nisi <u>omnium</u> divinarum humanarumque rerum cum <u>benevolentia</u> et <u>caritate</u> <u>consensio</u>*, Cic. *Amic.* 20) and on the basis of these words one might conclude that Lentulus has a special, maybe even unique place in Cicero's heart. And perhaps he did. But similiarly effusive statements can be found peppered throughout his correspondence, even with regard to people of whom we otherwise hear little or nothing. A certain Quintus Hippius, who appears only once in Cicero's letters, receives this compliment in a letter of recommendation to the local magistrates of an Italian town: "There are so many bonds joining Quintus Hippius to myself that no closer relationship exists than what he and I have" (*tantae mihi cum Q. Hippio causae necessitudinis sunt ut <u>nihil</u> possit esse coniunctius quam nos inter nos sumus, Fam.* 13.76).

Such, then, are the broad contours of *amor* and *amicitia* in Cicero's correspondence. Who are the recipients of his letters? Although we know from other sources that Cicero corresponded with women – one name we have is that of the wealthy Caerellia (see Chapter 1, pp. 92–93) – the surviving letters are almost all addressed to men. The one great exception consists in his wife Terentia, letters to whom are gathered as Book 14 of *Ad familiares*. In his reading of the first of these, sent from exile to Terentia back home in Rome, Erik Gunderson sketches the following scenario:

Cicero is in exile. Terentia turns out to be his "man on the spot." Where he is no longer the big man of the forum, she is made into his surrogate. Everybody's talk and letters tell him this, and his letter about those letters discourses of a discourse that assigns Terentia her role as *Cicero alter(a)*. This puts her, of course, in the position of a friend, but she is also a second self with whom Cicero disidentifies and whom he seeks to take in hand and control even as he sees himself in her and claims to leave her room to act. Can a wife be a friend? Should a wife be a friend?[101]

Let us look at the key moments of the letter in question, beginning with its opening sentence and ending with its seemingly hasty postscript.

Et litteris multorum et sermone omnium perfertur ad me incredibilem tuam virtutem et fortitudinem esse teque nec animi neque corporis laboribus defatigari. me miserum! te ista virtute, fide, probitate, humanitate in tantas aerumnas propter me incidisse, Tulliolamque nostram, ex quo patre tantas voluptates capiebat, ex eo tantos percipere luctus! nam quid ego de Cicerone dicam? qui cum primum sapere coepit, acerbissimos dolores miseriasque percepit. quae si, tu ut scribis, fato facta putarem, ferrem paullo facilius, sed omnia sunt mea culpa commissa, qui ab iis me *amari* putabam, qui invidebant, eos non sequebar, qui petebant. quod si nostris consiliis usi essemus neque apud nos tantum valuisset sermo aut stultorum *amicorum* aut improborum, beatissimi viveremus: nunc, quoniam sperare nos *amici* iubent, dabo operam, ne mea valetudo tuo labori desit. res quanta sit, intelligo, quantoque fuerit facilius manere domi quam redire; sed tamen, si omnes tribunos pl. habemus, si Lentulum tam studiosum, quam videtur, si vero etiam Pompeium et Caesarem, non est desperandum. de familia, quomodo placuisse scribis *amicis*, faciemus... non queo reliqua scribere – tanta vis lacrimarum est –, neque te in eundem fletum adducam; tantum scribo: si erunt in officio *amici*, pecunia non deerit; si non erunt, tu efficere tua pecunia non poteris ... fac valeas et ad me tabellarios mittas, ut sciam quid agatur et vos quid agatis. mihi omnino iam brevis exspectatio est. Tulliolae et Ciceroni salutem dic. valete. datum a. d. VI Kal. Decembr. Dyrrhachio. Dyrrhachium veni, quod et libera civitas est et in me officiosa et proxima Italiae. sed si offendet me loci celebritas, alio me conferam, ad te scribam. (Cic. *Fam.* 14.1)

In many people's letters and everyone's talk the news is reaching me that your courage and strength are unbelievable and that you are not allowing yourself to be worn down by the physical or mental stress. Poor me! That you, with your courage, trustworthiness, decency, and refinement, should have had to endure such troubles for my sake! That our little Tullia should now be suffering such grief from the very father who used to give her such delight! Not to mention our son – as soon as he came to the age of reason, great pain and suffering were his.

You say all of this was meant to be. Well, if I could believe that, the situation might be easier for me to bear. But no – this was all my fault. I thought I had the affection of those who were out to get me; I failed to follow those who were

---

[101] Gunderson 2007, p. 10. Gunderson detects here "a rare opportunity to see a Roman man and woman interacting as man and woman" (p. 8) – adding, however, the necessary qualification that "these letters are unidirectional, for we never hear back from Terentia," in which case one might ask how we can speak of an "interaction" at all. For another discussion of Terentia in Cicero's letters see Claassen 1996. For discussion of the experience of exile as it shapes Cicero's letters in general, see Jäger 1986, pp. 31–135, Hutchinson 1998, pp. 25–48.

looking for me. If we had only followed our own instincts and had not given such weight to the words of friends who were either idiots or bastards, our situation would be splendid right now. Anyway, since our friends are telling us that we should keep hope alive, I will try my best to keep my health from interfering with your labors. Of course I realize what a great task this is, and I realize how much easier it would have been to stay home than it will be to go back. Still, if we have all the tribunes of the people on our side, along with Lentulus (if he really supports us as much as it seems) and Pompey and Caesar too, there is no call for despair. As for the slaves, we will do what you say our friends think best …

I can't write any more, my tears are overwhelming and I don't want to make you cry too. I'll just say this: if our friends do their duty, money won't be lacking. If they don't, you won't be able to get by with your own money… Take care of yourself and send me couriers so that I can know what's going on and how you all are doing. At this point I don't have to wait long. Greet little Tullia and young Cicero for me. My best to you all!

November 26, Dyrrachium.

P.S. I have come to Dyrrachium because it is a free state, it owes me, and it is so close to Italy. But if the place turns out to be too crowded for my tastes, I'll go somewhere else and let you know.

To be sure, Terentia was representing Cicero's interests in his absence, and while it is certainly possible that Cicero, Terentia, or third parties posed themselves questions of the type "Is she acting like Cicero's friend?" or "Should she?" Cicero's own letter uses neither the language of *amicitia* nor the imagery of *alter ego* in connection with Terentia, but praises her *virtus, fortitudo, probitas, humanitas*, and *fides*. The last of these, of course, is an ideal closely associated with *amicitia*, but it is also a central ideal of marriage. Gunderson notes that these words "recall the excellences one would praise in a steadfast male political friend," and *virtus* and *fortitudo* are indeed masculine virtues whose appearance in women complicates their gendered status. Yet the suggestion that Cicero is casting Terentia as "a superlative wife, a man's man of a wife" and implicitly posing the question "if Terentia is a *Cicero altera*, is Cicero a *Terentia alter?*" is less persuasive. Rather than placing Terentia in the role of *alter ego* or *amicus*, Cicero's words worry about their children on the one hand, his (and Terentia's?) *amici* back in Rome on the other hand. Terentia undeniably plays a central role in this drama, but that role is not sketched with the language of *amicitia*, nor does Cicero take the step of addressing her as, say, *animi matrona virilis* (Ovid's words on Lucretia at *Fasti* 8.247).[102]

---

[102] Gunderson 2007, p. 11. For *virtus, fortitudo*, and masculine women, see Williams 2012.

Among the many male recipients of Cicero's letters, two special cases are his intimate friend Titus Pomponius Atticus and his slave and then freedman Tiro, special for nearly opposed reasons. As we have seen, Atticus is the man who, if any, modern readers would call Cicero's "best friend," but we have also seen that no such expression is found in Cicero's own letters, or indeed in any surviving Latin text (see Introduction, p. 30). How, then, does Cicero describe his relationship with Atticus? Not surprisingly, we find assertions of exclusivity and the formula "nothing is more X," but, as we have seen, the latter is precisely a formula, hardly limited to Atticus and in and of itself hardly to be taken literally.[103] Just as unsurprisingly, *amor* and *amare* appearly regularly and emphatically, but this too is by no means unique to Atticus.[104] One means Cicero has at his disposal for describing the special value of his relationship with Atticus is the powerful imagery of brother love. Another is the cumulative impact of description and valorization, independent of individual words or formulae, as in a letter written on January 20, 60 BC.

nihil mihi nunc scito tam deesse quam hominem eum quocum *omnia* quae me cura aliqua adficiunt una communicem, qui me *amet*, qui sapiat, quicum ego cum loquar nihil fingam, nihil dissimulem, nihil obtegam. abest enim frater ἀφελέστατος et *amantissimus*. †Metellus† non homo sed "litus atque aer" et "solitudo mera." tu autem qui saepissime curam et angorem animi mei sermone et consilio levasti tuo, qui mihi et in publica re *socius* et in privatis omnibus *conscius* et omnium meorum sermonum et consiliorum *particeps* esse soles, ubinam es? ita sum ab omnibus destitutus ut tantum requietis habeam quantum cum uxore et filiola et mellito Cicerone consumitur. nam illae ambitiosae nostrae fucosaeque *amicitiae* sunt in quodam splendore forensi, fructum domesticum non habent. itaque cum bene completa domus est tempore matutino, cum ad forum stipati gregibus *amicorum* descendimus, reperire ex magna turba neminem possumus quocum aut iocari libere aut suspirare *familiariter* possimus. qua re te exspectamus, te desideramus, te iam etiam arcessimus. multa sunt enim quae me sollicitant anguntque, quae mihi videor auris nactus tuas unius ambulationis sermone exhaurire posse. (Cic. *Att.* 1.18.1)

You should know that I miss nothing more than the person with whom I can share everything that causes me any anxiety; who loves me; who is wise; with

---

[103] *Att.* 5.1.5: *cum profectus eris cures ut sciam, sic habeas, nihil mehercule te mihi nec carius esse nec suavius*; *Fam.* 13.1.5: *nihil est illo mihi nec carius nec iucundius*. For other superlative expressions regarding Atticus see *Fam.* 5.5 (addressed to C. Antonius), *tui cupidus, nostri amantissimus*, and *Fam.* 13.18.2 (to Servius Sulpicius Rufus), *homine eo quem ego unice diligo*. See also *Att.* 1.17 with Konstan 1997, pp. 124–126.

[104] *Att.* 1.20.7 (May 60 BC): *si me amas, si te a me amari scis*; *Att.* 3.5 (58 BC): *tantum te oro ut, quoniam me ipsum semper amasti, ut eodem amore sis; ego enim idem sum. inimici mei mea mihi, non me ipsum ademerunt.*

whom I can speak without pretending, hiding, concealing anything. After all, my brother – so candid, loving – is not here either. Metellus [?] is not a human being but "beach and sky," "sheer solitude."

You, however, have so often relieved my worries and anxiety just by talking with me and giving your advice; you are my ally in political matters, you have intimate knowledge of all my private affairs, you share all my conversations and all my plans. Where are you now? I have been so abandoned by everyone that the only respite I can find is taken up by spending time with my wife, darling daughter, and sweet little son. Those ostentatious, tricked-out friendships I have certainly add shine to my reputation in the forum, but privately they bear no fruit. And so, when my house is nicely full in the morning, when I walk down to the forum surrounded by throngs of friends, in such a big crowd I can find not one man with whom I might freely joke or intimately sigh.

So then: I am waiting for you! I miss you! Come soon! There are so many things disturbing and weighing on me, but I do believe that your ears and a single one conversation while taking a walk would bring me relief.

Appealing to lofty ideals – in this case put into practice – of sharing, of caring, of pleasure, Cicero casts Atticus in a unique role, setting up distinctions between their relationship and others in Cicero's life: with his wife and children (implicitly, in some ways less rewarding than that which he enjoys with Atticus), with his brother Quintus (more or less on the same level), and with other kinds of *amicitiae* (advantageous socially but unrewarding privately). The distinction is potent and memorable, and corresponds to and no doubt informs those upon which Laelius insists in the *De amicitia* which Cicero dedicated to Atticus sixteen years later: "true and perfect friendship" (*vera et perfecta amicitia*) on the one hand, "common, ordinary, insubstantial" on the other (*vulgaris et mediocris, levis* and *communis*; Cic. *Amic.* 22; cf. 76, 77, 101).

Another man who has a unique role in Cicero's correspondence is Tiro, his slave, secretary, and companion who remained with him even after he was freed in 53 BC, and who after his former master's death may well have played a role in the eventual editing and publication of Cicero's letters.[105] As we have seen in Chapter 1, when Quintus Cicero congratulates his brother on freeing Tiro his language suggests that, for Quintus at least, one's slave could not also be one's *amicus* (*Fam.* 16.16: *nobis amicum quam*

---

[105] Cicero's letters to and about Tiro are gathered in Book 16 of the *Ad familiares*. Two of Tiro's own letters are cited by Aulus Gellius (*NA* 10.1.7, to an unknown recipient; 6.3.5, to Cicero's *familiaris* Q. Axius). See McDermott 1972 for a thorough review of the relationship between Cicero and Tiro, speculating that Tiro may have been Cicero's own son, born of a slave woman. See also Smadja 1976, Fitzgerald 2000, pp. 13–14, Citroni Marchetti 2000, pp. 80–83, Gunderson 2007, pp. 27–45.

servum esse maluisti). But how does Cicero himself describe his relationship with Tiro? Does he call it *amicitia*? As it happens, in the surviving correspondence Cicero never uses the word *amicus* to refer to or to address Tiro, whether in the four letters written while Tiro was still a slave (*Fam.* 16.10, 13, 14, 15) or subsequently. On the other hand, he does arguably activate the discourse of *amicitia* by using the imagery of the *alter ego*, assuring Tiro that "no one loves me who does not also love you."[106] And Cicero speaks the language of *amor* clearly enough. In one of several letters expressing concern at one of Tiro's recurring bouts of illness, sent by Cicero in November 50 BC in his own name as well as that of his brother, son, and nephew, we read the elegant reassurance: "We miss you even as we love you (*amemus*). Because we love you, we want to see you healthy; but because we miss you, we want to see you as soon as possible. Better the former, then!" Another letter on the same occasion speaks in the first person singular: "I know your thoughtfulness, your moderation, your love (*amorem*) for me. I realize that you will do everything possible in order to be with us again as soon as possible. My request, though: please don't be too hasty." A letter from about three yars later reiterates the point: "See to it that you come back happy and healthy: that way I will love (*amem*) not only you, but our Tusculan estate even more."[107]

Cicero's *amor* for Tiro was not, it seems, limited to letters. Pliny the Younger read an epigram attributed to Cicero in which the latter cast himself in the role of Tiro's *amans*, expecting his kisses and complaining – at night – that they never came. The possibility that the attribution was false must be kept in mind, though it has only rarely been raised. In any case, Pliny reads the epigram as Cicero's, calling it a *lascivus lusus* and using it as the inspiration for a poem of his own, which through its use of the terms *amores*, *blanditiae*, and *flammae* suggests the realm of Venus. Consequently, many readers of Pliny's poem understand Cicero's poem in turn to have expressed a specifically erotic desire, whether as a purely poetic stance or not.[108] But since we do not have Cicero's own words (if

---

[106] Cic. *Fam.* 16.4.4: *sic habeto, mi Tiro, neminem esse qui me amet, quin idem te amet*; cf. the different but related point at *Fam.* 16.7: *nemo nos amat qui te non diligit.*

[107] Cic. *Fam.* 16.1 (November 3, 50 BC): *nos ita te desideramus ut amemus; amor ut valentem videamus hortatur; desiderium ut quam primum; illud igitur potius* (Gunderson 2007, pp. 32–33, translates "our desire for you equals our love for you," but adds in n. 111 that "'love' of course may well be an over-translation"; the same is true of "desire"); *Fam.* 16.9: *tuam prudentiam, temperantiam, amorem erga me novi; scio te omnia facturum ut nobiscum quam primum sis; sed tamen ita velim, ut ne quid properes; Fam.* 16.19: *fac bellus revertare, <ut> non modo te sed etiam Tusculanum nostrum plus amem.*

[108] Plin. *Ep.* 7.4.6: *lascivum inveni lusum Ciceronis ... / nam queritur quod frauda mala frustratus amantem / paucula cenato sibi debita savia Tiro / tempore nocturno subtraxerit. his ego lectis / "cur*

indeed he wrote such a poem), and Pliny's label *lascivus lusus* is itself teasingly vague, key questions must remain unanswered. Did Cicero himself indeed use the word *amans*, or *amator*, or neither? Did he use the imagery of flames or invoke Venus? Did the poem create a scenario in which Tiro was still Cicero's slave? One thing we can say is that the kisses which clearly figured in the poem are in themselves polyvalent. We will return to their role in Fronto's correspondence below, but here it is worth noting that in a surviving letter to Tiro, Cicero's brother Quintus exuberantly evokes the kisses he looks forward to planting on Tiro's eyes in the midst of the forum.[109]

Among the many public figures with whom Cicero entered into and negotiated what some scholars call "political friendships" and which Cicero himself, writing privately to Atticus, calls *amibitiosae fucosaeque amicitiae* (*Att.* 1.18), I single out three, not least because the men in question had the greatest impact on public affairs and Cicero's own life: Pompey and Caesar, whose own alliance-cum-rivalry led to civil war and ultimately Caesar's ascendancy, and Marcus Antonius, whose complicated relationship with Cicero precipitated the latter's death.[110] Of and to Julius Caesar Cicero repeatedly writes of his *amor* and *amicitia*, here using the

post haec" inquam "nostros celamus amores / nullumque in medium timidi damus atque fatemur / Tironisque dolos, Tironis nosse fugaces / blanditias et furta novas addentia flammas?" Carcopino 1947, vol. 1 pp. 137–138, includes the epigram – whose authorship he questions – among the "accusations, aussi absurdes que monstrueuses," made by Cicero's enemies: incest with his daughter Tullia and "pédérastie" with his teacher M. Pupius Piso as well as with Tiro. Courtney 2003, p. 366, comments: "If the poem was genuine, Cicero probably conveyed by it no more than the affection expressed rather extravagantly by his brother [*Fam.* 16.27, see next note]; this could be interpreted by an adversary like Asinius Gallus *in malam partem*, just as [Sall.] *In Cic.* 2 distorts his affection for his daughter into an accusation of incest." In Roman terms, however, there is no significant parallel between father–daughter sexual relationships on the one hand and those between master and slave or patron and freedman on the other (cf. Sen. *Controv.* 4.pr.10 with Williams 2010, pp. 31–40, 104–109).

[109] Cic. *Fam.* 16.27 (December 44 BC): *te, ut dixi, fero <in> oculis. ego vos a. d. III K. videbo tuosque oculos, etiamsi te veniens in medio foro videro, dissaviabor. me ama et vale.* In the same letter, Quintus insults the consuls-elect Hirtius and Pansa as effeminate (*libidinum et languoris effeminatissimi animi plenos*): The masculinist stance is clearly not incompatible with Quintus' own kisses.

[110] See Spielvogel 1993 for an overview of the role of *amicitia* in Cicero's political alliances, above all with Caesar, Pompey, and Crassus in the period 59–50 BC. Another key figure, Caesar's assassin M. Junius Brutus, also appears as Cicero's *amicus* and object of his *amor*. In a letter to Atticus, Cicero notes that Messalla considered him to be Brutus' *alter ego* (*Att.* 1.15.2, *ad te tamquam ad alterum me proficiscens*). Elsewhere Cicero takes the stance of Atticus' rival for Brutus' affection, gladly yielding if Brutus is foolish enough to be influenced by a recent speech given by Gavius (*Att.* 6.3.7, May–June 50 BC): *huius nebulonis* [sc., Gavii] *oratione si Brutus moveri potest, licebit eum solus ames, me aemulum non habebis*); cf. *Att.* 6.2.7 (April 50 BC): *venio ad Brutum tuum, immo nostrum (sic enim mavis).* A much cited case of what is sometimes called "political friendship" is the exchange of letters between Cicero and Matius soon after Caesar's assassination (*Fam.* 11.27–28), which invite being read with the nearly contemporaneous *De*

imagery of burning, there that of the *alter ego*. In an especially fervently worded letter sent to his brother Quintus in September 54 BC, while the latter was on campaign with Caesar in Gaul, Cicero gushes about a letter he had received from Caesar (*suavissimae litterae*), places Caesar second in his affections after Quintus and his own children, and in what Henderson calls "an erotogenic lather of devotion to Caesar in a climax of simultaneous confession-cum-profession" declares himself to be *amore incensus*.[111] For Pompey Cicero likewise asserts both *amicitia* and *amor* throughout the ups and downs of their alliance. We have already seen the letter to Atticus in which by means of a simile he compares his experience with Pompey to the realm of experience denoted by the Greek phrase τὰ ἐρωτικά (*Att.* 9.10). Earlier, in a letter to Pompey himself in 62 BC, Cicero fulsomely affirms their *amicitia*, with skillful flattery comparing it to that between Scipio Aemilianus and Laelius (thus anticipating the configuration which later structured his *De amicitia*, the comparandi now however being Atticus and Cicero himself); asserts the right on that basis to speak openly; and expresses the hope of a solidification of their *amicitia* and of Pompey's recognition of the correctness and value of how he had handled the Catilinarian conspiracy.[112] Numerous others of Cicero's letters to and about Pompey speak of *amicitia* and *amor*, one of them teasingly describing the man as *nostri amores*, by means of the plural arguably once again speaking the language of τὰ ἐρωτικά.[113]

Finally, there is Marcus Antonius. Two of his letters to Cicero written in May 49 BC survive (*Att.* 10.8A, 10.10.2), but above all their epistolary relationship in the aftermath of Julius Caesar's assassination invites a closer look. In a letter written on April 22, 44 BC, Antony requests of Cicero a remarkable favor. He should publicly approve Antony's decision

---

amicitia, especially sections 36–43: see Combès 1958, Kytzler 1960, Hellegouarc'h 1963, pp. 47–48, Griffin 1997.

[111] See Cic. *Q fr.* 3.1.18 (*ille mihi secundum te et liberos nostros ita est, ut sit paene par. videor id iudicio facere – iam enim debeo –; sed tamen amore sum incensus*) with Henderson 2007 (quotation from p. 51). Cf. *Q fr.* 2.13.1 (*Caesaris tantum in me amorem*), 3.5.3 (*Caesaris amore, quem ad me perscripsit, unice delector*); *Fam.* 7.5.1 (*vide, quam mihi persuaserim te me esse alterum*). Discussions of Cicero's relationship with Caesar which focus on their correspondence include Boissier 1908, pp. 279–403, Carcopino 1947, vol. II, pp. 9–51, Lepore 1954, Lossmann 1962, Spielvogel 1993, Citroni Marchetti 2000.

[112] *Fam.* 5.7: *ac ne ignores quid ego in tuis litteris desiderarim, scribam aperte, sicut et mea natura et nostra amicitia postulat ... ut tibi multo maiori quam Africanus fuit me non multo minorem quam Laelium facile et in re publica et in amicitia adiunctum esse patiare.*

[113] See e.g. *Fam.* 1.8.2 (*tantum enim animi inductio atque mehercule amor erga Pompeium apud me valet*); *Att.* 2.23.2 (*noster amicus*), 2.19.2 (*Pompeius, nostri amores*). Among discussions of Cicero and Pompey see Lepore 1954, Rawson 1978, Spielvogel 1993, pp. 61–68, 77–86, and passim, Hutchinson 1998, pp. 148–162.

to recall Sextus Cloelius, a supporter of Cicero's archenemy Publius Clodius Pulcher (*Att.* 14.13A). Antony's argumentation focuses on Clodius' young son, openly appealing to the question of appearances in connection with *amicitia*. Please, writes Antony, give the young Clodius reason to believe that your conflict with his father was a matter of politics only, and that you have decided not to persecute his father's friends (*amicos paternos*) even though you could. Now that Clodius is long dead, let us work together to convince the young man that you will not continue your *inimicitiae* with his family. Antony's allusion to his own relationship with Cicero is coolly polite and transparently calculating. He makes no mention of his own feelings but appeals to Cicero's decency, wisdom, and affection for Antony (*amabiliter in me*), at the same time making a vague and therefore all the more sinister threat. Cicero surely does not want trouble in his old age.[114]

Distressingly enough for Cicero, Antony proceeded to read this letter aloud to the Senate – an act which Cicero later, as we will see, represented as a violation of some basic principles of *amicitia*. Meanwhile, Cicero's own private response to Antony, dated four days after the latter's letter, is graciously worded but just as calculating. He begins by wishing that Antony had made the request to him in person rather than by a letter "for one reason alone": that Antony might have perceived Cicero's *amor* for him directly, eye to eye. This is followed by a reassertion of this bond, "I have always held you in affection (*te semper amavi*)," and the formulaic but pointed claim that, especially in the current political crisis, "no one is dearer to me than you (*cariorem habeam neminem*)." Cicero then grants the request, colluding with Antony by giving him something to pass on to Clodius, whether or not anyone involved believed it, let alone whether or not it was true. Tell the young Clodius, Cicero writes, that my conflict with his father was indeed only a matter of politics; in fact, tell him that if his father were alive today, he and I would no doubt have patched over our differences. Cicero then ably counters Antony's not-so-veiled threats. Antony should not think that he is granting the request out of fear of "danger" or "strife," for Clodius is too young to be a source of the former and Cicero's own political standing (*dignitas*) is a shield against the latter.

---

[114] *Att.* 14.13A (April 22, 44 BC): *si humaniter et sapienter et amabiliter in me cogitare vis, facilem profecto te praebebis et voles P. Clodium, in optima spe puerum repositum, existimare non te insectatum esse, cum potueris, amicos paternos. patere, obsecro, te pro re publica videri gessisse simultatem cum patre eius, non contempsisse hanc familiam. honestius enim et libentius deponimus inimicitias rei publicae nomine susceptas quam contumaciae. me deinde sine ad hanc opinionem iam nunc dirigere puerum et tenero animo eius persuadere non esse tradendas posteris inimicitias ... arbitror malle te quietam senectutem et honorificam potius agere quam sollicitam.*

No, Cicero is granting the favor not of fear of danger – from Clodius, naturally, not from Antony – but rather "in order that you and I may become closer (*coniunctiores*) than we have been until now." The letter ends with the sharply double-edged assurance that Cicero will always undertake to support "whatever I think is in accordance with your desires and interests; I want you to take this to heart."[115]

About a month later, Cicero confides in a letter to Tiro that he still very much wishes to maintain his "longstanding and unsullied friendship" with Antony (*Antonii inveteratam sine ulla offensione amicitiam retinere sane volo, Fam.* 16.23.2, late May 44 BC). In early September, as the tides shifted yet again, Cicero began writing, delivering and publishing the sustained attacks on Antony which he called his *Philippics*, in the second of which he comes back to that fateful letter. He begins the speech by defending himself on an ethically if not politically serious charge that Antony had made against him: that he had violated their *amicitia* (*Phil.* 2.3: *de amicitia quam a me violatam esse criminatus est*). Cicero's defense combines simple refutation (he has not in fact violated their friendship) with a renewed attack (it is Antony who has done so). No matter how strained the situation, Cicero writes, I have always spoken of Antony as a decent friend does but now, after we had a falling out, he has publicized a private letter I sent him as a friend. Antony's action is a violation of all standards of good behavior in general and of *amicitia* in particular, and it counters a basic principle of letter-writing. In words that may give us pause as we come to the end of this reading of Cicero's correspondence, not intended for our ears or eyes, he pronounces that private letters serve as long-distance conversations amongst friends (*amicorum colloquia absentium*), and his language underscores the seriousness of the charge he makes against Antony by repeating the key term three times in close succession, throwing in an appeal to *vitae societas* for good measure.[116]

---

[115] *Fam.* 14.13B (April 26, 44 BC): *quod mecum per litteras agis unam ob causam mallem coram egisses. non enim solum ex oratione sed etiam ex vultu et oculis et fronte, ut aiunt, meum erga te amorem perspicere potuisses. nam cum te semper amavi primum tuo studio, post etiam beneficio provocatus, tum his temporibus res publica te mihi ita commendavit ut cariorem habeam neminem …puero quoque hoc a me dabis, si tibi videbitur, non quo aut aetas nostra ab illius aetate quicquam debeat periculi suspicari aut dignitas mea ullam contentionem extimescat, sed ut nosmet ipsi inter nos coniunctiores simus quam adhuc fuimus … ego quae te velle quaeque ad te pertinere arbitrabor semper sine ulla dubitatione summo studio faciam. hoc velim tibi penitus persuadeas.* Shackleton Bailey comments: "The fulsomeness of the first paragraph in particular goes considerably further than courtesy required or might excuse. Like most people who talk or write better than they think, the less genuine the note the more Cicero was apt to force it."

[116] Cic. *Phil.* 2.6–7: *quid est dictum a me cum contumelia, quid non moderate, quid non amice? … at etiam litteras, quas me sibi misisse diceret, recitavit homo et humanitatis expers et vitae communis*

These are strong words, but this is only one among many, much harsher attacks delivered across the fourteen *Philippics*, the last of which dates to September 21, 43 BC. The sequel is well known. As one of the newly established triumvirate, Antony saw to it that – *amicitia* and *amor* put aside, *inimicitiae* declared (Cic. *Phil.* 5.19) – Cicero's name was placed on the proscription lists, and so on December 7, 43 BC he met his death.

FRONTO'S LETTERS

Born around AD 100 in the city of Cirta (today Constantine in Algeria), Marcus Cornelius Fronto was a key figure in the literary and cultural scene at Rome in the second century AD. Widely admired as orator and advocate in his day and later seen as a second Cicero, Fronto moved at the highest levels of Roman society, among other things serving as tutor in Latin rhetoric to the designated successors of the Emperor Antoninus Pius, the two men known to history as Marcus Aurelius and Lucius Verus. Like Cicero's letters (which he deeply admired, recommending them to Marcus even more highly than Cicero's speeches), Fronto's surviving correspondence – a body of over two hundred letters to and from Antoninus, Marcus, and Lucius among many others – gives us an invaluable illustration of how the language of *amicitia* and *amor* might be used in the upper circles of Roman society in the writer's day in the speech genre of personal letters. And these were indeed personal. As in the case of Cicero's correspondence, most of Fronto's letters in general, and those to Marcus Aurelius in particular, seem to have been truly private in nature, written by one man for another's eyes only.[117]

---

ignarus. quis enim umquam, qui paulum modo bonorum consuetudinem nosset, litteras ad se ab amico missas offensione aliqua interposita in medium protulit palamque recitavit? quid est aliud tollere ex vita vitae societatem, tollere amicorum conloquia absentium? Habinek 1990, pp. 182–183, reads Cicero's *De amicitia*, in particular its emphasis on open criticism of one's *amici*, "in part as a legitimation of his own unconventional relationship with Antony."

[117] Discussions of Fronto and his correspondence include Champlin 1980, pp. 94–117, Cugusi 1983, pp. 241–264, Gaertner 1983 (seeing the correspondence with Marcus as having the function of *Unterrichtsprogramm*), Levi 1994, Rosen 1994, Schiatti 1995, L'Huillier 2002, Kasulke 2005, Fleury 2006, Richlin 2006 and 2006 (a monograph with the provisional title *Fronto + Marcus* is forthcoming), Freisenbruch 2007, Wei 2009. For Fronto's judgment on Cicero's letters see *Antonin.* 3.8.2 (*omnes autem Ciceronis epistulas legendas esse censeo mea sententia, vel magis quam omnis eius orationes: epistulis Ciceronis nihil est perfectius*). In what follows, I cite the text and numeration of van den Hout's revised 1988 Teubner edition; see van den Hout's preface for the tortuous history of this text, which first resurfaced in a seventh-century palimpsest discovered and published by Angelo Mai in 1815 after centuries of oblivion. Abbreviations for Fronto's letters are also as in van den Hout's edition.

Fronto's correspondence is pervaded by *amicitia*. Two letters inspired by two very different circumstances – one tricky, the other tragic – provide the occasion for declarations of his commitment to the ideals of Roman friendship. The first of these, written at some point between 146 and 158, has to do with an inheritance. Fronto had been named heir to five-twelfths of his friend Censorius Niger's estate – in a will which violently insulted the praetorian prefect Marcus Gavius Maximus, who happened, awkwardly enough, to be a close associate of the emperor Antoninus. After Censorius' death Fronto wrote the emperor a letter in which he justifies his decision to accept the inheritance, albeit in violation of the implicit rule that "when the prince abandons a friendship, the loyal courtier should do likewise." Fronto's tactic is to position himself as a loyal *amicus* to Censorius in the grand tradition: He will not abandon a friendship even when his friend has done something unadvisable or dangerous.[118] Another letter, written in 165 to Marcus Aurelius, now emperor, is inspired by the death of Fronto's young grandson. Soberly but proudly looking back on his own life, Fronto places *amicitia* at its center. In all his long life, he writes, he has never violated *fides*, but regularly behaved as an *amicus* should – even, he notes without going into detail, at great risk to himself. He delights, too, in his relationship with his brother, noting with pleasure that his brother in turn has experienced the *amicitia* of two emperors, first Antoninus Pius and now Marcus Aurelius.[119]

Fronto himself enjoyed the status of *amicus* to a succession of emperors, and not only in the sense of the semi-official title *amicus Caesaris*. Among those emperors, Marcus Aurelius had a unique role. As Edward Champlin puts it, "Two passions run through and unify Fronto's life as they do his letters: an obsession with rhetorical culture and a love for Marcus Aurelius."[120] These two passions are themselves intertwined.

---

[118] *Ad Pium* 3: *numquam ita animatus fui, imperator, ut coeptas in rebus prosperis amicitias, siquid adversi increpuisset, desererem.* Quotation from Champlin 1980, p. 101.

[119] *De nepote* 2.8: *nihil in longo vitae meae spatio a me admissum, quod dedecori aut probro aut flagitio foret; nullum in aetate agunda avarum, nullum perfidum facinus meum extitisse. contraque multa liberaliter, multa amice, multa fideliter, multa constanter saepe etiam cum periculo capitis consulta. quom fratre optimo concordissime vixi, quem patris vestri bonitate summos honores adeptum gaudeo, vestra vero amicitia satis quietu<m> et multum securum video.*

[120] Champlin 1980, p. 4. Some readers look for and find turning points in the relationship – for example, Marcus' alleged declaration of a shift from rhetoric to philosophy in AD 146 (*M. Caes.* 4.13), or his succession to the principate in 161 – but the language of the surviving letters shows few signs of such turning points. Rosen 1994, p. 128, sees "plötzlich ein Riß zwischen Lehrer und Schuler" in AD 146 but signficantly adds: "Ein Außenstehender hätte in ihrer weiteren Korrespondenz schwerlich einen Unterschied zu den vergangenen Jahren bemerkt." Since we are all by definition "outsiders" to Marcus and Fronto's relationship, all we have is the language of their correspondence, and that language shows no significant breaks over time. For

Questions of literary history and style, rhetorical practice and theory are a central topic of their correspondence, and equally central are reflections on their relationship itself, which is profoundly shaped by their roles as teacher and student. And "passion" is the right word. Fronto's correspondence with Marcus (which stretches from approximately 138, when the 17-year-old Marcus was adopted by Antoninus Pius, apparently to Fronto's own death five or six years after Marcus became emperor in 161) blends *amor* and *amicitia* in ways that strike many contemporary readers as unusual, even arresting. These letters draw attention to themselves, both because of who these two men were and because their language at times sounds to modern ears romantic or even erotic. And, as Amy Richlin has noted, we hear in this correspondence what we otherwise so rarely hear in the ancient textual tradition – the voice of the younger partner in an age-differentiated pairing, in this case a younger partner who happened to be the emperor's designated successor. In view of the range of responses to the possibilities of genital pleasures shared by teacher and student we find throughout the Greek and Latin textual tradition – from exaltation to nervous joking to condemnation – "when Marcus and Fronto write of themselves as each other's *erastes* – when Fronto writes to Herodes Atticus [Marcus' tutor in Greek rhetoric] that he is Herodes' *anterastes*, his rival for Marcus's favors – they cannot do so naively."[121]

Let us begin with endings. As in formal epistolary style in some modern languages (Italian and French, for example), the closing sentences of these letters attract accumulations of formulaic vocatives expressing respect,

---

skepticism regarding the notion that Marcus experienced a "sudden and total conversion" from rhetoric to philosophy, see Champlin 1980, pp. 118–130 (quotation from p. 121), with response at Rutherford 1989, pp. 103–107, and more generally Kasulke 2005. For the term *amicus Caesaris*, see Introduction, n. 111.

[121] Richlin 2006, pp. 8, 12–17 (quotation from p. 13). Cf. ibid. p. 124 n. 6: "No one knew better than Fronto that a metaphor, like a joke, can express its literal meaning within a framework that denies that this is what's being said." In other words, it is not enough to describe *Addit.* 8, in which Fronto casts himself as Marcus' *erastes* (see below), as "une sorte de jeu" (Grimal 1990, p. 153). There is much indeed that is ludic about this text and Marcus' response to it, but to say that is only the first step in interpretation. In addition to *amor* and *amicitia*, *philia* and *eros*, the Greek term *philostorgia* seems to have been an important element in both Fronto's and Marcus' language of love. In a letter to Lucius Verus, Fronto notes that the abstraction has no direct Latin equivalent and laments that he has never met anyone at Rome who possesses the quality (*Ad Verum* 1.6.7); Marcus closes one of his letters to Fronto with the bilingual sentence *vale, mi magister optime*, φιλόστοργε ἄνθρωπε (*De feriis Alsiensibus* 4.2), and in his only mention of Fronto in the *Meditations* writes that he learned from his teacher that Roman aristocrats are rather lacking in *philostorgia* (M. Aur. *Med.* 1.11, ἀστοργότεροί πώς εἰσιν). Elsewhere Marcus praises his own mother as *philostorgos* (*Medit.* 1.17.18) and evokes *philostorgia* as one of the qualities one should strive for if one wants be a manly Roman (*Medit.* 2.5, ὡς Ῥωμαῖος καὶ ἄρρην). See Grimal 1990.

affection, or both.[122] The most common vocatives we find are *domine* to Marcus and *magister* to Fronto, and naturally enough. In the polite language of the day *dominus*, rather like *Monsieur* and *Madame* in many registers of written French, was a respectful term covering relationships of all kinds (throughout the correspondence, Marcus refers to his own mother Domitia Lucilla as *domina mea*, his brother as *dominus meus*), while *magister* was a standard term denoting a teacher: Fronto is commemorated in his great-grandson's epitaph as orator, consul, and *magister imperatorum*.[123] Most often these vocatives are complemented with formulaic but not insignificant adjectives, frequently in the superlative: *magister iucundissime* and *domine dulcissime* are among the most common closing formulae. But the letter-endings offer much more than these vocatives. Letters written by the 22-year-old Marcus to Fronto during the latter's consulship draw attention to their temporary separation – Marcus was in Naples, while Fronto was taking care of official duties in Rome – and end with exuberant superlatives, with a melodramatic moment or two.

vale mi *amicissime*, vale mi *amantissime*, consul amplissime, magister *dulcissime*, quem ego biennio iam non vidi. nam quod aiunt quidam duos menses interfuisse, tantum dies numerant. eritne quom te videbo? (*M. Caes.* 2.8)[124]

desiderantissime homo et tuo Vero *carissime*, consul *amplissime*, magister *dulcissime*, vale mi semper, anima *dulcissima*. (*M. Caes.* 2.10)

vale mi magister *dulcissime*, homo *honestissime* et *rarissime*, suavitas et caritas et *voluptas* mea. (*M. Caes.* 2.16)

My best to you, best of friends and so affectionate, most eminent consul and dear teacher. It's been two years since I've seen you! Yes of course, some say it's only been two *months*, but they are just counting days. Will I ever see you?

I miss you so much. You mean so much to me, your true Verus, you eminent consul and dear teacher. My best wishes to you as ever, you delightful soul!

---

[122] For discussion of forms of address in the letters of Cicero, Seneca, and Pliny, especially in the closings (*subscriptiones*), see Corbinelli 2008, pp. 108–125, 145–153, 182–192.

[123] *CIL* 11.6334 (Pisaurum): *M. Aufidio Frontoni / pronepoti M. Corneli / Frontonis oratoris / consulis magistri / imperatorum Luci / et Antonini, nepoti{s} / Aufidi Victorini / praefecti urbis bis consulis / Fronto consul / filio dulcissimo*. For some comments on the terms *magister* and *dominus* see Richlin 2006, pp. 25–26.

[124] Van den Hout's note ad loc. points to the suggestive elasticity in the adjective *amans*. While it is morphologically an active participle, it can refer to the subject or the object of affection, or both; similarly *desiderantissime* in *M. Caes.* 2.10. Marcus' reaction to Fronto's absence stands in intriguing contrast to the admonitions of Cicero's Laelius: to attempt to prevent a friend from traveling for important business simply because one cannot endure the separation is to reveal a soft, implicitly womanish disposition unworthy of true friendship (Cic. *Amic.* 75: *saepe incidunt magnae res ut discedendum sit ab amicis; quas qui impedire volt, eo quod desiderium non facile ferat, is et infirmus est mollisque natura et ob eam ipsam causam in amicitia parum iustus*).

My best to you, dearest teacher, so honorable and so rare, such a source of delight and affection and pleasure for me.

Elsewhere, too, Marcus' language sounds rather like that of the passionate lovers subjected to the power of Venus we find in Latin literature across its history. Consider this letter-ending from four or five years later:

valebis mihi Fronto, ubiubi es, *mellitissime,* meus *amor,* mea *voluptas.* quid mihi tecum est? *amo* absentem. (*M. Caes.* 4.6)

All my best to you, Fronto, wherever you are: sweetest thing, my love, my delight. Why do I bother with you? I love someone who is absent.

Here the theme of absence, earlier exploited in the letters from Fronto's consulship, is expressed with a powerful concision which draws attention to a configuration of desire informing so many love-letters in so many times and places: *amo absentem.*[125] To be sure, Marcus' *mellitissime* finds a parallel in a letter of Cicero's to Atticus, in which he describes his own young son as *mellitus* (Cic. *Att.* 1.18.1), and Marcus himself elsewhere enthuses that not even his own mother has ever written him "anything so delightful and honeysweet" as what Fronto has just sent him (*M. Caes.* 2.5.2, *nihil umquam tam iucundum tamque mellitum eam ad me scripsisse*).[126] Yet the adjective also appears in Catullus' evocation of Lesbia's pet sparrow (Catull. 3.6: *nam mellitus erat suamque norat / ipsam tam bene quam puella matrem*) and of Juventius' eyes which he so desires to kiss (Catull. 48.1, *mellitos oculos tuos, Juventi*). Then there is this ending of a letter of Marcus' from the same period.

vale meum – quid dicam? quidquid dixero, satis non est. vale, *meum desiderium,* mea <*lux, mea*> *voluptas.* (*M. Caes.* 4.7.2)

Best to you, my – how to put it? Whatever I say will not be enough. Best to you, my longing, my darling, my delight.

The rhetorical tool of aposiopesis and the stance of helplessness are combined with a set of vocatives which find (if we accept Mai's supplement

[125] Altman 1982, pp. 13–15, points to "the letter's function as a connector between two distant points, as a bridge between sender and receiver" and thus its tendency to emphasize "either the distance or the bridge"; consequently, she notes, "the letter form seems tailored for the love plot, with its emphasis on separation and reunion," and it is no coincidence that a number of epistolary novels are "seduction novels."

[126] For a biographical sketch of Domitia Lucilla that emphasizes her close relationship with her son, see Hadot 1998, pp. lxxi–lxxv. One of the earliest surviving letters, written to Fronto by the approximately 18-year-old Marcus, concludes with some fervent language paralleling his affection for Fronto with that for his mother (*M. Caes.* 3.9.4: *vale, spiritus meus. ego non ardeam tuo amore, qui mihi hoc scripseris? quid faciam? non possum insistere. at mihi anno priore datum fuit hoc eodem loco eodemque tempore matris desiderio peruri. id desiderium hoc anno tu mihi accendis. salutat te domina mea*).

indicated above) a parallel in a letter from Cicero to his wife Terentia while in exile (Cic. *Fam.* 14.2.2, *hem, mea lux, meum desiderium*) and which, regardless of how the lacuna is filled, invite comparison with the words of Chrysis in Petronius' *Satyricon*, in one of several scenes in which she tries to consummate her burning desire for Encolpius.[127]

To be sure, Cicero's letters have shown us that the vocabulary of *amor* and *desiderium*, the imagery of yearning and burning, the implicit and explicit comparisons to the realm of what in Greek is called τὰ ἐρωτικά, were all characteristic of the speech genre of letters exchanged amongst Roman men of a certain standing. Still, most modern readers agree that the language of Marcus Aurelius' correspondence with Fronto, surpasses Cicero's – not to mention Pliny's! – in its insistent accumulations, its pathetic touches, its florid delicacy. But the next step in interpretation – what to *make* of this difference – has been taken in a variety of ways. One response has been simply to deny the erotic. Pierre Grimal assures his readers that matters are "easily explained" by Marcus' "affectionate nature" and by the familial, even pseudo-filial relationship he enjoyed with Fronto: "this affection is exclusively spiritual in nature and has nothing of the flesh."[128] Mario Attilio Levi speaks of "affectionate intimacy" and "friendliness," comparing the American usage of closing letters with the formula "Love" and ultimately seeing a "reciprocal love" comparable to that between Fronto and his own wife, or Marcus and his mother.[129] Another response is essentially non-committal. Klaus Rosen

---

[127] Petron. *Sat.* 139.4: "Now I've got you, just as I was hoping: you are the one I long for, you are my delight. The only way you can put out this flame is by dousing it with blood." (*teneo te, inquit, qualem speraveram: tu desiderium meum, tu voluptas mea, nunquam finies hunc ignem, nisi sanguine extinxeris*). The only thing missing from Marcus' letter is the imagery of burning and flames, but that is easy enough to find elsewhere in the correspondence. Cf. *M. Caes.* 1.3.1 (Fronto to Marcus: *ad quem tu tam fraglantes litteras mittis*), 1.7.3 (Fronto to Marcus: *quo poculo aut veneno quisquam tantum flammae ad amandum incussisset praeut tu me et facto hoc stupidum et attonitum ardente amore tuo reddidisti?*), 2.5.2 (Marcus to Fronto: *tanto amore lucentes … desiderio fraglantissimo incitaverint*).

[128] Grimal 1990, pp. 153–154: "Cela s'explique aisément, et par la nature affectueuse de Marcus et par les relations entretenues par Fronton avec la mère de son élève … Cette affection est d'ordre exclusivement spirituel et ne retient rien de charnel." Grimal adds that it may not be irrelevant that "Antonin bannissait de la cour l'amour des garçons." Behind this lies a fairly opaque remark by Marcus Aurelius in his *Meditations* to the effect that one of the things he learned from his adoptive father was τὸ παῦσαι τὰ περὶ τοὺς ἔρωτας τῶν μειρακίων (1.16.7). The phrase probably means that Marcus put an end to the court intrigues having to do with (τὰ περὶ) love affairs with young men of the kind alleged to have characterized the reigns of his predecessors Trajan and Hadrian (cf. *Hist. Aug.* Hadrian 4.5) – not such love affairs in themselves. In any case, Marcus' remark in his *Meditations*, composed late in life and alluding to more or less public actions, is of limited relevance to his earlier private correspondence with Fronto.

[129] Levi 1994, p. 263: "La corrispondenza continua a essere intonata a familiarità affettuosa, che, talvolta, ricorda la pur sbrigativa formula di amichevole saluto delle lettere americane, *Love*";

sees something more than a "conventionally affectionate epistolary style" or "set phrases," but goes no further than that, using the German language of both *Freundschaft* and *Liebe* without exploring either German or Latin terminology.[130] Yet another approach is taken by Pierre Hadot, who places Marcus Aurelius and Fronto in the tradition of philosophical student-teacher pairs joined in what he calls "l'amitié amoureuse," blending sincere affection with smiling irony and artifice.[131] Others downplay the issue by shifting the focus away from the central pair of Fronto and Marcus. Sebastiano Timpanaro writes that there is "no homosexual tendency – at least not a conscious one" in the correspondence between Fronto and *either* of his students, and that the key factor in *both* epistolary relationships is "not eroticism but affectation."[132] Similarly decentering the relationship between Marcus and Fronto, Pascale Fleury warns that modern readers too easily "misunderstand" the exuberant, playful qualities of the language of intimacy and affection used by these men and their contemporaries.[133] Finally, Edward Champlin rather surprisingly denies that the issue is even there, contrasting the "ultimately bland affection" of the correspondence between Marcus and Fronto with the "drama" of that with Lucius Verus.[134]

Yet another approach has been taken by Amy Richlin, who detects "a romantic interest" and reads the correspondence as a set of "passionate

---

p. 265: "Tutto il rapporto vuole essere fondato sul reciproco amore, giungendo a paragonare e misurare il proprio sentimento per il principe su quello per la consorte Crazia o su quello per colei *quae me genuit atque aluit.*"

[130] Rosen 1994, p. 124: "… widerlegen den Verdacht, daß es sich bei den Liebesbeteuerungen lediglich um einen konventionellen, herzlichen Briefstil handelte. Es waren nicht nur Floskeln, wenn Fronto an die Eifersuch von Marcus' Mutter dachte und Marcus mit Frontos Gemahlin Cratia in den Wettstreit um dessen Gunst treten wollte."

[131] Hadot 1998, p. cii: "… l'amitié amoureuse, dans laquelle il faut faire la part de l'affection sincère, de la communion d'esprit, de la convention littéraire, de l'ironie souriante et de l'artifice."

[132] Timpanaro 1987, p. 210 (emphasis added): "Nelle numerosissime smancerie e 'dichiarazioni d'amore' tra Frontone e *i suoi allievi Marco Aurelio e Lucio Vero* non si nota alcuna tendenza omosessuale, almeno non una tendenza consapevole: anche i bambini piccoli della famiglia imperiale ricevono baci a profusione, *oscula* e *savia* tra cui ormai non c'è differenza di significato, e la nota costante non è l'erotismo ma la leziosaggine."

[133] Fleury 2006, p. 27 (emphasis added): "Le lecteur moderne peut être surpris par l'expression et l'abandon avec lesquels Fronton exprime l'amour qu'il ressent *pour les jeunes Césars*, et les érudits ont souvent traité d'affectation sa tendresse. Cette impression s'explique, selon nous, par deux faits: d'une part, la mécompréhension moderne des terms servant à exprimer la familiarité et la proximité et, d'autre part, la propension qu'a Fronton d'aborder ces déclarations dans un esprit ludique, ce qui donne lieu parfois à des expansions rhétoriques qui semblent aux Modernes déplacées."

[134] Champlin 1980, p. 110: "The mercurial relations between the two men [Fronto and Lucius Verus] invest it with a drama absent from the ultimately bland affection of the exchanges with Marcus. Here protestations of love invariably accompany recriminations or explanations."

love letters." Even as she grants that this way of reading the correspondence may not convince everyone, Richlin sees Fronto and Marcus as
lovers. As a matter of biographical fact, it is certainly possible, and the
possibility only adds to these letters' interest. At the same time we are
confronted by a set of important, difficult questions. *How* do we define
friendship today, and who are "we"? What is "romantic" and what is
not? What kinds of physical expression can serve as criteria distinguishing friendship from love, friends from lovers, and why? The absence of
any explicit or even indirect reference to the sphere of experience denoted
by the periphrases *res veneriae* and τὰ ἀφροδίσια in the correspondence
between Marcus and Fronto, like the absence of any gossipy insinuations
in surviving ancient texts (such as the *Historia Augusta*, where we might
have expected to find them), raises another set of interesting questions. "If
there were to be a pederastic relationship between Fronto and his imperial
charge," Richlin suggests, "it would have to be careful and secret; letters
would be extremely risky; they would have to follow a strict code of plausible deniability. Arguably, that is exactly what we have in the Marcus–
Fronto letters."[135] Not unlike the range of conspiracy theories currently
enjoying such popularity, the argument does not permit counterargument in its own terms. If we fail to perceive something, it is not because it
is not there, but because we were meant not to perceive it. We may grant
the unknowability – what, after all, *can* we know about what goes on
behind certain scenes and facades? – even as we take it as an occasion to
pose other questions. Rather than asking what the relationship between
Marcus and Fronto *really was* as a point of biography and history, we can
read the letters the two of them exchanged, with an eye to how they represent and negotiate their relationship in and through language.

Let us, then, look more closely at the language. First, some small but
not insignificant points of lexicon and morphology. As we have seen
in Cicero's letters, the nouns *amor* and *desiderium* and corresponding
verbs do not directly correspond to English "love" and "desire," so easily

---

[135] Richlin 2006 (quotations from pp. 6, 17). The "risk" may be somewhat overstated. None less
than Julius Caesar had to put up with public ridicule regarding his relationship with King
Nicomedes that left nothing to the imagination: Caesar was called the "queen of Bithynia,"
Nicomedes "Caesar's fucker," and he was once described, more generally still, as "every woman's man and every man's woman" (Suet. *Iul.* 49–52: *Bithynica regina*; *pedicator Caesaris*;
omnium mulierum virum et omnium virorum mulierem). Caesar is reported to have been especially annoyed by the persistent talk of Nicomedes (Dio Cass. 43.20.1), but none of this had
any lasting impact on his public standing, let alone his political career. If anything, we might
conclude that after generations of autocracy, Marcus Aurelius' subjects would not have dared to
indulge in gossipmongering about the nature of his relationship with Fronto, even if they had
something on which to base it.

suggestive of the erotic; in the speech genre of letters, *amor* is often best translated with terms like "affection," *desiderium* with "missing you."[136] Furthermore, speakers of contemporary English, for whom "dearest" or "sweetest" almost inevitably evoke the realm of the romantic and in any case smack of the sentimental or hyperbolic, may be misled by the recurring use of the superlative suffix *-issimus* especially with adjectives like *carus, dulcis,* or *iucundus.* As we have also seen in Cicero's letters, exuberant expressions of affection, including the use of superlatives in *-issimus* and exclusive expressions such as "no one is more X," were standard features of the speech genre of Latin letter-writing. Here, too, a glance at usage patterns in contemporary Italian may be helpful; not by way of suggesting a direct correspondence (let alone historical continuity), but as a means of urging alertness to the role of vocatives and their superlatives in the verbal performance of relationships, and as a reminder of the uniqueness of each linguistic and cultural system. The vocative *caro mio* is easily exchanged between Italian-speaking men who in English would never call each other "my dear," and I have known of one very senior scholar writing to a junior colleague – whom he had never met – an email beginning with the address *carissimo.* To the recipient of this email the superlative, far from communicating heartfelt affection, marked a hierarchical moment, a performance of the older *barone* distributing his favors and generously making gestures of affection.

What do Fronto and Marcus write about their *amor*? One of Fronto's favorite exercises is to search for comparisons and similes. In a Greek letter to Marcus' mother Domitia Lucilla, he attempts a few in order to describe and justify his not having written her of late. Pointedly reminding her that he was busy composing a speech in praise of her husband, he offers a series of similes to describe himself. Fronto is like a hyena, stiff-necked and unable to turn his head from side to side; he is like a snake that darts forward; a weapon; a blast of wind; a straight line. He then cites the special power of similes drawn from the realm of *philia* or *eros*, trying out a comparison to Orpheus, who turned back because of his desire to see his wife and thus illustrates the dangers of distraction.[137] Temporarily abandoning the technique of comparison, Fronto

---

[136] When Fronto writes to Marcus, *me desiderato* (*M. Caes.* 3.21.3), even Richlin 2006 translates "miss me" (p. 127). Cf. *M. Caes.* 4.5: *valebis mihi magister carissime et dulcissime, quem ego, ausim dicere, magis quam ipsam Romam desidero* (I miss you more than I miss even Rome!).

[137] *M. Caes.* 2.3.2: τίς ἂν οὖν εἰκὼν εὑρεθείη πιθανή; μάλιστα μὲν ἀνθρωπίνη, ἄμεινον δὲ εἰ καὶ μουσική. εἰ δ'αὖ καὶ φιλίας ἢ ἔρωτος μετείη, μᾶλλον ἂν ἔτι ἡ εἰκὼν ἐοίκοι. For Fronto's pursuit of comparisons and similes (*imagines*, εἰκόνες) see Grimal 1990, pp. 156–158.

then observes that by composing a speech in honor of Antoninus he was, after all, doing something that could only bring pleasure to the emperor's wife and son. Quickly enough he returns to comparison, pointing out that in his speech he mentioned both the empress and her son by name, "just as lovers (*erastai*) name those dearest to them (*tous philtatous*) before taking a drink." This is not, of course, an assertion of erotic desire either for Marcus or for his mother, but the comparison itself and its passing juxtaposition are equally striking. As Richlin puts it, "it is odd to find Marcus's mother here along with him."[138]

Cultural anthropology teaches us that moments at which something strikes us as odd may be prompting us to look further. The question – as obvious as it is difficult to answer at a textual moment from the past like this – is whether what seems odd to us is also odd in its own intertwined contexts, personal and generic, linguistic and cultural. As we have seen, Domitia Lucilla is a key figure in her son's correspondence with Fronto and in the networks of intimacy it portrays; what of Fronto's passing comparison of his behavior to that of a lover? In another letter he develops the image further. Responding to the fact that Marcus, despite the extraordinary demands on his time and energy of late, has been sending him an average of more than one letter a day, Fronto writes: "When I got your letters, I experienced something like what a lover experiences (*simile patiebar quod amator patitur*) when he sees his darling (*delicias suas*) running to him along a rough and dangerous path." He then alludes to a staged version of the mythic story of the lovers Hero and Leander, in which "a girl in love (*amans puella*)" stands in a tower at night, holding a torch and waiting for "the young man who loves her (*amantem iuvenem*)" as he swims toward her. Pursuing the comparison, he continues that he would rather do entirely without Marcus, "even though I burn with love for you (*tametsi amore tuo ardeo*)," than allow him to undergo the perils of swimming to him at this hour of the night. "Turning from this tale to reality (*ut a fabula ad verum convertar*)," Fronto lets it out: He is anxious at the thought that he might add a further burden to all of Marcus' necessary toils by demanding that he constantly answer his letters.[139] That turn is worth our attention. The "reality (*verum*)" to which Fronto refers

---

[138] Richlin 2006, p. 94 n. 18 (cf. Richlin 2006, p. 126: Fronto's correspondence with Marcus' adoptive brother Lucius Verus "also has its odd moments"). *M. Caes.* 2.3.4: ἔπειτα δὲ καὶ ὑμῶν ἐμεμνήμην καὶ ὠνόμαζον δὲ ὑμᾶς ἐν τῷ συγγράμματι ὥσπερ οἱ ἐρασταὶ τοὺς φιλτάτους ὀνομάζουσιν ἐπὶ πάσῃ κύλικι (for the practice, see Pl. *Symp.* 214b and Cic. *Verr.* 2.1.66: *Graeco more bibere*).

[139] *M. Caes.* 3.14: *quas ego epistulas quom acciperem, simile patiebar quod amator patitur, qui delicias suas videat currere ad se per iter asperum et periculosum. namque is simul advenientem gaudet,*

is his desire that Marcus come to no harm because of Fronto's desire for contact, and their *amor* and *amicitia* are a part of this reality. What lies in the realm of fiction (*fabula*) is the story of Hero and Leander with its *amans puella* and *amans iuvenis*, along with the simile of the *amator* and his *deliciae*. Both mythic narrative and simile are, in short, figures for the *amor* which joins Marcus and Fronto – and that *amor* is embodied in the letters they write and send each other.[140]

Latin *amor* is so powerful because so flexible; if Fronto had written this letter in Greek, he might very well have used the language of *eros*. The conclusion is invited by another pair of letters exchanged by the two: a Greek text sent by Fronto and Marcus' response – in Latin, but with a few key words in Greek. Fronto's text (*Addit.* 8) takes the form of an *erotikos logos* which places itself in the tradition of Plato's *Phaedrus*, advancing the paradoxical argument that the best lover (*erastes*) for a beloved boy (*eromenos*) is one who is not in love (*ho mê erôn*). He thus implicitly casts himself as Marcus' *erastes* in the Greek tradition.[141] Marcus writes back in Latin saying, in essence, that Fronto won't get rid of Marcus so easily. Marcus joins in on Fronto's game, accepting its terms and entering into its world – but in another language, and with a surprising twist. In Marcus' Latin, Fronto's *eros* becomes *amor* and *hoi mê erôntes* are *non amantes* or *minus amantes*. No surprise there. Yet Marcus makes not only Fronto but himself the subject of the verb *amare*, and – this is the real twist – casts himself in the role of Fronto's *erastes*, using and transliterating the Greek word so as to leave no doubt on the point. He is switching the roles.

age perge, quantum libet, comminare et argumentorum globis criminare: numquam tu tamen *erasten* tuum, me dico, depuleris; nec ego minus *amare me Frontonem* praedicabo minusque *amabo*, quo tu tam variis tamque vehementibus

---

simul periculum reveretur. unde displicet mihi fabula histrionibus celebrata, ubi amans amantem puella iuvenem nocte lumine accenso stans in turri natantem in mare opperitur. nam ego potius te caruero, tametsi amore tuo ardeo, potius quam te ad hoc noctis natare tantum profundi patiar ... nunc ut a fabula ad verum convertar: id ego non mediocriter anxius eram, <ne> necessariis laboribus tuis ego insuper aliquod molestiae atque oneris inponerem ...

140 For the intertwining of love, desire, and letter-writing, see Altman 1982, Stewart 1984, Richlin 2006a, pp. 20–23 and passim.

141 See Fleury 2006, pp. 283–323, for a literary and thematic reading of the letter which sees it as enacting the superiority of rhetoric over philosophy; see Levi 1994, pp. 247–251 for the role of Greek culture and language in Fronto's correspondence. Elsewhere, addressing his fellow tutor Herodes (*M. Caes.* 2.1), Fronto writes that he was in love with some of his own teachers (ἤρων δὲ τοτὲ μὲν Ἀθηνοδότου τοῦ σοφοῦ, τοτὲ δὲ Διονυσίου τοῦ ῥήτορος) and casts Herodes and himself as rival lovers of the young Marcus Aurelius (ἀ<ν>τεραστὴς γὰρ εἶναι σοί φημι).

sententiis adprobaris *minus amantibus* magis opitulandum ac largiendum esse. ego hercule te it<a> *amore depereo* neque deterreor isto tuo dogmate ac, si magis eris aliis *non amantibus* opportunus et promptus, ego tamen *amabo* atque usque *amabo*. (*Addit.* 7.1)

Go ahead, make as many threats as you want, assail me with masses of arguments. But you will never get rid of your *erastes* – in other words, me. I will not stop saying that I love Fronto, or love him less, just because you demonstrate with such varied and vehement argumentation that one should be generous with and yield to those who are not in love. I am, by Hercules, passionate in my love for you and will not be deterred by the dogma you have set forth. Even if you are more yielding and compliant with others – who do not love you – I will love you anyway and will love you always.

Marcus then draws out the obvious if paradoxical implication. If he is *erastes*, then the older Fronto, his teacher, plays the role of *eromenos* – again the Greek word, this time not transliterated in the manuscript – and Marcus throws in some flame imagery for good measure.

ceterum quod ad sensuum densitatem, quod ad inventionis argutiam, quod ad aemulationis tuae felicitatem adtinet, nolo quicquam dicere te multo placentis illos sibi et provocantis Atticos antevenisse, ac tamen nequeo quin dicam. *amo* enim et hoc denique *amantibus* vere tribuendum esse censeo, quod victori<i>s τῶν ἐρωμένων magis gaude<rent. vi>cimus igitur, <vici>mus, inquam … illud equidem non temere adiuravero: si quis iste re vera Phaeder fuit, si umquam is a Socrate afuit, non magis Socratem Phaedri *desiderio* quam me per istos dies (dies dico? menses inquam) tui adspectus *cupidine arsisse*. tua epistula haec fecit ne ille †Diona† esset quin tantum *amet*, nisi confestim tuo *amore* corripitur. vale mihi maxima res sub caelo, gloria mea. sufficit talem magistrum habuisse. domina mea mater te salutat. (*Addit.* 7.2–4)

As for the density of ideas, the clever arrangement, the success of your argument, I don't really want to say that you beat those complacent and challenging Athenians, yet I can't help saying it. For I am in love and, after all, I do believe lovers ought to be allowed to rejoice all the more in the victories achieved by their *eromenoi*. So: we have won – won, I say! … I will freely swear to it: if that Phaedrus of yours ever really existed, and if he ever spent some time away from Socrates, Socrates did not miss Phaedrus any more than I did you all those days – what do I mean 'days'? 'months', rather – burning with desire to see you. Your letter brought it about that he did not love Dio so much (?) – unless he is immediately seized by love for you. All my best to you, the greatest thing under the sun, my pride and joy. It is enough to have had a teacher like you. The Lady my mother sends you her greetings.

We can, if we wish, read these paired texts in light of Fronto's practice of exploring comparisons. Our love, Fronto and Marcus are saying to each other, is *like* that which joins *erastai* and *eromenoi* in the Greek literary tradition. But the great mass of their Latin correspondence leaves no doubt on one point. Whatever it is, their *amor* is not metaphorical.

A pair of letters from the year 144 or 145 (*M. Caes.* 1.2, 1.3) shows us another way Marcus and Fronto might write to each other about their *amor*. Marcus addresses Fronto full of self-reproach. Although you are suffering terribly from gout, I am not dropping everything in order to come see you and massage your foot. Yet call me your *amicus*; am I really acting like one?[142] Fronto's response is warmly reassuring. You show me your *amor* and your *benevolentia* by the very fact of writing such ardent letters; your desire to run to me is precisely that which *amatores* feel. Your mother, Fronto continues, teasingly tells me she envies me for the affection you show me. Your *amor* for me is marvelous precisely because it does not stem from benefits given or received; it is so much more valuable than "those friendships which are warm with duties and service" (*istae amicitiae officiis calentes*), full of smoke and tears but quickly extinguished. Let's leave it that way, he concludes, and let others puzzle over the source of our *amor* the way some puzzle about the source of the Nile.[143]

This is fertile ground for those who perceive a strategy of covering up what today would be called a love affair.[144] The appeal to plausible deniability, as I have suggested, renders counterargument impossible, but I would draw attention to the ways in which Fronto's and Marcus' language fits smoothly into longstanding textual traditions not only of *amor* but also of *amicitia*. The assertion that "my soul has gone over to you," for example, found in the same letter and sometimes read as echoing a pederastically themed epigram by Quintus Lutatius Catulus and/or the Greek epigram that inspired it,[145] also invites being read in connection not only with erotic epigram but with one of the most proverbial of idealizing definitions of *amicitia*, to which Fronto and Marcus elsewhere appeal: "one

---

[142] *M. Caes.* 1.2.1: *et tu me amicum vocas, qui non abruptis omnibus cursu concitato pervolo?*

[143] *M. Caes.* 1.3.1–2: *quin etiam, quod est amatorum proprium, currere ad me vis et volare. solet mea domina parens tua interdum ioco dicere, se mihi quod a te tanto opere diligar invidere*; 1.3.5: *amicitiae istae officiis calentes fumum interdum et lacrimas habent et, ubi primum cessaveris, extinguuntur; amor autem fortuitus et iugis est et iucundus*; 1.3.10: *sine homines ambigant, disserant, disputent, coniectent, requirant ut Nili caput, ita nostri amoris originem.*

[144] Richlin 2006, p. 27 and p. 74, compares Catullus 7.

[145] *M. Caes.* 1.2.1: *at ego ubi animus meus sit, nescio; nisi hoc scio, illo nescio quo ad te profectum eum esse.* Catulus' epigram (opening with the couplet *Aufugit mi animus; credo, ut solet, ad Theotimus / devenit. sic est: perfugium illud habet*) is quoted at Gell. *NA* 19.9; see Courtney 2003, pp. 75–76, Perutelli 1990, Richlin 2006, p. 69. Yet the case for allusion is actually rather weak. The only verbal correspondence is the noun *animus*; instead of Catulus' metaphor of his soul as runaway slave (introduced by *perfugium* and continuing with *fugitivum* in the next line) Marcus uses the rather straightforward verb *proficiscor*; and the motif "soul crossing over" is hardly limited to this epigram (cf. Petron. *Sat.* 79: *et transfudimus hinc et hinc labellis / errantes animas*).

soul in two bodies." Cicero's Laelius observes that there is nothing more natural than that a human being should love himself and seek someone with whom he can "mingle his soul so that he can, as it were, make two souls into one" – and that someone is his *amicus*.[146] Fronto's distinction between the *amor* he shares with Marcus and other kinds of relationships, which he disparagingly invokes as *istae amicitiae officiis calentes*, recalls that made by Cicero between his own relationship of *amor* and *amicitia* with Atticus, whom he loves like a brother (Cic. *Att.* 1.5: *et nos ames et tibi persuadeas te a me fraterne amari*), and other, less intimate but politically and socially useful *amicitiae* (Cic. *Att.* 1.18: *illae ambitiosae nostrae fucosaeque amicitiae*). And Fronto's speculation on the sources or causes of their relationship, along with his delight that it is not based on benefits given or received but on the dazzling power of spontaneous affection (*amor fortuitus*), invites being read in connection with Laelius' words on his own *amicitia* with Scipio – their relationship, he proudly concludes, arose not out of a need for profit or because of the utility that undeniably flowed from it, but out of an awareness of the deeper enjoyment (*fructus*) that inheres in love (*amor*) itself – as well as with Laelius' praise of "the noblest and most natural kind of friendship: that which is sought in and for itself."[147]

Indeed, some letters of Fronto and Marcus suggest that the powerful, spontaneous, undeserved *amor* they share not only cannot be separated from *amicitia*, but ultimately is given its full meaning precisely because of that honorable bond. In one letter Marcus gushes of Fronto's letters as *benignissimae, verissimae, amicissimae*, proudly evokes Fronto's *amor* for himself, quotes a Greek phrase on the subject of *philoi*, and signs off with a sentence which by its very brevity draws attention to the highest of compliments it makes: "What can I call you but 'best of friends' (*amice optime*)?"[148] Another culminates with a brief exposure of the framework

---

[146] Marcus to Fronto: *M. Caes.* 3.10.1 (on your birthday I will pray not for you but for myself, *quia te iuxta ut memet ipsum amo*); perhaps also *M. Caes.* 3.7.1 (*quom tu quiescis et quod commodum valetudini sit tu facis, tum me recreas*: the final clause is emended by van den Hout to *tum me recreavi*). Fronto to Marcus: *M. Caes.* 5.44, *vale, domine, anima mea mihi potior* (cf. Hor. *Carm.* 2.17.5–8, quoted above, p. 192). Cic. *Amic.* 81: *quanto id magis in homine fit natura, qui et se ipse diligit et alterum anquirit, cuius animum ita cum suo misceat ut efficiat paene unum ex duobus*.

[147] Compare *M. Caes.* 1.3.6 (*quid quod neque adolescit proinde neque corroboratur amicitia meritis parta ut ille amor subitus ac repentinus?*) with Cic. *Amic.* 30–31: *sic amicitiam non spe mercedis adducti sed* quod omnius eius fructus in ipso amore inest *expetendam putamus*, and *M. Caes.* 1.3.5 (*at ego nihil quidem malo quam amoris erga me tui nullam extare rationem*) with Cic. *Amic.* 80: *pulcherrima illa et maxime naturali carent amicitia per se et propter se expetita*.

[148] *M. Caes.* 3.18: *quid ego de tuis litteris dicam benignissimis, verissimis, amicissimis? … ut ait nescio quis Graecus (puto Thucydides)*, τυφλοῦται γὰρ τὸ φιλοῦν περὶ τὸ φιλούμενον, *item tu partim meorum prope caeco amore interpretatus es. sed (tanti est me non recte scribere et te nullo meo merito,*

within which Marcus ponders and praises Fronto's attractions. Anyone who has a mind to think, eyes to see, or ears to hear should, Marcus writes, feel *amor* for Fronto, and that includes his colleague and rival Herodes. Using the terms we saw paired and ranked in Cicero's correspondence (above, p. 224), Marcus adds that he himself, insofar as he is Fronto's *amicus*, both experiences *amor* for him and is deeply fond of him (*vehementissime diligam*), while as his student he owes him *reverentia*.[149] For his part, Fronto elsewhere praises the elegance of a letter in which Marcus had voiced how much he missed hearing from his teacher, and takes the opportunity to pontificate on the theme of "absence makes the heart grow fonder," citing Socrates in the process. His conclusion: "The feeling of missing someone comes from love. Love (*amor*), then, increases when one misses someone (*desiderium*), and this is by far the best thing in friendship (*amicitia*)."[150] Letters like these suggest that *amicitia* could be set up as the master term of this relationship, the framework within which Marcus and Fronto live out and express their *amor* for each other.

Fronto's correspondence reminds us that *amor*, especially but not only in conjunction with *amicitia*, often lacks the connotational penumbra of passionate exclusivity that so frequently accompanies English "love." Fronto concludes a letter flattering Marcus on his ability to foster mutual affection (*amor mutuus*) amongst his friends and dependants, comparing him – he could not resist the technique! – to Orpheus, whose music brought together doves, wolves, and eagles. At the letter's end Fronto insists on his own *amor* for Marcus, opening up the range of his *amor* broadly indeed, but all of in and because of Marcus.

quo si quis umquam ingenio tantum valuit, ut *amicos* ac *sectatores* suos *amore* inter se *mutuo* copularet, tu hoc profecto perficies multo facilius, qui ad omnis virtutes natus es prius quam institutus … *amo* Iulianum (inde enim hic sermo defluxit), *amo* omnis qui te diligunt, *amo* deos qui te tutantur, *amo* vitam propter te, *amo* litteras tecum; <***> tuis mihi *amorem* tui ingurgito. (*M. Caes.* 4.1.1, 4)

sed solo tuo erga me amore laudare, de quo tu plurima et elegantissima ad me proxime scripsisti) ego, si tu volueris, ero aliquid. ceterum litterae tuae id effecerunt, ut quam vehementer me amares sentirem … vale mihi Fronto, quid dicam nisi amice optime? Marcus seems to have spectacularly misremembered the source of the Greek phrase – unless this is a private joke, or unless Haines' emendation of *Thucydides* to *Theophrastus* is correct. We will see in the next chapter that *amicus optimus* was an honorific formula in the speech genre of epitaphs; see also Introduction, p. 30.

[149] M. Caes. 4.2: et Herodes te amat et ego istic hoc ago, et qui te non amat, profecto neque ille animo intellegit neque oculis videt; nam de auribus nihil dico … nam cum te ut amicum vehementissime diligam, tum meminisse oportet quantum amorem amico, tantum reverentiae magistro praestare debere. vale mi Fronto carissime et supra omnis res dulcissime.

[150] M. Caes. 4.9: nam desiderium ex amore est. igitur amor cum desiderio auctus est, quod est in amicitia multo optimum.

So if anyone ever had the natural talent for brining together his friends and dependants in mutual affection, *you* will be able to do so – all the more easily because you were born to achieve every virtue even before being trained to do so ... I love Julianus (to return to the beginning of this conversation); I love everyone who is fond of you; I love the gods who watch over you; I love life because of you; I love literature together with you; <****> I take swigs of love for you.

A letter recommending Aemilius Pius to Passienus Rufus gives us a glimpse at further networks of *amor* and *amicitia* in Fronto's world.

> *ama* eum, oro te. cum ipsius causa hoc peto tum mea quoque, nam me etiam magis *amabis*, si cum Pio *familiarius* egeris. novit enim Pius nostra omnia et inprimis quam cupidissimus sim *amicitiarum* quom eiusmodi viris, qualis tu es, copulandarum. (*Amic.* 1.8)

Show him affection, please. I ask this both for his sake and for mine; you will show more affection to me as well if you are on familiar terms with Pius. He knows me very well indeed, and above all he knows how passionately fond I am of giving rise to friendships with men like you.

The imperative *ama* reminds us of a usage we saw in Cicero's correspondence, whereby *amare* can function as the verb corresponding to the noun *amicitia*. This is not a demand that Passienus should feel love for Pius, but a request that he treat him like an *amicus*.[151]

Not surprisingly, we find Fronto expressing *amor* for other members of the imperial family. In one revealing letter, Fronto explains to Marcus why he cannot claim to have experienced *amor* for the Emperor Hadrian even as he praised him lavishly in public. Rather than loving or feeling affection for Hadrian (*amare, diligere*), Fronto feared and revered him as he might a god, because *amor* requires both trust (*fiducia*) and a certain closeness (*familiaritas*), and his relationship with Hadrian lacked the former. Both qualities, however, are abundantly present in his relationship with the current emperor, Marcus' adoptive father, and thus: "I love and feel affection for (*amare, diligere*) Antoninus as I do the sun, the daylight, life, my soul; and I know that he loves me (*amari me ab eo*)."[152]

---

[151] Cf. Quintus' phrase *me ama* in a letter to Tiro (Cic. *Fam.* 16.27, above, p. 234). When Cato the Elder advises overseers (*vilici*) to make their masters' *amici* their own, he is not urging them to feel affection for those men, but to treat them in a certain way (Cato, *Agr.* 5.3: *amicos domini, eos habeat sibi amicos*).

[152] *M. Caes.* 2.4.1: *Hadrianum autem ... ut Martem Gradivom, ut Ditem patrem propitium et placatum magis volui quam amavi. quare? quia ad amandum fiducia aliqua opus est et familiaritate; quia fiducia mihi defuit, eo quem tantopere venerabar non sum ausus diligere. Antoninum vero ut solem ut diem ut vitam ut spiritum amo, diligo, amari me ab eo sentio.* In a letter to Claudius Julianus Naucellius, Fronto flatteringly combines an evocation of the ideal that *amici* are one soul in two bodies with the language of love and affection (*Amic.* 1.20: *a dominis nostris imperatoribus non propter aliud adamari me opto quam ut te quoque participem mei corporis et animi*

Responding to a letter in which Fronto describes his joy and *amor* upon seeing and hearing Marcus' baby sons, Marcus gushes that Fronto's letter had made his own children come alive to him, activating the discourse of *amicitia* by applying the figure of *alter ego* to his relationship with Fronto ("I saw my little boys when you saw them") but at the same time, by means of repeated imperatives and second-person indicatives, urging Fronto to continue in his *amor* – both for Marcus himself and for his sons.[153] Elsewhere Marcus recalls to Fronto how he and his mother shared their thoughts on their affection for Fronto and Fronto's wife Cratia respectively, wondering whose *amor* for whom was greater in a sort of lovers' dreamy contest to which Marcus throws in, for good measure, his love for Fronto's baby daughter.[154] Another of his letters to Fronto begins with the helpless exclamation "you have surpassed in your capacity for *amor* all *amatores* who have ever existed" and declares Fronto winner in an imaginary Greek athletic contest in *philia* (*ta Megala Philotesia*, "the Great Friendship Games"). Yet even as he asserts his own *amor* for Fronto, Marcus acknowledges that there is another whose *amor* for Fronto implicitly trumps all: Cratia, whose affection for her husband Marcus evokes with a sensual Plautine reminiscence of "a shower of love" soaking her dress and flowing into her very marrow.[155]

---

diligant). Van den Hout calls this "a rather unfortunate expression" without justifying the judgment, and adduces in comparison a reference to brother-love (Ter. *Ad.* 957: *tu germanus es pariter animo et corpore*).

[153] *Antonin.* 1.3 (Fronto to Marcus): *vidi pullulos tuos ... habeo enim quos pro te non oculis modo amem sed etiam auribus*; *Antonin.* 1.4 (Marcus to Fronto): *vidi filiolos meos, quom eos tu vidisti; vidi et te, cum litteras tuas legerem. oro te, mi magister, ama me ut amas; ama me sic etiam quo modo istos parvolos nostros amas. nondum omne dixi quod volo: ama me quo modo amasti. haec ut scriberem, tuarum litterarum mira iucunditas produxit.*

[154] *M. Caes.* 4.6 (written between AD 141 and 143 and concluding with the exuberant phrases cited above: *valebis mihi Fronto, ubiubi es, mellitissime, meus amor, mea voluptas. quid mihi tecum est? amo absentem): meus sermo hic erat: "quid existimas modo meum Frontonem facere?" tum illa: "quid autem tu meam Cratiam?" tum ego: "quid autem passerculam nostram Gratiam minusculam?" dum ea fabulamur atque altercamur, uter alterutrum vestrum magis amaret, discus crepuit, id est, pater meus in balneum transisse nuntiatus est ...* (Champlin 1980, p. 171 n. 83, calls this "an extraordinarily saccharine conversation.") The name of Fronto's wife is given as *Gratia* throughout the manuscript, but it is now generally agreed that this is an error for *Cratia*, i.e. Κρατεία (see van den Hout on p. 113.4).

[155] *M. Caes.* 2.5.1: *manus do: vicisti. tu plane omnis, qui umquam amatores fuerunt, vicisti amando. cape coronam atque etiam praeco pronuntiet palam pro tuo tribunali victoriam istam tuam:* M. Κορνήλιος Φρόντων ὕπατος νικᾷ, στεφανοῦται τὸν ἀγῶνα τῶν μεγάλων φιλοτησίων ... *ego vero te, qui minorem vim in amando possideo, magis amabo quam ullus hominum te amat, magis denique quam tu temet ipsum amas. iam mihi cum Cratia certamen erit, quam timeo ut superare possim. nam illius quidem, ut Plautus ait, "amoris imber grandibus guttis non vestem modo permanavit, sed in medullam ultro fluit".* The Plautine reference is either a paraphrase of *Mostell.* 138ff. or a quotation from a lost play. The remark that "I will love you even more than you love yourself" gives a glimpse at what to many modern readers will seem a rather alien conception of

Finally, the kisses: Fronto's letters are full of them, imagined and desired, given and received. The act of bringing one's lips to another's body is a notorious example of the way in which a single physical gesture can communicate a wide range of socially significant messages, both within and across cultural traditions. In the Latin textual tradition we find the kisses of elegiac poet-lovers, of Catullus and Lesbia or Juventius, of Propertius and Cynthia, of Martial and slave-boys; but we also find Catullus' poem to his *amicus* Veranius with his "delightful neck," Catullus' kisses on Veranius' eyes and mouth, and Quintus Cicero's fervently imagined greeting of Tiro, kisses planted on eyes in the midst of the forum. Then there is the practice scholars rather dryly call "social kissing" which had become widespread in Rome by the first century AD: often mouth to mouth, but we also hear of hands, chests, necks, eyes, and heads as objects of these kisses of greeting and respect.[156] What about the kisses exchanged between Marcus and Fronto? There is some memorable, even arresting talk in their private correspondence. In one letter Fronto evokes the pleasure of Marcus' kisses – and of their scent – and in another, attempting to explain why, embarrassingly enough, he had expressed a certain relief upon learning that not Marcus but Marcus' infant daughter was ill, he expatiates upon his *amor*. My dreams of you, he writes Marcus, never fail to include embraces and kisses, and when I pass images of you on the streets of Rome, I have the urge to blow kisses at them. To be sure, Fronto prefaces all of this with some hedging gestures – these are the private musings of gentlemen of leisure, the talk of kisses and dreams is playful, foolish, silly (*ludere, ineptire, frivolum*) – but he leaves no doubt that his affection for Marcus (*quanto opere te diligam*) is in itself a serious matter (*serium*).[157]

What to make of these kisses? Richlin asks the right question: "As with the convention of flowery language, the reader can look at letters Fronto wrote to other friends to see whether there is a difference between, on the one hand, Marcus's terms of endearment and the way Marcus and Fronto

love, especially when read against the backdrop of Christian ideals of selflessness; likewise with Marcus' exclamation of joy at the end of one of his letters: "Because I'm going to be seeing you, I love myself" (*M. Caes.* 5.20: *vale mi, omnia mea, magister. amo me quod te visurus sum*).

[156] Catull. 9.8–9 (*applicansque collum / iucundum os oculosque saviabor*); Cic. *Fam.* 16.27 (Quintus to Tiro): *tuosque oculos, etiamsi te veniens in medio foro videro, dissaviabor*. For an overview of kisses in Fronto's letters, see van den Hout on p. 67.14, and more generally Kroll 1931.

[157] *M. Caes.* 3.14.3: *quid est mihi osculo tuo suavius? ille mihi suavis odor, ille fructus in tuo collo atque osculo situs est; M. Caes.* 4.12.3–6: *non alienum tempus videtur de meo adversus te amore remissius aliquid tecum et liberalius fabulandi; nam ferme metu magno et pavore relevatis conceditur ludere aliquid atque ineptire … nunc ut frivolis finem faciam et convertar ad serium, hae litterae tuae cum primis indicio mihi fuerunt, quanto opere te diligam.*

talk about kisses and, on the other, how Fronto writes to other people."[158] Kisses and embraces in this correspondence are indeed by no means limited to Marcus and Fronto: Lucius Verus, for example, invokes Fronto's tight embraces and repeated kisses.[159] Particularly suggestive is a letter sent by Fronto to Marcus towards the end of his consulship in the summer of 143. Fronto makes the remarkable statement that he would lay down the office right now (!) in order to be able to be with Marcus in Naples, to embrace and kiss him, just as Cratia already enjoys the kisses of Marcus' mother. Domitia's *amor* for Cratia we have already seen (*M. Caes.* 4.6); here Fronto respectfully refers to his wife as the empress' *clienta*, thereby underscoring the crucial difference in status between the two women.[160] The two men's children, too, appear as recipients of meaningful kisses. Fronto reports that he has kissed his own young daughter on Marcus' behalf, asking that he do the same to his own daughter; each man thus becomes the vehicle of affection from his friend to his own daughter, and the kisses reassert the bond between the two friends themselves.[161] In the letter mentioned above, prompted by news that Marcus' infant daughter Faustina had been ill, Fronto imagines kissing the baby's tiny hands and chubby feet with even greater pleasure than Marcus' regal neck and charming mouth.[162]

A kiss could also be a formal gesture of respect that had to do less with feelings than with standing and status, privileges and alliances. Writing to Antoninus Pius on the anniversary of his accession, Fronto expresses the hope that next year he will be able to greet him with a double kiss to make up for the one he missed this year, kisses carefully located on the

---

[158] Richlin 2006, p. 19, adding: "I would argue that, yes, there is quite a difference."

[159] *Ad Verum* 1.4: *equidem videre te et arte complecti et multum exosculari videor mihi toto <****>.*

[160] *M. Caes.* 2.13.1–2: *mater enim tua particulas a te sibi missas cum clienta communicabit; neque est Cratia mea, ut causidicorum uxores feruntur, multi cibi. vel osculis solis matris tuae contenta vixerit. sed enim quid me fiet? ne osculum quidem usquam ullum est Romae residuum. omnes meae fortunae, mea omnia gaudia Neapoli sunt … ego vero etiam illud iuravero, me olim consulatu abire cupere, ut M. Aurelium conplectar.* Van den Hout glosses *clienta* "metaphorically the 'protégée,'" comparing Auson. 183.12, *adfectans esse clienta tibi.*

[161] *M. Caes.* 5.48: *filiae meae iussu tuo osculum dedi. numquam mihi tam suavis tamque saviata visa est. dominam saluta, domine dulcissime. vale et fer osculum matronae tuae.* Like others, Van den Hout understands *matronae tuae* to be an affectionate reference not to Marcus' wife but to his daughter, the "little lady." This letter, among others, disrupts any attempt to rigidly classify Latin words for kisses, regardless of Servius' report that "some people" distinguish among the terms *basium, osculum,* and *savium* (Serv. ad *Aen.* 1.256: *et sciendum osculum religionis esse, savium voluptatis, quamvis quidam osculum filiis dari, uxori basium, scorto savium dicant*; similarly Donat. Ter. *Eun.* 456; see Moreau 1978). Richlin 2006, pp. 26 and 89, glosses *savium* as an "erotic" or "French" kiss, raising the possibility that Fronto's language in this letter is joking.

[162] *M. Caes.* 4.12.7: *manus parvolas plantasque illas pinguiculas tum libentius exosculabor quam tuas cervices regias tuumque os probum et facetum.*

emperor's chest and hands and quite clearly a gesture of respect and homage, however much affection either man may have felt for the other.[163] Indeed, kissing the emperor, or receiving his kiss, could be a matter of palace intrigue. After Antoninus' death in 161, Fronto's relationship with Lucius Verus seems to have provoked envy in some quarters and Fronto and Lucius to have agreed on a strategic avoidance of displaying their friendship in public. In a letter datable to either 161–162 or 166–167, Fronto recalls with evident delight an occasion on which Lucius discreetly admitted him into his living quarters, there greeting him with a kiss on an especially significant part of his teacher's body.

> primum me intromitti in cubiculum iubebas, ita sine cuiusquam invidia osculum dabas, credo ita cum animo tuo reputans, mihi cui curam cultumque tradidisses oris atque orationis tuae, ius quoque osculi habendum, omnesque eloquentiae magistros sui laboris lege fructum cape<re> solitos in vocis aditu locatu<m>. morem denique saviandi arbitror honori eloquentiae datum. nam cur os potius salutantes ori admovemus quam oculos oculis aut frontes frontibus aut, quibus plurimum valemus, manus manibus, nisi quod honorem orationi impertimus? muta denique animalia oratione carentia osculis carent. hunc ego honorem mihi a te habitum <t>axo maximo et gravissimo pondere. (*Ad Verum* 1.7)

> First you gave orders that I should be admitted to your chamber; without arousing anyone's envy you then gave me a kiss. I suspect your thinking was that I, to whom you had entrusted the care and training of your mouth and speech, should also have the privilege of a kiss; and that all teachers of eloquence as a rule harvest the fruit of their labor, which is located at the origin of the voice. In short, I think that the custom of kissing arose as a means of honoring eloquence. After all, why do we put mouth to mouth when we greet each other, rather than eye to eye or forehead to forehead or (though this is the seat of our strength) hand to hand? We are bestowing honor on speech. The mute animals cannot speak – and do not kiss. And so I assign the honor you gave me a tremendous, a significant value.

Fronto's explanation of the historical origins of the mouth-kiss as form of greeting in imperial Rome is transparently tendentious but, in all their fulsomeness, his words point to something important about kisses throughout the Latin textual tradition and, as far as we can tell, in Roman social practice as well.[164] A kiss was a potent sign of a variety of relationships:

---

[163] *Ad Pium* 5: *suscepi vota et precatus sum uti anno insequenti bis te complecterer ista die, bis pectus tuum et manus exoscularer praeteriti simul et praesentis anni vicem persequens.*

[164] An episode narrated by Pliny in his panegyric of Trajan invites comparison. The emperor was compelled to dismiss a praetorian prefect who happened to be his *amicus*; as he bade him farewell in the port, he gave him a pointedly public kiss (Plin. *Pan.* 86.3: *prosecutus es enim nec*

of what poets might describe with the language of Venus and flames; of bonds of kinship and marriage; of *amicitia* across its entire range, from politically or socially beneficial alliance through affectionate intimacy. In short, kisses signified *amor*, elusive and flexible as always.

temperasti tibi, quo minus exeunti in litore amplexus, in litore osculum ferres). See Timpanaro 1987 for a contextualization of Fronto's letter which argues that the phrase *ius osculi* is "un prezio-sismo," modeled on the term *ius conubii* but corresponding to no comparable legal status.

CHAPTER 4

Friendship and the grave: the culture of commemoration

et absentes adsunt
et egentes abundant
et imbecilli valent
et, quod difficilius dictu est,
mortui vivunt.
(Cicero, *De amicitia* 23)

The absent are present, the poor are rich, the weak are strong, and – harder to say – the dead are alive.

I live in the present
speaking of myself
in the mouths of my friends;
I already hear them speaking
on the edge of my tomb.
(Derrida, *Politics of Friendship*)

Those who could read the Latin inscriptions marking the tombs which clustered along the roads leading in and out of ancient cities would regularly have come upon the words *amicus* and *amica*. Even today, attentive visitors to two of the few existing intact portions of Roman cemeteries – the Porta Nocera necropolis outside the walls of Pompeii (approximately 45 tombs datable to the period preceding the destruction of the city in AD 79) and the Isola Sacra necropolis between Portus and Ostia at the mouth of the Tiber (about 100 tombs datable to the late first through the early third centuries AD) – will notice the presence of *amicitia* in epitaphs commemorating the dead and the living and the ties that bound them, a presence that is as distinct as it is distinctively Roman. For, whereas more generally in the Western tradition burial practices and associated epitaphs have been a matter either for individuals or for family units structured around marriage and kinship, Romans were often buried in groups, individuals identified as *amici* not infrequently were members of these groups, and friends played a key role in Roman commemoration of the dead. One would hardly be aware of any of this from a reading of the Latin literary tradition or scholarly readings of that tradition; it is the aim of this chapter to show that a reading of Latin inscriptions significantly fills out our picture both of *amicitia* and of Roman commemorative practices.[1]

One of the most prominent of the funerary structures lining the street of tombs outside the Porta Nocera at Pompeii is a multistory aedicula tomb, excavated in October of 1954, whose centerpiece is a sculptural group of three individuals, now poignantly headless: a woman in the center, flanked by two men, each of whom is marked as a Roman citizen by the toga he wears (Tomb 23 OS; Figure 7).[2] Who are they? Who or what has brought them together to be commemorated in this configuration? For those who can decipher the inscriptions placed under the sculptures, a dramatic tale unfolds. Directly underneath the statues, a white marble plaque contains an inscription in red lettering which identifies the three individuals by name – each name conveniently placed beneath the corresponding statue. I first reproduce the inscription as it is laid out on the stone, followed by a transcription and translation.

P. VESONIVS Ɔ. L.	VESONIAE P. F.	M. ORFELLIO M. L.
	PATRONAE ET	FAVSTO AMICO
PHILEROS AVGVSTALIS		
VIVOS MONVMENT		
FECIT SIBI ET SVIS		

P. Vesonius (mulieris) l(ibertus) / Phileros augustalis / vivos monument(um) / fecit sibi et suis. // Vesoniae P(ubli) f(iliae) / patronae et // M(arco) Orfellio M(arci) l(iberto) / Fausto amico.

Publius Vesonius Phileros, freedman of a woman, Augustalis, while still alive dedicated this monument to himself and his own; to his patron Vesonia, daughter of Publius; and to Marcus Orfellius Faustus his friend, freedman of Marcus.

---

[1] See Petrucci 1998 and Guthke 2006 for overviews of epitaphs in the Western tradition, and Bray 2003 for epitaphs for friends, mostly in England. Studies of Greek commemorative practice include Kurtz and Boardman 1971, Morris 1992, Sourvinou-Inwood 1995, Garland 2001.

[2] Discussions of this tomb and its inscriptions include Ciprotti 1964, D'Ambrosio and De Caro 1983 (who date it to the first two quarters of the first century AD), Elefante 1985, Petersen 2006, pp. 77–80, Wallace-Hadrill 2008, pp. 48–53, Lepetz and Van Andringa 2011 (who speculate that Phileros had become "one of the most affluent freedmen in the city," p. 116).

Figure 7 The tomb commissioned by the freedman Publius Vesonius Phileros for himself, his former owner Vesonia, and his friend Marcus Orfellius Faustus

Spare as it is, this text provides the outlines of a narrative, and the labels PATRONAE and AMICO draw out its main themes. A freeborn woman named Vesonia, daughter of Publius Vesonius, owned a slave named Phileros, whom she at some point manumitted. After having amassed enough financial resources to do so, Phileros commissioned this impressive funerary monument for himself and his former owner, but also for a friend who, like Phileros, was a former slave – not of Vesonia, but of a man named Marcus Orfellius. After the inscription had been carved, Phileros was appointed to the office of *Augustalis* and had the title added to his inscription. It is perceptibly squeezed into the space available on the stone.[3] Seemingly at the same time and by the same rather less skilled stone-carver, the word *suis* was added to the final line of the first column of text, or else recarved to cover an earlier attempt. In any case, the formula *et suis*, found in countless Roman epitaphs, leaves room in the burial group for future but unspecified descendants, slaves, freedmen and freedwomen, or friends.[4]

Read together, the statuary group and the inscription underneath it tell a clear and not uncommon story. A wealthy freedman commissions a tomb for himself, and the statuary group he commissions places at its center not himself but the woman whom he memorializes as his former owner (*patrona*), to whom, like all freed slaves, he remained bound for life to fulfill certain duties (*officia*).[5] Standing at her right hand, Phileros memorializes himself visually in his citizen's toga and textually with the title of *Augustalis*, the combination underscoring his new status as freed

[3] For the *seviri augustales*, *augustales*, and *magistri augustales*, officials connected with the cult of Augustus who are not to be confused with the *flamines* or *sodales augustales*, see Duthoy 1978 (only about 10–15% of recorded cases are unambiguously freeborn citizens, the rest definitely or probably being freed slaves), Petersen 2006, pp. 57–83 (on the visibility of *augustales* in the material remains of Pompeii), Mouritsen 2011, pp. 248–261.

[4] D'Ambrosio and De Caro 1983, followed by Elefante 1985, p. 431 n. 1, state that *suis* was carved over a botched early attempt. When I viewed the inscription in June 2010, close study was impossible since it was affixed to the monument several meters above street level. The formula *sibi et suis* most often occurs as the final, open-ended phrase of an epitaph, but we also find the sequence *sibi et suis et* followed by names and (as in Phileros' inscription) *sibi et suis* followed directly by names without a linking conjunction. Examples of the former include *CIL* 10.2115 (Pozzuoli: *D(ecimus) Aterius Hermes / sibi et suis et Onesim(a)e / co(n)iugi suae et posteri(s)que eorum et Aterio Pr/isco nepoti*), of the latter *CIL* 10.1163 (Avellino: *Messia C(ai) f(ilia) monum(entum) fecit / sibi et suis, / C(aio) Oviedio T(iti) f(ilio) Tumulo et / C(aio) Oviedio C(ai) f(ilio) Luperco et / T(ito) Oviedio C(ai) f(ilio) Tumulo*).

[5] For the bond between freed slave (*libertus, liberta*) and former owner (*patronus, patrona*) and the importance of duties (*officia*) see Treggiari 1969, pp. 37–86, Fabre 1981, Gardner 1993, pp. 7–51, Mouritsen 2011. D'Ambrosio and De Caro 1983 observe that the statue representing Vesonia seems to have carried a torch in her right hand, thus evoking the "Ceres" type of portraiture and thereby heightening her prestige. Lepetz and Van Andringa 2011, p. 117, mistakenly identify Vesonia as the "patroness" of both Phileros and Faustus.

slave. At Vesonia's left stands Faustus, who, like Phileros, is commemorated as a citizen by the visual clue of the toga and as a freedman by the formula *M(arci) l(iberto)* in the text; that same text reveals that he is not primarily being commemorated in conjunction either with his former owner Marcus Orfellius or with Vesonia, but precisely as Phileros' friend. Statues and text together thus honor Phileros as dutiful freedman and generous friend, and Vesonia as a slave-owner who has earned – or at least received – the respect of one of her freedmen.[6]

Phileros' tomb memorializes two relationships structural to Roman society, one vertical (former owner to freed slave) and the other horizontal (*amicitia*). We will be seeing in this chapter that none of this is unusual. Women often took a central place in funerary commemorations; freed slaves frequently provided for the commemoration of their former masters; and the commemoration of friends was an integral feature of the landscape of Roman funerary practice.[7] What is strikingly unusual, however, is the second inscription that was subsequently placed beneath the first on a plaque affixed by five iron nails, one at each corner and one in the center, where there is a visible depression in the stone. This design was an integral part of the plan – the text was carved around the central nail and takes the depression into account – and speaks volumes to those who recognize its symbolism. Even to those who could not read the second inscription, its very form hinted that something here was unusual, even wrong. For both the nails and the impressionistic effect achieved by

---

[6] Wallace-Hadrill 2008 suggests that Phileros and his former owner Vesonia were a conjugal couple and that the 13-year-old Publius Vesonius Proculus and 20-year-old Vesonia Urbana named on two inscribed headstones were their children, while the 18-year-old Heliodorus was one of their slaves (similarly Hüttemann 2010, pp. 184–187; Lepetz and Van Andringan 2011, p. 117, assert that Proculus was Phileros' son). This is certainly possible as a matter of biographical fact, but what does the monument, as seen from the street on which it prominently stands, communicate about the relationships joining the three protagonists Phileros, Vesonia, and Faustus? Visually, the statuary group does not suggest a married couple – there is no *dextrarum iunctio* (see below, p. 346), indeed no physical contact at all between the woman and either of the men flanking her – but rather a triad. For some viewers this might have suggested a *patrona* and two of her freedmen; for others, a mother and her two sons; for others perhaps yet other configurations. For its part, the first inscription tells the story not of a married couple (see Weber 2008 for examples of epitaphs in which a freedman commemorates his former owner as both patron and wife, such as *CIL* 6.28815 from Rome: *C(aius) Vibius Hilarus / Vibiae Gratae / coniugi et patronae / carissumae suae fecit / et sibi*), not of a family or even of a *familia*, but of a woman and her freedman on the one hand, two friends on the other.

[7] Contrast Petersen 2006, p. 78: "This tomb was first and foremost his, while honoring his patroness and, *even more oddly*, his friend" (emphasis added). Petersen's study capably challenges any simplistic notion of "freedman art" or of a single and immediately identifiable "freedman style," but in general it has little to say about the *amicitia* joining freedmen to each other that is advertised in so many inscriptions.

the depression in the stone tablet at its center evoke the so-called *tabellae defixionis*: tablets on which curses were written, usually made of thin lead, often folded and pierced by nails.[8]

But who is being cursed in this stone version of a *defixio*, and why, and why is it attached so prominently to this tomb? To those who can read it, the text reveals quite a drama.

HOSPES PAVLLISPER MORARE
SI NON EST MOLESTVM ET QUID EVITES
COGNOSCE   AMICVM HVNC QVEM
SPERAVERAM MI ESSE AB EO MIHI ACCVSATO
RES SVBIECTI ET IVDICIA   INSTAVRATA DEIS
GRATIAS AGO ET MEAE   (nail)   INNOCENTIAE OMNI
MOLESTIA LIBERATVS SVM   QVI NOSTRVM MENTITVR
EVM NEC DI PENATES NEC INFERI RECIPIANT

hospes, paullisper morare, / si non est molestum, et quid evites / cognosce. amicum hunc quem / speraveram mi esse, ab eo mihi accusato/res subiecti et iudicia instaurata. deis / gratias ago et meae innocentiae: omni / molestia liberatus sum. qui nostrum mentitur, / eum nec Di Penates nec inferi recipiant.[9]

Stranger, stay a moment if it is no trouble to you, and learn what you should avoid. This man, whom I had hoped was my friend, suborned witnesses against me and initiated proceedings. I thank the gods and my own innocence; I was set free from all associated risks. Whoever of us is lying, may both the Household Gods and the gods below reject him.

While carefully avoiding naming names – perhaps a technique both for conveying scorn and for precluding any accusation of aggressive magical practices or desecration of a tomb – Phileros manages to cast Faustus as a liar and false friend who, by instigating legal proceedings against Phileros, had violated the principle of *fides* that should bind *amici* to each other. Both visually and verbally, this inscription drives home the point of Phileros' innocence – the central nail pierces the tablet between the key words MEAE and INNOCENTIAE – while its final words, prominently

---

[8] For discussion of curse-tablets with a selection of examples, see Gager 1992. Elefante 1985 draws the parallel between the second inscription and *defixiones*; Petersen 2006 focuses exclusively on the first of the two inscriptions, merely observing in a footnote that "the tomb displays another exterior inscription, which admonishes passersby" (p. 252 n. 72); Wallace-Hadrill 2008 discusses the second inscription but makes no mention of the nails and their possible implication.

[9] Wallace-Hadrill 2008, p. 50, comments: "The syntax is faltering, the sentence breathless, the cri-de-coeur rings loud and clear." But the syntax is regular (note the careful constructions *hunc ... ab eo ...* and *qui ... eum ...*; for *spero* plus present instead of future infinitive see *OLD* s.v. 2) and rather than a "cri-de-coeur" I read clear language coolly aiming its blow.

occupying the entire last line, amount to a curse wishing on Faustus the terrible fate of the unburied.[10]

There are two stories of *amicitia* here. The first, as we will see, is a common one: A man not only provides for a friend's burial but includes him in his own burial group, in an accompanying inscription honoring and perpetuating his memory and memorializing himself as dutiful, generous *amicus*. But the second story is as unusual among surviving Latin epitaphs as the first is usual. This is a story of the betrayal of *amicitia* by the very man who had received the honor of so prominent a funerary commemoration. And it is the story of a friend's response to betrayal. Unable or unwilling to go so far as to erase Faustus' presence from the publicly visible monument (for example by replacing his name in the inscription with someone else's and thereby rededicating the accompanying statue), Phileros commissioned a second inscription which purports to be a useful warning to passersby, but which is in effect a potent act of blame and exposure.[11]

This is dramatic enough. But for those who have access to the burial enclosure behind the streetside monument, the story continues.[12] Arranged around the enclosure are eighteen headstones or *columellae* of the humanoid shape particularly common in Pompeiian tombs, each marking the interment of cremated remains. Five of these are inscribed with names, and for those who can read them the plot thickens indeed. The cremated remains of Vesonia were placed in a vessel interred at a prominent spot in front of the streetside monument's rear side, covered over with a basalt slab and memorialized by an inscribed headstone; as often in such burials, a ceramic libation pipe leading into the grave pit enabled the pouring of libations to the deceased, and a fragmentary unguent flask found on the ground suggests that perfumed oil had been duly poured in Vesonia's honor. As for Phileros, an inscribed headstone marks his resting place,

---

[10] So Elefante 1985, who also suggests that the invocation of the gods of the household may be alluding to Faustus' violation of principles of hospitality and just possibly to his role as Phileros' *familiaris*.

[11] Wallace-Hadrill 2008, p. 50, observes: "In the end, Vesonius stands stripped to eternity of his pseudo-family, uncertain what to display to the outside world, to the passing *hospes*." I read the story somewhat differently, seeing less "uncertainty" on Phileros' part and more of an active decision, namely *not* to efface Faustus' name but to keep him there and thereby to expose him. See Carroll 2011 for discussion of a phenomenon comparable to official *damnatio memoriae* in a range of epitaphs. For an apparent example of the effacement of an *amicus* see *CIL* 5.5923 (Milan): *C. Cassius / Sopater linarius / sibi et Cassiae C.l. / Domesticae linar(iae) / {a} patronae et / Cassiae Suavi{i} l(ibertae) / et Cassiae Primigen(iae) l(ibertae).* Sartori 1994, p. 92, detects a further line, subsequently erased, which the Clauss–Slaby transcription reports as *[[et C[....]o amico]].*

[12] The following description of the tomb enclosure is based on Lepetz and Van Andringa 2011.

prominently situated behind Vesonia's in a central niche within the monument itself. His grave is not, however, centered in the space but occupies its right half. It was clearly designed to share the niche with another person's grave, and the conclusion that this other person was Faustus is practically irresistible. Such was the plan, but then came the drama: Faustus' role in a legal action against Phileros; the acquittal; the public repudiation of an erstwhile friend in a version of a curse tablet affixed to the streetside facade of a tomb. And what has been found within the tomb enclosure suggests a relentless follow-through in a more private and drastically concrete way. The vessel intended to hold Faustus' cremated remains alongside Phileros' in the central niche was backfilled; if a headstone had ever been inscribed, it was effaced; and the niche was redesigned to hold only one man's remains. Phileros seems to have done what he could to help make the final curse on the second inscription come true.

The Isola Sacra necropolis near the mouth of the Tiber served the nearby port community called, simply enough, Portus, which arose at the beginning of the second century AD in conjunction with Trajan's construction of a nearby canal and harbor. The cemetery grew and continued to be used through the third century AD, and was at some point thereafter abandoned. Significant portions of it were excavated in the 1930s; about 100 tombs are currently visible, and around 370 inscriptions have been catalogued. The surviving portion of the necropolis and the epitaphs that have been found in it well illustrate the role *amicitia* could and did play in Roman commemorative practices.[13] Walking amidst the tombs and browsing the hundred or so inscriptions still *in situ*, one finds a remarkably (and, as it turns out, typically) wide range of interpersonal relationships commemorated: above all those between husband and wife, parent and child, former owner and freed slave, but also the bonds of *amicitia*; also typical, as we will see, are those epitaphs which commemorate individuals without attaching any relational labels to their names at all. A striking feature of these epitaphs is the preponderance of individuals who are explicitly or implicitly commemorated as freed slaves. We will see below that freedmen and freedwomen are overrepresented in Latin epitaphs in general, but their predominance in the Isola Sacra necropolis, combined with the near total absence of epitaphs commemorating magistrates or even freedmen holding the title of *augustalis*, along with the

[13] For the Isola Sacra necropolis and its inscriptions see Calza 1940, Thylander 1951–1952, Baldassare 1987, Helttula 2007. The observations which follow are inspired by a day spent walking around the necropolis in June of 2010. My thanks to Pasquale for his kindness and to his marvelous dog Asia, who accompanied me into tombs 75 and 76.

relative modesty and uniformity of the tomb architecture, have led many to see this as a cemetery principally designed for the traders, merchants, and artisans, slave and freed, who lived and worked in the nearby port community.[14]

Even in this relatively small sample of epitaphs, *amicitia* is a distinct presence. One inscription, originally placed on the wall of a tomb in the third century, tells its readers that Publius Petronius Pelagius is honoring the memory of his *amicus incomparabilis* Marcus Aurelius Alexandrus Pius, who died at the age of thirty.[15] Another, found during the 1930 excavations but apparently not recorded at the time (unlike the inscription carved on the other side of the same stone, an epitaph commissioned by a veteran for himself, wife, son, daughter, stepdaughter, freed slaves and their descendants) communicates a simple message in somewhat coarse lettering.

D(is) M(anibus). / Nugasio b(ene) m(erenti) / et co(n)iugi eius / et filio feceru/nt *amici*. (Helttula 311)

To the spirits of the departed. To the well-deserving Nugasius, and to his wife and son. Given by friends.

Another epitaph, datable to the time of Trajan and thus from the earliest phase of the necropolis, is affixed to the exterior of tomb 62, the letters worn but still legible:

D(is) M(anibus) / L(uci) Sitti Crescentis. / P(ublius) Betilienus / Synegdemus / *amico merenti*. (Helttula 68)

To the spirits of the departed Lucius Sittius Crescens. Publius Betilienus Synegdemus [dedicated this] to his deserving friend.

The tomb is small and modest, a vaulted chest-tomb half buried in the earth and measuring only 130 × 90 centimeters. The quality of the inscription's lettering is not among the finest in this necropolis and the text occupies only the upper half of the stone. The lower half originally contained another inscription that was subsequently effaced. If we think of the inscriptions commissioned by Sopater of Milan or Phileros of Pompeii, we might well wonder whether behind this cancellation of someone's commemoration some drama lies – were it not for the fact that traces of the letters D.M. (the formula opening so many epitaphs) have been found

---

[14] Petersen 2006, pp. 184–226. Only one of Helttula's 372 inscriptions from the necropolis unambiguously commemorates a *sevir augustalis* (Helttula 245).

[15] Helttula 260: *D(is) M(anibus)* / *M(arci) Aureli Alexandr(i)* / *Pii. v(ixit) a(nnis) XXX m(ensibus)* / *VIII. / P(ublius) Petronius Pelagius / amico incom/parabili.*

at the bottom of the erased area, *upside down*. This suggests that the carver whom Synegdemus commissioned to create Crescens' epitaph re-used an earlier stone that had become available (with or without a connection either to the deceased or to Synegdemus), removing the existing inscription and turning the stone upside down so that the new epitaph in honor of Crescens might decently occupy the upper half of the surface.

As for Publius Betilienus Synegdemus, having commemorated his friend Crescens and himself in turn as generous *amicus*, he ended up being buried in the nearby tomb 64, commissioned by his wife Antiochis, a structure that is modestly low but in any case larger and distinctly more impressive than Crescens' resting place. The interior, measuring 200 × 200 centimeters, contains several rows of niches for cinerary urns in the walls; on the tomb's facade, an inscription – in distinctly higher-quality lettering than Synegdemus' commemoration of his friend – announces that his wife Betiliena Antiochis has commissioned this tomb for her husband, her former slaves and their descendants. A handsome funerary urn from the tomb bears an inscription identifying the ashes it contains as those of Synegdemus and Antiochis and the urn itself as a gift of a man named Marcus Cosconius Hyginus. The couple's names suggest that they were freed slaves of the same master, a certain Publius Betilienus, and we might be tempted to call Hyginus their friend and/or heir, but he does not commemorate himself with any label at all on the urn – which was in any case, unlike Antiochis' inscription on the exterior of their tomb, presumably not on public display.[16]

One of the largest of all excavated tombs in the necropolis – originally a single complex constructed around AD 125–130 or perhaps slightly earlier, and subsequently subdivided into what are now labeled tombs 75 and 76 – illustrates some further, equally typical commemorative configurations (see Figure 8 for an external view).[17] Its principal entrance – originally the only one – is surmounted by the following inscription, clearly carved in handsome letters, with the three men's names perceptibly larger than the rest of the text.

---

[16] Helttula 72: *Dis Manibus. / P. Betilieno Synegdemo / Betiliena Antiochis / coniugi bene merenti, / libertis libertabus posterisque / eorum fecit*; Helttula 73: *D. M. P. Betilieni / Synegdemi. et / Betilienae Antiochidi. / cura / M. Cosconi Hygini.*

[17] For detailed discussion of tombs 75 and 76 see Lazzarini 1991, pp. 67–107 (with attention to issues of law and the *ius inferendi* in particular), Helttula 2007, pp. 96–108. Petersen 2006, pp. 184–226 ("Family and Community at the Isola Sacra Necropolis"), says nothing about the inclusion of *amici* in this or other tombs in the necropolis, or about the legal category of *sepulcra familiaria* (below, n. 97).

Figure 8 Tombs 75 and 76 of the Isola Sacra necropolis

D   M
M COCCEIVS DAPHNVS
FECIT SIBI ET SVIS ET LIBERTIS LIBERTABVSQVE
POSTERISQVE EORVM ET
M ANTONIO AGATHIAE ET SVIS
ET LIBERTIS LIBERTABVSQVE POSTERISQVE EORVM ET
M VLPIO DOMITO ET SVIS
ET LIBERTIS LIBERTABVSQVE POSTERISQVE EORVM
PER FRONTE PEDES XL IN AGRO PEDES XL
(Helttula 82)

To the spirits of the departed. Marcus Cocceius Daphnus established this for himself and his own, and for his freedmen and freedwomen and their descendants; and for Marcus Antonius Agathias and his own, and for his freedmen and freedwomen and their descendants; and for Marcus Ulpius Domitus and his own, and for his freedmen and freedwomen and their descendants. 40 feet wide, 40 feet deep.

This is an impressive statement on the part of Marcus Cocceius Daphnus, who casts himself in the role of generous provider of burial and commemoration to an open-ended group of unnamed dependants. Found in many epitaphs, the formula *libertis libertabusque posterisque eorum*, often preceded by *sibi et (suis et)*, reminds us of one of the major responsibilities a slave-owner traditionally had in connection with his freed slaves: providing for their burial and even the burial of their descendants. Daphnus, however, also provides for two other men and their dependants. His relationship with Marcus Antonius Agathias and Marcus Ulpius Domitus is not given a label, but all three men's names suggest that they were freedmen or descendants of freedmen (in the case of Cocceius and Ulpius, connected with the households of the Emperors Nerva and Trajan respectively). We might speculate that they were each other's friends, or even that Agathias and Domitius could be called Daphnus' *clientes*, but the inscription commissioned by Daphnus, like Hyginus' for Antiochis and her husband Synegdemus, is not concerned to tell any such story. Their names, and his, are enough.

Above the entrance to the subsequently created subdivision on the left (now numbered tomb 76) stands the following inscription, placing not Daphnus but Agathias in the dominant position.

D(is) M(anibus). / M(arcus) Antonius Agathias / aediculam puram ex sepulchro / M(arci) Coccei Daphni, cuius heres est, / facta divisione inter se et coher(e)des suos, / adiecto de suo pariete medio et ostio libero / facto, fecit sibi et / [*several lines blank*] / libertis libertabusque posterisque eorum. (Helttula 92)

To the spirits of the departed. Marcus Antonius Agathias built an intact structure out of the tomb of Marcus Cocceius Daphnus, whose heir he is, after having divided up between himself and his fellow heirs. At his own expense he added a wall in the middle and opened up a door. He did this for himself and [*several lines blank*] his freedmen and freedwomen and for their descendants.

Amidst the flood of detail regarding who paid for what and what was built where, perhaps surprising to modern readers but typical of Latin inscriptions of all kinds, we learn that Agathias was one of Daphnus' heirs (and, although it would not have been visible to passersby on the street, one of the inscriptions inside the enclosure raises the possibility that he may have been Daphnus' son-in-law as well). It is striking that in this publicly visible inscription Agathias names no wife or children, not even by means of a vague *suis*; just as striking is the large space after the formulaic *sibi et*. It has been plausibly suggested that, when he commissioned the inscription, he left the space open for the names of an eventual wife or children but that, for whatever reason, the space was never filled.[18]

---

[18] Helttula 2007, pp. 96, 100, 105–106. For a comparable blank space see Helttula 38: *D. M. / Verria Zosime et / Verrius Euhelpistus / fecerunt sibi et /* [several lines blank] */ libertis libertabusque*

Passersby saw (and see) just those two prominent inscriptions placed over the entrances to the adjacent complexes 75 and 76. They alone, however, tell a perceptible story, one of a network of influence, protection, and display, emanating from Marcus Cocceius Daphnus and continuing on with one of his heirs, Marcus Antonius Agathias. Like those who are curious and lucky enough to gain access today, those who in the past went inside either or both enclosures – to leave offerings for the departed, to participate in the traditional rituals and banquets on anniversaries of death, or to participate in new buials – might read yet further stories. Within the subdivision set up by Agathias (tomb 76) numerous urns are set into niches along the walls, some of them still containing ashes and bone fragments, but none of them marked by inscriptions. These may well be the remains of Agathias' freedmen, freedwomen and their descendants promised burial in the exterior inscription. But one inscription, located above the entrance to a chamber at the back of the enclosure, in the right half of a space whose left half was never filled, reads as follows:

D(is) M(anibus). / M(arcus) Antonius / Pius Aemiliae / Maioric(a)e et / Cominio / Silva/no concessu in/trantib(us) parte dext(ra), / lib(ertis) liber(tabusque) pos(terisque) eor(um). (Helttula 93)

Marcus Antonius Pius to Aemilia Maiorice and Cominius Silvanus, by his concession, on the right side as one enters; and to his freedmen and freedwomen and their descendants.

Marcus Antonius Pius, who might possibly be Agathias' son, provides burial for and commemorates a woman and a man whose names communicate no relationship to Pius or Agathias or anyone else named in the inscriptions, not even a relationship of former owner and freed slaves. Maiorice and Silvanus may well have been Pius' friends, and they may well have been a married couple, but once again the inscription communicates none of this. Its concern is to perpetuate their names, locate them here, and commemorate Pius' generosity toward them, as well as to his freedmen and freedwomen and their descendants.[19]

posterisque eorum. That Agathias did indeed, at some point, marry and have children is suggested by an epitaph found inside tomb 75, recording the commemoration of Cocceia Doris by her grandson Marcus Antonius Callistianus, son of Marcus (Helttula 85). Doris may have been the fellow freedwoman and wife of the dedicator Daphnus; Agathias may have married a daughter of theirs and Callistianus may have been the son of this Cocceia and Agathias. The Marcus Antonius Pius who commissioned Helttula 93 (see below) may also have been Agathias' son. See discussion by Raija Veino at Helttula 2007, pp. 94–96.

[19] An inscription found in the left-hand part of the cella during the excavations of 1976–1979 but subsequently lost records that this same Pius granted burial to another person whose name communicates no connection: *D.M. / P. Ael(io) Trypho/ni, loc(um) conce/ssum [a] M. An/tonio Pio* (Helttula 94).

Entering tomb 75 through what was originally the only entrance to the undivided burial structure, we come into a spacious enclosure that is today luxuriantly overgrown. Here too the exterior walls are lined with niches containing cinerary urns, presumably many of them holding the remains of freedmen and freedwomen of Marcus Cocceius Daphnus and their descendants in turn; here too there is a central chamber at the back. Unlike tomb 76, however, here a few individual burials are visible, set apart in architectural elements within the enclosure and marked by their own inscriptions, datable to the Hadrianic period. One of these signals the resting place of Cocceia Doris, dedicated by her grandson Marcus Antonius Callistianus, who died at the age of twenty-one (Helttula 85). The inscription was evidently commissioned by someone else afterwards, but the names signal a family relationship to both Daphnus and Agathias. Another marks the tomb of Sextus Julius Armenius, covered by a black-and-white mosaic depicting Venus with a dove at her feet. Who was this man, and why is he buried and commemorated in a tomb enclosure designed not for Julii but for Cocceii and Antonii, and advertised as such? The brief inscription explains the connection:

D(is) M(anibus). / Cocceia Ty/che *Sexto / Iulio Armenio / amico b(ene) m(erenti) /* fecit. (Helttula 91; see Figure 9)[20]

To the spirits of the departed. Cocceia Tyche dedicated this to Sextus Julius Armenius, her well deserving friend.

Tyche was probably a descendant or freedwoman (or descendant of a freedwoman) of the Cocceius Daphnus who founded this complex.[21] So much is suggested, apart from her name, by the very fact that she took the initiative of including an apparently unrelated friend in this burial complex. Daphnus' original inscription at the entrance could be interpreted as granting the legal right to do so (*ius inferendi*) to those whom it includes in its formulaic language (*et suis et libertis libertabusque posterisque eorum*). As for Sextus Julius Armenius himself, we know nothing about him, other than that he found his resting place in the sepulchral complex associated with the family of his friend Cocceia Tyche, thanks to

---

[20] This inscription takes up only the left half of the available space. Was the other half originally planned to hold an inscription commemorating Cocceia Tyche herself? Or Armenius' wife, who ended up being commemorated in another inscription placed at the somewhat more prominent head side of the tomb?

[21] Suggested by Vainio in Helttula 2007, p. 105. An earlier, less persuasive suggestion was that Tyche is the same woman who is commemorated in an epitaph from Ostia as freedwoman of one Lucius Cocceius Adiutor and wife of the freedman Titus Manlius Bargathes (*CIL* 14.4865).

Figure 9 Epitaph in tomb 75 of the Isola Sacra necropolis

her initiative, and that he still rests there. But he is not alone, for another inscription attached to this tomb reads as follows:

D(is) M(anibus). / Iuliae Paullinae / coniugi ben(e) mer(enti) / Sex(tus) Iulius Armenius / fecit. (Helttula 90)

To the spirits of the departed. Sextus Julius Armenius dedicated this to Julia Paullina, his well deserving wife.

When Tyche commemorates Armenius as her *amicus*, she is not communicating that he was her lover. As I have argued in Chapter 1, in the formulaic language of inscriptions the relationship between *amica* and *amicus* is entirely parallel to that between *amicus* and *amicus*, *amica* and *amica*; the image of Venus, for its part, invites being read not as a symbol of Tyche's and Armenius' relationship but of that between Armenius and his wife Paullina, who still lie there together.[22] This configuration

---

[22] In 1940 Armenius' and Paullina's remains were apparently still in the tomb (Calza 1940, p. 331: "La piccola tomba contiene due corpi"). Calza 1940, pp. 174 and 177, concludes that Cocceia Tyche and Sextus Julius Armenius had lived together for many years and wonders whether the image of Venus signals a long-term concubinage; but, as Raija Vainio observes at Helttula 2007,

also illustrates the unpredictable arrangements and commemorations that could be found in burial complexes marked by dedications like Marcus Cocceius Daphnus'. Taking advantage of (or claiming) the *ius inferendi*, Cocceia Tyche included within the complex in which she herself was entitled to be buried a man who was not covered by any of the categories specified in Daphnus' inscription. That man in turn, once given a burial spot in the complex, not only provided one for his wife but set up an inscription which commemorated her to any and all who might later come into the enclosure, even though neither he nor she would appear to have been covered by the language of Daphnus' inscription.[23] All of this because of *amicitia*.

In fact, other inscriptions located within this enclosure commemorate individuals whose presence in the complex cannot be explained as easily as can Julia Paullina's. One epitaph datable to the Hadrianic period marks the burial of a freeborn woman named Maria Semproniana, commemorated by her father; no other Marii appear elsewhere in this tomb complex.[24] Two others commemorate slaves who died young and whose owners had no obvious connection to the Cocceii or Antonii; or rather, connections no doubt existed, but they are not described in the epitaphs. An inscription commissioned by Aelia Salviane commemorates her 6-year-old home-born slave Sabina, and another marks the burial of the 14-year-old Urbica, commemorated by the imperial slave Olympus, who records with touching precision that he had lived with Urbica for 1 year, 8 months, 22 days, and 3 hours.[25] Sabina's owner Aelia may have been

---

p. 105, "questo non possiamo dedurlo con certezza dall'epiteto *amicus*," and neither inscription uses the formula *cum quo vixit*. Thylander 1951–1952 claims without any evidence that not Paullina but Tyche was buried in this tomb together with Armenius, and describes the mosaic simply as representing "a nude woman." It may or may not be significant that the name *Armenius* is not otherwise attested in Ostia but is found in North African inscriptions, and that artistic tomb-coverings comparable to the Venus mosaic are also found in North Africa (Vainio in Helttula 2007, p. 104).

[23] Lazzarini 1991 persuasively argues that, unless the original inscription explicitly excluded certain individuals or categories of individual from burial, situations like this were always a potential result of such group dedications.

[24] Helttula 88: *Mariae M(arci) fil(iae) / Sempronian(a)e / M(arcus) Marius Iulianus / pater fecit*. The fact that her tomb was given and her burial commemorated by her father, and that she is there alone, suggests that she had no husband or children; what M. Marius Julianus' connection to the Cocceii or Antonii is remains unclear.

[25] Helttula 89: *D.M. / Sabinae / quae vixit ann(is) VI / m(ensibus) VIIII d(iebus) XX. / Aelia Salviane / vernae b(ene) m(erenti) fecit*; Helttula 87: *D.M. / Urbicae suae fecit / Olympus Matidiae / Aug(ustae) f(iliae) serv(us). cum qua vix(it) / anno I m(ensibus) VIII d(iebus) XXII h(oris) III. / quae decessit ann(orum) XIIII m(ensium) XI*. For the formula *cum qua vixit* see Chapter 1, p. 109. In view of the widespread understanding that young women became marriageable at menarche, the inscription commissioned by Olympus may be communicating that he had entered into a conjugal relationship with Urbica when she was 13 years old. In another epitaph from this tomb, the 19-year-old

related to the Publius Aelius Tryphonus who was given his burial place in tomb 76 by Marcus Antonius Pius (Helttula 94). Urbica's owner is not named, but may well have been the same woman who owned Olympus: *Matidia Augustae filia*, or Matidia minor, daughter of the emperor Trajan's niece. The fact that a slave of Matidia's used a space in this tomb complex to bury his young companion may hint at some high connections enjoyed by the Cocceii.

In addition to illustrating the variety of networks that could shape burial configurations and their commemoration in inscriptions, the Cocceius–Antonius complex reminds us of the risks of drawing conclusions when, as we usually must, we read inscriptions no longer *in situ* and with little or no knowledge of the physical context in which they were originally located. If the main inscription commissioned by Daphnus had survived out of its context and/or if Armenius' epitaph had not survived at all, we would not know that a man identified as an *amicus* of a member of the family found his resting place here. If Daphnus' inscription had survived out of its context, we would not know that the Sextus Julius Armenius whom it commemorates as a friend of Cocceia Tyche was buried in a complex set up by a male relative of the latter. If Armenius' epitaph for Paullina had survived out of its context, we would not know that this husband-to-wife dedication was part of a larger complex founded by someone evidently unrelated to either of them, to which they had access only because of a relationship that is described as *amicitia*. Read in their entirety, the inscriptions marking burials in tombs 75 and 76 reveal a variety of networks and a range of motivations for burial and commemoration which may surprise visitors or readers accustomed to think of graves as family affairs. They are, however, entirely typical of what we find across the Latin-speaking world. But while provision for ex-slaves, and even for their descendants, can readily be explained (if not explained away) by the centrality of the institution of slavery to Roman society, what about those friends?

TOGETHER IN DEATH

Death circles around Roman idealization of *amicitia*. In the Introduction and Chapter 2, for example, we have seen the interrelated motifs *contest of death* and *unity in death*. The mythic pair Orestes and Pylades were

---

Sabinia Attice is commemorated as the *coniunx* of Marcus Cocceius Onesimus, who records that he had lived with Attice (*cum qua vixit*) for six years and five months (Helttula 86).

honored and admired for their willingness to die in each other's stead ("I am Orestes!") while Nisus and Euryalus in fact die with each other, bodies intertwined, finding lasting rest together.[26] Nor was this a matter for myth only. Valerius Maximus' narratives of exemplary friends (above, p. 10) includes the pair Volumnius and Lucullus, who died in the turbulent events following Julius Caesar's assassination. Lucullus having been killed at Antony's orders because he had supported the assassins Brutus and Cassius, Volumnius begs Antony to be brought to his friend's corpse.

ductusque quo voluerat, dexteram Luculli avide osculatus, caput quod abscisum iacebat sublatum pectori suo adplicavit ac deinde demissam cervicem victori gladio praebuit. loquatur Graecia Thesea nefandis Pirithoi amoribus subscribentem Ditis se patris regnis commisisse: vani est istud narrare, stulti credere. mixtum cruorem amicorum et vulneribus innexa vulnera mortique inhaerentem mortem videre, haec sunt vera Romanae amicitiae indicia. (Val. Max. 4.7.4)

And once he was taken where he wanted to go, he passionately kissed Lucullus' right hand, picked up the head which had been severed and held it to his own chest, and then lowered his own neck in submission to the victor's sword. Let Greece tell of Theseus, yielding to Pirithous' wicked wishes and entrusting himself to the kingdom of Father Dis: that is for the foolish to narrate, the stupid to believe. But to see friends' blood mingled, wounds joined to wounds, death clinging to death: these are the true signs of Roman friendship.

Like Cicero's Laelius, meditating on Orestes and Pylades in the *De amicitia*, Valerius Maximus contrasts Greek myth and Roman reality and leaves no room for doubt as to which trumps which. Like Virgil's Nisus and Euryalus, these two Roman friends are joined together in death, body to body, head to chest. But what happened next?

The ideal according to which friends are a single soul divided into two bodies implicitly raises the possibility of a continuance of friendship beyond this life. And in the mythic narrative to which Valerius Maximus alludes, Theseus and Pirithous indeed travel together to the Underworld, symbolically dying together in a characteristically homosocial configuration. They undertake the journey in order that Pirithous may obtain the unobtainable Persephone as his bride. But the two men's souls are not united forever. Heracles is able to rescue Theseus from the Underworld – but not Pirithous. Does Roman idealizing of *amicitia* include the image

---

[26] Cic. *Fin.* 2.79: *aut, Pylades cum sis, dices te esse Orestem, ut moriare pro amico? aut, si esses Orestes, Pyladem refelleres?* 5.63: *qui clamores vulgi atque imperitorum excitantur in theatris, cum illa dicuntur: "ego sum Orestes", contraque ab altero: "immo enimvero ego sum, inquam, Orestes!"*; Verg. *Aen.* 9.444–445: *tum super exanimum sese proiecit amicum /confossus, placidaque ibi demum morte quievit.*

of two friends' souls still together after death, united in the next life as well as in this? Valerius Maximus stops short of this; what of Cicero's Laelius? In his reaction to Scipio's death, he lives up to the epithet *sapiens* so emphatically attributed to him; and he seems to know it. His mourning, he proclaims, is different from that of "most people," for he realizes that, by dying after a life full of honors, Scipio has not suffered any ill. Excessive mourning would thus be a sign of ill-will rather than friendly affection, and so Laelius boldly hopes – and from this he claims to derive satisfaction, not from being called *sapiens* – that the *amicitia* he shared with Scipio will live up to the proverb "true friendships are eternal," but with a crucial twist. Not the friendship itself, but its *memory* will last for ever.[27]

In his reluctance to consider what happens to friends' souls after death, Cicero's Laelius is not only reflecting a widespread reluctance to dogmatize about what happens after death that is widespread in Greek and Roman cultural traditions, which in general allowed for a variety of co-existing models, from the simple dissolution of the soul at death to elaborately differentiated narratives of an underworld. Seen from an even broader perspective, the silence about the fate of friends' souls is typical of the Western tradition in general, which has largely been silent on the question of whether friends' souls remain joined after death.[28] From Cicero's *De amicitia* to funerary inscriptions, the Latin textual tradition has little or nothing to say on this point. But what it does periodically say is as remarkable as it has been undernoticed. We will see that hundreds of surviving epitaphs memorialize individuals as *amici* and *amicae*, and that the logistics of burial arrangements often put these individuals in their lasting home together with their friends, often including them in what we

---

[27] Cic. *Amic.* 10: *non egeo medicina; me ipse consolor et maxime illo solacio, quod eo errore careo, quo amicorum decessu plerique angi solent. nihil mali accidisse Scipioni puto ...*; 14: *quocirca maerere hoc eius eventu vereor, ne invidi magis quam amici sit*; 15: *itaque non tam ista me sapientiae, quam modo Fannius commemoravit, fama delectat, falsa praesertim, quam quod amicitiae nostrae memoriam spero sempiternam fore.* Laelius himself later cites the proverb (32: *verae amicitiae sempiternae sunt*).

[28] Epstein 2006, p. 10, notes the significant silence in the Western tradition regarding the status of friendship in the afterlife, deliberately continuing it himself. In a striking exception, Aelred of Rievaulx prays that he may lie in God's bosom together with his friend Simon (*De spiritali amicitia: mihi quoque misero, qualicumque dilectori suo, in ipso sinu tuo cum ipso aliquando locum quietis indulge*); see discussion at Boswell 1980, pp. 221–226 and Bray 2003, pp. 254–261. The contradictory images of what happens to spouses after death disseminated in contemporary Western cultures are worth comparing. The formula "till death us do part," endorsed by many Christian rituals, envisions a union of souls only in this life and authorizes a widowed partner to remarry; at the same time, however, there is a widely circulated ideal of "eternal love" between spouses.

too easily call "family tombs," and sometimes placing two friends alone, side by side.

In other words, *amici* and *amicae* were often included in group burials whose configurations reflected and perpetuated the networks structuring Roman society; along with spouses, kin, and freed slaves, Romans not infrequently found their resting place in the company of others whose names are kept alive as their friends. Although historians and epigraphists have noted the phenomenon,[29] they have rarely explored its implications, but literary scholars have most often simply ignored it. "Epitaphs recording the deaths of friends are not common," a commentator on Martial writes; "it was unusual for friends to share a tomb, since tombs were generally family affairs."[30] Even a recent study of Roman funerary inscriptions, while noting that the regular presence of freed slaves in family burials points to a significant difference between the Roman *familia* and modern concepts of family, is silent on the point that individuals commemorated as *amici* not infrequently are included in these groups as well.[31] To be sure, epitaphs commemorating individuals as *amici* represent a small minority of surviving inscriptions, yet they were a distinct feature of the cultural and physical landscape in which Romans commemorated their dead. The Latin proverb which held that enmities should be mortal but friendship immortal will have rung true in more ways than one.[32]

FRIENDS AS COMMEMORATORS

Whereas Cicero's Laelius speaks in stirring but ultimately vague terms of immortalizing *amici* by keeping their memory alive, there were some distinctly concrete means of doing so. In a scene from Petronius' *Satyricon* (71–72), the ex-slave Trimalchio, addressing his dinner-guests as *amici* and making the equally pointed remark that slaves are people too, proclaims

---

[29] In the article on *amicus* in his 1895 *Dizionario epigrafico*, Ettore De Ruggiero observes that friends are not infrequently included in family burials along with relatives. More recent studies that acknowledge the presence of friends in group burials include Hesberg 1992, p. 15, and several of the essays in Peachin 2001.

[30] Howell 1980 1.93.

[31] Kolb and Fugmann 2008, p. 18. Theorization of the inclusion of friends in Roman group burials does not seem to have advanced significantly since Albertario 1941, p. 23 n. 2, who in passing speaks of a "dolce consuetudine che aveva dilatato l'ambito della *familia*." Fifty years later, Lazzarini 1991, p. 20, observes that "la deposizione, nel sepolcro 'esclusivo', di liberti ed amici era evidentemente compatibile con il culto privato familiare," but goes no further than that.

[32] Cic. *Rab. Post.* 32 (*neque me vero paenitet mortalis inimicitias, sempiternas amicitias habere*), *Amic.* 32 (*verae amicitiae sempiternae sunt*), Livy 40.46.12 (*vulgatum illud, quia verum erat, in proverbium venit: amicitias immortales, mortales inimicitias debere esse*). Cf. Fürst 1996, pp. 234–235.

that he has provided for the manumission of all his slaves in his will, and then reveals that he is commending his wife Fortunata to his friends (*omnibus amicis meis*). After causing his entire will to be recited, he turns to the question of his tomb, pointedly addressing Habinnas as his friend with an epithet that is, as we will see, commonly found in epitaphs: "How about it, my dear friend (*amice carissime*)? Will you build my tomb as I ordered you ... so that through your benefaction I may end up living after death?"[33]

There is a strong element of parody in this as in so much having to do with Trimalchio, but the parody is only effective if there is a backdrop of recognizable social realities. Central among them is the key role of *amici* in Roman funerary and commemorative practices. Other texts tell us, for example, that when full funeral rites were observed, a procession of both relatives and friends accompanied the corpse to the place of cremation or burial; that, when there was a cremation, both relatives and friends called upon the dead by name just before the pyre was lit; and that in the days, weeks, and months following the burial, both relatives and friends held meals and other ceremonies at the tomb on certain fixed occasions. We also read that if a person died without a will, or if a testator made no provision for who should take charge of the burial rites, Roman law left it to a friend to designate someone to do so, and it was clearly a widespread expectation that *amici* would be remembered in wills.[34]

And so we find a number of Latin inscriptions honoring the role of *amicitia* in burial and commemorative practices. An epitaph found along the Via Salaria outside of Rome praises Lucius Licinius Nepos for having given a final resting place for many of his friends and has him speak up, urging his friends to be generous in turn; the key term *amici* appears twice in rapid succession.[35] Others are more specific. An inscription from a columbarium in Rome in which a freedwoman commemorates herself and her husband, former slaves of the same master, records that their urns rest in a niche given by their mutual friend; an epitaph from Ostia announces

---

[33] Petron. *Sat.* 71–72: *amici, inquit, et servi homines sunt et aeque unum lactem biberunt, etiam si illos malus fatus oppresserit ... nam Fortunatam meam heredem facio, et commendo illam omnibus amicis meis ... quid dicis, inquit, amice carissime? aedificas monumentum meum quemadmodum te iussi?*

[34] For friends in funeral rites, see Toynbee 1971, pp. 46, 50, 51; for *amici* in wills, see Verboven 2002, p. 336. For overviews of Roman burial and commemorative practices, see Toynbee 1971, Reece 1977, Hopkins 1983, pp. 201–256, Hinard 1987 and 1995, Morris 1992, pp. 31–69 and 156–173, Pearce *et al.* 2000.

[35] *CIL* 6.9659 = *CIL* 6.33814 = *CLE* 1583: *(...) qui vivos / multis in futuram su(p)rem/a hospitia donavit amicis, / cuius in hospitio requiesc(ere)/nt, multis gratis (sic) / et amicis, quos roga/t ut quod eis superat suis / donent gratis, ne vendan/t.*

that the tomb of the 19-year-old Lucius Cacius Volusianus was set up by his parents on property given by his friend Gabinius Adiectus.[36] An epitaph from Rome announces that the deceased Sextus Julius Stratonicus had been given his burial site by two *amici*, Marcus Aurelius Fortunatus and Marcus Aurelius Alexander (all three names suggest the status of imperial freedman), adding that Stratonicus subsequently dedicated the tomb not only to himself but to his wife Clodia Mercurine and to his freedmen, freedwomen, and their descendants.[37] Epitaphs for soldiers often mention *amici*, whether fellow-soldiers or not. An inscription found near Paks in Hungary commemorates a North African soldier named Marcus Tullius Fortunatus along with his wife and their children in the name of Fabius Baritio, fellow-soldier, friend and heir of Fortunatus.[38] In greater detail still, an inscription from Rome commissioned by unnamed heirs (*heredes*) carefully announces that the bones of the soldier Sextius Naevius Verecundus have been shipped back to his home town of Verona but that this memorial marks the resting-place of his ashes; that a certain Cornelius composed its inscription; and that all of this was in honor of a deceased colleague and friend (*conlegae et amico*).[39] Finally, an inscription found in the Veneto and commissioned by Lucius Ragonius Quintianus, almost certainly the man of the same name who was consul in AD 182, reminds its readers that *amicitia* could create obligations that crossed generations.

C(aio) Sempronio / C(ai) f(ilio) Pap(iria) / Cassiano. / L(ucius) Ragonius / Quintianus / *amici filio* / t[est(amento)] fier[i] iussit. (*CIL* 5.1971 = Reali 49C; Oderzo; late second century AD)

---

[36] *CIL* 6.13871: *Caecia C(ai) l(iberta) Eulimene / C(aio) Caecio C(ai) l(iberto) Philaristo viro suo / et sibi fecit / D(ecimus) Cornelius Hilarus amicus / locum ollarum duarum dedit donavitque*; 14.705: *D(is) M(anibus) / L(ucio) Kacio Volusiano qui vixit an/nis XVIIII mens(e) I dieb(us) XXVI / Primitivianus et Volusia pa/rentes fecerunt loco con/cesso a Gabinio Adiecto amico optimo.*

[37] *CIL* 6.20278: *D(is) M(anibus). / Sex(to) Iulio Stratonico amico / optimo M(arcus) Aur(elius) Fortunatus / et M(arcus) Aur(elius) Alexander d{a}ede/runt donaveruntque …*

[38] *CIL* 3.3324: *D(is) M(anibus). / M(arcus) Tul(l)ius Fortuna(t)us / vet(eranus) c(o)h(ortis) D Mau(rorum) d(omo) Africa, / vix(it) an(nis) LXX. Sep(timiae) Dubita/[tae] con[iu]gi et fili(i)s eorum Fabius Baritio / [v]et(eranus) coh(ortis) eiusdem, heres ei(us). amico bene / mere[n]ti tit[ul]um.*

[39] *CIL* 6.2938: *Sex(to) Naevio / L(uci) f(ilio) Pub(lilia) / Verecundo sign(ifero) / coh(ortis) XIIII nato / Veronae. ossa / relata domum, / cinis hic adoperta / quiescit. heredes / titulum. versiculos / Cornelius epoi(esen) / conlegae et amico.* See Cugusi 1985, pp. 59–60 for brief discussion of this among other such signed verse inscriptions. The reading *epoi(esen)* is Mommsen's; others read *eroi* or the garbled cognomen of Cornelius. For the distinction between *ossa* and *cineres* cf. *CLE* 1062 (*[in terris] cineres alius lo[cus, hic h]abet ossa*) and *CIL* 6.15493 = *ILS* 7954 (*hic matris cineres sola sacravimus ara; / quae genuit Tellus, ossa tegit tumulo*) as well as *CIL* 6.21975 (*ossa dedi Terrae, corpus Volchano dedi/di*).

To Gaius Sempronius Cassianus, son of Gaius, of the Papiria tribe. Lucius Ragonius Quintianus provided this for the son of his friend in his will.

This text not only advertises Quintianus' connection with the elder Gaius Sempronius but, by declaring that Quintianus provided for this commemoration in his will, it portrays him as a dutiful friend.[40]

Occasionally we get glimpses at expectations, anxieties, even fears. An inscription from Rome announces that Calupius Daulicius Paetus has commissioned it for himself, his dependants and freedmen and women, and that he specified in his will that three named *amici* had the privilege of a joint *aedicula* within the tomb complex, while various other named persons might receive individual *aediculae*; the inscription includes an appeal to two of those whom he commemorates as his *amici* and fellow-freedmen, prohibiting them from allowing the tomb to be sold.[41] A text carved onto a stone sarcophagus found in Rome announces, in jerky grammar and poorly carved letters that spill outside of the panel designated for the inscription, that Lollia Valeria Maior has supplied the sarcophagus for herself and her husband Gaius Sicinius Olympius, who for his part asks his friends (*amici*) to see to it that he is indeed buried together with his wife.[42]

A late second-century AD inscription from a tomb complex erected outside the walls of Rome between the via Appia and the via Ardeatina for the freedmen of Gaius Bruttius Praesens (consul in the year 180) and of his son Lucius Bruttius Quintius Crispinus (consul seven years later) suggests how common the practice was of including friends in one's burial group – or, seen the other way around, of being commemorated in an epitaph as an *amicus* or *amica*. Commissioned by Praesens' freed slave Telesphorio and memorializing the gift of a plot by Praesens' son, this inscription announces Telesphorio's commemoration of himself along with one of his own freedmen whose name he specifies, and his "other freedmen and freedwomen and their descendants" who remain unnamed

---

[40] For *paterni amici* see Cic. *Fam.* 13.29.1, 13.38, 13.40, *Flac.* 14; Hor. *Sat.* 1.3.4–6 (*Caesar, qui cogere posset, / si peteret per amicitiam patris atque suam, non / quicquam proficeret*), Val. Max. 2.1.9; and consider the definition from the *Digest* quoted in the Introduction (*Digest* 50.16.223.1, above, p. 21).

[41] *CIL* 6.10236: *Calupius Daulicius Paetus fecit sibi et [suis] / [et liber]tis libertabusque suis posterisq(ue) eorum, et leg[avit] / [Marcioni(?) et] Philemoni et Helladi amicis ius unius aedicul(ae), et / <G>ru<p>o et Apollonio [et] <P>elopi col(libertis) meis sing(ulis) ius singul(arum) aedicul(arum), / et Tropidi et S<y>ntrop<h>o Crescentis ius singular(um) aedicul(arum). T(ito) Marcio / et Philemo, amici et colliberti, fidei vestrae conmitto ne / quis vendat aut abalienet …*

[42] *Notizie degli Scavi di Antichità* 1953, 234: *D(is) M(anibus) Lollia Valeria / Maior conpara/bit sibi et co(n)iugi. / Gaius Sicinius Olym/pius. et Gaius Sicinius / Olympius petet amicos / suos ut cum co(n)- / iuge sua / ponatur.*

and unspecified. There is no mention of wife or children, and the epitaph ends on a note of apology.

D(is) M(anibus) / C(ai) Brutti Telesphorionis C(ai) Brutti Praesen/tis c(larissimae) m(emoriae) v(iri) II co(n)s(ulis) lib(erti) Numidae ipsius. loco si/bi donato a L(ucio) Bruttio Quintio Crispino fili/o eius, co(n)s(uli) patrono. vivus sibi fecit et Cari/co lib(erto) suo et ceteris libertis libertabus/que suis posterisque eorum omnium / futurorum. hoc monumentum ex mea / frugalitate feci et e[i]s qui supra scri/pti sunt. *ceteri amici, ignoscetis*: hoc monu/mentum hospitem non recip<i>t. <b>ene valetis. (*CIL* 6.7582; Rome)

To the spirits of the departed. Gaius Bruttius Telesphorion, Numidian and freedman of Gaius Bruttius Praesens of glorious memory, twice consul; the plot was given him by Lucius Brutius Quintius Crispinus the son of Praesens, himself consul and patron. While still alive, [Telesphorio] dedicated this to himself, to Caricus his freedman, and to his other freedmen and freedwomen and all their future descendants. I have dedicated this tomb from my own savings, for those whose names are written above. All other friends, do forgive me! This tomb cannot hold a guest. Farewell.

Telesphorio's burial plot will not include those he calls "guests (*hospites*)" and whom other epitaphs commemorate as *amici*. But what he describes as a question of financial resources and space was also, of course, often a matter of choice. Many hundreds of inscriptions from around the Latin-speaking world suggest that Telesphorio had good reason to ask for forgiveness.

LATIN EPITAPHS: HOW MANY, WHEN, WHERE, WHO?

Of the over 400,000 Latin inscriptions that have been published to date, an estimated 300,000–320,000 have the function of commemorating the dead, and it is a characteristic of Latin epitaphs that the deceased is frequently commemorated not as a sole individual or half of a married couple but as participant in one or more relationships of various kinds, thereby memorialized as a social actor located within a particular lineage or network.[43] Standard formulae commemorate freeborn men and women with the names of their fathers ("son of" or "daughter of" being reserved for the freeborn), freed slaves with the names of their former owners ("freedman of" or "freedwoman of"), and slaves with the names of their current

[43] Cf. Ariès 1985, Meyer 1990, Bodel 2001. See Häusle 1980 for a survey of themes like *memoria* and *monumentum* in Greek, Latin, and Aramaic inscriptions. In this chapter I leave to the side so-called "dedicatory inscriptions" in honor of *amici* or *amicae* not marking burials but, for example, identifying a commemorative statue. Examples include *CIL* 5.4129 (Gambara in Gallia Cisalpina), 6.1363 (Rome), 14.363 (Ostia Antica), *AE* 1998.734 (Carmona, near Seville).

owners ("slave of") – although, unfortunately enough for attempts at compiling thorough statistics, the use of these formulae decreased markedly beginning in the second century AD. In addition to these vertical relationships, and cutting across all status distinctions, many epitaphs indicate horizontal relationships; above all those created by marriage, but also *amicitia*.

Searches of the Clauss–Slaby database of over 404,000 Latin inscriptions for the various relational labels used in them reveal some consistent patterns.[44] We find 19,215 occurrences of *co(n)iu-*, 6,466 of *uxor*, and 3,918 of *marit-*, yielding a total of 29,599 occurrences of labels referring to spouses; 5,274 occurrences of *patronus* or *patrona*; 1,922 of *amicus, amica*, or *amicitia*; 896 of *contubernalis*; and 149 of *concubina*. Searches of smaller, geographically defined samples in the database confirm the pattern. A search of the more than 40, 000 inscriptions from the city of Rome yields 10,771 occurences of *maritus, uxor*, and *coniunx*; 1,707 of *patronus* and *patrona*; 782 of *amicus, amica, amicitia*; 401 of *contubernalis*; 48 of *concubina*. Searches of other available resources tell the same story. The printed index to volume VI of the *Corpus Inscriptionum Latinarum*, covering most but not all inscriptions from the city of Rome, reports about 7,000 occurrences of *coniunx, maritus*, and *uxor*; about 1,500 of *patronus* and *patrona*; more than 500 of *amicus, amica*, and *amicitia*; 331 of *contubernalis*; and 36 of *concubina*. In a far smaller sample, among the 371 inscriptions from the Isola Sacra necropolis catalogued in Helttula 2007 we find 97 occurrences of *coniunx, maritus, marita*, or *uxor*; 14 of *patronus* or *patrona*; 4 of *amicus*; 2 of *contubernalis*; and none of *concubina*.

Numbers like these tell us, of course, little or nothing about the relative value amongst Latin speakers of the relationships to which the words refer, nor even about how widespread or perceptible they were as social realities. We cannot conclude on this basis that friends were far less important to them than their spouses or patrons, or that friends were fifteen times more important than concubines. What we can say is that *in inscriptions* references to *amicitia* were far less frequent than those to marriage, more frequent than those to the conjugal bond known as *contubernium*, and far more frequent than those to concubinage.[45] Above all, we can conclude

---

[44] Because this database occasionally duplicates inscriptions, and in this case a handful of the results of a search for *amic-* are the proper name *Amicus*, we cannot insist on the precise figures; furthermore, the database includes inscriptions of all kinds, not just epitaphs (which make up 75–80% of all surviving inscriptions). Still, the statistics given above are useful as an approximate indicator of absolute numbers and relative frequency.

[45] Cf. Bodel, 2001, p. 34: "No one would conclude from the relative paucity of tombstones erected to parents at Rome that mothers and fathers were unimportant in the Roman family, since too

that an appeal to *amicitia* was an entirely thinkable option in commemoration, one which passersby who could read them would regularly find
in epitaphs, and one which was clearly integrated into commemorative
practices, evidently taken for granted as a possibility.

Apart from special cases like the Porta Nocera or Isola Sacra inscriptions, found *in situ* in archaeological contexts that allow more or less precise dating, assigning a date to a Latin epitaph, and indeed to any Latin
inscription, can be a tricky matter. Except for those naming magistrates
and other individuals who can be assigned dates on the basis of external
evidence, most inscriptions can be identified only in broad terms on the
basis of the lettering, nomenclature, or archaeological context in which
the stone was found. Specialists often content themselves with such indications as "Republican" (in fact quite rare), "late first century," or "second/
third century." In any case, there is a clearly identifiable pattern in what
has been called the Latin "epigraphic habit." The dedication of inscriptions on an appreciable scale began in the first century BC, grew steadily
over the course of the first and second centuries AD, reached a noticeable
peak around the turn of the second to third centuries, and then fell off
sharply during the third century. Various explanations for the curve have
been offered, none universally accepted. But the undisputed fact is that
the great majority of Latin inscriptions can be dated only vaguely, most of
them to the period ranging from the late first to the late second centuries
AD, and, unless otherwise indicated, that can be assumed as the rough
dating of the epitaphs cited in what follows.[46]

Where are these inscriptions found? The city of Rome is not surprisingly the area with the highest concentration of surviving examples, followed by North Africa (partially because the climate favors preservation);
within Italy, Rome is followed by Campania. But Latin inscriptions have
been found everywhere there were people speaking the language, and it
is clear that wherever there were people speaking Latin, they were commissioning inscriptions which commemorated friends.[47] Within this
overall pattern of distribution, can we detect any variation in the relative
frequency of inscriptions mentioning *amici*? No overall statistic is available, but samples taken from geographically defined samples across the

---

much literary, legal and artistic evidence points to the opposite conclusion." For the terms *contu-*
bernalis and *concubina* see Introduction, n. 26, and chapter 1, nn. 39 and 54.
[46] For the Roman epigraphic habit see MacMullen 1982, Meyer 1990, Bodel 2001. Typically, Reali
1997, p. 242, concludes that more than 75 percent of his sample of inscriptions from Gallia
Cisalpina mentioning *amici* and *amicae* are datable "al 1 e/o 11 secolo d.C."
[47] Bodel 2001, p. 8.

Roman Empire make it clear that wherever Latin inscriptions were being commissioned, these included commemorations of *amici*. Thanks to the work of Mauro Reali we can be less subjective with regard to epitaphs from the Italian peninsula. Reali has catalogued 161 inscriptions using the terms *amicus* and *amica* from Cisalpine Gaul and included photographs of over 100 of them, as well as 163 such inscriptions from the rest of Italy apart from the city of Rome; almost all of his 324 inscriptions are epitaphs. Among many other findings that emerge from Reali's work is the fact that the proportion of inscriptions which mention *amici* is markedly higher both in the city of Rome and in the urbanized areas of Cisalpine Gaul (1 out of 80) than it is in the rest of the Italian peninsula (1 out of 200), and he proposes a few explanations for this noticeable discrepancy. Rome and Cisalpine Gaul were the most urbanized and prosperous areas of ancient Italy, and Rome was home to a disproportionately high number of soldiers and veterans. These men were frequently given burial and commemorated not by family members or spouses (soldiers were officially forbidden from marrying until AD 212) but by their fellow-soldiers, who identified themselves with such labels as *contubernalis, commanipularis, sodalis,* and, precisely, *amicus* (see below, pp. 300–301).

Where were epitaphs erected? Rural burials of all kinds have left few traces, and within the cities, the masses of the poor were given no individual burial at all. Their bodies were anonymously disposed of, many of them unceremoniously dumped into trenches or pits such as one found on the Esquiline in Rome, sometimes along with animal cadavers.[48] Only the more decorous types of burial, which presupposed some financial means, were usually accompanied by some form of textual commemoration. In the simplest of these, the cremated remains were placed in amphorae or other kinds of jars buried in groups or rows and sometimes marked with the name of the departed and date of death.[49] Burials within *columbaria* – vaulted structures containing anywhere from several dozen to two or three thousand cinerary urns placed in niches lining the walls – were usually marked by inscriptions, either on the container itself or on a plaque

---

[48] Hor. *Sat.* 1.8.14–16 alludes to mass graves on the Esquiline. In 1876 Lanciani found a section of a trench on the Esquiline outside the Servian walls that contained a mass of human and animal remains; he estimated that there were originally around 24,000 bodies. See Bodel 1994, p. 42: "Lanciani's figure is perhaps exaggerated, but we have no reason to doubt that a quantity of human and animal carcasses had at some point been dumped indiscriminately into part of the *fossa* just north of the Esquiline gate, perhaps when whatever public disposal facilities were located in the vicinity had been filled to capacity."

[49] See *CIL* 6.8211–8397 for some examples excavated in Rome in 1732. The Isola Sacra necropolis includes amphorae half-buried in the earth, containing ashes but marked by no inscriptions.

placed in the wall below the niche in which the container was installed.[50] For their part, individual tombs or private complexes were almost always marked with inscriptions recording names and relationships.

The surviving epitaphs do not, however, give us an unmediated picture of the overall contours of the societal settings in which they were commissioned. Not everyone received lasting monuments or textual commemoration, and the differences between those who did and those who did not do not easily map onto gender or social distinctions. The few necropoleis which survive partially intact, for example, make it clear that not everyone who was buried in such tombs was mentioned in an accompanying inscription. In tomb 75 of the Isola Sacra necropolis, for example, over 170 funerary urns were found, but the publicly visible inscriptions above the two entrances name only three individuals (Marcus Cocceius Daphnus, Marcus Antonius Agathias, and Marcus Ulpius Domitus) and those inside the enclosure bring the total of individuals both named and commemorated as being buried in the complex to 13; although some inscriptions inside the complex seem to have been lost, their total number cannot have been extremely high. The implication is important and can be generalized. Many, perhaps most, people who found their final resting place within a permanent sepulchral complex were not individually commemorated by name in an inscription.[51] In short, the surviving burial monuments and associated inscriptions do not give us a fully representative picture of commemorative practices or social networks at every level of Roman society. With that precaution in mind, however, we can consider distribution patterns within those inscriptions that do survive, and what we find is often of interest.

When discussing a society so strongly differentiated in terms of gender and juridical status as that of the Romans, questions of *who* commissioned these inscriptions *for whom* are of fundamental importance. Women are in the minority but a distinct presence in Latin inscriptions – somewhat more prominently, as we have seen, in Cisalpine Gaul and Spain than

---

[50] For an overview of the term *columbarium* (literally, "dovecote," in ancient texts describing a variety of structures with holes or niches in a wall, in modern scholarship a term for a type of communal tomb) and a brief survey of examples from Rome, see Caldelli and Ricci 1999, pp. 59–68. For inscriptions found in *columbaria* see *CIL* 6.3926–8397, 33062–33710, 37301–37740; *ILS* 7872–7947; Hasegawa 2005. Some of these structures were apparently built by and for *collegia funeraticia* or burial clubs, whose members paid dues in order that their burial and commemoration might be seen to by the organization: see Hopkins 1983, pp. 211–217, Hasegawa 2005, pp. 81–88. *CIL* 14.2112 spells out the membership rules of a club from Lanuvium.

[51] See Eck 1987, especially pp. 65–68, 73–74, citing the Vatican necropolis. Morris 1992, p. 166, points out that since the entire complex has not been preserved intact, we cannot be certain that all inscriptions have survived; but this does not contradict Eck's basic point.

elsewhere. They are not only commemorated in inscriptions dedicated in turn by both men and women, but they commissioned inscriptions commemorating themselves, their husbands, children, freedmen and freedwomen, patrons, slaves, and male and female friends. On the point of juridical status, the threefold distinction among freeborn Romans (*ingenui* and *ingenuae*), slaves (*servi* and *servae* or *vernae*), and freed slaves or "freedmen and freedwomen" (*liberti* or *libertae*) is fundamental to any reading of epitaphs. But it is worth emphasizing that these categories in turn do not easily align with economic ones – some freedmen became quite wealthy, some freeborn Roman (perhaps especially in the city) were desperately poor, and some privileged slaves themselves owned slaves – nor is there any straightforward correlation among social standing, economic means, burial practice, and inscriptional commemoration. Some freeborn urban poor ended up in anonymous mass graves while, as we will see, not a few slaves were commemorated in epitaphs and even commissioned some themselves, and a letter of Pliny's shows that some freeborn Romans with considerable financial means chose not to erect tombs commemorating themselves.[52]

That said, one fact is striking. Inscriptions dedicated by and to individuals who are explicitly identified as slaves, though very much in the minority, are hardly a rarity. Here too some regional variation has been detected – commemorations by and of slaves are proportionately more commonly found in Italy than elsewhere[53] – but the very fact that slaves could and did participate in the culture of commemorating friends is worth emphasizing. The impression one easily gains from reading Latin literature, sometimes uncritically adopted in the scholarship too, is that *amicitia* was a matter for Roman citizens;[54] surviving epitaphs complicate the picture by showing how partial it is. The question of slave marriage is comparable. From the perspective of Roman law, slaves could not participate in the full form of marriage known as *conubium*, nor could they have legitimate children. Any offspring of slaves generally belonged to the

---

[52] Plin. *Ep.* 9.19.6–8; cf. 6.10 (Pliny implies that the decision against having a funerary monument was unusual and perhaps ostentatious).

[53] Saller and Shaw 1984 see a hint at the relative importance of slavery in different parts of the ancient Mediterranean, but Morris rightly counters: "The only thing it tells us for sure is that slaves did not put up or receive tombstones very often in the western provinces" (Morris 1992, p. 161).

[54] Cf. Spielvogel 1993, p. 7: "*Amicitia* bezeichnet nämlich sowohl das freundschaftliche Verhältnis zwischen *cives Romani* als auch zwischen dem römischen Volk und fremden Städten sowie Nationen." Reali 1997, p. 235, acknowledges the presence of slaves amongst epitaphs commemorating *amici* but surmises that "l'*amicitia* – così come l'abbiamo veduta – fosse davvero una relazione difficile da contrarre e gestire in assenza della libertà individuale."

master. Yet the body of surviving inscriptions amply demonstrates that many slaves put up funerary inscriptions commemorating, precisely, their spouses and children as *coniuges* and *filii*.[55]

A much discussed characteristic of Latin epitaphs is the noticeable prominence of freed slaves. In an important study published in 1961, Lily Ross Taylor reported that in a sample of Republican-era epitaphs from the city of Rome, 75 percent of individuals with explicitly identified status are freedmen and freedwomen, as are about 37 percent of a sample from the rest of Italy.[56] In Mauro Reali's sample of inscriptions from Cisalpine Gaul, over 38 percent of named *amici* are certainly or probably freedmen, and for the rest of Italy excluding the city of Rome he reports a figure slightly over 22 percent.[57] To be sure, we cannot know exactly what proportion of the entire population in any given area, whether the city of Rome, Cisalpine Gaul with its smaller cities, or all of Italy, consisted of freed slaves; and many inscriptions fail to identify the status of the individuals they name. In fact, unambiguous markers – such as the patronymic formula reserved for freeborn citizens (*Marci filius, Publi filia*) or the labels *libertus* and *liberta* identifying freed slaves as such – were increasingly omitted after the first century AD, precisely when the western portion of the Roman Empire witnessed an explosion of the epigraphic habit. As a result, the category called *incerti* in some samples actually represents the majority of cases, the Latin term dignifying the troublesome fact that the inscriptions in question tell us nothing certain about the juridical status of the individuals named.[58]

In the absence of explicit markers of status, how in fact can we make *any* conclusions, however tentative? Epigraphists have developed a set of criteria but are keenly aware that in any given case they may not be sufficient to establish certainty. Servile status is probably signaled by the use of single names of a type otherwise known to have been frequently given to slaves, and freed status is strongly suggested by such factors as

---

[55] Flory 1978, Saller 2001.

[56] Taylor 1961, p. 128. Her explanations for the discrepancy are that "the slaves who had the skills necessary to win freedom probably had a better chance in the city"; that "freedmen, not slaves, were eligible for free grain distribution in the capital"; and that "masters are reported to have brought their slaves to Rome and to have freed them in order to have them fed by the state" (pp. 128–129, citing Dio Cass. 39.24.1).

[57] For the higher proportion of freedmen in commemorations of *amici* in Cisalpine Gaul than in the rest of Italy. Reali 1997, p. 234, sees an explanation in the trading and other economic opportunities provided by prosperous small cities like Aquileia, Pola, and Patavium.

[58] Cf. Taylor 1961, pp. 118–119, identifying as *incerti* about 66 percent of a sample of thousands of epitaphs from the city of Rome taken from *CIL* 6. On the basis of their names, however, she concludes that the majority of these were actually freed slaves (p. 123).

Readership 289

cognomina known to have been common slave names, the holding of the office *sevir augustalis*, and combinations with other similar names.[59] The risk of circularity in any individual case is clear, but as indications of probabilities and overall patterns these indications are persuasive, and so it is generally agreed that there is a "massive overrepresentation" of freedmen and freedwomen in epitaphs. The most widely accepted explanation for this overrepresentation is that freed slaves had a greater need for a public staging of social identity.[60] Funerary inscriptions provided an effective forum for advertising their newly acquired citizen status. Men in particular could record their *tria nomina* and any offices they may have held, most characteristically that of a *sevir augustalis*. A similar story seems to be told by the archaeological record. On the one hand, freedmen like the baker Eurysaces in Rome erected prominent, sometimes rather sumptuous funerary monuments that openly proclaimed their status; on the other hand we find regular, even monotonous facades, often with rows of portraits, lined up along streets of tombs, in a pattern which became common in the first century AD and which seems above all to locate the deceased as members of a group which constituted its own kind of new elite.[61] Since, unlike freeborn Romans, freed slaves had no legal ancestors, no fathers or mothers or siblings to memorialize along with themselves, it may not be coincidental that other kinds of relationship are frequently memorialized in their epitaphs: the vertical relationships joining them to their former owners (*patronus, patrona*) and their own freed slaves in turn (*libertus, liberta*), and the horizontal relationships joining them to fellow freedmen and freedwomen of the same master (*conlibertus, conliberta*), but also to those who are commemorated as *amici* and *amicae*.

READERSHIP

How many people were able to read these epitaphs? Although we cannot know exact percentages, only a minority of the people who walked by the tombs lining streets leading in and out of Roman cities were capable of reading the inscriptions placed on them. Yet one epitaph anticipates that

---

[59] For summary of the issues see Mouritsen 2011, pp. 120–126. In the sample of columbaria inscriptions catalogued at Hasegawa 2005, pp. 73–80, the most common slave names are, in descending order of frequency, Felix, Eros, Hilario/Hilarus, Faustus/Faustio, Phileros, Antigonus, Antiochus, and Iucundus for males, and Secunda, Erotis, (H)elpis, Hilara, Prima, and Iucunda for females. For the predominance of freedmen amongst the *seviri augustales*, see above, n. 3.

[60] Cf. Taylor 1961, pp. 129–130, Morris 1992, p. 166 ("massive over-representation"), Hesberg 1992, pp. 273–275, Reali 1997 passim and pp. 261–262, Mouritsen 2005, Mouritsen 2011, pp. 120–141.

[61] Hesberg 1992, pp. 38–39, 47; for Eurysaces' tomb see Petersen 2006, pp. 84–120.

those unable to read it themselves will ask others to read it aloud for them, and more generally it is worth keeping in mind that there are different levels of literacy. Many people may have been able to decipher names on inscriptions even if they were not capable of reading more complex texts.[62] In any case, there was a widespread assumption that those who had the ability to do so would frequently stop to read the texts inscribed on and near tombs. Petronius' Trimalchio stipulates that a sundial be set up at his tomb, so that those who stop to see what time it is will see his name whether they want to or not, and one epitaph rather challengingly asks, "Why are you all standing here and reciting the inscription on my tomb?"[63]

The tomb complex in the Isola Sacra necropolis illustrates another important point. Announcements of group burials legible to the general public did not always tell the whole story. Although the large inscription commissioned by Cocceius Daphnus and placed above the main entrance does not provide for this possibility, Cocceia Tyche saw to the burial of a male friend within the complex, and he in turn provided for the burial of his wife there, although she seems to have had no other connection to the Cocceii or Antonii. There is every reason to think the pattern typical. Among the tombs that have been found along the Via Cornelia in Rome, Mausoleum K has a publicly visible plaque announcing that Gaius Valerius Herma has dedicated the tomb to his wife, daughter and son as well as to his freedmen and freedwomen and their descendants, but includes niches in its interior which are marked by plaques identifying not only those described in the main inscription but also an *amicus* who, as the text carefully specifies, was provided a burial place by two members of the family.[64] Mausoleum F, which seems never to have had a publicly visible inscription above its entrance, houses the funerary urns of freedmen and family members of the Tullii and Caetenni, almost all of them

---

[62] *Supplementum italicum* n.s. 4: 78–84, no. 58, vv. 42–43: *titulumque quicumque legerit aut lege[ntem] auscultarit.* For questions related to literacy see Harris 1989, Beard *et al.* 1991, Bowman and Woolf 1994, Johnson and Parker 2009; in connection with inscriptions, Bodel 2001, pp. 15–19. Woolf 1997 reminds us that because of their frequent use of abbreviations and symbols, even in antiquity not all inscriptions would have been instantly legible to those who could otherwise read Latin; one had to learn how to read them.

[63] Petron. *Sat.* 71.11: *horologium in medio, ut quisquis horas inspiciet, velit nolit, nomen meum legat; CIL* 8.9513 = *ILS* 8144 (Caesarea Mauretaniae): *quid statis et recitatis titulum monumenti mei?* Cf. Prop. 4.7.83–84: *hic carmen media dignum me scribe columna, / sed breve, quod currens vector ab urbe legat.* For an overview of inscriptions which appeal to their readers, see Häusle 1980, pp. 41–63.

[64] Feraudi-Gruénais 2003, no. 36: *C. Valerius Herma fecit et / Flaviae T.f. Olympiadi co(n)iugi et / Valeriae Maximae filiae et C. Valerio / Olympiano filio et suis libertis / libertabusque posterisq(ue) eorum*; 45: *cui locum obt(ulerunt) Valerii Philumenus et Galatia amico bene merenti.*

commemorated with such labels as *coniunx*, *filius*, or *patronus*; but one inscription commemorates a man and woman as friends (*amici*) of one of the Tullii.[65] And finally, inscriptions placed inside a burial enclosure or columbarium would, of course, have been visible only to those who entered these internal spaces, many of which were designed in such a way as to have been essentially private, meant for those who were visiting to honor their dead with offerings and libations, or participating in a new burial. Even to those who entered these spaces, the epitaphs were not always easily visible. It is clear that some of the inscriptions placed within columbaria, for example, were located in hard-to-see places.[66]

Yet whatever their original location, and however many or few people might actually have read them, epitaphs are, like all texts, acts of communication which represent themselves as such. Like Greek epitaphs before them, many Latin inscriptions directly address passersby, creating an imagined dialogue between the living and the dead which not infrequently draws on discourses of friendship. Among those whom the inscribed departed address from the realm of the dead we find unnamed *amici*. The epitaph of Gaius Silicius Romanus Thagorensis and Erucia Victoria from Rome ends with an address to their friends and parents (*amici et parentes*), praying that the gods will treat them well and that they may come safe, sound, and happy to the funeral feast. An inscription from Ostia commemorating Aulus Livius Strato, his wife, children, freedmen and freedwomen and their descendants, ends with a cryptic phrase addressed to *amici*. And a verse epitaph from Rome for a Flavius Agricola establishes a link between living and dead in an even more specific way. The dear departed addresses passersby, observing that he enjoyed his wine in life and encouraging them – *amici* who are distinctly marked as male – to follow his example, adding in the pleasures of Venus while they're at it.[67] Texts like these give their own twist to performances of *amicitia*, one familiar from other languages and cultures as well. An address to a stranger or strangers as "my friend(s)" is a verbal gesture, like a smile or open arms, urging or asserting a connection, casting the speaker in the role of one who is experienced in the ways of friendship.

---

[65] Feraudi-Gruénais 2003, no. 24: *D(is) M(anibus) / Aureli Gigantis / et Papiriae / Profuturae / eius. Tullius / Hermadion amicis / b(ene) m(erentibus)*.

[66] The point is emphasized by Eck 1987.

[67] *CIL* 6.26554 (*amici et parentes*); *CIL* 14.380 (*amici, hoc at securos*; Dessau glosses *huc ad securos venietis*); *CIL* 6.17985a = 6.34112 = *CLE* 856; line 4, *nec defuit umqua(m) Lyaeus*; lines 12–15: *amici, qui legitis, moneo, miscete Lyaeum / et potate procul redimiti tempora flore / et venereos coitus formosis ne denegate puellis: / cetera post obitum terra consumit et ignis* (lines 12–15).

LABELS AND LAYOUT

What about us today, generally reading these inscriptions so drastically out of context, almost never at the tomb and usually not even looking at a stone on display in a museum, but deciphering a transcription or photograph in a printed volume or on a website? How might we read epitaphs naming *amici*, and epitaphs in general? What are we looking for, and to what extent can we expect to find it?

Whether in prose or verse, epitaphs simultaneously illustrate the constraints and the possibilities of speech genres. Much of their power derives from the fact that they refer to what is simultaneously the most individual and the most universal of human experiences, and that they do so in formulaic language which nonetheless often manages to communicate something specific about the individual – above all, by the simple but effective means of naming names. For those of us accustomed to the range of Greek and Latin personal names we find in the literary tradition, many of the names memorialized in the epitaphs are new and unfamiliar; to us (and no doubt to many native Latin speakers who were born and spent their entire lives in Rome) some of them sound odd and others downright foreign. For their part, the adjectives and nouns attached to these names invite being read less as complete and objective reports on the deceased than as acts of self-presentation. Richard Saller reminds us that "the epitaphs were inscribed to perpetuate the memory of the deceased into future generations and to represent his or her closest relationships to passersby who had no knowledge of the burial ritual," and I would add that the epitaphs also perpetuate the memory of those who *commissioned* them. The bonds which they commemorate are not necessarily or exclusively the "closest relationships" the deceased enjoyed in life, but those which he or she, or whoever commissioned the inscription, decided to commemorate, for whatever reasons.[68]

Words like *amicus*, then, invite being interpreted as labels which could be attached to names in epitaphs for a variety of reasons, emotional, tactical or other, to which we only sometimes have access. We must read them – and their absence – with care. As we will see, not a few epitaphs include names without attaching any relational label to them at

---

[68] Saller 2001, p. 101. Bodel 2001, p. 34, aptly speaks of "the epigraphic bias." Cf. Morris 1992, p. 159: "They do not tell us as much about brute demographic 'realities' as about what Roman buriers thought *ought* to be said in such a context." See Alföldy and Panciera 2001 for Latin inscriptions as *Selbstdarstellung*; Feraudi-Gruénais 2003 warns against over-using the term.

all. Consider this inscription from a columbarium along the Via Aurelia outside Rome.

C(aius) Curtius C(ai) l(ibertus) Lucrio fecit / sibi et Curtiae C(ai) l(ibertae) Turanni/di libertae suae, et libertis / libertabusque suis posterisque / eorum, et L(ucio) Cominio Heleno. (*CIL* 6.7786; Rome)

Gaius Curtius Lucrio, freedman of Gaius, dedicated this to himself and to his freedwoman Curtia Turannis, freedwoman of Gaius, and to his freedmen and freedwomen and their descendants, and to Lucius Cominius Helenus.

This epitaph memorializes Lucrio as the former slave of a man named Gaius Curtius and Turannis as the former slave of Lucrio, but communicates nothing about who Lucius Cominius Helenus was and in particular what his relationship to Lucrio was. His name suggests, but not conclusively, that he too was a freed slave, but if so, his former master was not Lucrio but a man named Lucius Cominius. The inscription commissioned by Lucrio is not concerned to give a label to their relationship; the very fact that Helenus' name is on the list is enough. We may speculate that the two men were friends, and there is a good chance that in life they called each other *amici*, but Lucrio's provision of burial for and commemoration of Helenus will not be reflected in any statistics related to the commemoration of friends in Latin inscriptions. And there are hundreds, perhaps thousands, of other inscriptions like this one.

A marble plaque from Rome with first-century AD inscriptions on both sides announces the commemoration of a woman by two men; the names of all three suggest they were freed slaves or perhaps the children of freed slaves, but in any case of different masters. The two inscriptions are different in a small but important detail.

[*side A*] D(is) M(anibus) / Aufidiae Epiteu/xis. Ti(berius) Claudius / Hermes tutor / et T(itus) Flavius Her/mes amicus / bene merenti / fecerunt.
[*side B*] D(is) M(anibus) / Aufidiae Epi/teuxis. T(itus) Flavi/us Hermes, / Ti(berius) Claudius H/ermes tutor / b(ene) m(erenti) fecerunt. (*CIL* 6.12839 = *CIL* 10.2129, Rome)[69]

To the spirits of the departed. For Aufidia Epiteuxis. Tiberius Claudius Hermes her guardian and Titus Flavius Hermes her friend dedicated this to a deserving woman.

To the spirits of the departed. For Aufidia Epiteuxis. Titus Flavius Hermes and Tiberius Claudius Hermes her guardian dedicated this to a deserving woman.

---

[69] The form *Epiteuxis* is either an irregular genitive form (Solin 2003, p. 1304) or an error for the dative *Epiteuxi*.

Claudius Hermes' name comes first on one side, Flavius Hermes' on the other, and even more importantly, while the former commemorates himself as Aufidia's *tutor* in both texts, the latter memorializes himself as her *amicus* in only one. We can only guess as to why two versions of Epiteuxis' epitaph were carved and if there is any significance to the differences between them, but in any case this double inscription is a valuable reminder of the limitations on our ability to interpret epitaphs imposed by the precariousness of survival. If only the inscription on Side B had survived, for example, we would have no hint that the relationship between Flavius Hermes and Aufidia Epiteuxis was memorialized with any label at all, let alone one so meaningful as *amicus*.

Before turning to a survey of the various configurations we find in epitaphs commemorating *amici* and *amicae*, some recurring characteristics of their formulaic language are worth considering. First is a point made in the Introduction: Whereas in literary texts *amicus* has a set of near-synonyms (*necessarius*, *sodalis*, *familiaris*), the inscriptions overwhelmingly use the label *amicus* or *amica*. The much more rarely occurring *sodalis* most often signifies a member of a formally constituted organization called a *sodalitas* or *sodalicium*, and the labels *necessarius* and *familiaris* are found hardly at all. Second, the repertoire of epithets accompanying the noun *amicus* is distinctly limited, the most common of them being *optimus*, *carus* or *carissimus*, *bene merens*, and *incomparabilis*, with some regional distinctions in relative frequency.[70] These formulaic qualifiers may or may not give an accurate picture of the relationship as it was lived by the parties involved or perceived by others, but we can look to them for further glimpses at ideals, and sometimes we even see them: *bene merens*, for example, illustrates the open workings of exchange (one deserves to be treated well because one has done a favor or service). Yet the significant fact is that these epithets are not specific to friendship, for the same adjectives also typically modify *coniunx* and other relational terms. Epitaphs are full of commemorations of *optimus frater*, *carissimus filius*, *patrona bene merens*, and so on. It is, in other words, hard to identify any specific adjective or formula as constitutive or even characteristic of the commemoration of *amici*. It is arguably the noun itself that bears the weight and has the function.

---

[70] The attempt by Reali 1997, p. 196, to distinguish among these epithets (*optimus* and *bene merens* as belonging to an "ethical" sphere and *carus* to an "affective" sphere) is not convincing, and Reali himself notes that such distinctions cannot be rigidly insisted upon in any case.

The order and arrangement of words on the stone frequently repays close attention. A verse inscription from Umbria illustrates some possibilities.

> Q. Petronio / Birroni[o]. /
> [P]arva quidem mo/[nu]menta tibi pro / munere vitae
> feci/[m]us et tumulo teximus / [os]sa levi.
> sed quoniam / [viv]a[e] facis est erepta vo/lup<t>as,
> testatur titulus / pignus amicitiae.
> si / datur extinctis men/tem retinere priorem, /
> respice, Birroni, *munus / amicitiae. /*
> vixit annis XXXXIII, / die(bu)s XXXIX. /
> C. Helvius / Ianuarius.
>
> (*CIL* 11.5927 = *CLE* 1102 = Reali 128It; Umbertide)

To Quintus Petronius Birronius.
We set up this monument, small though it is, in tribute to your life (?)
and covered your bones with a light mound.
The pleasure of your living flame has been taken away from us,
but the inscription gives witness to a pledge of friendship.
If the departed are allowed to hold on to earlier memories,
Birronius, take note of this gift of friendship!
He lived 43 years and 39 days.
Gaius Helvius Januarius.[71]

This text self-referentially meditates on the point that both the tomb and the inscription itself are concrete signs of the obligations that can come with Roman friendship. Repetitions are structural to the message: *pro munere vitae* and *munus amicitiae* frame the poem; *vitae* in line 1 is echoed both by the phrase *vivae facis … voluptas* in line 3[72] and by the formulaic *vixit* in the prose conclusion; the phrases *pignus amicitiae* and *munus amicitiae* are in identical metrical positions, closing the second and third of the three couplets. But the layout and varying size of the lettering also contribute to the message. The inscription begins with the name of the deceased written in large letters over two lines:

Q PETRONIO
BIRRONI[O]

---

[71] The reading and interpretation of certain details in this inscription are controversial. Apart from the problem in line 3 (see next note), what are we to make of the plural verbs *fecimus* and *teximus* in view of the fact that only one man is identified as the dedicator? Is this a poetic plural, or did more than one person contribute to the erection of the tomb (*monumenta*) but only Januarius takes credit for the inscription (*titulus*)? What is the meaning of the phrase *pro munere vitae*?

[72] The phrase is puzzling and the text may be corrupt, but the adjective *vivae* seems secure. Rejecting the alternative reading *vivae faciest (faciei est)* without further explanation (*non placet*), Bücheler explains *vivae facis* thus: *fax sideris et vitae, amoris et studii, rogi et sepulcri quorsum hic dicta sit non clare perspicitur, putes ad vivum amorem significandum.*

The poem follows, written in smaller letters and arranged at the end as follows:

RESPICE BIRRONI MVNVS
AMICITIAE

After two prose lines taken up with the traditional indication of Birronius' lifespan, the text concludes with the name of the dedicator, once again in larger letters and once again spread out over two lines.

C HELVIVS
IANVARIVS

The visual emphasis is thus squarely placed on the names of deceased and dedicator and on the relationship linking them. The *cognomina* of the two men and the key noun *amicitiae* are the only words in the inscription that take up entire lines by themselves, and, in a type of ring composition, their names frame the whole. The final and climactic word of the poem, *amicitiae*, is given a double emphasis: visually (for those who casually look at the stone without reading it closely, or those with limited literacy) and metrically (for those who have the ability and go to the effort of reading the poem).

COMMEMORATIVE CONFIGURATIONS: A TYPOLOGY

In what follows, I present and interpret examples of a considerable body of epitaphs using the language of *amicitia* whose existence has gone largely unnoticed outside of specialist studies of epigraphy. Among various possible ways of organizing the material, I have chosen the following:

1 Individual commemoration of friends
   (a) dedicated by an individual
   (b) dedicated by more than one person
2 Commemoration of friends as part of a group
   (a) along with dedicator's spouse, children and/or kin
   (b) along with dedicator's freed slaves
   (c) along with dedicator's spouse, children and/or kin, and freed slaves
   (d) along with dedicator's former master
3 Commemoration of unnamed friends
4 Commemoration of friends at the center of a burial group
5 Commemoration of two individuals as friends

Throughout, I pay attention to the formal features just described (layout on stone, placement and order of words) and, as in the preceding chapters, to configurations of gender. Throughout, too, I suggest that we be alert to the processes of reading such texts and attentive to the ways in which epitaphs, carved in stone and meant to last, by commemorating bonds of *amicitia* perpetuate them. And, presenting and reading these inscriptions at multiple removes from their original context, I suggest we keep in mind the possibilities raised by those found *in situ* in the Porta Nocera and Isola Sacra cemeteries, illustrating the larger and more complex networks of interpersonal relationships in which epitaphs commemorating someone as an *amicus* or *amica* might take their place.

Type 1: Individual commemoration of a friend

Hundreds of surviving Latin epitaphs announce the burial of an individual alone and commemorate him or her using the language of *amicitia* instead of, or together with, that of kinship and marriage. In such epitaphs the memory both of the deceased and of those who commissioned the inscriptions is kept alive: the deceased as worthy of the label *amicus*, the survivors as loyal friends. It has been argued that inscriptions like these are also sending the message that those who commissioned them were heirs of the deceased, and in many cases this was probably true; but I stay with the language of the texts, considering which lenses they use in order to project the relationship between honored dead and honoring survivors. For one who commissioned an epitaph to cast himself in the role of heir (*heres*), bound by the provisions of a will and responsibly fulfilling his duty, is one thing; to commemorate the departed and/or oneself with the symbolically richer if not so neatly definable language of *amicitia* is another.[73]

The range of individuals memorialized with such language is broad indeed. On the axis of gender, women are underrepresented yet distinctly present in the role of both deceased and commemorator. The full range of juridical status is represented, from freeborn citizens to slaves, freed slaves being particularly prominent; in these individual commemorations, soldiers, too, make a frequent appearance. On the axis of age, the great majority of epitaphs commemorating individuals with the language

---

[73] Saller 1994, p. 98, argues that "the arrangement of burial was widely interpreted as tantamount to acceptance of the inheritance of the deceased"; Bodel 2001 is skeptical. See Verboven 2002, pp. 183–223, for discussion of inheritance and legacies in connection with kinship and friendship.

of *amicitia* refer to adults, but a number of inscriptions keep alive the memory of deceased children or adolescents with the language of *amicitia*. An epitaph from Lyon marks the burial of the 6-year-old Gaius Martius Valerius, also known as Viventius. Commissioned by his parents Toutedo and Aterita – the nomenclature suggests that they were Gauls who had obtained Roman citizenship – it records not only their grief but that of his friends (*ab amicis qui amissionem eius flagitant*).[74] An epitaph for a 7-year-old found near Trilj, Croatia, announces in an elegiac couplet that it was commissioned by his friend (*fidus amicus*) and then adds some words in prose, consoling the boy's mother.[75] The epitaph of the 13-year-old Quintus Caecilius Marcianus of Rome was dedicated by his friend Rufus, and an epitaph from Ameria announces that the 16-year-old Marcus Antonius Agrippinus, who had in his youth already held the office of priest (*sacerdos*), was being commemorated by his *amicus* Gaius Nunnius Victor.[76]

A stone found in Hispellum in Umbria is carved with the following inscription commemorating the infant Melanthus, whose name suggests that he was a slave:[77]

Melantus / mensum XIIII, / *dulcis amicis*, carus suis. / qui neminem offen(dit) / nisi quom est mortu(u)s. (*CIL* 11.5325; Hispellum)

Melanthus, 14 months old, a delight to his friends, loved by his own. He never hurt anyone except by dying.

The formulaic appeal to friendship in the epitaph of this fourteen-month-old suggests the high value placed on friendship. In all its spareness – those who commissioned it do not even name themselves – this epitaph incisively illustrates the peculiar power that epitaphs can have for those who read them, wherever or whenever.

---

[74] *CIL* 13.11205 (Lyon): *D(is) M(anibus) et memoriae aeternae / C(ai) Marti Valeri qui et / Viventi vano signo / cognominatus ani/mae innocentissi/mae et infanti dulcis/simo et desiderantissi/mo non solum a paren/tibus sed et ab amicis qui / amissionem eisi̱us flagi̱tant. q(ui) vixit annis VI / m(ense) I d(iebus) X, ut subita valetudin[e] / sit abreptus. C(aius) Martius / Toutedo et Mercator(ia) / Ateurita parentes mi/serrimi amisso filio / fecer(unt) et sibi vivi posue/runt et sub ascia dedika/verunt. bene vale, / anima dulcissima.*

[75] *CIL* 3.2722=3.9729 (Tilurium): *C(aius) Laberius f(ilius) / [---]es ann(orum) VII / h(ic) s(itus) e(st). / hunc titulum posuit tibi fidus amicus: ultuma / quae potui debita pers[o]lui. / non dolere, mater, faciundum fuit. properavit / aetas, voluit hoc astrum meum. vale et priores / aetate te tollant hunc luctum tibi.*

[76] *CIL* 6.13758 (Rome): *Sacr(um) / Q. Caec(ili) / Marciani / q(ui) v(ixit) an(nis) XIII. / Rufus amic(o)*; *CIL* 11.4379 = Reali 121It (Ameria): *M. Antonio / Agrippino / sacerdoti. / vixit annis XVI / mensibus XI et / diebus [...]. fecit / C. Nunnius / Victor / amicus.*

[77] See King 2000 for an overview of Roman epitaphs for infants.

Type 1a: Commemorated by an individual

Some epitaphs for sole individuals using the language of *amicitia* announce that they have been commissioned by one person. We have seen that women fully participated not only in the culture of commemoration but in the discourse of *amicitia* within the speech genre of inscriptions, and so it is no surprise to find epitaphs commemorating a woman as *amica*, whether of a man or of a woman.

D(is) M(anibus). / Settidi/ae Calli/tyche po/suit aram / *amicae caris(simae)* / Aeli[a] Chre/ste. (*CIL* 5.232 = Reali 6C; Pola; second or perhaps third century AD)

Iuliae / Chreste / A[g]a[t]ho / *amicae / bene / merenti*. (*CIL* 3.2387; Salona)

To the spirits of the departed. For Settidia Callityche. Aelia Chreste dedicated this altar to her dearest friend.

To Julia Chreste. Agathon to his well-deserving friend.

An even larger number of sole commemorations of friends were commissioned by men for their *amici*, and we find the usual range of juridical status and geographical distribution. The following examples from the city of Rome are typical:

Q(uinto) Annio Apto, / vix(it) ann(is) XXXV. / C(aius) Antonius Herma / *amico bene merenti* / fecit. (*CIL* 6.11704)

D(is) M(anibus). / fecit Aurel(ius) / Isidorus / *amico suo* / Mullicio / Callinico. (*CIL* 6.13134a)

To Quintus Annius Aptus, who lived 35 years. Gaius Antonius Herma dedicated this to his deserving friend.

To the spirits of the departed. Aurelius Isidorus dedicated this to his friend Mullicius Callinicus.

Sole commemoration of *amici* of this kind have been found everywhere Latin inscriptions were being set up, from Dalmatia in the east to Spain in the west.

L(ucio) Fabio L(uci) f(ilio) Gal(eria) / Capitoni / *amico optumo*. / L(ucius) Aelius / Rocianus. (*CIL* 2.1324; Medina in Spain)

D(is) M(anibus) s(acrum). / Cn(aeus) Iulius Cn(aei) f(ilius) / Maturus (quattuor) vir / a[e]d(ilicia) pot(estate), q(uaestor) p(ecuniae) a(limentariae). / vixit ann(is) XLVII. / Pontilius Caedi/mnus *amico*. (*CIL* 10.47 = Reali 92 It; Vibo Valentia)

To Lucius Fabius Capito, son of Lucius, of the tribe Galeria, his excellent friend. Dedicated by Lucius Aelius Rocianus.

Sacred to the spirits of the departed. Gnaeus Julius Maturus, son of Gnaeus, quattuorvir with the authority of an aedile, quaestor pecuniae alimentariae; he lived 47 years. Pontilius Caedimnus dedicated this to his friend.

Inscriptions from the Iberian peninsula in particular give us passing hints at how local populations might participate in Latin-language discourse of *amicitia* and Roman commemorative practices by commissioning Latin inscriptions in honor of friends. Often the names are the mixture of Latin nomina and sometimes Greek cognomina typical of Roman citizens and freedmen around the Empire:

M(arco) Aquilio / Aquilino / an(norum) XXXV. / L(ucius) Porcius / Severus / *amico optimo.* (*CIL* 2.3754; Valencia, second century AD)

L(ucio) Scribonio / Euphemo / seviro aug(ustali). / L(ucius) Rubrius / Eutyches / *amico.* (*CIL* 2.3743; Valencia, second half of first century AD)

To Marcus Aquilius Aquilinus, aged 35. Lucius Porcius Severus to his excellent friend.

To Lucius Scribonius Euphemus, *sevir augustalis.* Lucius Rubrius Eutyches dedicated this to his friend.

Sometimes, however, we find Celtic names and abbreviations which, because of our extremely partial knowledge of the language, complicate interpretation but give us a glimpse at locally inflected usage, for example the use of a genitive plural to denote one's group of origin.

D(is) M(anibus). / Doidero / Arc(a)n(u)n (?) Bo/deri f(ilio) Vad(iniensi) / an(norum) XXX. Turanto / Bodeccun / *amico suo* / posuit. / h(ic) s(itus) e(st). (*AE* 1986.389; Vellila de Valdoré)[78]

[Ca]esilius / [M]alceno / [Ma]elonis / [f(ilio)] *amico* / *[su]o* st(a)t(u)i(t). (*AE* 1990.520; Ibahernando, province of Cacérès)[79]

To Doideros of the Arcanes (?), son of Boderos, of Vadines, aged 30. Turanto of the Bodecces (?) erected this for his friend. He lies buried here.

Caesilius erected this for Malcenus, son of Maelon, his friend.

An especially common type of epitaph found around the Roman Empire commemorates a soldier, his status communicated by the formulaic *militavit annis* ... ("served in the army for ... years"), by military titles, or the simple label *miles,* "soldier." Many are commemorated by fellow-soldiers in epitaphs which, by using labels like *contubernalis* or *commanipularis,* hold the spotlight on their shared military experience; but many are commissioned by a man who, whether or not he was a fellow-soldier,

---

[78] The inscription, accompanied by an image of a horse, is carved into a stele. ARCNN perhaps stands for *Arcanun,* the ending being a genitive plural of a suprafamilial group (cf. *Bodeccun*); *Turanto,* nominative, is attested at *CIL* 2.5721.

[79] The final letters of this inscription have also been interpreted as the formulaic Latin abbreviation S.T.T.L.: *s(it) t(ibi) t(erra) l(evis),* "may the earth lie lightly upon you."

commemorates either himself or the deceased with the label *amicus*, often with such epithets as *bene merens* or *optimus*.[80] Others invoke not (or not only) the ideal of friendship but also the legality of inheritance and the duties that came with it by using two meaningful labels: *heres* and *amicus*. That a soldier might end up being given a burial monument by a man who commemorates himself as heir and friend of the deceased was so common an arrangement that we find the formula *(heres) amico optimo faciundum curavit* ([his heir] commissioned this for his excellent friend) not infrequently abbreviated as *(H).A.O.F.C.*[81]

Although we would hardly know it from reading Latin literature, not only were slaves not excluded from the culture of commemoration, but those who had the financial resources to participate in it did so quite actively. Epitaphs commissioned by slaves in order to commemorate fellow-slaves are by no means a rarity, and in not a few of them we find the language of *amicitia*.

Dis Man(ibus) Restituti / C(ai) Bellici Natalis ser(vi) / grammatici. Plocamio / *amico amantissimo* fecit. (*CIL* 6.9450; Rome, first century AD)[82]

Primigenio / imp(eratoris servo) / Epidectus / Spendontis / disp(ensator) *amico*. (*CIL* 5.96 = Reali 1C; Pula, Croatia; probably first century AD)

To the spirits of Restitutus, slave of Gaius Bellicus Natalis, language teacher. Plocamio erected this for her most loving friend.

To Primigenius, the emperor's slave. Epidectus, slave of Spendon and steward, [dedicated this] to his friend.

In Restitutus' epitaph the honorific label *amico* is given greater weight by the accompanying superlative *amantissimo*, while in the inscription in honor of the imperial slave Primigenius it completes an A-B-A arrangement found in many inscriptions: the name of the deceased (here in the dative), the name of the commemorator (here in the nominative), and

---

[80] For *contubernalis*, *commilito*, and *commanipularis* in soldiers' inscriptions, see Lendon 2006; for friendships among soldiers, see Ricci 2001 (noting that of a sample of 155 inscriptions referring to soldiers' friendships, only nine evoke friendship with civilians), Phang 2001, pp. 113–114, 159–164, 262–295, Busch 2005. For soldiers' inscriptions from the city of Rome see *CIL* 6.2550–3650, 37181–37300; those using the label *amicus* include *CIL* 6.2440, 2521, 2524, 2590, 2622, 2642, 2643, 2701, 2724, 2746, 2975, 2981, 3135, 3176, 3190, 3192, 3203, 3209, 3214, 3222–3225, 3235, 3237, 3241, 3253, 3357; those using both *amicus* and *contubernalis* or *commanipularis* include *CIL* 6.2552, 6.2571, 2614, 2628, 2924. Such inscriptions have been found all around the Empire; examples include *CIL* 3.322 (Calchedon in Pontus and Bithynia), *CIL* 2.3180 (Valeria), *CIL* 2.4156 (Tarraco), *AE* 1995.1260 (Bánom in Pannonia Superior, today Hungary, early third century AD).

[81] Examples from the city of Rome include *CIL* 6.3178, 3199, 3220, 3230, 3271, 3272, 3290.

[82] Solin 2003, p. 1235, cites *Plocamio* in this inscription and the fragmentary *CIL* 6.24296 as a woman's slave name corresponding to the masculine *Plocamus*.

then a label for the deceased (here again in the dative) which honors both parties and motivates the existence of the inscription.

The burial complex in Rome known as the *monumentum familiae Statiliorum*, actively used from the late first century BC into the first century AD, housed the remains of hundreds of slaves and freedmen of that branch of the Statilii represented most prominently by Titus Statilius Taurus, consul in 26 BC; the complex may have been founded by his son of the same name, consul in 11 BC. Over 400 epitaphs naming 657 different individuals have survived, carved into plaques marking the location of funerary urns.[83] Some of these use the language of *amicitia*, telling sketchy but suggestive stories about relationships among the slaves of a prominent Roman household. One plaque, for example, was commissioned by Lucius Norbanius Quadratus' slave Amerimnus for the 30-year-old Modestus, a former slave of Norbanius whom Amerimnus commemorates as his dear friend (*amico suo carissimo*). Another epitaph from this complex, an example of type 1b, is worth citing here because of its eloquently simple evocation of the relationships that could be commemorated among slaves in this household (Figure 10). It marks the resting place of the ashes of Optata the doorkeeper, slave of Pansa, dedicated by her unnamed friends (*amici*).[84]

A plaque found in structure N of the complex (Figure 11) stands out not only for the relative sumptuousness of its decoration (its scheme of wreaths and flowers, arranged around a central opening for pouring libations to the dead, is unique among surviving plaques from this complex) but also for its richer language and prominent location. Of the more than four hundred surviving epitaphs, it is one of only fourteen designed to be placed not near a niche in a wall but on a podium. The text itself is artistically carved, albeit with slightly irregular spacing, and, for those who can read it, it is marked by an elegiac couplet and a noticeable (some readers might say heavy-handed) accumulation of alliteration and assonance.

> hic est ille situs, / qui qualis *amicus* / *amico*
> quaque fide / fuerit, mors fuit indicio. //
> f(unus) f(ecit). //
> Faustus Erotis / dispensatoris vicarius.
> (*CIL* 6.6275; Rome)

---

[83] See Caldelli and Ricci 1999 and Hasegawa 2005, pp. 57–61.

[84] *CIL* 6.6487 (Caldelli and Ricci 1999, no. 247, fig. 220): *Modesto / L(uci) Norbani Quadrati l(iberto), / vix(it) a(nnis) XXX. / Amerimnus Norbani / amico suo carissimo*; *CIL* 6.6326 (Caldelli and Ricci 1999, no. 342, fig. 206): *Optata, Pa(n)saes / ostiaria. fecerunt / amici.*

Figure 10 Columbarium plaque from the *monumentum familiae Statiliorum* in Rome, commissioned for the slave Optata by unnamed friends

> Here he lies:
> the kind of friend to friend he was,
> and how trustworthy he was,
> his death proved.
> He performed the funeral rites.
> Faustus, under-slave of the steward Eros.

Faustus is memorialized as a *vicarius*, a slave's slave, whose master Eros, like Epidectus of Pula, held the position of *dispensator*, steward or financial manager, thought to have ranked fairly high in the hierarchy of household slaves and perhaps more likely to have had slaves of his own.[85] With its array of alliterations and assonances (*qui qualis, amicus amico, fide fuerit, funus fecit Faustus*, the latter set emphasized by the abbreviation F.F.), this epitaph commemorates Faustus as an especially admirable friend, hinting at a moving story of *amicitia* between one slave and another who was subordinate to him, a story that involved the circumstances of Faustus' death.

---

[85] Faustus' master is almost certainly himself commemorated at *CIL* 6.6274, in honor of Eros the *dispensator*, slave of Titus Statilius Posidippus. Posidippus seems to have been one of the most prominent freedmen of the Statilii, owned at least three other *dispensatores* besides Eros and may have held the position himself. See Merola 1990 for thorough discussion of *vicarii* (pp. 136–140 for this and other relevant epitaphs from the *monumentum Statiliorum*) and Hasegawa 2005, pp. 37–38 and 57–61 for the position of *dispensator* in this household in general and in connection with Posidippus in particular. The phrase *funus facere* ("to celebrate a funeral": *TLL* s.v. *funus* 6.1603.9–12) appears in another epitaph from this complex (*CIL* 6.6486: *Modestus / Eunus funus feci[t]*); in Faustus' epitaph the implied subject seems to be Eros.

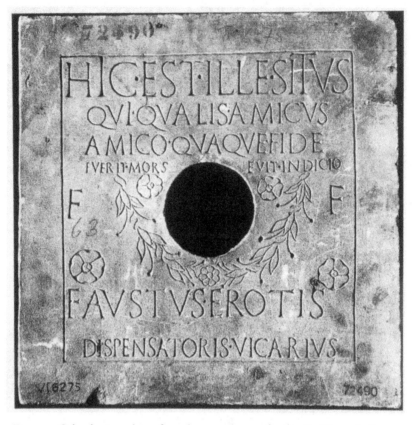

Figure 11 Columbarium plaque from the *monumentum familiae Statiliorum* in Rome, commissioned by the under-slave Faustus for his master, the slave Eros

Did he, for example, die while protecting Eros? In any case, the deceased is memorialized as an ideal friend not only by means of the phrase *amicus amico* (friend to a friend) but by the evocation of the concept of *fides*, and even by the juxtaposition of the two men's names, larger than most of the rest of the text and placed underneath the opening for libations: FAVSTVS EROTIS.

The evidently proverbial phrase *amicus amico* (and variations on it) has been found in other epitaphs – including yet another from the *monumentum familiae Statiliorum* and a Christian epitaph from Rome which dates itself to the year AD 469 – as well as literary texts ranging from comedy to Petronius.[86] Likewise, the evocative couplet carved at the top of the plaque turns out to be a poetic building-block of a kind we see elsewhere in inscriptions and graffiti, available for use, re-use, and adapation as needed.[87] Another epitaph from Rome – of uncertain date but, as it happens, for a slave as well – contains the same poem with only minor variations:

> Rufioni Rutiliae / servo dedit / C(aius) Vehilius Albanus. /
> hic est ille situs, qui qualis *amicus amicis* /
> quaque fide vixit, mors fuit indicium.
> (CIL 6.25570 = CLE 1000)

> To Rufio, slave of Rutilia, given by Gaius Vehilius Albanus.
> Here he lies:
> the kind of friend to friends he was,
> and with what trust he lived,
> his death proved.

Reading Rufio's epitaph together with Faustus' reveals, apart from some minor variations in syntax and word choice, one potentially significant detail above all. Faustus is praised for his fidelity to a friend (*amicus amico*), Rufio as a "friend to friends (*amicus amicis*)." We learn nothing more specific about the circumstances of either man's death, and even this detail can be read in two opposing ways: The plural suggests that Rufio surpasses Faustus in his commitment to *amicitia*; or it means that Rufio's epitaph is vaguely generic, while Faustus' bears the weightiness of specificity.

Both of these men were slaves, and Faustus a sub-slave at that. Rufio, however, is commemorated by a man whose triple name communicates that he is a Roman citizen, whether born as such or a freed slave; and the epitaph carefully specifies that Rufio belonged not to Albanus but to a woman named Rutilia. This, then, is a story of *amicitia* between a Roman citizen and someone else's slave. Other epitaphs confirm that *amicitia* could be and was evoked as the bond joining slaves not only to

---

[86] *CIL* 6.6609 (*monumentum Statiliorum*): *quoat vixit, vixit suaviter. / T(itus) Statilius Tauri / lib(ertus) Eros Parra, vixit probe, / pudenter, amicus amico, placuit / suis. have et tu, vale et tu. fecit / Hetereia P(ubli) l(iberta) Chreste viro suo; CLE* 689 = *ILCV* 3114: *hic Lucianus cum bona pace / quiescit, innoce(n)s mansuetus / mites l(a)etus, cum amicis amicus, / vixit annis pl(us) m(inus) L nulla manente / querella. / depositus est in pace die [---] K(a)l(endas) Septembres Flabio Marciano et [Z] enone v(iris) [cl(arissimis) cons(ulibus)]*; Plaut. *Curc.* 332, *Mil.* 660; Ter. *Phorm.* 562; Petron. *Sat.* 43–44; and Otto 1890, p. 23.

[87] For such building-blocks in poetic graffiti from the walls of Pompeii, see Wachter 1998 and Williams (forthcoming).

other slaves but to free men and women as well. We have already seen one example from the Statilii complex in Rome: Quadratus' slave Amerimnus memorializes as his *amicus* the freedman Modestus, former slave of the same owner (*CIL* 6.6487). An epitaph found in the vicinity of Pola announces that it was commissioned by a slave in honor of his friend, an imperial freedman.

T(ito) Flavi[o] / Aug(usti) l(iberto) / Heliad[i] / Dionysiu[s] / Spur(i) Enni R[ufi?] (servus) / *amico*. (Reali 9C; late first century AD)

To Titus Flavius Helias, freedman of the emperor. Dionysius, slave of Spurius Ennius Rufus (?), dedicated this to his friend.

An inscription from Spain commemorates the same configuration of *amicitia* seen in Rufio's epitaph – between a Roman citizen and someone else's slave – and in this case it is the slave himself who has commissioned the epitaph.

M(arcus) Aemilius / M(arci) f(ilius) Optatus / Longus h(ic) s(itus) e(st). / Suavis D(ecimi) Val(erii) Stabilion(is) (servus) / *memor amicitiae* hoc / munus supremum dat. (*CIL* 2.1753; Cadiz)

Here lies Marcus Aemilius Optatus Longus, son of Marcus. Suavis, slave of Decimus Valerius Stabilio, mindful of their friendship, gives this final gift.

This text, formulated in language fully typical of the speech genre of epitaphs,[88] has equally typical functions. Above all, of course, it commemorates the man whose name comes first: the deceased Marcus Aemilius Optatus Longus, carefully memorialized as freeborn by means of the formulaic M.F., "son of Marcus." But it also perpetuates the memory of Suavis, who provided the monument; it reminds its readers that such a gesture can be expected of *amici*; it advertises that Suavis, though a slave, enjoyed a relationship of *amicitia* with a freeborn man; and, by giving the name of Suavis' master, it keeps this instance of *amicitia* distinct from the master–slave relationship.

How indeed is the relationship between slaves and *their own masters* commemorated in the formulaic language of epitaphs evoking friendship or affection? The adjective *amans* appears to be the term of choice. We find inscriptions memorializing an *amantissimus dominus* and a *fidelissimus et amantissimus servus*, and, in an interesting reversal of how we

---

[88] For *memor amicitiae* in an epitaph marking the commemoration of the deceased by a friend, see *CIL* 8.2170 (near Theueste, today El Ksour in Tunisia). The phrase *supremum munus* is found in inscriptions commemorating friends as well as spouses, referring either to the monument as a whole or to the inscription in particular: see *CIL* 10.174 = *CLE* 405.3 (Potenza), *CIL* 3.2964 = 9148 = 13895 = *CLE* 1141 (Salona).

might expect the qualities to be invoked, an epitaph from Capua for the slave Hilarus memorializes him for his affection for his master and his dutifulness to his friends (*amans domini, obsequens amicis*). But I have not yet found a single example of the commemoration of the relationship between a slave and his or her master in which the term *amicus* appears, apart from Faustus' epitaph from the Statilii complex in Rome, but Faustus' master is himself a slave. In general, although the sample is too small to be conclusive, it would seem that the language of *amicitia* was largely avoided in representations of the relationship between master and slave in the speech genre of inscriptions.[89]

Type 1b: Commemorated by more than one person
In Chapter 1 we considered epitaphs for women who are commemorated alone as the *amica* of two or more others – men, women, or both. Examples include the following:

D(is) M(anibus). / Maeliae / Liberali. / Ti(berius) Claudius / Menodorus / et Clodia Primi/genia fecerunt / *amicae carissi/mae et b(ene) m(erenti)*, / mihique poste/risque meis. / in fr(onte) p(edes) XVI / in ag(ro) p(edes) XVIIII. (*CIL* 6.7648; Rome)

To the spirits of the dead. To Maelia Liberalis. Tiberius Claudius Menodorus and Clodia Primigenia dedicated this to their dearest and well-deserving friend, to myself and my descendants. 16 feet wide, 19 feet deep.

Among jointly commissioned epitaphs in honor of individual men, we find the usual range in juridical status, from slave to free.

D(is) M(anibus). / have, Plautiane. fecit / Euporas conserv(us) / *et Clemens amicus* / bene merenti. vixit / annis XXIII, mens(ibus) XI, die(bus) XXIII. (*CIL* 11.6276 = Reali 130It; Fano)

Sedato Arre/ni f(ilio) an(norum) XXIII. / *Valerius Elaes/us Fusci f(ilius) Vxs/amensis et Elc/uius Modes/tinus Emerite(n)s/is amici.* (*AE* 1995.861; Tardemézar, Spain)

D(is) M(anibus). / Sentio / Celeri. / Dom(itia) Aphro/disia et Vir(ius) / Stephanus / *amico b(ene) m(erenti)* p(osuerunt). (*CIL* 3.2522; Salona)

D(is) M(anibus). / Atimeto / medico. / Basileus / et Partheno/paeus / Faustinae / Aug(ustae) servi / ab ornamen/tis *amico / bene merenti* / fecerunt. (*CIL* 6.8896; Rome)

---

[89] *CIL* 10.7612 (Cagliari): *L(ucio) Iulio Pon/ticlo nego/tianti Galli/cano Primus / serbus amantis/simo domino posuit*; *CIL* 3.328 = 3.6987 (Nicomedia): *servo / fidelissimo et sui amantissimo / t(itulum) m(emoriae) p(osuit)*; *CIL* 10.4167 (Capua): *Hilari Clodi / M(arci) s(ervi) o(ssa) h(ic) s(ita) s(unt). / vixsit annos / XXII. amans / domini, opseq(u)ens amicis.* Burton 2004, p. 215, observes that in Plautus' comedies, while we certainly find *amicitia* between slaves, "nowhere are slaves constructed as *amici* of their masters and vice-versa."

To the spirits of the dead. Hail, Plautianus! Euporas, fellow slave, and Clemens, friend, dedicated this to a deserving man. He lived 23 years, 11 months, 23 days.

To Sedatus, son of Arrenus, 23 years old. [Dedicated by] Valerius Elaesus of Uxama, son of Fuscus, and Elcuius Modestinus of Emerita, his friends.

To the spirits of the dead: to Sentius Celer. Domitia Aphrodisia and Virius Stephanus erected this monument to their deserving friend.

To the spirits of the dead: to Atimetus the physician. Basileus and Parthenopaeus, slaves of the empress Faustina in charge of her jewelry, dedicated this to a well-deserving friend.

In epitaphs like these, the relationship *between* the individuals who have commissioned the inscription is given no explicit label. To be sure, by commemorating themselves as the *amici* of the departed, Elaesus and Modestinus come close to representing themselves as each other's *amici*, but that is only an implication. Domitia Aphrodisia and Virius Stephanus may or may not have been a conjugal couple, but the inscription they commissioned says nothing on the point. And while Euporas memorializes himself as Plautianus' fellow slave (*conservus*), Clemens calls himself Plautianus' *amicus*, leaving open such questions as whether he too was a slave, and what relationship, if any, he had to Euporas. What is emphasized in all such texts is the bond of *amicitia* which joined them to the dear departed, the living as dutiful and the dead as deserving friends.

Sometimes *amicitia* is invoked together with one or more other relationships, the deceased being perpetuated in several roles simultaneously. A number of epitaphs for men, commissioned jointly by the widow and a male friend, and once again hinting at or openly communicating status ranging from slave to freeborn, memorialize the confluence of what are arguably the two most important bonds that a Roman man might establish in life and advertise in death – marriage to a woman and *amicitia* with a man.

D(is) M(anibus). / P(ublio) Rubrio / Hilaro. / P(ublius) Vettius / Gemellus / *amico optimo* et / Rubria / Glymene / coniugi b(ene) m(erenti) / fecerunt. (*CIL* 6.5336; Rome)

D(is) M(anibus). / L(ucio) Annio C(ai) f(ilio) / Mino, qui / vixit an/nis p(lus) m(inus) XLV, / C(aius) Iulius Cr/es[t]us *amic/o* et coniu/nx coniugi / b(ene) m(erenti) f(ecerunt). (*CIL* 10.5437 = Reali 71It; Aquinum)

To the spirits of the dead: to Publius Rubrius Hilarus. Publius Vettius Gemellus dedicated this to his excellent friend, and Rubria Clymene to her deserving husband.

To the spirits of the dead: to Lucius Annius Minus, son of Gaius, who lived for about 45 years. Gaius Julius Chrestus dedicated this to his friend, and his wife to her deserving husband.

It is particularly striking that the name of Lucius Annius Minus' wife does not even appear. She is a cipher, the spouse commemorating her spouse (compare the expressive juxtaposition *coniunx coniugi* with the formula *amicus amico* cited above) taking second place to the fully announced Gaius Julius Chrestus, who commemorates his *amicus*.

Other inscriptions announce the joint commemoration of a man by his wife, child, and an *amicus*, thus memorializing the deceased as husband, father, and friend,[90] and a handful, commissioned by an *amicus* of the deceased along with one of his slaves, perpetuate his memory as deserving friend and decent master.

Dis Manibus. / C(aio) Iulio Lygdamo. / vix(it) ann(is) XXVIII / mens(ibus) X dieb(us) XX. / fecerunt / C(aius) Rustius Epictetus / *amico dignissimo* / *bene merenti* et / Severus domino dignissim(o). (*CIL* 6.5327; Rome)

To the spirits of the departed. To Gaius Julius Lygdamus, who lived 28 years, 10 months, 20 days. Gaius Rustius Epictetus dedicated this to his worthy and deserving friend, Severus to his worthy master.

It is likely that both the deceased and his friend Epictetus were former slaves themselves – albeit not of the same master – but thanks to the slave Severus' participation in this commemoration, Lygdamus' epitaph emphasizes his roles as *amicus* and *dominus*. Other epitaphs, memorializing the deceased as brother and friend, locate the deceased in the two most highly valued of relationships joining Roman men.

L(ucio) Atilio L(uci) l(iberto) / Saturnino annor(um) XL, domo / Fl(avia) Scarbantia, interfec(to) / a latronibus in<tr>usis. / Atilius Tertius frater / et Statius Onesimus / amico. / loc(o) gratuit(o) dat(o) ab / Clodia Tertia. (*Inscr. Aq.* 861 = Reali 26C; Aquileia)[91]

D(is) M(anibus). / G(aio) Laelio G(ai) f(ilio) Iugu/ndo et Laelius / Paullinus fratri / piissimo, vixit ann(is) / LV, bene merenti. / C(aius) Disinius Verus *amico* / *meren(ti)*. (*CIL* 11.2052 = Reali 141It; Perugia)

For Lucius Atilius Saturninus, son of Lucius, aged 40 years, from Flavia Scarbantia, killed by thieving intruders. His brother Atilius Tertius dedicated

---

90 E.g. *CIL* 6.2371 (Rome), 9.4009 (Alba Fucens).
91 The stone reads *inrtusis* in the fourth line; at *ILS* 8507 Dessau corrects this to *in Rutsis,* but Reali 1997 more persuasively suggests *intrusis* (cf. Italian *intrusi,* "intruders"). See Gunnella 1995 for the theme of sudden or premature death in epitaphs.

this, and Statius Onesimus to his friend, on property given as a gift by Clodia Tertia.

To the spirits of the dead. To Gaius Laelius Iucundus, son of Gaius. Laelius Paullinus dedicated this to his devoted brother, who lived 55 years, well-deserving; and Gaius Disinius Verus to his deserving friend.

Whereas such inscriptions have the function not only of memorializing the deceased and locating him in key social networks, but also of publicizing the generosity and dutifulness of those who commissioned them, epitaphs dedicated by nameless friends place the emphasis squarely on the deceased as someone who had *amici* loyal, dutiful, and generous enough, and with sufficient financial means, to dedicate a funerary monument to him. We cannot know in any given case whether these "friends" constituted a coherent and recognizable group (those, say, who could also be called *clientes*, or fellow-members of a guild, professional association, or burial club), but the language of these epitaphs itself makes its point simply and clearly: They are *amici*.[92] An example from Spain brings the point across in language displaying the highest possible compression, abbreviation, and formularity.

D(is) M(anibus) s(acrum). / C(aio) Clodio / Victorin/o annor(um) / XX. amici. / h(ic) s(itus) e(st). s(it) t(ibi) t(erra) l(evis). (*CIL* 2.3332; Tugia)

Sacred to the spirits of the dead. To Gaius Clodius Victorinus, aged 20. His friends dedicated this. He is buried here. May the earth lie lightly upon you.

One inscription from Rome meditates on the commemoration of the deceased by his *amici* in a poem of irregular but recognizably dactylic meter, and another lets its readers know that the 60-year-old Gaius Allidius Hermas is missed and mourned by his *amici*: "whatever he said, he was a delightful friend."[93] An epitaph from Sicca in Tunisia for a young man named Pilarus is dedicated by his father, describing the deceased as lamented by his *amici* as well as by his parents;[94] and one from Ravenna

---

[92] It is a commonplace in the Latin literary tradition that it was socially effective to appear in public or make one's way to the forum surrounded by groups of men who could be called companions, friends, and/or clients, and whose anonymous mass was precisely the point. See Cic. *Att.* 1.18 (*cum ad forum stipati gregibus amicorum descendimus*); Mart. 2.18.5, 2.57.5, 2.74 (*greges togatorum*), 3.7.2, 3.46.1, 6.48.1, 10.74.3; Juv. 1.46–48, 141–143, 10.44–46. For burial clubs, see above, n. 50.

[93] *CIL* 6.1951 (Rome): *hic ego Murinus praeco Felix, cui tales amici / complerunt animos ut post me nome<n> haberem*; *CIL* 6.11464 (Rome): *C(aio) Allidio Hermae, / qui quidquid dixit / dulcis amici{i}s erat. / hunc quoque post mortem / deflemus amici. / vixit annis LX.*

[94] *Inscriptiones latines de la Tunisie* (Paris 1944) 1610 (Sicca): *Pilarum sacravit hunc pater / ipse, quem aetatis flosculo / leti crudeli iniuria / amici cum parentibus / raptum geminis affectibus / [vide]rent et flerent simul.*

announces the commemoration of the approximately 27-year-old Aurelius Germanio by his unnamed brothers and friends (*fratres et amici*).[95]

A poem inscribed on a funerary altar found near Seville and perhaps originally from the ancient town of Salpensa commemorates a young man – probably although not certainly a slave[96]– as beloved friend, and the young man's name, poignantly appropriate in the poetic commemoration of a friend, is Pylades.

> Pylades Anni Novati patris (servus?) / h(ic) s(itus) e(st). /
> subductum primae Pyladen haec ara iuventae /
> indicat, exemplum non leve amicitiae. /
> nanq(ue) sodalicii sacravit turba futurum /
> nominis indicium nec minus officii. /
> dicite, qui legitis, solito de more sepulto: /
> pro meritis, Pylades, sit tibi terra levis.
>
> (CIL 2.1293 = CLE 1103; Salpensa)

> Here lies Pylades, (slave of?) Annius Novatus the elder.
> This altar tells of Pylades taken from us in youth,
> an example of friendship not trivial.
> A throng of comrades dedicated this lasting sign
> of his name, and of their dutifulness too.
> You who read this, speak to the buried as custom would have it:
> "For all your merits, Pylades, may the earth lie lightly upon you."

Speaking in the voice of an anonymous throng of friends who wish to keep Pylades' memory alive, this inscription combines standard poetic diction, epitaphic formulae, with a metrical irregularity or two, but shows a perfect correspondence (by no means the norm) between line divisions on the stone, and an eloquently self-conscious use of the formulaic language of poetic epitaphs. A self-referential evocation of the function of the object on which the text is inscribed (*haec ara ... indicat*) makes use of the concept of *exemplum* in order to look ahead to its future status as testimony and model, and the address to the passersby in the final couplet builds up to the concluding formula *sit tibi terra levis*, marked as a stereotypical formula (*solito de more*). And yet, for all its emphatic eloquence, this text does not seek to keep alive the memory of those who committed it. They remain a nameless *turba*, a noun which reminds us that a side

---

[95] *ILCV* 2706b (Ravenna): *fratres et amici / Aurelio / Germanioni / qui <v>ixi<t> annis / plus / minus / XXIVII / in place.*

[96] Following Bücheler in his *CLE* note, I understand the superscription to signify that Pylades is the slave of the elder Annius Novatus, not his son. For the slave and freedman name *Pylades* see Solin 2003, pp. 561–562.

effect of the use of the plural *amici* is to leave open the question of how many there were. Both the namelessness and the unspecified number of the friends intensifies the aura around the deceased.

Type 2: Commemoration of friends as part of a group

Roman burial practices stand out for the frequency with which the dead are buried and commemorated in groups whose composition extends well beyond the triad consisting of husband, wife, and children. The Cocceius–Antonius complex in the Isola Sacra necropolis reminds us that many surviving inscriptions commemorating an individual alone may originally have been part of some larger burial group, but even among the hundreds of thousands of epitaphs surviving outside their original context, many explicitly commemorate groups and record for posterity the relationships structuring them. The most commonly memorialized bonds are those between husband and wife, parent and child, but as our examples from Pompeii and the Isola Sacra have illustrated, these are very often accompanied by freed slaves and their descendants (*libertis libertabusque posterisque eorum*), and sometimes by *amici* and *amicae* as well. In such group commemorations, as in individual commemorations, we find both men and women in the roles of both commemorated and commemorator; here too we find slaves participating in the intertwined cultures of commemoration and *amicitia*; here too, former slaves seem to be overrepresented.

The inclusion in group commemorations otherwise structured around kinship and marriage of freed slaves *and their descendants*, and perhaps above all of friends, has important but underexplored implications. Can such group burials even be called, as they sometimes are, "family tombs"?[97] What do we mean by "family"? It is well known that the Latin word *familia* by no means covers the same semantic space as modern words like *family*, *Familie*, or *famiglia*. The Latin term includes both the freeborn children (*liberi*) and the household slaves (*famuli*) of the man

---

[97] Whatever we might mean by "family tomb," it is not the same as the technical term *sepulcrum familiare*. In the language of Roman law this term designated a tomb whose possession remained within the *familia*, a status that was often but not always signaled in accompanying inscriptions by means of the formula *hoc monumentum heredem non sequitur/sequetur* in order to distinguish it from a *sepulcrum hereditarium*, whose ownership passed to named heirs. Both types might provide for burial and commemoration of "family members," however we define the term. See *Digest* 11.7.5 (*familiaria sepulcra dicuntur, quae quid sibi familiaeque suae constituit; hereditaria autem, quae quis sibi heredibusque suis constituit, vel quod pater familias iure hereditario adquisiit*) and Lazzarini 1991 for detailed discussion.

called *pater familias*; whether or not his wife was a part of his *familia* was and is a tricky question; *familia* itself sometimes denotes the household slaves as a group, and only them.[98] On the other hand, the substantivized adjective *familiaris* is, as we have seen, a near-synonym for *amicus* in many speech genres of Latin literature, but precisely *not* in the formulaic language of inscriptions, and in some contexts it could even, like *famulus*, denote a slave.[99] The linguistic overlaps are suggestive. I do not wish to imply that a Roman's friends were normatively considered a part of his or her *familia*, still less that they were in any significant way analogous to his or her slaves. On the contrary, the two relationships arguably existed in a dialectical tension, slavery being based on dependence and possession, *amicitia* on interdependence and sharing. But I would emphasize the ways in which the groupings and boundaries suggested by the Latin vocabulary are different from those in other languages, English in particular. On the one hand, at least partially depending on the speech genre in which an utterance participated, one's *familiares* could either be one's friends or one's slaves; on the other hand, we find nothing like the alliterative English phrase "friends and family" in extant Latin texts – the collocation *amici et familia* is not attested.

   In what follows I offer an overview of epitaphs which commemorate the following burial configurations: (2a) friends along with the dedicator's spouse and/or children or other kin; (2b) friends along with the dedicator's freedmen and freedwomen; (2c) friends along with the dedicator's spouse and/or children or other kin, as well as his or her freedmen and freedwomen; (2d) friends along with dedicator's former owner (*patronus* or *patrona*), with or without the dedicator's spouse and children. Within each type, epitaphs are organized by size of the commemorative group, beginning with groups consisting of the dedicator, a friend, and some third person (usually but not always the dedicator's spouse); then groups of three plus unnamed dependants commemorated by means of the formulae *suis* or *posteris* or *libertis libertabusque posterisque eorum*; and finally groups of four or more.

---

[98] See Saller 1984 and Saller 2000 for overviews. Saller 1994, pp. 74–101, reviews usage patterns of the words *domus* and *familia*: the latter sometimes refers to those under the authority of the *paterfamilias* (thus often excluding, for example, the wife), sometimes more broadly to all those living in a household (thus including the wife), sometimes only to the household slaves. Both ancient and modern etymologies take *familia* to be related to an Italic root meaning "slave" (Latin *famulus*): see Paul. Fest. 77.11 (among the Oscans, *servus famel nominabatur, unde et familia vocata*) and Ernout and Meillet 2001 s.v. *famulus*.

[99] Sen. *Ep.* 47.14 describes the usage as archaic but still surviving in the mime plays of his day.

As usual, the geographical distribution and variety of juridical status are equally broad. Whether commissioned by men or women, most
of these epitaphs include the dedicator him- or herself, a configuration
marked by the formulaic *sibi et.* Most are commissioned by a single person, but some are in the name of two, a few in the name of three. Among
those commissioned by two people, I have found none commissioned by
two women. Although the configuration must have been possible, it was
evidently so rarely done that it has left no traces. A few were commissioned by two men. We may be tempted to understand them as pairs of
friends, but the epitaphs place no label on their relationship with each
other. Most double commissions are in the name of a man and a woman;
again, while some or many of these may have lived as conjugal couples,
the inscriptions they commission do not communicate this, instead
memorializing them as people who together provided for burial of friends
and dependants. As in all epitaphs, finally, we sometimes find individuals
commemorated with no relational label at all attached to their name. In
some such cases readers can (and often do) reconstruct possible connections on the basis of the nomenclature, but those who commissioned the
inscriptions were content to memorialize those in question not as spouses,
friends, or as anything else, but simply in their individuality by means of
their names alone, whose bareness arguably lends even greater emphasis
to their inclusion in the memorial group.

Type 2a: Spouse, children, and/or kin
In the *monumentum familiae Statiliorum* of Rome we find a clumsily and
thus all the more movingly worded epitaph in which a slave woman commemorates her 5-year-old son along with a male slave whom she calls her
"constant friend."

Epaphrae Tauri (servo) unctori. facit mulier / infelix amori suo dulcissimo filio
/ *et amico continenter.* Cladus Elates / filius, vixit annos V, dies XVIII. (*CIL 6.
6378*; Rome, first century AD)[100]

For Epaphra, slave of Taurus, masseur. An unhappy woman dedicated this to
her darling, her sweet son, and to her constant friend. Cladus, son of Elate, lived
5 years and 18 days.

---

[100] The *CIL* entry quotes Mommsen's description of Elate as *mulier haec pietate animi magis quam
sermonis elegantia conspicua.* In another, more simply worded epitaph from this tomb the boy is
commemorated alone (*CIL 6.6379: Cladus Elate(s) f(ilius) / vixit ann(is) V d(iebus) XIIX*). For the
slave and thus freedman name Epaphra ('Επαφρᾶς) see Solin 2003, pp. 349, 1475; for *Cladus*, pp.
1196–1197; for *Elate*, pp. 1170–1171.

Other epitaphs include friends in a group consisting of three named individuals. In an inscription from Rome, a man commemorates himself – carefully noting his freeborn status – along with his freedwoman wife and someone else's freed slave whom he calls his *amicus*:

C(aius) Fundanius C(ai) f(ilius) / Rufus sibi et / Valeriae (mulieris) l(ibertae) Hedone / uxori *et* / *Q(uinto) Farsuleio Q(uinti) l(iberto)* / *Zetho* / *amico suo*. (*CIL* 6.18724; Rome)

Gaius Fundanius Rufus, son of Gaius, to himself and to his wife Valeris Hedone, freedwoman of a woman, and to his friend Quintus Farsuleius Zethus, freedman of Quintus.

A Latin epitaph found in Greece commemorates the same configuration – a man dedicates the inscription to himself, his wife, and a man identified as his *amicus*[101] – and one found in Pannonia likewise announces a soldier's commemoration of himself, his wife, and a male friend (*amicus*).[102] In an epitaph from Rome a man and a woman announce their commemoration of themselves in the company of a female friend.

Diis Manibus. / C(aius) Poppaeus Vale(n)s et / Poppaea Ilias fecerunt / sibi et Avianiae Charidi / *amicae suae carissimae*. (*CIL* 6.39780; Rome)

To the spirits of the dead. Gaius Poppaeus Valens and Poppaea Ilias dedicated this to themselves and to Aviania Charis their dear friend.

Valens' and Ilias' names suggest they were former slaves of the same master or same family. They perhaps formed a conjugal couple, perhaps not, but the inscription they commissioned does not communicate that; instead it communicates that they are buried together with Charis, whom they memorialize as their *amica*.

Other epitaphs commemorating three named individuals use formulaic expressions to communicate that unnamed dependants or descendants may find their final resting place here as well. In two examples from Rome we find a woman commissioning a monument for herself, her husband, and a female friend (*amica*), along with an open-ended provision for eventual descendants (*posterisque suis*).[103] In another, we find a woman

---

[101] *Inscriptiones Latinae in Graecia Repertae* (ed. M. Sasel Kos, Faenza 1979) 85 (Argos; the inscription is repeated on the stone): *[L(ucius) Naevius Cal]listus sibi et Veneriae coniug(i) / [et L(ucio) Aeli]o Camo amico optimo. / [in fronte c]um taberna ped(es) in agro ped(es).*

[102] *CIL* 3.4148 (Lendava, Pannonia superior): *C(aius) Iulius / Severinus / vet(eranus) leg(ionis) I Adiut(ricis) / viv(us) fecit sibi et / Straboniae Victo/rinae coniugi pien/tissimae annor(um) XXXIX / et C(aio) Ulpio Licinio / amico optimo.*

[103] *CIL* 6.16684 (Rome): *Cusinia Hygia / fecit sibi et / A(ulo) Fulvio Clymen[o] / coniugi suo caris/simo sibi, et / Umbriciae Hediae / amicae sibi caris/simae, posterisque suis*; *AE* 2001.317 (Rome): *[D(is)]*

commemorating herself along with her 18-year-old son – whose freeborn status and father's name she memorializes – but also another man whom she commemorates as *amicus optimus*, by means of the formula *et suis* creating the possibility that other dependants will be buried here too.

Dis Manibus. / C(aio) Hirtio C(ai) f(ilio) Quirin(a) / Materno, / ann(os) nato XVIII mens(es) VII, / Hirtia Egloge filio / pientissimo fecit, et sibi et suis / *et Q(uinto) Favio Maximo / amico optimo*. (*CIL* 6.19503; Rome)

To the spirits of the dead. To Gaius Hirtius Maternus, son of Gaius, of the tribe Quirina, who lived 18 years and 7 months. Hirtia Egloge dedicated this to her devoted son and to her own, and to Quintus Fabius Maximus her excellent friend.

In another epitaph from Rome rather insistently using flattering formulae, a man commemorates himself along with his wife (*coniugi carissimae de se bene merenti*) and his male friend (*amico pientissimo*), using the formula *posterisque suis* to make room for unnamed descendants.[104]

Commemorative groups of this kind often consist of four or more named invididuals. An epitaph from Milan was commissioned by a woman who commemorates herself, her husband, a woman whom she identifies as her *amica*, and two others – a man and a woman – with no label at all.

V(iva) f(ecit) / Afreia Attis / sibi et C(aio) Atilio / Victori viro / suo *et Volumniae / Monad(ae) amicae* / [et] M(arco) Albucio Prisco / et Se[xti]ae Severai. / h(oc) m(onumentum) h(eredem) n(on) s(equetur). (*CIL* 5.5936 = Reali 116C; Milan; first–second century AD)

While still alive, Afreia Attis commissioned this for herself, for her husband Gaius Atilius Victor, for her friend Volumnia Monas, for Marcus Albucius Priscus and for Sextia Severa. This tomb will not be passed on to the heir.

Among those commissioned by men and commemorating groups of four or more, some identify the dedicator and the departed as freeborn Roman citizens:

V(ivus) f(ecit) / L(ucius) Lannus / Primi f(ilius) sibi et / C(aio) Lanno fr(atri) / et Tertullae / Tordinae uxori, / Lannae Firmae f(iliae), / C(aio) [Corn]elio / Succ[es]so [a]m[i]co. (*CIL* 5.3655 = Reali 68C; Verona; second half of first century AD)

<hr />

M(anibus) / [...C]attien(o) / [R]estitut(o). / Flavia Fe/licula co/n(iugi) b(ene) m(erenti) f(ecit) / sib(i) / poster(isque) / suis et An/nulenae / Melitine am/icae optimae.

[104] *CIL* 6.24545 (Rome): *D(is) M(anibus). / Pompeiae Ianuariae, / quae vixit annis XXXXV. / L(ucius) Pompeius Apollonius / coniugi carissimae de se bene / merenti fecit et sibi posteris/que suis et / Ti(berio) Claudio Primo / amico pientissimo.*

While still alive, Lucius Lannus the son of Primus dedicated this to himself and to Gaius Lannus his brother and Tertulla Tordina his wife; to Lanna Firma his daughter; and to Gaius Cornelius Successus his friend.

An epitaph from Libarna in northern Italy illustrates one of the ways in which the discourse of *amicitia* might not only be enshrined in a text carved in stone but materially influence the composition of burial groups.

C(aio) Catio L(uci) f(ilio) Maec(ia) / Martiali scribae, / vixit ann(os) XVIII, / L(ucio) Catio C(ai) f(ilio) Severo / patri, / C(aio) Virio C(ai) f(ilio) Fido / avo, / Muciae P(ubli) f(iliae) Quartae / aviae, / *C(aius) Lucretius Genialis* / *amicus* / sibi et / Valeriae uxori // f(aciendum) c(uravit). // tu qui legisti nomina / nostra, vale. (*CIL* 5.7430 = Reali 139C; Libarna, first or second century AD; Figure 12)[105]

To Gaius Catius Martialis the scribe, son of Lucius, of the tribe Maecia, who lived 18 years; to his father Lucius Catius Severus, son of Gaius; to his grandfather Gaius Virius Fidus, son of Gaius; to his grandmother Mucia Quarta, daughter of Publius. Their friend Gaius Lucretius Genialis commissioned this for himself and his wife Valeria. You who have read our names, farewell!

Gaius Lucretius Genialis has commissioned an inscription commemorating his 18-year-old friend Gaius Catius Martialis along with Martialis' father, grandfather, and grandmother, the bonds joining them to Martialis being prominently communicated by the words PATRI, AVO, and AVIAE, each centered in its own line of the inscription. Culminating the series of labels is AMICVS, referring to Genialis himself. There follow the prominent letters F and C to the left and right, abbreviating the formulaic phrase *faciendum curavit*, "saw to its being done"; between them are two lines in smaller, much less prominent letters specifying that Genialis has also included himself in the burial, along with his wife. The inscription carefully specifies that Martialis is a freeborn man, but says nothing about Genialis' own status. If he was a freedman, his name shows that he was not a former slave of the Catius family, but the most salient point is made by the single word *amicus*.

Some epitaphs explicitly note the status of the dedicator as freed slave, such as one from Rome, commissioned by a former slave with the distinctly non-Latin looking name Theuda:

---

[105] The comments on this epitaph at Reali 1997, p. 119, illustrate the subjective nature of more than a few attempts to assign a date to Latin inscriptions: "La grafia elegante e regolare si presta ad una datazione al I/II sec. d.C., non ostandovi l'onomastica dei personaggi: una certa tendenza alla verbosità converrebbe, però, al II."

Figure 12 Epitaph commissioned by Gaius Lucretius Genialis for his 18-year-old
friend Gaius Catius Martialis; Martialis' father, grandfather, and
grandmother; and Genialis himself along with his wife Valeria

C(aius) Fonteius Capitonis [l(ibertus)] / Th[e]uda sibi et / C(aio) Fonteio
Capitonis l(iberto) / Phoenice fratri, / Fonteiae C(ai) et (mulieris) l(ibertae)
Primae / collibertae, / *Nireo amico*, Fonteiae Aethre, / C(aio) Fonteio Montano /
[---] (*CIL* 6.18523; Rome)

Gaius Fonteius Theuda, freedman of Capito, dedicated this to himself; to his brother Gaius Fonteius Phoenix, freedman of Capito; to his fellow-freedwoman Fonteia Prima, freedwoman of Gaius and a woman; to his friend Nireus; to Fonteia Aethre; to Gaius Fonteius Montanus (…)

In others, although status is not made explicit, the names suggest freedman or occasionally even slave status.

D(is) M(anibus). / Phileteni, q(uae) et / Mammeni, coniu/gi incomparabi/li karissimae, / et Hermione fil(iae) / dulcissimae, q(uae) v(ixit) / a(nnos) III m(enses) VI, fecit / et sibi et suis / Hermes, *et* / *T(ito) Iul(io) Achillaeo a/mico.* (*CIL* 6.24103; Rome)[106]

M(arcus) Catius Donatus / v(ivus) f(ecit) sibi et Attiae / Samati(a)e cariss[i]/mae contubern(ali), / Catiae Primigeniae / sorori suae, et / [T]i(berio) Claudio Trophim(o) / (et) Hyacintho, socior(um) / p(ublici) p(ortorii), *amicis suis,* et / posteris / et C(aio) Caecinae / Fidenti. (*CIL* 5.8361 = Reali 17C; Aquileia, first century AD)

D(is) M(anibus). / C(aius) Curtius / Agathemer / VIvir sibi et / Lorei(a)e Prisci/ll(a)e coniugi / mihi carissim(a)e / *et Q(uinto) Cassio* / *Valeriano et* / *Toriae Olympi/di amicis caris.* / loca duo et ceteri/sque meis v(ivus) f(ecit). (*CIL* 5.3395 = Reali 63C; Verona, first/second centuries AD)

To the spirits of the departed. To Philete, also known as Mamme, his incomparable and beloved wife, and to Hermione his darling daughter, who lived 3 years and 6 months. Hermes dedicated this to them and to himself and his own, and to Titus Julius Achillaeus his friend.

Marcus Catius Donatus dedicated this while still alive to himself and to Attia Samatia his dear spouse; to Catia Primigenia his sister; to his friends Tiberius Claudius Trophimus and Hyacinthus, associates in the customs tax office; and to his descendants; and to Gaius Caecina Fidens.

To the spirits of the departed. Gaius Curtius Agathemer the *sevir* [dedicated this] to himself – and to my dearest wife, and two burial places for my dear friends Quintus Cassius Valerianus and Thoria Olympis, and for all my other dependants. He dedicated this while still alive.

Some epitaphs advertise even larger groups, even more generous provision. An impressive inscription from Aquileia announces that Marcus Tullius Anteros, almost certainly a freedman, has dedicated a burial plot to himself and and his friends (*et amicis suis*), whereupon there follows a list of no fewer than twenty names. The first on the list is a woman memorialized as Anteros' conjugal partner (*contubernalis*) and nearly all of the rest

---

[106] To the datives *Phileteni* and *Mammeni* compare the form *Mnemeni*, dative of *Mneme* attested in at least one inscription (Solin 2003, p. 1335).

are explicitly labeled as freedmen or freedwomen: but the freeborn status
of one man and one woman is carefully indicated.[107]

Perhaps slightly less impressive but equally typical is a second-century
AD epitaph found near Brescia:

M(arcus) Terentius / Pyramus / IIIIIIvir aug(ustalis), / *L(ucio) Appio Aphobeto
/ IIIIIIviro aug(ustali) (iterum) / gratuito, amico,* / Terentiae Piste / s[oror]i, /
Messia[e---]cusae / u[xor]i, / *P(ublio) Postumio Primioni,* / *Postumiae Quartae
a(micis) b(ene) m(erentibus).* (*CIL* 5.4480 = Reali 95C; near Brescia, second century AD)

Marcus Terentius Pyramus the *sevir augustalis* [dedicated this] to Lucius Appius
Aphobetus, twice *sevir augustalis,* his friend, as a gift; to his sister Terentia Piste;
to his wife Messi[a] (…)ecusa; and to Publius Postumius Primio and Postumia
Quarta his well-deserving friends.

After the opening self-advertisement comes Aphobetos, the man whom
Pyramus memorializes as his *amicus,* accompanied by the most detailed
set of labels; then come Pyramus' sister and wife, identified as such; and
finally a man and a woman, perhaps a conjugal couple but perhaps not,
whom he likewise memorializes as his *amici.* Names, titles, and labels are
neatly set out, line by line, culminating with the phrase *amicis bene merentibus,* so formulaic that it is abbreviated A.B.M. The inscription configures everyone it mentions in relationship to Pyramus, thus placing him
at the apex of the relationships just as he is literally at the top of the text,
advertising his responsibility and generosity.[108]

An inscription from Padua cited in Chapter 1 announces that Lucius
Cosius Donatus memorializes himself, his wife, two men whom he calls
his *amici* along with their respective wives, two women identified as his
amicae, and three further invididuals (two men and a woman) who are
given no labels at all (*CIL* 5.2937). In an epitaph from Aquileia, a man
commemorates his freeborn mother, and along with her his wife and four
other individuals, three men and a woman, called his *amici intimi.*[109]

---

[107] *Inscr. Aq.*1567 = Reali 33C (Aquileia): *M. Tullius Anteros / locum sepulturae sibi et / amicis suis
dedere, eis qui infr(a) s(cripti) s(unt): / Titiae (mulieris) l(ibertae) Melpomene cont(ubernali)
Anterotis, / T(ito) Betutio T(iti) l(iberto) Karo … / T(ito) Kanio T(iti) f(ilio) Proculo, / Petroniae
L(uci) f(iliae) Procile …*

[108] In the *CIL* entry Mommsen notes that although he inspected the inscription himself, he was
not able to see the two last lines since the bottom of the stone was buried under the floor, but
he rejects the argument that the final lines were invented by earlier transcribers. For epitaphs
explicitly memorializing pairs of individuals both as married couple and as *amici* of the person
who commissioned the inscription, see *CIL* 5.4438 (discussed in Chapter 1), 5.8295, 6.13871.

[109] *CIL* 5.1436 = Reali 35C (Aquileia, perhaps late first century AD): *Sex(tus) Valerius / Valerianus
v(ivus) f(ecit) si[bi] / et Valeriae Sex(ti) f(iliae) Secun[dae] / matri et patronae, / Cossutiae*

Finally, an inscription from Milan reminds us of the limitations on what such texts can tell us.

C(aius) Calventiu[s] / Campanus / sibi et / Cassiae Pollae / coniugi / carissimae /et Calventio Calvo fil(io) / IIIIIIvir(o) iun(iori) / et C(aio) Cassio / Sextilio
amico, / Cassiae Satullae / socerae, / C(aio) Cassio / Masuinni f(ilio) / socero.
(*AE* 1969–1970.201 = Reali 131C; Milan; first century AD)

Gaius Calventius Campanus dedicated this to himself and Cassia Polla his dear wife; to his son Calventius Calvus, junior *sevir*; to his friend Gaius Cassius Sextilius; to his mother-in-law Cassia Satulla and his father-in-law Gaius Cassius, son of Masuinnus.

Reali suggests that Campanus' friendship with Sextilius may have led to his marriage to Sextilius' relative Polla; but it could just as well have been the other way around, that Campanus only came to know Sextilius after having married Polla. We cannot know, and the inscription is not concerned to communicate such information. Instead, it perpetuates the memory of the interconnections between Gaius Calventius Campanus and his wife's family, advertises his own generosity in providing for their commemoration, and uses the language of *amicitia* as it does so.

Type 2b: Freed slaves
Inscriptions of this type make no reference to the dedicators' spouses or children. At the time the inscription was commissioned, perhaps there were none, or perhaps they received commemoration in some other inscription. In any case, such epitaphs have the effect not only of honoring the deceased as worthy of inclusion in one's group, but of memorializing those who commissioned the inscriptions as responsible *patroni* or *patronae* and faithful *amici* and *amicae*. But there is more. Those who dedicated them were setting up and commemorating their own burial group on the basis of something other than marriage and kinship: on the bonds of *amicitia* and those linking former slave to former master. Epitaphs like these in some cases broaden and complicate our views of the kinds of households that could be created and lived in, and in all cases of the burial groups that could be commemorated for posterity in the Latin-speaking world. These burial groups were extended and lasting households that were not structured and, more importantly, not

Ih[-]eni con[iugi] / optimae et amicis inti[mis] / C(aio) Cornelio Aviticiano / Corneliae Fortun[ata]e / et C(aio) Urvinio Abascanto / [...]io Claro [...]. Unusually, Valerianus commemorates Secunda not only as his mother but as his *patrona* or former owner. He was presumably born to her and a male slave, and thus himself a slave at birth who was at some point given his freedom by his mother.

represented, on the basis of the husband–wife–child triad, and the epitaphs bring home the point that those called *amici* and *amicae* were often
prominent members of these groupings. In those cases in which a man
and a woman appear as joint dedicators, we may, if we wish, read them as
conjugal couples, but if so, in most cases we would be reading "between
the lines." The inscriptions commissioned by these pairs communicate
nothing explicitly on the point of their own relationship. Instead, like
the epitaph commissioned by two men, Apollodorus and Dionysius of
Rome (*CIL* 6.25876, see below), such texts memorialize the pair in the
first instance as two individuals who together provided for the burial and
commemoration of friends and dependants.

A few epitaphs of this type commemorate precisely three individuals.
An inscription from Rome announces the threefold commemoration by
the slave Trypho of himself, a woman named Daphne (seemingly another
slave), and a male friend (*amicus*) whose name suggests that he is a freed
slave, but of another former master.[110] Others set up a group of three but
make open-ended provision for descendants and dependants.

D(is) M(anibus). / L(ucius) Baebilius Euryal(us) / et Valeria Lais vivi fec(erunt) /
sibi et libertis liberta/busque suis *et amico* / *Statio Crescenti.* / aditum ad sepul/
crum et unam dio[---] / [---] (*CIL* 3.2245; Salona)

D(is) M(anibus). / C(aius) Vibius Felix et / Claudia Agele / fecer(unt) sibi et suis /
posterisq(ue) eor(um) *et* / *M(arco) Iulio Paulino* / *amico de se b(ene) m(erenti).* / in
fr(onte) p(edes) II s(emissem) in agr(o) p(edes) II s(emissem). / posterisq(ue) eius.
(*CIL* 6.28802; Rome)

To the spirits of the departed. Lucius Baebilius Euryalus and Valeria Lais, still
alive, dedicated this to themselves and their freedmen and freedwomen, and to
their friend Statius Crescens. The approach to the tomb (…)

To the spirits of the departed. Gaius Vibius Felix and Claudia Agele dedicated
this to themselves and their own and their descendants; and to Marcus Julius
Paulinus their well-deserving friend. 2½ feet wide, 2½ feet deep. And to his
descendants.

Most epitaphs of this type commemorate groups of four or more, including a friend or friends along with the dedicators' freedmen and freedwomen. In view of their larger number, it may be helpful to organize
these by the number of dedicators.

Some are commissioned by one person who sometimes identifies his
or her status. In an epitaph from Como, Quintus Secundienus Restitutus

---

[110] *CIL* 6.27687 (Rome): *Trypho Pontiaes (servus) sibi et Dapne et / Q(uinto) Herennio Amarantho
amico. // Rufio sibi et Chloridi et / Aul(a)e filiae, vix(it) an(nis) IV.*

uses a full set of formulae to identify himself as a freeborn Roman citizen and commemorates himself, his parents, and a man who, last on the list and perhaps a freedman – but if so, not of Restitutus himself – is emphatically memorialized as *amicus optimus.*

V(ivus) f(ecit) / Q(uintus) Secundienus Q(uinti) f(ilius) / Ouf(entina) Restitutus / VIvir sibi et / Q(uinto) Secundieno Q(uinti) f(ilio) / Ouf(entina) Restituto / patri VIvir(o) et / Russienae L(uci) f(iliae) / Secundae matri / et / *L(ucio) Publicio Thalamo / amico optimo.* (*AE* 1995.618 = Reali 108C; Como; first–second century AD)

While still alive, Quintus Secundienus Restitutus, son of Quintus, of the tribe Oufillena, sevir, [dedicated this] to himself; and to his father Quintus Secundienus Restitutus, son of Quintus, of the tribe Oufillena, sevir; and to his mother Russiena Secunda, daughter of Lucius; and to Lucius Publicius Thalamus, his excellent friend.

An epitaph from Padua was likewise commissioned by a freeborn man in honor of himself, his freedman and fellow heir, a man to whom he attachs the label *amicus*, and a woman to whom he attaches no label at all. The names of these last two suggest they are former slaves, but the inscription does not make the point explicitly.[111] An epitaph found in Rome was commissioned by a woman – probably a freed slave – named Magnia Tyche, for herself, for three individuals whom she identifies as *carissimi sui* and whose names suggest that they too were freed slaves (two of them perhaps previously belonging to the same owner as Tyche), for her own unspecified freedmen and freedwomen and their descendants, and – in what seems to have been a later addition – to a man and a woman whom she commemorates as her *amici fidelissimi.*[112]

Among other group epitaphs commissioned by individuals, we find Quintus Volusius Victorinus commemorating his parents and two *amici* (a man and a woman); Gaius Erucius Faustus, explicitly commemorating himself as a freedman and memorializing his fellow freedman Oceanus as well as his *amicus* Eros, former slave of another master; a freedman named Agathemerus commemorating himself along with his *amicus bonus* Hermia (freed slave of another master), Philodamus (former slave of

---

[111] *CIL* 5.2844 = Reali 57C (Padua, second century AD): *V(ivus) f(ecit) / L(ucius) Aelius L(uci) f(ilius) / Fab(ia) Macer / VIvir sibi et / L(ucio) Aelio Antigon(o) / lib(erto) consorti / et P(ublio) Saltio Mystico / amico, / Saltiae Euthy/ciae. / h(oc) m(onumentum) h(eredem) n(on) s(equetur).*

[112] *CIL* 6.21852 (Rome): *D(is) M(anibus). / Magnia Tyche fecit sibi / et karis(simis) suis T(ito) Magnio Ani/ceto et T(ito) Magnio Euthycho et / Q(uinto) Tillio Figuliano bene merenti/bus, / et libertis libertabusque pos/terisque eorum. h(uic) m(onumento) d(olus) m(alus) a(besto). / item Ti(berio) Claudio Honorato et Claudiae / Marcellae / amicis fidelissimis. vasa obrendaria dua ite<m> / ol(l) iaria tria introeuntibus parte dexteri/ore fecit et donavit.*

Hermia's own master), and his own freed slave Iucundus; and a freedman named Quadratus commemorating himself, his own freedwoman Grata, and two other freed slaves whom he memorializes as his *amici*.[113] In an epitaph from Rome Gaius Clodius Euphemus memorializes Lucius Agrius Fortunatus as his *optimus et sanctissimus amicus*, along with Vitulus and Fortunata, two *alumni* or slaves whom he raised as his foster-children. In an indirect glimpse at the varieties of household structures that could arise in conjunction with slavery and manumission, the nomenclature suggests that they were not Euphemus' slaves but Fortunatus', and that Euphemus and Fortunatus themselves were former slaves.[114] Commemorating an even larger group is an an inscription cited in Chapter 1, in which a freedman of the emperor who had held the office *a cura amicorum* generously provides for and commemorates three other imperial freedmen (one woman and two men), an imperial slave who had not been freed, his own formulaically open-ended freedmen and freedwomen and their descendants, and two other individuals – a man and a woman whose names show that they were not imperial freedmen or slaves – as his *amici* (*CIL* 6.8799).

Among group epitaphs commissioned jointly by two individuals, those commissioned by male–female pairs in some cases may *imply* conjugal bonds between the two, but they usually do not memorialize themselves as such, but rather in their role of *amici* to the departed. In an inscription from Aquiliea, a man and a woman jointly commemorate a male friend along with a 1-year-old infant who may well have been their child, yet they do not memorialize that fact or place any label on their relationship.

T(itus) Vettidius / Cladus et / Octavia Cn(aei) l(iberta) / Italia / vivi fecerunt / sibi et suis l(ibertis) l(ibertabusque). / Ampliatus anniculus / et dier(um) VII / hic situs est. / et C(aio) Dindio Zenonis / lib(erto) Ianuario / amico. / loc(us) moni(menti) q(uo)q(uo)ver(sus) / ped(es) XXII. (*Inscr. Aq.* 1618 = Reali 37C; Aquileia, first century AD)

Titus Vettidius Cladus and Octavia Italia, freedwoman of Gnaeus, while still alive dedicated this to themselves and their freedmen and freedwomen. Ampliatus, just one year old and 7 days, is buried here. Also dedicated to their friend Gaius Dindius Januarius, freedman of Zeno. The tomb reaches 22 feet in each direction.

---

[113] *CIL* 6.24097 (Rome); *CIL* 10.2389 = *AE* 1980.234 = *AE* 1988.338 (Pozzuoli, first century AD); *CIL* 5.6059 (Milan); *CIL* 5.5850 (Milan).

[114] *CIL* 6.17369 (Rome): *C(aius) Clodius Euphemus / L(ucio) Agrio [F]ortunato / optimo et sanctissimo amico / et L(ucio) Agrio Vitulo et / Agriae Fortunatae / alumnis suis / karissimis, sibiq(ue) et / suis posterisque eorum s(upra) s(cripti) / sunt, lib(ertis) libertabusq(ue) / eorum omnium q(ui) s(upra) s(cripti) s(unt).*

The language of the epitaph in itself communicates nothing more about the relationship between Cladus and Italia than does the following, commissioned by two men whose names suggest that they may have been freed slaves of the same master.

V(ivi) f(ecerunt). D(is) M(anibus). / C(ai) Satri Apollodorus et / Dionysius sibi et / Pontiae Saturninae / piae sanctae fideli(ssimae) castissimae et / libertis libertabusque suis / posterisque eorum et / Pontiaes Saturninaes libertis / libertabusque eius posterisque eorum, *et / Piritheo amico bono* c[...]a[...]oii[...]co. (*CIL* 6.25876; Rome)

Dedicated while they were still alive. To the spirits of the departed. Gaius Satrius Apollodorus and Gaius Satrius Dionysius to themselves; and to Pontia Saturnina, devoted, respectable, faithful and chaste; and to their freedmen and freedwomen and their descendants; and to the freedmen and freedwomen of Pontia Saturnina and their descendants; and to their good friend Piritheus (...)

Here too we find teasing glimpses at networks and possibly even household structures. Apollodorus and Dionysius commemorate no wives or children, but rather a woman to whose name they attach an impressive series of honorific epithets: *piae sanctae fidelissimae castissimae.* They do not call her their former owner (*patrona*) and indeed their names suggest that their former owner was named Gaius Satrius. Was Pontia his wife? Or did Apollodorus and Dionysius include her, along with their friend Piritheus, in their own burial group for other reasons, inaccessible to us? Finally, an epitaph from Ostia shows that such inscriptions could even be commissioned by *three* individuals. The slaves Callinice, Trophimus, and Eleutheris dutifully record their master's name (Caecilius Victor) as they commemorate themselves and their descendants along with two individuals whose names suggest they were freed slaves: Aurelia Euphrosyne, memorialized as their sister (*sorori piissimae*), and Valerius Eutychus, memorialized as their friend (*amico optimo*).[115]

Type 2c: Freed slaves, spouse, children, and/or kin

Some epitaphs memorialize friends as part of a larger group, usually including the dedicators themselves, and interweaving the two kinds of relationship informing the epitaphs we have reviewed above. The dedicators, many of them former slaves themselves, commemorate their spouses and friends along with their own freed slaves. Some of these memorialize

---

[115] *ISOstiense* 120: *si qu(i)s hoc mo[numentum ven]/dider(it) aut do[no deder(it) in]/fer(et) aer(ario) popul[i---] // D(is) M(anibus). / Aureliae E[u]phrosy/n(a)e sorori piissimae / et Valerio Eutycho / amico optimo fece/runt Callinice et Tro/phimus et Eleutheris / Caecili Victoris servi, / et sibi posterisq(ue) suorum.*

the individuals by name, using the formula *libertis libertabusque posterisque eorum* to potentially open up the group to further dependants and their descendants. In an epitaph from Rome we find a woman commemorating, first, her female friend, and then her husband and herself:

Dis Manibus. / Sergia Marcella / fecit *Flaviae Proc(u)lae* / *amicae pientissimae* / et Flavio Theodoro / coniugi suo, et sibi et suis, / libertis libertabusque / posterisque eorum. (*CIL* 6.26337; Rome)

To the spirits of the dead. Sergia Marcella dedicated this to Flavia Procula her devoted friend and to Flavius Theodorus her own husband; to herself and her own; to her freedmen and freedwomen and their descendants.

Another from Rome contains two distinct commemorations, the second of them announcing that a woman has purchased the plot for herself, her husband, and a male friend (*amico carissimo*).[116] Among epitaphs commissioned by men, we find some in which the dedicator commemorates himself, his wife, and a male friend, adding formulae providing for descendants and/or freed dependants.

L(ucius) Sestius / Sotericus sibi / et Sestiae Priscae / collibertae et / coniugi suae bene / merenti, cum qua / vixit annis XXX, / de qua nihil doluit / nisi morte. / et *T(ito) Titio Basso amico* / *suo*, homini optimo / et singularis exempli. / et libertis libertabusque / suis posterisque eoru(m). / in fronte p(edes) XII in agro p(edes) XII. (*CIL* 6.26467a; Rome)

Lucius Sestius Sotericus [dedicated this] to himself; to his fellow-freedwoman and well-deserving wife Sestia Prisca, with whom he lived for 30 years, suffering no grief from her except when she died; and to his friend Titus Titius Bassus, an excellent man of unique character; and to his freedmen and freedwomen and their descendants. 12 feet wide, 12 feet deep.

In an inscription from Ostia commemorating this configuration we find the addition of a clause specifically prohibiting the kind of subsequent additions to the burial group that we have seen in the Cocceius complex in the nearby Isola Sacra necropolis.

M(arcus) Aurelius Secundus fecit / sibi et Iuliae Aphrodite / coniugi suae carissimae / et *Aurelio Romano amico* / *suo*, libertis libertabusque pos/terisque eorum. si quis autem / post obitum nostrum extra/nium corpus inferre voluerit, da/vit aerari(o) populi sestertia (quinquaginta milia) n(umero). / in fronte p(edes) n(umero) XV, in agro p(edes) n(umero) XIII. (*CIL* 14.667 = Reali 7It; Ostia)

---

[116] *CIL* 6.15299 (Rome): *D(is) M(anibus)* / *Scantia* / *Venusta emit* / *sibi et Scantio* / *Proto coniugi suo* / *et Ti(berio) Claudio* / *Regillo amico* / *carissimo. intrantibus* / *parte dexteriore dimidia.* / *libertis libertabusque* / *posterisque eorum.*

Marcus Aurelius Secundus dedicated this to himself, to his dear wife Julia Aphrodite, to his friend Aurelius Romanus, and to his freedmen and freedwomen and their descendants. If after our decease anyone should bring in a body that does not belong here, he will pay fifty thousand sesterces to the public treasury. Fifteen feet across, thirteen feet deep.

The appeal to a notion of "belonging" implicit in the phrase *extraneum corpus* was no doubt open to interpretation.

Among epitaphs honoring commemorative groups of four or more named individuals, we find some that were jointly commissioned by two people. In one, a man and woman commemorate their son (*filio dulcissimo*) along with a male friend of theirs (*amico optimo*).[117] Another, in honor of Viria Vitalis, was jointly commissioned by her husband and her father, who – in words that may have been added later – also commemorate a man named Gaius Virius Argaeus as *amicus optimus*. Whether this communicates that he was the friend of Viria herself, of her father, of her husband, or of any or all of them is not clear, but what is clear is that the epitaph ends with an evocation of *amicitia*.[118] Most commemorations of groups larger than three, however, were commissioned by individuals; as usual, both male and female, freeborn and freed. Among epitaphs commissioned by women we find one in which Publicia Alexandria commemorates herself, her two sons, and a male friend (*amico carissimo*); one in which Quintilia Fortunata commemorates herself, her daughter, a former slave of the same master (*conliberto*), and a female friend (*amicae carissimae*); and one in which Octavia Faustina commemorates herself, her son Pomponius Faustinus, her *filiaster* (stepson or illegitimate son) Sextus Cornelius Verus, and Verecundus her *amicus incomparabilis*.[119] In an epitaph found at Arles, Valeria Urbana commemorates herself in her role as priestess, along with her husband, a female friend, and one of her freedwomen. The words are laid out on the stone such that the labels (VIRO, AMICAE, and LIBERTAE) pile up on the viewer's right, on one side of a relief portrait of the deceased.

[117] *CIL* 6.38683 (Rome): *D(is)* / *M(anibus)*. / *in* / *f(ronte)* / *p(edes)* / *III* / *in* / *a(gro)* / *p(edes)* / *III.* // *C(aius) Octavius Secundus* / *et Aemil(i)a Eutycis C(aio) Oc/tavio Sabino f(ilio) dulci/ssimo qui v(ixit) an(nos) III m(enses) V, / et C(aio) Fabio Maximo ami(co)* / *opt(imo) et sibi et suis pos/terisque suis lib(ertis) libertabusq(ue).*

[118] *CIL* 6.29027 (Rome): *D(is) M(anibus).* / *Viriae Vitali fecerunt* / *L(ucius) Larsinius Sabinus* / *con-iugi karissimae* / *et pientissimae et* / *C(aius) Virius Successus pater.* / *quae vix(it) ann(os) XXXVII m(enses) VIII d(ies) XIX.* / *et sibi et suis lib(ertis) lib(ertabus) poster(is)q(ue) eor(um) et* / *C(aio) Virio Argaeo amico optimo.*

[119] *CIL* 6.25147 (Publicia Alexandria), 6.25287 (Quintilia Fortunata), 6.23342 (Octavia Faustina, who seems to be communicating that she had been married twice, but neither husband is named). For *filiaster* see Watson 1989, Friedl 1996, p. 147.

Valeria Urbana antistis sibi / et Sex(to) Mantio / Eroti viro / *et Octaviae Hilarae amicae* / et Charidi libertae. (*CIL* 12.708; Arles)

Valeria Urbana the priestess dedicated this to herself, and to Sextus Mantius Eros her husband, and to Octavia Hilara her friend, and to Charis her freedwoman.

And a first-century AD epitaph from Novara cited in Chapter 1 was commissioned by a freedwoman and records her commemoration of as many as eleven individuals (*CIL* 5.6516 = Reali 136C; Figure 4). Among epitaphs commissioned by men we find Gaius Purellius Papia, who had held the office of *augustalis* at Allifae, commemorating himself, his *concubina*, a colleague, and a male friend (*amico*); Titus Flavius Daphnus commemorating a female slave named Prima who died at the age of 12, along with himself, his wife Euphrosyne, a male relative (*cognatus*) named Lucius Laberius Hermes, and his friend Cassia Synethe (*amicae optimae*); the freedman Marcus Satrius Valens commemorating himself, his wife, son, daughter, and a male friend (*amico*); the freeborn Lucius Mettius Primus, trumpeter in the army, commemorating himself along with his wife and daughter, one of his freedwomen, his friend (*amico*) Campester, freed slave of another man, and the freeborn Gaius Domitius Raptus, to whom no relational label is attached; the freeborn soldier Gaius Apponius Novellus commemorating himself along with his wife and two sons and his friend (*amico*) Tiberius Julius Onager, who lived 47 years; Sextus Valerius Alcides commemorating himself, his wife, three *amici*, and three former slaves, one of them identified as his special favorite (*delicata*).[120]

One inscription from the city of Rome naming four individuals and datable to the third century AD is of interest for its explicit exclusion of an individual by name – not unparalleled, but fairly rare in surviving epitaphs. It begins by announcing the commemoration of Marcus Antonius Encolpius, his wife Cerellia Fortunata, and his freedman Athenaeus, along with the formulaic freedmen and freedwomen, but then explicitly excludes Encolpius' son Athenio, who is forbidden any and all access to the tomb or burial within it. Penalties are even laid down for anyone who in the future should attempt to bury Athenio or any of his descendants here. Why? As in Phileros of Pompeii's second inscription, a drama is hinted at, but details are spare: "Because he denied that I was his father after having done me much wrong." On the other hand, Aulus Laelius

---

[120] *CIL* 9.2368 (Gaius Purellius Papia; Allifae), 6.18404 = 6.25029 (Titus Flavius Daphnus; Rome), *Inscriptiones Latinae quae in Iugoslavia repertae et editae sunt* 2.682 (Marcus Satrius Valens; Salona), *CIL* 11.1218 (Lucius Mettius Primus; Piacenza), 6.2902 (Gaius Apponius Novellus; Rome), 5. 2180 (Sextus Valerius Alcides; Altinum).

Apelles, Encolpios' *cliens carissimus* who stood by him "in such a catastrophe," may choose any sarcophagus he wishes; and, after a Greek poem denying the existence of the traditional Underworld (there is no ferryman Charon, no river to cross, no three-headed Cerberus) this remarkable epitaph ends with some slightly jumbled Latin prose reiterating Apelles' name, reasserting his right to burial, and, in the text's final two words, memorializing him as *amicus optimus*.[121]

Type 2d: Former masters

In the preceding inscriptions, men and women provide for and memorialize the burial of their friends along with their freed slaves, often in the company of the dedicator's spouse, children, or other kin. But we find the bond created by manumission commemorated in the other direction as well. Here, as with Vesonius Phileros' tomb from Pompeii, it is the freed slave who commemorates a friend or friends in the company of his or her former owner (*patronus, patrona*) and often others, related to him or her by kinship or marriage, or sometimes commemorated as his or her fellow freed slaves.

Among those including the dedicator's spouse is one from Alba Fucens in which Aulus Nonius Obsequens commemorates himself, his wife, his patron, and a man he prominently memorializes both as a freeborn citizen and as his *amicus optimus*.

L(ucio) Oblicio L(uci) f(ilio) Pal(atina) Fauno / IIIIvir(o) aed(ili) amico optimo, / A(ulo) Nonio A(uli) f(ilio) Fab(ia) Rufo IIIIvir(o) i(ure) d(icundo) patron(o), / A(ulus) Nonius Opsequens VIvir aug(ustalis) sibi et / Manliae Lupercae coniugi fecit. (CIL 9.3942; Alba Fucens)

To Lucius Oblicius Faunus, son of Lucius, of the tribe Palatina, *quattuorvir* and aedile, excellent friend; and to Aulus Nonius Rufus, son of Aulus, of the tribe Fabia, *quattuorvir iure dicundo* and patron. Aulus Nonius Opsequens, *sevir augustalis*, dedicated this to himself and to Manlia Luperca his wife.

An inscription from Como announces Gaius Plinius Calvus' commemoration of himself, his wife, his son and daughter, son-in-law, grandson, former owners (a man and a woman), brother, and finally an *amicus*. The relationships are carefully laid out, the respective labels coming at the

---

[121] *CIL* 6.14672: ... *ideo quia me pos(t) multas iniurias parentem sibi a<b>negaverit. / et A(ulo) L<a>elio Apeliti clienti karissimo. quem <v>oluerit do<n>ationis causa sarcofa/gum eligat sibi, (pr) opter quod in tam ma(g)na clade non me reliquerit, cuius beneficia (h)abeo... / Olo Lelio Apelleti uno sarc{h}ofago. itum ambitum habere de<b>e<bi>t.* amico optimo. See Lazzarini 1991, pp. 20–21. Another example of an exclusion by name comes from the Isola Sacra necropolis: *libertis libertabusque poste / risque eorum, praeter Panara / tum et Prosdocia(m)* (Helttula 133).

end of the lines, the last of them being AMICO alone.[122] An even larger group is commemorated by Publius Laelius Lucifer in an epitaph found at Interocrium (today Antrodoco) in Latium. He memorializes himself, his 23-year-old son, two wives (one freeborn, one a former slave), one of his freedwomen, a stepson, and finally a friend (*amico optimo*), former slave of another master.[123] Among epitaphs commissioned by freedwomen, we find two fragmentary inscriptions from Milan: one in which a Novellia commemorates herself, her former owner, her husband, and a woman she identifies as her *amica*, along with some others whom we can no longer identify; and another in which Plinia Donata commemorates, among others, her patron, her children, and Gaius Publicius Italus, her *amicus*.[124]

Others, like that commissioned by Phileros of Pompeii, make no mention of a spouse, though some of them commemorate sons and daughter. An inscription from Aquileia datable to the mid-first century AD and commissioned by the freedwoman Betutia Fusca commemorates herself, her former owner (a veteran from Vienne in southern France), another former slave of the same owner, and a man named Marcus Salvius Primus whom she identifies as her *amicus*.[125] An inscription from Rome begins as the epitaph for a 4-year-old child, and proceeds to announce that it was commissioned by the child's mother in honor not only of her son but also of her patron and a male friend.

Vix(it) an(nis) IV / men(sibus) IV. / D(is) M(anibus) / M(arci) Turrani Benedicti / fecit Turrania / Onesime mater et sibi et / M(arco) Turranio Secundo / patrono suo de se b(ene) m(erenti) / et suis libertis liberta/busq(ue) posterisq(ue) eor(um)

[122] *CIL* 5.5300 (Como): *V(ivus) f(ecit) / C(aius) Plinius / Calvos VIvir / sibi et Plinis / Successae uxori, / Chrysiadi et / Successori f(iliis), / L(ucio) Casticio L(uci) f(ilio) Ouf(entina) / Catullo IIIIvir(o) / aed(ilicia) pot(estate) genero, / L(ucio) Casticio L(uci) f(ilio) Ouf(entina) / Maximo nepot(i), / Plinis Tharsae et / Verecundae pat(ronis), / Plinio Cerdoni fr(atri), / Plinio Phaenomen(i) / amico.*

[123] *CIL* 9.4653 (Interocrium): *P(ublius) Laelius Lucifer sibi et / P(ublio) Laelio P(ubli) f(ilio) Entello, vixit an(nos) XXIIII, / Egnatiae C(ai) f(iliae) Megisteni coniugi, / Antistiae L(uci) l(ibertae) Sabinae coniugi, / Laeliae P(ubli) l(ibertae) Atticeni Laeli Entelli, / C(aio) Egnatio Cereali filiastro, / C(aio) Albio C(ai) l(iberto) Diadumeno amico optimo, / posterisq(ue) suis fecit. / in agro p(edes) XXXVI in fr(onte) p(edes) XVIII. h(oc) m(onumentum) h(eredem) non s(equetur).* For *filiaster* see above, n. 119.

[124] *CIL* 5.6054 (Milan): *V(iva) f(ecit) / Novellia / [---]noe sibi et / memoriae / [---] Novelli Agilis / patroni opt(imi) et / [---] Novelli Euhodi / mariti opt(imi) et / [---]Iuniae Myrtil[---] / amic(ae) opt(imae), Domi[---] / [---] Agili[---];* *CIL* 5.6068 = Reali 123C (Milan, second century AD): *[Q(uinto) Plinio --- et] / [Pliniae Q(uinti) fil(iae)] / Secundae / et Pliniae Q(uinti) f(iliae) Maxima[e], / Plinia Q(uinti) l(iberta) Donata / patrono idem viro / et fili(i)s suis / et C(aio) Poblicio [It]alo / amico.*

[125] *AE* 1988.583 = Reali 39C (Aquileia, mid-first century AD): *Betutia Sex(ti) l(iberta) Fusca / v(iva) f(ecit) sibi et / Sex(to) Betutio Sex(ti) f(ilio) Vol(tinia) / Vianna, patrono sig(nifero) / leg(ionis) VIIII, vet(erano), et / Sex(to) Betutio Sex(ti) l(iberto) Secundo conlib(erto) / et M(arco) Salvio Primo amico.*

et / *M(arco) Lollio Athenagorae* / *amico fidelissimo* / in [---m(ensibus)---] III
d(iebus) III. (*CIL* 6.27799; Rome)

He lived 4 years and 4 months. To the spirit of Marcus Turranius Benedictus.
Turrania Onesime his mother dedicated this to him and to herself, and to Marcus
Turranius Secundus her patron, who treated her well, and to her own freedmen
and freedwomen and their descendants, and to Marcus Lollius Athenagoras her
faithful friend ... 3 months and 3 days.

Among those commissioned by men, an epitaph from Milan announces
the freedman Acceptus' commemoration of himself, his former owner, a
fellow-freedman of the same master, and a friend named Gaius Lucilius
Florus.[126] An inscription from Aquileia datable to the first half of the first
century AD was commissioned by a man and a woman in honor of their
patron, their daughter, two women who seem to have been their own
former slaves, and in the midst of them a man whom they memorialize –
even before his death – as their *amicus*.[127] Peculiarly touching because of
its awkward lettering and lapses in grammar is an epitaph from Rome,
datable to the Republican period, in which the freedman Salvius proclaims that he has commissioned the epitaph at his own expense for his
former owner Gaius Lollius Phileros (himself a former slave), for Salvius
himself, and for four others who are carefully identified both as freedmen
and freedwomen and as his *amici*.

C(aius) Lol(l)ius C(ai) l(ibertus) Pileros. / C(aius) Lol(l)ius C(ai) l(ibertus)
Salvius / libertus de sua / pecunia faciund(um)/ coeravit patron(o) / et sibi *ami-
cisque:* / *Volminia (mulieris) l(iberta) Salvia,* / *Galio M(arci) l(iberto) Euclida, Galia
(sic)* / *M(arci) l(iberto) H<e>dylo, Popnia Q(uinti) l(iberta) Fausta.* / in fr(onte)
p(edes) XVI, in ag(ro) p(edes) XX. (*CIL* 6.21470; Rome)

Gaius Lollius Phileros, freedman of Gaius. Gaius Lollius Salvius, freedman of
Gaius, a freedman, commissioned this at his own expense for his patron and for
himself, and for his friends: Volminia Salvia, freedwoman of a woman, Galius
Euclides, freedman of Marcus, Galius Hedylos, freedman of Marcus, Popnia
Fausta, freedwoman of Quintus. 16 feet wide, 20 feet deep.

A funerary monument displayed in the amphitheater in Capua but
reported as coming from S. Angelo in Formis combines a relief sculpture

---

[126] *CIL* 5.6100 (Milan): *V(ivus) f(ecit)* / *M(arcus) Sulpicius M(arci) l(ibertus)* / *Acceptus* / *sibi et* /
M(arco) Sulpicio Acasto / *patrono,* / *Eroti Cinnamo* / *conlibertis patroni,* / *et* / *C(aio) Lucilio Floro*
amico.

[127] *Inscr. Aq.* 587 = Reali 20C (Aquileia, first half of first century AD): *Sex(to) Caesernio* / *Libano*
patron(o) / *Sex(tus) Caesernius Cedrus* / *IIIIIIvir et* / *Caesernia Sex(ti) l(iberta) Prima v(ivi)*
f(ecerunt), / *Caeserniae Iridi f(iliae),* / *Caeserniae Iucundae v(ivae),* / *L(ucio) Plancio Antae amico*
v(ivo), / *S[ex(to) Ca]esernio Diodoto conlib(erto) v(ivo),* / *C[a]eserniae Venustae lib(ertae) v(ivae),* /
l(ibertis) l(ibertabus)q(ue) suis.

of four persons – two men on the left, wearing togas, and on the right a man in a toga joining his right hand with that of a woman in a veil – with an inscription. Sculpture and inscription tell two related but slightly different stories. The sculpture group communicates that four people are being commemorated, all of them Roman citizens; the combination of *dextrarum iunctio* and veil signals that the couple at the right are husband and wife; the other two men might be friends, relatives, or patrons. The inscription surrounding the sculpture group names not four but five individuals:

[*above the sculpture group*] M(arco) Equitio / M(arci) l(iberto) Primo // M(arco) Equitio / M(arci) l(iberto) Hilaro // M(arco) Equitio / M(arci) M(arci) l(iberto) Dardano // Cassiae M(arci) [l(ibertae?)] / Rufae.

[*below the sculpture group*] Primus l(ibertus) patro(no) suo et sibi et sueis *et* / P(ublio) Aulio (mulieris) l(iberto) Secundo amico fecit. (*AE* 1989.161 = *AE* 1994.428 = *AE* 2002.+265; Capua, early first century AD)

To Marcus Equitius Primus, freedman of Marcus. To Marcus Equitius Hilarus, freedman of Marcus. To Marcus Equitius Dardanus, freedman of Marcus and Marcus. To Cassia Rufa, freedwoman of Marcus.

Primus the freedman erected this for his patron, for himself and his own, and for his friend Publius Aulius Secundus, freedman of a woman.

For those who can read the words, the alignment of the first four names above the respective sculptures identifies the two men on the left as Primus and Hilarus, both of them freed slaves of a Marcus Equitius, and the married couple as Dardanus (former slave who had been jointly owned by two men named Marcus Equitius – most obviously, Primus and Hilarus themselves) and Rufa (former slave of a certain Marcus Cassius). The text below the sculpture adds a fifth name, announcing that Primus has dedicated this monument to "his and his own" and to his former master – not, however, specifying which Marcus Equitius that is – and also to Secundus, freedman of a woman named Aulia, whom Primus includes in the group and memorializes as his *amicus*.[128]

Type 3: Unnamed friends

Some epitaphs make open-ended provision for unnamed *amici* in conjunction with burial groups of various sizes and types.

---

[128] D'Isanto 1994, p. 186, asserts that Dardanus is the *patronus* of Primus and Hilarus without giving reasons, but perhaps on the basis of the fact that in the text underneath the sculpture, *Primus* and *patrono* align with the first two statues. In an earlier publication D'Isanto had interpreted the two figures on the left to be children and had not taken account of the second part of the inscription.

A(ulus) Terentius A(uli) l(ibertus) / Antiochus sibi / *et amicis sueis*. (*CIL* 6.27161; Rome)

Locum C(ai) Calvisi / Bacchi. sibi et / fratri *et amicis*. (*CIL* 6.14275; Rome)

V(ivus) f(ecit) / C(aius) Arrius C(ai) f(ilius) / Optatus / sibi et suis / et / C(aio) Arrio C(ai) f(ilio) / Clementi / filio suo et / T(ito) Saufeio M(arci) f(ilio) / *et amicis et* / *sodalibus* / *carpentari(i)s*. / v(ir) d(evotus). / in f(ronte) p(edes) XXXXI / ret(ro) p(edes) XXXXX. (*AE* 1927.129; Padova)

C(aius) Laecanius Simon[i]s lib(ertus) Catagraphus sibi et suis, / Laecaniae Prophasi coniugi, Laecaniae Ephyre [f(iliae)] et lib(ertae), / Gra[p]te fil(iae) et Tryphaenae fil(iae), Rhodope f(iliae), / Heo fil(io), Hedynoe fil(iae), Sulpiciae Damale / Tryph(a)enae matri meae, Diogeni fratr[i] meo, / *et amicis caris(simis) meis*. qui volent hoc venire / suo quisque die, veniant et requiescant. (*CIL* 5.182 = Reali 4C; Pula, probably second century AD)[129]

Aulus Terentius Antiochus, freedman of Aulus, to himself and his friends.

The plot of Gaius Calvisius Bacchus. For himself, his brother, and his friends.

While still alive, Gaius Arrius Optatus, son of Gaius, dedicated this to himself and his own, and to his son Gaius Arrius Clemens, son of Gaius, and to Titus Saufeius, son of Marcus, and to his friends and carpenter colleagues. A dutiful man. 41 feet wide, 50 feet deep.

Gaius Laecanius Catagraphus, freedman of Simon, [dedicated this] to himself and to his own; to Laecania Prophasis his wife, to Laecania Ephyre his daughter and freedwoman, to Grapte his daughter and Tryphaena his daughter, to Rhodope his daughter, to Heos his son, to Hedynoe his daughter, to Sulpica Damale Tryphaena my mother, to Diogenes my brother, and to my dear friends. Those who wish to come here, each on their appointed day, shall come and rest.

Epitaphs like these raise some important and only partially answerable questions. Since there was no legally recognized act or verifiable fact of birth or status that defined an individual as someone's *amicus*, anyone who claimed to have been the dedicator's friend could theoretically claim to be covered by such inscriptions and thus to have the right to a burial place within the accompanying complexes.[130]

---

[129] The shift from third person (*sibi et suis*) to first person (*matri meae*) finds parallels in a number of inscriptions. For the final provision, see Reali 1997, p. 30, and Lazzarini 1991, p. 23.

[130] One way of regulating the matter, however loosely, is hinted at by the provision in *CIL* 6.21808 from Rome: *Maesius Hylas* / *sibi et suis,* / *lib(ertis) libertabusq(ue) eorum, et amicis* / *set degnis*. Whether *sed* is restrictive ("but only the deserving ones") or intensive ("the really worthy ones"), this seems to be granting a right of approval (or refusal) to the person or persons who inherited legal control over the tomb: see Lazzarini 1991, p. 22 with n. 44.

Type 4: Friends at the center

That two or even three people might be commemorated at the center of a burial group whose membership will grow with time is a message communicated by many epitaphs, and the configurations of that core vary. Most frequent are married couples (in one inscription we read of two married couples together),[131] and pairs joined by bonds of kinship are by no means uncommon. A second- or third-century AD Latin epitaph from Dalmatia with accompanying portrait busts of two women commemorates them as Aurelia Marcellina and her 18-year-old daughter Marcella, buried along with Marcellina's unnamed descendants.[132] Sometimes the inscription specifies no relationship at all. A late second-century AD epitaph found at Mentana, commissioned by three men whose names suggest that they were freed slaves but of three different owners, places them at the center of a burial group consisting of their descendants, freedmen, and freedwomen. While the three men may well have been friends, their epitaph but places no label on their relationship.[133]

The bond of *amicitia* is named in some group epitaphs of this type, although the deceased are not themselves commemorated as each other's friends. An epitaph from Rome announces that Publius Aelius Epaphroditus has set up a tomb for himself along with two sons of unnamed friends (*amicorum filiis*) – the nomenclature suggests they were all slaves and freedmen of the same man or family – along with *their* descendants, not his.[134] In a late first-century AD inscription found near a catacomb along the via Appia, Tiberius Julius Nepos, who had married into the family of the Statilii (whose slaves and freedmen were buried in the columbarium discussed above), commemorates himself, his freedmen

---

[131] Among many examples of married couples at the center of groups (*et suis*; *et posteris*; *libertis libertabusque*) see, from Ostia alone, *CIL* 14.849, 1153, 1157, 1318; for two couples together, see *CIL* 14.1232 (Portus).

[132] *AE* 1994.1362 (Delminium in Dalmatia, late second/early third century AD, with portrait busts of two women): *D(is) M(anibus). / Aur(elia) Marcel/lina mater / Aur(eliae) Marcel/lae fil(iae) pientis/simae defunc/tae ann(orum) XVIII, / sibi et post(eris) / suis p(osuit)*.

[133] *AE* 1986.60 (Mentana, late second century AD): *D(is) M(anibus). / L(ucius) Sempronius Demetrius / et C(aius) Allius Stefan<u>s et / Aurelius Crescentio fe/cerunt sibi et suis libertis libertabus/que posterisque eorum*.

[134] Three men are named and the possibility of others is raised, yet an accompanying Greek phrase underscores that "two people lie here": two young men commemorated by a man who memorializes himself as their fathers' friend. *CIL* 6.34234 (Rome): *D(is) M(anibus) / P(ublio) Aelio Epaphrodito vix(it) / ann(os) XXV et P(ublio) Aelio / [Epaphro?]ditiano vix(it) / ann(os) XX. fec(it) / P(ublius) Aelius / Epaphroditus / amicorum fili(i)s / carissimis et sibi p(osterisque) eor(um). / [ἐν τῷ]δε τόπῳ κεῖνται δύο*.

and freedwomen, along with the freedmen and freedwomen of his wife –
but also his friend (*amicus dulcissimus*) Gaius Julius Hilarus along with
the latter's freedmen and freedwomen: a broad sweep and generous statement on Nepos' part.[135] A third-century AD epitaph from Parma commissioned by Gaius Valerius Aeclanius marks the burial of three women
whose names suggest they were former slaves, but not of the same owners;
the only relationship given a label is that between Aeclanius and the third
of the three women, commemorated as his *amica*.[136]

Sometimes, however, we find friendship at the very center of the commemorative group, in epitaphs which communicate that two or more
individuals, joined to each other by *amicitia* and nothing more (or
less), are sharing a tomb. An inscription from Rome quoted in Chapter
1 announces Agrilia Piste's commemoraton of herself and three female
friends.

Agrilia Piste, quae et / Pompusidia, f(ecit) *Valeriae / Trophime et Vi(c)toriae /
Erotario et Muciae / Ianuariae amicabus / optimis*, et sibi et / posterisq(ue) eorum.
(*CIL* 6.7671; Rome, second century AD)

Agrilia Piste, also called Pompusidia, dedicated this to Valeria Trophima,
Victoria Erotarion, and Mucia Januaria her excellent friends, and to herself, and
to their descendants.

These four women, whose names suggest that they were freed slaves
of four different masters, are not alone. The provision for descendants
leaves open the possibility that any or all of them have, or might some
day have, children and perhaps husbands too, but the primary message
of the inscription is loud and clear: Agrilia Piste, like Marcus Cocceius
Daphnus of the Isola Sacra necropolis (above, p. 269), is setting herself up
as the basis of an open-ended burial group at the center of which she herself lies in the company of three other women. But unlike Daphnus, who
puts no label on his relationships with Agathias and Domitus, in this text
which she has had carved into stone Piste names the bond which joins her
to Trophime, Erotarion, and Januaria as *amicitia*.

---

[135] *CIL* 6.20149: *D(is) M(anibus) / Ti(berius) Iulius Nepos se vibus conparav/it sibi et suis libert(is)
liberta(bus) posterisq(ue) / eorum itemque et Statiliis liberti(s) / libertabus co(n)iugis suae quond/am
et C(aio) Iulio Hilaro amico dulcissi/mo et liber(tis) liberta(bus) eius in portion/e locorum duorum et
iud{e}ici sicu(t) / donationi ei factae continetur*. See Caldelli and Ricci 1999, appendix 3, n. 38.

[136] *CIL* 11.1101 = 1114: *C(aius) Valer/ius Aeclan/ius posuit. / D(is) M(anibus). / Pesceni/ae Pauli/n(a)e et
Se/rtoriae / Tert(iae) e[t De?]/metriae / Hermon/ini ami/c(a)e b(ene) m(erenti)*. Editors have generally expanded the abbreviation B.M. to the plural *bene merentibus*, making it refer to Paulina
and Tertia as well as Hermonis, but I suggest reading the singular *bene merenti*.

A number of epitaphs tell a similar story, but cast only two individuals as friends and protagonists, at the center of an open-ended commemorative group. Sometimes these are opposite-sex pairs:

D(is) M(anibus). / Ulpiae Vitali fecit P(ublius) Fufi/cius Felix *amicae suae fide/lissimae*, quae sibi morie(n)s fidem / servavit; et sibi, libertis liber/tabusque suis posterisque eorum. (*CIL* 6.29409; found in Florence, but thought to originate from Rome)

D(is) M(anibus) / T(itus) Aelius Euangelus fecit sibi / *et Aeliae Telesphoridi ami-cae / optimae* et lib(ertis) libert(abus)q(ue) p(osterisque) eorum. (*CIL* 6.34237; Rome)

To the spirits of the departed. Publius Fuficius Felix dedicated this to Ulpia Vitalis his faithful friend, who was faithful to him in death; and to himself, his freedmen and freedwomen, and their descendants.

To the spirits of the departed. Titus Aelius Euangelus dedicated this to himself and to Aelia Telesphoris his excellent friend, and to his freedmen and freed-women and their descendants.

As I argue in Chapter 2, regardless of what these individuals' relation-ships actually were or may have been perceived to be, the language of their epitaphs is not commemorating them as conjugal couples. Instead, these inscriptions are directly comparable to those which commemorate same-sex pairs of friends and place them at the center of a burial group. The following examples illustrate the usual range in juridical status from possible slaves or freedmen and freedwomen to those explicitly commem-orated as freeborn citizens.

Domitiae Vitali fec(it) / Obulnia Tertia *amicae / pientissimae* et sibi et / libertis libertabusque suis. (*CIL* 6.17041; Rome)

D(is) M(anibus). / Eusynetus / Pithano / *amico / carissimo / b(ene) m(erenti)* f(ecit) et / sibi et suis. (*AE* 1977.75; Rome, second century AD)

L(ucius) Pomponius / Extricatus / v(ivus) f(ecit) sibi et suis / et C(aio) Appio Vivano / *amico b(ene) m(erenti)*. / in fr(onte) p(edes) VI / in ag(ro) p(edes) VI. (*CIL* 3.2475 = 3.8635; Salona)

C(aius) Parredius / Amaranthus / sibi *et C(aio) Licinio C(ai) f(ilio) / Co[l(lina)] Macro amico* / et suis. / in fr(onte) XIII in ag(ro) p(edes) XX. (*CIL* 11.4144; Narni)

To Domitia Vitalis. Obulnia Tertia dedicated this to her devoted friend and to herself, and to her freedmen and freedwomen.

To the spirits of the dead. Eusynetus dedicated this to Pithanus his dear friend, well-deserving, and to himself and his own.

Lucius Pomponius Extricatus, while still alive, dedicated this to himself and his own, and to Gaius Appius Vivanus his deserving friend. Six feet wide, six feet deep.

Gaius Parredius Amaranthus dedicated this to himself and to his friend Gaius Licinius Macrus, son of Gaius, of the tribe Collina, and to his own. Thirteen feet wide, twenty feet deep.

Epitaphs like these invite a few questions, unanswerable in any given case but worth asking.[137] The formulaic *et suis* in some of these epitaphs leaves open the possibility of future descendants, but the absence of spouses' names is noticeable. At the time the inscription was commissioned, were these individuals not married, or were their spouses commemorated in another inscription? Did any of these pairs share a home, like Laelius and Scipio (Cic. *Amic.* 103), or like the young men mentioned in the epitaph for Allia Potestas (*CIL* 6.37965), or like Lupus and Aper of Iuvanum, who grew up as slaves in the same household and were commemorated together in a joint epitaph to which we will return (*CIL* 11.188 = *CLE* 1210)? Did any of these pairs, commemorated as *amici* and *amicae*, call each other *frater* and *soror*?

The inscriptions communicate nothing on these points. Their language is generically spare but the implications particularly eloquent. Quartina and Marcella, Extricatus and Vivanus, Amaranthus and the freeborn Gaius Licinius Macrus – these and other pairs of friends formed the core of open-ended burial groups which made room for others, whether the freed slaves of one or an open-ended *sui*. There must have been further instances of comparable and yet other kinds of arrangements, but even this handful of inscriptions opens our eyes to the wide range of possible configurations in burial groups and commemorative practices among Romans. More often than has been acknowledged, Roman burials and the inscriptions marking them perpetuated the memory of and thereby enacted the ties not only of kinship, marriage, or slavery, but of nothing more nor less than *amicitia*.

Type 5: Just friends

What, finally, of that particularly eloquent possibility, that two persons might be buried together and alone? No freedmen or freedwomen, no open-ended *sui*, but just the two of them; commemorated not as kin, spouses or former slaves but as *amici*, no more and no less. We have already seen one famous case of two friends finding their resting place

---

[137] Further examples of the configuration of two friends at the center of an open-ended burial group include *CIL* 6.2493 (Rome, two men, one of them a soldier), 6.12370 (Rome, two men), 12.3679 (Nimes, two women), *Il lapidario Zeri di Mentana* (Rome 1982) 1.183 (Rome, two men).

next to each other. Dying not long after Maecenas, Horace was put to rest in a tomb next to his friend's. Suetonius' description of the arrangement implies two separate monuments, each presumably marked by a commemorative text which may or may not have made reference to the other. Still, what passersby on the Esquiline saw, and what Suetonius' text itself communicates, is that two men who called each other *amici* in life rested next to each other (*iuxta*) in death.[138]

That two friends might share a single tomb has long been a possibility in the Western tradition – rare enough, but not quite invisible. Homer tells of Patroclus' ghost coming to Achilles in order to urge that their bones be mingled in a single urn (*Iliad* 23.83–93), and centuries later the medieval narrative of Amys and Amylion culminates with the narration of how the two friends' bodies miraculously moved in order to lie next to each other.[139] Focusing on England in particular, Alan Bray has shown that the joint burial of two friends was rather more common than previously thought. Claiming to have just scratched the surface, and only in England at that, Bray issues a welcome challenge: These joint burials "are not fortuitous to a history of friendship – they are its fault line."[140]

Among the very few hints at this fault line we find in the literary tradition surviving from ancient Rome is an epigram by Martial fervently celebrating the joint burial of two centurions.

> Fabricio iunctus fido requiescit Aquinus,
> qui prior Elysias gaudet adisse domos.
> ara duplex primi testatur munera pili:
> plus tamen est, titulo quod breviore legis:
> *iunctus uterque sacro laudatae foedere vitae;*
> *famaque quod raro novit, amicus erat.*
> (Mart. 1.93)

> Aquinus rests here, united with his faithful Fabricius,
> and rejoices that he went first to the Elysian dwellings.
> A double altar testifies to the rank of *primus pilus*,
> but more important is what you read in a briefer inscription:
> "Each was united to the other in the sacred bond of a praiseworthy life,
> and, a thing rarely heard of, each was a friend."

The opening couplet emphasizes the bond of *amicitia* joining Fabricius and Aquinus with traditional imagery. The key terms *iunctus* and *fido* and

---

[138] Suet. *Vita Hor.*: *humatus et conditus est extremis Esquiliis iuxta Maecenatis tumulum.*
[139] Compare a phrase from the *Vita sanctorum Amici et Amelii*: *quos Deus sicut unanimi concordia et dilectione in vita coniunxit, ita et in morte eos separari noluit.* See Hyatte 1994, Bray 2003, p. 94.
[140] Bray 2003, p. 253; cf. p. 304: "There are many more."

the motif of the contest in death are, as we have seen, common to Roman idealization of friends, but also of brothers and spouses. In the second couplet we read that the two men were centurions, and that they are commemorated in an inscription on a double altar specifying their (relatively high) rank the contrast with what follows suggests that this is a fairly long prose epitaph indicating their names, ages, and years in military service. Yet Martial assigns greater importance (*plus tamen est*) to the second and briefer inscription in verse which he quotes in the third and final couplet of his own composition. Here the emphasis is not on Fabricius' and Aquinus' status or achievements, but on the strength of the bond that joined them in life and death and on the rarity of so strong a friendship. Note the slightly pleonastic *iunctus uterque*, echoing and reinforcing *iunctus* in the opening verse, and *sacrum foedus* is reminiscent of Catullus' *aeternum hoc sanctae foedus amicitiae* (109.6), discussed in the previous chapter. Aquinus' and Fabricius' shared military experience fades into the background as the quoted inscription and Martial's epigram simultaneously build up to the final two words in which the key term appears for the first and only time: *amicus erat*. It is easy to imagine these two men calling each other *frater*. Whether Martial's epigram is describing a real tomb or is rather an epideictic exercise on the traditional theme of epitaphs, it represents Aquinus and Fabricius' tomb as an entirely possible reality. Although Latinists commenting on the poem have suggested or stated outright that such an arrangement was rare and unusual, and that tombs were "generally family affairs,"[141] the epitaphs presented in this chapter tell, as we have seen, another story. *Amici* and *amicae* regularly appear as members of burial groups of various sizes and configurations which are structured around various other kinds of relationship: parent–child and husband–wife, but also patron–freed slave. But what of burials and commemorations *à deux*?

Many surviving funeral momuments – relief portraits, inscriptions, or both – commemorate the burial of two individuals together and alone, and in those cases in which inscriptions survive we find a wide variety

---

[141] Citroni ad Mart. 1.93: "Che due amici di famiglie diverse si facessero seppellire l'uno accanto all'altro era un fatto assai raro"; Howell 1980: "It was unusual for friends to share a tomb, since tombs were generally family affairs." Howell cites as a parallel for Martial's Aquinus and Fabricius a joint epitaph for two soldiers (*CIL* 5.936–937). These two soldiers are not, however, commemorated as friends but as brothers, and they are far from alone: L. Titius commemorates himself, his *concubina*, his son, his daughter, and a *delicata* named Veneria; his brother Quintus commemorates himself, his wife, his son, and an unidentified Venusta; both add a formula providing for their freed slaves and the latters' descendants. See Henriksén 2006 for an overview of poetic epitaphs in Martial.

of combinations that might surprise the modern viewer or reader, accustomed to think of double burials as more or less exclusively the prerogative of conjugal couples. Among Roman double burials, to be sure, the majority are husband and wife,[142] and Ovid's narrative of Pyramus and Thisbe, joined by passionate *amor* (and a hint of *amicitia*) but prevented by their fathers from marrying, culminates with the theme of these star-crossed young lovers' joint burial: a lasting gesture made at the request of Thisbe, about to follow her lover in death, one that makes up – almost – for what was denied them in their short lives.[143] Apart from the bonds of marriage, desired or obtained, numerous epitaphs for two commemorate the bonds of blood: parent and child above all, but also, as we have seen in Chapter 2, grandmother and granddaughter (*CIL* 11.4978).[144] A number of epitaphs were commissioned to mark the joint burial of two brothers, two sisters, or brother and sister. One of them, evidently commemorating a brother and sister who had been slaves of different owners, is carved into a large marble altar. Its verbal simplicity ("For Marcus Antonius Anteros and his sister Cassia Melete") eloquently complements the rich decoration consisting of rams' heads, garlands, Gorgons, griffins, and dolphins.[145]

Double commemorations were by no means limited to married couples or kin. Not surprisingly, the bonds created by the institution of slavery structured not a few double burials and their commemoration. We find epitaphs memorializing master and slave, former master and freed slave, together and alone.[146] Aulus Allius' epitaph in honor of his beloved freed slave Potestas envisions that he will join her when his time comes, though he does not quite openly speak of a joint burial (*CIL* 6.37965, line 39:

---

[142] Thousands of examples of husband–wife joint commemoration survive, many of them concisely but effectively expressing the motif "two as one" by means of the verbs *iungere*, *sociare* and their compounds, the adverb *iuxta*, or the adjective *communis*. Examples include *CIL* 5.1721 (Aquileia), 11.1122 = *CLE* 1273 (Parma), *CLE* 68 (Rome), *CLE* 1302 (Fano), *CLE* 1969 (Madauros), *CLE* 2107B (Madauros).

[143] Ov. *Met.* 4.55–166, culminating with this line: *quodque rogis superest, una requiescit in urna.* *Amor* pervades the narrative from its opening lines (59–60: *notitiam primosque gradus vicinia fecit: / tempore crevit amor*) to Thisbe's dying words, wishing for the joint burial (156: *ut quos certus amor, quos hora novissima iunxit, / componi tumulo non invideatis eodem*). The hint at *amicitia* comes in the narrative of their communicating through a crack in the wall (76–77: *nec sumus ingrati: tibi nos debere fatemur, / quod datus est verbis ad amicas transitus aures*).

[144] Mother and son: *CIL* 3.11095, 5.2647; mother and daughter: *CIL* 2.2977, 6.14307, 14.2737; father and daughter: *CIL* 6.13824; father and son: *CIL* 3.10591.

[145] *CIL* 6.11964: *Dis Manibus. / M(arco) Antonio Anteroti / et Cassiae Meleteni / sorori.* Other brother–sister epitaphs include *CIL* 6.11961, 20987, 27805, 8.9048; epitaphs for two brothers include *CIL* 6.7419 (= *CLE* 1016), 6.7426, 9.3473 (= *CLE* 186), *CLE* 305, 416, 1824.

[146] Master and slave: *CIL* 3.2491, 6.9290; former master and freed slave: *CIL* 5.3791, 6.37301, 6.37456, 6.38421 (the freedman bearing the apt name Amicus).

qui sine te vivit, cernit sua funera vivos; 46: *cumque ad te veniam, mecum comitata sequetur*). That two freed slaves might find their resting place together and be commemorated as such is illustrated by a visually and verbally eloquent epitaph found in Ravenna which combines a brief prose introduction with a poem in (almost perfect) elegiac couplets.

delphinus	*Medusa*	*delphinus*
protome	*protome*	

DVO IVVAN LVPI ET APRI
VNA IVVANIAE DOMVS
HOS PRODVXIT ALVMNOS
LIBERTATIS OPVS CONTVLIT VNA DIES
NAVFRAGA MORS PARITER RAPVIT
QVOS IVNXERAT ANTE
ET DVPLICES LVCTVS
SIC PERINIQVA DEDIT

duo Iuvan(ensium) Lupi et Apri. /
una Iuvaniae domus / hos produxit alumnos, /
libertatis opus contulit una dies. /
naufraga mors pariter rapuit / quos iunxerat ante, /
et duplices luctus / sic periniqua dedit.
(*CIL* 11.188 = *CLE* 1210; Ravenna)[147]

[The monument] of two from Iuvanum: Lupus and Aper.
One home in Iuvanum raised them as foster-children,
one day gave them the gift of freedom.
Death in a shipwreck together took away those whom it had joined,
and so, most unjustly, brought about a double grief.

---

[147] I give Bormann's 1888 *CIL* text, which he based on autopsy. In his *Anthologia veterum latinorum epigrammatum et poematum* (ed. H. Meyer, Leipzig 1835, vol. II, p. 1233), Pieter Burman reports earlier readings of the poem's first line (*una iuventutis*; *una iuvenilis*; *una Iuvavonis*), claiming that the Roman settlement on the site of Salzburg (*municipium Claudium Iuvavum*; see *CIL* 3.5530–5561 for some inscriptions found there) was called not only *Iuvavo* or *Iuvavia* but also *Iuvania* or *Iuvanum*, though he cites no evidence for the latter spelling. In his 1897 *CLE* text Bücheler follows Bormann in printing *Iuvaniae*, suggesting that it refers to Salzburg even as he acknowledges that that town's name was usually spelled with -v- rather than -n-. It is more likely that Lupus and Aper came from the Italian town *Iuvanum*, about 30 km inland from the Adriatic in today's Abruzzo and find spot of at least eighty-five inscriptions in Clauss–Slaby's database; perhaps they died in a shipwreck near Ravenna. Before the eighteenth century Lupus and Aper's epitaph had been stored inside the structure known as La Rotonda, just possibly on the site of an ancient lighthouse (cf. Paolo Gamba Ghiselli, *Lettera sopra l'antico edificio di Ravenna detto volgarmente La Rotonda*, 1765).

While the text places no label on their relationship, both its imagery and that of the visual decoration strongly suggest ideals of *amicitia*. The motif of union in life and death is given powerful expression both by visual means – the symmetrically arranged composition of two dolphins framing two portrait busts with a Gorgon's head in the center – and by textual devices: the prominent appearance of DVO as the first word and DVPLICES LVCTVS in the penultimate line, the repetition of the point that Lupus and Aper died together (*pariter, iunxerat*), the recurring language of ones and twos (*duorum, una domus, una dies, duplices luctus*). The somewhat puzzling phrase *quos iunxerat ante*, given visual prominence by taking up an entire line, is perhaps communicating that Lupus and Aper were not only figuratively joined in death (*mors pariter rapuit*) but literally died in each other's arms, like a male–female slave pair commemorated in an epitaph from Vercelli, or even tied themselves to each other during the storm, like Giton and Encolpius in Petronius' *Satyricon*.[148] Reading this monument's visual and verbal imagery together with Petronius' narrative and Martial's epigram on the centurions Fabricius and Aquinus, we might find ourselves wondering whether Lupus and Aper referred to each other as *amicus*, or *frater*, or both; but the inscription – whoever may have commissioned it – uses no specific label, expressing its message by means of the language of *alumni* (almost brothers, but not quite), ones and twos, unity in death.

A considerable number of double epitaphs send no explicit message at all about the bond that linked the two individuals, simply and thus all the more eloquently recording the two names alone. Sometimes, to be sure, there is a hint at a story – numerous plaques marking niches in columbaria mark the resting place of two slaves, whether of the same or different owners.[149] Pairings of man and woman raise the usual question whether they constituted a conjugal couple. Whatever the subjective experience or recognized status of their relationship may have been in life, in death such pairs are commemorated together by means of the simple juxtaposition of their names, the wording no different from that which

---

[148] *CIL* 5.6700 (Vercelli; Mommsen reports that he himself saw only a fragment containing the final three lines but records earlier transcriptions of the first part in italics): *D.M. / Philumeni / et Eutychiae / Menander / et Vestina domini / iuvenum / bene merentium / qui cum simul / quietem sani petissent / in complexu / pari exanimes / inventi sunt*; Petron. *Sat.* 114 (the parallel is suggested by Bücheler in *CLE*).

[149] From the *monumentum Liviae* see *CIL* 6.4257 (*Amomo / Bibuli. // Iuliae / Natali / Bibuli*) and 6.3942 (*Antiochus / Liviae / atriensis. // Myrtilus / Caesaris / Diogenianus*); from the *monumentum Marcellae* see 6.4423 (*Epaphra / Marcellae / argentarius. // Thyrannus / topiarius / Marcellae*).

commemorates same-sex pairs. Consider, for example, the following col-umbarium plaques from the so-called *monumentum Marcellae* along the Via Appia outside of Rome, the first two commemorating male–female pairs, the third a pair of men, all three of them probably freed slaves of the same owner.

M(arcus) Valerius / Nedymus. // Valeria / Fausta. (*CIL* 6.4667)

P(ublius) Porcilius / Celsus. // Porcilia / Thallusa. (*CIL* 6.4640)

C(aius) Publilius / Carpus. // C(aius) Publilius / Eros. (*CIL* 6.4645)

Other columbarium plaques commemorate two men together without any relational labels, but the nomenclature communicates that they are not freedmen of the same former owner.[150] Outside of columbaria con-texts the issue is the same. In an epitaph found at Altinum, a freeborn man and woman of different families are jointly commemorated in an epitaph which applies no label to their relationship:

C(aius) Murius C(ai) filius / sibi et / Potiae M(arci) f(iliae) / Secundae. (CIL 5.2245; Altinum)

Gaius Murius, son of Gaius, to himself and to Potia Secunda, daughter of Marcus.

How different is this from inscriptions and monuments commemorating two women or two men together? Two examples from southern France invite consideration. A monument found at Saint-Genis-des-Fontaines combines a portrait pair of two women with an inscription which identi-fies them as freeborn but not obviously related:

Tertulla L(uci) / Catupris f(ilia) // Lucia L(uci) / Vassedonis f(ilia). (*CIL* 12.3031 = *AE* 1995.1053)

Tertulla, daughter of Lucius Catupris. Lucia, daughter of Lucius Vassedo.

An elaborate cinerary urn, most likely dating from the second century AD, found at Cimiez (Cimella) in present-day Nice, boasts a richly sym-metrical decoration emphasizing duality and balance. There are two pairs of birds – one pair pecking at a festoon of oak leaves and acorns, the other eating from a basket of fruit – and two heads of Bacchus with harpies under each. For those who can read it, there is also the simple announce-ment of two men's names:

---

[150] E.g. *CIL* 6.4957: *M'. Fulvius / Auctus. // C. Mamilius / Demetrius*; 6.12363: *P(ublius) Arrenus P(ubli) l(ibertus) / Fortunatus. // L(ucius) Quirinius / Tuscus*; 6.11974: *M(arcus) Antonius / M(arci) l(ibertus) / Cinnamus. // Q(uintus) Peccellius / Q(uinti) l(ibertus) / Celer.*

D(ecimi) Albicci Licini. // Antoni Liberalis. (*CIL* 5.7925 = 6.11300)[151]

Whether or not any or all of the individuals commemorated in these inscriptions called each other *amici* or *amicae* in life, whether or not ancient readers of the inscriptions assumed that they did so, these brief commemorative texts content themselves with making the point that two people have found their resting place together. An admittedly random sampling of *CIL* turns up no examples of two unrelated women named on a joint columbarium plaque (for a mother and daughter, see *CIL* 6.5190). It would seem, them, that women whose remains were placed in columbaria usually ended up being commemorated with a man. But, as we have seen, the entire body of epitaphs from around the Roman Empire make it abundantly clear that this was not true of women who received or gave themselves more costly and prestigious burials.

Some inscriptions for two use labels which configure the deceased in a relationship of *amicitia* not with each other, but with the person who commissioned the inscription.

C(aius) Ofilli[us] / C(ai) l(ibertus) Amemptus / fecit / Cn(aeo) Sentio Thallo et / Sentiae / Aprili / *amicis suis / bene merentibus*. (*CIL* 14.3808 = Reali 35It; Tibur)[152]

D(is) M(anibus). / Q(uintus) Trebonius Gra/phicus donavit / *amicis carissimis* / L(ucio) Camerio Attico / et L(ucio) Camerio Euty/cho d(e)f(unctis). (*CIL* 6.38980; Rome)

D(is) M(anibus). / L(ucius) Arr(ius) Lo[gi]smus fecit filiae / [---vix(it) an(nis)---] / men(sibus) VIII, d(iebus) XVIII, et Arr(io) / Protioni *amico*, vix(it) ann(is) / XXV. (*CIL* 10.7047 = Reali 156It; Catania)[153]

L(ucio) Statorio / Bathyllo / IIIIIIvir(o) patron(o), / P(ublio) Messio P(ubli) f(ilio) / Calvioni *amico*, / L(ucius) Statorius / Trophimus IIIIIIvir / aug(ustalis) cum Naevia Secunda / uxsore. / in f(ronte) p(edes) XVI / in ag(ro) p(edes) XX. (*CIL* 11.6831 = Reali 155C; Bononia; first century AD)

Gaius Ofillius Amemptus, freedman of Gaius, dedicated this to Gnaeus Sentius Thallus and Sentia Aprilis, his well-deserving friends.

---

[151] The *nomen* Albiccius is well attested in the Maritime Alps region but not in Rome. The urn was purchased by the British Museum in 1786. A description quoted at *CIL* 5.7925 strikingly de-emphasizes the imagery of duality, speaking merely of "varie figure d'uccelli et altri animali."

[152] The *CIL* description indicates that this was carved on to a marble cippus which contains a cavity for the ashes of the deceased, who are oddly described in the singular rather than the plural: *cippus marmoreus in superiore parte excavatus ad recipiendos cineres defuncti*.

[153] The *CIL* editor suggests reading *Erotioni* instead of *Protioni*. Solin 2003, p. 1122, has only one attestation of the name *Protio*, whereas *Erotion* is common enough as both masculine and feminine name (p. 363).

To the spirits of the dead. Quintus Trebonius Graphicus gave this monument to his dear departed friends Lucius Camerius Atticus and Lucius Camerius Eutychus.

To the spirits of the dead. Lucius Arrius Logismus dedicated this to his daughter [... who lived ... years], 8 months and 18 days, and to his friend Arrius Protio, who lived 25 years.

To Lucius Statorius Bathyllus, *sevir*, his former master; and to his friend Publius Messius Calvio, son of Publius. Lucius Statorius Trophimus, *sevir augustalis*, dedicated this together with his wife Naevia Secunda. 16 feet wide, 20 feet deep.

To be sure, there are often direct or indirect clues to the relationships between the two deceased individuals. Atticus and Eutychus may well have been freed slaves of the same masters, Thallus and Aprilis likewise (and perhaps a conjugal couple at that). But those are just hints, and sometimes the text does not even hint. What relationship, if any, existed between Logismus' daughter and his friend and possibly fellow-freedman Protio, or between Trophimus' former master Bathyllus (himself perhaps a freed slave) and his freeborn friend Publius Messius Calvio? The inscriptions locate these individuals solely in networks linking them to the men who commissioned them, who thereby memorialize themselves as dutiful fathers, freedmen, friends.

Inscriptions sent their message, of course, only to those who could read them. The message that two people were buried and commemorated together could be sent to a much wider audience by means of relief portraits. Sculptures depicting male–female pairs are often read as conjugal couples, the same-sex pairings as former slaves of the same master, but surviving inscriptions have shown us that other commemorative configurations were entirely possible, for example, parent and child, brother and sister, freedman and former master, and, as we will see, *amici*.[154] When portrait sculpture is accompanied by text, the words of the latter sometimes complement the message sent by the former. A funerary altar found in Modena communicates visually that two men, both of them literate Roman citizens, are buried together; the accompanying inscription tells

[154] In her catalogue of ninety-two funerary reliefs from the city of Rome and environs, Kleiner 1977 cites thirty-four double commemorations: twenty-four male–female pairs, seven pairs of men, three pairs of women. Kleiner cautiously concludes that "we may assume that, in most cases, members of the same sex portrayed together are *conliberti*" (p. 35). Five of her ten same-sex examples are accompanied by inscriptions, and while three of them indeed commemorate the pair as former slaves of the same master, one speaks of freedman and patron, another of mother and daughter.

those who can read it that they served together as soldiers.[155] Sometimes, however, the text complicates the picture. An elegant funerary monument from a columbarium outside Rome combines the image of two men in their togas, right hands joined in the gesture known as the *dextrarum iunctio*, symbolic of various relationships sealed by *fides*, especially – but not exclusively – marriage, hospitality, and *amicitia*.[156] The image, then, sends the message that two Roman citizens are being commemorated together, and that they were linked by a significant social bond. But then there is the inscription.

Dis Manibus. / [*wreath*] / C(aius) Iulius Hermes / vix(it) ann(is) XXXIIII m(ensibus) V / dieb(us) XIIII. / C(aius) Iulius Andronicus / conlibertus fec(it) / bene merenti de se. (*CIL* 6.5326; Rome)

To the spirits of the departed. Gaius Julius Hermes, who lived 34 years, 5 months, 14 days. Gaius Julius Andronicus his fellow freedman dedicated this to him; he deserved it.

The text records that both Andronicus, who commissioned it, and Hermes were former slaves, perhaps imperial slaves; in this case, then, the gesture of *dextrarum iunctio* seems to be sealing the bond between *conliberti*. Yet the text designates this as the resting place of Hermes *alone*. The implication is worth keeping in mind. A relief sculpture of two people together, while clearly memorializing the bond that joined them in life, does not necessarily mark a shared resting place.[157]

Among monuments commemorating two women, an example from Capua combines a bas-relief sculpture of two women joining their right hands in the *dextarum iunctio* with the following inscription:

Dexsonia Selemio (*sic*) sibi et / Philemae suae ama[n]tis(s)i{u}mae. (*CIL* 10.4110; Capua)[158]

Dexonia Selenio, to herself and to her loving Philema.

The nomenclature of the text suggests that Dexonia Selenio is a freed slave and that Philema is either her slave or a freedwoman, whether of Selenio herself or someone else; the fact that the two figures are in no

---

[155] *AE* 1986.238 (a marble altar with one man on each side, each wearing a toga and holding a scroll in his hand): *M. Numisius / Castor sibi et / Q. Velucio Vero / contubern(ali) / t(estamento) p(oni) i(ussit)*.
[156] For the *dextrarum iunctio* see Freyburger 1986, pp. 167–176 (marriage), 177–185 (*amicitia*), 185–193 (hospitality).
[157] Andronicus may have provided for other people's burial as well. On a marble urn from the same columbarium is found an inscription in which a man by the same name commemorates his freedman Epagathus (*CIL* 6.5325).
[158] See Chioffi 2005, p. 120 (no. 130).

way visually differentiated from each other, for example in clothing or hair style, might be interpreted as sending a message that the two women are on the same social level. On the other hand, at least one monument depicting two women, both wearing a veil and clasping right hands, is accompanied by an inscription identifying one as the freed slave of the other; and we have seen that *amans* and *amantissimus* not only appear in epitaphs commemorating an affectionate relationship between master and slave, but may have been the term of choice to describe that bond, since the language of *amicitia* was apparently unavailable. Read as a whole, the monument communicates that two women are being commemorated together and alone; whatever bond linked them in life, it is described for posterity in terms neither of kinship nor of dependence, but of affection (*amantissimae*).[159]

Another monument displaying two women joining right hands is datable to the second half of the first century AD; the accompanying inscription communicates that they were both freed slaves of a woman named Fonteia.

Fonteia (mulieris) l(iberta) Eleusis. h(uic?) o(lla?) dat(a?) a Fonteia (mulieris) l(iberta) Helena. (*CIL* 6.18524; Rome; British Museum Sculpture 2276)

Fonteia Eleusis, freedwoman of a woman. She was given an urn by (?) Fonteia Helena, freedwoman of a woman.

The monument has provoked some discussion, not only because of the unparalleled and somewhat opaque abbreviated text in the middle of the inscription but also because the relief was visibly recarved in antiquity. The figure on the left, corresponding to Eleusis, seems originally to have been a man and the first half of the inscription seems to have been recarved as well.[160] One reading of this monument, partially driven by the false assumption that the gesture of *dextarum iunctio* could *only* signify a married couple, is that Eleusis and Helena were an erotically bonded couple. This is not impossible, and it is also quite possible that the two

---

[159] For attestations of the slave (and thus freedwoman) name *Philema* see Solin 2003, p. 1347; for the slave (and thus freedwoman) name *Selenio*, see ibid. pp. 415–416. For *amans* and *amantissimus* describing slaves and their owners, see above, n. 89. For an inscription commemorating a freedwoman and her *patrona*, see *CIL* 12.891 from Arles: *[Tur]raniae Sexst(i) l(ibertae) / [Ph]ilemationi C(h)ia l(iberta) / [si]bi et patronae / viva fecit.*

[160] The abbreviation has been expanded on the Clauss–Slaby website as *h(aec) o(llae?) dat(ae)*; Stupperich 1983 supports the suggestion *h(uic) o(lla) data*. The most likely of the hypotheses put forward in explanation of the recarving is that the monument was originally designed to commemorate Helena together with her husband and that subsequently, for whatever reasons, the figure on the left was recarved to represent a woman, the monument now used to commemorate Helena together with her fellow freedwoman Eleusis.

women called each other *amica* while alive. But the monument itself communicates neither of these things. The only relationship evoked by the text is that of fellow-freedwomen, and the portrait sculpture is polyvalent. A monument found at Arles, for example, combines a sculptural pair of veiled women joining right hands in the *dextrarum iunctio* with an inscription identifying the two as a freeborn woman and her former slave. Here the gesture might suggest the bond of *officium* joining former owners and their freed slaves, the bond commemorated in Phileros' monument at Pompeii, for himself, his *patrona* Vesonia, and his presumed friend Faustus.[161]

And so we come to epitaphs for two individuals buried together and alone which, like Martial's poem on the joint tomb of two centurions, use the language of *amicitia* to describe and honor the bond which joined them. In Chapter 1 we considered inscriptions commemorating male–female pairs with the language of *amicitia*, such as the following:

Terentiae Martiae / [Se]x(tus) Attius Flavius / *amicae* et animae / inconparabili / [e]t sibi vivus. (*CIL* 12.2010; Vienne)

D(is) M(anibus) s(acrum). / C(aius) Tadius Vic/torinus / Processae / *amicae bene* / *merenti* et / sibi. (*CIL* 9.2973 = Reali 97It; Iuvanum)

To Terentia Martia. Sextus Attius Flavius [dedicated this] to his friend, a unique spirit, and to himself while still alive.

Sacred to the spirits of the dead. Gaius Tadius Victorinus [dedicated this] to his well-deserving friend Processa and to himself

While inscriptions like these are usually read as referring to conjugal couples who were not united in full matrimony or *iustum conubium*, I have argued that, however any given relationship may have been experienced or perceived in life, in the epitaphs commissioned to commemorate these individuals in death, the terms *amicus* and *amica* in themselves communicate nothing more nor less than what they do in same-sex configurations. There is every reason to suppose that joint commemorations of two women as *amicae* were among possible configurations, and a fragmentarily

---

[161] *CIL* 12.793: *Cornelia L(uci) f(ilia) Sedata / sibi et Corneliae / Optatae l(ibertae) annoru(m) XX / piae viva fecit.* Brooten 1996, p. 59, makes too much of the clasped right hands, oversimplifying when she calls the *dextrarum iunctio* "the classic gesture of married persons"; she concludes that "the relief and the inscription allow for several interpretations, one of which is that the two women had lived in a relationship that they considered comparable to a Roman marriage." The discussion in D'Angelo 1990 is flawed by a lack of understanding of the formulaic language of Latin epitaphs and the very meaning of the category "freedwoman"; and the argument that, like Tryphaena and Tryphosa in a New Testament passage discussed, "Helena and Eleusis are related names" because "Helena may recall one of the requirements of the [Eleusinian] mysteries, which was knowledge of the Greek tongue" is quite unconvincing.

preserved epitaph from Brescia may do just that, although its fragmentary state and abbreviated wording makes certainty impossible; still, the extreme rarity of surviving examples suggests that it was not a common configuration.[162] And what of pairs of male *amici* commemorated together and alone, like Martial's Fabricius and Aquinus? I have found six surviving epitaphs which memorialize precisely this configuration but whose existence has gone quite unnoticed in the scholarship.

D(is) M(anibus). / C(aio) Pompusidio / Fructo / fecit sibi *et / Atilio Marti/ali amico / b(ene) m(erenti)*. (*AE* 1988.104; Rome, second half of second century AD)[163]

D(is) M(anibus). / Pompeius Pom/peianus sibi *et / Rufio Pudenti / amico bene me/renti* fecit. (*CIL* 6.24497; Rome)[164]

V(ivus) f(ecit) / P(ublius) Alfius / Serenus / sibi *et / T(ito) Calventio / Firmo / amico bon[o]*. (Pais, *Corporis Inscriptionum Latinarum Supplementa Italica* 519 = Reali 62C with illustration; found at Baone, about 25 km southwest of Padova; late first century AD; Figure 13)

Q(uintus) Pompeius Lucr[io] / sibi *et / C(aio) Novellio Crescen[ti] / amico*. (*CIL* 5.3704 = Reali 71C with illustration; Verona, Museo Maffeiano; first–second century AD; Figure 14)

Q(uintus) Lucilius / Charinus / sagarius / Mediolanensis, VIvir Mediolani, sibi *et / Q(uinto) Sulpicio Celado / amico*. / in fr(onte) p(edes) XII, in agr(o) p(edes) XIIII. (*CIL* 9.5752 = Reali 117It; Ricina)

P(ublius) Aemilius P(ubli) f(ilius) Masculus, / militavit in coh(orte) V pr(aetoria). / A(ulus) Timinius Daphnus / *amico b(ene) m(erenti)* / fecit / et sibi. (*CIL* 6.2554; Rome)

To the spirits of the departed. Gaius Pompusidius Fructus dedicated this to himself and to Atilius Martialis his deserving friend.

To the spirits of the departed. Pompeius Pompeianus dedicated this to himself and to Rufius Pudens his deserving friend.

While still alive, Publius Alfius Serenus [dedicated this] to himself and to Titus Calventius Firmus his good friend.

---

[162] *CIL* 5.4628 = Reali 88C (Brescia): ---/ *Iuventia / Longina / amic(o vel –ae) / dulcissim(o vel –ae) et sib(i) / [---] / h(oc) m(onumentum) h(eredem) n(on) s(equetur)*. Because the endings are abbreviated, the gender is not unambiguously expressed. The illegible line in the middle might well have contained the abbreviated formula *libertis libertabusque posterisque eorum*.

[163] That Fructus' name is in the dative rather than the nominative case is probably a carver's error of a not unparalleled type; alternatively one could understand a full stop after his name: "For Gaius Pompusidius Fructus. He dedicated this to himself and to his deserving friend Atilius Martialis."

[164] Pompeianus' name is common enough, and Rome large enough, that this is probably not the same man as the Quintus Pompeius Pompeianus who dedicated an epitaph to himself and his parents (*CIL* 6.24498).

Figure 13 Epitaph commissioned by Publius Alfius Serenus for himself and
his friend Titus Calventius Firmus

Quintus Pompeius Lucrio [dedicated this] to himself and to Gaius Novellius
Crescens his friend.

Quintus Lucilius Charinus, cloak salesman from Milan and *sevir* at Milan,
[dedicated this] to himself and to Quintius Sulpicius Celadus his friend. 12 feet
wide, 14 feet deep.

Figure 14 Epitaph commissioned by Quintus Pompeius Lucrio for himself
and his friend Gaius Novellius Crescens

Publius Aemilus Masculus, son of Publius, who served in the fifth praetorian cohort. Aulus Timinius Daphnus dedicated this to his well-deserving friend and to himself.

To this list we might add the following epitaph found at Verona, commissioned by the slave Novicius for himself and a man whose name suggests he was a freed slave of the same family, and who is commemorated as Novicius' *sodalis*.

[*image of a rose flanked by two dolphins*] V(ivus) f(ecit). / Novicius / Rabutiorum (servus) / sibi *et* / *P(ublio) Rabutio Glago / sodali*. (*CIL* 5.3679; Verona)

While still alive, Novicius, slave of the Rabutii, [dedicated this] to himself and to his comrade Publius Rabutius Glagus.

The term might be communicating that the two men belonged to a club or *sodalicium*, but it might also be a rare instance in this speech genre of the use of the noun as a near-synonym of *amicus*. In any case, in all its direct simplicity, the epitaph communicates that the two men have found a resting place together.

Even in this small sample the range in social status among those who commissioned these joint commemorations for themselves and a friend is notable – from the slave Novicius, who dedicates a joint tomb for himself and Glagus, perhaps a freed slave of the same household, to the cloak salesman Quintus Lucilius Charinus, whose name suggests freedman status, to Publius Aemilius Masculus, who is explicitly memorialized as a freeborn citizen. The variety of effect created by word choice and order and layout on the stone is equally worth noting. The epitaph for Serenus and Firmus, roughly contemporary with Martial's epigram on the joint tomb of Fabricius and Aquinus, was executed with particular care, the text surrounded by an oval border and surmounted with two dolphins, its lettering of high quality, regular and clear:

V F
P ALFIVS
SERENVS
SIBI ET
T CALVENTIO
FIRMO
AMICO BON[O]

The epitaph for Pompeius Lucrio and Novellius Crescens is carved with a simple symmetry that commemorates the two men and the bond that links them with a spare eloquence.

Q POMPEIVS LVCR[IO]
SIBI ET
C NOVELLIO CRESCENTI
AMICO

The epitaph from Verona communicates symmetry and duality in much the same way, with the addition of visual means as well.

[*dolphin*] [*rose*] [*dolphin*]
V F
NOVICIVS
RABVTIORVM
SIBI ET
P RABVTIO GLAGO
SODALI

The inscription from Ricina places Charinus' name first and weighs it down with non-abbreviated indications of his profession and office; then comes Celadus, accompanied only by the eloquently simple label *amico*:

Q LVCILIVS
CHARINVS
SAGARIVS
MEDIOLANENSIS
VI VIR MEDIOLANI
SIBI ET
Q SVLPICIO CELADO
AMICO
IN FR P XII IN AGR P XIIII

The inscription commissioned by Timinius Daphnus shows the opposite order.

P AEMILIVS P F MASCVLVS
MILITAVIT IN COH V PR
A TIMINIVS DAPHNVS
AMICO   B M
FEC [*image of dish*]   IT
ET   SIBI

First comes the full name of his friend Masculus, with the formula P. F. ("son of Publius") memorializing his status as freeborn Roman citizen; the next line commemorates him as a soldier; then come Daphnus' name, followed by the invocation of *amicitia*; the specification that this memorial is also for Daphnus himself (*et sibi*) comes a quiet but effective finale.

These inscriptions have barely been noticed, their implications hardly pursued. These seven are almost certainly the tip of an iceberg, and in any case their very existence shows that this was a thinkable and knowable commemorative constellation. As Bray asks about joint burials of friends in England: "Why have these monuments played so little part in

our understanding of the past? Why have we not *seen* them before?"[165]
The same question might be posed of the sarcophagus for two men, traditionally identified as brothers but unaccompanied by an inscription, discussed at the end of Chapter 2. And another question worth asking is
whether and how they differ from epitaphs commemorating male–female
pairs, together and alone, with the language of *amicitia* (see above). If my
reading of the language of such inscriptions is not found persuasive, or if,
independently of the possible denotation of the formulaic labels used in
their epitaphs, we speculate that some, most, or or all of the pairs being
commemorated in such inscriptions did indeed constitute conjugal couples, what is to stop us from reading commemorations of male pairs the
same way? After all, the labels available for communicating a conjugal
or sexual bond between man and woman in this speech genre were not
available in the case of male couples. The masculine *concubinus*, in the literary tradition referring to a man's sexual partner (cf. Catullus 61), is not
found among the over 400,000 inscriptions in the Clauss–Slaby database
and, as we have seen, in the language of inscriptions a man's *contubernalis*
is his fellow-soldier, one who shared a tent or *taberna*.

In the end, however, instead of asking ultimately unanswerable questions about the relationship between, say, Pompeianus and Pudens or
Lucrio and Crescens while they were alive, I suggest that we stay with
the language of the texts commemorating them after death and heed the
speech genre in which they are participating. If we do this, what we see is
that these relationships are being projected to future readers not through
the lens of sexual partnership or spousehood but through that of *amicitia*,
with all the ideals that connotes and invokes: sharing and union, reciprocity and goodwill, *fides* and *amor*. Because they name just two names,
epitaphs like these are particularly effective illustrations of how epitaphs
in general can effectively convey their message. The combination of spare
formulae and irreducible individuality effected by names and epithets
draws attention in a uniquely powerful way to the intersection of language, representation, and experience in the commemoration of interpersonal bonds. To the extent that we continue to read and talk and write
about them, these epitaphs perpetuate some of the possibilities of Roman
friendship to this day.

---

[165] Bray 2003, p. 304. Reali 1997 includes three of these epitaphs in his catalogue and illustrates
two of them, but offers no commentary on their interest or significance. For a parallel among
Christian epitaphs in Rome, see *ICUR* 4.9408 (fourth century AD, from the crypta S. Cornelii):
Genuarus / placuid se uni/ter poni cum a/micum suum Sibi/rinu.

Works cited

Adams, James N. 1982. *The Latin Sexual Vocabulary*. London.

  1983. "Words for 'Prostitute' in Latin." *Rheinisches Museum* 126: 321–358.

  1984. "Female Speech in Latin Comedy." *Antichthon* 18: 43–77.

  1995. "The Language of the Vindolanda Writing Tablets: An Interim Report." *Journal of Roman Studies* 85: 86–134.

  2003. *Bilingualism and the Latin Language*. Cambridge.

Albanese, Bernardo. 1962. "La struttura della *manumissio inter amicos*." *Annali del Seminario Giuridico dell'Università di Palermo* 29: 5–103.

  1963. "*L'amicitia* nel diritto privato romano." *Ius* 1–2: 130–147.

Albertario, Emilio. 1941. "*Sepulchra familiaria* e *sepulchra hereditaria*." In *Studi di diritto romano*, vol. II, pp. 1–28. Milan.

Alföldy, Géza and Silvio Panciera, eds. 2001. *Inschriftliche Denkmäler als Medien der Selbstdarstellung in der römischen Welt*. Stuttgart.

Altman, Janet. 1982. *Epistolarity: Approaches to a Form*. Columbus.

Ariès, Philippe. 1985. *L'homme devant la mort*. Paris.

Arkins, Brian. 1982. *Sexuality in Catullus*. Hildesheim.

Assmann, Jan. 2011. *Cultural Memory and Early Civilization: Writing, Remembrance, and Political Imagination*. Cambridge.

Augoustakis, Antony, and Carole Newlands. 2007. "Statius' *Silvae* and the Poetics of Intimacy." *Arethusa* 40: 117–125.

Austen, Jane. *Love and Friendship*. With a foreword by Fay Weldon. Hesperus Classics, London. 2003.

Austin, J. L. 1975. *How To Do Things With Words*. 2nd edn. Cambridge, Mass.

Austin, Lucy. 1946. "The Caerellia of Cicero's Correspondence." *Classical Journal* 41: 305–309.

Bagnall, Roger and Raffaella Cribiore. 2006. *Women's Letters from Ancient Egypt, 300 BC – AD 800*. Ann Arbor.

Bakhtin, Mikhail. 1981. *The Dialogic Imagination: Four Essays*. Trans. Michael Holquist. Austin.

  1986. *Speech Genres and Other Late Essays*. Trans. Vern W. McGee. Austin.

Baldassare, Ida. 1987. "La necropoli dell'Isola Sacra (Porto)." In Hesberg and Zanker 1987, pp. 125–138.

Bannon, Cynthia J. 1997. *Brothers of Romulus: Fraternal "Pietas" in Roman Law, Literature, and Society*. Princeton.

Bartsch, Shadi. 2006. *The Mirror of the Self: Sexuality, Self-Knowledge, and the Gaze in the Early Roman Empire*. Chicago.

Bassnett, Susan. 2002. *Translation Studies*. 3rd edn. New York and London.

Beall, Stephen. 2001. "*Homo fandi dulcissimus*. The Role of Favorinus in the *Attic Nights* of Aulus Gellius." *American Journal of Philology* 122: 87–106.

Beard, Mary, et al., eds. 1991. *Literacy in the Roman World*. Ann Arbor.

Bellincioni, Maria. 1984. "Amicizia." *Enciclopedia Virgiliana* I, pp. 135ff. Rome.

Bettini, Maurizio. 1992. *Il ritratto dell'amante*. Turin.

Biewer, Carolin. 2006. *Die Sprache der Liebe in Shakespeares Komödien. Eine Semantik und Pragmatik der Leidenschaft*. Heidelberg.

Biguenet, John and Rainer Schulte, eds. 1989. *The Craft of Translation*. Chicago and London.

Birley, Anthony. 2002. *Garrison Life at Vindolanda: A Band of Brothers*. Stroud.

Bloom, Allan. 2000. *Shakespeare on Love and Friendship*. Chicago.

Bloomer, W. Martin. 1992. *Valerius Maximus and the Rhetoric of the New Nobility*. London.

Bodel, John. 1994. *Graveyards and Groves: A Study of the Lex Lucerina*. Cambridge, Mass.

    ed. 2001. *Epigraphic Evidence: Ancient History from Inscriptions*. London and New York.

Boehringer, Sandra. 2007. *L'homosexualité féminine dans l'antiquité grecque et romaine*. Paris.

Boissier, Gaston. 1908. *Cicéron et ses amis. Étude sur la société romaine au temps de César*. 14th edn. Paris. (Engl. trans. *Cicero and his Friends*, trans. Adnah David Jones, New York 1897.)

Boswell, John. 1980. *Christianity, Social Tolerance, and Homosexuality*. Chicago.

    1994. *Same-Sex Unions in Premodern Europe*. New York.

Bourdieu, Pierre. 1977. *Outline of a Theory of Practice*. Trans. Richard Nice. Cambridge.

Bowman, Alan. 1994. "Letters and Literacy on Rome's Northern Frontier." In Bowman and Woolf 1994, pp. 109–125.

Bowman, Alan, and David Thomas. 1994. *The Vindolanda Writing-Tablets (Tabulae Vindolandenses II)*. London.

    1996. "New Writing-Tablets from Vindolanda." *Britannia* 27: 299–328.

    2003. *The Vindolanda Writing-Tablets (Tabulae Vindolandenses III)*. London.

Bowman, Alan, and Greg Woolf, eds. 1994. *Literacy and Power in the Ancient World*. Cambridge.

Bowman, Alan, David Thomas, and J. N. Adams. 1990. "Two Letters from Vindolanda." *Britannia* 21: 33–52.

Bray, Alan. 2003. *The Friend*. Chicago and London.

Breed, Brian W. 2006. *Pastoral Inscriptions: Reading and Writing in Virgil's "Eclogues."* London.

Brink, Laurie and Deborah Green, eds. 2008. *Commemorating the Dead: Texts and Artifacts in Context*. Berlin and New York.

Brooten, Bernadette J. 1996. *Love between Women: Early Christian Responses to Female Homoeroticism.* Chicago.

Brunt, P. A. 1988. "*Amicitia* in the Late Roman Republic." In *The Fall of the Roman Republic and Related Essays*, pp. 351–381. Oxford. (First published in *PCPS* 11 [1965]: 1–20.)

Burgess, Dana L. 1986. "Catullus c. 50: The Exchange of Poetry." *American Journal of Philology* 107: 576–586.

Burton, Paul. 2004. "*Amicitia* in Plautus: A Study of Roman Friendship Processes." *American Journal of Philology* 125: 209–243.

Busch, Alexandra. 2005. "Kameraden bis in den Tod? Zur militärischen Sepulkraltopographie im kaiserzeitlichen Rom." In Richard Neudecker und Paul Zanker, eds., *Lebenswelten. Bilder und Räume in der römischen Stadt der Kaiserzeit*, pp. 101–112. Wiesbaden.

Butler, H. E. and E. A. Barber, eds. 1933. *The Elegies of Propertius.* Oxford.

Bütler, Hans-Peter. 1970. *Die geistige Welt des jüngeren Plinius. Studien zur Thematik seiner Briefe.* Heidelberg.

Butler, Judith. 1990. *Gender Trouble: Feminism and the Subversion of Identity.* New York.

Byrne, Shannon. 2004. "Martial's Fiction: Domitius Marsus and Maecenas." *Classical Quarterly* 54: 255–265.

Cairns, Francis. 2006. *Sextus Propertius the Augustan Elegist.* Cambridge.

Caldelli, Maria Letizia. 2001. "*Amicus/-a* nelle iscrizioni di Roma. L'apporto dell'epigrafia al chiarimento di un sentimento sociale." In Peachin 2001, pp. 21–30.

Caldelli, Maria Letizia, and Cecilia Ricci. 1999. *Monumentum familiae Statiliorum.* Rome.

Calza, Guido. 1940. *La necropoli del Porto di Roma nell'Isola Sacra.* Rome.

Camps, W. A., ed. 1961. *Propertius: Elegies, Book 1.* Cambridge.

Carcopino, Jérôme. 1947. *Les secrets de la correspondance de Cicéron.* Paris.

Carlon, Jacqueline. 2009. *Pliny's Women: Constructing Virtue and Creating Identity in the Roman World.* Cambridge.

Carroll, Maureen. 2011. "*Memoria* and *damnatio memoriae*: Preserving and Erasing Identities in Roman Funerary Commemoration." In Carroll and Rempel 2011, pp. 65–90.

Carroll, Maureen and Jane Rempel, eds. 2011. *Living through the Dead: Burial and Commemoration in the Classical World.* Oxford.

Castrén, Paavo and Henrik Lilius, eds. 1970. *Graffiti del Palatino*, vol. II: *Domus Tiberiana.* Helsinki.

Champlin, Edward. 1980. *Fronto and Antonine Rome.* Cambridge, Mass., and London.

Chevallier, Raymond. 1983. *La romanisation de la Celtique du Pô.* Rome.

Chioffi, Laura. 2005. *Museo Provinciale Campano di Capua. La raccolta epigrafica. Le iscrizioni latine: cortili, sale, depositi.* Capua.

Cimma, Maria Rosa. 1976. *Reges socii et amici populi Romani.* Milan.

Ciprotti, Pio. 1964. "Inscriptiones nonnullae nondum editae in Italia repertae." *Helikon* 4: 303–307.

Citroni Marchetti, Sandra. 2000. *Amicizia e potere nelle lettere di Cicerone e nelle elegie ovidiane dall'esilio*. Florence.

Claassen, Jo-Marie. 1996. "Documents of a Crumbling Marriage: The Case of Cicero and Terentia." *Phoenix* 50: 208–232.

Clark, John R., and Anna Lydia Motto. 1993. "Seneca on Friendship." *Atene e Roma* 38: 91–98.

Clausen, Wendell. 1994. *A Commentary on Virgil's Eclogues*. Oxford.

Coleman, Robert, ed. 1977. *Vergil: Eclogues*. Cambridge.

Combès, Robert. 1958. "Cicéron et Matius. 'Amitié' et politique à Rome." *Revue des Études Latines* 36: 176–187.

ed. 1993. *Cicéron. Lélius de l'amitié*. Paris.

Connors, Catherine. 1998. *Petronius the Poet: Verse and Literary Tradition in the Satyricon*. Cambridge.

Conte, Gian Biagio. 1986. *The Rhetoric of Imitation*. Trans. Charles Segal. Ithaca.

Corbinelli, Silvia. 2008. *Amicorum colloquia absentium. La scrittura epistolare a Roma tra comunicazione quotidiana e genere letterario*. Naples.

Cotton, Hannah. 1985. "*Mirificum genus commendationis*: Cicero and the Latin Letter of Recommendation." *American Journal of Philology* 106: 328–334.

1986. "The Role of Cicero's Letters of Recommendation: *Iustitia* versus *gratia*?" *Hermes* 114: 443–460.

Courtney, Edward. 1995. *Musa lapidaria: A Selection of Latin Verse Inscriptions*. Atlanta.

2003. *Fragmentary Latin Poets*. Rev. edn. Oxford.

Crook, J. A. 1955. *Consilium Principis*. Cambridge.

Cugusi, Paolo. 1983. *Evoluzione e forme dell'epistolografia latina nella tarda repubblica e nei primi due secoli dell'impero*. Rome.

1985. *Aspetti letterari dei Carmina latina epigraphica*. Bologna.

Curchin, Leonard A. 1994. "The Celtiberian Vocable *kar* in Two Inscriptions from Central Spain." *Zeitschrift für Papyrologie und Epigraphik* 103: 229–230.

D'Ambrosio, Antonio, and Stefano De Caro. 1983. *Un impegno per Pompei. Fotopiano e documentazione della Necropoli di Porta Nocera*. Milan.

D'Angelo, Mary Rose. 1990. "Women Partners in the New Testament." *Journal of Feminist Studies in Religion* 6: 65–70.

Dench, Emma. 2005. *Romulus' Asylum: Roman Identities from the Age of Alexander to the Age of Hadrian*. Oxford.

Deniaux, Élizabeth. 1993. *Clientèle et pouvoir à l'époque de Cicéron*. Rome.

Derrida, Jacques. 1997. *Politics of Friendship*. Trans. George Collins. London and New York.

Deutscher, Guy. 2010. *Through the Language Glass: Why the World Looks Different in Other Languages*. New York.

Devere, Heather. 2000. "Reviving Greco-Roman Friendship: A Bibliographic Review." In Preston King and Heather Devere, eds., *The Challenge to Friendship in Modernity*, pp. 149–187, Portland and London.

Dickey, Eleanor. 2002. *Latin Forms of Address from Plautus to Apuleius*. Oxford and New York.

D'Isanto, Gennaro. 1994. "Rilettura di un'iscrizione cristiana di Capua." *Zeitschrift für Papyrologie und Epigraphik* 101: 183–186.

Dixon, Suzanne. 1992. *The Roman Family*. Baltimore and London.

　　2001. *Reading Roman Women: Sources, Genres and Real Life*. London.

Dover, Kenneth J. 1978. *Greek Homosexuality*. London.

Dugas, Laurent. 1894. *L'amitié antique d'après les moeurs populaires et les théories des philosophes*. Paris.

　　1914. *L'amitié antique*. 2nd edn. Paris.

Dupont, Florence and Thierry Éloi. 2001. *L'érotisme masculin dans la Rome antique*. Paris.

Duthoy, Robert. 1978. "Les Augustales." *Aufstieg und Niedergang der römischen Welt* II. 16.2: 1254–1309.

Dutsch, Dorota. 2008. *Feminine Discourse in Roman Comedy: On Echoes and Voices*. Oxford.

Dyck, Andrew. 1979. "On the Composition and Sources of Cicero, *De officiis* 1.50–58." *Classical Antiquity* 12: 77–84.

Eck, Werner. 1987. "Römische Grabinschriften. Aussageabsicht und Aussagefähigkeit im funerären Kontext." In Hesberg and Zanker 1987, pp. 75–83.

El Murr, Dimitri. 2001. *L'amitié*. Paris.

Elefante, Maria. 1985. "Un caso di *defixio* nella necropoli pompeiana di Porta Nocera?" *Parola del passato* 40: 431–443.

Ellis, Robinson. 1889. *A Commentary on Catullus*. Oxford.

Ernout, Alfred and Antoine Meillet. 2001. *Dictionnaire étymologique de la langue latine. Histoire des mots*. Reprint of 4th edn. with additions by Jacques André. Paris.

Epstein, David. 1987. *Personal Enmity in Roman Politics 218–43 BC*. London.

Epstein, Joseph. 2006. *Friendship: An Exposé*. Boston.

Fabre, Georges. 1981. *Libertus. Recherches sur les rapports patron–affranchi à la fin de la république romaine*. Rome.

Faderman, Lillian. 1981. *Surpassing the Love of Men: Romantic Friendship and Love between Women from the Renaissance to the Present*. New York.

Farrell, Joseph. 2001. *Latin Language and Latin Culture: From Ancient to Modern Times*. Cambridge.

Fedeli, Paolo, ed. and transl. 1988. *Properzio: Elegie*. Florence.

Fedeli, Paolo, 2005. *Properzio. Elegie, Libro II*. Cambridge.

Fehr, Beverley. 1996. *Friendship Processes*. Thousand Oaks, Calif., and London.

Feraudi-Gruénais, Francesca. 2003. *Inschriften und "Selbstdarstellung" in stadtrömischen Grabbauten*. Rome.

Ferrua, Antonio. 1972. "Iscrizioni dell'Italia inferiore." *Epigraphia* 34: 131–148.

Fiore, Benjamin. 1997. "The Theory and Practice of Friendship in Cicero." In Fitzgerald 1997, pp. 59–76.

Fischer, Edith. 1973. *Amor und Eros. Eine Untersuchung des Wortfeldes "Liebe" im Lateinischen und Griechischen*. Hildesheim.

Fitzgerald, John T., ed. 1996. *Friendship, Flattery and Frankness of Speech: Studies on Friendship in the New Testament World*. Leiden.

1997. *Greco-Roman Perspectives on Friendship*. Atlanta.

Fitzgerald, William. 1995. *Catullan Provocations: Lyric Poetry and the Drama of Position*. Berkeley.

2000. *Slavery and the Roman Literary Imagination*. Cambridge.

Fleury, Pascale. 2006. *Lectures de Fronton. Un rhéteur latin à l'époque de la Seconde Sophistique*. Paris.

Fliedner, Heinrich. 1974. *Amor und Cupido. Untersuchungen über den römischen Liebesgott*. Meisenheim.

Flory, Marleen. 1978. "Family in *familia*: Kinship and Community in Slavery." *American Journal of Ancient History* 3: 78–95.

Fogazza, Donatella, ed. 1981. *Domiti Marsi testimonia et fragmenta*. Rome.

Fögen, Thorsten. 2004. "Gender-Specific Communication in Graeco-Roman Antiquity." *Historiographica Linguistica* 2/3: 199–276.

Fordyce, C.J. 1961. *Catullus: A Commentary*. Oxford.

Forsyth, Phyllis Young. 1977. "The Irony of Catullus 100." *Classical World* 70: 313–317.

Foucault, Michel. 1994. "De l'amitié comme mode de vie." In *Dits et écrits*, vol. IV: *1980–1988* (ed. D. Defert and F. Ewald), pp. 163–167. Paris.

Fowler, Don. 2000. "Epic in the Middle of the Wood: *Mise en Abyme* in the Nisus and Euryalus Episode." In Alison Sharrock and Helen Morales, eds., *Intratextuality: Greek and Roman Textual Relations*, pp. 89–114. Oxford.

Fraisse, Jean-Claude. 1974. *Philia. La notion d'amitié dans la philosophie antique*. Paris.

Freisenbruch, Annelise. 2007. "Back to Fronto: Doctor and Patient in his Correspondence with an Emperor." In Morello and Morrison 2007, pp. 235–256.

Freyburger, Gérard. 1986. *Fides. Étude sémantique et religieuse depuis les origines jusqu'à l'époque augustéenne*. Paris.

Friedl, Raimund. 1996. *Der Konkubinat im kaiserzeitlichen Rom*. Stuttgart.

Fürst, Alfons. 1996. *Streit unter Freunden. Ideale und Realität in der Freundschaftslehre der Antike*. Stuttgart.

Gaertner, Hans. 1983. "Ein Kronprinz und sein Lehrer." In Peter Neukam, ed., *Struktur und Gehalt*, pp. 25–49. Munich.

Gager, John, ed. 1992. *Curse Tablets and Binding Spells from the Ancient World*. Oxford.

Gardner, Jane. 1986. *Women in Roman Law and Society*. London.

1993. *Being a Roman Citizen*. London.

Garland, Robert. 2001. *The Greek Way of Death*. 2nd edn. London.

Gaudemet, Jean. 1982. "Note sur les *amici principis*." *Romanitas: Christianitas. Untersuchungen zur Geschichte und Literatur der römischen Kaiserzeit*, pp. 42–60. Berlin.

Geertz, Clifford. 1983. *Local Knowledge: Further Essays in Interpretive Anthropology*. New York.

Gelzer, Matthias. 1969. *The Roman Nobility*. Oxford.

Giangrande, Giuseppe. 1980. "An Alleged Fragment of Gallus." *Quaderni urbinati di cultura classica* 5: 141–152.

Gibson, Bruce, ed. 2006. *Statius: Silvae 5*. Oxford.

Gibson, Roy K. 1995. "How to Win Girlfriends and Influence Them: *Amicitia* in Roman Love Elegy." *Proceedings of the Cambridge Philological Society* 41: 62–82.

Gillis, Daniel. 1983. *Eros and Death in the "Aeneid."* Rome.

Gold, Barbara. 1987. *Literary Patronage in Greece and Rome*. Chapel Hill.

Goldhill, Simon. 2006. "Antigone and the Politics of Sisterhood." In Vanda Zajko and Miriam Leonard, eds., *Laughing with Medusa: Classical Myth and Feminist Thought*, pp. 141–161. Oxford.

Goold, G. P., ed. and trans. 1999. *Propertius: Elegies*. London and Cambridge, Mass.

Greenblatt, Stephen. 1990. *Learning to Curse: Essays in Early Modern Culture*. New York-London.

Greene, Ellen. 1998. *Erotics of Domination: Male Desire and the Mistress in Latin Love Poetry*. Baltimore.

Gregori, Gian Luca. 2001. "*Amici Brixiani*." In Peachin 2001, pp. 31–40.

Grewing, Farouk, ed., 1998. *Toto notus in orbe. Perspektiven der Martial-Interpretation*. Stuttgart.

Griffin, Miriam. 1997. "From Aristotle to Atticus: Cicero and Matius on Friendship." In Jonathan Barnes and Miriam Griffin, eds., *Philosophia Togata II: Plato and Aristotle at Rome*, pp. 86–109. New York and Oxford.

Grimal, Pierre. 1990. "Ce que Marc-Aurèle doit à Fronton." *Revue des Études Latines* 68: 151–159.

Gruen, Erich. 1982. "Greek *pistis* and Roman *fides*." *Athenaeum* 60: 50–68.

Gunderson, Erik. 1997. "Catullus, Pliny and Love Letters." *Transactions of the American Philological Association* 127: 201–232.

2000. *Staging Masculinity: The Rhetoric of Performance in the Roman World*. Ann Arbor.

2007. "S.V.B.E.V." *Classical Antiquity* 26: 1–48.

Gunnella, Adda. 1995. "Morti improvvise e violente nelle iscrizioni latine." In Hinard 1995, pp. 9–22.

Guthke, Karl Siegfried. 2006. *Sprechende Steine. Eine Kulturgeschichte der Grabschrift*. Göttingen.

Habinek, Thomas. 1990. "Towards a History of Friendly Advice: The Politics of Candor in Cicero's *De amicitia*." *Apeiron* 23: 165–185.

Hadot, Pierre, ed. 1998. *Marc Aurèle. Écrits pour lui-même*. Vol. 1. With the collaboration of Concetta Luna. Paris.

Haggerty, George E. 1998. *Unnatural Affections: Women and Fiction in the Later 18th Century.* Bloomington.

Hall, Jon. 2009. *Politeness and Politics in Cicero's Letters.* Oxford.

Halperin, David M. 1990. *One Hundred Years of Homosexuality, and Other Essays on Greek Love.* New York and London.

2002. *How To Do the History of Homosexuality.* Chicago.

Hardie, Philip. 1994. *Virgil, Aeneid: Book IX.* Cambridge.

Harris, William. 1989. *Ancient Literacy.* Cambridge, Mass.

Hasegawa, Kinuko. 2005. *The Familia Urbana during the Early Empire: A Study of Columbaria Inscriptions.* Oxford.

Häusle, Helmut. 1980. *Das Denkmal als Garant des Nachruhms. Beiträge zur Geschichte und Thematik eines Motivs in lateinischen Inschriften.* Munich.

Häussler, Ralph. 2002. "Writing Latin – From Resistance to Assimilation: Language, Culture and Society in Northern Italy and Southern Gaul." In Alison Cooley, ed., *Becoming Roman, Writing Latin? Literacy and Epigraphy in the Roman West*, pp. 61–76. Portsmouth, R.I.

Häussler, Reinhard. 1968. *Nachträge zu A. Otto, Sprichwörter und sprichwörtliche Redensarten der Römer.* Hildesheim.

Heldmann, Konrad. 1976. "Ciceros *Laelius* und die Grenzen der Freundschaft. Zur Interdependenz von Literatur und Politik 44/43 v.Chr." *Hermes* 104: 74–103.

Hellegouarc'h, Joseph. 1963. *Le vocabulaire latin des relations et des partis politiques sous la République.* Paris.

Helttula, Anne, ed. 2007. *Le iscrizioni sepolcrali latine nell'Isola Sacra.* Rome.

Henderson, John. 2007. "…when who should walk into the room but… Epistoliterarity in Cicero, *Ad Q fr.* 3.1." In Morello and Morrison 2007, pp. 37–85.

Henriksén, Christer. 2006. "Martial's Modes of Mourning: Sepulchral Epitaphs in the *Epigrams.*" In Ruurd Nauta, Harm-Jan van Dam, and Johannes J. L. Smolenaars, eds., *Flavian Poetry*, pp. 349–367. Leiden.

Hermand, Jost. 2006. *Freundschaft. Zur Geschichte einer sozialen Bindung.* Cologne.

Hermann, Alfred. 1959. *Altägyptische Liebesdichtung.* Wiesbaden.

Hesberg, Henner von. 1992. *Römische Grabbauten.* Darmstadt.

Hesberg, Henner von, and Paul Zanker, eds. 1987. *Römische Gräberstraßen. Selbstdarstellung, Status, Standard.* München.

Heslin, Peter. 2005. *The Transvestite Achilles.* Cambridge.

Hexter, Ralph. 1992. "Sidonian Dido." In Ralph Hexter and Daniel Selden, eds., *Innovations of Antiquity*, pp. 332–384. New York.

Heyworth, Stephen J. 2007. *Cynthia: A Companion to the Text of Propertius.* Oxford.

Hinard, François, ed. 1987. *La mort, les morts et l'au-delà dans le monde romain.* Caen.

1995. *La mort au quotidien dans le monde romain.* Paris.

Hingley, Richard. 2005. *Globalizing Roman Culture: Unity, Diversity and Empire.* London.

Hodge, R. I. V. and R. A. Buttimore. 1977. *The Monobiblos of Propertius.* Cambridge.

Hofmann, Johann Baptist. 1951. *Lateinische Umgangssprache.* 3rd edn. Heidelberg.

Holford-Strevens, Leofranc. 2003. *Aulus Gellius: An Antonine Scholar and His Achievement.* Oxford.

Hollis, Adrian. 2007. *Fragments of Roman Poetry, c. 60 BC – AD 20.* Oxford.

Hopkins, Keith. 1983. *Death and Renewal.* Cambridge.

Horsfall, Nicholas. 1985. "CIL VI 37965 = CLE 1988 (Epitaph of Allia Potestas): A Commentary." *Zeitschrift für Papyrologie und Epigraphik* 61: 251–272.

Howell, Peter. 1980. *A Commentary on Book One of the Epigrams of Martial.* London.

Hutchinson, Gregory. 1984. "Propertius and the Unity of the Book." *Journal of Roman Studies* 74: 99–106.

1998. *Cicero's Correspondence: A Literary Study.* Oxford.

Hüttemann, Arno. 2010. *Pompejanische Inschriften. Der heutige Bestand vor Ort im Stadtgebiet und in den Nekropolen.* Stuttgart.

Hyatte, Reginald. 1994. *The Arts of Friendship: The Idealization of Friendship in Medieval and Early Renaissance Literature.* Leiden.

Jäger, Wolfgang. 1986. *Briefanalysen. Zum Zusammenhang von Realitätserfahrung und Sprache in den Briefen Ciceros.* Frankfurt am Main.

Jakobson, Roman. 1959. "On Linguistic Aspects of Translation." In Reuben A. Brower, ed., *On Translation,* pp. 232–239. Cambridge, Mass.

Janan, Micaela. 1991. "'The Labyrinth and the Mirror': Incest and Influence in *Metamorphoses* 9." *Arethusa* 24: 239–256.

2001. *The Politics of Desire: Propertius IV.* Berkeley and London.

Johnson, William and Holt Parker, eds. 2009. *Ancient Literacies: The Culture of Reading in Greece and Rome.* Oxford and New York.

Kaster, Robert A. 2005. *Emotion, Restraint, and Community in Ancient Rome.* Oxford and New York.

Kasulke, Christoph Tobias. 2005. *Fronto, Marc Aurel und kein Konflikt zwischen Rhetorik und Philosophie im 2. Jh. n. Chr.* Munich and Leipzig.

Katz, Jonathan. 2001. *Love Stories: Love between Men before Homosexuality.* Chicago.

Keay, Simon and Nicola Terrenato, eds. 2001. *Italy and the West: Comparative Issues in Romanization.* Oxford.

Keith, Alison. 2008. *Propertius: Poet of Love and Leisure.* London.

Kennedy, Duncan. 1987. "*Arcades ambo:* Vergil, Gallus and Arcadia." *Hermathena* 14: 47–59.

1993. *The Arts of Love: Five Studies in the Discourse of Roman Love Elegy.* Cambridge.

Kent, Dale. 2009. *Friendship, Love and Trust in Renaissance Florence.* Cambridge, Mass.

Keulen, Wytse. 2009. *Gellius the Satirist: Roman Cultural Authority in "Attic Nights."* Leiden.

Kierdorf, Wilhelm. 1987. "Freundschaft und Freundschaftskündigung. Von der Republik zum Prinzipat." In Gerhard Binder, ed., *Saeculum Augustum*, vol. 1: *Herrschaft und Gesellschaft*, pp. 223–245. Darmstadt.

Kilpatrick, Ross S. 1986. *The Poetry of Friendship: Horace, Epistles 1.* Edmonton.

Kim, Jin-ok. 2003. *Charlotte Brontë and Female Desire.* New York.

King, J. J. 1980. "The Two Galluses of Propertius' Monobiblos." *Philologus* 124: 212–230.

King, Margaret. 2000. "Commemoration of Infants on Roman Funerary Inscriptions." In G. J. Oliver, ed., *The Epigraphy of Death: Studies in the History and Society of Greece and Rome*, pp. 117–154. Liverpool.

Kleijwegt, Marc. 1998. *"Extra fortunam est quidquid donatur amicis*: Martial on Friendship." In Grewing 1998, pp. 256–277.

Kleiner, Diana. 1977. *Roman Group Portraiture: The Funerary Reliefs of the Late Republic and Early Empire.* New York.

Knight, Gillian. 2005. "Friendship and Erotics in the Late Antique Verse Epistle: Ausonius and Paulinus Revisited." *Rheinisches Museum* 148: 361–403.

Kolb, Anne and Joachim Fugmann. 2008. *Tod in Rom. Grabinschriften als Spiegel römischen Lebens.* Mainz.

Konstan, David. 1997. *Friendship in the Classical World.* Cambridge.

Korhonen, Kuisma. 2006. *Textual Friendship: The Essay as Impossible Encounter. From Plato and Montaigne to Levinas and Derrida.* Amherst, N.Y.

Kroll, Wilhelm. 1931. "Kuss." *RE* suppl. v, pp. 511–520.

ed. 1989. *C. Valerius Catullus.* 7th edn. Stuttgart.

Kuefler, Matthew, ed. 2006. *The Boswell Thesis: Essays on Christianity, Social Tolerance, and Homosexuality.* Chicago.

Kurtz, Donna and John Boardman. 1971. *Greek Burial Customs.* London.

Kytzler, Bernhard. 1960. "Beobachtungen zu den Matius-Briefen." *Philologus* 104: 48–62.

Labate, Mario. 1995. "Petronio, *Satirico* 80–81." *Materiali e discussioni* 35: 165–175.

Lakmann, Marie-Luise. 1997. "Favorinus von Arelate. Aulus Gellius über seinen Lehrer." In Beate Czapla, Tomas Lehmann, and Susanne Liell, eds., *Vir bonus dicendi peritus. Festschrift für Alfons Weische*, pp. 233–243. Wiesbaden.

Landolfi, Luciano. 2008. "Venere, Amore, gli Amorini nell'elegia di Properzio. Uno sguardo d'insieme." In Santini and Santucci 2008, pp. 97–154.

Langlands, Rebecca. 2006. *Sexual Morality in Ancient Rome.* Cambridge.

Laser, Günter, ed. 2001. *Quintus Tullius Cicero, "Commentariolum petitionis."* Darmstadt.

Lazzarini, Sergio. 1991. *Sepulcra familiaria. Un'indagine epigrafico-giuridica.* Padova.

Lee, Guy, trans. 1994. *Propertius: Poems.* Oxford.

Lendon, Jon E. 2006. "*Contubernalis, commanipularis* and *commilito* in Roman Soldiers' Epigraphy: Drawing the Distinction." *Zeitschrift für Papyrologie und Epigraphik* 157: 270–276.

Lepetz, Sébastien and William Van Andringa. 2011. "*Publius Vesonius Phileros vivos monumentum fecit*: Investigations in a Sector of the Porta Nocera Cemetery in Roman Pompeii." In Carroll and Rempel 2011, pp. 110–133.

Lepore, Ettore. 1954. *Il princeps ciceroniano e gli ideali politici della tarda Repubblica*. Napoli.

Levi, Mario Attilio. 1994. *Ricerche su Frontone*. Rome.

Lewis, C. S. 1960. *The Four Loves*. London.

L'Huillier, Marie-Claude. 2002. "Fronton et ses amis. L'orateur dans la cité." In Stéphane Ratti, ed., *Antiquité et citoyenneté*, pp. 293–306. Besançon.

Lloyd, Geoffrey E. R. 1992. "Methods and Problems in the History of Ancient Science." *Isis: Journal of the History of Science Society* 83: 564–577.

Lombardi Vallauri, Luigi. 1974. *Amicizia, carità, diritto. L'esperienza giuridica nella tipologia delle esperienze di rapporto*. Milan.

Lossmann, Friedrich. 1962. *Cicero und Caesar im Jahre 54. Studien zur Theorie und Praxis der römischen Freundschaft*. Wiesbaden.

Lowrie, Michèle. 2007. "Horace and Augustus." In Stephen J. Harrison, ed., *The Cambridge Companion to Horace*, pp. 77–92. Cambridge.

Lucarelli, Ute. 2007. *Exemplarische Vergangenheit. Valerius Maximus und die Konstruktion des sozialen Raumes in der frühen Kaiserzeit*. Göttingen.

Ludwig, Paul. 2002. *Eros and Polis: Desire and Community in Greek Political Theory*. Cambridge.

Luftig, Victor. 1993. *Seeing Together: Friendship between the Sexes in English Writing, from Mill to Woolf*. Stanford.

Lyne, R. O. A. M. 1980. *The Latin Love Poets from Catullus to Horace*. Oxford. 1987. *Further Voices in Vergil's Aeneid*. Oxford.

Lyons, John. 1995. *Linguistic Semantics: An Introduction*. Cambridge.

MacCary, William T. 1985. *Friends and Lovers: The Phenomenology of Desire in Shakespearean Comedy*. New York.

MacFaul, Tom. 2007. *Male Friendship in Shakespeare and his Contemporaries*. Cambridge.

Macleod, C. W. 1973. "Parody and Personalities in Catullus." *Classical Quarterly* 23: 294–303.

MacMullen, Ramsay. 1982. "The Epigraphic Habit in the Roman Empire." *American Journal of Philology* 103: 233–246.

Makowski, John F. 1989. "Nisus and Euryalus: A Platonic Relationship." *Classical Journal* 85: 1–15.

Marcus, Sharon. 2007. *Between Women: Friendship, Desire and Marriage in Victorian England*. Princeton.

Matter, E. Ann. 2006. "My Sister, My Spouse: Woman-Identified Women in Medieval Christianity." In Kuefler 2006, pp. 152–166

Mattingly, David. 2011. *Imperialism, Power, and Identity: Experiencing the Roman Empire*. Princeton.

Mauser, Wolfram and Barbara Becker-Cantarino, eds. 1991. *Frauenfreundschaft – Männerfreundschaft. Literarische Diskurse im 18. Jahrhundert*. Tübingen.

McDermott, Emily. 1982. "Horace, Maecenas, and Odes 2.17." *Hermes* 110: 211–228.

McDermott, William C. 1972. "M. Cicero and M. Tiro." *Historia* 21: 259–286.

McDowell, Andrea G. 1999. *Village Life in Ancient Egypt: Laundry Lists and Love Songs*. Oxford.

Mencacci, Francesca. 1996. *I fratelli amici. La rappresentazione dei gemelli nella cultura romana*. Venezia.

Merola, Francesca Reduzzi. 1990. *Servo parere. Studi sulla condizione giuridica degli schiavi vicari e dei sottoposti a schiavi nelle esperienze greca e romana*. Camerino.

Méthy, Nicole. 2007. *Les lettres de Pline le Jeune. Une représentation de l'homme*. Paris.

Meyer, Elizabeth. 1990. "Explaining the Epigraphic Habit in the Roman Empire: The Evidence of Epitaphs." *Journal of Roman Studies* 80: 74–96.

Michel, Jacques. 1962. *Gratuité en droit romain*. Brussels.

Millar, Fergus. 1977. *The Emperor in the Roman World*. London.

Miller, Paul Allen. 1994. *Lyric Texts and Lyric Consciousness: The Birth of a Genre from Archaic Greece to Augustan Rome*. London.

  2004. *Subjecting Verses: Latin Love Elegy and the Emergence of the Real*. Princeton.

Milnor, Kristina. 2009. "Literary Literacy in Roman Pompeii: The Case of Vergil's *Aeneid*." In William A. Johnson and Holt N. Parker, eds., *Ancient Literacies*, pp. 288–319. Oxford and New York.

Morgan, Teresa. 2007. *Popular Morality in the Early Roman Empire*. Cambridge.

Moorton, Richard. 1990. "Love as Death: The Pivoting Metaphor in Vergil's Story of Dido." *Classical World* 83: 153–166.

Moreau, Philippe. 1978. "*Osculum, basium, savium*." *Revue de Philologie* 52: 87–97.

Morello, Ruth and Andrew Morrison, eds. 2007. *Ancient Letters: Classical and Late Antique Epistolography*. Oxford.

Morris, Ian. 1992. *Death-Ritual and Social Structure in Classical Antiquity*. Cambridge.

Mouritsen, Henrik. 2005. "Freedmen and Decurions: Epitaphs and Social History in Imperial Italy." *Journal of Roman Studies* 95: 38–63.

  2011. *The Freedman in the Roman World*. Cambridge.

Moussy, Claude. 1966. *Gratia et sa famille*. Paris.

Mueller, Hans-Friedrich. 2002. *Roman Religion in Valerius Maximus*. London and New York.

Munday, Jeremy. 2001. *Introducing Translation Studies: Theories and Applications*. New York and London.

Murphy, M. Lynne. 2003. *Semantic Relations and the Lexicon: Antonymy, Synonymy, and Other Paradigms*. Cambridge.

Narducci, Emanuele. 1989. "Le ambiguità della *amicitia*." In *Modelli etici e società. Un'idea di Cicerone*, pp. 79–110. Pisa.

Nauta, Ruurd. 2002. *Poetry for Patrons: Literary Communication in the Age of Domitian*. Leiden.

Navarro Antolín, Fernando, ed. and comm. 1996. *Lygdamus*. Brill.

Newman, John Kevin. 1990. *Roman Catullus*. Hildesheim.

Nicholson, Nigel. 1999. "Bodies without Names, Names without Bodies: Propertius 1.21–22." *Classical Journal* 94: 143–161.

Nisbet, Robin and Margaret Hubbard. 1991. *A Commentary on Horace: Odes Book II*. Oxford.

Nörr, Dieter. 1991. *Die "fides" im römischen Völkerrecht*. Heidelberg.

Nussbaum, Martha. 2002. "Eros and Ethical Norms: Philosophers Respond to a Cultural Dilemma." In Martha Nussbaum and Juha Sihvola, eds., *The Sleep of Reason: Erotic Experience and Sexual Ethics in Ancient Greece and Rome*, pp. 55–94. Chicago.

Oliensis, Ellen. 1997. "The Erotics of *amicitia*: Readings in Tibullus, Propertius, and Horace." In Judith Hallett and Marilyn Skinner, eds., *Roman Sexualities*, pp. 151–171. Princeton.

Oppermann, Irene. 2000. *Zur Funktion historischer Beispiele in Ciceros Briefen*. Munich.

Orgel, Stephen. 1996. *Impersonations: The Performance of Gender in Shakespeare's England*. Cambridge.

Oschema, Klaus, ed. 2007. *Freundschaft oder "amitié"? Ein politisch-soziales Konzept der Vormoderne im zwischensprachlichen Vergleich (15.-17. Jahrhundert)*. Berlin.

Osiek, Carolyn. 2008. "Roman and Christian Burial Practices and the Patronage of Women." In Brink and Green 2008, pp. 243–270.

Otto, August. 1890. *Sprichwörter und sprichwörtliche Redensarten der Römer*. Leipzig.

Oulton, Carolyn. 2007. *Romantic Friendship in Victorian Literature*. Aldershot, UK, and Burlington, Vt.

Packard, Chris. 2005. *Queer Cowboys and Other Erotic Male Friendships in Nineteenth-Century American Literature*. New York.

Palma, Antonio. 1988. *Iura vicinitatis. Solidarietà e limitazioni nel rapporto di vicinato in diritto romano dell'età classica*. Turin.

Pangallo, Alessandro. 1976. "Domizio Marso contro Bavio." *Maia* 28: 29–33.

Pangle, Lorraine Smith. 2003. *Aristotle and the Philosophy of Friendship*. Cambridge.

Pani, Mario. 1993. "Le raccomandazioni nell'epistolario di Plinio." In *Potere e valori fra Augusto e Traiano*, pp. 141–157. Bari.

Papanghelis, Theodore D. 1987. *Propertius: A Hellenistic Poet on Love and Death*. Cambridge.

Parca, Maryline. 2001. "Local Languages and Native Cultures." In Bodel 2001, pp. 57–72.

Parker, Barbara L. 1987. *A Precious Seeing: Love and Reason in Shakespeare's Plays.* New York.

Peachin, Michael, ed. 2001. *Aspects of Friendship in the Graeco-Roman World.* Portsmouth, R.I.

Pearce, John, Martin Millett, and Manuela Struck, eds. 2000. *Burial, Society and Context in the Roman World.* Oxford.

Perutelli, Alessandro. 1990. "Lutazio Catulo poeta." *Rivista di filologia e di istruzione classica* 118: 257–281.

Petersen, Lauren. 2006. *The Freedman in Roman Art and Art History.* Cambridge.

Petrain, David. 2000. "Hylas and Silva: Etymological Wordplay in Propertius 1.20." *Harvard Studies in Classical Philology* 100: 409–421.

Petrucci, Armando. 1998. *Writing the Dead: Death and Writing Strategies in the Western Tradition.* Trans. Michael Sullivan. Stanford.

Phang, Sara Elise. 2001. *The Marriage of Roman Soldiers (13 B.C. – A.D. 235): Law and Family in the Imperial Army.* Leiden.

Pincus, Matthew. 2004. "Propertius's Gallus and the Erotics of Influence." *Arethusa* 37: 165–196.

Pizzolato, Luigi. 1993. *L'idea di amicizia nel mondo antico classico e cristiano.* Torino.

Powell, Jonathan. 1990. *Cicero: Laelius on Friendship, and the Dream of Scipio.* Warminster.

  1995. "Friendship and its Problems in Greek and Roman Thought." In D. Innes, H. Hine, and C. Pelling, eds., *Ethics and Rhetoric: Classical Essays for Donald Russell on his Seventy-Fifth Birthday*, pp. 31–45. Oxford.

Prado-Vilar, Francisco. 2011. "Tragedy's Forgotten Beauty: The Medieval Return of Orestes." In Jaś Elsner and Janet Huskinson, eds., Life, Death, and Representation: Some New Work on Roman Sarcophagi, pp. 83–118. Oxford.

Price, Anthony. 1989. *Love and Friendship in Plato and Aristotle.* Oxford.

Pucci, Pietro. 1961. "Il carme 50 di Catullo." *Maia* 13: 249–256.

Putnam, Michael. 1985. "Possessiveness, Sexuality, and Heroism in the *Aeneid*." *Vergilius* 31: 1–21.

  2006. *Poetic Interplay: Catullus and Horace.* Princeton.

Quinn, Kenneth. 1973. *Catullus: The Poems.* 2nd edn. London.

Rabinowitz, Nancy and Lisa Auanger, eds. 2002. *Among Women: From the Homosocial to the Homoerotic in the Ancient World.* Austin.

Raccanelli, Renata. 1998. *L'amicitia nelle commedie di Plauto. Un'indagine antropologica.* Bari.

Ramdohr, Friedrich Wilhelm Basilius von. 1798. *Venus Urania. Über die Natur der Liebe, über ihre Veredelung und Verschönerung.* Leipzig.

Rauh, Nicholas. 1986. "Cicero's Business Friendships: Economics and Politics in the Late Roman Republic." *Aevum* 60: 3–30.

Raval, Shilpa. 2001. "'A Lover's Discourse': Byblis in *Metamorphoses* 9." *Arethusa* 34: 285–311.

Rawson, Beryl. 1974. "Roman Concubinage and Other *de facto* Marriages." *Transactions of the American Philological Association* 104: 279–305.

1978. *The Politics of Friendship: Pompey and Caesar.* Sydney.

Reali, Mauro. 1997. *Il contributo dell'epigrafia latina allo studio dell'*amicitia*. Il caso della Cisalpina.* Florence.

Reece, Richard, ed. 1977. *Burial in the Roman World.* London.

Rees, Roger. 2007. "Letters of Recommendation and the Rhetoric of Praise." In Morello and Morrison 2007, pp. 149–168.

Reitzenstein, Richard. 1912. *Zur Sprache der lateinischen Erotik.* Heidelberg.

Ricci, Cecilia. 2001. "L'amicizia tra soldati: le truppe urbane." In Peachin 2001, pp. 41–50.

Richlin, Amy. 2006a. *Marcus Aurelius in Love.* Chicago and London.

2006b. "Fronto + Marcus: Love, Friendship, Letters." In Kuefler 2006, pp. 111–129.

Rimell, Victoria. 2002. *Petronius and the Anatomy of Fiction.* Cambridge.

Rizzelli, Giunio. 1995. "Il dibattito sulle ll. 28–29 dell'elogio di Allia Potestas." *Studia et documenta historiae et iuris* 61: 623–655.

Rogers, Robert S. 1959. "The Emperor's Displeasure: *amicitiam renuntiare.*" *Transactions of the American Philological Association* 90: 224–237.

Rosati, Gianpiero. 2008. "Il rivale, o il triangolo del desiderio." In Santini and Santucci 2008, pp. 251–272.

Rosen, Klaus. 1994. "Marc Aurel und Fronto. Eine Freundschaft zwischen Macht und Kultur." In Klaus Rosen, ed., *Macht und Kultur im Rom der Kaiserzeit*, pp. 121–135. Bonn.

Rosenmeyer, Patricia. 2001. *Ancient Epistolary Fictions: The Letter in Greek Literature.* Cambridge.

Ross, David. 1975. *Backgrounds to Augustan Poetry: Gallus, Elegy and Rome.* Cambridge.

Rouland, Norbert. 1979. *Pouvoir politique et dépendance personnelle dans l'Antiquité romaine. Genèse et rôle des rapports de clientèle.* Brussels.

Rowland, Robert J. 1970. "Cicero's *necessarii.*" *Classical Journal* 65: 193–198.

Rumpf, Lorenz. 1996. *Extremus labor. Vergils 10. Ekloge und die Poetik der Bucolica.* Göttingen.

Rundel, Tobias. 2005. "*Mandatum* zwischen *utilitas* und *amicitia.*" *Perspektiven zur Mandatarhaftung im klassischen römischen Recht.* Münster.

Rutherford, R. B. 1989. *The "Meditations" of Marcus Aurelius: A Study.* Oxford.

Saller, Richard. 1982. *Personal Patronage under the Early Empire.* Cambridge.

1984. "*Familia, domus,* and the Roman Conception of the Family." *Phoenix* 38: 336–355.

1989. "Patronage and Friendship in Early Imperial Rome: Drawing the Distinction." In Andrew Wallace-Hadrill, ed., *Patronage in Ancient Society*, pp. 49–62. London and New York.

1994. *Patriarchy, Property and Death in the Roman Family*. Cambridge.

2000. "Family and Household." *Cambridge History of the Ancient World*, 2nd edn. Vol. XI, pp. 855–874. Cambridge.

2001. "The Family and Society." In Bodel 2001, pp. 95–117.

Saller, Richard, and Brent Shaw. 1984. "Tombstones and Roman Family Relations in the Principate: Civilians, Soldiers and Slaves." *Journal of Roman Studies* 74: 124–156.

Santini, Carlo and Francesco Santucci, eds. 2008. *I personaggi dell'elegia di Properzio*. Assisi.

Sapir, Edward. 1956. *Culture, Language and Personality*. Selected and edited by David G. Mandelbaum. Berkeley and Los Angeles.

Sartori, Antonio. 1994. *Guida alla sezione epigrafica delle raccolte archeologiche di Milano*. Milan.

Schalow, Paul Gordon. 2007. *A Poetics of Courtly Male Friendship in Heian Japan*. Honolulu.

Schiatti, Serafino. 1995. "Frontone maestro imperiale." In *Storia, letteratura e arte a Roma nel secondo secolo d.C.*, pp. 277–293. Florence.

Schukraft, Beate. 2007. "Homosexualität im Alten Ägypten." *Studien zur Altägyptischen Kultur* 36: 297–331.

Screech, Michael A., ed. and trans. 2004. *Michel de Montaigne: On Friendship*. London.

Sedgwick, Eve Kosofsky. 1985. *Between Men: English Literature and Male Homosocial Desire*. New York.

Segal, Charles. 1970. "Catullan *otiosi:* The Lover and the Poet." *Greece and Rome* 17: 25–31.

Serrano Delgado, José Miguel. 1987–1988. "La aportación de la epigrafía para el conocimiento de la *amicitia*. Relación de dipendencia en el alto imperio." *Habis* 18–19: 345–365.

Shannon, Laurie. 2002. *Sovereign Amity: Figures of Friendship in Shakespearean Contexts*. Chicago and London.

Sharrock, Alison. 2000. "Constructing Characters in Propertius." *Arethusa* 33: 263–284.

Shaw, Brent. 1997. "Ritual Brotherhood in Roman and Post-Roman Society." *Traditio* 52: 327–355.

Sherwin-White, A. N. 1966. *The Letters of Pliny: A Historical and Social Commentary*. Oxford.

Simpson, William Kelly et al., eds. 1973. *The Literature of Ancient Egypt: An Anthology of Stories, Instructions, and Poetry*. New Haven.

Skidmore, Clive. 1996. *Practical Ethics for Roman Gentlemen: The Work of Valerius Maximus*. Exeter.

Skinner, Marilyn. 1997. "*Ego mulier:* The Construction of Male Sexuality in Catullus." In Judith Hallett and Marilyn Skinner, eds., *Roman Sexualities*, pp. 129–150. Princeton.

Smadja, Élisabeth. 1976. "Esclaves et affranchis dans la correspondence de Cicéron. Les relations esclavagistes." *Annales littéraires de l'Université de Besançon* 187: 73–109.

Smith, Bruce R. 1991. *Homosexual Desire in Shakespeare's England: A Cultural Poetics*. Chicago.

Solin, Heiki. 2003. *Die griechischen Personennamen in Rom*. 2nd edn. Berlin.

Sourvinou-Inwood, Christiane. 1995. *"Reading" Greek Death to the End of the Classical Period*. Oxford.

Spielvogel, Jörg. 1993. *Amicitia und res publica. Ciceros Maxime während der innenpolitischen Auseinandersetzungen der Jahre 59–50 v.Chr*. Stuttgart.

Spisak, Art L. 1998. "Gift-Giving in Martial." In Grewing 1998, pp. 243–255.

2007. *Martial: A Social Guide*. London.

Steinmetz, Fritz-Arthur. 1967. *Die Freundschaftslehre des Panaitios*. Wiesbaden.

Stewart, Susan. 1984. *On Longing*. Baltimore.

Stok, Fabio. 2008. *"Amici/amicitia* in Properzio." In Santini and Santucci 2008, pp. 213–232.

Stowers, Stanley. 1986. *Letter Writing in Greco-Roman Antiquity*. Philadelphia.

Stupperich, Reinhard. 1983. "Zur *dextrarum iunctio* auf frühen römischen Grabreliefs." *Boreas. Münstersche Beiträge zur Archäologie* 6: 143–250.

Syme, Ronald. 1939. *The Roman Revolution*. Oxford.

Taylor, Lilly Ross. 1961. "Freedmen and Freeborn in the Epitaphs of Imperial Rome." *American Journal of Philology* 82: 113–132.

Thomas, Keith. 2009. *The Ends of Life: Roads to Fulfilment in Early Modern England*. Oxford.

Thomson, Douglas F. S. 1998. *Catullus*. Toronto.

Thylander, Hilding. 1951–1952. *Inscriptions du Port d'Ostie*. Lund.

Timpanaro, Sebastiano. 1987. "Il *ius osculi* e Frontone." *Maia* 39: 201–211.

Tobin, Robert. 2000. *Warm Brothers: Queer Theory and the Age of Goethe*. Philadelphia.

Todd, Janet. 1980. *Women's Friendship in Literature*. Columbia.

Toynbee, Jocelyn. 1971. *Death and Burial in the Roman World*. Ithaca.

Trapp, Michael. 2003. *Greek and Latin Letters: An Anthology*. Cambridge.

Treggiari, Susan. 1969. *Roman Freedmen during the Late Republic*. Oxford.

1981a. "Concubinae." *Papers of the British School at Rome* 49: 59–81.

1981b. *"Contubernales* in *CIL* 6." *Phoenix* 35: 42–69.

1991. *Roman Marriage: Iusti Coniuges from the Time of Cicero to the Time of Ulpian*. Oxford and New York.

Treu, Kurt. 1972. "Freundschaft." *Reallexikon für Antike und Christentum* 8: 418–434.

Van Dam, Harm-Jan. 1984. *Statius, "Silvae" Book II: A Commentary*. Leiden.

Van den Hout, Michael P. J. 1999. *A Commentary on the Letters of M. Cornelius Fronto*. Leiden.

Van Sickle, John. 2004. *The Design of Virgil's Bucolics*. 2nd ed. London.

Venuti, Lawrence. 2004. *The Translation Studies Reader*. 2nd edn. London.

Verboven, Koenraad. 2002. *The Economy of Friends: Economic Aspects of* amicitia *and Patronage in the Late Republic*. Brussels.

Vicinus, Martha. 2004. *Intimate Friends: Women Who Loved Women, 1778–1928*. Chicago and London.

Vinson, Martha. 1992. "Party Politics and the Language of Love in the Lesbia Poems of Catullus." In Carl Deroux, ed., *Studies in Latin Literature and Roman History*. Vol. VI, pp. 163–180. Brussels.

Voelke, André-Jean. 1961. *Les rapports avec autrui dans la philosophie grecque d'Aristote à Panaetius*. Paris.

Wachter, Rudolf. 1998. "*Oral poetry* in ungewohntem Kontext. Hinweise auf mündliche Dichtungstechnik in den pompejanischen Wandinschriften." *Zeitschrift für Papyrologie und Epigraphik* 121: 73–89.

Walde, Alois and J. B. Hofmann. 1938. *Lateinisches etymologisches Wörterbuch*, vol. I. 3rd edn. Heidelberg.

Wallace-Hadrill, Andrew 2008. "Housing the Dead: The Tomb as House in Roman Italy." In Brink and Green 2008, pp. 39–77.

Watson, C. Lindsay. 2003. *A Commentary on Horace's Epodes*. Oxford.

Watson, Patricia. 1989. "*Filiaster: Privignus* or 'Illegitimate Child'?" *Classical Quarterly* 39: 536–548.

Weber, Ekkehard. 2008. "*Libertus et coniunx.*" In Peter Mauritsch *et al.*, eds., *Antike Lebenswelten. Konstanz, Wandel, Wirkungsmacht*, pp. 367–380. Wiesbaden.

Weber, Thomas. 1988. *Fidus Achates. Der Gefährte des Aeneas in Vergils Aeneis*. Frankfurt.

Webster, Jane and Nicholas Cooper, eds. 1996. *Roman Imperialism: Post-Colonial Perspectives*. Leicester.

Weeks, Jeffrey. 2007. *The World We Have Won. The Remaking of Erotic and Intimate Life*. London and New York.

Weeks, Jeffrey, Brian Heaphy, and Catherine Donovan, eds. 2001. *Same-Sex Intimacies: Families of Choice and Other Life Experiments*. London and New York.

Wegner, Michael. 1969. *Untersuchungen zu den lateinischen Begriffen socius und societas*. Göttingen.

Wei, Ryan. 2009. "The Exercise of Friendship in the High Roman Empire." D.Phil. thesis. Oxford.

West, David. 1998. *Horace, Odes II: Vatis Amici*. Oxford.

White, Peter. 1975. "The Friends of Martial, Statius and Pliny, and the Dispersal of Patronage." *Harvard Studies in Classical Philology* 79: 265–300.

1978. "*Amicitia* and the Profession of Poetry in Early Imperial Rome." *Journal of Roman Studies* 68: 74–92.

1993. *Promised Verse: Poets in the Society of Augustan Rome*. Cambridge, Mass.

2007. "Friendship, Patronage, and Horatian Sociopoetics." In Stephen J. Harrison, ed., *The Cambridge Companion to Horace*, pp. 195–206. Cambridge.

2010. *Cicero in Letters: Epistolary Relations of the Late Republic*. Oxford.

Wilfong, Terry. 2002. "Friendship and Physical Desire: The Discourse of Female Homoeroticism in Fifth-Century CE Egypt." In Rabinowitz and Auanger 2002, pp. 304–329.

Williams, Craig A. 1995. "Greek Love at Rome." *Classical Quarterly* 45: 517–539.

2004. *Martial, "Epigrams": Book Two.* Oxford and New York.

2008. "Friends of the Roman People: Some Remarks on the Language of *amicitia.*" In Altay Coşkun, ed., *Freundschaft und Gefolgschaft in den auswärtigen Beziehungen der Römer,* pp. 29–44. Frankfurt am Main.

2010a. *Roman Homosexuality.* 2nd edn. Oxford and New York.

2010b. "*Cessamus mimum componere?* Performances of Gender in Petronius' *Satyricon.*" In Marco Formisano and Therese Fuhrer, eds., *Gender-Inszenierungen in der antiken Literatur,* pp. 25–44. Trier.

2012. "Perpetua's Gender: A Latinist Reads the *Passio Perpetuae et Felicitatis.*" In Jan Bremmer and Marco Formisano, eds., *Perpetua's Passions: Multidisciplinary Approaches to the Passio Perpetuae et Felicitatis,* pp. 54–77. Oxford.

Forthcoming. "Graffiti." In Thomas Hubbard, ed., *A Companion to Graeco-Roman Sexualities.* Oxford.

Williams, Gareth. 1994. *Banished Voices.* Cambridge.

Williams, Gordon. 1968. *Tradition and Originality in Roman Poetry.* Oxford.

1980. *Figures of Thought in Roman Poetry.* New Haven and London.

1990. "Did Maecenas Fall from Favor? Augustan Literary Patronage." In Kurt Raaflaub and Mark Toher, eds., *Between Republic and Empire: Interpretations of Augustus and his Principate,* pp. 258–275. Berkeley.

Williams, Mark. 1988. "Catullus 50 and the Language of Friendship." *Latomus* 47: 69–73.

Winkler, John J. 1990. *The Constraints of Desire: The Anthropology of Sex and Desire in Ancient Greece.* New York and London.

Wiseman, Timothy Peter. 1987. "*Pete nobiles amicos.* Poets and Patrons in Late Republican Rome." In Barbara Gold, ed., *Literary Patronage in Greece and Rome,* pp. 73–86. Austin.

1995. *Remus: A Roman Myth.* Cambridge.

Woolf, Greg. 1997. "Beyond Romans and Natives." *World Archaeology* 28: 339–350.

1998. *Becoming Roman: The Origins of Provincial Civilization in Gaul.* Cambridge.

Wray, David. 2001. *Catullus and the Poetics of Roman Manhood.* Cambridge.

Yourcenar, Marguerite. 1981. *Anna soror.* Paris.

Index of passages discussed

General index

CPSIA information can be obtained
at www.ICGtesting.com
Printed in the USA
LVHW080054110319
610000LV00010BB/156/P